"Peterson conducts a full-orbed tour of christology, particularly highlighting the often neglected role of Christ's resurrection in our salvation. Peterson writes with a pastor's heart, as is evident in the biblical fidelity and remarkable clarity that marks this work."

Thomas R. Schreiner, James Buchanan Harrison Professor
of New Testament Interpretation, The Southern Baptist Theological Seminary

"Robert Peterson has produced a comprehensive study of Christ's saving work that puts the cross at the center, but also shows how it is part of a wider plan. He shows how the atonement must be seen in the context of Christ's whole life and ministry without compromising the essential truth of his penal substitutionary sacrifice for us. This is a refreshing and insightful study, which is much needed at the present time and deserves to be widely read."

Gerald Bray, Research Professor of Divinity,
Beeson Divinity School, Samford University

"Dr. Peterson told me in correspondence, 'my work is not [systematic theology] as much as laying biblical foundations for systematics.' Well, people can define terms as they like. But I think *Salvation Accomplished by the Son* is systematic theology at its very best. It deals with doctrines of systematic theology by bringing them into closest proximity with the biblical texts that justify them. That is the kind of systematics of which we need much more. This is the book to which, after Scripture itself, I would first turn to explore any question about Jesus's incarnation, atonement, or resurrection."

John M. Frame, Professor of Systematic Theology and Philosophy,
Reformed Theological Seminary, Orlando

"At the heart of evangelicalism is the simple affirmation 'Jesus saves.' Theologian Robert Peterson shows us that this affirmation is both simple enough for a child's faith and profound enough for a scholar's erudition. In this sweeping and comprehensive study, Peterson not only unpacks the full scope of Christ's saving work, from first advent to second; he pastorally applies this to the believer so that the result is not bone-dry theology, but heart-melting doxology. I left this book with a new desire to sing, 'Jesus saves!'"

Sean Michael Lucas, Senior Minister,
The First Presbyterian Church, Hattiesburg, Mississippi

"At the center of Christianity is a crucified and risen Savior—a person, event, and picture so profound and massive, we have the sixty-six books of the Bible to unpack it. In this book, trusted and reliable guide Robert Peterson leads us deep into the rich contours of the atoning work of Christ. This is theology as it's supposed to be: biblically informed at every turn, historically aware and enriched, culturally engaged, and pastorally presented—all leading us to worship the slain and risen Lamb."

Stephen J. Nichols, Research Professor of Christianity and Culture, Lancaster Bible College

"Nothing should be of greater interest to a believer than the person and work of Jesus Christ. The precious and intricate theology involved in salvation and the glory and nature of Christ excite the deepest affections. In Robert Peterson's *Salvation Accomplished by the Son* you will find the most satisfying food for your soul as he navigates the riches of christology and soteriology with deep insight and piercing simplicity. These pages have fueled my worship and motivated my love for Jesus. Read this book and you will bask in the glory of the Son."

Rick Holland, Senior Pastor, Mission Road Bible Church, Prairie Village, Kansas

"Robert Peterson has given us a wonderful summation of the Bible's witness to the Son's saving work. This book is methodical, thorough, and accessible. It skirts atonement theories and fashionable trends to get at Christ's atoning actions and roles. We learn that the gospel message is not flat and simplistic but multi-dimensional, nuanced, and rich. This book is an extended embodiment of the ancient invitation to 'behold the Lamb of God, who takes away the sin of the world.'"

Robert W. Yarbrough, Professor of New Testament, Covenant Theological Seminary

"There are many works dealing with Christ's work of redemption, usually focusing on Jesus's dying on the cross to save his people from their sins. While this is an important aspect of Christ's saving work, it is not the complete picture. Dr. Peterson, in examining nine saving events of Christ and six scriptural aspects of his work, presents a more complete picture of Christ's saving work. This study not only presents Christ's work with careful exegesis, but also magnifies the grace and mercy of God as they are seen in Christ's work of salvation. This is a valuable and important contribution to soteriology."

Van Lees, Pastor, Covenant of Grace Church, St. Charles, Missouri

SALVATION

ACCOMPLISHED BY THE

SON

Other Crossway Books by Robert A. Peterson

The Deity of Christ (coeditor)
The Glory of God (coeditor)
Suffering and the Goodness of God (coeditor)

SALVATION
ACCOMPLISHED BY THE
SON

The Work of Christ

ROBERT A. PETERSON

WHEATON, ILLINOIS

Cover design: Smartt Guys Design
Cover photo: Fine Art Photography Library, London / Art Resource, New York
Interior design and typesetting: Lakeside Design Plus

First printing 2012
Printed in the United States of America

Unless otherwise indicated, Scripture quotations are from the ESV® Bible (*The Holy Bible, English Standard Version*®), copyright © 2001 by Crossway. Used by permission. All rights reserved.

The Scripture quotation marked CEV is taken from the *Contemporary English Version*. Copyright © 1995 by American Bible Society. Used by permission.

The Scripture quotation marked JB is from *The Jerusalem Bible*. Copyright © 1966, 1967, 1968 by Darton, Longman & Todd Ltd. and Doubleday & Co., Inc.

Scripture quotations marked NASB are from *The New American Standard Bible*®. Copyright © The Lockman Foundation 1960, 1962, 1963, 1968, 1971, 1972, 1973, 1975, 1977, 1995. Used by permission.

Scripture quotations marked NIV are from the *Holy Bible, New International Version*®. Copyright © 1973, 1978, 1984 Biblica. Used by permission of Zondervan. All rights reserved. The "NIV" and "New International Version" trademarks are registered in the United States Patent and Trademark Office by Biblica. Use of either trademark requires the permission of Biblica.

The Scripture quotation marked NRSV is from *The New Revised Standard Version*. Copyright © 1989 by the Division of Christian Education of the National Council of the Churches of Christ in the U.S.A. Published by Thomas Nelson, Inc. Used by permission of the National Council of the Churches of Christ in the U.S.A.

Scripture quotations marked RSV are from *The Revised Standard Version*. Copyright © 1946, 1952, 1971, 1973 by the Division of Christian Education of the National Council of the Churches of Christ in the U.S.A.

The Scripture quotation marked TNIV is taken from the *Holy Bible, Today's New International Version*. TNIV®. Copyright © 2001, 2005 by International Bible Society. Used by permission of Zondervan. All rights reserved.

All emphases in Scripture quotations have been added by the author.

Hardcover ISBN:	978-1-4335-0760-1
ePub ISBN:	978-1-4335-2360-1
PDF ISBN:	978-1-4335-0761-8
Mobipocket ISBN:	978-1-4335-0762-5

Library of Congress Cataloging-in-Publication Data
   Peterson, Robert A., 1948–
      Salvation accomplished by the Son: the work of Christ / Robert A. Peterson.
         p. cm.
      Includes bibliographical references and indexes.
      ISBN 978-1-4335-0760-1 (hc)
         1. Atonement. 2. Jesus Christ—Priesthood. I. Title.
   BT265.3.P44 2012
   232'.3—dc23

                                  2011025564

Crossway is a publishing ministry of Good News Publishers.

SH	24	23	22	21	20	19	18	17	16	15	14	13	12
14	13	12	11	10	9	8	7	6	5	4	3	2	1

I warmly dedicate this volume
to professor James Pain of Drew University,
my doctoral mentor, counselor, and friend.

Contents

Acknowledgments   11

Introduction   12

Part One: Events

Introduction to Jesus's Saving Events   21

1 Christ's Incarnation   27

2 Christ's Sinless Life   41

3 Christ's Death   61

4 Christ's Resurrection   117

5 Christ's Ascension   151

6 Christ's Session   183

7 Christ's Pentecost   206

8 Christ's Intercession   227

9 Christ's Second Coming   251

Part Two: Pictures

Introduction to the Pictures of Jesus's Saving Events   273

10 Christ Our Reconciler   276

11 Christ Our Redeemer   313

12 Christ Our Legal Substitute   362

13 Christ Our Victor   413

14   Christ Our Second Adam   463

15   Christ Our Sacrifice   500

     Conclusion   550

     Appendix: The Extent of the Atonement   566

     Bibliography   576

     General Index   588

     Scripture Index   601

Acknowledgments

I have many people to thank for helping me on this project:

Mary Pat Peterson, for her prayers and unwavering support.

The congregation of Country Bible Church, in Bunker Hill, Illinois, for their prayers.

The administration of Covenant Theological Seminary, for graciously granting me a sabbatical.

Allan Fisher, Jill Carter, and the rest of Crossway's team, for their support, aid, and encouragement.

Larry and Sydney Catlett, for making my sabbatical more productive.

Nick and Ellen Pappas, for inviting me to spend many hours writing in their "farm house" in Bismarck, Missouri.

Logan Almy, for drafting the chapter on Christ's intercession.

K. J. Drake, for drafting the chapter on Christ's ascension.

Kyle Dillon, for preparing the bibliography and more.

Jack Collins, for much expert advice on the Old Testament, graciously given.

Chris Morgan for offering theological insight and counsel.

Brad Matthews and Marcus Johnson, for commenting on the manuscript.

Thom Notaro, Dorothy Carroll, Beth Ann Brown, Mary Ruth Murdoch, and Elliott Pinegar, for editing and proofreading.

Rick Matt, for editing the bibliography.

Mark Menninga, Kyle Dillon, K. J. Drake, and Mary Pat Peterson, for reading the manuscript.

James C. Pakala, library director, and Steve Jamieson, reference and systems librarian, of the J. Oliver Buswell Jr. Library at Covenant Theological Seminary, for professional and gracious research assistance.

Introduction

Every religion and ideology has its visual symbol, which illustrates a significant feature of its history or beliefs. The lotus flower . . . is now particularly associated with Buddhism. Because of its wheel shape it is thought to depict either the cycle of birth and death or the emergence of beauty and harmony out of the muddy waters of chaos.

Ancient Judaism avoided visual signs and symbols, for fear of infringing the second commandment which prohibits the manufacture of images. But modern Judaism has adopted the so-called Shield or Star of David, a hexagram formed by combining two equilateral triangles. It speaks of God's covenant with David that his throne would be established for ever and that the Messiah would be descended from him.

Islam, the other monotheistic faith which arose in the Middle East, is symbolized by a crescent, at least in West Asia. Originally depicting a phase of the moon, it was already the symbol of sovereignty in Byzantium before the Muslim conquest.

Christianity, then, is no exception in having a visual symbol. The cross was not its earliest, however.[1]

These words of John Stott set Christianity's symbol in the context of those of other world religions. He goes on to say that the earliest Christian symbols included the peacock (symbolizing immortality), the dove, the athlete's victory garland, and especially, the fish, which when spelled in Greek letters (*ichthys*) was an acronym for "Jesus Christ, Son of God, Savior."[2]

Stott notes that believers had a wide range of possibilities from which to choose the symbol of Christianity. He lists seven:

---

[1]John R. W. Stott, *The Cross of Christ* (Downers Grove, IL: InterVarsity, 1986), 20.
[2]Ibid.

- the manger in which Jesus was laid at birth
- the carpenter's bench at which he worked
- the boat from which he taught in Galilee
- the apron that he wore to wash his disciples' feet
- the stone that was rolled from the mouth of his tomb
- the throne that he shares with the Father
- the dove, which symbolizes the Spirit's coming at Pentecost[3]

But bypassing all these, Christians chose Christ's cross as their emblem. On the one hand, this is amazing because the cross spoke of crucifixion, which was regarded with horror in the ancient world. It is probably the most vicious method of execution because it delayed death, sometimes for days, to maximize torture. On the other hand, in light of Paul's sentiment, "But far be it from me to boast except in the cross of our Lord Jesus Christ" (Gal. 6:14), they chose well. Why? Because the cross describes where the work of salvation was accomplished.

This book is all about that work. Actually, I will soon argue that Christians would have better chosen the cross *and* the stone rolled from Jesus's tomb! But believers did choose the cross as their symbol, and for good reasons.

Christ's saving work is profound, massive, and magnificent. It is profound because of the identity of the One who performed it. The mystery of the incarnation of the Son of God lends to the mystery of his saving work. This book assumes a high christology. It begins "from above" with the second person of the Trinity in heaven becoming a genuine human being in Jesus of Nazareth. "The Word became flesh" (John 1:14). God did this through the Holy Spirit's miraculous conception of Jesus's humanity in the womb of the Virgin Mary. As a result "the child to be born will be called holy—the Son of God" (Luke 1:35). The profundity of Christ's work is traceable to the profundity of his person.

Christ's work is also massive, so massive that not even a big book can exhaust its meaning. And it is magnificent because of its wondrous effects. These include pleasing God himself, defeating God's enemies, and rescuing all of God's people and the creation itself. My goals are to show something of the profundity, massiveness, and magnificence of the work of Christ for us sinners.

At this point, readers might be asking a very good question: Why should I read this book? I will give four answers that I hope will be sufficient.

---

[3]Ibid., 21.

Christ's Death Is Debated

Evangelical Christians are debating the significance of Christ's death as never before. As exhibit A, consider the 2006 volume *The Nature of the Atonement*.[4] In that book four evangelical scholars set forth their understanding of Christ's atonement, to which the other three respond with critique. Gregory A. Boyd defends the Christus Victor view, maintaining that Christ in his death and resurrection won a mighty victory over Satan and the demons. Thomas R. Schreiner defends penal substitution, according to which Christ's death satisfied God's justice and paid the penalty for our sins. Bruce R. Reichenbach defends the healing view, explaining the atonement in terms of healing and restoration. Joel B. Green defends the kaleidoscopic view, holding that no one model or metaphor of the atonement is sufficient to explain the significance of Christ's death. This is not the time for me to enter into these debates; my purpose now is simply to point to their existence.

It is not only scholars who are debating the meaning of the work of Christ. *The Lost Message of Jesus*, written by Steve Chalke and Alan Mann in 2003, set off a firestorm in their native England.[5] In their book, Chalke, a high-profile evangelical personality in Britain, and Mann rejected penal substitution. The matter had been debated in scholarly circles for years, but *The Lost Message of Jesus* alerted the people in the churches. Defenders of penal substitution entered the fray. The result was so much concern among evangelicals that various meetings were held to address the issue, especially the 2005 London Symposium on the Theology of the Atonement, which led to the publication in 2008 of *The Atonement Debate*.[6]

The debates concerning views of Christ's death point to the need for guidance. It is my hope that this book might provide some of that guidance.

Christ's Resurrection Is Neglected

A second reason why readers ought to read this book is evangelicals' failure to teach that Jesus's death *and resurrection* save sinners. I. Howard Marshall, in the preface to *Aspects of the Atonement: Cross and Resurrection in the Reconciling of God and Humanity*, affirms that Christ's death saves. Then he perceptively

---

[4]James Beilby and Paul R. Eddy, eds., *The Nature of the Atonement: Four Views* (Downers Grove, IL: IVP Academic, 2006).

[5]Steve Chalke and Alan Mann, *The Lost Message of Jesus* (Grand Rapids: Zondervan, 2003).

[6]Derek Tidball, David Hilborn, and Justin Thacker, eds., *The Atonement Debate* (Grand Rapids: Zondervan, 2008). For the full story of *The Lost Message of Jesus* and the responses it engendered, see David Hilborn, "Atonement, Evangelicalism and the Evangelical Alliance: The Present Debate in Context," in *The Atonement Debate*, 15–33.

underlines "the (often neglected) place of the resurrection of Christ in this saving action."[7] This is so true. Of course, evangelicals confess belief in Jesus's resurrection from the dead. This confession usually takes two forms. First, evangelicals affirm the historicity of Christ's resurrection over against liberal denials. This is an apologetic use of the resurrection. Second, they stress the resurrection as proving the efficacy of the cross. We know that Jesus's death saves because he is alive. These two strategies are sound. But they are incomplete.

Even the great book by Stott *The Cross of Christ*, which is required reading in my theology classes and from which I quoted to begin this essay, minimizes the saving significance of Jesus's resurrection.[8] In fact, it is difficult to find evangelical Christians who are exceptions to this rule.[9]

Scripture, however, teaches that Jesus's resurrection (never to be separated from his cross) is essential to his saving work. Three times in the Gospel of Mark Jesus predicts that his ministry would lead to Jerusalem, where he would die and rise (8:31; 9:31; 10:32–34). Twice in John's Gospel Jesus predicts his resurrection (2:19–22; 10:17–18) and twice he teaches that his resurrection saves (11:25–26; 14:19). The apostles' preaching in Acts mentions Jesus's crucifixion, but emphasizes his resurrection (2:24, 32; 3:15; 4:1–2, 10; 5:30; 13:33, 34, 37; 17:2–3, 18, 31).

Paul summarizes the gospel that he preached with these words: "For I delivered to you as of first importance what I also received: that Christ died for our sins in accordance with the Scriptures, that he was buried, that he was raised on the third day in accordance with the Scriptures" (1 Cor. 15:3–4). A little later he writes, "And if Christ has not been raised, your faith is futile and you are still in your sins" (v. 17). And repeatedly in his letters he broadcasts the saving impact of Jesus's resurrection (Rom. 4:25; 5:10; 10:9–10; 1 Cor. 15:14–22, 47–49; Eph. 2:4–7; Col. 1:18).

Please do not misunderstand: Jesus's crucifixion is an indispensable part of the gospel. I only want to urge that so is his resurrection. We must follow Scripture and hold together the salvific importance of our Lord's cross and empty tomb. Two chapters especially will help us: one on Jesus's resurrection and one on his role as second Adam.

Christ's Death and Resurrection Are Part of His Story

A third reason for reading this volume is that Jesus's death and resurrection do not stand alone. They are part of the greatest story ever told. They are preceded

---

[7] I. Howard Marshall, *Aspects of the Atonement: Cross and Resurrection in the Reconciling of God and Humanity* (London: Paternoster, 2007), viii.

[8] Stott, *The Cross of Christ*, 237–39.

[9] One is Richard Gaffin, *Resurrection and Redemption*, 2nd ed. (Phillipsburg, NJ: P&R, 1987).

by his incarnation and sinless life. His becoming a genuine human being and living victoriously are essential prerequisites for his death and resurrection. If he had not become one of us, he could not have died in our place. If he had sinned, his death could not have rescued others; he would have needed rescue himself.

Christ's cross and empty tomb are followed by his ascension, session (sitting at God's right hand), pouring out the Spirit at Pentecost, intercession, and second coming. These are the five essential results of his death and resurrection. Without them the salvation that he accomplished would not have been delivered to us. It would not have touched our lives now and in the future.

We only understand Jesus's saving death and resurrection properly within the framework of his story. I do not know of a resource that explains how each of the events in Jesus's story is redemptive. That is, until now. The first half of the book is devoted to a biblical exposition of Christ's nine saving events:

- incarnation
- sinless life
- death
- resurrection
- ascension
- session
- Pentecost
- intercession
- second coming

Christ's Death and Resurrection Are Interpreted by Pictures

Fourth, events are not self-interpreting, not even God's events. People living in the ancient Near East upon hearing of Yahweh's deliverance of the Israelites from Egyptian bondage would not automatically have believed that Israel's God was the only true and living God. They would have interpreted the exodus within the framework of their own worldview. Most would have concluded that Yahweh was stronger than the gods of Egypt, but few would have asked to receive circumcision and to join God's covenant people. To understand the exodus aright, they would have needed God's verbal revelation explaining its significance.

It is the same for the greatest events in history—Jesus's death and resurrection. People could have stood at the foot of Jesus's cross and not understood its meaning. In fact, some people did (Matt. 27:39–43)! Events do not interpret themselves; they need words to explain them. In his grace, therefore, God not only acts in history, but also explains the significance of his actions. Scripture, that is to say, is deed-word revelation.[10] This is also true for Christ's saving accomplishment. God not only acts in Jesus's cross and empty tomb to accomplish salvation; he also paints pictures that explain that saving work for us.

I confess that years ago as a doctoral student studying the work of Christ, I came to realize that I had only two pictures in mind. I knew that Christ had offered himself as a sacrifice and that he had paid the penalty for our sins. Then reading the Reformers opened my eyes to other pictures of his work. In addition to recording Jesus's nine events, Scripture also paints pictures that interpret the saving import of those events. There are many such pictures in the Bible, but I count six major pictures and devote a chapter to each:

- Christ our reconciler
- Christ our Redeemer
- Christ our legal substitute
- Christ our Victor
- Christ our second Adam
- Christ our sacrifice

I invite readers to accompany me on a journey as we explore Jesus's nine events and view Scripture's six pictures.

---

[10]See George Eldon Ladd, *A Theology of the New Testament* (Grand Rapids: Eerdmans, 1974), 31–32.

PART *One*

———————————— ✾ ————————————

E V E N T S

Introduction
to Jesus's Saving Events

We Are Not Saved by Our Works

Scripture repeatedly says that we cannot merit God's favor by our good deeds. Though it is sometimes overlooked, this is the message of the Old Testament.

> If you, O Lord, should mark iniquities,
>   O Lord, who could stand? (Ps. 130:3)

> Enter not into judgment with your servant,
>   for no one living is righteous before you. (Ps. 143:2)

> We have all become like one who is unclean,
>   and all our righteous deeds are like a polluted garment. (Isa. 64:6)

The New Testament also abundantly testifies to the fact that we cannot merit salvation by our good works.

> And by him everyone who believes is freed from everything from which you could not be freed by the law of Moses. (Acts 13:39)

> For by works of the law no human being will be justified in his sight, since through the law comes knowledge of sin. (Rom. 3:20)

> A person is not justified by works of the law but through faith in Jesus Christ, so we also have believed in Christ Jesus, in order to be justified by faith in Christ and not by works of the law, because by works of the law no one will be justified. (Gal. 2:16)

For by grace you have been saved through faith. And this is not your own doing; it is the gift of God, not a result of works, so that no one may boast. (Eph. 2:8–9)

But when the goodness and loving kindness of God our Savior appeared, he saved us, not because of works done by us in righteousness, but according to his own mercy, by the washing of regeneration and renewal of the Holy Spirit. (Titus 3:4–5)

God, who saved us and called us to a holy calling, not because of our works but because of his own purpose and grace, which he gave us in Christ Jesus before the ages began, . . . (2 Tim. 1:8–9)

We Are Saved by Jesus's Works

Scripture is clear—we cannot rescue ourselves from our sins. It is just as clear that Jesus Christ saves. Jesus himself said, "I am the way, and the truth, and the life. No one comes to the Father except through me" (John 14:6). His apostles proclaimed the same message. Listen to Peter: "This Jesus is the stone that was rejected by you, the builders, which has become the cornerstone. And there is salvation in no one else, for there is no other name under heaven given among men by which we must be saved" (Acts 4:11–12). And hear Paul: "Believe in the Lord Jesus, and you will be saved, you and your household" (Acts 16:31).

Robert Letham asks a good question and gives it a good answer:

What do we mean by "the work of Christ"? In short, we refer to all that Christ did when he came to this earth "for us and our salvation," all that he continues to do now that he is risen from the dead and at God's right hand, and all that he will do when he returns in glory at the end of the age.[1]

This is correct. In its broadest sense the work of Christ is vast in scope, stretching from his incarnation to his second coming. And my goal is to explore something of that vastness, but first things first. I must ask, What do people usually mean when they speak of the work of Christ? The expected answer is that Jesus died on the cross to save his people from their sins. While this answer is correct, it is incomplete. Listen as Paul gives his most famous summary of the gospel that he preached: "For I delivered to you as of first importance what I also received: that Christ died for our sins in accordance with the Scriptures, that he was buried, that he was raised on the third day in accordance with the Scriptures" (1 Cor. 15:3–4).

---

[1] Robert Letham, *The Work of Christ*, Contours of Christian Theology (Downers Grove, IL: InterVarsity, 1993), 18–19.

Jesus's Death and Resurrection Are His Main Saving Deeds

Jesus's crucifixion saves, but not apart from his empty tomb. A Savior who remained in the grave would not be a Savior. And Jesus's resurrection saves, but not apart from his cross. The two are inseparable in God's plan and should be inseparable in our thinking. What are the two most important of Christ's redemptive events? His death and resurrection.

Jesus himself predicted his two key saving events:

> And he began to teach them that the Son of Man must suffer many things and be rejected by the elders and the chief priests and the scribes and be killed and after three days rise again. (Mark 8:31; see also 9:31; 10:33–34)

> For this reason the Father loves me, because I lay down my life that I may take it up again. No one takes it from me, but I lay it down of my own accord. I have authority to lay it down, and I have authority to take it up again. This charge I have received from my Father. (John 10:17–18; see also 2:19)

Paul, in Romans, also joins Christ's death and resurrection:

> If you confess with your mouth that Jesus is Lord and believe in your heart that God raised him from the dead, you will be saved. For with the heart one believes and is justified, and with the mouth one confesses and is saved. (Rom. 10:9–10)

Many times Paul combines Jesus's death and resurrection as his primary saving events: Romans 4:25; 2 Corinthians 5:15; and Philippians 3:10. Luke does the same in Acts 2:22–24, as do the writer to the Hebrews in 1:3 and the apostle Peter in 1 Peter 1:11.

Jesus Performed Nine Saving Deeds

Unequivocally, Scripture highlights Jesus's death and resurrection when it speaks of his saving accomplishment. It does, however, paint a fuller picture and mentions seven *additional* aspects of Christ's saving work:

- *incarnation*
- *sinless life*
- death
- resurrection
- *ascension*
- *session*
- *Pentecost*

- *intercession*
- *second coming*

Brief definitions are in order. The *incarnation* is the Son of God's becoming a human being by a supernatural conception in Mary's womb. Christ's *sinless life* is his living from birth to death without sinning in thought, word, or deed. His *ascension* is his public return to the Father by "going up" from the Mount of Olives. His *session* is his sitting down at God the Father's right hand after his ascension. *Pentecost*, as much Christ's saving work as any other event on the list, is his pouring out the Holy Spirit on the church in newness and power. His *intercession* includes his perpetual presentation in heaven of his finished cross work and his prayers on behalf of his saints. His *second coming* is his return in glory at the end of the age to bless his people and judge his enemies.

New Testament writers frequently mention these nine saving events of Christ. I will cite one sample passage for each of the seven events other than the crucifixion and resurrection.

Jesus's incarnation saves. The incarnation of the Son of God is an essential precondition for his saving work, as Paul shows in Philippians 2:5–9:

> Christ Jesus, who, though he was in the form of God, did not count equality with God a thing to be grasped, but made himself nothing, taking the form of a servant, being born in the likeness of men. And being found in human form, he humbled himself by becoming obedient to the point of death, even death on a cross. Therefore God has highly exalted him and bestowed on him the name that is above every name.

Jesus's sinless life saves. Jesus's living a sinless life is necessary for him to be our Savior, as the writer to the Hebrews teaches (while mentioning Christ's ascension): "Since then we have a great high priest who has passed through the heavens, Jesus, the Son of God, let us hold fast our confession. For we do not have a high priest who is unable to sympathize with our weaknesses, but one who in every respect has been tempted as we are, yet without sin" (Heb. 4:14–15).

Jesus's ascension saves. Jesus's ascension is also a part of his saving work, as Paul testifies in a confession of faith (combined with his incarnation and resurrection):

> Great indeed, we confess, is the mystery of godliness:
>
> > He was manifested in the flesh,
> >   vindicated by the Spirit,
> >   seen by angels,

> proclaimed among the nations,
>   believed on in the world,
>   taken up in glory. (1 Tim. 3:16)

Jesus's session saves. Jesus's session belongs to his saving events, as the writer to the Hebrews reminds us:

> And every priest stands daily at his service, offering repeatedly the same sacrifices, which can never take away sins. But when Christ had offered for all time a single sacrifice for sins, he sat down at the right hand of God. . . . For by a single offering he has perfected for all time those who are being sanctified. (Heb. 10:11–12, 14)

Jesus's work at Pentecost saves. Pentecost is as much a part of Jesus's saving work as his death and resurrection, and Peter affirms its importance in his Pentecost sermon (along with Jesus's resurrection, ascension, and session): "This Jesus God raised up, and of that we all are witnesses. Being therefore exalted at the right hand of God, and having received from the Father the promise of the Holy Spirit, he has poured out this that you yourselves are seeing and hearing" (Acts 2:32–33).

Jesus's intercession saves. Jesus's intercession is a vital saving event, as Hebrews reveals: "He holds his priesthood permanently, because he continues forever. Consequently, he is able to save to the uttermost those who draw near to God through him, since he always lives to make intercession for them" (Heb. 7:24–25).

Jesus's second coming saves. Jesus's second coming is the final aspect of his saving work, as Hebrews 9:28 explains, juxtaposing it with his atoning death: "So Christ, having been offered once to bear the sins of many, will appear a second time, not to deal with sin but to save those who are eagerly waiting for him."

Scripture Gives Many Combinations of Jesus's Saving Deeds

The New Testament puts Jesus's saving events in many combinations. In addition to the passages cited above, Paul brings together Christ's resurrection and session (Eph. 1:20–21), his resurrection, session, and second coming (Col. 3:1–4), his resurrection and second coming (1 Thess. 1:10), his death, resurrection, and second coming (1 Thess. 4:14), and his incarnation, crucifixion, and resurrection (2 Tim. 2:8).

Moreover, there are two passages that each include four saving events (in addition to Acts 2:32–33, quoted above). First, Paul joins Jesus's crucifixion, resurrection, session, and intercession: "Who is to condemn? Christ Jesus is the one who died—more than that, who was raised—who is at the right hand of

God, who indeed is interceding for us" (Rom. 8:34). Second, the apostle Peter unites Christ's cross, resurrection, ascension, and session.

> For Christ also suffered once for sins, the righteous for the unrighteous, that he might bring us to God, being put to death in the flesh but made alive in the spirit . . . through the resurrection of Jesus Christ, who has gone into heaven and is at the right hand of God, with angels, authorities, and powers having been subjected to him. (1 Pet. 3:18, 21–22)

The classic statement of the breadth of Christ's saving work is John Calvin's hymn of praise to Christ:

> If we seek salvation, we are taught by the very name of Jesus that it is "of him" [1 Cor. 1:30]. If we seek any other gifts of the Spirit, they will be found in his anointing. If we seek strength, it lies in his dominion; if purity, in his conception; if gentleness, it appears in his birth. For by his birth he was made like us in all respects [Heb. 2:17] that he might learn to feel our pain [cf. Heb. 5:2]. If we seek redemption, it lies in his passion; if acquittal, in his condemnation; if remission of the curse, in his cross [Gal. 3:13]; if satisfaction, in his sacrifice; if purification, in his blood, if reconciliation, in his descent into hell; if mortification of the flesh, in his tomb; if newness of life, in his resurrection; if immortality, in the same; if inheritance of the Heavenly Kingdom, in his entrance into heaven; if protection, if security, if abundant supply of all blessings, in his Kingdom; if untroubled expectation of judgment, in the power given him to judge. In short, since rich store of every kind of goods abounds in him, let us drink our fill from this fountain, and from no other.[2]

Conclusion

The New Testament writers regard Jesus's death and resurrection as the central acts of history. His cross and empty tomb are redemptive. The same writers regard two prior events as necessary preconditions to his death and resurrection—his incarnation and sinless life. And they regard five subsequent events as necessary results of his death and resurrection—his ascension, session, Pentecost, intercession, and second coming. Christ's saving accomplishment, then, with a narrow focus, consists of his death and resurrection. But when viewed with a broader lens, it includes everything from his incarnation to his return. It is good for us to study each of his nine redemptive deeds. And that is exactly what the following nine chapters do. Each chapter will trace one event through Scripture and then summarize what part that event plays in Christ's saving work.

---

[2]John Calvin, *Institutes of the Christian Religion*, ed. John T. McNeill, trans. Ford Lewis Battles, 2 vols. (Philadelphia: Westminster, 1960), 1:527–28 (2.16.19).

Incarnation
Sinless Life
Death
Resurrection
Ascension
Session
Pentecost
Intercession
Second Coming

Chapter 1

Christ's Incarnation

Now it was of the greatest importance for us that he who was to be our Mediator be both true God and true man. . . . Since our iniquities, like a cloud cast between us and him, had completely estranged us from the Kingdom of Heaven, no man, unless he belonged to God, could serve as the intermediary to restore peace. But who might reach to him? Any one of Adam's children? No, like their father, all of them were terrified at the sight of God. . . . What then? The situation would surely have been hopeless had the very majesty of God not descended to us, since it was not in our power to ascend to him. Hence, it was necessary for the Son of God to become for us "Immanuel, that is, God with us," and in such a way that his divinity and our human nature might by mutual connection grow together. . . . In undertaking to describe the Mediator, Paul then, with good reason, distinctly reminds us that He is man: "One mediator between God and men, the man Jesus Christ."[1]

Calvin is correct. The Mediator had unique qualifications. He had to be both God and man to save us sinners. He had to be God because only God could save us. He had to become man because the work of salvation had to be performed by a human being for human beings. How God became a man is the subject of this chapter. Orthodox christology begins from above with God the Son, the second person of the Trinity, who, according to the

---

[1]John Calvin, *Institutes of the Christian Religion*, ed. John T. McNeill, trans. Ford Lewis Battles, 2 vols. (Philadelphia: Westminster, 1960), 1:464 (2.12.1).

Apostles' Creed, "was conceived by the Holy Spirit, and born of the Virgin Mary."

Jesus's incarnation saves. It does not save in and of itself, by the mere fact of God's becoming a man. It does not save apart from Christ's death and resurrection. But it is an essential prerequisite for those saving events. We will investigate the Old Testament, the Synoptic Gospels, the Gospel of John, and the Epistles before drawing conclusions.

Old Testament Background

Isaiah 7:14

Seven hundred years before Messiah's birth, Isaiah prophesied: "Therefore the Lord himself will give you a sign. Behold, the virgin shall conceive and bear a son, and shall call his name Immanuel" (Isa. 7:14). It is difficult to understand how this prophecy relates to its historical context in evil King Ahaz's day, and faithful interpreters disagree. Some favor a single fulfillment view that understands Isaiah 7:14 as only predicting the coming of Christ. Others favor a double fulfillment view that understands the verse as finding an immediate fulfillment in Ahaz's day and a long-range fulfillment in Christ. We cannot here deal with the issue in detail.[2]

The important point is that Matthew regards it as a prophecy of Christ's virgin birth:

All this took place to fulfill what the Lord had spoken by the prophet:

> "Behold, the virgin shall conceive and bear a son,
>   and they shall call his name Immanuel"

(which means, God with us). (Matt. 1:22–23)

Although critical Old Testament scholars have questioned whether *almah* should be translated "virgin" in Isaiah 7:14, conservatives generally agree that in that context it means "a young woman who is unmarried and sexually chaste,"[3] and there is no doubt that the Greek word Matthew uses (παρθένος, *parthenos*, following the LXX) only means "virgin."

---

[2] Raymond Ortlund's note on Isa. 7:14 in the *ESV Study Bible* describes both single fulfillment and double fulfillment views, and notes that faithful interpreters are found on both sides of the debate.
[3] Ibid.

Isaiah 9:6

Later, Isaiah foretold that the Messiah would be a divine-human ruler over Israel (and the world) who would bring peace and reign forever:

> For to us a child is born,
>> to us a son is given;
> and the government shall be upon his shoulder,
>> and his name shall be called
> Wonderful Counselor, Mighty God,
>> Everlasting Father, Prince of Peace. (Isa. 9:6)

Alec Motyer's words deserve quotation:

> The emphasis falls not on what the child will do when grown up but on the mere fact of his birth. . . . He is *born* as from human parentage and *given* as from God. . . . The decisions of a king make or break a kingdom and a kingdom designed to be everlasting demands a wisdom like that of the everlasting God. In this case, like God because he is God, *the Mighty God* (*ʾel gibbor*), the title given to the Lord himself in 10:21–22. . . . God has come to birth, bringing with him the qualities which guarantee his people's preservation (wisdom) and liberation (warrior strength).[4]

Isaiah looked forward and saw the coming one, who was to be virgin born, even God himself entering into human life. He would sit on David's throne forever and bring freedom to Israel and the nations (Isa. 9:7). Although we cannot be certain how much Isaiah understood when "the Spirit of Christ in" him "predicted the . . . Christ" (1 Pet. 1:11), the prophet saw dimly the things promised "and greeted them from afar" (Heb. 11:13).

The Event in the Synoptic Gospels

Before Jesus's birth, God announces to Israel that he will send the promised Redeemer. The priest Zechariah, John the Baptist's father, filled with the Spirit, prophesies that in sending John as the forerunner of the Messiah, God

> has visited and redeemed his people
> and has raised up a horn of salvation. (Luke 1:68–69)

---

[4] J. Alec Motyer, *The Prophecy of Isaiah: An Introduction and Commentary* (Downers Grove, IL: Inter-Varsity, 1993), 101–2, italics original.

Mary in her Magnificat rejoices that in sending the Promised One, God "has helped his servant Israel, in remembrance of his mercy" in fulfillment of Old Testament promises (v. 54). Astonishingly, the glory of God shines on poor shepherds in their fields at night, and an angel of the Lord announces to them, "For unto you is born this day in the city of David a Savior, who is Christ the Lord" (2:11).

Before Jesus's birth, God proclaims concerning Mary, "That which is conceived in her is from the Holy Spirit," and the newborn is to be named Jesus (Matt. 1:20; Luke 1:31). Why? The angel of the Lord's reassuring words to Joseph link the Messiah's name to his mission: "She will bear a son, and you shall call his name Jesus, for he will save his people from their sins" (Matt. 1:21). "Jesus" means "the Lord saves."

The godly Simeon was told by God that he would live to see the Messiah. He does that very thing when he holds the eight-day-old baby Jesus in his arms and blesses God,

> My eyes have seen your salvation . . .
> a light for revelation to the Gentiles,
>   and for glory to your people Israel. (Luke 2:30, 32)

The aged prophetess Anna remained in the temple worshiping night and day. And when Jesus was presented in the temple, "at that very hour she began to give thanks to God and to speak of him to all who were waiting for the redemption of Jerusalem" (v. 38).

So, God brings an amazing message to those who have ears to hear his words and eyes to see his kingdom: the baby Jesus is the Savior. He saves not as a baby, however, but as an adult, who will live a sinless life, die on a cross, and rise to live again.

Teaching in the Gospel of John

Jesus Is the Light

The prologue to John's Gospel is justly famous. It introduces many themes that the rest of the Gospel develops. But its main theme is the incarnation of the Son of God. John does not call him the Son right away, but rather the Word and the light. John uses a literary form known as a chiasm to highlight the incarnation. Regular parallelism follows the pattern AB AB or ABC ABC, and so on, in which letters stand for ideas. Inverted parallelism, or chiasm, reverses the pattern: AB BA or ABC CBA, and so forth. John's prologue forms a chiasm using the pattern AB BA.

The Son of God is called "the Word" in verse 1 and "the light" in verse 7. If John were following regular parallelism, he would first speak of the incarnation in terms of the Word becoming flesh and next in terms of the light coming into the world. Instead, he reverses the order. Verse 9 says, "The true light, which enlightens everyone, was coming into the world." Then verse 14 says, "And the Word became flesh and dwelt among us."

Here is the pattern:

A The Word (v. 1)

   B The light (v. 7)

   B The light comes into the world (v. 9)

A The Word becomes flesh (v. 14)

By using this pattern John rivets readers' attention on the incarnation. He shows that the incarnation was to bring salvation to humankind. When he writes, "The true light was coming into the world" (John 1:9), he pictures the world as dark, devoid of the knowledge of God. Christ comes as the light, the divine-human illuminator, who enlightens everyone with whom he comes in contact in his earthly ministry. Jesus as the light brings saving knowledge to all who believe in him, although sadly many reject him (vv. 10–11).

The grand illustration of this is when Jesus, the light of the world (John 8:12; 9:5), gives physical and spiritual sight to a man born blind. The former blind man believes in Jesus, worships him, and enjoys the forgiveness of sins found in him (9:38–41). But for those who reject Jesus, his light blinds them and hardens them in their sins (vv. 40–41).

John's favorite way of showing Jesus as the light is to present him as the revealer of the invisible Father. As such the Son brings messages from the Father into the world. The Son reveals the Father so well that to believe in the Son's word is to believe in the Father and gain eternal life: "Truly, truly, I say to you, whoever hears my word and believes him who sent me has eternal life. He does not come into judgment, but has passed from death to life" (John 5:24).

Jesus's role as revealer and light is made plain in John 12:44–50:

> Whoever believes in me, believes not in me but in him who sent me. And whoever sees me sees him who sent me. I have come into the world as light, so that whoever believes in me may not remain in darkness. If anyone hears my words and does

not keep them, I do not judge him; for I did not come to judge the world but to save the world. The one who rejects me and does not receive my words has a judge; the word that I have spoken will judge him on the last day. For I have not spoken on my own authority, but the Father who sent me has himself given me a commandment—what to say and what to speak. And I know that his commandment is eternal life. What I say, therefore, I say as the Father has told me.

Of course, the saving knowledge that Jesus the revealer imparts is not apart from his saving death and resurrection. He himself teaches: "I am the good shepherd. The good shepherd lays down his life for the sheep" (John 10:11), and "I lay down my life that I may take it up again" (John 10:17). A crucial part of the revealer's message is that he must die and be raised from the dead on behalf of his people.

Jesus Is the Word

John also portrays the Son as the preincarnate Word. In this role the Son was face-to-face with the Father before creation. He was also equal with the Father as the phrase "the Word was God" demonstrates.[5] In addition, he was the Father's agent in creating everything, as the affirmations and denials in John 1:1–3 show. This same eternal Word "became flesh and dwelt among us." The second person of the Trinity became a flesh-and-blood human being. Furthermore, he lived among his fellow human beings for thirty-three years, three and a half of which were devoted to public ministry. As a result the apostles and other witnesses saw "his glory, glory as of the only Son from the Father, full of grace and truth." That is, the incarnate Word revealed in his humanity divine qualities of glory, grace, and faithfulness as John points out in 2:11 and 11:4, 40.

Jesus received a divided response from humankind (his creatures and covenant people Israel). Most "did not know him" and "did not receive him" (John 1:10, 11). "But to all who did receive him, who believed in his name, he gave the right to become children of God" (v. 12). Even as we use words to reveal our inmost thoughts, so God used the Word, his unique Son, to reveal his mind as well (v. 18). The Word came as the Savior, and all who believed in him were freed from their bondage to sin (8:34, 36) and adopted into the family of God. The incarnate Word is the God-man who "from his divine fullness" gives "grace upon grace" to needy sinners (1:16).

---

[5]For discussion, see D. A. Carson, *The Gospel According to John*, The Pillar New Testament Commentary (Grand Rapids: Eerdmans, 1991), 117.

Once more, it is important to remember that the incarnate Word does not save apart from the cross and empty tomb. Indeed, the Word is also "the Lamb of God, who takes away the sin of the world" (John 1:29) by giving himself as a sacrifice. The Word made flesh is the one who predicted his resurrection when he said of the temple that was his body, "Destroy this temple, and in three days I will raise it up" (2:19).

Teaching in the Epistles

If the Gospels tell the story and provide some theological interpretation of it, the Epistles assume the Gospels' story and provide much theological interpretation. So it is that Paul speaks of the incarnation when explaining God's intention to redeem his new covenant people.

Galatians 4:4–5

> But when the fullness of time had come, God sent forth his Son, born of woman, born under the law, to redeem those who were under the law, so that we might receive adoption as sons.

Paul has been speaking of three covenants: the Abrahamic covenant, the Mosaic covenant coming 430 years later and subordinate to it, and the new covenant in Christ, which fulfilled the promise made to Abraham (Gal. 3:16–29). Now Paul speaks of the arrival of the One who ratifies the new covenant: "But when the fullness of time had come, God sent forth his Son" (4:4). Paul views the incarnation from the perspective of heaven; it involved God's sending his Son into the world.

Viewed from the perspective of earth, the Son was "born of woman" (v. 4). This succinctly speaks of the Christ's virginal conception in Mary's womb and subsequent birth. Why did God send his Son into the world to be born of Mary? The next words provide a hint: he was "born under the law" (v. 4). Paul means that the Messiah was a Jewish boy, whose birth obligated him to keep the law of God's covenant people. And that is what Jesus did, perfectly, his whole life.

Next Paul connects the incarnation with its purpose—redemption: "God sent forth his Son, born of woman, born under the law, to redeem those who were under the law" (v. 4). The purpose of the incarnation was to facilitate redemption. For the Son to redeem us, he had to become one of us. No incarnation, no redemption. But the good news is: *incarnation*, and therefore redemption.

The apostle gives an important result of redemption—adoption. The Son came "so that we might receive adoption as sons" (Gal. 4:4). "Adoption is an act of God's free grace, whereby we are received into the number and have a right to all the privileges of the sons of God."[6] Paul thus mentions Christ's redeeming work but does not expand on it. He did that in the previous chapter: "Christ redeemed us from the curse of the law by becoming a curse for us" (3:13). That is, the Son endured the penalty of the law, condemnation on the accursed cross, in order to redeem all Jews and Gentiles who believe in him.

The purpose of the incarnation was to bring about redemption, which involved Christ's bearing in his person the law's threat of judgment, so that his people might become the sons and daughters of the living God.

Philippians 2:5–8

After calling for unity in surrounding texts (1:27; 4:2), Paul exhorts his beloved Philippians to unity in 2:1–4:

> So if there is any encouragement in Christ, any comfort from love, any partici-
> pation in the Spirit, any affection and sympathy, complete my joy by being of
> the same mind, having the same love, being in full accord and of one mind. Do
> nothing from rivalry or conceit, but in humility count others more significant
> than yourselves. Let each of you look not only to his own interests, but also to
> the interests of others.

What is the apostle's strategy to promote unity in the Philippian congregation? He urges them to follow Christ's example of humility in their dealings
with one another.

> Have this mind among yourselves, which is yours in Christ Jesus, who, though he
> was in the form of God, did not count equality with God a thing to be grasped,
> but made himself nothing, taking the form of a servant, being born in the like-
> ness of men. And being found in human form, he humbled himself by becoming
> obedient to the point of death, even death on a cross. (Phil. 2:5–8)

This is Scripture's boldest statement of Jesus's two states, the state of humiliation (from birth to burial) and the state of exaltation (from resurrection to
return). Paul begins and ends this section with references to Christ's deity.
First, he says that Christ existed "in the form of God" (v. 6), something only
true of God himself. He ends this section (vv. 10–11) with an allusion to Isaiah
45:22–25, where God himself says, "I am God, and there is no other" (Isa. 45:22).

---

[6]Westminster Shorter Catechism, 34.

Paul applies directly to Jesus what Isaiah said was true of God alone. He regards Jesus as equal with God.

Within this picture frame of affirmations of Christ's equality with God, Paul speaks volumes about the condescension of God. He paints a vivid picture of the incarnation and its effects. The divine Son "humbled himself," "made himself nothing." Does this mean that he divested himself of his divinity, as some have taught, taking the words "he emptied [ἐκένωσεν, *ekenōsen*] himself" literally as an "emptying" of some divine attributes? No, because the very next words show that Paul's language here is metaphorical. The Son "emptied himself" ["made himself nothing," ESV] by "taking the form of a servant." This is how God condescended—he became a servant. And Paul does not have an angelic servant in mind, for he says that the Son was "born in the likeness of men" (Phil. 2:7). The One who existed in "the form of God" took "the form of a servant." Almighty God became a servant! He did this when he was born in human likeness.

But even this is not the full extent of the Son's humiliation. He also "humbled himself by becoming obedient to the point of death, even death on a cross" (v. 8). What condescension! God the Creator became one of his human creatures and then not a king or a prince, but a bondslave. He humbled himself by obeying his Father unto death to fulfill his mission. And not just any death, but a scandalous death by crucifixion!

So, the apostle Paul interprets the incarnation of the Son of God as a great act of condescension, an act that led to his crucifixion. It was also an act that led to his exaltation as the next three verses so eloquently testify.

> Therefore God has highly exalted him and bestowed on him the name that is above every name, so that at the name of Jesus every knee should bow, in heaven and on earth and under the earth, and every tongue confess that Jesus Christ is Lord, to the glory of God the Father. (Phil. 2:9–11)

The state of humiliation is followed by Christ's triumphant state of exaltation (vv. 9–11). God does not leave his Son on the cross but highly exalts him (v. 9). This includes everything from Jesus's resurrection to his future return. A discussion of these glorious things will have to wait for a later chapter.

Now the question begs to be asked, why? Paul answers in another epistle: "God shows his love for us in that while we were still sinners, Christ died for us" (Rom. 5:8). In context Paul portrays the incarnate Son as the great example of love and humility. Christ's example is powerful. He counted the Philippians (and the rest of his people) as more significant than himself (cf. Phil. 2:3). They were not more significant, but he counted them so when he loved them and gave himself for them. In addition, he was looking not only to his own interests, but also to the interests of others (v. 4), namely, the Philippians and all other believers.

Paul wants Euodia and Syntyche (4:2) and the rest of the congregation to remember the reason they are in the congregation—because of Christ's monumental act of humility and love. Paul wants them to follow Christ's selfless example. In doing this, they will promote unity in their church.

Hebrews 2:9, 14–15, 16–17

No chapter of Scripture teaches the incarnation more emphatically than Hebrews 2. This chapter contains at least three major pictures of Christ's saving work, divinely given interpretations of the meaning of the Savior's death and resurrection. I will not develop these three pictures now but rather note that each one is preceded by an affirmation of the incarnation.

> But we see him who for a little while was made lower than the angels, namely Jesus, crowned with glory and honor because of the suffering of death, so that by the grace of God he might taste death for everyone. (Heb. 2:9)

The writer to the Hebrews quotes Psalm 8, which, within a frame of praise to God for his majesty, celebrates the creational blessings of Adam and Eve. Two blessings are singled out: the glory and honor with which our first parents were endowed and their dominion over the animal kingdom (Ps. 8:4–6, quoted in Heb. 2:6–8). After quoting the psalm, the author refers to Jesus. Though Psalm 8 originally referred to Adam and Eve, what it says pertains to Jesus in his incarnation. He too "for a little while was made lower than the angels" (Heb. 2:9). He, the second person of the Holy Trinity, became a man so as to be "crowned with glory and honor because of the suffering of death, so that by the grace of God he might taste death for everyone" (v. 9).

Jesus is here portrayed as "the last Adam" and "the second man" (1 Cor. 15:45, 47). He is only the second human being created as God intended—in fellowship with him and without sin (Eve is not included in the Bible's headship theology). And he is "the last Adam" because he does what no one before him or after him could do; as the unique Redeemer he has no successor. Via his death and resurrection he restores the creational blessings of glory and honor and dominion forfeited by the first Adam in his fall. And it is his incarnation that makes all of that possible.

The author of Hebrews introduces a second picture of Christ's saving work with another reference to the incarnation:

Since therefore the children share in flesh and blood, he himself likewise partook of the same things, that through death he might destroy the one who has the power of death, that is, the devil, and deliver all those who through fear of death were subject to lifelong slavery. (Heb. 2:14–15)

This is the Christus Victor theme, made famous by Gustaf Aulén's book, which gave its name to this atonement motif.[7] God the Son comes into his world to fight and overcome his and his people's enemies: Satan, the demons, sin, the grave, death, hell, and the world understood as an organized system of evil opposed to God (1 John 2:15). How does he win this mighty victory? Through his victorious life, death, resurrection, exaltation to heaven, and return.

What is the essential prerequisite for all of this to occur? The incarnation of the Son of God, of course. Because the people he came to save "share in flesh and blood, he himself likewise partook of the same things" (Heb. 2:14). The Son, a divine title for Christ according to Hebrews 1, partook of human flesh and blood in his incarnation. The Son of God truly became a son of Adam.

Why? The writer gives two reasons: to defeat the Devil and deliver those fearful of God's wrath: "that through death he might destroy the one who has the power of death, that is, the devil, and deliver all those who through fear of death were subject to lifelong slavery" (vv. 14–15). By his death on the cross Christ, our champion, vanquishes his ancient foe and redeems his people. The Devil is a usurper who uses death to terrorize poor sinners. Christ overcomes the strong man and frees his prisoners (Matt. 12:28–29). Once more we underscore the key fact: it is the incarnation that brings the Son from heaven to earth so he can be Christus Victor.

The writer to the Hebrews introduces yet a third picture of the atonement by speaking of the incarnation again:

For surely it is not angels that he helps, but he helps the offspring of Abraham. Therefore he had to be made like his brothers in every respect, so that he might become a merciful and faithful high priest in the service of God, to make propitiation for the sins of the people. (Heb. 2:16–17)

The dominant picture of Christ the Savior in Hebrews is neither that of second Adam nor that of Victor, but Christ as the great High Priest and sacrifice. Already in chapter 1 the author has introduced this picture in a few words: "After making purification for sins, he sat down at the right hand of the Majesty on

---

[7]Gustaf Aulén, *Christus Victor: An Historical Study of the Three Main Types of the Idea of the Atonement*, trans. A. G. Hebert (1931; repr., New York: Macmillan, 1969).

high" (1:3). And Scripture's grandest exposition of Christ as priest and sacrifice occurs in Hebrews 7–10.

Perhaps this theme is put last in chapter 2 to give it prominence; readers are left with it still before their eyes as they begin chapter 3. The important point at present is to see that it too begins with the incarnation. After saying that Christ came to save human beings, not angels, the writer specifies, "Therefore he had to be made like his brothers in every respect, so that he might become a merciful and faithful high priest" (Heb. 2:17).

Hebrews 1 teaches that to be our great High Priest Christ had to be divine. Hebrews 2 adds that to be our great High Priest Christ had to become human. As the divine-human priest, the Son of God made "propitiation for the sins of the people" (v. 17). Here Christ's sacrifice is a propitiation, not only expiating believers' sin (Heb. 9:26), but also enabling God to maintain his moral integrity and save sinners.

In Hebrews 2 then, the writer presents Jesus's work of salvation using three pictures. Christ is second Adam, Victor, and priest. The writer introduces each picture by telling of the incarnation. Plainly, it is the essential precondition for Jesus's cross and empty tomb.

Connecting the Dots: Christ's Incarnation Saves

Gordon Fee's highlighting of the crucial importance of the incarnation for Pauline theology introduces our summary of the teaching of all of Scripture that Christ's incarnation is essential for salvation:

> Paul clearly understood Christ the Savior himself to be divine; he was not simply a divine agent. . . . Thus the full deity of Christ is never something Paul argues for; rather, it is the constant presupposition of everything that he says about Christ as Savior. . . . To be sure, Paul speaks only rarely of the "Son of God who loved me and gave himself for me" (Gal. 2:20); but the very fact that in this case he identifies Christ as "the Son of God" suggests that what overwhelms Paul about such love is not simply Christ's death on his behalf. What lies behind such language is the overwhelming sense that the preexistent, and therefore divine, Son of God is the one who by incarnation as well as crucifixion "died for me." To put the matter another way, the deity of Christ is therefore for Paul no small matter; it is rather of central significance to his understanding of, and devotion to, his Lord.[8]

---

[8]Gordon D. Fee, *Pauline Christology: An Exegetical-Theological Study* (Peabody, MA: Hendrickson, 2007), 511–12.

As Isaiah prophesied, the virgin-born Immanuel, even God himself, would enter human life, rule on David's throne forever, and liberate Israel and the nations (Isa. 7:14; 9:6). In the fullness of time, God does a startling thing—in mercy he sends a baby to redeem his people from their sins, both believing Jews and Gentiles. Incredibly, an angel from heaven appears with God's glory shining at night and announces to lowly shepherds, "For unto you is born this day in the city of David a Savior, who is Christ the Lord" (Luke 2:11).

John presents Jesus as the light coming into the world and the Word become flesh (John 1:9, 14). He is God incarnate who reveals the invisible Father to human beings. And, in fulfillment of Jesus's own prophecies, he later lays down his life and takes it up again (10:17–18).

Paul testifies that "God sent forth his Son, born of woman . . . to redeem those who were under the law" so we might become the children of God (Gal. 4:4–5). He who existed in "the form of God" took "the form of a servant, being born in the likeness of men" so he could die on the cross. As a result "God has highly exalted him" in his resurrection and ascension and will universally exalt him when he comes again (Phil. 2:6–7, 9).

After teaching the Son's deity in chapter 1, Hebrews 2 puts great emphasis on the saving significance of his partaking of flesh and blood. In order for him to fulfill his roles of second Adam, Victor, and priest, it was necessary for him to become a genuine human being (Heb. 2:9, 14, 17).

So then, does Christ's incarnation save? The answer depends on what exactly is being asked. Does Christ's incarnation save in and of itself? The answer is no. Salvation does not come automatically to humankind when the eternal Son of God becomes a man. But does Christ's incarnation save as the essential precondition for the saving deeds that follow? The answer is yes. Only a divine-human Redeemer would do. If the Son had not become a human being, he could not have lived a sinless human life, died, and risen again to deliver his people. He could not have ascended, sat down at God's right hand, poured out the Holy Spirit, interceded for his own, and come again. To perform these saving works, he had to become one of us. In that important sense, Christ's incarnation saves.

Philip Edgcumbe Hughes memorably underscores the nexus between the incarnation and Christ's saving work:

> But Bethlehem is not the whole story. The birth that took place there was not an end in itself but a means to an end. The end to which Bethlehem was a means was Calvary, and unless Bethlehem is seen in direct relationship to Calvary its true purpose and significance are missed. The cradle was the start of the road that led to the cross; and the purpose of Christ's coming was achieved not in the cradle

but on the cross. . . . Thus Jesus declared of himself that "the Son of Man came . . . *to give his life as a ransom for many*" (Mk. 10:45), and St. Paul proclaimed that "Christ Jesus came into the world *to save sinners*" (1 Tim. 1:15).[9]

Bethlehem is not the whole story, but it is the essential beginning of the story. The center of the story is Jesus's death and resurrection. But between the incarnation and the death and resurrection lies Jesus's sinless life, the subject of the next chapter.

---

[9]Philip Edgcumbe Hughes, *The True Image: The Origin and Destiny of Man in Christ* (Grand Rapids: Eerdmans, 1989), 219, italics original.

Incarnation
Sinless Life
Death
Resurrection
Ascension
Session
Pentecost
Intercession
Second Coming

Chapter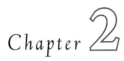

Christ's Sinless Life

This sinlessness [of Christ] involves two elements.

First, Christ was free of actual sin. He betrays no consciousness of guilt. He never prays for forgiveness. He never confesses short-coming. On the contrary, all he did, thought or said conformed exactly to the will of God. He fulfilled all righteousness (Mt. 3:15).

Secondly, he was free from inherent sin. Nowhere in the structures of his being was there any sin. Satan had no foot-hold in him. There was no lust. There was no affinity with sin. There was no proclivity to sin. There was no possibility of temptation from within. In no respect was he fallen and in no respect was his nature corrupt.

Until the nineteenth century this was the virtually unanimous confession of the church.[1]

Donald Macleod is correct: the sinlessness of Christ was the historic position of the Christian church until the Enlightenment. This fact prompts two questions this chapter will seek to answer: Does Scripture teach the sinlessness of Christ? If so, what theological significance does Christ's sinlessness have?

---

[1]Donald Macleod, *The Person of Christ*, Contours of Christian Theology (Downers Grove, IL: InterVarsity, 1998), 221–22.

Jesus's Sinlessness Is Predicted in the Old Testament

The Old Testament in numerous passages predicts events in Jesus's life and ministry. At least one of them predicts his sinless life on earth after the incarnation and before his death and resurrection.

Isaiah 53

Seven hundred years before Jesus's coming, Isaiah prophesies his death and resurrection in this famous song about the Servant of the Lord, the Messiah. He also predicts some details of his earthly life. The message of the Servant's saving accomplishment will appear almost too good to be true.

> Who has believed what he has heard from us?
>   And to whom has the arm of the Lord been revealed? (Isa. 53:1)

There are a number of reasons why this message is hard to believe. One is the obscurity of the Servant.

> For he grew up before him like a young plant,
>   and like a root out of dry ground. (v. 2)

Jesus's fellow Galileans do not immediately believe that he is the Messiah (see Matt. 13:53–58). In addition, the Servant does not possess a royal bearing, as many Jews expected the Messiah to have.

> He had no form or majesty that we should look at him
>   and no beauty that we should desire him. (Isa. 53:2)

Furthermore, the majority response of the covenant people to their Messiah is not one of welcome and joy.

> He was despised and rejected by men;
>   a man of sorrows, and acquainted with grief;
> and as one from whom men hide their faces
>   he was despised, and we esteemed him not. (vv. 3–4)

Isaiah also, in two places in the Servant Song, prophesies that Messiah will be sinless. This involves not transgressing in action or speech, reflecting his righteous character. First, when Isaiah predicts that Messiah will die with wicked men, he also foretells his purity in deed and word:

> And they made his grave with the wicked
>> and with a rich man in his death,
> although he had done no violence,
>> and there was no deceit in his mouth. (v. 9)

Peter quotes this verse when encouraging his readers to follow Jesus's example of suffering unjust punishment patiently (1 Pet. 2:21–23). How difficult it is not to return evil for evil but to keep one's tongue in such circumstances! And that is exactly what Isaiah said that the Servant would do. And he did.

In fact, a few verses later, when discussing the Servant's suffering and bearing the sins of many, Isaiah testifies to a holy use of Messiah's tongue:

> He poured out his soul to death . . .
> yet he bore the sin of many,
>> and makes intercession for the transgressors. (Isa. 53:12)

Even while dying a horrible death and bearing others' sins, he prays for them. That is remarkable, indeed.

Second, when predicting that the Servant's work will be the basis for the justification of sinners, Isaiah describes the Servant's character in one powerful word:

> By his knowledge shall the righteous one, my servant,
>> make many to be accounted righteous,
>> and he shall bear their iniquities. (v. 11)

Isaiah calls him "the *righteous* one, my servant," and that prediction accords exactly with the New Testament portrait of him.

It is striking that in the most famous of Old Testament passages predicting Messiah's death and resurrection, the prophet Isaiah predicts that the coming Servant of the Lord will be righteous in character and will demonstrate that by not sinning in deed or speech.

Jesus's Sinlessness Is Revealed in the New Testament

All parts of the New Testament testify that the incarnate Son of God was without sin: the Gospels, Acts, Pauline Epistles, General Epistles, and Revelation.

The Gospels

Luke. In response to Mary's question, the angel Gabriel explains to her how she, a virgin, will conceive: "The Holy Spirit will come upon you, and the power of the Most High will overshadow you; therefore the child to be born will be called holy—the Son of God" (Luke 1:35). The Virgin Mary will conceive due to a miracle of the Holy Spirit within her womb. The result? Even before Jesus's birth, God announces that he will be the holy Son of God.

Mark. One evidence of the Gospels' authenticity is that they present the disciples' gradually coming to understand who Jesus is. On more than one occasion the Father speaks from heaven, declaring the identity of his beloved Son (Matt. 3:17; 17:5). It is true that Peter, in his famous declaration, confesses, "You are the Christ, the Son of the living God" (Matt. 16:16). But it is also true that Peter does not arrive at this conclusion on his own; as Jesus declares, "Flesh and blood has not revealed this to you, but my Father who is in heaven" (v. 17). The Gospels record the disciples' struggling to understand who Jesus is, often taking one step forward and two backward.

It is ironic that the demons have a better understanding of Christ than the disciples prior to his resurrection. We see this in an early encounter between Jesus and a man with an unclean spirit. As soon as the man meets Jesus, the evil spirit within him cries out: "What have you to do with us, Jesus of Nazareth? Have you come to destroy us? I know who you are—the Holy One of God" (Mark 1:24). In keeping with the views of contemporary magical texts, scholars believe that these words are the demon's attempt to control Jesus by speaking his name. But Jesus will have none of it. He rebukes the demon, silences him, and commands him to come out of the possessed man. And the demon obeys, amazing the disciples (vv. 25–28). Noteworthy is that the demons acknowledge Jesus's sinlessness when they claim to know who he is and address him as "the Holy One of God" (Mark 1:24).

John. The Gospel of John also testifies to Jesus's moral purity. Jesus scandalizes a crowd by teaching two things that they consider outrageous: apparent cannibalism and God's control over who comes to Jesus. As a result most of the crowd leaves him "and no longer walked with him" (John 6:66). Jesus asks the twelve disciples frankly, "Do you want to go away as well?" (v. 67). Peter, their spokesman, replies: "Lord, to whom shall we go? You have the words of eternal life, and we have believed, and have come to know, that you are the Holy One of God" (vv. 68–69). Here again, Peter speaks better than he knows (this may be John's version of Peter's confession of Matt. 16:16). But he speaks the truth: they will follow Jesus even when his words are incomprehensible. Why? His words are revelation from God because Jesus is "the Holy One of God."

In John 8, Jesus engages in a pitched battle with the Jewish leaders. They keep claiming that they, descendants of Abraham, do not need to believe in Jesus. He acknowledges their physical descent from Abraham but denies that Abraham is their spiritual father. To the contrary, their deeds reveal their true paternity all too well: "You are of your father the devil" (John 8:44). In this charged atmosphere, Jesus speaks daringly: "Which one of you convicts me of sin?" (v. 46). I do not recommend this approach for you or me! But it works coming from Jesus's lips. The reason is simple—he is the incarnate Son of God, and as the God-man, he never sins, not even when provoked by his sworn enemies.

The Acts of the Apostles

Acts 3:14. Acts frequently bears witness to the sinlessness of the Christ. After Peter heals a lame man in Jesus's name outside the temple in Jerusalem, a crowd gathers. Peter takes no credit for the healing. Instead, he acknowledges the God of Abraham, Isaac, and Jacob, who, he says addressing his fellow Jews, "glorified his servant Jesus, whom you delivered over and denied in the presence of Pilate" (Acts 3:13). Peter does not relent but continues to confront his hearers: "But you denied the Holy and Righteous One, and asked for a murderer to be granted to you" (v. 14). Peter uses hard words because he loves his fellow Jews and desires for them to see their need of a Savior so that they might come to him for salvation. And in so doing, he labels Jesus "the Holy and Righteous One" (v. 14), thereby confessing his moral spotlessness.

Acts 4:27, 30. Apostolic miracles and preaching stir up the crowds in Jerusalem, which in turn stirs up the wrath of the Jewish leaders. They arrest the apostles and bring them before the Sanhedrin for questioning. Their strategy is simple: threaten the apostles so they will stop preaching Jesus. But the apostles refuse to be cowed, and they preach Jesus to the Jewish leaders instead. After more threats, the leaders release the apostles, who gather with other believers for prayer (Acts 4:1–23).

The apostles praise God for foretelling in Psalm 2 the Jewish and Gentile opposition to his "holy servant Jesus" that led to his crucifixion (Acts 4:25–27). They pray for boldness: "And now, Lord, look upon their threats and grant to your servants to continue to speak your word with all boldness, while you stretch out your hand to heal, and signs and wonders are performed through the name of your holy servant Jesus" (Acts 4:29–30). The Savior is described in various ways in the book of Acts, but here twice in short compass the apostles pray to God concerning his "holy servant Jesus" (Acts 4:27, 30).

Acts 7:52. The martyr Stephen, near the very end of the sermon that leads to his death, accuses his hearers of emulating their forefathers' sins: "As your fathers did, so do you" (Acts 7:51). He recalls the history of the Israelites' persecuting the Old Testament prophets. Then he mentions the Messiah: "And they killed those who announced beforehand the coming of *the Righteous One*, whom you have now betrayed and murdered" (v. 52).

Acts 22:14. After being rescued by a Roman tribune and his soldiers from being beaten by a Jewish mob, Paul is granted permission to address the people in Hebrew. He recounts Jesus's appearing to him on the Damascus Road, his being blinded, and his being taken to Damascus. There a disciple named Ananias granted sight to Paul (who was still known as Saul) and told him, "The God of our fathers appointed you to know his will, to see the Righteous One and to hear a voice from his mouth; for you will be a witness for him to everyone of what you have seen and heard" (Acts 22:14–15). Here Ananias, like Stephen, called Jesus "the Righteous One" because of his godly character.

The Pauline Epistles

The apostle Paul joins the chorus of New Testament authors who confess Jesus's sinless perfection. In 2 Corinthians 5:18–21 he expounds the doctrine of reconciliation, alternating two emphases. First, he speaks of Christ's ministry of peacemaking (reconciliation) through his death and resurrection: "God . . . through Christ reconciled us to himself; . . . in Christ God was reconciling the world to himself, not counting their trespasses against them" (2 Cor. 5:18–19). Second, he speaks of God's giving us a ministry of announcing Christ's work of reconciliation: "God . . . gave us the ministry of reconciliation; . . . entrusting to us the message of reconciliation. Therefore, we are ambassadors for Christ, God making his appeal through us. We implore you on behalf of Christ, be reconciled to God" (vv. 18–20).

Paul concludes this section with a famous verse: "For our sake he made him to be sin who knew no sin, so that in him we might become the righteousness of God" (v. 21). Gordon Fee speaks of this verse, using Martin Luther's words, as containing a "happy exchange" for believing sinners: "This is the great exchange: and it could happen for Paul only because the sinless one was nonetheless truly one of us and he came to know our sinfulness not by his own experience of it but by bearing the weight of it in his death on the cross."[2] We were filled with sin that is put to Christ's spiritual bank account: "He made him to be sin." In turn, Christ's righteousness is credited to us "so that in him we might become the righteousness of God."

---

[2]Gordon D. Fee, *Pauline Christology: An Exegetical-Theological Study* (Peabody, MA: Hendrickson, 2007), 331.

How is this possible? It is made possible by the part of 2 Corinthians 5:21 that I omitted. The verse describes Christ as "him . . . who knew no sin." That is another way of saying that he lived a sinless life and accrued righteousness that can be credited to believers. In post-Reformation Reformed orthodoxy, this has been called Christ's "active obedience" to distinguish it from Christ's "passive obedience," his sufferings on the cross. Because "passive" today connotes passivity, I prefer to refer to the two aspects as Christ's "lifelong obedience," and his obedience "to the point of death, even death on a cross" (Phil. 2:8). When Paul speaks of Jesus as "him . . . who knew no sin," he teaches that his lifelong obedience (along with his death on the cross) is the basis of our justification. The apostle thus specifically connects Jesus's sinless life with our salvation.

Paul Barnett's pithy summary deserves citation:

> This verse makes powerful assertions about Christ, his life and death. It points first to the sinlessness of his incarnate life ("he knew no sin") and then to his sin-laden death ("[God] made him sin"). It is to be inferred that the efficacy of his death arises from the sinlessness of his life. Because in his death God "made" *this* sinless man sin for us, those who are "in him" by faith commitment "became the righteousness of God."[3]

The General Epistles

The General Epistles lay heavy emphasis on Christ's sinlessness.

Hebrews. The writer to the Hebrews accentuates Christ's deity in chapter 1 and his humanity in chapter 2, and brings them both together in terms of Christ's priesthood in 4:14–16:

> Since then we have a great high priest who has passed through the heavens, Jesus, the Son of God, let us hold fast our confession. For we do not have a high priest who is unable to sympathize with our weaknesses, but one who in every respect has been tempted as we are, yet without sin. Let us then with confidence draw near to the throne of grace, that we may receive mercy and find grace to help in time of need.

When the writer calls Jesus "the Son of God," he is ascribing deity to him since he uses "Son of God" as a divine title (Heb. 4:14; cf. 1:8; 3:6). He also underlines Christ's deity when he says that he, unlike other high priests, "has passed through the heavens" (4:14).

---

[3]Paul Barnett, *The Second Epistle to the Corinthians*, The New International Commentary on the New Testament (Grand Rapids: Eerdmans, 1997), 313–14.

The author also ascribes humanity to Christ when he presents him as sympathetic to us in our weaknesses. Why is he sympathetic? Because Jesus "in every respect has been tempted as we are" (v. 15). The next words are vital: Jesus has been tempted just as we are "yet without sin" (v. 15). Not only does his divine nature set him apart from every other high priest in Israel. But his humanity also sets him apart—because it is sinless. He has been tried and found true.

The fact that deity and sinless humanity combine in the person of Christ has enormous implications for our salvation. The writer exhorts us boldly to approach the throne of God in heaven, a throne of majesty and awesome holiness. Such a description of God's throne should drive us away in fear. But because of Christ's priestly offering of himself, that majestic throne has become "a throne of grace," which we approach "with confidence" (v. 16). What do we find there? Mercy and grace: "that we may receive mercy and find grace to help in time of need" (v. 16). Christ is able to give us grace because he is divine. He offers us mercy because his sinless humanity enables him to sympathize with his people. Once again, Scripture teaches the saving significance of Christ's sinless life.

Uniquely in Scripture, three times Hebrews says something that at first appears shocking—that Jesus was "made perfect":

> For it was fitting that he, for whom and by whom all things exist, in bringing many sons to glory, should make the founder of their salvation perfect through suffering. (Heb. 2:10)

> Although he was a son, he learned obedience through what he suffered. And being made perfect, he became the source of eternal salvation to all who obey him, being designated by God a high priest after the order of Melchizedek. (Heb. 5:8–10)

> For the law appoints men in their weakness as high priests, but the word of the oath, which came later than the law, appoints a Son who has been made perfect forever. (Heb. 7:28)

Because the third passage merely mentions the Son having been "made perfect" (7:28), and the first passage connects that idea with suffering but tells us no more (2:10), the key lies in understanding the second passage—Hebrews 5:8–10—where the idea is developed.

The preceding verse focuses our attention on Christ's humanity: "In the days of his flesh, Jesus offered up prayers and supplications, with loud cries and tears, to him who was able to save him from death, and he was heard because of his reverence" (Heb. 5:7). This speaks, of course, of Gethsemane where Jesus, overwhelmed with sorrow, poured out his heart to the Father (see Matt. 26:36–46).

The Father answered the Son's prayer, not by removing the cross, but by raising him from the dead. Jesus's being made perfect concerns his human struggles and culminates in the cross.

How was the incarnate Son "made perfect"? Certainly, nothing was lacking in his divine nature. And his humanity was always without sin. In what sense, then, did he need to be made perfect? A hint is provided when Hebrews 2:10 says that God made Christ "perfect through suffering." This idea is expanded when Hebrews 5:8 says that Jesus "learned obedience through what he suffered." The Son was made perfect when, over the course of his earthly life, he learned to obey the Father, especially by enduring suffering.

An illustration will help. Imagine that in the first-century *Jerusalem Gazette* a listing appears in its "Help Wanted" section for the job of Redeemer of the world. There are three requirements for the job. First, the applicant must be God; no others need apply. That would narrow the job pool to three. Second, the applicant must also have become man. That would exclude all but one.

The point of the passages in Hebrews that teach that the incarnate Son was made perfect is found in the third qualification in the job description for Redeemer. Not only must the applicant be God incarnate; he must also have on-the-job experience. Although Jesus's humanity was never sinful, in God's plan it must be tried and found true. God did not send his Son to earth as a thirty-three-year-old to die and be raised. He sent him as an infant in order for him to experience human life, with all of its trials and temptations, triumphantly.

It is critical to note the purpose for the Son's being made perfect, that is, experientially qualified to be Savior by learning obedience through suffering. "And being made perfect, he became the source of eternal salvation to all who obey him, being designated by God a high priest after the order of Melchizedek" (Heb. 5:9–10). Jesus's sinless life was necessary for him to become "the source of eternal salvation" for every believer. His proven sinlessness enabled him to die and rise to save sinners. It qualified him to offer himself as a sacrifice in his ministry as our great "high priest after the order of Melchizedek."

In many ways Hebrews shows the superiority of Christ as High Priest to the Aaronic high priests. One way is his sinlessness: "He has no need, like those high priests, to offer sacrifices daily, first for his own sins and then for those of the people, since he did this once for all when he offered up himself" (Heb. 7:27). Levitical priests had to make sacrifices for their own sins; Christ did not because he had no sins. The quotation contains a second difference too: Aaronic high priests offered daily sacrifices, but Christ offered himself "once for all."

The author to the Hebrews extols the sinless Christ now ascended to heaven: "For it was indeed fitting that we should have such a high priest, holy, innocent, unstained, separated from sinners, and exalted above the heavens" (v. 26). Here the author describes Christ in five ways. The last pertains to his present position as heavenly High Priest: "exalted above the heavens." The first four again drive home his perfection of character; he was "holy, innocent, unstained, separated from sinners." In this manner, the writer shows that Jesus's sinless earthly life, culminating in his atoning death and resurrection, is an essential prerequisite for his present heavenly ministry.

F. F. Bruce's comments on this passage form a fitting conclusion to my treatment of Hebrews as a whole:

> The new priesthood is better because the new priest is Jesus. Jesus, who endured sore temptations on earth; Jesus, who poured out His heart in earnest prayer to God; Jesus, who learned by suffering how hard the way of obedience could be; . . . Jesus, who offered up His life to God as a sin-offering on their behalf—this same Jesus is the unchanging high priest and helper of all who come to God through Him. "Such a high priest does indeed fit our condition" (NEB). He has the unique qualification of having experienced the full force of temptation without once yielding to it. There is no question of His fitness to appear in the presence of God; He is the Holy One of God, free from all guile and defilement.[4]

Indeed, because the Son of God was tried, tested, and found blameless, he is able as our great High Priest to offer the unique sacrifice of himself on earth and then to take that offering into the presence of his Father in heaven to avail perpetually for his people.

1 Peter. In two passages the apostle Peter also affirms the moral excellence of Jesus Christ. First, in 1 Peter 2:21–23, Peter exhorts his persecuted readers, should God call them to do so, to suffer as Christians, following Jesus's example:

> For to this you have been called, because Christ also suffered for you, leaving you an example, so that you might follow in his steps. He committed no sin, neither was deceit found in his mouth. When he was reviled, he did not revile in return; when he suffered, he did not threaten, but continued entrusting himself to him who judges justly.

Jesus is first of all Savior, as Peter affirms in the very next verse: "He himself bore our sins in his body on the tree, that we might die to sin and live to righteousness" (1 Pet. 2:24). But after one trusts him as Savior, one also is to follow

---

[4]F. F. Bruce, *The Epistle to the Hebrews*, The New International Commentary on the New Testament (Grand Rapids: Eerdmans, 1964), 156.

his example. In this context, we are to follow Jesus's example of suffering injustice patiently. Specifically, Christ "committed no sin, neither was deceit found in his mouth" (v. 22, citing Isa. 53:9). He refused to return reviling for reviling, but trusted God instead. Peter calls upon his readers to do the same. Jesus's sinless life not only qualifies him to die and rise as our Savior; it also sets a standard for the lives of believers.

Peter also teaches Jesus's sinlessness in 1 Peter 3:18: "For Christ also suffered once for sins, the righteous for the unrighteous, that he might bring us to God." Peter teaches much about Jesus's atonement. First, it is costly: it entailed suffering for the Son of God. Second, it is unique: Jesus suffered once for all time. Third, it is saving: Jesus suffered to "bring us to God," to close the breach that separated us from him. Fourth, and most importantly for our present purposes, it is substitutionary. Jesus died *for* sinners; he died in their place.

Notice Peter's language: "For Christ also suffered once for sins, *the righteous for the unrighteous*, that he might bring us to God." Peter uses first the singular and then the plural number. He writes "the righteous *one* for the unrighteous *ones*." Christ is the righteous one, the sinless one, the holy one, who dies for his people. His sinless life gives moral power to his death; it enables him to deliver others, even all who believe in him.

1 John. In five different ways in his first epistle John teaches that Jesus's earthly life was sinless. John writes to dissuade his readers from sinning. "But if anyone does sin, we have an advocate with the Father, Jesus Christ the righteous" (1 John 2:1). Jesus not only saves his people once and for all time; he also represents them before God the Father every day of their lives. He does so as "Jesus Christ the righteous" who makes "propitiation for our sins" (vv. 1–2). His righteous character enables him to make propitiation and to serve as advocate.

The Christians to whom John writes have been bruised by false teachers who, when they failed to persuade the Christians to accept false doctrines about Christ and the Christian life, rejected and abandoned the believers. John writes to assure (1 John 5:13) and strengthen these believers. In contrast with the antichrists, who have plagued the churches with false teaching, John assures his readers, "You have been anointed by the Holy One, and you all have knowledge" (1 John 2:20). The believers have been anointed with the Holy Spirit and are capable of recognizing and rejecting false teaching because "his anointing teaches you about everything" (v. 27). Christ is "the Holy One" who granted these believers the Spirit and who guides them in the truth. Christ's character is holy.

John rejoices in the Father's love, which makes us his children and gives us a glorious hope: "Beloved, we are God's children now, and what we will be has not yet appeared; but we know that when he appears we shall be like him, because we shall see him as he is" (1 John 3:2). We are presently members of God's family by grace through faith in his unique Son. But we have not seen anything yet! When Christ returns, our character will be made to resemble his. This will occur when we are granted the beatific vision—the seeing of God that fills the beholder with joy.

What will our character be like in that day? We will be holy. In fact, even now, "everyone who thus hopes in him purifies himself as he is pure" (1 John 3:3). The pure Christ will bring our character into conformity with his sinless one at the second coming. In the meantime such an awe-inspiring prospect motivates us to purity of thought, word, and deed.

John distinguishes between "the children of God" and "the children of the devil" (1 John 3:10). How can we tell them apart? True believers do not keep on sinning as they did before coming to know Christ (vv. 6–7). John does not want his readers to be deceived: "Whoever makes a practice of sinning is of the devil, for the devil has been sinning from the beginning" (v. 8). The Devil's children are evident and so are God's: "No one born of God makes a practice of sinning" (v. 9).

The Devil's children reflect his character, and God's children reflect the character of their Father. John gives a number of reasons why God's sons and daughters do not practice sin. The most important one is: "You know that he appeared to take away sins, and in him there is no sin. No one who abides in him keeps on sinning" (1 John 3:5–6). Christ came into the world to die and "take away sins." One essential qualification for his making atonement is that "in him there is so sin" (v. 5). Once more we see that his sinless character enables him to save sinners by dying for them.

John starkly says: "Little children, let no one deceive you. Whoever practices righteousness is righteous, as he is righteous" (1 John 3:7). This is the fifth time that John says the equivalent of "Jesus Christ is righteous." Here his atonement secures both justification and ongoing sanctification. For believers to live in sin is to act as if Christ did not die for their sins! It is to dishonor him and his saving work.

The Book of Revelation

Each of the seven letters to the churches in Revelation 2–3 begins with a description of the living Christ, taken from the vision of him in chapter 1.

> To the angel of the church in Ephesus write: "The words of him who holds the seven stars in his right hand, who walks among the seven golden lampstands . . ." (2:1)

And to the angel of the church in Smyrna write: "The words of the first and the last, who died and came to life . . ." (2:8)

And to the angel of the church in Pergamum write: "The words of him who has the sharp two-edged sword . . ." (2:12)

And to the angel of the church in Thyatira write: "The words of the Son of God, who has eyes like a flame of fire, and whose feet are like burnished bronze . . ." (2:18)

And to the angel of the church in Sardis write: "The words of him who has the seven spirits of God and the seven stars . . ." (3:1)

And to the angel of the church in Philadelphia write: "The words of the holy one, the true one, who has the key of David, who opens and no one will shut, who shuts and no one opens . . ." (3:7)

And to the angel of the church in Laodicea write: "The words of the Amen, the faithful and true witness, the beginning of God's creation . . ." (3:14)

Taken together these descriptions reveal much about Christ. Our interest is in the sixth description, which begins Christ's letter to the church at Philadelphia: "The words of the holy one, the true one, who has the key of David, who opens and no one will shut, who shuts and no one opens" (Rev. 3:7). Christ speaks as "the holy and true one," one characterized by moral purity and faithfulness. Thus, from the beginning of the New Testament story—Mary's being told that her child "will be called holy" (Luke 1:35)—to its end—"the words of the holy one" (Rev. 3:7)—Christ is consistently portrayed as the holy, sinless one.

And here again his perfect life qualifies him to save sinners, for he "has the key of David, who opens and no one will shut, who shuts and no one opens" (Rev. 3:7). As on every other page of Revelation, this verse relies heavily on Old Testament imagery, in this case "the key of David" from Isaiah. To summarize a complicated matter: "The whole group of ideas thus concerns entry to the house of David, the kingdom, the city, and temple of God."[5] Therefore, when John depicts Jesus as unalterably opening or closing with the key of David, he means that Jesus alone has authority to irreversibly admit or exclude people from the kingdom of God. Those who believe in "the holy one, the true one" he saves forever, but those who reject him he casts into hell forever.

---

[5] Michael Wilcock, *The Message of Revelation*, The Bible Speaks Today (Downers Grove, IL: InterVarsity, 1975), 55.

Jesus's Sinlessness Is the Unambiguous Teaching of Scripture

Isaiah predicted that the coming Servant of the Lord would do "no violence," and that there would be "no deceit in his mouth." Consequently, he, "the righteous one, my servant," would

> make many to be accounted righteous,
> and he shall bear their iniquities. (Isa. 53:9, 11)

The New Testament reveals that the incarnate Son of God was the long-awaited coming one, who would bring redemption to Israel and the nations.

Putting together all of the evidence for Jesus's sinlessness yields an impressive result. Whether we investigate the parts of the New Testament, the aspects of his life, his character, or various witnesses, the result is the same—he is the holy one whose sinless life qualifies him to rescue sinners.

All Parts of the New Testament

All parts of the New Testament testify that to accomplish that saving work, the Son/Servant was without sin: the Gospels, Acts, Pauline Epistles, General Epistles, and Revelation.

The Gospels

> The child to be born will be called holy—the Son of God. (Luke 1:35)

> What have you to do with us, Jesus of Nazareth? Have you come to destroy us? I know who you are—the Holy One of God. (Mark 1:24)

> Lord, to whom shall we go? You have the words of eternal life, and we have believed, and have come to know, that you are the Holy One of God. (John 6:68–69)

The Acts

> But you denied the Holy and Righteous One, and asked for a murderer to be granted to you. (Acts 3:14)

> For truly in this city there were gathered together against your holy servant Jesus, whom you anointed, both Herod and Pontius Pilate, along with the Gentiles and the peoples of Israel. (Acts 4:27)

> And now, Lord, look upon their threats and grant to your servants to continue to speak your word with all boldness, while you stretch out your hand to heal, and

signs and wonders are performed through the name of your holy servant Jesus. (Acts 4:29–30)

As your fathers did, so do you. . . . And they killed those who announced beforehand the coming of the Righteous One, whom you have now betrayed and murdered. (Acts 7:51–52)

The God of our fathers appointed you to know his will, to see the Righteous One and to hear a voice from his mouth; for you will be a witness for him to everyone of what you have seen and heard. (Acts 22:14–15)

The Pauline Epistles

For our sake he made him to be sin who knew no sin, so that in him we might become the righteousness of God. (2 Cor. 5:21)

The General Epistles

For we do not have a high priest who is unable to sympathize with our weaknesses, but one who in every respect has been tempted as we are, yet without sin. (Heb. 4:15)

He committed no sin, neither was deceit found in his mouth. When he was reviled, he did not revile in return; when he suffered, he did not threaten, but continued entrusting himself to him who judges justly. (1 Pet. 2:22–23)

For Christ also suffered once for sins, the righteous for the unrighteous, that he might bring us to God. (1 Pet. 3:18)

But if anyone does sin, we have an advocate with the Father, Jesus Christ the righteous. (1 John 2:1)

You have been anointed by the Holy One, and you all have knowledge. (1 John 2:20)

Everyone who thus hopes in him purifies himself as he is pure. (1 John 3:3)

You know that he appeared to take away sins, and in him there is no sin. No one who abides in him keeps on sinning. (1 John 3:5–6)

Little children, let no one deceive you. Whoever practices righteousness is righteous, as he is righteous. (1 John 3:7)

The Revelation

> And to the angel of the church in Philadelphia write: "The words of the holy one, the true one, who has the key of David, who opens and no one will shut, who shuts and no one opens. . . ." (Rev. 3:7)

There is no question, then, that the writers of the New Testament think that Jesus's sinlessness is very significant. From the Gospels through Revelation they agree that the One who accomplishes redemption by his death and resurrection is holy and without sin.

Aspects of His Life

Examining various aspects of Jesus's life yields the same result—his righteousness is underscored by many texts.

Before birth: God announces that he will be the holy Son of God (Luke 1:35).

In Word: Isaiah prophesies, "There was no deceit in his mouth" (Isa. 53:9). Likewise, Peter affirms, ". . . neither was deceit found in his mouth. When he was reviled, he did not revile in return; when he suffered, he did not threaten" (1 Pet. 2:22–23).

In Deed: Paul teaches, "For our sake he made him to be sin who knew no sin, so that in him we might become the righteousness of God" (2 Cor. 5:21). The writer to the Hebrews explains, "For we do not have a high priest who is unable to sympathize with our weaknesses, but one who in every respect has been tempted as we are, yet without sin" (Heb. 4:15). Peter preaches, "He committed no sin. . . . but continued entrusting himself to him who judges justly" (1 Pet. 2:22–23).

Every aspect of the earthly life of the Son of God demonstrates that he is sinless.

His Character

It is no surprise, then, that the New Testament repeatedly testifies to his pure and holy character:

- "the Holy and Righteous One" (Acts 3:14)
- "your holy servant Jesus" (Acts 4:27)
- "your holy servant Jesus" (Acts 4:30)
- "the Righteous One" (Act 7:52)
- "the Righteous One" (Acts 22:14)
- "the righteous" (1 Pet. 3:18)
- "Jesus Christ the righteous" (1 John 2:1)
- "the Holy One" (1 John 2:20)

- "he is pure" (1 John 3:3)
- "in him there is no sin" (1 John 3:5–6)
- "he is righteous" (1 John 3:7)
- "the holy one" (Rev. 3:7)

Various Witnesses

Diverse personalities testify to his moral uprightness.

Demons. Encountering Jesus, the unclean spirit within a man cries out: "What have you to do with us, Jesus of Nazareth? Have you come to destroy us? I know who you are—the Holy One of God" (Mark 1:24).

Disciples. Peter, spokesperson for the Twelve, testifies: "Lord, to whom shall we go? You have the words of eternal life, and we have believed, and have come to know, that you are the Holy One of God" (John 6:68–69).

Enemies. When locked in a verbal battle with the Jewish leaders who opposed him, Jesus exclaims, "Which one of you convicts me of sin?" (John 8:46).

Whether human beings or fallen angels, whether friends or foes, the witnesses agree—Jesus of Nazareth is the holy one of God.

Scripture Connects Jesus's Sinlessness and Saving Accomplishment

The answer, then, to the first question asked at the beginning of this chapter—Does Scripture teach the sinlessness of Christ?—is an emphatic *yes*. Philip Hughes draws attention to the progression, indispensability, and costliness of Jesus's sinless life:

> The perfection of Jesus, then, was not just a perfection of being but a perfection of becoming: the former was sustained by the latter, as progressively he consolidated what he was and had to be. But in no sense was the perfecting of Jesus a progress from imperfection to perfection. Had he at any time been imperfect, or had he even momentarily lapsed into disobedience, he would have failed in all that he came to be and do; he would have become as the first Adam became; incompetent then to save others, he would himself have been in need of salvation. . . . The incarnation was not a comfortable excursion or an enjoyable interlude. We do not consider sufficiently its extreme costliness in suffering and anguish to him who is the eternal Son of God and Image after which we are formed; nor do we remind ourselves, as we constantly should, that the perfection of obedience which he established through suffering was not for his but for our sake, "for us men and for our salvation."[6]

---

[6]Philip Edgcumbe Hughes, *The True Image: The Origin and Destiny of Man in Christ* (Grand Rapids: Eerdmans, 1989), 331.

It is time to address the second question: What theological significance does Christ's sinlessness have? Scripture resounds with the truth that Jesus Christ is sinless, and it tells us why this is so important: because only the righteous one is qualified to perform the work of redemption.

> By his knowledge shall the righteous one, my servant,
>   make many to be accounted righteous,
>   and he shall bear their iniquities. (Isa. 53:11)

For our sake he made him to be sin who knew no sin, so that in him we might become the righteousness of God. (2 Cor. 5:21)

For we do not have a high priest who is unable to sympathize with our weaknesses, but one who in every respect has been tempted as we are, yet without sin. Let us then with confidence draw near to the throne of grace, that we may receive mercy and find grace to help in time of need. (Heb. 4:15–16)

And being made perfect, he became the source of eternal salvation to all who obey him, being designated by God a high priest after the order of Melchizedek. (Heb. 5:9–10)

For Christ also suffered once for sins, the righteous for the unrighteous, that he might bring us to God. (1 Pet. 3:18)

But if anyone does sin, we have an advocate with the Father, Jesus Christ the righteous. (1 John 2:1)

You know that he appeared to take away sins, and in him there is no sin. No one who abides in him keeps on sinning. (1 John 3:5–6)

The words of the holy one, the true one, who has the key of David, who opens and no one will shut, who shuts and no one opens. (Rev. 3:7)

This is an impressive array of passages. Both the prophet Isaiah and the apostle Paul connect the Servant of the Lord's holiness to justification. The prophet says that the righteous Servant will justify many "and he shall bear their iniquities" (Isa. 53:11). The apostle agrees when he teaches that the One "who knew no sin" so identified with our sin as "to be sin" for this purpose: that in spiritual union with him "we might become the righteousness of God" (2 Cor. 5:21).

The writer to the Hebrews connects Jesus's tested moral purity to his office of High Priest. He is a sympathetic priest because he has been tried and found true—"without sin." Consequently, we can come to him who now sits enthroned in heaven and receive grace and mercy from his hand (Heb. 4:15–16). He gives grace because he is divine. He gives mercy because he is a human who was tempted in every way as we are and was found sinless. As the experientially qualified High Priest in the order of Melchizedek, he is thus "the source of eternal salvation" to all believers (Heb. 5:8–10).

Peter links the Son of God's righteousness to his role as Mediator: "For Christ also suffered once for sins, the righteous for the unrighteous, that he might bring us to God" (1 Pet. 3:18). As the sole godly one, he suffers in the place of the ungodly ones. The result? Because he is the morally spotless Mediator, he brings them to God.

John joins the sinless Christ to his people's sins. John does not want his readers to sin, but when they do he comforts them with the knowledge that "we have an advocate with the Father, Jesus Christ the righteous" (1 John 2:1). The purpose of the Son's first coming was to die on the cross "to take away sins." He could perform such an astounding work only because "in him there is no sin." As a result, those who know him as Savior and continue to love him "do not keep on sinning" the way they did before they came to know him (1 John 3:5–6).

The last book of Scripture records solemn words "of the holy one, the true one, who has the key of David." With this key he "opens and no one will shut, . . . shuts and no one opens" (Rev. 3:7). That is, holy Jesus alone has authority to irreversibly admit or exclude people from the final kingdom of God.

Therefore in different contexts with different words at different times and for different purposes, Isaiah, Paul, the author of Hebrews, Peter, and John all proclaim the same message. Only the sinless Son of God can be the Savior of the world.

Robert Letham insightfully summarizes the message of this chapter and points us toward the following chapters:

> There is the consistent witness of the New Testament to Jesus' sinlessness. . . . To a man, the New Testament writers regard it as beyond dispute. To be sure, Jesus is fully human: there could be no salvation unless the Word had become flesh. But did full and true humanity require sinfulness? The answer to that must be no. Just as Adam, when created, was fully human and yet sinless, so the second Adam who took Adam's place not only started his life without sin but continued so. Adam was tempted in a beautiful garden and succumbed. The second Adam was tempted in a bleak desert and yet triumphed (Mt. 4:1–10; Lk. 4:1–12). Again, the ultimate goal of our salvation is seen as final deliverance from sin and its consequences. Life and righteousness will replace death and condemnation. Will we be less than

fully human for that? In fact the reverse will be true. We shall be fulfilled as men and women, remade in the image of God. The assumption in the New Testament that Christ's true humanity involves complete sinlessness is in harmony with the basic anthropological and soteriological teaching of the whole Bible.[7]

Indeed, the incarnation and sinless life of the Son of God are essential prerequisites for the redemption of Adam's fallen sons and daughters. The incarnation was essential for the work of salvation to be accomplished; it was necessary for the Son of God to become a man to save his people from their sins. Likewise, Christ had to live a sinless life in order to accomplish redemption. A sinner is unable to rescue sinners. Only a sinless Savior will do. In that regard, the sinless life of the Lord Jesus Christ saves, as John Stott emphasizes:

> His obedience was indispensable to his saving work. "For just as through the disobedience of the one man the many were made sinners, so also through the obedience of the one man the many will be made righteous" (Rom. 5:19). If he had disobeyed, by deviating an inch from the path of God's will, the devil would have gained a toehold and frustrated the plan of salvation. But Jesus obeyed; and the devil was routed. . . . Thus he refused either to disobey God, or to hate his enemies, or to imitate the world's use of power. By his obedience, his love and his meekness he won a great moral victory over the powers of evil. He remained free, uncontaminated, uncompromised. The devil could gain no hold on him, and had to concede defeat.[8]

As indispensable as the incarnation and Christ's sinless life are, they do not save by themselves. Rather, they are essential preconditions for Christ's central saving events—his death and resurrection. These events are the subjects of the next two chapters.

---

[7]Robert Letham, *The Work of Christ*, Contours of Christian Theology (Downers Grove, IL: InterVarsity, 1993), 114–15.
[8]John R. W. Stott, *The Cross of Christ* (Downers Grove, IL: InterVarsity, 1986), 235.

Incarnation

Sinless Life

Death

Resurrection

Ascension

Session

Pentecost

Intercession

Second Coming

Chapter 3

Christ's Death

God's love to sinners was expressed by *the gift of His Son to be their Saviour*. The measure of love is how much it gives, and the measure of the love of God is the gift of His only Son to be made man, and to die for sins, and so to become the one mediator who can bring us to God. No wonder Paul speaks of God's love as "great," and passing knowledge! (Eph. 2:4; 3:19). Was there ever such costly munificence? Paul argues that this supreme gift is itself the guarantee of every other: "He that spared not his own Son, but delivered him up for us all, how shall he not with him also freely give us all things?" (Rom. 8:32). The New Testament writers constantly point to the Cross of Christ as the crowning proof of the reality and boundlessness of God's love.[1]

J. I. Packer's words ring true, and so it is imperative that we treat Jesus's death (together with his resurrection, the subject of the next chapter) as the centerpiece of his saving work. There is so much biblical material that this chapter must be selective. When the Gospels record the event of Christ's death, they primarily cite two Old Testament passages—Psalm 22 and Isaiah 53. We will investigate these passages as important background for the New Testament interpretation of the death of the Messiah.

---

[1]J. I. Packer, *Knowing God* (Downers Grove, IL: InterVarsity, 1973), 114, italics original.

Old Testament Foreshadowings

Psalm 22

The twenty-second psalm is written in the genre of lament, the most common category in the Psalter. In laments the psalmists cry to the Lord for help in distressed situations. So it is here, where the innocent psalmist is anguished due to terrible suffering and mocking. In light of the New Testament's use of this psalm in the crucifixion story of Jesus, it is proper to view it as speaking in the first place of an individual innocent Old Testament sufferer, David, and in the second place of Jesus, the son of David and innocent sufferer par excellence.

Jack Collins succinctly points out the ways that Matthew 27 employs Psalm 22 to refer to Jesus's crucifixion: "Matthew 27:35 echoes Ps. 22:18 (dividing the garments by lot); Matt. 27:39 echoes Ps. 22:7 (wagging heads); Matt. 27:43 echoes Ps. 22:8 (the derisive challenge for God to rescue him); and Matt. 27:46 cites Ps. 22:1 (Jesus crying out)."[2] Indeed, Jesus dies with a loud cry of the words of Psalm 22:1, "My God, my God, why have you forsaken me?" (Matt. 27:46).

The early church correctly saw this psalm's two main themes—David's persecution by his enemies and his subsequent vindication—as also describing Jesus's dreadful suffering and death and his subsequent resurrection. His suffering on the cross is graphically described by verse 16: "They have pierced my hands and feet." His vindication begins following the declaration that God has heard his cry for help in verse 24: "From you comes my praise in the great congregation" (v. 25). The vindicated Messiah will lead the congregation in worship as Hebrews 2:12 explains, putting Psalm 22:22 in the resurrected Jesus's mouth:

> I will tell of your name to my brothers;
>   in the midst of the congregation I will sing your praise.

And, as Psalm 22 predicts, this will include redeemed Gentiles.

> All the ends of the earth shall remember
>   and turn to the LORD,
> and all the families of the nations
>   shall worship before you. (v. 27)

---

[2] I am grateful to my colleague Jack Collins for his insightful summary of this psalm's message in the *ESV Study Bible*.

Isaiah 53

The Old Testament passage that reflects most profoundly on the redemptive death of the Messiah is Isaiah 52:13–53:12. This is the fourth of Isaiah's Servant Songs. The dominant theme of this song is suffering—terrible suffering.

> His appearance was so marred, beyond human semblance,
>> and his form beyond that of the children of mankind. (52:14)

> He was despised and rejected by men;
>> a man of sorrows, and acquainted with grief;
> and as one from whom men hide their faces
>> he was despised, and we esteemed him not. . . .
> But he was wounded . . . ;
>> he was crushed. . . .
> He was oppressed, and he was afflicted. . . .
> By oppression and judgment he was taken away. (53:3, 5, 7, 8)

The Servant suffers horribly, enduring despising, rejection, grief, being wounded and even "crushed," oppression, affliction, and being assaulted beyond recognition. It is important to ask concerning this terrible suffering, was it deserved? The first answer is no, for the Servant

> . . . had done no violence,
>> and there was no deceit in his mouth. (v. 9)

The Servant did not sin in word or deed. In fact, his character could be summed up in this description: he is "the righteous one, my servant" (v. 11).

But matters become complicated when we ask again, was the Servant's suffering deserved? This is true because of these words:

> Yet it was the will of the LORD to crush him;
>> he has put him to grief. (v. 10)

God willed the appalling suffering of his righteous Servant! How can we square this with God's righteous character? The answer lies in another major theme of this Servant Song, that of vicarious suffering.

> But he was wounded for our transgressions;
>> he was crushed for our iniquities;
> upon him was the chastisement that brought us peace,
>> and with his stripes we are healed.

> . . . and the LORD has laid on him
>   the iniquity of us all. (vv. 5–6)

>   . . . who considered
> that he was cut off out of the land of the living,
>   stricken for the transgression of my people? (v. 8)

>   . . . and he shall bear their iniquities. (v. 11)

>   . . . yet he bore the sin of many. (v. 12)

The innocent Servant suffers willingly: "He poured out his soul to death" (v. 12). He does so as a Sin-Bearer in the place of others; he takes the punishment that they deserve. The Servant's substitutionary death has amazing results. His death accomplished justification; it makes "many to be accounted righteous" (v. 11). His death is "an offering for guilt" (v. 10), which according to Leviticus makes "atonement" and procures forgiveness (Lev. 5:16, 18). As such it sanctifies ("sprinkles") "many nations" (Isa. 52:15).

Alan Groves's conclusions to his study of Isaiah 53 bear repeating:

> Isaiah 53, therefore, is using the language of "bearing guilt" in a unique and most unusual fashion. If the foregoing argument is correct, then for the Servant to "bear guilt" is for him to make atonement. . . . It is precisely by means of the revelation of the *extraordinary* nature of the purification of which Isaiah spoke that the prophecy makes its most distinctive contribution to redemptive history. . . . The Torah knew no atonement that produced the universal and permanent purification envisioned in Isaiah. . . . Rather, it would be accomplished by a *new* thing (Is 48:7) . . . the astounding suffering of one righteous Israelite (Is 52:13–53:12), who bore the sins of others.[3]

The Servant's vicarious death also wins a great victory. We see this in the structure of the Servant Song. Amazingly, the central section treating the horrible suffering of the Servant is hemmed in by bookends that speak of his exaltation.

> Behold, my servant shall act wisely;
>   he shall be high and lifted up,
>   and shall be exalted. (52:13)

---

[3] J. Alan Groves, "Atonement in Isaiah 53," in *The Glory of the Atonement*, ed. Charles E. Hill and Frank A. James III (Downers Grove, IL: InterVarsity, 2004), 87–89, italics original.

> Therefore I will divide him a portion with the many,
>> and he shall divide the spoil with the strong. (53:12)

The suffering Servant will be victorious. His humiliation will be followed by exaltation. The song more than hints at his resurrection.

> When his soul makes an offering for guilt,
>> he shall see his offspring; he shall prolong his days. (v. 10)

The suffering Servant lives after dying. Alec Motyer, an expert in Isaiah, agrees:

> He who was crushed under the will of the LORD lives as the executor of that will. In 14:9–17 Isaiah depicted earth's royalty in Sheol, clutching their now meaningless dignities, actually weak, as are the rest, and with their pretensions in life exposed as pitiable foibles. Death has dethroned them. In the case of the Servant, however, death ushers him into sovereign dignity and power, with his own hand administering the saving purposes of the Lord, and as victor taking the spoil (verse 12).[4]

Other Old Testament Passages

Old Testament scholars understand other texts to predict the death of the Messiah. I will merely list some of them here:

> And after the sixty-two weeks, an anointed one shall be cut off and shall have nothing. And the people of the prince who is to come shall destroy the city and the sanctuary. Its end shall come with a flood, and to the end there shall be war. Desolations are decreed. (Dan. 9:26)[5]

> And I will pour out on the house of David and the inhabitants of Jerusalem a spirit of grace and pleas for mercy, so that, when they look on me, on him whom they have pierced, they shall mourn for him, as one mourns for an only child, and weep bitterly over him, as one weeps over a firstborn. (Zech. 12:10; cf. John 19:37)

> "Awake, O sword, against my shepherd,
>> against the man who stands next to me,"
>>> declares the LORD of hosts.
> "Strike the shepherd, and the sheep will be scattered." (Zech. 13:7; cf. Matt.
>> 26:31)

---

[4]J. Alec Motyer, *The Prophecy of Isaiah: An Introduction and Commentary* (Downers Grove, IL: Inter-Varsity, 1993), 440–41.

[5]Though most Old Testament scholars take this as a prediction of Jesus's crucifixion, not all do; cf. John E. Goldingay, *Daniel*, Word Biblical Commentary (Dallas: Word, 1987), 266–68.

The Event in the Synoptic Gospels

What the Old Testament foreshadowed came to pass in the life and death of Jesus of Nazareth. Once more we must be selective, omitting incidental references to the crucifixion. Here we will examine those passages in which Jesus says that he came to die, those in which he predicts his death, and those that tell of his death on the cross.

He Came to Die

Simon Gathercole has called attention to passages where Jesus states the purpose of his coming.[6] Two of these set the stage for our discussion:

> And when Jesus heard it, he said to them, "Those who are well have no need of a physician, but those who are sick. I came not to call the righteous, but sinners." (Mark 2:17; see also Matt. 9:13; Luke 5:32)

> For the Son of Man came to seek and to save the lost. (Luke 19:10)

Jesus came to heal the spiritually sick, to call sinners, and to seek and save the lost. But how does he do these things? The answer is found in the most famous Synoptic passage telling the purpose of his coming.

The ransom saying (Mark 10:45). The most famous Synoptic ransom saying is also one of the most debated texts in the New Testament. I will not enter the debates, but treat it as the very voice of Jesus.[7] James and John make an outrageous request—to sit at Jesus's right and left hands in the future kingdom (Mark 10:35–37). Jesus gently rebukes them, informing them that they do not know what they are asking and that it is the Father's role to assign such places of honor (vv. 38–40). The other ten disciples do not fare any better but are "indignant at James and John" (v. 41).

Jesus seizes the occasion as a teachable moment and tells them that they are thinking the way unsaved people think—insisting on their rights and dominating those under them. His kingdom will not be made of such things: "But it shall not be so among you. But whoever would be great among you must be your servant, and whoever would be first among you must be slave of all" (vv. 43–44). Jesus teaches the principle of servant leadership. And his next words reveal that

---

[6]Simon J. Gathercole, *The Pre-existent Son* (Grand Rapids: Eerdmans, 2006), 148–76.

[7]For a short treatment, see William L. Lane, *Commentary on the Gospel of Mark*, The New International Commentary on the New Testament (Grand Rapids: Eerdmans, 1974), 383–85; for a long treatment see Scot McKnight, *Jesus and His Death: Historiography, the Historical Jesus, and Atonement Theory* (Waco, TX: Baylor University Press, 2005), esp. 159–71, 239, 356–60.

he exemplifies it: "For even the Son of Man came not to be served but to serve, and to give his life as a ransom for many" (v. 45). He, the Lord of glory, could have exercised his rights to be received with honor, as was proper. But he did not. Instead, he came as a Servant, and the epitome of his service was "to give his life as a ransom for many" (v. 45).

Simon Gathercole, in arguing for Jesus's preexistence, studies this text to understand the purpose of his first advent and concludes: "His present earthly life is to be one of service, by contrast to what might otherwise be expected. . . . The second part of the purpose expressed in Mark 10:45 is that his death (the sense of 'giving life') is to accomplish the release of many others who are in some kind of enslavement."[8] "Some kind of enslavement" indeed! That would be bondage to sin, from which Jesus delivers all who believe in him (John 8:34–36).

The transfiguration (Luke 9:30–31). Luke's version of the transfiguration account is pregnant with theological meaning. Here we focus on two verses: "And behold, two men were talking with him, Moses and Elijah, who appeared in glory and spoke of his departure, which he was about to accomplish at Jerusalem" (Luke 9:30–31). Moses and Elijah, representing the Law and the Prophets, respectively, appear with Jesus on "the holy mountain" (2 Pet. 1:18). Key for our purposes is the topic of their discussion: "Moses and Elijah . . . spoke of his *departure*, which he was about to accomplish at Jerusalem" (Luke 9:31). The word translated "departure" is the Greek ἔξοδος (*exodos*), which indeed speaks in the New Testament of departure from this life in death, as in Peter's death (2 Pet. 1:15).

Because Jesus is "about *to accomplish*" his exodus "at Jerusalem," the word takes on an additional meaning, a typological one referring also to the great redemptive event of the Old Testament—the exodus from Egypt (the meaning it also has in Heb. 11:22).[9] The Law and the Prophets personified spoke with Jesus of his departure from this world, which would constitute an exodus that he would accomplish in the holy city. This is one way in which Luke shows that Jesus's death would be redemptive. It is the grand redemptive event to which the Old Testament exodus pointed. Here, as in Mark 10:45, Jesus's death leads to deliverance of others. His death was so important that he predicted it for his disciples in plain words.

---

[8]Gathercole, *The Pre-existent Son*, 167.
[9]William F. Arndt and F. Wilbur Gingrich, *A Greek-English Lexicon of the New Testament and Other Early Christian Literature*, 2nd ed. (Chicago: University of Chicago, 1979), 276.

He Predicted His Death

On three different occasions, Jesus predicted his arrest, death, and resurrection:

> And he began to teach them that the Son of Man must suffer many things and be rejected by the elders and the chief priests and the scribes and be killed, and after three days rise again. (Mark 8:31; see also Matt. 16:21; Luke 9:22)

> For he was teaching his disciples, saying to them, "The Son of Man is going to be delivered into the hands of men, and they will kill him. And when he is killed, after three days he will rise." (Mark 9:31; see also Matt. 17:22–23; Luke 9:44)

> See, we are going up to Jerusalem, and the Son of Man will be delivered over to the chief priests and the scribes, and they will condemn him to death and deliver him over to the Gentiles. And they will mock him and spit on him, and flog him and kill him. And after three days he will rise. (Mark 10:33–34; see also Matt. 20:18–19; Luke 18:32–33)

The Synoptic Gospels present Jesus as a prophet who both preached the Word of God to his contemporaries and also predicted many things, including the Jews' rejection of their Messiah (Matt. 23:37–38), the destruction of the temple (Matt. 24:2), his betrayal (Matt. 26:20–25), his return (Matt. 24:30–31), the last judgment (Matt. 25:31–36), and the final kingdom of God (Matt. 19:28). But most importantly, Jesus predicted his death and resurrection as the three passages above reveal.

It is helpful to view the details of the above passages from Mark in table form (table 1).

Table 1. Jesus's prediction of his death and resurrection in Mark's Gospel

Text	Suffering	Delivered to Jews	Rejected by Jews	Condemned	Delivered to Gentiles	Mocked	Flogged	Killed	Will Rise
8:31	x		x					x	x
9:31		x						x	x
10:33–34		x		x	x	x	x	x	x

Jesus, the great prophet of God, foretold that he would suffer much, be delivered to the Jewish authorities, and be rejected and condemned (by trial) by them. He foretold that he would be delivered over to Gentiles (for trial), mocked (including being spat upon), flogged, and put to death. He also foretold that he would rise from the dead. Jesus thus foretold his death and resurrection. Next we consider the Gospel accounts of his death.

He Died

The four Gospels record the death of Jesus:

> Now from the sixth hour there was darkness over all the land until the ninth hour. And about the ninth hour Jesus cried out with a loud voice, saying, "Eli, Eli, lema sabachthani?" that is, "My God, my God, why have you forsaken me?" And some of the bystanders, hearing it, said, "This man is calling Elijah." And one of them at once ran and took a sponge, filled it with sour wine, and put it on a reed and gave it to him to drink. But the others said, "Wait, let us see whether Elijah will come to save him." And Jesus cried out again with a loud voice and yielded up his spirit. (Matt. 27:45–50)

> And when the sixth hour had come, there was darkness over the whole land until the ninth hour. And at the ninth hour Jesus cried with a loud voice, "Eloi, Eloi, lema sabachthani?" which means, "My God, my God, why have you forsaken me?" And some of the bystanders hearing it said, "Behold, he is calling Elijah." And someone ran and filled a sponge with sour wine, put it on a reed and gave it to him to drink, saying, "Wait, let us see whether Elijah will come to take him down." And Jesus uttered a loud cry and breathed his last. And the curtain of the temple was torn in two, from top to bottom. And when the centurion, who stood facing him, saw that in this way he breathed his last, he said, "Truly this man was the Son of God!" (Mark 15:33–39)

> It was now about the sixth hour, and there was darkness over the whole land until the ninth hour, while the sun's light failed. And the curtain of the temple was torn in two. Then Jesus, calling out with a loud voice, said, "Father, into your hands I commit my spirit!" And having said this he breathed his last. Now when the centurion saw what had taken place, he praised God, saying, "Certainly this man was innocent!" And all the crowds that had assembled for this spectacle, when they saw what had taken place, returned home beating their breasts. And all his acquaintances and the women who had followed him from Galilee stood at a distance watching these things. (Luke 23:44–49)

> After this, Jesus, knowing that all was now finished, said (to fulfill the Scripture), "I thirst." A jar full of sour wine stood there, so they put a sponge full of the sour wine on a hyssop branch and held it to his mouth. When Jesus had received the sour wine, he said, "It is finished," and he bowed his head and gave up his spirit. (John 19:28–30)

The four Gospels unitedly testify to the death of Jesus Christ. And they each provide hints as to the redemptive significance of his death. Table 2 shows what they have in common and where they differ.

Table 2. Shared testimony of Jesus's death in the Gospels

	Matthew	Mark	Luke	John
Darkness	x	x	x	
"My God, my God, why have you forsaken me?"	x	x		
Yielded up spirit	x			x
Breathed his last		x	x	
Temple curtain torn		x	x	
Centurion testifies		x	x	
"Into your hands I commit my spirit."			x	
"I thirst."				x
"It is finished."				x

All four Gospels include the fact that Jesus gave up his spirit or breathed his last. This means that he willed to die. He gave himself in death. The three Synoptics record the fact that darkness covered the land of Israel for three hours. "The darkness that 'came over the land' from noon till 3:00 P.M. (that is what 'sixth hour' and 'ninth hour' refer to) was a sign of judgment and/or tragedy."[10] God was judging the people of Israel and their land for rejecting their Messiah. But at the same time, the darkness indicated a judgment on Jesus, as the cry of dereliction shows.

This terrible cry appears in Matthew and Mark: "My God, my God, why have you forsaken me?" (translated from Aramaic). Ultimately incomprehensible, this loud cry of abandonment revealed that a deep judgment was taking place. The eternal fellowship between the Father and Son was interrupted as the Son became the Sin-Bearer.

Mark and Luke record that the curtain into the Most Holy Place, or Holy of Holies, was torn in two, demonstrating the efficacy of Christ's death. The way into the Most Holy Place was now opened so that believers "with confidence draw near to the throne of grace" (Heb. 4:16). In addition, Mark indicates that the curtain was torn "from top to bottom" (Mark 15:38), showing that this was an act of God, not human beings. In this vivid way, God proclaimed that Christ crucified had given believers access to the very presence of God.

In Mark and Luke the attending centurion testified to the innocence (Luke 23:47) and identity of "the Son of God" (Mark 15:39). God thus underlines the truth that Jesus died undeservedly. He did not die for his own sins, for he had none; he died for the sins of others.

---

[10]D. A. Carson, *Matthew*, The Expositor's Bible Commentary (Grand Rapids: Zondervan, 1984), 577.

Luke alone records that Jesus committed his spirit into the Father's hands. This too shows that Jesus died willingly. It also shows that the awful bearing of sin was past. "My God, my God, why have you forsaken me?" (Matt. 27:46) is replaced with, "Father, into your hands I commit my spirit!" (Luke 23:46). Joel Green aptly argues:

> Employing this psalm [Ps. 31:5], Jesus manifests his own faith in the sovereign God whom, he believes, will rescue him from the hands of his enemies. In light of the coupling of death and resurrection in Jesus' passion predictions . . . we may hear in Jesus' prayer his faith in the God who raises from the dead.[11]

John alone records two sayings of Jesus on the cross. "I thirst" (John 19:28) fulfills Scripture, and "It is finished" (v. 30) "triumphantly announces the completion of his mission entrusted to him by the Father at what may be considered the lowest point in his life, his death by crucifixion."[12]

It remains for the rest of the New Testament, especially the Epistles and the Revelation, to unfold the full meaning of the cross. But already the Gospels themselves more than hint at its redemptive significance through the natural phenomenon of darkness, the words of Jesus and the centurion, Jesus's action of willing to die, and God's action of tearing the temple's curtain in two.

Teaching in the Gospel of John

The Fourth Gospel engages in more interpretation of the death of Jesus than do the Synoptic Gospels. John paints at least seven pictures of Christ's saving accomplishment.

The Son of Man Lifted Up

Jesus saves as the Son of Man lifted up. After Jesus says, "And I, when I am lifted up from the earth, will draw all people to myself," John defines this image for us: "He said this to show by what kind of death he was going to die" (John 12:32–33). Jesus will be crucified, that is, physically "lifted up" on a cross. At the same time, two things suggest a figurative meaning. First, preceding these verses, Jesus says, "The hour has come for the Son of Man to be glorified" (v. 23). His death will, in some sense, glorify him. And second, the result of his being

---

[11]Joel B. Green, *The Gospel of Luke*, The New International Commentary on the New Testament (Grand Rapids: Eerdmans, 1997), 826.

[12]Andreas J. Köstenberger, *John*, Baker Exegetical Commentary on the New Testament (Grand Rapids: Baker Academic, 2004), 551.

lifted up is to "draw all people to" himself (v. 32); Jesus's terrible crucifixion will have positive results—people being drawn to him.

According to John, then, Jesus's "lifting up" involves literal crucifixion and figurative exaltation. It is as if the worst his enemies can do to him only begins his return to the Father. His seeming defeat accomplishes a great victory. And this is in keeping with the most commonly suggested Old Testament background for Jesus's being lifted up.

> Behold, my servant shall act wisely;
> 　he shall be high and lifted up,
> 　and shall be exalted. (Isa. 52:13)

Isaiah's most famous Servant Song—in chapter 53—begins with words not of suffering but of exaltation. The suffering Servant will be victorious. John's Gospel teaches the same truths when it tells of Jesus's saving death as the Son of Man lifted up.

John uses this picture of Christ's saving work when he presents him crucified as the antitype to Moses's lifting up the bronze serpent in the wilderness. Jesus says:

> Truly, truly, I say to you, we speak of what we know, and bear witness to what we have seen, but you do not receive our testimony. If I have told you earthly things and you do not believe, how can you believe if I tell you heavenly things? No one has ascended into heaven except he who descended from heaven, the Son of Man. And as Moses lifted up the serpent in the wilderness, so must the Son of Man be lifted up, that whoever believes in him may have eternal life. (John 3:11–15)

Jesus underscores his hearers' unbelief when he says that he (as the Father's witness) has spoken of regeneration, a divine work occurring on earth, but they will not believe. Their unbelief hinders his communicating heavenly realities to them. No human being has gone to God and returned with divine mysteries. Jesus is uniquely qualified to reveal such mysteries because he alone has come from the Father into the world.

Jesus then teaches that Moses's lifting the bronze serpent is a type of Christ's being lifted up: "And as Moses lifted up the serpent in the wilderness, so must the Son of Man be lifted up" (John 3:14). In Numbers 21, God sent venomous snakes among the Israelites in the wilderness to punish them for speaking ill of him and his servant Moses (Num. 21:4–6). After they repented, Moses prayed for them and, in obedience to God's word, made a bronze snake and put it on a pole. "And if a serpent bit anyone, he would look at the bronze serpent and live" (v. 9).

As I have written elsewhere:

"Just as Moses lifted up the serpent in the desert, so the Son of Man must be lifted up, that everyone who believes in him may have eternal life" (John 3:14–15). John 3:18 warns us that all who have not trusted Christ for salvation already stand condemned before God—a worse malady than the snake bites of Numbers 21! Here too, however, is a better remedy—the saving death of the Son of Man. Moses raised a bronze serpent, and all who looked to it were delivered from the snakes. Similarly, Jesus was to be raised up in crucifixion so that all who look to him would be delivered from eternal condemnation.[13]

The Good Shepherd

Jesus saves as the Good Shepherd who dies and rises for his sheep.

I am the good shepherd. The good shepherd lays down his life for the sheep. He who is a hired hand and not a shepherd, who does not own the sheep, sees the wolf coming and leaves the sheep and flees, and the wolf snatches them and scatters them. He flees because he is a hired hand and cares nothing for the sheep. I am the good shepherd. I know my own and my own know me, just as the Father knows me and I know the Father; and I lay down my life for the sheep. And I have other sheep that are not of this fold. I must bring them also, and they will listen to my voice. So there will be one flock, one shepherd. For this reason the Father loves me, because I lay down my life that I may take it up again. No one takes it from me, but I lay it down of my own accord. I have authority to lay it down, and I have authority to take it up again. This charge I have received from my Father. (John 10:11–18)

In contrast to the false shepherds of Israel's past (Ezek. 34:2–4) and present (John 9:28–29, 34, 40–41), Jesus is "the good shepherd" (10:11, 14). The false shepherds flee when the sheep are threatened (vv. 12–13). By contrast, Jesus loves the Father and loves his sheep and sticks by them. He has a personal relationship with his people, described as reciprocal knowledge, akin to that between the Father and the Son (v. 14).

What does the Good Shepherd do for his people? He "lays down his life for the sheep" (vv. 11, 15). He gives himself in death for them. Jesus underlines the voluntariness of his self-giving: "No one takes it from me, but I lay it down

---

[13]Robert A. Peterson, *Getting to Know John's Gospel: A Fresh Look at Its Main Ideas* (Phillipsburg, NJ: P&R, 1989), 94.

of my own accord" (v. 18). How should we construe this self-offering? D. A. Carson argues that the answer is in terms of sacrifice:

> The words "for (*hyper*) the sheep" suggest sacrifice. The preposition, itself ambiguous, in John always occurs in a sacrificial context. . . . In no case does this suggest a death with merely exemplary significance; in each case the death envisaged is on behalf of someone else. The shepherd does not die for his sheep to serve as an example. . . . No, the assumption is that the sheep are in mortal danger; that in their defence the shepherd loses his life; that by his death they are saved. That, and that alone, is what makes him *the good shepherd*.[14]

Carson is correct. Jesus, the Good Shepherd, lays down his life in sacrifice to rescue his sheep from grave danger.

Furthermore, Jesus includes his resurrection as a part of his saving work: "I lay down my life that I may take it up again" (v. 17). Jesus's death and resurrection fulfill the Father's plan of salvation: "I have authority to lay it down, and I have authority to take it up again. This charge I have received from my Father" (v. 18). It is noteworthy that here Jesus raises himself from the grave.[15] The Good Shepherd dies and rises to save his sheep, both Jew and Gentile (v. 16), from their sins.

The Lamb of God

Jesus saves as the Lamb of God who takes away sins. The sacrificial system plays a vital role in the Old Testament. Countless animals were sacrificed in conjunction with the various Levitical offerings. Against this background, John the Baptist, upon seeing Jesus approaching, proclaims, "Behold, the Lamb of God, who takes away the sin of the world!" (John 1:29). The next day, when he sees Jesus, John says similar words: "Behold, the Lamb of God!" (v. 36).

Scholars have reached very different conclusions when they have sought the Old Testament background for John's words identifying Jesus as God's Lamb. The most common suggestions include the Passover lamb, the lamb led to slaughter in Isaiah 53:7, the lamb of the daily sacrifices, the scapegoat, and the guilt offering.[16] The inability of scholars to agree and the fact that John's statement is general rather than specific lead me to another conclusion. I agree with Leon Morris:

---

[14]D. A. Carson, *The Gospel According to John*, The Pillar New Testament Commentary (Grand Rapids: Eerdmans, 1991), 386, italics original.

[15]In Scripture, only in John 2:19–22 and 10:17–18 is Jesus said to raise himself from the dead.

[16]See Leon Morris, *The Gospel According to John*, The New International Commentary on the New Testament (Grand Rapids: Eerdmans, 1971), 144–47, for discussion of these views and more.

The fact is that a lamb taking away sin, even if it is distinguished as God's Lamb, is too indefinite a description for us to pin-point a reference. . . . But it seems more probable that of set purpose he used an expression which cannot be confined to any one view. He is making a general allusion to sacrifice. . . . All that the ancient sacrifices foreshadowed was perfectly fulfilled in the sacrifice of Christ.[17]

Jesus's death "takes away the sin of the world!" (John 1:29); that is, as the culmination of all of the Old Testament sacrifices, it is an atoning death that brings forgiveness to everyone who believes. By "the world" John, contrary to first-century Jewish expectation, proclaims that this Lamb's death would bring forgiveness to believing Jews and Gentiles alike. Jesus's sacrificial death "is completely adequate for the needs of all men. Right at the beginning of his Gospel John points us forward to the cross and to the significance of the cross."[18]

The Priestly Sacrifice

Jesus saves as the one who consecrates himself as both priest and sacrifice. Previously, Jesus said that the Father consecrated him and sent him into the world (John 10:36). Now, in his justly famous High Priestly Prayer, he petitions the Father in behalf of his disciples: "Sanctify them in the truth; your word is truth. As you sent me into the world, so I have sent them into the world. And for their sake I consecrate myself, that they also may be sanctified in truth" (John 17:17–19). Although the ESV uses "consecrate" and not "sanctify" for Jesus, the same word is used for both the disciples' sanctification and his (in John 10:36; 17:19). Why? As is his custom, John forces readers to think, for at first glance this is confusing.

A key lies in remembering that the Old Testament teaches that both priest and sacrifice had to be set apart as holy to the Lord. The end of Exodus describes the consecration of Aaron and his sons:

Then you shall bring Aaron and his sons to the entrance of the tent of meeting and shall wash them with water and put on Aaron the holy garments. And you shall anoint him and consecrate him, that he may serve me as priest. You shall bring his sons also and put coats on them, and anoint them, as you anointed their father, that they may serve me as priests. And their anointing shall admit them to a perpetual priesthood throughout their generations. (Ex. 40:12–15)

---

[17]Ibid., 147–48.
[18]Ibid., 148.

Before Deuteronomy 15 speaks of sacrificing firstborn male animals, it speaks of dedicating them to the Lord. Sanctification precedes sacrifice.

> All the firstborn males that are born of your herd and flock you shall dedicate to the Lord your God. You shall do no work with the firstborn of your herd, nor shear the firstborn of your flock. . . . But if it has any blemish, if it is lame or blind or has any serious blemish whatever, you shall not sacrifice it to the Lord your God. (Deut. 15:19, 21)

John presents Jesus, whom the Father sanctified and sent into the world (John 10:36), as dedicating himself both as High Priest and as sacrifice in his death on the cross, when he prays, "And for their sake I consecrate myself, that they also may be sanctified in truth" (17:19). Notice that Jesus's consecration is the basis for that of his disciples. His atoning death sanctifies them; it sets them apart as holy to the Lord. And in verse 17, he prays that God would use his Word as a means of their ongoing sanctification: "Sanctify them in the truth; your word is truth." And even as the Father set Jesus apart and sent him into the world (10:36), so he now sets apart his disciples and sends them into the world: "As you sent me into the world, so I have sent them into the world" (17:18).

Jesus sanctifies himself to God as both priest and sacrifice and thereby sanctifies his people and sends them into the world with a mission—to bring the good news of Jesus's saving sacrifice to a lost world.

The Victor

Jesus saves as the mighty Victor who delivers his people by defeating their enemies.

The Gospel of John is filled with conflict. Although Jesus's temptation by Satan in the wilderness and Jesus's exorcisms of demons are absent from the Fourth Gospel, these absences serve only to heighten the big and final battle—at the cross. The instigation for Judas's betrayal of Jesus is from the Evil One himself: "During supper, when the devil had already put it into the heart of Judas Iscariot, Simon's son, to betray him" (John 13:1–2). And the Devil not only inspires Judas for his evil deed; he also empowers him, as Jesus foretells: "Then after he [Judas] had taken the morsel, Satan entered into him. Jesus said to him, 'What you are going to do, do quickly'" (13:27).

Make no mistake—the cross is the critical battleground in the warfare between God and Satan, between good and evil. As Jesus views the cross approaching, here is how he interprets it: "The ruler of this world is coming. He has no claim on me, but I do as the Father has commanded me, so that the world may know that I love the Father" (John 14:30–31). Remember, the Father commanded that Jesus die and arise. For Jesus said concerning his life: "No one takes it from me, but I lay it down of my own accord. I have authority to lay it down, and I have authority to take it up again. This charge I have received from my Father" (10:18).

Jesus is also convinced that at the cross Satan will be vanquished: "Now will the ruler of this world be cast out" (12:31); "The ruler of this world is judged" (16:11). Jesus our champion not only will defeat the prince of darkness but also cause his kingdom to fall. First John best defines the "world" as God's enemy:

> Do not love the world or the things in the world. If anyone loves the world, the love of the Father is not in him. For all that is in the world—the desires of the flesh and the desires of the eyes and pride in possessions—is not from the Father but is from the world. And the world is passing away along with its desires, but whoever does the will of God abides forever. (1 John 2:15–17)

Note that John says that "the world is passing away." In John's Gospel Jesus specifies when this will occur: "Now is the judgment of this world; now will the ruler of this world be cast out" (John 12:31). And when Jesus prepares his own for struggles in the world, he declares: "I have said these things to you, that in me you may have peace. In the world you will have tribulation. But take heart; I have overcome the world" (John 16:33).

Jesus is our conquering hero who defeats the enemies—the Devil, the world, and more—by dying for sinners and rising again in victory.

The One Dying for the Nation

Jesus saves as the one who dies for Israel and for all of God's children. Irony is a key feature of the style of the Fourth Gospel. Repeatedly characters in the story say words that are true in ways they never intended—but God did.[19] Nowhere is irony more evident than in the unintended meaning of the high priest Caiaphas's words:

> So the chief priests and the Pharisees gathered the Council and said, "What are we to do? For this man performs many signs. If we let him go on like this, everyone will believe in him, and the Romans will come and take away both our place and our nation." But one of them, Caiaphas, who was high priest that year, said to them, "You know nothing at all. Nor do you understand that it is better for you

---

[19]Raymond E. Brown, *The Gospel According to John (i-xii)*, Anchor Bible (Garden City, NY: Doubleday, 1966), cxxxvi.

that one man should die for the people, not that the whole nation should perish."
(John 11:47–50)

The Jewish leaders are disturbed by Jesus's popularity. They fear that if it continues to grow, it might lead to insurrection with consequent Roman intervention. The result? The Romans might destroy the temple and Israel itself. Caiaphas, the high priest that fateful year, speaks rudely and straightforwardly: "It is better for you that one man should die for the people, not that the whole nation should perish" (v. 50). Caiaphas has no intention of predicting Jesus's atonement. His statement is one of political expediency. He means, "Let's kill Jesus and bring his whole movement to a halt so the Romans won't come and destroy our nation."

But God has other intentions for Caiaphas's words, according to John's editorial comment: "He did not say this of his own accord, but being high priest that year he prophesied that Jesus would die for the nation, and not for the nation only, but also to gather into one the children of God who are scattered abroad" (vv. 51–52). Irony of ironies! God causes the murderous words of the high priest to predict the atonement of the Messiah, whom the words were designed to destroy! Jesus will die for the nation and also "to gather into one the children of God who are scattered abroad" (v. 52). That is, Jesus will die to unite believing Jews and Gentiles into one people of God.

Caiaphas's words work, but not with the results that he expected. John explains: "So from that day on they made plans to put him to death" (v. 53). The Jewish leaders kill their Messiah, but that act inadvertently contributes to the salvation of the world! God uses the wrath of men to praise him. Indeed, the high priest speaks God's truth: Jesus is the one who will die for the people and for all of God's children.

The Grain of Wheat, Dying

Jesus saves as the grain of wheat that, by dying, bears much fruit. When Greeks (Gentiles from anywhere in the Greek-speaking world) come to Jerusalem with an interest in the Jewish Passover, they ask to talk to Jesus (John 12:20–21). When the word reaches him, he apparently avoids the question and instead says: "The hour has come for the Son of Man to be glorified. Truly, truly, I say to you, unless a grain of wheat falls into the earth and dies, it remains alone; but if it dies, it bears much fruit" (vv. 23–24).

The "hour" of which Jesus speaks is a wonderful and complicated theme of the Fourth Gospel. For our purposes it is sufficient to note that previous references to the hour were future and now become present. We see this in John 13:1: "Now before the Feast of the Passover . . . Jesus knew that his hour had come to depart out of this world to the Father" (cf. 12:27; 17:1). Jesus's "hour" is the appointed time for him to die, rise, and ascend to the Father. This is the time for Jesus's glorification, including even the cross, because the cross begins his return to the Father.

In this context Jesus speaks of the grain of wheat dying. He uses the language of appearance, in which a seed "dies," that is, disappears from view, when it is planted in the earth. When it "dies" it bears much fruit. Jesus tells this parable about himself. He is the grain of wheat which, dying, bears much fruit. His disciples will only later understand that the "much fruit" of which Jesus speaks includes Gentiles. So, Jesus does not ignore the Greeks, but includes them in discussion of the results of his saving death. Beasley-Murray is pithy: "So surely as a grain of wheat must be buried if it is to yield fruit for man, so the Son of Man must give himself in death if he is to produce a harvest of life for the world."[20]

With his next words Jesus applies the parable to his disciples: "Whoever loves his life loses it, and whoever hates his life in this world will keep it for eternal life" (John 12:25). The disciples too are to be "grains of wheat" who are to "die," lose themselves in Christ's service, and thereby gain eternal life. Jesus's next words further explain: "If anyone serves me, he must follow me; and where I am, there will my servant be also. If anyone serves me, the Father will honor him" (v. 26).

Jesus, like a planted grain of wheat, dying will produce a plentiful harvest, saving many Jews and Gentiles.

Teaching in the Acts of the Apostles

The emphasis of Acts is not on Jesus's death but on his resurrection and exaltation.[21] The apostles are chiefly witnesses of Christ's resurrection (Acts 1:22; 3:15). Jesus's resurrection certifies his lordship, as Peter testifies on the day of Pentecost (2:36). His resurrection and exaltation are proofs that through him God offers the forgiveness of sins (5:30–31). Indeed, it is as the resurrected one that Christ forgives the sins of all who repent and believe in him (3:26).

The death of Christ is mentioned frequently in Acts. The apostles teach that Christ's death fulfilled God's plan. Peter preaches that Jesus was "delivered up according to the definite plan and foreknowledge of God" (Acts 2:23). The believers together pray to God acknowledging that what Herod and Pilate

---

[20]George R. Beasley-Murray, *John*, Word Biblical Commentary (Waco, TX: Word, 1987), 211.
[21]Jesus's resurrection is mentioned in the following places: Acts 1:22; 2:24–36; 3:15, 26; 4:10, 33; 5:30; 10:40; 13:30, 33, 34, 37; 17:3, 31; 26:22–23. His exaltation is mentioned in 2:33; 5:31.

conspired to do to Jesus only accomplished "whatever your hand and your plan had predestined to take place" (Acts 4:27–28). This was because Jesus's arrest, condemnation, and crucifixion fulfilled the words of Psalm 2:1–2.

The Christ Must Suffer

Repeatedly Acts teaches that Christ had to suffer in order to fulfill the predictions of the Old Testament. One passage will summarize others. After God healed a lame beggar through Peter, the apostle proclaimed, "What God foretold by the mouth of all the prophets, that his Christ would suffer, he thus fulfilled" (Acts 3:18; cf. 13:27; 17:3; 26:22–23).

Although Acts contains many references to the Messiah Jesus's suffering, it does not explain the saving significance of his death as clearly as the writings of John, Paul, the author to the Hebrews, or Peter do. Instead, Luke accents the saving significance of Jesus's resurrection, as already noted.

Jesus Is the Suffering Servant of the Lord

Acts does contain at least three hints of the saving significance of Jesus's death. First, Acts identifies Jesus with the suffering Servant of the Lord in Isaiah 53. The Ethiopian treasurer, who was reading Isaiah 53:7–8, queries Philip the evangelist, "About whom, I ask you, does the prophet say this, about himself or about someone else?" (Acts 8:34). Philip does not hesitate to reply: "Then Philip opened his mouth, and beginning with this Scripture he told him the good news about Jesus" (v. 35). Acts, then, understands Christ's person and work in terms of Isaiah 53.

Since the subject of Isaiah 53 is the suffering Servant of the Lord, and since Acts 8:34–35 identifies the sufferer of Isaiah 53 as Jesus, this sheds light on the passages in Acts that speak of Christ as God's "servant." In the passages quoted below, the speaker is indicated in parentheses:

> The God of Abraham, the God of Isaac, and the God of Jacob, the God of our fathers, glorified his servant Jesus, whom you delivered over and denied in the presence of Pilate. (Peter, Acts 3:13)

> God, having raised up his servant, sent him to you first, to bless you by turning every one of you from your wickedness. (Peter, Acts 3:26)

> For truly in this city there were gathered together against your holy servant Jesus, whom you anointed, both Herod and Pontius Pilate, along with the Gentiles and the peoples of Israel. (believers, Acts 4:27)

And now, Lord, look upon their threats and grant to your servants to continue to speak your word with all boldness, while you stretch out your hand to heal, and signs and wonders are performed through the name of your holy servant Jesus. (believers, Acts 4:29–30)

Luke's references in Acts to Jesus as "the Righteous One" are also reminiscent of Isaiah 53, this time pointing to verse 11, which reads,

> By his knowledge shall the righteous one, my servant,
>> make many to be accounted righteous,
>> and he shall bear their iniquities.

(Notice that Isaiah equates "the Righteous One" and the Lord's "servant.") Peter, Stephen, and Ananias, the believer who ministered to Saul of Tarsus after his conversion on the Damascus road, all refer to Jesus as "the Righteous One."

But you denied the Holy and Righteous One, and asked for a murderer to be granted to you. (Peter, Acts 3:14)

And they killed those who announced beforehand the coming of the Righteous One, whom you have now betrayed and murdered. (Stephen, Acts 7:52)

The God of our fathers appointed you to know his will, to see the Righteous One and to hear a voice from his mouth; for you will be a witness for him to everyone of what you have seen and heard. (Ananias, Acts 22:14–15)

None of these seven passages, which identify Jesus with the Servant of the Lord and righteous one of Isaiah 53, explains the saving significance of Jesus's death. But their pointing to the most powerful Old Testament passage to treat that theme is suggestive of the redemptive significance of his death. That theme, of course, is explicitly drawn out of Isaiah 53 by other New Testament authors.[22]

Jesus Was Put to Death by Hanging on a Tree

A second hint of the saving significance of Jesus's death is found in the two places where Peter says that the Jewish leaders put Jesus to death "by hanging him on a tree" (Acts 5:30; 10:39) and a third where Paul speaks of his being taken "down from the tree" (13:29). The background for these sayings is Deuteronomy 21:22–23:

---

[22]Mark 9:12; Luke 24:26; 1 Pet. 1:11; 2:25.

And if a man has committed a crime punishable by death and he is put to death, and you hang him on a tree, his body shall not remain all night on the tree, but you shall bury him the same day, for a hanged man is cursed by God. You shall not defile your land that the LORD your God is giving you for an inheritance.

In Acts, the apostles use the language of hanging on a tree to describe Jesus's death on the cross. They do not, however, draw out the theological implications of this fact—that Jesus was accursed when he died for sinners. It would remain for Paul to do so in his letter to the Galatians: "Christ redeemed us from the curse of the law by becoming a curse for us—for it is written, 'Cursed is everyone who is hanged on a tree'" (Gal. 3:13, citing Deut. 21:23). G. B. Caird comments, "Surely no Christian preacher would have chosen to describe the death of Jesus in terms which drew attention to the curse of God resting on the executed criminal, *unless he had first faced the scandal of the Cross and had come to believe that Jesus had borne the curse on behalf of others.*"[23]

Jesus Purchased the Church with His Blood

A third hint of the saving significance of Jesus's death is more than a hint; it is an intimation. This occurs when Paul admonishes the Ephesian elders, "Pay careful attention to yourselves and to all the flock, in which the Holy Spirit has made you overseers, to care for the church of God, which he obtained with his own blood" (Acts 20:28). This is an example of what the church fathers called the communication of attributes of the person of Christ. Scripture, designating Christ by a divine title, ascribes to him a quality pertaining to his human nature—"blood," that is, being susceptible to death. The communication of attributes underlines the unity of the person of Christ because it brings his human and divine natures together in an arresting manner.

Key for our present purposes is what Christ is said to do: as God incarnate he "purchased" the church with his own blood.[24] This is the language of redemption with an emphasis on the redemption price, as Morris points out: "Here the imagery is that of purchase. The Church is bought, as in a commercial transaction, with the blood of Christ. . . . What he means is the Church became Christ's own at great cost. For our salvation Christ shed his blood."[25] Christ is our Redeemer who delivered us from bondage by his blood—his violent death on the cross.

---

[23]Dennis E. Johnson, *The Message of Acts in the History of Redemption* (Phillipsburg, NJ: P&R, 1997), 148, citing G. B. Caird, *The Apostolic Age* (London: Duckworth, 1955), 40, italics added by Johnson.
[24]Some manuscripts read "Lord" instead of "God." This matters little because both are divine titles.
[25]Leon Morris, *The Cross in the New Testament* (Grand Rapids: Eerdmans, 1965), 140–41.

We began our survey of Acts by saying that it accentuates Christ's exaltation, including his resurrection, more than his death. Now, after examining what Acts says about Christ's death, we return to our starting place—his exaltation. But this time we stress that our Lord's exaltation means a great victory for him and his people. Repeatedly, Acts presents Jesus's death as the unjust verdict of the leaders of God's covenant people and then juxtaposes it with his resurrection as God's just verdict, which reverses the sinful judgment of man:

This Jesus . . . you crucified and killed by the hands of lawless men. God raised him up, loosing the pangs of death, because it was not possible for him to be held by it. (Acts 2:23–24)

Let all the house of Israel therefore know for certain that God has made him both Lord and Christ, this Jesus whom you crucified. (2:36)

The God of Abraham, the God of Isaac, and the God of Jacob, the God of our fathers, glorified his servant Jesus, whom you delivered over and denied in the presence of Pilate. (3:13)

But you denied the Holy and Righteous One, and asked for a murderer to be granted to you, and you killed the Author of life, whom God raised from the dead. To this we are witnesses. (3:14–15)

Those who live in Jerusalem and their rulers, because they did not recognize him nor understand the utterances of the prophets, which are read every Sabbath, fulfilled them by condemning him. . . . They asked Pilate to have him executed. . . . But God raised him from the dead. (13:27–28, 30)

This theme of reversal—sinful people condemning God's Christ but God overturning their verdict by raising and exalting him to his own right hand in heaven—again points to God's plan of salvation being accomplished, not by human design or strength, but by the mighty power of God through Christ the Redeemer.

Teaching in the Pauline Epistles

The death of Christ is a nonnegotiable part of the gospel that Paul preached and for which he would have died: "Christ died for our sins in accordance with the Scriptures . . . he was buried . . . he was raised on the third day in accordance with the Scriptures" (1 Cor. 15:3–4). Paul says much about the saving significance of

Christ's death, and if we were not so familiar with his words, we would realize
how shocking many of them are:

> Now if we have died with Christ, we believe that we will also live with him. (Rom. 6:8)

> He who did not spare his own Son but gave him up for us all, how will he not also
> with him graciously give us all things? (Rom. 8:32)

> For I decided to know nothing among you except Jesus Christ and him crucified.
> (1 Cor. 2:2)

> I have been crucified with Christ. It is no longer I who live, but Christ who lives
> in me. (Gal. 2:20)

> But far be it from me to boast except in the cross of our Lord Jesus Christ, by which
> the world has been crucified to me, and I to the world. (Gal. 6:14)

> . . . Christ Jesus, who, though he was in the form of God, did not count equality
> with God a thing to be grasped, but made himself nothing, taking the form of a
> servant, being born in the likeness of men. And being found in human form, he
> humbled himself by becoming obedient to the point of death, even death on a
> cross. (Phil. 2:5–8)

In fact, Paul says so much about Christ's cross that we must be selective.[26]
The second part of this book has six chapters treating the main biblical pictures
that interpret Christ's saving accomplishment. In order not to be too repetitive
we will study seven passages here while merely listing nine others that will be
dealt with in later chapters.[27]

Romans 3:24–26

> . . . Christ Jesus, whom God put forward as a propitiation by his blood, to be
> received by faith. This was to show God's righteousness, because in his divine
> forbearance he had passed over former sins. It was to show his righteousness
> at the present time, so that he might be just and the justifier of the one who has
> faith in Jesus.

---

[26]Rom. 3:24–26; 4:25; 5:6–10; 6:3–10; 7:4; 8:2–4, 32, 34; 14:9, 15; 1 Cor. 1:17–18, 23; 2:2; 8:11; 10:16;
15:3, 14–15; 2 Cor. 4:10; 13:4; Gal. 2:20; 6:14; Eph. 1:7; 2:13–16; Phil. 2:8; 3:10; Col. 1:20, 22; 2:14, 20;
1 Thess. 4:14; 5:10; 2 Tim. 2:11.
[27]Rom. 4:24–25; 8:3–4; 1 Cor. 6:19–20; 2 Cor. 5:18–20, 21; Gal. 1:4; Eph. 2:13–16; Col. 1:19–22; Titus
2:13–14.

In his purpose statement for the epistle to the Romans, Paul says that he will explain the gospel, which proclaims the revelation of the saving righteousness of God to all believers (Rom. 1:16–17). But he does not immediately do so. Instead, he says that "the wrath of God is revealed from heaven" against rebels (v. 18). It is only after showing humankind's universal need for salvation that the apostle returns to his theme: "But now *the righteousness of God* has been manifested" (3:21).

Furthermore, this righteousness is needed by all, "for all have sinned and fall short of the glory of God" (v. 23). Does generic faith in God save or does saving faith have a more specific content? The answer is that faith that saves is "faith in Jesus Christ for all who believe" (v. 22). What is the basis of this saving righteousness given to believers? It is Christ's works of redemption and propitiation (vv. 24–26). Paul simply mentions redemption and does not discuss it. We will postpone discussion of it until our study of Ephesians 1:7 in this chapter and the subsequent full chapter devoted to it.

If Paul only mentions redemption, he unfolds the meaning of propitiation. It is helpful at this point to distinguish propitiation and expiation. Both are accomplishments of Jesus's death on the cross but they point in different directions and have different aims. Propitiation is directed toward God and expiation is directed toward sin. Propitiation is the turning away of God's wrath, and expiation is the putting away of sin.

The publication of C. H. Dodd's *The Bible and the Greeks* in 1935 led to a "critical orthodoxy" that overturned the traditional understanding of the words translated "propitiation."[28] Dodd argued, largely on linguistic and theological grounds, that the word in Romans 3:25 should be rendered "means of expiation" and concerned Christ's work to cover or forgive sins. He insisted that the idea of propitiation was pagan in origin, conjuring up notions of vindictive deities who in rage demanded blood, and that it was unworthy of God. Dodd's work has been answered effectively by Leon Morris and Roger Nicole, among others.[29]

Before giving my view, I will affirm that Scripture teaches that Christ's death accomplishes the expiation of sin (e.g., in Heb. 9:26). But that is not the issue; the issue is what the meaning of ἱλαστήριον (*hilastērion*) is in Romans 3:25. Before making my case I want to distance the biblical portrayal of propitiation from pagan notions. In pagan ideas humans make fickle gods willing to forgive by appeasing (propitiating) them by various means. In Scripture a holy and lov-

---

[28]C. H. Dodd, *The Bible and the Greeks* (London: Hodder & Stoughton, 1935). The words are ἱλάσμος (*hilasmos*, 1 John 2:2; 4:10), ἱλάσκεσθαι (*hilaskesthai*, Heb. 2:17), and ἱλαστήριον (*hilastērion*, Rom. 3:25).
[29]Leon Morris, *The Apostolic Preaching of the Cross*, 3rd ed. (Grand Rapids: Eerdmans, 1965), 155–78; Roger Nicole, "C. H. Dodd and the Doctrine of Propitiation," *Westminster Theological Journal* 17 (1955): 117–57.

ing God takes the initiative and propitiates his own justice by bearing the brunt of his wrath against sin to freely forgive his rebellious creatures.

For two reasons I understand *hilastērion* in Romans 3:25 as propitiation and not merely expiation. First, the whole context of Romans has built up to this point, as I summarized above. The gospel is the revelation of God's saving righteousness (1:16–17). God has revealed his wrath against sinners (1:18–3:20). In 3:21 Paul returns to his announced theme—the revelation of God's saving righteousness. But if verses 25–26 do not teach that God's wrath was satisfied in Christ's cross, then where did the wrath of 1:18–3:20 go? How is it that 5:1 announces that believers have "peace with God through our Lord Jesus Christ"? How is that possible if God has not spent his holy hatred against sin? The answer is that God has punished Christ with the wrath we sinners all deserve. Douglas Moo reasons cogently: "When to the linguistic evidence we add the evidence of the context of Rom. 1–3, where the wrath of God is an overarching theme (1:18; cf. 2:5), the conclusion that *hilastērion* includes reference to the turning away of God's wrath is inescapable."[30]

Second and more importantly, 3:25–26 speak of propitiation and not merely expiation because of the meaning of these verses themselves. Key to understanding the passage is the redemptive historical distinction between "former sins" and "the present time" (vv. 25, 26). God publicly displayed Jesus as a *hilastērion* in his blood because in his patience "he had passed over *former sins*" (v. 25). Paul means that up until the time of Jesus's crucifixion, God forgave sins without actually having made atonement for them. The animal sacrifices were a picture of the gospel, and God really forgave Old Testament believers (see, e.g., Ps. 103:12). But "it is impossible for the blood of bulls and goats to take away sins" (Heb. 10:4). In his mercy God forgave the Old Testament saints without actually having made atonement. He forgave Old Testament believers on the basis of the work of Christ to come. But in the meantime, every time a sacrifice was performed, God wrote an IOU to himself, so to speak, looking forward to his actually making atonement through the blood of Christ (cf. Heb. 9:15). Paul tells us that that is what Christ did "at the present time." Christ had to die in order for God to maintain his moral integrity, to "settle accounts" that he had made with himself prior to Christ's death.

That is why Romans 3:25–26 says, "God put forward [Christ Jesus] as a propitiation by his blood. . . . to show God's righteousness," and "It was to show his righteousness at the present time, so that he might be just and the justifier of

---

[30]Douglas J. Moo, *The Epistle to the Romans*, The New International Commentary on the New Testament (Grand Rapids: Eerdmans, 1996), 235.

the one who has faith in Jesus." Although the meaning of "righteousness" here is debated, Moo argues convincingly that

> "his righteousness" must have reference to some aspect of God's character that might have been called into question because of his treating sins in the past with less than full severity, and that has now been demonstrated in setting forth Christ as "the propitiatory." . . . [It means] God's "consistency" in always acting in accordance with his character.[31]

The problem is not what so many assume today—how could a loving God condemn anyone?[32] That question is easily answered by reading the first three chapters of the Bible, or the first three chapters of Romans. A holy God could condemn the world for its rebellion. The biblical problem is a much more difficult one—how could a holy God maintain his moral integrity and forgive sinners? The answer is by putting forward Christ "as a propitiation in his blood." God settled accounts accumulated in the Old Testament; he satisfied his holy anger against sin by pouring that anger against Christ, who willingly gave himself for his people.[33]

The results are fantastic. God maintains his moral integrity as God and at the same time saves everyone who believes in his Son. In fact, Christ secured "an eternal redemption" that brings an "eternal inheritance" (Heb. 9:12, 15). Thus it is "at the present time" that we learn that God forgave "former sins" on the basis of Christ's work to come.

This passage is of great importance because of its programmatic place in Paul's argument in Romans. When Paul begins to actually explain the revelation of God's saving righteousness to sinners, he mentions redemption and elucidates propitiation.

Romans 5:10

> For if while we were enemies we were reconciled to God by the death of his Son, much more, now that we are reconciled, shall we be saved by his life.

This is the shortest of the four reconciliation passages in Paul. We will study the others—2 Corinthians 5:18–20; Ephesians 2:13–16; and Colossians 1:19–22—

---

[31] Ibid., 240. See the discussion beginning on p. 238.

[32] For an accessible and brief presentation of hell, see Christopher W. Morgan and Robert A. Peterson, *What Is Hell?*, Basics of the Faith (Phillipsburg, NJ: P&R, 2010).

[33] See the excellent treatment of this passage by D. A. Carson, "Atonement in Rom 3:21–26," in Hill and James, *The Glory of the Atonement*, 119–39.

in the chapter "Christ Our Reconciler." This passage appears in a section of Romans giving the benefits of justification. In Romans 5:1–5 Paul lists these benefits: peace with God (v. 1), joy (v. 2), hope (vv. 2–5), and God's love (v. 5). Then in verses 6–11 he repeats the same benefits in reverse order: God's love (vv. 6–8), hope (vv. 9–10), joy (v. 11), and peace with God (v. 11). The benefits thus fall into a pattern. An inverted parallelism or chiasm follows the form ABCD DCBA, where the letters stand for ideas. Here are the benefits laid out in a diagram:

A Peace with God (v. 1)

  B Joy (v. 2)

    C Hope (vv. 2–5)

      D God's love (v. 5)

      D God's love (vv. 6–8)

    C Hope (vv. 9–10)

  B Joy (v. 11)

A Peace with God (v. 11)

In verses 9–10, then, Paul draws his readers' attention to the hope of final salvation. He does this in two ways: first, in terms of justification, and then in terms of reconciliation (in vv. 9 and 10, respectively). Twice Paul employs a Jewish argument from the more difficult to the less difficult. He uses the words "much more" to signal his use of this argument. In verse 9 he argues in terms of justification, and in verse 10 in terms of reconciliation.

Paul uses shorthand in verse 9 and longhand in verse 10. The full argument involves an "if" clause followed by a "then" clause, and we find both types of clauses in verse 10. But verse 9 only has a "then" clause. Paul expects his readers to provide an "if" clause from the preceding verses: If, when we were condemned before a holy God, he justified us through the death of his Son. . . . "Since, therefore, we have now been justified by his blood, much more shall we be saved by him from the wrath of God" (v. 9). Paul uses "wrath" to refer to hell, as he frequently does in his writings.[34]

Paul argues from the harder to the easier: if God did the harder thing—justified guilty sinners—he will surely do the easier thing—keep saved to the

---

[34]He also uses "wrath" to refer to hell in Rom. 1:18; 2:5, 8; 3:5; 9:22; 12:19; Eph. 2:3; 5:6; Col. 3:6; 1 Thess. 1:10; 2:16; 5:9. See Douglas J. Moo, "Paul on Hell," in Christopher W. Morgan and Robert A. Peterson, eds., *Hell Under Fire* (Grand Rapids: Zondervan, 2004), 91–109.

end those he has justified. This is a powerful argument for God's preservation of his saints. God did the incredible and declared the unrighteous righteous through Christ. Now he will do the expected—he will stand by his previous verdict and not condemn his justified people.

For the sake of emphasis, Paul repeats a similar argument designed to assure his readers of final salvation. But now he refers to salvation as reconciliation instead of justification. "For if while we were enemies we were reconciled to God by the death of his Son, much more, now that we are reconciled, shall we be saved by his life" (Rom. 5:10). This time Paul writes in longhand, giving both "if" and "then" clauses: if when we were God's enemies he made us his friends by his Son's death, now that we are his friends he certainly will keep us saved by his Son's resurrection. Here Paul does not state what we shall be saved from, but he has already told us in verse 9—God's wrath.

Reconciliation is the only picture of Christ's saving work in our study that lacks an Old Testament background. In fact, it appears only in the four Pauline passages listed at the beginning of this section. Its background is alienation—"we were enemies" of God due to our sins (v. 10). Reconciliation means peacemaking. God, the offended party, takes the initiative and makes peace between himself and the alienated offenders—us. But more than God's initiative is necessary for reconciliation to occur. God must accomplish the work of reconciliation.

Who is the peacemaker? This peace must be brought about by God but also by a human being. The reconciler must be God because only God can restore the rebels (Col. 1:19–20). The reconciler must be a man because death is necessary and God in heaven cannot die. The reconciler is Christ, God incarnate; "he himself is our peace," as Paul says (Eph. 2:14). How does he accomplish this? In Colossians, Paul explains that Christ reconciles by "making peace by the blood of his cross" (Col. 1:20) and "in his body of flesh by his death" (Col. 1:22). Romans is more concise: "We were reconciled to God by the death of his Son" (Rom. 5:10). I will conclude by rehearsing the point of Romans 5:10: "For if while we were enemies we were reconciled to God by the death of his Son, much more, now that we are reconciled, shall we be saved by his life." God, who made enemies into friends through Christ's death (and resurrection), will keep his friends unto final salvation through Christ's (death and) resurrection.

Romans 5:18–19

Therefore, as one trespass led to condemnation for all men, so one act of righteousness leads to justification and life for all men. For as by the one man's disobedience the many were made sinners, so by the one man's obedience the many will be made righteous.

This passage is the culmination of Paul's famous Adam-Christ parallel in Romans 5. A brief summary of the apostle's argument is in order. He begins to make a comparison that he does not complete: "Therefore, just as sin came into the world through one man, and death through sin, and so death spread to all men because all sinned—" (Rom. 5:12). The dash indicates that the flow of thought is interrupted. Paul intends to compare Adam's disastrous effects on the human race with Christ's salutary effects on his people. But he does not finish the comparison. Instead, in the next two verses he demonstrates that only Adam's sin can explain the domination of sin over the human race from the fall in Eden to the giving of the law at Sinai.

Next Paul lays the foundation for the completion, in verses 18–19, of the unfinished comparison begun in verse 12: "Adam, who was a type of the one who was to come" (v. 14). In certain respects Adam is a type, a prefiguring, an acted prophecy, of Christ, the coming one. Both have tremendous effects upon others. The destinies of the whole human race are viewed in relation to Adam and Christ. Indeed, Christ is "the last Adam . . . the second man" (1 Cor. 15:45, 47).

There are fundamental similarities between Adam and Christ. But before explaining these, Paul feels it necessary to underscore dissimilarities between the two. Adam's one sin brings death; Christ brings grace and eternal life (Rom. 5:15). Adam's one sin brings condemnation; Christ's grace brings justification (v. 16). Adam's one sin brings the reign of death; Christ brings a reign of life to believers (v. 17).

Having set a sufficient distance between Adam and Christ, Paul now proceeds to build upon their basic similarity to complete the comparison begun in verse 12. "Therefore, as one trespass led to condemnation for all men, so one act of righteousness leads to justification and life for all men" (v. 18). Adam's one sin brought God's verdict of condemnation to humanity. His original sin makes all guilty before God. Elsewhere in the passage, Paul explains that the consequence of Adam's sin is physical and spiritual death (vv. 12, 14, 15, 17). His thought is thus that Adam's sin led to condemnation, which led to death.

Christ, the second Adam, also has enormous effect upon his race, his people, but, unlike the first Adam's, the effect is positive: ". . . so one act of righteousness leads to justification and life for all men" (v. 18). The second Adam stands over against the first Adam. Christ's "one act of righteousness," because it corresponds to Adam's "one trespass," refers to something Christ did, namely, his death on the cross. Christ's death produces the opposite of the condemnation brought on by

Adam's primal sin—"justification," God's verdict of righteousness. Paul unbalances the equation when he adds to justification "and life for all men," thereby emphasizing the greatness of Christ's accomplishment. Christ's cross brings God's declaration of righteousness, which in turn brings eternal life. His thought is thus that Christ's one act of righteousness leads to justification, which leads to life.

Paul basically repeats the thought of verse 18 in verse 19: "For as by the one man's disobedience the many were made sinners, so by the one man's obedience the many will be made righteous." Adam's disobedience, his original sin, caused his race to become sinners. By contrast, Christ's obedience causes his race to become righteous in God's sight. While not denying Christ's lifelong obedience, Paul here focuses on Christ's "becoming obedient to the point of death, even death on a cross" (Phil. 2:8). The effects of the two Adams upon their respective races can be expressed thus:

Adam's disobedience ➡ many were made sinners.
Christ's obedience ➡ many will be made righteous.

Universalists claim that when Paul writes "so one act of righteousness leads to justification and life for all men" (v. 18), he teaches that everyone will be saved.[35] But this is a selective use of the evidence, for Paul says "by the one man's obedience *the many* will be made righteous" in the very next verse. Is the apostle contradicting himself in the space of two verses, teaching that all, not merely many, are affected by the two Adams in verse 18 and that many, but not all, are affected by them in verse 19? Of course not. The key is to note that Paul is not comparing "all men" with "the many." Rather, he is contrasting the two Adams and their huge effects upon their respective races. Adam brings woe to his race, and Christ salvation to his. It is not "all" opposed to "many" in verses 18–19. It is "one trespass" of one man affecting "all men" and "one act of righteousness" of one man affecting "all men" in verse 18. It is "one man's disobedience" bringing condemnation and "one man's obedience" bringing justification in verse 19. We cannot look to these verses for the number of the lost or redeemed, for it is not Paul's purpose to give those numbers here. He does that elsewhere, indicating that everyone is fallen in Adam and all believers are saved by Christ.

In sum, Paul presents Christ as the second and last Adam, whose "one act of righteousness," his "obedience" unto death on the cross, is the basis for God's justifying sinners (who believe) and granting them eternal life.

---

[35]For a brief refutation of universalism, see Robert A. Peterson, *Hell on Trial* (Phillipsburg, NJ: P&R, 1995). For a fuller refutation, see J. I. Packer, "Universalism: Will Everyone Ultimately Be Saved?," in Morgan and Peterson, *Hell Under Fire*, 169–94.

Galatians 3:13

> Christ redeemed us from the curse of the law by becoming a curse for us—for it is written, "Cursed is everyone who is hanged on a tree."

This verse is located in a section of the epistle dominated by the ideas of "curse" and "blessing." Old Testament background includes the Israelites' rehearsing the blessings and curses of the law on Mount Ebal and Mount Gerazim, respectively (Deut. 27:12–28:68). God wanted the people to know that, depending on their obedience or disobedience to God's law, they would reap the blessings or curses contained therein. God's words of blessing and curse were viewed as dynamic and powerful. In contrast to our culture's view of words as trivial, Scripture portrays God's words as dynamic.

> For as the rain and the snow come down from heaven
>> and do not return there but water the earth,
> making it bring forth and sprout,
>> giving seed to the sower and bread to the eater,
> so shall my word be that goes out of my mouth;
>> it shall not return to me empty,
> but it shall accomplish that which I purpose,
>> and shall succeed in the thing for which I sent it. (Isa. 55:10–11)

> For the word of God is living and active, sharper than any two-edged sword, piercing to the division of soul and of spirit, of joints and of marrow, and discerning the thoughts and intentions of the heart. (Heb. 4:12)

In Scripture God's word is powerful and effective. So it is in Galatians 3:7–14, where Paul instructs his readers concerning the blessings of the Abrahamic covenant and the curses of the law. Notice the numerous uses of "blessed"/"blessing" and "curse"/"cursed" (italicized here):

> Know then that it is those of faith who are the sons of Abraham. And the Scripture, foreseeing that God would justify the Gentiles by faith, preached the gospel beforehand to Abraham, saying, "In you shall all the nations be *blessed.*" So then, those who are of faith are *blessed* along with Abraham, the man of faith.
> For all who rely on works of the law are under a *curse*; for it is written, "*Cursed* be everyone who does not abide by all things written in the Book of the Law, and do them." Now it is evident that no one is justified before God by the law, for . . . . Christ redeemed us from the *curse* of the law by becoming a *curse* for us—for it is written, "*Cursed* is everyone who is hanged on a tree"—so that in Christ Jesus

the *blessing* of Abraham might come to the Gentiles, so that we might receive the promised Spirit through faith. (Gal. 3:7–11, 13–14)

Note that the passage begins and ends with blessing and that between the blessing is much emphasis on cursing (five occurrences). How does Paul define the blessings and the curses? The blessings are the fulfillment of the promises that God made to Abraham when he entered into covenant with him. Paul cites part of Genesis 12:3: "In you shall all the nations be blessed" (Gal. 3:8). He views that promise as fulfilled in the gospel's coming to the Gentiles. He says Christ died for us "so that in Christ Jesus the blessing of Abraham might come to the Gentiles" (v. 14). And then he defines one of the blessings: "so that we might receive the promised Spirit through faith" (v. 14). The blessings of the Abrahamic covenant are the blessings of the gospel, including a relationship with God through Christ, receiving the Holy Spirit, eternal life, and all that they entail.

Paul does not allow us to guess what he means by the curse. It is the threat of the punishment that will be meted out to all lawbreakers: "Cursed be everyone who does not abide by all things written in the Book of the Law, and do them." It is within this context of blessing and curse that Paul teaches that "Christ redeemed us from the *curse* of the law by becoming a *curse* for us" (v. 13). Richard Longenecker helpfully explains, enlisting the words of Martin Luther:

> The thought involved here is that of "an exchange curse" . . . as Klaus Berger calls it . . . or more expansively, M. Luther: "Thou Christ art my sin and my curse, or rather, I am thy sin, thy curse, thy death, thy wrath of God, thy hell; and contrariwise, thou are my righteousness, my blessing, my life, my grace of God and my heaven."[36]

Verse 13 is as strong a statement of Christ's being our legal penal substitute as is found in Scripture. Paul cites Deuteronomy 21:23, which curses the executed person whose body is left hanging on a tree, to prove that Christ died the death of an accursed man: "For it is written, 'Cursed is everyone who is hanged on a tree'" (Gal. 3:13). Christ took the penalty that we lawbreakers deserved—he became a curse—in order that we might gain the blessing of eternal life. He died an accursed death on the tree to rescue us from the punishment of the law.[37]

---

[36]Richard N. Longenecker, *Galatians*, Word Biblical Commentary (Nashville: Nelson, 1990), 121.

[37]I reject Hans Boersma's interpretation of this passage in his prestigious book, *Violence, Hospitality, and the Cross* (Grand Rapids: Baker, 2004), 172, whereby he interprets it in terms of the nation of Israel instead of individual Jews and Gentiles.

Ephesians 1:7

> In him we have redemption through his blood, the forgiveness of our trespasses,
> according to the riches of his grace.

Ephesians 1:3–14 is one long sentence in Greek. Paul gives structural indicators that divide it into sections: "to the praise of his glorious grace" (v. 6) and what appears to be shorthand for it, "to the praise of his glory" (vv. 12, 14). The resultant divisions have a Trinitarian theme.

1:3–6: The Father's election
1:7–12: The Son's redemption
1:13–14: The Holy Spirit as seal

Our concern is with the central section, the only one that mentions Christ's saving work in the first fourteen verses. Paul says that in Christ "we have redemption through his blood" (v. 7). All of the salvific blessings come to us "in Christ," that is, by union with him. His work does not benefit us as long as he remains outside of us, but when we are spiritually joined to him by faith, his benefits become ours. Paul begins Ephesians 1:3–14 praising the Father for uniting us with his Son and thereby granting us all blessings: "Blessed be the God and Father of our Lord Jesus Christ, who has blessed us in Christ with every spiritual blessing in the heavenly places" (v. 3).

When Paul writes, "We have redemption through his blood" (v. 7), he points to the redemption price. We cannot do a full study of redemption based on this verse alone; many other passages must be taken into account. We will do so in a later chapter devoted to "Christ Our Redeemer." For now it will suffice to list the three aspects of redemption given by Morris, who has conducted such a study:

- "The state of sin out of which man is to be redeemed."
- "The price which is paid. . . . Christ has paid the price of our redemption. . . . He is our Substitute."
- "The resultant state of the believer. . . . the liberty of the sons of God."[38]

John Stott describes this third aspect in another way: "It draws attention to the person of the redeemer who has proprietary rights over his purchase. Thus Jesus' lordship over both church and Christian is attributed to his having bought us with his own blood."[39]

---

[38] Morris, *The Apostolic Preaching of the Cross*, 61–62.
[39] John R. W. Stott, *The Cross of Christ* (Downers Grove, IL: InterVarsity, 1986), 181.

Morris and Stott summarize Scripture's teaching on redemption well. We were in bondage to sin (Gal. 4:4–7). Christ redeemed us through his blood (Eph. 1:7). As a result, we enjoy the freedom of God's sons and daughters (Gal. 4:7–9; 5:1), and we gladly acknowledge Christ's lordship over us (1 Cor. 6:18–20).

Ephesians 1:7 specifies the redemption price—"redemption through his blood." Although some have sought to define "blood," occurring in such a context, as the release of life and the like, Morris has shown definitively that this is an error. Rather, after studying "blood" in the whole of Scripture, he concludes, "Thus it seems tolerably certain that in both the Old and New Testaments the blood signifies essentially the death."[40] The blood of Christ, which redeems, is his violent death on the cross.

Paul describes an important benefit of redemption when he speaks of "redemption through his blood, the forgiveness of our trespasses." Here is the central aspect of Christian freedom purchased by Christ—forgiveness. The Redeemer's cross work has bought us out of slavery to sin with the result that our sins are pardoned and our consciences are clean before God. All of this, of course, is "according to the riches of his grace" (v. 7). It is no wonder that the redeemed will cry out,

> Worthy are you . . .
> for you were slain, and by your blood you ransomed people for God
>   from every tribe and language and people and nation. (Rev. 5:9)

Ephesians 5:2

> And walk in love, as Christ loved us and gave himself up for us, a fragrant offering and sacrifice to God.

Paul exhorts the Ephesians "to put off [their] old self, which . . . is corrupt through deceitful desires . . . and to put on the new self, created after the likeness of God in true righteousness and holiness" (Eph. 4:22–24). He then proceeds to apply the pattern of taking off and putting on to several areas: take off falsehood and put on the truth (v. 25); take off sinful anger and put on being angry while not sinning (vv. 26–27); take off stealing and put on working (v. 28); take off corrupt talk and put on edifying talk (v. 29); take off anger and clamor and put on kindness and forgiveness (vv. 31–32).

These last two verses deserve quotation, as they lead into 5:1–2: "Let all bitterness and wrath and anger and clamor and slander be put away from you, along

---

[40]Morris, *The Apostolic Preaching of the Cross*, 126. His entire treatment is valuable (pp. 112–28).

with all malice. Be kind to one another, tenderhearted, forgiving one another, as God in Christ forgave you" (4:31–32). Speaking of kindness, tenderheartedness, and forgiveness leads Paul to speak of love. This is especially so because he uses God's forgiveness in Christ as the measure of Christians' willingness to forgive each other when wronged.

This leads the apostle to write, "Therefore be imitators of God, as beloved children" (5:1). God's love for us in putting us into his family motivates us to imitate God and to love one another. Next Paul writes, "And walk in love, as Christ loved us" (v. 2). His thought moves from imitating God to imitating Christ. Believers are to live lives of love because Christ first loved them.

It is easy for Paul, when speaking of Christ's love for his people, to think of his sacrificial death. So, he writes, "And walk in love, as Christ loved us and gave himself up for us, a fragrant offering and sacrifice to God" (v. 2). Christ's love is epitomized in his voluntary death on behalf of his own. He "gave himself up for us" because he "loved us." And this self-giving is described in the terms of Old Testament sacrifice: "a fragrant offering and sacrifice to God." As Old Testament food offerings were sometimes described as having "a pleasing aroma to the LORD" (e.g., Lev. 1:9; Gen. 8:21), so the apostle describes Christ's priestly sacrifice of himself as "a fragrant offering and sacrifice to God." Christ's self-offering is pleasing to God. God favorably accepts the self-sacrifice of his beloved Son.

We easily think of Hebrews when we think of Christ as our sacrifice, but the idea is here in Ephesians 5:2 too: "Christ loved us and gave himself up for us, a fragrant offering and sacrifice to God." Jesus's death on the cross is a priestly sacrifice. And although Paul does not develop the idea here, elsewhere Scripture teaches that this is the ultimate sacrifice, which saves believers eternally.

Colossians 2:13–15

And you, who were dead in your trespasses and the uncircumcision of your flesh, God made alive together with him, having forgiven us all our trespasses, by canceling the record of debt that stood against us with its legal demands. This he set aside, nailing it to the cross. He disarmed the rulers and authorities and put them to open shame, by triumphing over them in him.

Paul depicts two maladies from which unsaved people suffer, including his readers in Colossae before they came to faith in Christ—spiritual death and uncleanness: "[You] were dead in your trespasses and the uncircumcision of your flesh" (v. 13). And God, in his grace, heals their maladies. The remedy for spiritual death is regeneration: "God made [you] alive together with him"

(v. 13). The remedy for spiritual uncleanness is full pardon for sin: ". . . having forgiven us *all* our trespasses" (v. 13).

If we ask how God does this, Paul answers, "by canceling the record of debt that stood against us with its legal demands" (v. 14). "Record of debt" translates χειρόγραφον (*cheirographon*), which means a handwritten note of indebtedness. Paul adds that the record of debt opposes us "with its legal demands." A comparison with the only other place where Paul uses this word sheds light on its use here. There the expression "the law of commandments expressed in *ordinances*" (Eph. 2:15) shows that it refers to the Ten Commandments.

Humankind signed, as it were, a handwritten note admitting its failure to keep God's commandments. This record of debt "stood against us" because it condemned us; it exposed us as lawbreakers. Paul says that God forgave us "by canceling the record of debt that stood against us with its legal demands." The word "cancel" here means blot out or erase the debt. Is Paul teaching that God merely looked the other way, so to speak, and did not hold us responsible for our disobedience to his law? Of course not, for the next words explain how God canceled our moral debt: "This he set aside, nailing it to the cross" (Col. 2:14).

Here is a vivid picture of legal penal substitution. God forgave our sins by nailing our bond of indebtedness, consisting of our failure to keep the Ten Commandments, to the cross of his Son. The imagery here is the Roman practice of nailing to crosses the charges for which the crucified were being executed (see John 19:19). Moo captures the thrust:

> In causing him to be nailed to the cross, God (the subject of the verb) has provided the full cancellation of the debt of obedience that we had incurred. Christ took upon himself the penalty that we were under because of our disobedience, and his death fully satisfied God's necessary demand for due punishment of that disobedience.[41]

In the next verse, Paul abruptly shifts imagery: "He disarmed the rulers and authorities and put them to open shame, by triumphing over them in him." "The rulers and authorities" are angels in Paul's letters, here evil angels or demons because God defeats them (cf. Col. 1:15; Eph. 6:12). God is portrayed as our mighty champion, who through Christ defeats and humiliates the demons. The word rendered "disarmed" is literally "stripped." Paul is saying either that God stripped his demonic foes of their weapons or that he stripped them of their clothes. The picture is one of a Roman victory parade in which the victors

---

[41]Douglas J. Moo, *The Letters to the Colossians and to Philemon*, The Pillar New Testament Commentary (Grand Rapids: Eerdmans, 2008), 211–12.

would march in pride and the conquered enemies would cringe in defeat. Paul may be picturing the enemies as being paraded naked before the conquerors' wives and children, adding to their humiliation. At least he is saying that God disarmed them.

God "put them to open shame" (Col. 2:15). The word used here occurs elsewhere in the New Testament only in Matthew 1:19, where godly Joseph determines to divorce Mary quietly because he was "unwilling *to put* her *to shame.*" Almighty God openly humiliated the demons. Furthermore, in keeping with the Roman triumphal march imagery, Paul says that God disarmed the demons and shamed them "by triumphing over them in him."

The Greek word at the end of Colossians 2:15 is ambiguous, meaning that God triumphed either in *him* or in *it*, a reference to the cross. The NIV adopts "the cross," and the ESV "him." It seems to me that whichever option is chosen, it implies the other. God triumphed over the demons in the Christ (of the cross). Or God triumphed over the demons in the cross (of the Christ). Either way, it is Jesus crucified who accomplished God's mighty victory over the demons.

In the space of two verses, then, Paul combines the legal penal and Christus Victor views of the atonement. Christ pays our moral debt, and God in him vanquishes our demonic enemies. We will further explore the relation between these two verses in the chapter "Christ Our Victor."

Teaching in the General Epistles

The General Epistles also have much to teach us concerning Jesus's saving death.

Hebrews

Hebrews is famous for its presentation of Christ as High Priest and sacrifice. These themes will be the primary focus of the chapter "Christ Our Sacrifice."[42] Here I will treat two passages in Hebrews: the brief introduction of the sacrificial theme in chapter 1 and the multiple images of Christ's saving work in chapter 2.

Hebrews 1:3

> Long ago, at many times and in many ways, God spoke to our fathers by the prophets, but in these last days he has spoken to us by his Son, whom he appointed the heir of all things, through whom also he created the world. He is the radiance of the glory of God and the exact imprint of his nature, and he upholds the universe by the word of his power. After making purification for sins, he sat down at

---

[42]There we will study Hebrews 1:3; 2:17–18; 7:23–27; 9:11–28; and 10:10–14.

the right hand of the Majesty on high, having become as much superior to angels as the name he has inherited is more excellent than theirs. (Heb. 1:1–4)

Hebrews 1, as clearly as anywhere in Scripture, presents Christ's threefold office of prophet, priest, and king. The Son of God is the great prophet, for "in these last days he [God] has spoken to us by his Son" (Heb. 1:2). Preeminently in Hebrews 1, Christ is the King who "sat down at the right hand of the Majesty on high" as co-regent, who (unlike the angels) bears the royal and divine title of "Son," and who has a "throne," a "scepter," and a "kingdom" (vv. 3, 5, 8). In fact, the first chapter of Hebrews mainly treats Christ's coronation as heavenly King at his session at God's right hand. Although Hebrews 1 first mentions Christ's prophetic office and largely concerns his royal office, in one phrase it introduces what will become a major theme of the epistle—Christ's office of High Priest: "After making purification for sins, he sat down at the right hand of the Majesty on high" (v. 3).

This text, anticipating the powerful teaching in chapters 9 and 10, magnifies Christ's saving accomplishment. It is a key text on the atonement because it affirms that Jesus made "purification for sins." The author views sin as defiling and in need of cleansing. Christ's death on the cross washes away sin and brings forgiveness to everyone who believes. These words contain three truths concerning Jesus's saving death and resurrection.

First, Hebrews 1:3 teaches that Christ's atonement is *final* because, unlike any Old Testament priest, after finishing his priestly service he sat down. Verses from chapter 10 provide inspired commentary on 1:3:

> And every priest stands daily at his service, offering repeatedly the same sacrifices, which can never take away sins. But when Christ had offered for all time a single sacrifice for sins, he sat down at the right hand of God, waiting from that time until his enemies should be made a footstool for his feet. For by a single offering he has perfected for all time those who are being sanctified. (Heb. 10:11–14)

The tabernacle and temple contained furniture, but none suitable for sitting. While serving, Old Testament priests never sat. This was one indication that their sacrifices were provisional, that they could "never take away sins" (10:11). If they had taken away sin, they would have ceased being offered (10:2). The Old Testament offerings cried out for a future sacrifice to deal with sin once and for all. The Son of God made that very sacrifice when he offered himself. And—astonishingly from an Old Testament perspective—"when Christ had offered for all time a single sacrifice for sins, he *sat down* at the right hand of God" (v. 12). His session showed the finality of his priestly work.

Second, Hebrews 1:3 teaches that Christ's atonement is *perfect* because of where he sat down: "After making purification for sins, he sat down at the right hand of the Majesty on high" (1:3). When Christ finished his atoning work, he ascended and sat down at God's right hand, the chief place of authority and honor in the universe. The Father's granting the Son such a position is the Father's way of showing that the Son's work of atonement is complete and perfect. Nothing can be added. For this reason the former sacrifices, offered at the command of God, have ceased.

> For Christ has entered . . . into heaven itself, now to appear in the presence of God on our behalf. Nor was it to offer himself repeatedly, as the high priest enters the holy places every year with blood not his own, for then he would have had to suffer repeatedly since the foundation of the world. But as it is, he has appeared once for all at the end of the ages to put away sin by the sacrifice of himself. (9:24–26)

Christ's finished, perfect sacrifice brings the Old Testament offerings to a halt, and because it is perfect, it is also efficacious.

Third, Hebrews 1:3 teaches that Christ's atonement is *effective* because of where he sat down. When he sat at the right hand of "the Majesty on high," Christ had satisfied all of God's requirements to make atonement. His priestly sacrifice made "purification for sins." That is why the author says later in his letter that Christ secured an "eternal redemption" and "by a single offering he has perfected for all time those who are being sanctified" (Heb. 9:12; 10:14). David A. deSilva captures well the author's meaning: "The exaltation of the Son is the present reality that the addressees should consider. It is the proof of the efficacy of his ministry of mediation and guarantee of God's favor for those who approach God through the Son."[43]

Hebrews 2:8–9, 14–15, 17

> At present, we do not yet see everything in subjection to him. But we see him who for a little while was made lower than the angels, namely Jesus, crowned with glory and honor because of the suffering of death, so that by the grace of God he might taste death for everyone. . . .
>
> Since therefore the children share in flesh and blood, he himself likewise partook of the same things, that through death he might destroy the one who has the

---

[43]David A. deSilva, *Perseverance in Gratitude: A Socio-Rhetorical Commentary on the Epistle "to the Hebrews"* (Grand Rapids: Eerdmans, 2000), 91.

power of death, that is, the devil, and deliver all those who through fear of death were subject to lifelong slavery. . . . Therefore he had to be made like his brothers in every respect, so that he might become a merciful and faithful high priest in the service of God, to make propitiation for the sins of the people.

Hebrews 2 has one of the most concentrated and extensive treatments of Christ's saving work in Scripture. It will reappear numerous times in later chapters dealing with the metaphors that explain Christ's saving deeds. Here I will survey the author's presentation of three successive atonement motifs.

Jesus, the second and last Adam. The Son's incarnation establishes a solidarity between him and humankind that enables him to act as their representative. As shown in the chapter on the incarnation, that event is the trigger of the three atonement motifs corresponding to the three parts of the quotation above. The first motif presents Jesus as the second and last Adam in light of the author's quotation of Psalm 8:4–6:

> What is man, that you are mindful of him,
>   or the son of man, that you care for him?
> You made him for a little while lower than the angels;
>   you have crowned him with glory and honor,
>   putting everything in subjection under his feet. (Heb. 2:6–8)

In its context the psalm speaks of our first parents, Adam and Eve, and of their creational blessings of honor and dominion. The writer summarizes Psalm 8:6–8: "Now in putting everything in subjection to him, he left nothing outside his control" (Heb. 2:8). Under God, Adam and Eve's dominion was total. But, alas, although this was the situation at creation, "at present, we do not yet see everything in subjection to him" (v. 8). The fall ruined humankind's exercise of dominion, and now people abuse one another and the rest of God's creation.

The situation seems hopeless because all human beings are tarnished by the curse of sin. Who can rescue fallen humankind? The author answers: "But we see him who for a little while was made lower than the angels, namely Jesus, crowned with glory and honor because of the suffering of death, so that by the grace of God he might taste death for everyone" (v. 9). This psalm is not messianic, that is, it does not predict the Messiah. But at his incarnation, Jesus steps into Psalm 8, so to speak. When the Son of God becomes a human being, the words of the psalm that originally described Adam and Eve now pertain to him. By virtue of his incarnation, Jesus is the "last Adam," the "second man"

(1 Cor. 15:45, 47). In this way, he "for a little while was made lower than the angels" (Heb. 2:9).

Why? The answer lies close at hand: "We see him who for a little while was made lower than the angels, namely Jesus, crowned with glory and honor because of the suffering of death, so that by the grace of God he might taste death for everyone" (v. 9). Jesus became a man so that he could experience "the suffering of death." As the second Adam he was able to "taste death for everyone" and thereby reverse the curse on our first parents and their race. As a result, he now is "crowned with glory and honor." Consequently, God the Father, because of the death and exaltation of Jesus his Son, brings "many sons to glory" (v. 10), restoring the original creational "glory and honor" (Ps. 8:5; Heb. 2:7).

Peter T. O'Brien's words are apt: "In an amazing way Jesus fulfills God's design for creation and displays what had always been intended for all humankind. He is the one in whom the primal glory and sovereignty are restored."[44]

Jesus, the Victor. The second atonement motif presents Jesus as the Victor. Again, the writer to the Hebrews begins with the incarnation: "Since therefore the children share in flesh and blood, he himself likewise partook of the same things" (Heb. 2:14). By becoming a human being, Jesus shared in humanity. Why did he become a man? He did so "that through death he might destroy the one who has the power of death, that is, the devil, and deliver all those who through fear of death were subject to lifelong slavery" (vv. 14–15).

The Son of God became a human being so that he could die on the cross. His death accomplishes two goals. First, it destroys the Devil. Second, it delivers his people from hell. The Devil "has the power of death" as the usurper who deceived Adam and Eve and occasioned the fall. Jesus's death vanquishes the Evil One, by already depriving him of his power, and will one day result in his being cast into "the lake of fire and sulfur" to suffer eternal punishment (Rev. 20:10).

By his death the Son also delivers "all those who through fear of death were subject to lifelong slavery" (Heb. 2:15). The "death" spoken of here is not mere physical death, but spiritual death that involves the "fear" that "has to do with punishment" (1 John 4:18). Such fear of death enslaves those who do not know the Lord. Christ the Redeemer, through his death and resurrection, delivers from this bondage all who believe in him. He is his people's mighty champion.

---

[44]Peter T. O'Brien, *The Letter to the Hebrews*, The Pillar New Testament Commentary (Grand Rapids: Eerdmans, 2010), 101.

Jesus, the great High Priest. The third atonement motif presents Jesus as the great High Priest. We thus end our survey of Hebrews where we began in 1:3, with Christ our priest, a theme that will take precedence in the rest of the author's christological exposition. Once more the author starts with the incarnation: "Therefore he had to be made like his brothers in every respect, so that he might become a merciful and faithful high priest in the service of God" (Heb. 2:17). We needed a great High Priest who was both divine and human, namely "Jesus" (the name given him at birth), "the Son of God" (a divine title from Hebrews 1 on) (Heb. 4:14). The writer emphasized the Son's deity in chapter 1, and as we have seen by the repeated references to the incarnation, his humanity in chapter 2. We thus have a High Priest who perfectly meets our need. As the God-*man* he is able to "sympathize with our weaknesses" and as the *God*-man he is able to grant us "mercy and grace to help in time of need" (4:15–16). As the divine-human priest he is "holy, innocent, unstained, separated from sinners, and exalted above the heavens" (7:26).

What works does Jesus, our great High Priest, perform? He makes "propitiation for the sins of the people" and "is able to help those who are being tempted" (2:18). That is, he saves by virtue of his once-for-all-time cross work and ongoing intercession. His making atonement on the cross here is translated in two different ways. Some render "to make expiation" (e.g., rsv) and others "to make propitiation" (e.g., esv). For reasons given in my exposition of Romans 3:24–26, I agree with O'Brien (citing Koester): "The notion of atonement has to do with the restoration of a relationship marred by sin, and this encompasses both expiation, the removal of sin, and propitiation, the averting of divine wrath."[45]

Jesus not only has made atonement but continues to serve as High Priest in heaven itself. The writer explains: "For because he himself has suffered when tempted, he is able to help those who are being tempted" (Heb. 2:18). On the basis of his death and resurrection he saves "to the uttermost those who draw near to God through him, since he always lives to make intercession for them" (7:25). He appears before the Father on our behalf, presenting his sacrifice and pleading our case.

Hebrews 2, then, brings together three themes to describe Christ's saving accomplishment. He is the second Adam, who in his suffering of death and his exaltation restores the creational glory and dominion forfeited by our first parents in the fall. He is the mighty Victor, who attains two goals: "that by his death Jesus might break the power of the evil tyrant who held sway over death; and, second, that through this same death he might rescue those who had been

---

[45]Ibid., 122.

enslaved."[46] And, he is our great High Priest, who has made atonement on the cross and continues to make intercession in heaven "to help those who are being tempted" (2:18).

First Peter

The apostle Peter also testifies to the saving significance of Jesus's death in a number of passages.

1 Peter 1:1–2

> To those who are elect . . . according to the foreknowledge of God the Father, in the sanctification of the Spirit, for obedience to Jesus Christ and for sprinkling with his blood . . .

In his first letter's salutation Peter speaks of Spirit-wrought sanctification that results in obedience to Jesus Christ. This is the initial sanctifying work of the Spirit, in which he sets sinners apart for God, constituting them saints. This initial sanctification is "for obedience to Jesus Christ," that is, it results in obedience to Christ. The obedience of which Peter speaks is evangelical obedience, faith in Jesus.[47] It too has results—sprinkling with Jesus's blood, which means cleansing due to his death. Ramsey Michaels is correct: "To be sprinkled with Jesus' blood was to be cleansed from one's former way of living and released from spiritual slavery by the power of his death."[48]

To summarize: Peter teaches that the Spirit constitutes sinners saints and as a result (though simultaneously) they obey the gospel, that is, believe in Jesus, and are cleansed by his atoning death.

1 Peter 1:18–19

> . . . knowing that you were ransomed from the futile ways inherited from your forefathers, not with perishable things such as silver or gold, but with the precious blood of Christ, like that of a lamb without blemish or spot.

Because this passage will figure prominently in the chapter "Christ Our Redeemer," I will treat it briefly here. Returning to his pilgrim motif (1 Pet.

---

[46]Ibid., 114.

[47]At times Peter uses "obedience" and "obey" to speak of obeying the command to believe on Christ (1:22; 3:1), and hence accepting Christ, and "disobey" to speak of disobeying the gospel command, and hence rejecting Christ (4:17).

[48]J. Ramsey Michaels, 1 Peter, Word Biblical Commentary (Waco, TX: Word, 1988), 12–13.

1:1; cf. 2:11), Peter tells Christians to live in the fear of God the Father: "And if you call on him as Father who judges impartially according to each one's deeds, conduct yourselves with fear throughout the time of your exile" (1:17). He gives another reason for careful living: "knowing that you were ransomed from the futile ways inherited from your forefathers, not with perishable things such as silver or gold, but with the precious blood of Christ, like that of a lamb without blemish or spot" (vv. 18–19). This is the language of redemption. It implies a state of bondage—they needed to be delivered "from the futile ways," a reference to their prior worship of false gods. And that deliverance did not come cheap—even "silver or gold" would not accomplish it. No, a much more precious ransom price was paid: "the precious blood of Christ." Once more "blood" speaks of Christ's saving death. Here Jesus is likened to "a lamb without blemish or spot" (v. 19). Frequently, the Old Testament stipulates that sacrificial animals had to be "without blemish" (Ex. 12:5; Lev. 1:3, 10; 3:1, 6, etc.). Thomas Schreiner says wisely: "Animals were without defect physically, but Peter's point was that Jesus was sinless (cf. 2:22). He was a perfect sacrifice because of his perfect life."[49] So, Peter highly esteems Christ's atonement and rejoices that it redeems.

1 Peter 2:21–24

> For to this you have been called, because Christ also suffered for you, leaving you an example, so that you might follow in his steps. He committed no sin, neither was deceit found in his mouth. When he was reviled, he did not revile in return; when he suffered, he did not threaten, but continued entrusting himself to him who judges justly. He himself bore our sins in his body on the tree, that we might die to sin and live to righteousness. By his wounds you have been healed.

Peter exhorts his readers to suffer, following Christ's example (1 Pet. 2:21–23; cf. Isa. 53:9, 7). The thought of Christ's suffering on the cross easily leads the apostle to use more redemptive language. Jesus is not only our example of suffering; he is our suffering Savior whose unique suffering saves us. "He himself bore our sins in his body on the tree, that we might die to sin and live to righteousness" (1 Pet. 2:24; cf. Isa. 53:4, 11). Peter does not say that Christ "offered" our sins on the tree, but that he "bore" them to or on the tree. Peter paints a picture of Jesus carrying our sins away in his death.

When Peter says "tree," he alludes to Deuteronomy 21:23. "It becomes in the New Testament an almost technical word for the cross of Jesus (Acts

---

[49]Thomas R. Schreiner, *1, 2 Peter, Jude,* The New American Commentary (Nashville: Broadman and Holman, 2003), 86.

5:30; 10:39; Gal. 3:13),", Michaels affirms.[50] Perhaps Peter alludes to the curse of the Deuteronomy passage, but his emphasis is not there "but rather on the removal of sins which the cross of Christ accomplished."[51] We should not miss Peter's ethical purpose: "He himself bore our sins in his body on the tree, that we might die to sin and live to righteousness." God desires holy lives in his people, and that was one reason he gave his Son to die for them.

When Peter says, "Christ also suffered *for you*" (1 Pet. 2:21), he underlines the substitutionary character of Christ's death. He does so again: "By his wounds you have been healed" (v. 24; cf. Isa. 53:5), returning to Isaiah 53. Peter Davids agrees: "This fact [substitution] is further underlined in the last clause of the verse (now shifting to Isa. 53:5), that his wounds (the welts and bruises one would have as a result of a blow with a fist or whip) have brought healing to us."[52] Peter's point is the same as Isaiah's—Christ's death saves.

1 Peter 3:18

> For Christ also suffered once for sins, the righteous for the unrighteous, that he might bring us to God.

After encouraging his readers to suffer for doing good, Peter returns to the subject of Christ's suffering. His teaching is straightforward: "For Christ also suffered once for sins, the righteous for the unrighteous" (v. 18). When Jesus calls us to suffer, this is not something beyond his own experience. He also suffered. In that way our suffering is like his, and Peter implies that Christ is our example in suffering.

But Christ's suffering is unlike ours in more than one way. He suffered "once," and that suffering was momentous, which is not true of our suffering. Michaels is correct:

> Although the specific contrast in Hebrews between the sufficiency of Christ's sacrifice "once for all" and the inadequacy of the repeated animal sacrifices of the OT priestly system is lacking in 1 Peter, ἅπαξ (*hapaks*) does connote sufficiency and completeness. Christ's suffering is over, its purpose fully accomplished.[53]

---

[50]Michaels, *1 Peter*, 148.
[51]Ibid.
[52]Peter H. Davids, *The First Epistle of Peter*, The New International Commentary on the New Testament (Grand Rapids: Eerdmans, 1990), 113.
[53]Michaels, *1 Peter*, 202.

The most important difference between our suffering and his is that, unlike ours, his is redemptive. "Christ also suffered once for sins." Peter elaborates: "the righteous for the unrighteous." The Greek is instructive: "the righteous one for the unrighteous ones." Jesus died for sinners. He died in their place. Peter Davids is to the point: "Christ's substitutionary death for those who deserved death comes across clearly."[54]

What is the purpose of Christ's death? "Christ also suffered once for sins, the righteous for the unrighteous, that he might bring us to God" (v. 18). Christ died a redemptive death for those who were far away from God to lead them to God. He died as Mediator of the new covenant, as the only intermediary between God and human beings. Once more Davids deserves quotation: "Jesus died in order that, so to speak, he might reach across the gulf between God and humanity and, taking our hand, lead us across the territory of the enemy into the presence of the Father who called us."[55]

In sum, Peter presents Christ's death as saving in that his shed blood cleanses (1:2) and redeems (1:19), he carries our sins away from us to the tree (2:24), his wounds on the cross heal us (2:24), and he dies in our place to join us to God (3:18).

First John

John's first epistle has important things to say about Jesus's atoning death. I will treat three passages.[56]

1 John 1:7

> But if we walk in the light, as he is in the light, we have fellowship with one another, and the blood of Jesus his Son cleanses us from all sin.

This verse precedes three verses teaching that Christians must honestly face their sins:

> If we say that we have no sin, we deceive ourselves, and the truth is not in us. If we confess our sins, he is faithful and just to forgive us our sins and to cleanse us from all unrighteousness. If we say that we have not sinned, we make him a liar, and his word is not in us. (1 John 1:8–10)

To pretend that we as believers are sinless is to engage in self-deception, to reject God's word, and to call God a liar. God takes sin seriously. And so should we.

---

[54]Davids, *The First Epistle of Peter*, 136.
[55]Ibid.
[56]First John 3:5–8 will be treated in the chapter "Christ Our Victor."

That is why 1 John 1:9 is wedged between the two other verses above: if believers keep honest accounts with God and daily confess their sins, they will daily experience his forgiveness and cleansing.

But what about when Christians obey God's truth and do not sin, when they "walk in the light," as John puts it? What is the basis for their standing with God then? "If we walk in the light, as he is in the light . . . the blood of Jesus his Son cleanses us from all sin" (1 John 1:7). Even when we are not conscious of sinning against the Lord, the basis of our relationship with him is "the blood of Jesus his Son." And even when we walk in the light, that blood "cleanses us from all sin." This "means that in the cross of Christ our sin is effectively and repeatedly . . . removed," as Smalley says.[57] Jesus's blood purifies us from the beginning to the end. There is no other atonement. And as a result of Christ's saving death, "we have fellowship with one another" as fellow believers (1:3 has already said that "our fellowship is with the Father and his Son Jesus Christ").

Robert Yarbrough's comments on the word "cleanses" in "the blood of Jesus his Son cleanses us from all sin" (1 John 1:7) are edifying:

> The word for "cleanses" (καθαρίζω, katharizo) is found only here and in 1:9 in all the Johannine writings. By contrast, it is common in the Synoptics (eighteen occurrences), expressing the outcome of Jesus's healing and saving touch and word (e.g., Matt. 8:3). . . . Paul uses the word three times, once to exhort believers in their duty (2 Cor. 7:1) and twice to describe the saving work of God's Word (Eph. 5:26) or God's Son (Titus 2:14). Hebrews uses the word to denote . . . what Christ achieved. . . . John's use of this word shows that his doctrine of Christ's work is well within the flow of what is claimed for Jesus in his earthly life by Gospel writers and what was taught about the power of his death in a wide range of early churches.[58]

It is comforting to note that "the blood of Jesus his Son cleanses us from *all* sin" (1 John 1:7). Christ's is an efficacious atonement, and therefore ours is a joyful life (v. 4).

1 John 2:2

> He is the propitiation for our sins, and not for ours only but also for the sins of the whole world.

---

[57]Stephen S. Smalley, *1, 2, 3 John*. Word Biblical Commentary (Waco, TX: Word, 1984), 25.
[58]Robert W. Yarbrough, *1–3 John*, Baker Exegetical Commentary on the New Testament (Grand Rapids: Baker Academic, 2008), 58.

John carefully crafts his argument. God is absolute light, complete purity and truth (1:5). Let no one claim to walk with God while living in sin and error (v. 6). Those who live in holiness and truth are the ones whom Christ's atonement saves (v. 7). Let no one claim to be without sin; rather, Christians should confess their sins daily to receive forgiveness and cleansing (vv. 8–10). John speaks plain words; he writes to keep God's children from sinning. But if they slip, they have "an advocate with the Father, Jesus Christ the righteous" (2:1). The word translated "advocate" (παρακλήτος, *parakletos*) appears only in John's writings, here and in his Gospel at 14:16, 26; 15:26; and 16:7. There in the Gospel Jesus promises to send the Holy Spirit as a legal advocate, mediator, or intercessor to help the disciples when he returns to the Father. John applies the same word to Jesus here. "John's readers have such an advocate [in the legal sense], mediator, or intercessor with the Father in the event that they sin."[59]

In this context, John writes, "He is the propitiation for our sins, and not for ours only but also for the sins of the whole world" (1 John 2:2). It is not difficult to discern the connection between this verse and the preceding. What makes Jesus's intercessory ministry before the Father in heaven so powerful is his resurrection, and ascension, and especially his atoning death.

We return to the controversial matter as to whether *hilasmos* (and related words) should be translated "expiation" (so the NIV, "the atoning sacrifice for our sins") or "propitiation" (so ESV).[60] Because we dealt with this issue in our handling of Romans 3:24–26, I will only point interested readers to literature and quote Robert Yarbrough, with whose conclusions I agree:

> While Jesus's death certainly has the effect of expiating sin (wiping away its penalty), it is difficult to avoid the impression that it also propitiates (turns away the wrath of) God's promised punishment of sin and sinners whose transgressions are not atoned for on the last day—a day of condemnation spoken of by Jesus in John 12:48.[61]

I will postpone to an appendix the matter of the extent of the atonement—whether Christ died to save all or only the elect—and this text in relation to that topic. Here I will only quote the balanced conclusion of Yarbrough:

---

[59]Ibid., 76.

[60]Ἱλαστήριον (*hilasterion*) occurs in Rom. 3:25, ἱλάσκεσθαι (*hilaskesthai*) in Heb. 2:17, and ἱλάσμος (*hilasmos*) in 1 John 2:2; 4:10.

[61]Yarbrough, *1–3 John*, 78. For a full discussion, see D. L. Akin, *1, 2, 3 John*, New American Commentary (Nashville: Broadman and Holman, 2001), 82–84. For the view that only expiation is involved, see J. Painter, *1, 2, and 3 John*, Sacra Pagina 18 (Collegeville, MN: Liturgical Press, 2002), 146–47. For the view that propitiation is also involved, see Smalley, *1, 2, 3 John*, 40.

Jesus's ministry as ἱλάσμος, 1 John 2:2 goes on to say, extends beyond the sins of the "we" of John and his readers to "those of the whole world." . . . There is a universal dimension to Christ's death for sins . . . in the same sense that God's promise to Abraham has a universal horizon: "All peoples on earth will be blessed through you" (Gen. 12:3 NIV). . . . It is not warranted to conclude from this, however, that all individuals in the world will be redeemed by Christ's death for sin. . . . Amid the wideness of the atonement's scope . . . there is at the same time an undeniable particularity.[62]

John writes to promote holiness in his readers, but knows that Christians still sin (1 John 1:8, 10). He graciously points to God's provision in Christ, who serves as heavenly Mediator, intercessor, and legal advocate based on his cross work (2:1). That cross work satisfied God's justice and put away the sins of believers (2:2). It also demonstrated God's love as nothing else, as our next passage reveals.

1 John 4:9–14

In this the love of God was made manifest among us, that God sent his only Son into the world, so that we might live through him. In this is love, not that we have loved God but that he loved us and sent his Son to be the propitiation for our sins. Beloved, if God so loved us, we also ought to love one another. No one has ever seen God; if we love one another, God abides in us and his love is perfected in us.

By this we know that we abide in him and he in us, because he has given us of his Spirit. And we have seen and testify that the Father has sent his Son to be the Savior of the world.

After vigorous teaching concerning testing the spirits, John urges his readers to love one another and thereby gain assurance that they have been regenerated (1 John 4:7–8). John knows that Christian love is rooted in God's love in Christ: "In this the love of God was made manifest among us, that God sent his only Son into the world, so that we might live through him" (v. 9). The Father's initiative in sending his Son into a world that hated him is the source of the love believers have for one another.

In fact, ultimately love is vertical and not horizontal; that is, God's love precedes and precipitates ours. This love comes down; it does not first of all go up: "In this is love, not that we have loved God but that he loved us" (v. 10). We are not believers because we chose to love God. What distinguishes us from unbelievers is not our superior spirituality whereby we were inherently moved

---

[62] Yarbrough, *1–3 John*, 79–80.

to love God. To the contrary, true love begins not with our love for God but with his love for us.

What is the epitome of God's love for us? John has a ready answer: "In this is love . . . that he loved us and sent his Son to be the propitiation for our sins" (v. 10). Once more we return to the idea of propitiation. We have seen it in Romans 3:25, where we treated it in detail, in Hebrews 2:17, and in 1 John 2:2. It will feature prominently in the chapter "Christ Our Legal Substitute." Here I merely summarize: Christ's death accomplished many things, including turning away God's wrath and expiating our sins. John's main point is that Christ's atonement is the most emphatic demonstration of what God's love is.

"Beloved, if God so loved us, we also ought to love one another" (1 John 4:11). John ties God's love in Christ to the love between Christian brothers and sisters. The invisible God has manifested himself in his love by sending his Son to be our Savior. "The expression of God's love among believers is important because it renders visible the God who in himself cannot be seen," Yarbrough states.[63] When we come to know his love and consequently love one another, God becomes "visible" and his love attains its goal (is "perfected") in his people (v. 12). And our continuing to enjoy God's love and to love him in return is evidence of the work of God's Spirit in our lives (v. 13).

John rounds out this section by returning to the idea, expressed in verse 10, that the Father sent the Son to save: "And we have seen and testify that the Father has sent his Son to be the Savior of the world" (v. 14). As in the opening verses of the epistle, "we" refers primarily to the apostles. John knew Jesus before and after his resurrection and was a witness of his crucifixion (John 19:26). Smalley is right: "The essential meaning here of the statement that Jesus is 'savior' is that, as the exalted Christ and Son of God (cf. [1 John] 2:22–23), he brings release from sin (cf. [1 John 4] v. 10) and therefore spiritual life (cf. v. 9b)."[64]

To summarize: 1 John presents Christ's death as "the blood of Jesus his [the Father's] Son," which "cleanses us from all sin" (1 John 1:7) and "the propitiation for our sins, and . . . for the sins of the whole world" (2:2; 4:10). Jesus's atoning death purifies his people, propitiates God's wrath, and expiates sin.

The Book of Revelation

In five passages Revelation paints the vivid picture of Jesus the Lamb who was slain and who saves his people by his blood.

---

[63]Ibid., 245.
[64]Smalley, *1, 2, 3 John*, 253.

Revelation 1:5–6

To him who loves us and has freed us from our sins by his blood . . . be glory and dominion forever and ever.

In the greeting to the seven churches, following the prologue to the book, John prays: "Grace to you and peace from him who is and who was and who is to come, and from the seven spirits who are before his throne, and from Jesus Christ the faithful witness, the firstborn of the dead, and the ruler of kings on earth" (Rev. 1:4–5). John appeals to the only one who can bestow grace and peace—God himself. God is the holy Trinity of the Father (he "who is and who was and who is to come"), the Holy Spirit ("the seven spirits who are before his throne"), and the Son.

The Son is "Jesus Christ the faithful witness, the firstborn of the dead, and the ruler of kings on earth" (v. 5). "The faithful witness" speaks of Jesus's being the truth (John 14:6), the great prophet, who was trustworthy unto death. "The firstborn of the dead" refers to Jesus's resurrection after his crucifixion. "The ruler of kings on earth" speaks of Jesus's cosmic rule following his exaltation to God's right hand. John thus refers to Christ's three offices of prophet ("the faithful witness"), priest (implied in the reference to Christ's death in "the firstborn of the dead"), and king ("the ruler").

Mentioning Christ's threefold office prompts John immediately to break into a doxology: "To him who loves us and has freed us from our sins by his blood . . . be glory and dominion forever and ever" (Rev. 1:5–6). Jesus is worthy of everlasting praise because of his great love shown in dying for believers. The reference to "his blood" harkens back to Old Testament priests' making atonement for sins by the sprinkling of blood. Jesus's sacrificial death delivers Christians by freeing them from their sins. Robert Mounce is perceptive: "The love of Christ is a continuing relationship which in point of time expressed itself in the redemptive act of Calvary. This release was purchased by the blood of Christ."[65]

Revelation 5:6

And between the throne and the four living creatures and among the elders I saw a Lamb standing, as though it had been slain, with seven horns and with seven eyes, which are the seven spirits of God sent out into all the earth.

---

[65]Robert H. Mounce, *The Book of Revelation*, The New International Commentary on the New Testament (Grand Rapids: Eerdmans, 1977), 71.

John weeps because no one is found worthy to open the scroll of judgment in God's right hand. An elder comforts him: "Weep no more; behold, the Lion of the tribe of Judah, the Root of David, has conquered, so that he can open the scroll and its seven seals." John presents Christ as the Victor who has conquered and as David's descendant. Capable interpreters have taken "the Root of David" to speak of the Messiah as the origin of David, but Gregory Beale shows that it is probably better taken to mean David's descendant.[66]

Our concern, however, is with "the Lion of the tribe of Judah" who "has conquered." John appeals to Jacob's prophecy concerning Judah in Genesis 49:9, with its symbol of the king of the beasts, to present Christ as the champion of his people. Christ overcomes our enemies and thereby delivers us. John develops this idea elsewhere in the Apocalypse, but only here relates it to Christ's saving work (Rev. 6:16; 17:14; 19:15–21).

John is told to behold the Lion, but, surprisingly, when he looks he sees not a Lion but a Lamb. "And between the throne and the four living creatures and among the elders I saw a Lamb standing, as though it had been slain, with seven horns and with seven eyes, which are the seven spirits of God sent out into all the earth" (5:6). This is the dominant symbol for Christ in Revelation—the Lamb. In fact, in all of its twenty-eight occurrences in Revelation but one—a simile in 13:11—it is a symbol for Christ the Redeemer. What is the significance of John's looking for a Lion but seeing the Lamb? Beale answers: "Christ as a Lion overcame by being slaughtered as a Lamb, which is the critical event in ch. 5."[67] His seven horns denote great strength, and seven eyes, great wisdom.

The Lamb slain is, of course, Christ crucified. As such he is found worthy to open the sealed book of judgment. As such he is worshiped by living creatures, elders, and innumerable angels (vv. 7–13). Their song of praise draws our interest:

> Worthy are you to take the scroll
>   and to open its seals,
> for you were slain, and by your blood you ransomed people for God
>   from every tribe and language and people and nation,
> and you have made them a kingdom and priests to our God,
>   and they shall reign on the earth. (vv. 9–10)

---

[66]G. K. Beale, *The Book of Revelation*, The New International Greek Testament Commentary (Grand Rapids: Eerdmans, 1999), 1146–47. For the interpretation of "the Root of David" as origin, see George R. Beasley-Murray, *The Book of Revelation*, New Century Bible Commentary (London: Marshall, Morgan, and Scott, 1974), 432, as reported in Beale, 1146n78.

[67]Beale, *The Book of Revelation*, 352.

The Lamb alone is worthy to open the scroll. He "was slain," or "slaughtered,"[68] a reference to Christ's bloody crucifixion. By the Lamb's "blood" he "ransomed people for God." This is a clear reference to redemption. Implied is the state of bondage out of which people need to be redeemed. The redemption price is the sacrificial death of Christ, the Lamb of God.

Christ's redemptive death is efficacious to redeem; it actually ransoms people for God. Furthermore, it is for all, for people from "every tribe and language and people and nation." His death does not save everyone, but saves all of God's people from every people group, tongue, ethnicity, and political entity. The result is that the ransomed people belong to God as a kingdom of priests. John thus presents the church as the new Israel, seeing the purposes for Old Testament Israel's existence (Ex. 19:5–6)—to be a kingdom of priests and a holy nation—fulfilled in Christ's redeemed people, including believing Jews and Gentiles.

This is the key text in the Revelation on Christ's atonement. The ones that follow build on it, and I will treat them briefly.

Revelation 7:14

> They have washed their robes and made them white in the blood of the Lamb.

The saints are described in this manner. This speaks of Christians being cleansed through Christ's sacrificial death. "The idea of making robes white by washing them in blood is a striking paradox," Mounce explains. "It is the sacrifice of the Lamb upon the cross which supplies white garments for the saints."[69]

Revelation 12:11

> And they have conquered him by the blood of the Lamb and by the word of their testimony, for they loved not their lives even unto death.

John pictures a great war in heaven with the archangel Michael and his angels fighting a dragon, which is identified as the Devil and Satan (v. 7). The Devil is defeated and cast out of heaven into the world, at which point victory is announced: "Now the salvation and the power and the kingdom of our God and the authority of his Christ have come, for the accuser of our brothers has been thrown down, who accuses them day and night before our God" (v. 10). Although this means warfare on earth, there is rejoicing in heaven over the

---

[68]Greek, σφάζω (sphazō), "to slaughter," in Arndt and Gingrich, *A Greek-English Lexicon of the New Testament*, 796.
[69]Mounce, *The Book of Revelation*, 174.

saints. Here is their testimony: "And they have conquered him by the blood of the Lamb and by the word of their testimony, for they loved not their lives even unto death" (v. 11). Martyred believers defeat the Devil by "the blood of the Lamb," the atoning sacrifice of Christ. Beale is direct: "The saints' status in heaven has been legitimized finally by Christ's suffering on the cross."[70] This is not to minimize the saints' perseverance, even unto death, but to place the ultimate praise where it belongs—with the Lamb.

Revelation 13:8

> And all who dwell on earth will worship it, everyone whose name has not been written before the foundation of the world in the book of life of the Lamb who was slain.

That great enemy of God known as the beast from the sea, a counterfeit christ, utters blasphemies and makes war on the saints, causing people to worship it and the dragon (Rev. 13:1–7). In fact, "all who dwell on earth will worship it, everyone whose name has not been written before the foundation of the world in the book of life of the Lamb who was slain" (v. 8).

The book of life serves as the census register of the city of God. This book records the names of those chosen for salvation because "only those who are written in the Lamb's book of life" will enter the eternal city of God (21:27). God will protect them from eternal death (3:5), the beast's deceptions (17:8), and the lake of fire (20:15).

By describing it as "the Lamb's book of life" (21:27) and "the book of life of the Lamb who was slain" (13:8), John indicates that the book belongs to Jesus by virtue of his having made atonement for the sins of his people. Here as in the other four passages, Jesus is the Lamb who was slain, who died as a priestly sacrifice to purify sinners.

Connecting the Dots

We have traced the redemptive significance of Jesus's death from the Old Testament foreshadowings through the Synoptic Gospels, the Gospel of John, Acts, the Pauline Epistles (Romans, Galatians, Ephesians, and Colossians), the General Epistles (1 Peter, 1 John, and Hebrews), and Revelation. One way to summarize our research is briefly to anticipate the six pictures of Christ's saving accomplishment that will appear in later chapters. I will list representative

---

[70] Beale, *The Book of Revelation*, 663.

passages from the various sections of Scripture studied that correspond to the pictures. The fact that Christ as reconciler has only one passage listed and Christ as second Adam only two is insignificant. I will treat more passages in the chapters devoted to those pictures.

Christ is our legal substitute. We were condemned by the law before a righteous God. Christ on the cross suffers the penalty of the law in our place that we might be justified (Isa. 53:11; Rom. 3:25–26; Gal. 3:13; Col. 2:14; 1 Pet. 3:18; 1 John 2:2; 4:10).

Christ is our Victor. We were opposed by Satan and his demons, foes far more powerful than we. Christ becomes one of us to defeat these enemies in his death (and resurrection) (Isa. 52:13; 53:12; John 12:31; Col. 2:15; Heb. 2:14–15).

Christ is our Redeemer. We were enslaved to sin, but Christ, by paying the ransom price in his death, delivers us from bondage unto the liberty of the sons and daughters of God (Mark 10:45; Luke 9:31; Acts 20:28; Eph. 1:7).

Christ is our reconciler. We were alienated from God due to our sins. Christ dies to make peace between God and us and to bring us back into fellowship with God (Rom. 5:10).

Christ is our second Adam. In the fall of our first father Adam, we lost honor and dominion and became subject to death and condemnation. In the incarnation, the Son of God becomes the second man, the last Adam, who by his obedience unto death (and his resurrection) restores the creational benefits and justifies us (Rom. 5:18–19; Heb. 2:9).

Christ is our sacrifice. We were defiled by sin and unable to approach God. Christ, our great High Priest, offers himself as a unique sacrifice to God, cleansing us of sin and enabling us to come into God's presence with reverence and boldness (Isa. 52:15; 53:10; John 1:29, 36; 17:19; Eph. 5:2; Heb. 1:3; 2:17; 1 Pet. 1:2; 1:18–19; 2:24; 1 John 1:7; Rev. 1:5; 5:6; 7:14; 12:11; 13:8).

Incarnation

Sinless Life

Death

Resurrection

Ascension

Session

Pentecost

Intercession

Second Coming

Chapter 4

Christ's Resurrection

It is a remarkable fact that there are many monographs on the theology of the death of Christ, but very few, by comparison, on the theology of his resurrection. Within the latter group of writings, attention has mostly been devoted to the historicity of the resurrection of Christ, and to its significance in relation to the future resurrection of believers. Interest also centers on the role of the resurrection in relation to the present new life of believers. But how is it a saving event? Indeed, is it a saving event?[1]

The resurrection of the Lord Jesus Christ saves. The very heart of Christ's saving accomplishment is his death and resurrection. When Paul summarizes the gospel, he includes both: "For I delivered to you as of first importance what I also received: that Christ died for our sins in accordance with the Scriptures, that he was buried, that he was raised on the third day in accordance with the Scriptures" (1 Cor. 15:3–4). Notice that both Christ's death and resurrection are "in accordance with the Scriptures," that is, predicted in the Old Testament. Where does the Old Testament predict Jesus's resurrection from the dead?

Old Testament Background

Though there are more candidates for this position than we have time to explore, we will examine three passages.

---

[1] I. Howard Marshall, *Aspects of the Atonement: Cross and Resurrection in the Reconciling of God and Humanity* (London: Paternoster, 2007), 68.

Psalm 16:8–11

When God's Old Testament people sing the sixteenth psalm, they commit themselves to the Lord and his care for this life and the next. The last four verses focus Israel's attention on joy in God's presence after death:

> I have set the LORD always before me;
>> because he is at my right hand, I shall not be shaken.
> Therefore my heart is glad, and my whole being rejoices;
>> my flesh also dwells secure.
> For you will not abandon my soul to Sheol,
>> or let your holy one see corruption.
> You make known to me the path of life;
>> in your presence there is fullness of joy;
>> at your right hand are pleasures forevermore. (Ps. 16:8–11)

Although faithful Israelites, singing this psalm, expressed their hope for the future, the words of the last four verses predict the resurrection of Christ, the holy one without peer, as both Peter and Paul attest.

Peter in his Pentecost sermon, after speaking of Christ's crucifixion, affirms his resurrection. His proof? David's words in Psalm 16:

> I saw the Lord always before me,
>> for he is at my right hand that I may not be shaken;
> therefore my heart was glad, and my tongue rejoiced;
>> my flesh also will dwell in hope.
> For you will not abandon my soul to Hades,
>> or let your Holy One see corruption.
> You have made known to me the paths of life;
>> you will make me full of gladness with your presence. (Acts 2:25–28)

Peter continues to drive his point home, insisting that David died and was buried, and that his tomb remains. "Being therefore a prophet, . . . he foresaw and spoke about the resurrection of the Christ, that he was not abandoned to Hades, nor did his flesh see corruption. This Jesus God raised up, and of that we all are witnesses" (Acts 2:29–32).

Paul too regards David's words as a prophecy of Jesus's resurrection. Preaching at Antioch in Pisidia, after the apostle speaks of Jesus's death, he announces Jesus's resurrection using Psalms 2 and 16. Our concern is with his citation of the latter:

And as for the fact that he raised him from the dead, no more to return to corruption, he has spoken in this way, . . .

> "You will not let your Holy One see corruption."

For David, after he had served the purpose of God in his own generation, fell
asleep and was laid with his fathers and saw corruption, but he whom God raised
up did not see corruption. (Acts 13:34–37)

The apostles Peter and Paul, then, proved the resurrection of Jesus to their
Jewish audiences by appealing to the words of Psalm 16.

Isaiah 53:10

Isaiah 53 is the single most amazing Old Testament prophecy of the person and
work of Christ. It is difficult to find anywhere else in Scripture such strong and
repeated affirmations of Jesus's substitutionary atonement as those that appear
in verses 5–6, 10–12.

Isaiah ascribes the Servant's suffering to the will of God. The Servant voluntarily suffers, as these words show: "He poured out his soul to death" (v. 12).
In suffering he endures oppression (vv. 7–8). By doing so he fulfills the plan of
God. Furthermore, the Servant gives himself up to death as a guilt offering, a
sacrifice for sins "when his soul makes an offering for guilt . . ." (v. 10). Isaiah
thus predicts what is more fully explained in Hebrews 9–10: "He has appeared
once for all at the end of the ages to put away sin by the sacrifice of himself"
(Heb. 9:26), and "We have been sanctified through the offering of the body of
Jesus Christ once for all" (Heb. 10:10).

What is not always noticed, however, is that this great Servant Song also
predicts the resurrection of the Servant.

> Yet it was the will of the LORD to crush him;
>   he has put him to grief;
> when his soul makes an offering for guilt,
>   he shall see his offspring; he shall prolong his days;
> the will of the LORD shall prosper in his hand. (Isa. 53:10)

These words prophesy Christ's resurrection: "He shall see his offspring; he
shall prolong his days" (v. 10). The expression "to prolong one's days" (v. 10) and
similar expressions occur in the Old Testament twenty-one times. With one possible exception (Ps. 23:6), they always refer to earthly life being lengthened. But
the use of "he shall prolong his days" in Isaiah 53:10 is without parallel because

it is here used of a person who first died. It thus speaks of the prolongation of the Servant's life after death—that is, his resurrection. Bruce Waltke agrees: "In other words, Messiah must first die a vicarious death bearing the iniquities of Israel and then be raised from the dead to his glory."[2]

The words of Alec Motyer, who has devoted his life to the study of Isaiah, deserve our attention:

> The guilt offering has been made; what remains now is the gathering of the family (all those for whom the reparation was made) and the Servant lives on, vested with authority to see that this is done. The Old Testament testified uniformly that the dead are alive, and in this sense it is no surprise to find the Servant alive after death. But things are said about him after death that set him apart from all others. Jacob, for example, "sees his children" (29:23) like the Servant "sees his seed" ([53:]10c), but Jacob does so as a mere watcher from the sidelines of history. Not so the Servant! He who was crushed under the will of the LORD lives as the executor of that will. In 14:9–17 Isaiah depicted earth's royalty in Sheol, clutching their now meaningless dignities, actually weak, as are the rest, and with their pretensions in life exposed as pitiable foibles. Death has dethroned them. In the case of the Servant, however, death ushers him into sovereign dignity and power, with his own hand administering the saving purposes of the Lord, and as victor taking the spoil ([Isa. 53] verse 12).[3]

Motyer captures Isaiah's message. The suffering Servant of the Lord lives after death and wields authority. His exerting authority is seen in the words "the will of the LORD shall prosper in his hand" (v. 10), that is, by the Servant's personal agency. The Lord's will is that his Servant should die as a sacrifice for sins and then "see his offspring," his children. The Servant is the personal agent who causes the Lord's will to flourish by accomplishing God's plan through his death and resurrection. In fact, the end of the Servant Song portrays him who lives after death "as victor taking the spoil" (v. 12).[4]

Jonah 1:17

After God commissioned Jonah to preach to the city of Nineveh, an enemy of Jonah's Israel, the reluctant prophet took a boat in the opposite direction (1:1–3).

---

[2]Bruce K. Waltke, *An Old Testament Theology* (Grand Rapids: Zondervan, 2007), 889.
[3]J. Alec Motyer, *The Prophecy of Isaiah: An Introduction and Commentary* (Downers Grove, IL: Inter-Varsity, 1993), 440–41.
[4]Ibid., 440.

And the LORD appointed a great fish to swallow up Jonah. And Jonah was in the belly of the fish three days and three nights. (Jonah 1:17)

A mighty storm threatened the ship, and the pagan sailors cast lots to see who on board was the cause. The lot fell on Jonah, who confessed that his rebellion against the Lord was to blame. Reluctantly they threw Jonah overboard and the storm ceased (1:15). A great fish swallowed up Jonah, but when the Lord commanded the fish, it vomited Jonah on the shore, and he preached to Nineveh as he had been instructed to do in the first place.

Jesus draws a parallel between Jonah's adventure and his own saving work. When the Jewish leaders ask him to perform a sign, he is not pleased: "An evil and adulterous generation seeks for a sign, but no sign will be given to it except the sign of the prophet Jonah. For just as Jonah was three days and three nights in the belly of the great fish, so will the Son of Man be three days and three nights in the heart of the earth" (Matt. 12:39–40).

Jonah appeared to die and live again when he was swallowed and later regurgitated by the great fish. Jesus himself teaches that Jonah's experience in the fish anticipates his death and resurrection. By Jewish reckoning, a part of a day counts as that day. Jesus's crucified body was put into Joseph of Arimathea's tomb on Friday, where it remained until Sunday morning. Part of Friday, all of Saturday, and part of Sunday constitute three days. Thus when we look back at the Old Testament story of Jonah with the twenty-twenty hindsight Jesus provides, we learn that the prophet's experience looks forward to Jesus's death and resurrection.

The Event in the Gospels

In all four Gospels Jesus predicts his resurrection from the dead: Matthew 16:21; 17:22–23; 20:18–19; Mark 8:31; 9:31; 10:32–34; Luke 9:22; 18:31–33; John 2:19–22; 10:17–18.

The four Gospels also unite in including the resurrection of Jesus near the end of their versions of his story. In the Synoptic Gospels, the women who go to anoint Jesus's body with spices meet angels instead, who tell them good news.

"Do not be afraid, for I know that you seek Jesus who was crucified. He is not here, for he has risen, as he said. Come, see the place where he lay. Then go quickly and tell his disciples that he has risen from the dead, and behold, he is going before you to Galilee; there you will see him. See, I have told you." So they departed quickly from the tomb with fear and great joy, and ran to tell his disciples. And behold, Jesus met them and said, "Greetings!" And they came up and took hold of his feet and worshiped him. Then Jesus said to them, "Do not be afraid; go and tell my brothers to go to Galilee, and there they will see me." (Matt. 28:5–10)

"Do not be alarmed. You seek Jesus of Nazareth, who was crucified. He has risen; he is not here. See the place where they laid him. But go, tell his disciples and Peter that he is going before you to Galilee. There you will see him, just as he told you." And they went out and fled from the tomb, for trembling and astonishment had seized them, and they said nothing to anyone, for they were afraid. (Mark 16:6–8)

"Why do you seek the living among the dead? He is not here, but has risen. Remember how he told you, while he was still in Galilee, that the Son of Man must be delivered into the hands of sinful men and be crucified and on the third day rise." And they remembered his words, and returning from the tomb they told all these things to the eleven and to all the rest. (Luke 24:5–9)

John's Gospel includes a complementary account of Mary Magdalene, who after seeing the angels, encounters Jesus, whom she mistakes for a gardener:

But Mary stood weeping outside the tomb, and as she wept she stooped to look into the tomb. And she saw two angels in white, sitting where the body of Jesus had lain, one at the head and one at the feet. They said to her, "Woman, why are you weeping?" She said to them, "They have taken away my Lord, and I do not know where they have laid him." Having said this, she turned around and saw Jesus standing, but she did not know that it was Jesus. Jesus said to her, "Woman, why are you weeping? Whom are you seeking?" Supposing him to be the gardener, she said to him, "Sir, if you have carried him away, tell me where you have laid him, and I will take him away." Jesus said to her, "Mary." She turned and said to him in Aramaic, "Rabboni!" (which means Teacher). Jesus said to her, "Do not cling to me, for I have not yet ascended to the Father; but go to my brothers and say to them, 'I am ascending to my Father and your Father, to my God and your God.'" Mary Magdalene went and announced to the disciples, "I have seen the Lord"—and that he had said these things to her. (John 20:11–18)

Teaching in the Gospel of John

The Fourth Gospel goes beyond the Synoptic Gospels in two areas pertaining to Jesus's resurrection. Here alone in Scripture Jesus raises himself from the dead.

Jesus answered them, "Destroy this temple, and in three days I will raise it up." The Jews then said, "It has taken forty-six years to build this temple, and will you raise it up in three days?" But he was speaking about the temple of his body. When therefore he was raised from the dead, his disciples remembered that he had said this, and they believed the Scripture and the word that Jesus had spoken. (John 2:19–22)

For this reason the Father loves me, because I lay down my life that I may take it up again. No one takes it from me, but I lay it down of my own accord. I have authority to lay it down, and I have authority to take it up again. This charge I have received from my Father. (John 10:17–18)

John's Gospel also provides more theological interpretation of Jesus's resurrection than the Synoptics do. This is most evident in two passages.

John 11:23-27

Jesus's good friend Lazarus has died, and when his sisters Martha and Mary greet Jesus separately, they use the same words: "Lord, if you had been here, my brother would not have died" (John 11:21, 32). Little do they know that Jesus has deliberately waited for his friend to die in order to display God's glory and strengthen believers' faith (vv. 4, 6, 15).

Martha, after speaking the words quoted above, expresses more confidence in Jesus: "But even now I know that whatever you ask from God, God will give you" (v. 22). We do not know what she had in mind, but Jesus replies: "Your brother will rise again" (v. 23). Martha reflects good Jewish theology: "I know that he will rise again in the resurrection on the last day" (v. 24).

Jesus's reply is shocking: "I am the resurrection and the life" (v. 25). He identifies himself with the great future event of God—the resurrection of the dead. And he adds that *he* is the eternal life. What do these stunning words mean? I will answer by appealing to a broad theme in the Fourth Gospel and then by interpreting the words that immediately follow in John 11:25.

The broad theme is that of Jesus as the life-giver. This does not refer to his laying down his life for his sheep, which indeed he does (John 10:11–18). Rather, it refers to his bestowing eternal life on those who are spiritually dead. John's portrait of Jesus as life-giver begins even before his incarnation when the Word, as God's agent in creation, gave life to all things: "All things were made through him, and without him was not any thing made that was made" (1:3). It is no surprise, then, that as the incarnate Word, Jesus gives eternal life to believers: "But to all who did receive him, who believed in his name, he gave the right to become children of God" (1:12).

Jesus, the Son of God, is life-giver throughout John's Gospel. After healing a man who was lame for thirty-eight years, Jesus says, "For as the Father raises the dead and gives them life, so also the Son gives life to whom he will" (5:21).

In the most famous "I am" saying, "Jesus said to him, 'I am the way, and the truth, and *the life*'" (14:6). He is the life—the Good Shepherd who promises his sheep, "I give them eternal life, and they will never perish" (10:28).

This magnificent theme of the Son as life-giver forms the background for Jesus's words concerning dead Lazarus: "I am the resurrection and the life" (John 11:25). His next words help us: "Whoever believes in me, though he die, yet shall he live, and everyone who lives and believes in me shall never die" (vv. 25–26). It is easy to know generally what Jesus's words mean—he gives eternal life, especially as the risen one. But it is difficult to explain them exactly.

Perhaps the best explanation is that of C. H. Dodd: the two parts of the "I am saying" go with the two parts of the saying that follows, respectively: "I am the resurrection. . . . Whoever believes in me, though he die, yet shall he live." And "I am the life. . . . Everyone who lives and believes in me shall never die" (vv. 25–26).[5] As the resurrection, Jesus will raise believers in him who experience physical death; at his voice they will come out of their graves "to the resurrection of life" (5:28–29). Because he is the life, those who while alive physically trust Jesus as Savior will not experience the second death (hell).

When Jesus asks Martha, "Do you believe this?" she answers, "Yes, Lord; I believe that you are the Christ, the Son of God, who is coming into the world" (11:26–27). Martha's positive response anticipates the Gospel's purpose statement: "Now Jesus did many other signs in the presence of the disciples, which are not written in this book; but these are written so that you may believe that Jesus is the Christ, the Son of God, and that by believing you may have life in his name" (20:30–31).

With the words "Lazarus, come out," Jesus, "the resurrection and the life," raises his friend from the tomb as proof that he is now giver of eternal life and as a token of his power to raise the dead to everlasting life on the last day (John 11:43–44).

John 14:18–20

In his famous farewell discourse, Jesus tells his disciples that he will leave them and return to his Father in heaven (John 14:12). He promises to send them the Holy Spirit, who will be with them forever (vv. 16–17). Next Jesus says: "I will not leave you as orphans; I will come to you. Yet a little while and the world will see me no more, but you will see me. Because I live, you also will live. In that day you will know that I am in my Father, and you in me, and I in you" (vv. 18–20).

---

[5]C. H. Dodd, *Interpretation of the Fourth Gospel* (Cambridge: Cambridge University Press, 1953), 365.

Jesus promises to appear to his disciples—although not to unbelievers—after his death. Commentators debate the meaning of "that day" in verse 20. Some think it refers to "Jesus' coming to his followers in the Spirit . . . at Pentecost."[6] D. A. Carson explains why "that day" is better understood as referring to Jesus's resurrection:

> After all, the time when the disciples come to recognize that Jesus is in the Father and the Father is in him is *that day* (v. 20) when Jesus has risen from the dead: that is the "coming" in view. The consequence of Jesus' rising from the dead is new life for the disciples, new eschatological life mediated by the Spirit: *Because I live, you also will live.*[7]

According to John, believers already have this eternal life and will enjoy it more fully in the age to come (John 3:36; 12:25). Why is this true? Jesus declares, "Because I live, you also will live" (14:19). F. F. Bruce explains that Jesus's "resurrection life guaranteed unending life to his people because by faith they were united to the Living One, and would draw their life from him."[8]

John presents Jesus's resurrection, inseparable from his death, as a saving event indeed; it brings us eternal life now and guarantees our everlasting life after the resurrection of the dead.

The Event and Teaching in the Acts of the Apostles

The Apostles Emphasize Jesus's Resurrection

Jesus's resurrection lies at the heart of the apostles' preaching. The apostles, of course, announce that Jesus was crucified. But their repeated emphasis in Acts is on his resurrection. We hear this from their lips in sermons and prayers.

> Peter: "This Jesus God raised up, and of that we all are witnesses" (Acts 2:32; see also Acts 2:24; 3:15; 4:1–2, 10; 5:30).

> Stephen: "He called out, 'Lord Jesus, receive my spirit'" (Acts 7:59).

> Paul: "And Paul went in, as was his custom, and on three Sabbath days he reasoned with them from the Scriptures, explaining and proving that it was necessary for

---

[6] Andreas J. Köstenberger, *John*, Baker Exegetical Commentary on the New Testament (Grand Rapids: Baker Academic, 2004), 439.

[7] D. A. Carson, *The Gospel According to John*, The Pillar New Testament Commentary (Grand Rapids: Eerdmans, 1991), 501.

[8] F. F. Bruce, *The Gospel of John* (Grand Rapids: Eerdmans, 1983), 303.

the Christ to suffer and to rise from the dead, and saying, 'This Jesus, whom I proclaim to you, is the Christ'" (Acts 17:2–3; see also Acts 13:33, 34, 37; 17:18, 31).

Peter and Paul Proclaim that the Risen Christ Saves

Both Peter and Paul teach the saving significance of Jesus's resurrection in Acts.

Peter. After citing Psalm 16 as a prophecy fulfilled in Jesus's resurrection, Peter teaches his hearers that the pouring out of the Spirit at Pentecost is the work of this risen Christ:

> This Jesus God raised up, and of that we all are witnesses. Being therefore exalted at the right hand of God, and having received from the Father the promise of the Holy Spirit, he has poured out this that you yourselves are seeing and hearing. . . . Let all the house of Israel therefore know for certain that God has made him both Lord and Christ, this Jesus whom you crucified. (Acts 2:32–33, 36)

The listeners understand the saving significance of Jesus's resurrection very well: "Now when they heard this they were cut to the heart, and said to Peter and the rest of the apostles, 'Brothers, what shall we do?'" (Acts 2:37). At which point Peter points them to Christ and they believe and are baptized (vv. 38–41).

After hearing a lame beggar, Peter, standing before the Sanhedrin, is careful not to take the glory himself: "Let it be known to all of you and to all the people of Israel that by the name of Jesus Christ of Nazareth, whom you crucified, whom God raised from the dead—by him this man is standing before you well" (Acts 4:10). Peter gives glory to Christ, whom he exalts as "the stone that was rejected by you, the builders, which has become the cornerstone" (v. 11).[9] Next the apostle tells the saving significance of Jesus's (death and) resurrection, concluding, "And there is salvation in no one else, for there is no other name under heaven given among men by which we must be saved" (vv. 10–12).

Paul. Peter is not the only apostle in Acts to preach that Jesus's resurrection saves. Paul does the same. As is his custom, in the synagogue at Antioch in Pisidia he takes advantage of the opportunity given visitors to speak and rehearses God's dealings with Israel until the time of David. Paul then says, "Of this man's offspring God has brought to Israel a Savior, Jesus, as he promised" (Acts 13:23). After explaining Jesus's execution and burial, Paul preaches, "but God raised him from the dead" and Jesus appeared to many, including the apostles, who are now witnesses of his resurrection.

---

[9]Jesus taught Peter this interpretation of Ps. 118:22 (see Matt. 21:42).

Paul cites Psalms 2 and 16 as Old Testament prophecies of Jesus's resurrection. He then affirms the significance of that singular event: "Let it be known to you therefore, brothers, that through this man forgiveness of sins is proclaimed to you, and by him everyone who believes is freed from everything from which you could not be freed by the law of Moses" (Acts 13:38–39). Jesus is a (crucified and) living Savior who forgives the sins of those who repent and delivers them from legalism.

Teaching in the Pauline Epistles

Romans 4:25

If a hundred pastors were asked what Jesus did to justify sinners, they would almost unanimously answer, "die in our place." And they would be correct. Paul presents the basis of God's declaring believing sinners righteous as "a propitiation by his blood" (Rom. 3:25–26) and as his "one act of righteousness" (Rom. 5:18).

The pastors' answer is correct as far as it goes. But there is one passage in Paul—even in Romans—that they would have overlooked, Romans 4:24–25: "Jesus our Lord . . . was delivered up for our trespasses and raised for our justification." In what sense was Jesus "raised for our justification"? He died in our place. Was he raised in our place? If he saved us as our substitute in his death, how can we express the way that he saves us in his resurrection?

Paul has just spoken of justification, even of God's crediting righteousness to Abraham when he believed God (Rom. 4:22). The apostle notes that God's dealings with Abraham were not merely specific to him; they pertain to us as well (v. 23). Indeed, God's saving righteousness in Christ will also "be counted to us who believe in him who raised from the dead Jesus our Lord" (v. 24). Again we ask, what is the connection between Jesus's resurrection and our justification?

Paul explains: Christ "was delivered up for our trespasses" (Rom. 4:25). Jesus died for our sins. He was our substitute who died the death that we deserved to die in order to save us from that death, even the judgment of God. The next part of the verse tells that Jesus was more than our substitute: he was "raised for our justification" (v. 25). After careful reflection on the meaning of this neglected verse, I. Howard Marshall summarizes:

> First, it follows that, in the event of crucifixion and resurrection, it is inadequate to think of Christ purely as substitute. Substitution means that Christ acts instead of us, and does something that, as a result of his doing it, we do not

need to do. We do *not* have to bear the eternal consequences of our sin because Christ has done so. But the same cannot be said of resurrection. Christ is not raised instead of us, but so that we might share his resurrection. He is raised for us, for our benefit, on our behalf, in order that what has happened in him may be recapitulated in us, by what has happened in him being extended to us as we are joined to him by faith.[10]

Marshall makes an important contribution to our investigation into Jesus's resurrection as a saving event. Jesus's accomplishment is so great that we need many concepts to understand it, even in part. He died as our substitute, as our last chapter showed repeatedly. But he also saves us as our resurrected representative—as the One who lives on our behalf. His resurrection saves us as he, who died for us, is freed from death by God. "Thus the raising of Jesus by God the Father is seen to be an essential part of his saving act, and is not simply a way of proclaiming to humanity that the price of sin has been paid. If Christ had not been raised, we would still be in our sins."[11]

Romans 5:10

> Since, therefore, we have now been justified by his blood, much more shall we be saved by him from the wrath of God. For if while we were enemies we were reconciled to God by the death of his Son, much more, now that we are reconciled, shall we be saved by his life. (Rom. 5:9–10)

Arguing for God's preservation of believers, Paul twice employs a Jewish argument from the more difficult to the less difficult. In verse 9 he argues in terms of justification, and in verse 10 in terms of reconciliation. If God did the harder thing—justified guilty sinners—he will surely do the easier thing—keep saved to the end those he has justified.

For emphasis, Paul repeats a similar argument for preservation. But now he refers to salvation as reconciliation instead of justification. "For if while we were enemies we were reconciled to God by the death of his Son, much more, now that we are reconciled, shall we be saved by his life" (Rom. 5:9–10). If when we were God's enemies he made us his friends by his Son's death, now that we are his friends he surely will keep us saved by his Son's resurrection.

It is clear that Paul refers to Christ's cross twice in Romans 5:9–10 when he speaks of "his blood" and "the death of his Son." But to what does the apostle

---

[10]Marshall, *Aspects of the Atonement*, 91–92.
[11]Ibid., 97.

refer when he speaks of our being saved "by his life"? Thomas Schreiner is correct: "A reference to the resurrection of Christ is certainly intended."[12]

Paul's references to Christ's blood in verse 9 and his life in verse 10 do not divide the accomplishment of salvation between his death and resurrection. Rather, reminiscent of 4:25, "Christ's death and resurrection are inseparable in effecting salvation."[13] As a result, either one, as a synecdoche (a figure of speech in which a whole stands for a part, or, as in this case, a part for the whole), could stand for Christ's whole saving accomplishment.

Here again Paul points to Christ's (death and) resurrection as work that brings about the salvation of his people.

Romans 10:8–13

Paul has a burden for his fellow Israelites and prays that God might save them (Rom. 10:1). He laments that their zeal for God is not combined with knowledge (v. 2). They have sought to establish their own righteousness based on the law instead of submitting to God's righteousness based on faith in Christ (vv. 3–7).

In this they misunderstand the Old Testament. It teaches, as the apostles do, that salvation comes from believing the message (v. 8). Paul summarizes the New Testament message that he proclaims: "If you confess with your mouth that Jesus is Lord and believe in your heart that God raised him from the dead, you will be saved" (v. 9). This is in keeping with the Old Testament principles that "everyone who believes in him will not be put to shame," and "everyone who calls on the name of the Lord will be saved" (Rom. 10:11, 13; Isa. 28:16; Joel 2:32).

What does Paul mean when he requires verbal confession of Jesus's lordship and heartfelt faith in his resurrection for salvation (Rom. 10:9)? It is important to note that Paul is not giving two different steps that people must take to be saved. Confessing and believing are two different ways of talking about a positive response to Christ as he is offered in the gospel.[14] And calling on the name of the Lord (v. 13) is yet another way of talking about confessing Christ and believing in him; it does not give another condition for salvation.

When Paul writes, "If you confess with your mouth that Jesus is Lord," he reflects the commonly held conviction that people must believe that Jesus is Lord to be saved (1 Cor. 12:3; 16:22) and that Jesus was appointed Lord at his resurrection (Acts 2:36; Phil. 2:9–11). When the apostle says, "If you . . . believe

---

[12] Thomas Schreiner, *Romans*, Baker Exegetical Commentary on the New Testament (Grand Rapids: Baker Academic, 1998), 264.

[13] Ibid.

[14] So Douglas J. Moo, *The Epistle to the Romans*, The New International Commentary on the New Testament (Grand Rapids: Eerdmans, 1996), 657.

in your heart that God raised him from the dead, you will be saved" (Rom. 10:9), he teaches that Jesus's resurrection is a part of the gospel and that belief in his resurrection, therefore, is necessary for salvation (cf. 1 Cor. 15:3–4). The next verse helps us: "For with the heart one believes and is justified, and with the mouth one confesses and is saved." Faith that saves is "with the heart"—that is, heartfelt, sincere—and confession of Christ is necessary for salvation.

In Romans 10:9–10, then, Paul shows that Christ's resurrection saves when he insists that faith in it is necessary for salvation. Some are surprised that Paul mentions faith in Christ's resurrection but does not mention his crucifixion. In at least one place where Paul spells out the gospel in detail, 1 Corinthians 15:3–4, he mentions both.

1 Corinthians 15:3–4, 14–22

Paul's fullest summary of the gospel that he preaches includes Christ's death and resurrection: "For I delivered to you as of first importance what I also received: that Christ died for our sins in accordance with the Scriptures, that he was buried, that he was raised on the third day in accordance with the Scriptures." The apostle knows that some truths are more important than others. He includes the gospel among the most important truths. He regards it "as of first importance" (v. 3).

This is the message that he delivers to others because it is the one he "received" from Christ. Here Paul writes the gospel in longhand, including both the cross and empty tomb. Many times, he and the other apostles use shorthand, mentioning only the one or the other. John Calvin wisely explains:

> Whenever mention is made of his death alone, we are to understand at the same time what belongs to his resurrection. Also, the same synecdoche applies to the word "resurrection": whenever it is mentioned separately from death, we are to understand it as including what has to do especially with his death.[15]

Christ's death and resurrection are so essential to Christianity and so inseparable that when the Bible speaks of either one of them, we are to infer the other as well.

Furthermore, Paul teaches that Christ's resurrection is as necessary for our salvation as his crucifixion. In 1 Corinthians 15:12–19 he candidly contemplates what results would follow if Christ were not raised from the dead. His list is impressive:

---

[15]John Calvin, *Institutes of the Christian Religion*, ed. John T. McNeill, trans. Ford Lewis Battles, 2 vols. (Philadelphia: Westminster, 1960), 1:521 (2.16.13).

And if Christ has not been raised, then our preaching is in vain and your faith is in vain. . . . And if Christ has not been raised, your faith is futile and you are still in your sins. Then those also who have fallen asleep in Christ have perished. If in Christ we have hope in this life only, we are of all people most to be pitied. (1 Cor. 15:14, 17–19)

If Jesus's resurrection had not occurred, the apostles' preaching would be a waste of time and effort. In addition, the faith of their hearers would be as big a waste. If Christ were still in the tomb, disastrous results would obtain for living and dead believers. Living believers would still be in their sins (v. 17). Those who trust Christ for salvation would in fact not be forgiven at all. Dead believers would "have perished." Though they died trusting Christ to save them, if he were a dead savior, he could not deliver them. If he were not risen, they would have died and gone to hell. In sum, "if in Christ we have hope in this life only, we are of all people most to be pitied" (v. 19).

Paul's frank ruminations are harrowing. We rejoice that "in fact Christ has been raised from the dead, the firstfruits of those who have fallen asleep" (v. 20). The fact that Jesus is the "firstfruits" means that more are to come. Indeed, Jesus's resurrection is the cause of his people's being raised to eternal life: "For as by a man came death, by a man has come also the resurrection of the dead. For as in Adam all die, so also in Christ shall all be made alive" (vv. 21–22). Paul contrasts the first and second Adams. Adam's sin in the garden brought death to the human race (Rom. 5:12). Christ, "the last Adam," "the second man" (1 Cor. 15:45, 47), brings resurrection to all who are united to him by grace through faith. And he does so as the (crucified and) risen one. His resurrection means resurrection and everlasting life to believers. It saves.

1 Corinthians 15:47–49

Later in the same chapter Paul again teaches that Jesus's resurrection saves, as he once more contrasts Adam and Christ:

The first man was from the earth, a man of dust; the second man is from heaven. As was the man of dust, so also are those who are of the dust, and as is the man of heaven, so also are those who are of heaven. Just as we have borne the image of the man of dust, we shall also bear the image of the man of heaven.

God made Adam from the dust of the ground and his name reminds him of that fact (ground is *adamah* in Gen. 2:7). When the Son of God became a human being in the incarnation, he came down "from heaven" (1 Cor. 15:47).

Paul's point is that the people associated with the two Adams resemble them. Since Adam's fall human beings are "of the dust": we bear Adam's resemblance in that, because he sinned and died, so do we. But in Christ, we "are of heaven" (v. 48). That is, "we shall also bear the image of the man of heaven" (v. 49). In context that means we will be raised imperishable, in glory, and in power (vv. 42–43), just as Christ was. We will resemble Christ the second and last Adam, who is also our head; because he is alive, we are assured a glorious resurrection.

Ephesians 2:4–7

Paul combines Jesus's resurrection with regeneration in this passage. He digs a deep pit for sinners by describing our unsaved condition as involving spiritual death, lostness, devotion to Satan, and worldliness, and as deserving God's wrath (Eph. 2:1–3). Against this horrible background the apostle accentuates God's compassion: "But God, being rich in mercy, because of the great love with which he loved us, even when we were dead in our trespasses, made us alive together with Christ" (vv. 4–5). God made those who were spiritually dead "alive." And this is the epitome of grace; it illustrates well the fact that "by grace you have been saved" (v. 5).

How did God cause those who were "dead in the trespasses and sins" (v. 1) to be "made alive"? The answer is that he "made us alive together with Christ . . . and raised us up with him" (vv. 5–6). This is Pauline language of union with Christ. It is his favorite way of speaking of God's application to sinners of the salvation wrought by Christ. God joined us to Christ in his (death and) resurrection and gave us spiritual life.

The visible revelation of the new heavens and new earth awaits the return of Christ and the resurrection of the dead. In the meantime, because Jesus died and rose again, the new age has dawned. Because of Jesus's resurrection God regenerates sinners. He gives them life of the age to come, here and now. They still live in mortal bodies and die. But the day will come when their resurrected bodies will be immortal, imperishable, glorious, powerful, and dominated by the Holy Spirit (1 Cor. 15:42–44, 52–53).

Colossians 1:18

In the Christ hymn of Colossians 1, Paul powerfully attests to the risen Christ's ability to save. The apostle first shows Christ's preeminence over creation (vv. 15–17). He holds first place in this realm because he visibly revealed God in his incarnation, he was God's agent in creation, he is heir of all (vv. 15–16), he is eternal, and he performs the work of providence (v. 17).

Christ also is preeminent over his church: "And he is the head of the body, the church" (v. 18). As a human head controls its body, so Christ rules his church. Paul's next words are at first obscure: "He is the beginning" (v. 18). The beginning of what? His statement above, that by Christ "all things were created, in heaven and on earth" (v. 16), provides a clue. It takes readers back to Genesis 1:1: "In *the beginning*, God created the heavens and the earth." Christ is Lord over the creation because it is his creation; in the beginning he was God's agent in creating all. He is Lord over his church because it too is a part of his creation, or rather, his re-creation; *he* is the new beginning, the source of the church's eternal life.

"He is the beginning," then, portrays Christ as the beginning, the source of life for the church, over which he is head. In what capacity is he the church's beginning? As "the firstborn from the dead" (v. 18). It is Jesus's powerful resurrection from the dead that enables him to be Lord over the church, to rule it as head, and to give life to each of its members. It is no surprise, then, that Paul follows immediately with these words: "that in everything he might be preeminent" (v. 18). "Everything" corresponds to the two spheres just discussed: the creation (vv. 15–17) and the re-creation (v. 18), of which the church is a part. Paul presents Christ as Lord of all and as Savior of his church by virtue of his (death and) resurrection.

Teaching in the General Epistles

Hebrews 7:16, 24–25

Repeatedly the writer to the Hebrews shows the superiority of Christ's high priesthood to that of the Old Testament priests. They became priests on the basis of their descending from Aaron. Christ came as a priest of a different order—that of Melchizedek. Furthermore, he became "a priest, not on the basis of a legal requirement concerning bodily descent, but by the power of an indestructible life" (Heb. 7:16). As proof the writer quotes his favorite Old Testament text concerning Christ's priesthood: "You are a priest forever, after the order of Melchizedek" (Ps. 110:4). The emphasis is on the word "forever," and the "indestructible life" of Hebrews 7:16 refers to Christ's resurrection.

No Old Testament priest could be a priest forever, because each grew old and died. Therefore, there had to be many of them: "The former priests were many in number, because they were prevented by death from continuing in office" (Heb. 7:23). By contrast, Christ "holds his priesthood permanently, because he continues forever" (v. 24). Of course, this is another reference to his resurrection. And the writer links Jesus's resurrection to his role as priest.

The following statement is as clear as any in Scripture that Jesus's resurrection saves: "Consequently, he is able to save to the uttermost those who draw near to God through him, since he always lives to make intercession for them" (Heb. 7:25). It is common knowledge that Jesus as our great High Priest had to die as a sacrifice for our sins. It is not common knowledge that he also had to rise to save us. His crucifixion and resurrection save.

He "saves to the uttermost" because he is alive to "make intercession" for believers. In context, this refers to his presenting his priestly sacrifice in the heavenly tabernacle, God's very presence. Christ's sacrifice is perpetually present in heaven because he is alive after dying for our sins! The result? Believers need not fear rejection by God because Christ's all-sufficient sacrifice keeps them saved.

1 Peter 1:3

Peter praises God the Father: "Blessed be the God and Father of our Lord Jesus Christ! According to his great mercy, he has caused us to be born again to a living hope" (1 Pet. 1:3). The reason for Peter's praise is the Father's role in our regeneration. We most readily think of the Holy Spirit when we think of regeneration, and that makes sense because he is the person of the Trinity who quickens us, who moves us from death to life (John 3:8).

However, the Father and Son have roles to play in our receiving eternal life from God, too. The Father is the instigator, who in mercy causes us to be born again. His action is "through the resurrection of Jesus Christ from the dead" (1 Pet. 1:3). It is Jesus's resurrection that supplies the power for the new life. His resurrected life is the source of the eternal life that the Spirit applies to us according to the Father's merciful plan.

The result of the Trinity's causing us to be born again is a living hope in life after death. Life after death involves "an inheritance that is imperishable, undefiled, and unfading, kept in heaven for you" (v. 4). Unlike every inheritance on earth, our heavenly inheritance is without ruin, sin, or loss of glory; also it cannot be lost since it is "reserved."

1 Peter 1:18–21

After urging his readers to pursue holiness, Peter reminds them of the cost of their redemption: "knowing that you were ransomed . . . with the precious blood of Christ, like that of a lamb without blemish or spot" (1 Pet. 1:18–19). Christ is God's ultimate spotless, sacrificial lamb, who by his death "takes away the sin of the world" (John 1:29).

In Pauline fashion, Peter contrasts Christ in God's eternal plan with Christ revealed in time and space: "He was foreknown before the foundation of the world but was made manifest in the last times for the sake of you" (1 Pet. 1:20). He "was made manifest," of course, in his incarnation.

He best demonstrates that he came for their sake in his role as the Mediator between God and human beings: You "through him are believers in God" (v. 21). Christ's crucifixion comes readily to mind when we think of him as Mediator. Peter mentions another event that is an integral part of Christ's mediatorial work: "God . . . raised him from the dead and gave him glory, so that your faith and hope are in God" (v. 21). Christ the Mediator died and arose in glory. The result is that believers' "faith and hope are in God" (v. 21). Their faith is not a figment of their imagination but resides firmly in the true and living God.

Teaching in the Book of Revelation

The Revelation too speaks of Christ's resurrection in at least three places.

Revelation 1:4–5

> John to the seven churches that are in Asia:
> Grace to you and peace from . . . Jesus Christ the faithful witness, the firstborn of the dead, and the ruler of kings on earth.

John is writing to seven churches in the first-century province of Asia Minor. He names them in chapters 2–3. Revelation is, among other things, a letter, and as a part of John's salutation he prays that God the holy Trinity would grant grace and peace to his readers. Our concern is with "Jesus Christ the faithful witness, the firstborn of the dead, and the ruler of kings on earth." We offer a brief summary of these titles, which are drawn from the Old Testament.

Jesus is described as one who was a faithful witness to the Father, even though it meant persecution unto death.[16] John mentions this role of Jesus to motivate the churches to which he writes also to persevere in faithful witness to God, regardless of the consequences. He also describes Jesus as "the firstborn from the dead." As in Colossians 1:18 (and Ps. 89:27), so here "firstborn" means first in rank and privilege. Christ occupies the highest position because of his resurrection from the dead. As we will see, John expands on the significance of Jesus's resurrection for the church in Revelation 1:18 and 3:14. Here he explains its cosmic significance: as a result of the resurrection, Jesus is "the ruler of kings

---

[16]John draws on Old Testament background from Ps. 89:27, 37 and Isa. 43:10–13.

on earth."[17] The risen one is sovereign Lord over all earthly rulers. Although this truth is not universally acknowledged now, one day it will be.

Revelation 1:17–18

> When I saw him, I fell at his feet as though dead. But he laid his right hand on me, saying, "Fear not, I am the first and the last, and the living one. I died, and behold I am alive forevermore, and I have the keys of Death and Hades."

John is overwhelmed with the vision of the exalted Christ in verses 13–16 and collapses, but Christ graciously comforts him. When Jesus says, "I am the first and the last," he employs Old Testament language used by God himself to teach his eternity. This occurs three times in Isaiah:

> I, the LORD, the first,
>> and with the last; I am he. (Isa. 41:4)

> Thus says the LORD, the King of Israel
>> and his Redeemer, the LORD of hosts:
> "I am the first and I am the last;
>> besides me there is no god." (Isa. 44:6)

> I am he; I am the first,
>> and I am the last. (Isa. 48:12)

Jesus thus identifies himself with God from the Old Testament and in so doing teaches that he is the eternal one.

In addition, Christ proclaims: "I am . . . the living one. I died, and behold I am alive forevermore" (Rev. 1:17–18). He not only shares God's attribute of eternity; he has died on the cross and has been raised from the dead. As such he is "the living one." Having died once, he is "alive forevermore." Death has no more power over him. In fact, because of his death and mighty resurrection he can say truly, "I have the keys of Death and Hades" (v. 18). That is, "through the victory of the resurrection Christ became king even over the realm of the dead in which he was formerly imprisoned. Now, not only is he no longer held in death's bonds but he also holds sway over who is released and retained in that

---

[17] I acknowledge a debt to Gregory Beale's outstanding work *The Book of Revelation*, New International Greek Testament Commentary (Grand Rapids: Eerdmans, 1999), 191.

realm."[18] In other words, as the crucified and risen one, Jesus is humankind's Savior and Judge.

Revelation 2:8

As is his custom in the letters to the seven churches, John addresses the church's "angel": "And to the angel of the church in Smyrna write: 'The words of the first and the last, who died and came to life.'" Our interest lies not in the details of the letter, but in the description of Christ. Once more Christ is referred to in the Old Testament language of eternity—"the first and the last." Moreover, he is the one "who died and came to life." Here again we are reminded of his death and resurrection.

Revelation 3:14

In the letter to the church in Laodicea, the Revelation's most important words concerning Christ's resurrection appear: "Write: 'The words of the Amen, the faithful and true witness, the beginning of God's creation.'" As in 1:4, Jesus is referred to as "the faithful witness," this time with the added adjective "true." The title "Amen," which precedes, means the same thing: Jesus is the "Amen" to God's promises.

What does Jesus mean when he refers to himself as "the beginning of God's creation"? The majority of interpreters understand this in the sense of Colossians 1:15–16[19]—Christ is the Father's agent in the creation of the heavens and the earth.[20] This accords with the Bible's teaching generally, that of the Revelation more specifically, and even this context in particular. But another interpretation also meets these three criteria, and others. Gregory Beale has convinced me that Jesus here refers not to the original creation but to the new creation.

There are several reasons for this. First, the word "Amen" in Revelation 3:14 refers to Isaiah 65:16:

> So that he who blesses himself in the land
>   shall bless himself by the God of truth,

---

[18]Ibid., 215.

[19]For example, see Robert H. Mounce, *The Book of Revelation*, The New International Commentary on the New Testament (Grand Rapids: Eerdmans, 1977), 124–25.

[20]Of course, neither here nor elsewhere does the Revelation teach that Christ is the first creature of God, as the ancient Arians and contemporary Jehovah's Witnesses claim. Rather, he is the eternal God, "the first and the last," according to 1:17–18; 2:8; 21:6; 22:13. For an outstanding presentation of the deity of Christ in Revelation, see Andreas J. Köstenberger, "The Deity of Christ in John's Letters and the Book of Revelation," in *The Deity of Christ*, ed. Christopher W. Morgan and Robert A. Peterson, Theology in Community (Wheaton, IL: Crossway, 2011).

and he who takes an oath in the land
    shall swear by the God of truth;
because the former troubles are forgotten
    and are hidden from my eyes.

Many commentators rightly conclude that Isaiah 65:16 is the source of the word "Amen" in Revelation 3:14.[21] In fact, the words translated "the God of truth" are literally "the God of Amen" in Hebrew and could be understood as a name—Amen. If so, then Isaiah 65:16 and Revelation 3:14 are the only two verses in the entire Bible that use "Amen" as a name. The very next verse in Isaiah reveals what the blessings of verse 16 are:

For behold, I create new heavens
    and a new earth,
and the former things shall not be remembered
    or come into mind. (Isa. 65:17)

So because the Old Testament antecedent to Revelation 3:14 (Isa. 65:16) is immediately followed by the first Old Testament reference to the new heavens and earth, it makes sense that Revelation 3:14 also speaks to that theme.

Second, the next words of Revelation 3:14, "the faithful and true witness," recall 1:5, which speaks of "Jesus Christ the faithful witness." "Witness" is used five times in the Revelation, and three of those uses refer to martyrs and human witnesses to Jesus: 2:13; 11:3; 17:6. The only two places where "witness" refers to Jesus are 1:5 and 3:14. This is one way that John points readers of 3:14 back to 1:5. Indeed, Revelation 3:14 further explains Christ's title in 1:5, which has to do not with creation but with Christ's earthly ministry, crucifixion, and resurrection. Therefore, 3:14 too deals with redemption, not creation.

Third, the expression in Revelation 1:5, "the firstborn of the dead," harkens back to Colossians 1:18: "He is the beginning, the firstborn from the dead." And the words immediately preceding in Colossians speak not of creation but of the church, a part of God's new creation: "And he is the head of the body, the church."

For these three reasons and more,[22] we are to interpret Jesus's self-description in Revelation 3:14—"the beginning of God's creation"—as an expansion of the reference to Jesus's resurrection in 1:5—"the firstborn of the dead." That is, as he who died and arose Jesus is "the beginning of God's creation." Jesus is the

---

[21]Beale adduces "weighty evidence that the Isaiah text is the *primary* source for the titles in Rev. 3:14." *The Book of Revelation*, 299–301.

[22]See the extended discussion in ibid., 297–301.

one who has been raised from the dead and as the resurrected one inaugurates the new creation of God. Thus the words in Revelation 1:5 and 3:14 teach that there is a sense in which the "new heaven and new earth," which will only be consummated in Revelation 21–22, are already here. Jesus lives and has begun the new age already. He gives eternal life now to all who believe in him.

Christ's Resurrection Saves

We are ready to summarize a neglected and vital truth: combined with his crucifixion, Jesus's resurrection saves. Many passages of Scripture testify to the saving significance of his resurrection in general terms:

> Jesus Christ of Nazareth . . . whom God raised from the dead. . . . And there is salvation in no one else, for there is no other name under heaven given among men by which we must be saved. (Acts 4:10, 12)

> You . . . through him are believers in God, who raised him from the dead and gave him glory, so that your faith and hope are in God. (1 Pet. 1:20–21)

> I died, and behold I am alive forevermore, and I have the keys of Death and Hades. (Rev. 1:18)

These verses ascribe a general saving significance to Jesus's resurrection. But how specifically does it save?

- Christ's resurrection brings justification and forgiveness.
- Christ's resurrection establishes peace with God.
- Christ's resurrection inaugurates the new creation.

Christ's Resurrection Brings Justification and Forgiveness

Justification. When Paul gives the basis for God's declaring sinners righteous in Romans, he points primarily to the cross of Christ. In Romans 3:25–26 the basis of justification is "Christ Jesus, whom God put forward as a propitiation by his blood." In Romans 5:18–19 the basis of justification is Christ's "obedience" unto death, his "one act of righteousness." Paul focuses on the cross, but docs not omit Jesus's resurrection.

In one passage in Romans the apostle brings together the cross and empty tomb. Righteousness "will be counted to us who believe in him who raised from the dead Jesus our Lord, who was delivered up for our trespasses and raised for our justification" (Rom. 4:23–25). Here dealing with "our trespasses" and "our justification" are not two separate blessings, but one way of talking about the same blessing—free justification. Justification can be expressed as the positive imputation of righteousness to the believing sinner (Rom. 4:3–5; 5:18–19; 2 Cor. 5:21). It can also be expressed as the nonimputation of sin to the same (Rom. 4:6–7). So when Paul says Jesus "was delivered up for our trespasses," he means that his atoning death was necessary for our justification. When he says that Jesus was "raised for our justification," he means that Jesus's triumphant resurrection was necessary for our justification. Both Jesus's death and his resurrection are necessary for sinners to be justified before a holy God.

Jesus's death is the basis of our justification in that he, our substitute, died in our place, paying the penalty that we could never pay. He also saves us as our resurrected Lord and representative—as the one who lives on our behalf. This is true in at least two senses. First, Christ's resurrection testifies to the efficacy of his death, as C. E. B. Cranfield explains: "For what was necessitated by our sin was, in the first place, Christ's atoning death, and yet, had His death not been followed by His resurrection, it would not have been God's mighty deed for our justification."[23] Second, Jesus's resurrection saves us as he who died for us is freed from death by God. His saving death and saving resurrection are the reasons that God will free us from death too. James Dunn clarifies: "The link between justification and Jesus' resurrection . . . underscores its point—that the justifying grace of God is all of a piece with his creative, life-giving power."[24] As we will see, his resurrection is the basis and guarantee of our resurrection to eternal life on the last day.

Forgiveness of sins. Because Jesus's death *and* resurrection combine to constitute the basis of our justification, Paul announces to his hearers in Pisidian Antioch: "God has brought to Israel a Savior, Jesus, as he promised. . . . but he whom God raised up did not see corruption. Let it be known to you therefore, brothers, that through this man forgiveness of sins is proclaimed to you" (Acts 13:23, 37–38). With these words Paul is not detracting from the saving value of Jesus's atonement. Rather, he is teaching an additional truth—the saving value of Jesus's resurrection. Specifically, Jesus's (death and) resurrection is the basis for the apostolic message of the "forgiveness of sins" (v. 38).

Similarly, when Paul contemplates what would be true if Christ had not risen from the grave, he emphasizes, "And if Christ has not been raised, your faith is

---

[23]C. E. B. Cranfield, *The Epistle to the Romans*, The International Critical Commentary (Edinburgh: T&T Clark, 1975), 252.

[24]James D. G. Dunn, *Romans 1–8*, Word Biblical Commentary (Dallas: Word, 1988), 241.

futile and you are still in your sins" (1 Cor. 15:17). Why would that be the case? Anthony Thiselton answers: "Without the resurrection of Christ, Christ's death alone has no atoning, redemptive, or liberating effect in relation to human sin."[25] It is because Jesus our divine-human representative not only died in our place but also lives as Victor over sin and the grave that he saves to the end all who come to God through him.

A priestly sacrifice in heaven. A related truth is taught in Hebrews 7:23–25. Unlike the Old Testament priests who died and were succeeded by their descendants, Christ "holds his priesthood permanently" (Heb. 7:24). Why? "Because he continues forever" as the risen one. "Consequently, he is able to save to the uttermost those who draw near to God through him, since he always lives to make intercession for them" (Heb. 7:25). The intercession spoken of here is not Christ's heavenly ministry of praying for the saints according to the will of God, as the Holy Spirit prays (Rom. 8:27). That is taught in Romans 8:34: "Christ Jesus is the one who died—more than that, who was raised—who is at the right hand of God, who indeed is interceding for us."

The intercession of Hebrews 7:25 does not exclude Christ's ministry of prayer, but its focus lies elsewhere, on his priestly ministry of making atonement for sins by shedding his blood. The following context makes this clear: "He has no need, like those high priests, to offer sacrifices daily, first for his own sins and then for those of the people, since he did this once for all when he offered up himself" (v. 27). Once more the writer contrasts Christ's superior priesthood and sacrifice with their inferior Old Testament precursors. The Levitical priests, as sinners, every day had to offer sacrifices for themselves and for the people. But the sinless Christ "once for all" time made the singular sacrifice "when he offered up himself" for sinners on the cross (v. 27).

So, when the writer says, "He is able to save to the uttermost those who draw near to God through him, since he always lives to make intercession for them" (Heb. 7:25), he means that Jesus saves his people forever because he continually presents his priestly sacrifice in God's presence in heaven. The atonement that he made once for all on Calvary's cross avails forever because as the resurrected one he holds a permanent priesthood "by the power of an indestructible life" and "continues forever" (Heb. 7:16, 24). Bruce underscores this truth:

> It is true that Christ did die, and that this death was the essential priestly offering for man's sins; but his death was not the termination of his priesthood, or the

---

[25] Anthony C. Thiselton, *The First Epistle to the Corinthians*, The New International Greek Testament Commentary (Grand Rapids: Eerdmans, 2000), 1220.

moment of its transition from him to someone else, for he rose from the grave, victor over death, and now continues as our sole and ever living high priest.[26]

So, Jesus is our High Priest who saves by his death *and* resurrection.

Christ's Resurrection Establishes Peace with God

In addition to bringing justification and forgiveness Jesus's (death and) resurrection also bring peace with God—reconciliation. Paul accents Christ's saving work in Romans 5:9–10 by speaking of justification and reconciliation. At first glance it appears that he connects Jesus's cross with justification—"we have now been justified by his blood"—and Jesus's resurrection with reconciliation—"now that we are reconciled, shall we be saved by his life." Closer inspection, however, reveals that the apostle is crediting Jesus's death and resurrection as the combined ground of both our justification *and* our reconciliation.

This is proved by quoting verse 10 in full: "For if while we were enemies we were reconciled to God by the death of his Son, much more, now that we are reconciled, shall we be saved by his life." Here Paul attributes reconciliation to Christ's death and final salvation to his (resurrection) life. We are reconciled and finally saved by both Christ's death and his resurrection. It is not obvious, however, *how* Christ's resurrection saves.

Schreiner helps us:

> How does the life of Christ save from eschatological wrath? It is instructive to recall the parallels between Rom. 5:1–11 and 8:18–39 at this point. More specifically, 8:33–34 poses two arguments as to why believers can be assured that they will not be condemned on the day of judgment. The first reason is that God has accomplished justification, and he will not accuse those whom he has vindicated. Second, believers are assured that they will escape condemnation since for their sake Christ died, was raised to life from the dead and intercedes. So too, in 5:10 the "life of Christ" probably designates both his resurrection and his intercessory work for believers. . . . The reference to Christ's death and resurrection also recalls 4:25, where both the death and resurrection of Christ are constitutive elements of the believer's justification. Christ's death and resurrection are inseparable in effecting salvation.[27]

Schreiner is correct. We must not separate what God has put together, and he has put Jesus's death and resurrection inseparably together. Together they

---

[26]F. F. Bruce, *A Commentary on the Epistle to the Hebrews*, The New International Commentary on the New Testament (Grand Rapids: Eerdmans, 1977), 269.
[27]Schreiner, *Romans*, 267.

describe Christ's saving work. But usually Scripture mentions only one of them and expects us to infer the other. This is the case in Romans 5:9, where Jesus's "blood" justifies. Sometimes, however, Scripture mentions both Jesus's death and his resurrection. This is the case in Romans 5:10, which ascribes reconciliation to his "death" and ultimate salvation to "his life." How exactly does his resurrection save us in the end? The answer involves rehearsing what we have already discussed: his resurrection assures justification and forgiveness, and guarantees Christ's permanent priesthood. The answer also anticipates the next section, which highlights the great significance of Christ's resurrection in inaugurating the new creation and all that comes with it now and in the future.

Christ's Resurrection Inaugurates the New Creation

The most prominent way that Jesus's (death and) resurrection saves is by bringing about God's new creation. This can be viewed profitably from at least three perspectives: that of the new birth now, that of our future resurrection, and that of the new heavens and new earth.

It Brings the New Birth and Eternal Life Now

John, Paul, and Peter all teach that Jesus's resurrection brings new life in regeneration to sinners now.

John 11:25–26. Jesus utters haunting words to Lazarus's sister Martha: "I am the resurrection and the life. Whoever believes in me, though he die, yet shall he live, and everyone who lives and believes in me shall never die."

As outlined earlier in this chapter, John's theme of Jesus as life-giver forms the background for his words.[28] The incarnate Son of God gives eternal life to all who believe in him. There I argued that C. H. Dodd best explains these difficult verses. Following his lead yields an elliptical form of verse 25: "I am the resurrection: Whoever believes in me, though he die, yet shall he live." Jesus will raise believers in him who experience physical death—at his voice they will come out of their graves "to the resurrection of life" (5:28–29). He is the life-giver who will give resurrection life to his people on the last day.

Also following Dodd, a similar ellipsis of verses 25–26 yields, "I am the life: Everyone who lives and believes in me shall never die." Persons who trust Jesus as Savior in life will not experience the second death (hell). That is because Jesus the life-giver gives them eternal life now as a gift: "I give them eternal life, and they will never perish, and no one will snatch them out of my hand. My Father,

---

[28]See pp. 123–24.

who has given them to me, is greater than all, and no one is able to snatch them out of the Father's hand" (John 10:28–29).

With the words, "Lazarus, come out," Jesus, "the resurrection and the life," raises his friend from the tomb as proof that he is now giver of eternal life and as a token of his power to raise the dead to everlasting life on the last day (John 11:43–44). D. A. Carson captures these truths: "Just as he not only gives bread from heaven (6:27) but is himself the bread of life (6:35), so also he not only raises the dead on the last day (5:21, 25ff.) but is himself the resurrection and the life. There is neither resurrection nor eternal life outside of him."[29]

Ephesians 2:4–7. Against a background of terrible human rebellion and sin, Paul extols God's love: "But God, being rich in mercy, because of the great love with which he loved us, even when we were dead in our trespasses, made us alive together with Christ" (vv. 4–5). God in grace made those who were spiritually dead "alive." God causes us who were spiritually dead to be "made alive" by spiritually uniting us to Christ in his resurrection. P. T. O'Brien aptly summarizes Paul's thought:

> At the very time when we were spiritually dead *God made us alive with Christ.* . . . Paul's readers have come to life with Christ, who was dead and rose again; their new life, then, is a sharing in the new life which he received when he rose from the dead. It is only in union with him that death is vanquished and new life, an integral part of God's new creation, received.[30]

The appearing of the new heavens and new earth awaits Christ's second coming and the resurrection of the dead. But because Jesus died and rose again, God already regenerates sinners. He gives them now the eternal life characteristic of the age to come. Now we have eternal life in mortal bodies. On that day, again because of Jesus's resurrection, God will transform our lowly bodies to be like the resurrected body of the Son of God in glory, power, and immortality.

1 Peter 1:3. In the midst of praise, Peter ascribes roles in regeneration to the Father and the Son. First the Father: "Blessed be the God and Father of our Lord Jesus Christ! According to his great mercy, he has caused us to be born again to a living hope" (1 Pet. 1:3). The Father in mercy causes us to be born again. He is the divine planner of regeneration that issues in our sure hope—our confidence of future salvation.

---

[29]Carson, *The Gospel According to John*, 412.

[30]Peter T. O'Brien, *The Letter to the Ephesians*, The Pillar New Testament Commentary (Grand Rapids: Eerdmans, 1999), 167, italics original.

The Father plans for us to be born again "through the resurrection of Jesus Christ from the dead" (v. 3). It is Jesus's resurrection that unleashes divine power that causes our regeneration to new life. His resurrected life is the source of the eternal life that the Spirit applies to us now according to the Father's gracious plan. Peter Davids speaks precious truth: "Because Jesus really did shatter the gates of death and exists now as our living Lord, those who have committed themselves to him share in his new life and can expect to participate fully in it in the future."[31]

John, Paul, and Peter, therefore, each point to Christ's resurrection from the dead as the source of believers' present possession of eternal life. Because Jesus loved us, gave himself for us, and conquered death by rising from the dead, we are regenerated now. This is in anticipation of our future resurrection unto final salvation, which also is the result of Jesus's resurrection.

It Causes Our Resurrection

Christians believe in the resurrection from the dead but do not always realize its full import. It is one of Scripture's most important ways of talking about our final salvation. Our resurrection *is* our final salvation. We will be raised to eternal life on the new earth in glorious, imperishable, immortal, and powerful bodies that are filled with the Holy Spirit (Phil. 3:21; 1 Cor. 15:42–43, 52–53). Why? Because "Christ died for our sins . . . [and] was raised on the third day" (1 Cor. 15:3–4).

1 Corinthians 15:20–22. After frankly discussing the disastrous consequences if Christ were not raised, Paul exclaims, "In fact Christ has been raised from the dead" (1 Cor. 15:20). He calls the risen Christ "the firstfruits of those who have fallen asleep" (v. 20). The fact that Jesus is the "firstfruits" means that there are more to come—Jesus's resurrection is the cause of believers' being raised to eternal life: "For as by a man came death, by a man has come also the resurrection of the dead. For as in Adam all die, so also in Christ shall all be made alive" (vv. 21–22). Paul contrasts the two Adams. The first Adam's sin in the garden brought death to his race (Rom. 5:12). The (death and) resurrection of the second Adam brings resurrection to his race—all who are spiritually joined to him by faith. His resurrection means resurrection and eternal life to believers. In this way it saves. Gordon Fee's summary deserves quotation:

> Paul means that those who are "in Christ," those who have entered the new humanity through grace by means of his death and resurrection, will just as cer-

---

[31]Peter H. Davids, *The First Epistle of Peter*, The New International Commentary on the New Testament (Grand Rapids: Eerdmans, 1990), 52.

tainly "be made alive"; they will be raised from the dead in the *shared life* of the risen One. Thus Christ is the firstfruits; he is God's pledge that all who are his will be raised from the dead. The inevitable process of death begun in Adam will be reversed by the equally inevitable process of "bringing to life" begun in Christ.[32]

1 Corinthians 15:47–49. The apostle again contrasts Adam and Christ later in 1 Corinthians 15 in order to show that Jesus's resurrection saves.

> The first man was from the earth, a man of dust; the second man is from heaven. As was the man of dust, so also are those who are of the dust, and as is the man of heaven, so also are those who are of heaven. Just as we have borne the image of the man of dust, we shall also bear the image of the man of heaven. (1 Cor. 15:47–49)

God made the first man from the dust of the ground and named him "Adam" (the word "ground" in Gen. 2:7 is *adamah*). The Son of God came down "from heaven" (1 Cor. 15:47) when he became a human being. Paul teaches that the people associated with the two Adams resemble them. Because of Adam's fall human beings are "of the dust": we follow our father Adam in sin and death. But in Christ, believers "are of heaven" (v. 48). "From heaven" means "grounded in the reality of God and the new creation."[33] Paul's point is that "we shall also bear the image of the man of heaven" (v. 49). This means that we will be raised in resurrection bodies (vv. 42–43), just as Christ was. We will be made like Christ, the second and last Adam. Because he is alive, we are assured resurrection to eternal life and glory. Once more, Jesus's resurrection rescues us from the effects of the fall. It means life instead of death, righteousness instead of sin, glory instead of humiliation.

It Inaugurates the New Heavens and New Earth

Christ's (atoning death and) resurrection brings regeneration and eternal life now. It causes the resurrection of believers to eternal life on the last day. In addition, it has cosmic effects. Jesus's resurrection inaugurates the new heavens and new earth.

The Bible begins, "In the beginning, God created the heavens and the earth" (Gen. 1:1). Its last two chapters begin, "Then I saw a new heaven and a new earth, for the first heaven and the first earth had passed away" (Rev. 21:1). How do we get from the story's beginning—the creation of the heavens and earth—to

---

[32]Gordon D. Fee, *The First Epistle to the Corinthians*, The New International Commentary on the New Testament (Grand Rapids: Eerdmans, 1987), 751, italics original.
[33]Thiselton, *The First Epistle to the Corinthians*, 1288.

the story's end—the revelation of the new heaven and earth? Of course, the fall intervened and made a new heaven and earth necessary. But how does God bring it about? How will "the creation itself . . . be set free from its bondage to corruption and obtain the freedom of the glory of the children of God?" (Rom. 8:21). This will occur through the Son of God's death and resurrection.

Colossians 1:19–20. Paul gives Christ's qualifications to be the reconciler of all things: "For in him all the fullness of God was pleased to dwell" (Col. 1:19). Colossians 2:9 provides inspired commentary on this text: "In him the whole fullness of deity dwells bodily." Christ is God incarnate, the God-man. Because of that, "God was pleased . . . through him to reconcile to himself all things, whether on earth or in heaven, making peace by the blood of his cross" (1:19–20).

The big question is, what does Paul mean by "all things" in this verse? In the immediate context he uses the expression four times: "For by him *all things* were created, in heaven and on earth, visible and invisible, whether thrones or dominions or rulers or authorities—*all things* were created through him and for him. And he is before *all things*, and in him *all things* hold together" (1:16–17). Each time the meaning is the same—all created reality. The preincarnate Son created "all things" (v. 16, twice). He is eternal; he existed before "all things" (v. 17). And he performs the divine work of providence: "in him all things hold together" (v. 17).

Therefore, when verse 20 says that he reconciled "all things," we would expect the meaning to be the same—Christ reconciled all created reality. This conclusion is confirmed by the very next words, "God was pleased . . . through him to reconcile to himself all things, whether on earth or in heaven" (v. 20). These words are an echo of those in verse 16: "By him all things were created, in heaven and on earth." Even as Christ created everything in heaven and earth, so he reconciles everything in heaven and earth.

In this context "all things" that Christ reconciled more specifically includes angels, saved human beings, and the heavens and earth. That angels are involved is indicated by the way verse 16 explains "all things in heaven and on earth," as "visible and invisible, whether thrones or dominions or rulers or authorities." By these expressions the apostle designates angels (see 1 Cor. 15:24; Eph. 1:21; 6:12; Col. 2:15). But in what sense did Christ reconcile angels? Scripture teaches that the unfallen angels do not need salvation and that there is no salvation for the fallen angels. For these reasons scholars speak of Christ's reconciling angels as his defeating and subjugating them in order to maintain his peaceable kingdom. A key text here is Colossians 2:15, where after speaking of the cross in the previous verse, Paul writes, "He disarmed the rulers and authorities and put them to open shame, by triumphing over them in him."

Human beings too are reconciled, as the two verses immediately following Colossians 1:20 demonstrate: "And you, who once were alienated and hostile in mind, doing evil deeds, he has now reconciled in his body of flesh by his death, in order to present you holy and blameless and above reproach before him." The Colossian believers are a sample of the persons whom Christ reconciles.

When Paul, then, writes that God through Christ reconciled "to himself all things, whether on earth or in heaven," he means that believers were saved, demons subjugated, and the heaven and earth delivered from the curse. I cannot improve on Douglas Moo's summary:

> Colossians 1:20 teaches, then, not "cosmic salvation" or even "cosmic redemption," but "cosmic restoration" or "renewal." Through the work of Christ on the cross, God has brought his entire rebellious creation back under the rule of his sovereign power. . . . God's work in Christ has in view a reclamation of the entire universe, tainted as it is by human sin (Rom. 8:19–22). That fallen human beings are the prime objects of this reconciliation is clear from the New Testament generally and from the sequel to this text ([Col. 1] vv. 21–23). But it would be a serious mistake (not always avoided) to limit this "reconciling" work to human beings.[34]

What did Christ do to accomplish this astounding feat—the reconciliation of all things? Paul tells us: "making peace by the blood of his cross" (Col. 1:20). He specifically mentions Christ's cross. Does he thereby intend to exclude Christ's resurrection? No, for immediately before speaking of Christ's qualifications to be reconciler he says that "he is the beginning, the firstborn from the dead" (v. 18). He means, as we explained earlier in this chapter, that Christ is the beginning, the source, of God's new creation in his role of "the firstborn from the dead," holding the highest rank as the resurrected one.[35] We conclude that Christ crucified and risen is the peacemaker.

One point needs clarification. When Paul speaks of Christ's reconciling "all things" and that includes human beings, does he teach universalism, the idea that all men and women will be saved? No, for four reasons. First is the near context in Colossians 1. Both before and after Colossians 1:19–20 Paul indicates that salvation involves a change of moral sphere. Had the Colossians not undergone this change, their sins would not be forgiven (vv. 13, 21). Second

---

[34]Douglas J. Moo, *The Letters to the Colossians and to Philemon*, The Pillar New Testament Commentary (Grand Rapids: Eerdmans, 2008), 137.
[35]See pp. 132–33.

is the teaching of the entire epistle. In 3:6, Paul announces that "the wrath of God is coming" against rebellious human beings. Third is the teaching of Paul's epistles as a whole. In Romans 2 he says that the lost will inherit "wrath and fury" and "tribulation and distress" (vv. 8, 9). In 2 Thessalonians, "those who do not know God. . . . will suffer the punishment of eternal destruction" (1:8–9). Fourth is the teaching of the whole New Testament. Jesus warns in Matthew 25:46 of "eternal punishment," and the end of the biblical story includes human beings outside the city of God, in the lake of fire, suffering the second death of eternal separation from the joy of God (Rev. 21:8; 22:15).

Revelation 3:14. If our treatment of this verse is correct, it is another passage that teaches that Christ inaugurates the new heaven and earth. Here Jesus refers to himself as "the beginning of God's creation." Though the majority of interpreters understand this as teaching that Christ is the Father's agent in creation, I am convinced that Jesus here refers not to the original creation but to the new creation. Earlier I gave three reasons for this, which I summarize here.

First, Isaiah 65:16 is the source of the word "Amen" in Revelation 3:14. In fact, as we saw, these are the only two verses in the entire Bible that could be understood to use "Amen" as a name. The very next verse in Isaiah says,

> For behold, I create new heavens
>   and a new earth,
> and the former things shall not be remembered
>   or come into mind.

Therefore, because the Old Testament antecedent to Revelation 3:14 (Isa. 65:16) is immediately followed by the first Old Testament reference to the new heavens and earth, it supports the conclusion that Revelation 3:14 also speaks of that idea.

Second, the next words of Revelation 3:14, "the faithful and true witness," point readers back to 1:5, which speaks of "Jesus Christ the faithful witness." "Witness" is used five times in the Revelation, and three of those uses refer to martyrs and human witnesses to Jesus (2:13; 11:3; 17:6). The only two places where "witness" refers to Jesus are 1:5 and 3:14. This is John's way of telling readers to interpret 3:14 in light of 1:5. Revelation 3:14 further explains Christ's title in 1:5, which treats not creation but Jesus's preaching, death, and resurrection. Revelation 3:14 also treats redemption, not creation.

Third, the expression in Revelation 1:5, "the firstborn of the dead," takes us back to Colossians 1:18: "He is the beginning, the firstborn from the dead." And the words that immediately precede in Colossians speak not of creation but of the church, a part of God's new creation: "And he is the head of the body, the church."

Therefore, we are to interpret Jesus's description of himself in Revelation 3:14—"the beginning of God's creation"—as an elaboration of the reference to his resurrection in 1:5—"the firstborn of the dead." In a word, "His resurrection is viewed as the beginning of the *new* creation."[36] This means that he alone who died and arose is "the beginning of God's creation." Jesus is the one who is alive after dying and, as the living one, launches the new creation of God. Thus the words in Revelation 1:5 and 3:14 teach that there is a sense in which the "new heaven and new earth," which will only be consummated in Revelation 21–22, are already here.

The crucified and resurrected Christ already has begun the new age. He gives eternal life now to all who believe in him by regenerating them. He will raise them from the dead to eternal life in resurrected bodies when he comes again. And one of the magnificent fruits of his death and resurrection is the revelation of the new heaven and new earth, of which the prophets and apostles spoke (Isa. 65:17; 66:22; 2 Pet. 3:13).

Jesus saves. This chapter and the last have set forth the heart of his saving accomplishment—his death and resurrection. Previously, we saw that the incarnation and sinless life of our Lord were essential preconditions for the cross and empty tomb. The next chapter begins a series of five that explore ramifications of his death and resurrection that are also parts of his saving work.

---

[36] Beale, *The Book of Revelation*, 298, italics original.

Incarnation
Sinless Life
Death
Resurrection
Ascension
Session
Pentecost
Intercession
Second Coming

Chapter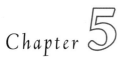

Christ's Ascension

Heaven is the place and sphere from where the universe is sustained and ruled; heaven is the place and sphere from where salvation goes forth into the world of space and time. For God's salvation to be a universal and everlasting salvation, the incarnate Son, Jesus the Messiah, returned to heaven where he could be the source of salvation everywhere to all who believe. From heaven, through the agency of the Holy Spirit . . . the incarnate Son preaches the Word of God, builds up God's church, and continues the divine work that began in the restricted area of Palestine.[1]

Most Christians have never considered the saving significance of Christ's ascension, the theme of Peter Toon's quotation above. We have seen in the previous chapter that Christ's resurrection is essential to his work as the Redeemer of humanity. While the resurrection is often neglected in discussions of Christ's saving work, it still remains an important point of worship and meditation for the church today. This is much less the case with the event we will discuss in this chapter, the ascension of Christ. We confess our belief in the ascension in the Apostles' Creed:

And [we believe] in Jesus Christ our Lord, who was conceived of the Holy Spirit, born of the virgin Mary, suffered under Pontius Pilate, was crucified, died, and was buried. He descended into hell, and on the third day he rose

---

[1] Peter Toon, *The Ascension of Our Lord* (Nashville: Nelson, 1984), xiii.

again and ascended into heaven and sat down at the right hand of God the Father Almighty.

Unfortunately, many Christians today neglect the doctrine of the ascension. Perhaps this neglect is due to the fact that although Christians confess belief in the ascension of Christ, they do not understand the ascension's place in the work of Christ or its effect on their lives. The Bible, however, teaches that the ascension is a saving event. Peter proclaims this in Acts 5:30–31: "The God of our fathers raised Jesus, whom you killed by hanging him on a tree. God exalted him at his right hand as Leader and Savior, to give repentance to Israel and forgiveness of sins."

In this chapter we will survey the relevant texts on the ascension and seek to understand better this event in relationship to Christ's saving work as a whole. We will see three key points regarding the ascension's significance: the ascension is the linchpin of Christ's saving work bridging his earthly and heavenly ministries, an essential part of his sacrificial work as he presents his perfect sacrifice before the Father, and a fuller realization of the reconciliation between God and man as Christ represents humanity in the presence of the Father.

We begin our study of the saving significance of the ascension in the Old Testament.[2]

Background for the Ascension in the Old Testament

As we turn to the Old Testament background for the ascension of Christ, we must keep two scriptural truths in mind. First, Christ himself is the trajectory and fulfillment of the Old Testament. Christ comes as the long-expected offspring of Abraham, the epitome of the law, the Davidic King, and the prophesied Messiah, and because of this, foreshadows of him are present throughout the Old Testament in more ways than direct prophecy. Second, the Old Testament witness to the coming Messiah was, while profound and multifaceted, a shadowy outline of the full glory that would be revealed. Christ's breaking into redemptive history came in fulfillment of the Old Testament promise but with a posture and a mission that defied expectations. Thus, as we turn to investigate the Old Testament texts pointing to the ascension, we seek to understand properly these passages in their original context and the import they bear upon our subject.

---

[2]Works consulted for this chapter include: Gerrit Scott Dawson, *Jesus Ascended: The Meaning of Christ's Continuing Incarnation* (Phillipsburg, NJ: P&R, 2004); Douglas Farrow, *Ascension and Ecclesia* (Grand Rapids: Eerdmans, 1999); and Toon, *The Ascension of Our Lord*.

Psalm 68

Psalm 68 praises God for his past faithfulness in redeeming and preserving his people throughout their history, calling them to remember and live in light of this faithfulness in the present while awaiting his ultimate triumph. There is scholarly debate surrounding the interpretation of particular features of this text, but three themes are clear.

First, this psalm emphasizes the victory of God over his enemies. This is evident from the opening verse:

> God shall arise, his enemies shall be scattered;
>> and those who hate him shall flee before him!

The victory of God is repeated throughout, including in verses 11–14, 17, 20–22, and 30. As the people sang this psalm in worship, they were to call to mind the power of their God by which they were formed and continued to prosper. This leads to the second theme: God's care and provision for his people. This is especially prominent in verses 4–7, which recall God's provision for the Israelites in the wilderness after he brought them out of Egypt. We see this theme again in verse 19, where the psalmist declares,

> Blessed be the Lord,
>> who daily bears us up;
>> God is our salvation.

The final theme is the glory of God. In fact, it is within the context of this glory that the other two themes are couched. Verse 4 declares that the people are to "sing praises to his name" and "exult before him." As the psalm progresses, even the surrounding mountains are said to envy the mount God has chosen as his dwelling place, presumably Mount Zion (vv. 15–16). God's taking up of this dwelling is described as a great procession: he enters his sanctuary accompanied by musicians dancing and praising the Lord (vv. 24–27). In response to this glory, humanity, kings, and even nations are said to offer gifts to the Lord (vv. 18, 29, 31–32). Therefore, despite some of the trickier details, Psalm 68 can be seen to celebrate God's victory over his enemies, God's provision for his people, and his surpassing glory.

Verse 18 is of particular interest for understanding the ascension of Christ, because Paul quotes it in Ephesians 4:8:

> You ascended on high,
>> leading a host of captives in your train

and receiving gifts among men,
even among the rebellious, that the LORD God may dwell there.

This verse likely describes the Lord setting his dwelling place on Mount Zion (see vv. 15–16) as he condescended to be truly present with his people. The theme of victory is evident as he leads a host of captives with him; also apparent is his glory as men present him gifts, and immediately following in verse 19 the Lord's provision is extolled. These factors demonstrate that verse 18 presents the three main themes of the psalm itself. This insight will be essential as we turn to Paul's use of this verse later in the chapter.

Psalm 110:1

The LORD says to my Lord:
"Sit at my right hand,
until I make your enemies your footstool."

Psalm 110 begins in a rather striking way; we are welcomed into a conversation between "the LORD" (Yahweh, the covenant name for God in the Hebrew) and another Lord whom he addresses. Kidner argues that a better rendering of verse 1 from the Hebrew is "the oracle of Yahweh to my lord."[3] Therefore we see that this first verse is a proclamation by God to "my Lord." The identity of this second lord is not given, but the title of the psalm, "A Psalm of David,"[4] seems to point us away from understanding this figure as David or any of his earthly heirs. For David to refer to himself seems unlikely, and even more so with regard to one of his earthly heirs. David was the head of his kingly line, and it would be unthinkable for him to express deference and honor to one of his descendants. Therefore, this second Lord is one who is superior to David and also takes the throne that has been promised to David's offspring (2 Sam. 7); this could only refer to the Messiah.

Although the New Testament indicates that verses from the Psalms are predictive of the coming Messiah, and sometimes David or another psalmist is a type of the coming one, few psalms are entirely messianic. However, Psalm 110 is an exception. If any psalm should be understood as messianic, it is this one. This is demonstrated by the New Testament usage of Psalm 110, which is quoted more often than any other. Jesus himself quotes this

---

[3]Derek Kidner, *Psalms 73–150*, Tyndale Old Testament Commentaries (London: Inter-Varsity, 1975), 427.
[4]The authenticity of which Jesus himself endorses in Mark 12:36. For a discussion of the authenticity of the titles to the Psalms, see Derek Kidner, *Psalms 1–72*, Tyndale Old Testament Commentaries (London: Inter-Varsity, 1975), 47–49.

psalm as he challenges the Pharisees' understanding of the coming Messiah. He poses a riddle to them: How can David, in the power of the Spirit, call the Messiah his Lord while he is also his descendant? The Pharisees cannot answer, and from that time on no one dared to ask him any question (Matt. 22:41–46 and parallels). The Gospel authors never answer this riddle directly, but the reader is expected to wrestle with and understand it in light of the life of Jesus as a whole: he is the Messiah.

Not only does Jesus interpret Psalm 110 as fulfilled in himself; the author of Hebrews also makes extensive use of Psalm 110:4, which says,

> The LORD has sworn
>> and will not change his mind,
> "You are a priest forever
>> after the order of Melchizedek."

In Hebrews 7 we are told that Christ is the priest forever in the order of Melchizedek, and on that basis he can offer the more perfect sacrifice.[5] Therefore this psalm powerfully declares the unique identity of the Messiah as Lord of David and priest in the order of Melchizedek. In the New Testament both of these roles are ascribed to Jesus.

Psalm 110:1 is of particular interest for our study of the ascension because Peter quotes it in the context in his Pentecost sermon.

> For David did not ascend into the heavens, but he himself says,

>> "The Lord said to my Lord,
>> Sit at my right hand,
>>> until I make your enemies your footstool" (Acts 2:34–35)

I will discuss the importance of this verse when we come to Acts, but we can see from Peter's citation that this text is fulfilled only at Jesus's ascension.

There are three implications that we can draw from the connection between Psalm 110 and the ascension. First, the destination of Christ's ascension is the right hand of God, the Father, the place of greatest honor and authority. He ascends not merely into heaven or into the clouds, but to the dwelling place of God. Second, the ascension is connected to kingship. Christ's ascension marks him as the true Davidic King, who is greater than his father David. I will explain this theme further in the chapter on Christ's session. Third, the ascension is

---

[5]We will more fully discuss Melchizedek and the ascension in Hebrews later in this chapter.

connected to Christ's victory over his enemies. Christ by his selfless sacrifice won the definitive triumph over the powers on the cross, but the cross is the beginning of that victory, not the end. As Christ takes his rightful place seated at the right hand of God, he also awaits the culmination of his triumph when all his enemies will be placed under his feet in subjection.

Summary

The Old Testament reveals to the people of God the messianic promise that God will send one into the world to redeem his people from oppression and lead them into victory. Although the glory of this promise is developed throughout the Old Testament, it remains veiled. As the Old Testament closes, the promise is still enigmatic and unfulfilled. The Messiah will come in glory and take his place at the right hand of God, fulfilling the Davidic kingship (Psalm 110; Dan. 7:13–14); he will also be the suffering Servant of Isaiah 53, despised and rejected by men.

The believer before the time of Christ was left with this riddle: How could the Christ come to rule all things and yet be crushed for the iniquities of the people? How could he both approach the Ancient of Days and sit at his right hand while also being considered stricken, smitten by God, and afflicted? From an Old Testament perspective it is extremely difficult to answer these questions, but with God's further revelation through his unique Son, Jesus Christ, we see these two strains of the messianic promise come together. After Christ's death and burial he triumphantly rises from the dead, and with the ascension he transitions from his state of humiliation—his earthly ministry, suffering, and death—to his state of exultation—his heavenly session, sending of the Spirit, and intercession. Therefore, while the ascension is not explicitly predicted in the Old Testament, its necessity can be seen once the fuller revelation of Christ has come.

Background for the Ascension in the Gospels

John 6:61–62

> But Jesus, knowing in himself that his disciples were grumbling about this, said to them, "Do you take offense at this? Then what if you were to see the Son of Man ascending to where he was before?"

This statement by Jesus comes at a very volatile time in his ministry. The day before, he performed the miraculous feeding of the five thousand and then crossed over the Sea of Galilee with his disciples, although he took an unusual route for part of the journey (John 6:1–21). Seeing that he and his disciples have gone, the crowd follows after them, but Jesus knows that their motives are based not on faith but instead on a desire for more bread and miraculous signs (vv. 26–31). Therefore he tells them that they should not seek bread that perishes, but the bread that comes down from heaven, and that this bread is Jesus himself (vv. 32–40).

By this statement Jesus makes a startling claim: that he himself has come down from heaven. His words incite the crowd to murmur, and they question his authority to make such a claim. Jesus replies that he has been sent by the Father for this task (vv. 41–50). Then he pushes it a step further: "Truly, Truly, I say to you, unless you eat the flesh of the Son of Man and drink his blood, you have no life in you" (v. 53). As he goes on to explain, we see that Jesus declares that it is only through an intimate spiritual union with him that one can partake of the benefits of his flesh and blood, namely, the salvation he will accomplish at the cross (vv. 54–59). This is too much for the crowds to take, so they protest, "This is a hard saying; who can listen to it?" (v. 60). In this context Jesus evokes his future ascension on high: "But Jesus, knowing in himself that his disciples were grumbling about this, said to them, 'Do you take offense at this? Then what if you were to see the Son of Man ascending to where he was before?'" He makes clear that the people do not believe because they do not see by the Spirit, who comes only by the will of the Father, but that they rely on mere human understanding (vv. 63–65). This is the final straw for the crowds, who then abandon Jesus, leaving only the Twelve. So what does this account reveal about the ascension?

Although this statement is brief, it tells the purpose of Jesus's ascension. The crowd's lack of understanding of his identity and mission causes them to become hostile to his extraordinary claims. In response, he invokes his coming ascension, and Carson is correct to say that, given the flow of the story, its purpose is to increase the offense.[6] This is an indictment on the crowd's lack of faith and understanding. They prefer the filling of their stomachs to knowing the Son of Man who came down from heaven. But apart from this we observe that Jesus sees his ascension as the confirmation of his incarnation and redemptive mission.

Jesus's question to the crowd is not answered; it merely causes them to abandon his teaching. However, the answer they should have given is, "If we see the Son of Man returning to where he was before, then we will know that he is who

---

[6]D. A. Carson, *The Gospel According to John*, The Pillar New Testament Commentary (Grand Rapids: Eerdmans, 1991), 300–301.

he says he is." The crowd does not see this as a possibility because their eyes
have not been opened by the Father. But as readers of this text we are called to
understand that this Jesus who descended from heaven will also ascend into
heaven, and that this will show that he is the Son of God.

John 7:39; 16:4–7

> Now this he said about the Spirit, whom those who believed in him were to
> receive, for as yet the Spirit had not been given, because Jesus was not yet glori-
> fied. (7:39)

> I did not say these things to you from the beginning, because I was with you.
> But now I am going to him who sent me, and none of you asks me, "Where are
> you going?" But because I have said these things to you, sorrow has filled your
> heart. Nevertheless, I tell you the truth: it is to your advantage that I go away, for
> if I do not go away, the Helper will not come to you. But if I go, I will send him
> to you. (16:4–7)

These two texts reveal one of the key purposes behind the ascension: that
Christ would send the Spirit at Pentecost. The first reference to this in the
Gospel comes as John's comment clarifying Jesus's statement in 7:38, regarding
one who believes in him, that "out of his heart will flow rivers of living water."
The main point is that the living water is the Holy Spirit, the bringer of life,
but John also states that the reason the Spirit has not yet come is "because
Jesus was not yet glorified" (v. 39). Christ's glorification in this verse does not
indicate his ascension specifically but speaks of the events surrounding the
crucifixion as a whole, including the ascension.[7] John did not get this idea
on his own, but was taught it by Jesus himself, whose says more about the
Spirit in John 16.

In John 13–17, which is commonly called the Upper Room Discourse,
we are given an intimate picture of the final night that Jesus spent with his
disciples. They have retired to a room in Jerusalem to celebrate the Passover
meal, and Jesus takes this opportunity to give them final instruction and
encouragement as his arrest and subsequent crucifixion draw near. In this
final hour Jesus reveals that he will soon leave them, and he knows that they
do not fully understand and are disheartened by his words. Jesus has just
finished telling them that the world will hate them just as it has hated him,
and they can expect opposition and even death as they seek to continue his

---

[7]Andreas J. Köstenberger, *John*, Baker Exegetical Commentary of the New Testament (Grand Rapids:
Baker Academic, 2004), 241.

ministry. He wants them to understand the difficulties that lie before them, but he also assures them that they will not be left alone. After he ascends into heaven, he will send the Spirit who will lead them and convict the world of sin. We see from this text that the ascension was necessary that Christ might send the Holy Spirit at Pentecost.

John 20:17

> Jesus said to her, "Do not cling to me, for I have not yet ascended to the Father; but go to my brothers and say to them, 'I am ascending to my Father and your Father, to my God and your God.'"

It is Easter morning and Mary and the other women have come to properly prepare Jesus's body for burial, only to find the tomb empty. Upon discovering this, Mary rushes back to the disciples, fearing that his body has been stolen. Then Peter and John race to the tomb and find it as she has said, but seeing nothing further, they return to their homes.

Mary stays behind weeping. In her anguish she is slow to realize what has happened, even when two angels appear and ask why she is troubled. Then she turns and sees Jesus, but she does not recognize him, thinking that he is only the gardener. Mary pleads with him to tell her where they have taken the body, not yet understanding that the one whom she seeks is before her. Then he calls her name, and she exclaims "Teacher," recognizing him at last. Jesus then says, "Do not cling to me, for I have not yet ascended to the Father; but go to my brothers and say to them, 'I am ascending to my Father and your Father, to my God and your God.'" With these words Christ declares to her that he has not come back to stay permanently, but that his mission will continue. Although he has been raised from the dead, the work of redemption is not done, nor will it continue as it did before the cross and resurrection. Christ points her to the next stage in his saving work and appoints her to tell the disciples this news.

Christ indeed rose victorious from the grave that first Easter morning, but that was not to be the end of his redemptive work, as this text shows. Through the resurrection he was changed, and he would not return to his itinerant ministry; instead he would ascend to his Father. This text shows us that Christ himself viewed his ascension as an essential next step in his work. As aptly described by Douglas Farrow, "Jesus' ascension, in other words, is for John the next decisive step in the liturgy of atonement after the shedding of his blood on the cross, a step he is able to take by virtue of the grace and power of his resurrection."[8] We will continue to unpack how this was so by looking at the event of the ascension itself.

The Event of the Ascension in Luke-Acts

Luke 24:50–53

Then he led them out as far as Bethany, and lifting up his hands he blessed them. While he blessed them, he parted from them and was carried up into heaven. And they worshiped him and returned to Jerusalem with great joy, and were continually in the temple blessing God.

Acts 1:6–11

So when they had come together, they asked him, "Lord, will you at this time restore the kingdom to Israel?" He said to them, "It is not for you to know times or seasons that the Father has fixed by his own authority. But you will receive power when the Holy Spirit has come upon you, and you will be my witnesses in Jerusalem and in all Judea and Samaria, and to the end of the earth." And when he had said these things, as they were looking on, he was lifted up, and a cloud took him out of their sight. And while they were gazing into heaven as he went, behold, two men stood by them in white robes, and said, "Men of Galilee, why do you stand looking into heaven? This Jesus, who was taken up from you into heaven, will come in the same way as you saw him go into heaven."

Luke is the only biblical author who provides us with an account of the ascension proper, and, as if making up for the others' omission, he narrates the event twice, both at the end of his Gospel and at the beginning of Acts. The first thing to note with these two accounts is that they are a narration of the same event with differing levels of detail and different rhetorical purposes. Some critical scholars have attempted to find discrepancies here, but no serious problems exist. The narrative structure is fundamentally the same, the accounts take place at the same location with different levels of specificity, and they can easily be fitted into the same chronology. But given that these two texts record the same event, why the double account?

To answer this question we must consider the purpose of Luke's two-volume work, which we call the Gospel of Luke and the Acts of the Apostles. In Acts 1:1–2, Luke explains, "In the first book, O Theophilus, I have dealt with all that

---

[8]Douglas Farrow, "Ascension and Atonement," in *The Theology of Reconciliation*, ed. Colin E. Gunton (London: T&T Clark, 2003), 71.

Jesus began to do and teach, until the day when he was taken up." In his Gospel, Luke set out to present an orderly account of the earthly ministry of the Lord, and because of this we can understand the ascension as the end of that story. Jesus gives his disciples final words of encouragement and promise (Luke 24:46–49), leads them out of Jerusalem, and blesses them (vv. 50–51); while doing this he ascends (v. 51), and the disciples return to Jerusalem rejoicing.

This ends one stage in the story, and Luke's telling of the event shows us as much by portraying it as the fitting resolution after his death and resurrection. In vindication of his life and death after the resurrection, Christ is raised into heaven, and the correct response is blessing God and worship (v. 53). But there are hints in this account that the story does not end here. When Jesus speaks to the disciples, he commands them to wait in Jerusalem "until you are clothed with power from on high" (v. 49), and tells them that they will be his witnesses to the nations. So at the close of Luke, the disciples, as well as the readers, are left in a position of wondering how these things will come about.

Luke answers this question as he continues the story in his second book. Some have said that if in Luke we have what Jesus began to do and teach (Acts 1:1), then in Acts we have what Jesus continued to do and teach as the early church was formed and spread.[9] Although this statement is too simple, the point is useful. Acts does not shift the focus from the work of God through Jesus to the work of the church, but instead tells of the work of God through Jesus as he grows his kingdom despite challenges both internal and external.[10] Luke starts his second book by narrating the ascension again, but this time not as the end but as the beginning of the story. The placement of the ascension at the beginning of Acts shows that it is foundational to all that follows in the book.

Whereas the account in Luke's Gospel leaves us wondering how the promises to the apostles will be fulfilled, Acts gives us the account from a slightly different, more detailed, perspective, and then spends the rest of the book showing how the message of the Messiah went forth, starting with Pentecost in chapter 2. Therefore the dual ascension accounts in Luke and Acts help us to understand that the ascension is the great linchpin of Christ's saving work. For at the ascension, Christ's earthly ministry, his humiliation, comes to an end, and the heavenly ministry, his exaltation, begins.

Viewing the ascension account in Acts as a beginning helps us to understand the exchange between Jesus and the disciples immediately before he ascends. This interchange clarifies the nature of Christ's messiahship. In Acts 1:6 the

---

[9] E.g., F. F. Bruce, *The Acts of the Apostles* (Grand Rapids: Eerdmans, 1951), 66.

[10] Hans Bayer, "Acts and Paul" (lecture presented at Covenant Theological Seminary, St. Louis, Missouri, November 15, 2010).

disciples come to Jesus with a question: "Lord, will you at this time restore the kingdom of Israel?" This is not in itself a bad question. The disciples have come to understand that Jesus is the Messiah and have finally accepted that this will entail that he be put to shame, crucified, and resurrected as he predicted (Luke 9:21–22; 43–45; 18:31–34). But this question seems to indicate that they still do not fully understand what kind of Messiah Jesus is.

First, it seems likely that the disciples have in mind Jesus's overturning the Roman authority and reestablishing the Davidic monarchy. The expectation of a military messiah who would defeat the national foes of Israel and reestablish her prosperity was common in first-century Judaism. But apart from their militaristic focus, the question also reveals a nationalistic focus. Luke has gone to great lengths in his Gospel to establish that Jesus is for Gentile as well as Jew, especially in the accounts of the miracles where he intentionally records Jesus's healing non-Jewish people. The disciples' question seems to miss the point that Jesus's mission is not merely for Israel but for the entire world. Therefore, even though the disciples have come to believe that Jesus has to suffer the cross and be resurrected, they now expect that Jesus will be the militaristic Messiah who will redeem the Israelite nation.

Jesus's answer comes not so much as a rebuke as a two-part corrective addressing the issues discussed above. First he says, "It is not for you to know times or seasons that the Father has fixed by his own authority" (Acts 1:7). By this Jesus corrects the apostles' messianic expectation. He shows that the restoration of Israel will not come either at the time or in the manner that they are expecting, but will be far greater than they can imagine because it is by the Father's authority and power, not that of men. Then he corrects their nationalistic tendencies, saying, "But you will receive power when the Holy Spirit has come upon you, and you will be my witnesses in Jerusalem and in all Judea and Samaria, and to the end of the earth" (v. 8). Jesus reiterates that he has not come for the sake of the Jewish people alone, but that the Messiah has come for all nations, starting in Jerusalem and spreading outward to the ends of the earth.

Jesus then punctuates his response by ascending into heaven in verse 9. This ascension demonstrates that Jesus's messianic role is not one of earthly conqueror or national defender. His throne is not on the earth, nor is his reign executed through earthly means. He is Lord over all things, and his kingdom will not be constrained by geography or ethnicity. Jesus ascends on high to take up his reign as the Davidic King, as foretold in Psalm 110, and to conduct the advance of his kingdom from there. In this way the ascension is a dramatic statement of Christ's universal kingship.

There is one final thing in this account that is pertinent to understanding the ascension: in the ascension Christ does not abandon his human nature. As the apostles stand there gawking after seeing their Lord and teacher ascend into the heavens, two angels appear. These messengers call to the disciples, "Men of Galilee, why do you stand looking into heaven? This Jesus, who was taken up from you into heaven, will come in the same way as you saw him go into heaven" (Acts 1:11). Again, this demonstrates that the ascension is not the end of Christ's work but another step toward the final realization of salvation at the second coming; but it also shows that Christ ascended body and all. If we skip to the end of the story in Revelation 21, we see that the consummation of the story is not all God's people going to heaven but heaven itself descending and the God-*man* Jesus reigning as King.[11]

Therefore, if Christ's return is a physical return, then, based on this verse, his ascension was just as physical. This means that right now, there is a man, a full flesh-and-body man still marked with the wounds of his crucifixion, sitting at the right hand of the Father as Lord and King over all the earth. Jesus does not shuck off his human nature but ascends as both God and man into the very presence of the Father as a representative of humanity. Can this be explained fully? Not in full, certainly. Christ's dwelling in heaven with a physical body is a glorious mystery that should cause us to worship and marvel.

Reflections on the Ascension in Acts

Acts 2:32–36

> This Jesus God raised up, and of that we all are witnesses. Being therefore exalted at the right hand of God, and having received from the Father the promise of the Holy Spirit, he has poured out this that you yourselves are seeing and hearing. For David did not ascend into the heavens, but he himself says,
>
> > "'The Lord said to my Lord,
> > Sit at my right hand,
> > until I make your enemies your footstool.'
>
> Let all the house of Israel therefore know for certain that God has made him both Lord and Christ, this Jesus whom you crucified."

Our first reflection on Christ's ascension is in Peter's Pentecost speech. On the day of Pentecost the disciples are gathered together, and the Holy Spirit comes upon them from heaven, leading them to speak in the native languages

---

[11] We lack space to defend this here, but see the chapter on the second coming and N. T. Wright, *Surprised by Hope* (New York: Harper One, 2008).

of the diverse people present (Acts 2:1–6). Some are amazed at this occurrence, but others scoff and dismiss the disciples as drunk (vv. 7–13). Peter, functioning as the spokesman for the disciples, responds that these men are not drunk, but rather God has fulfilled the promise he gave to the prophet Joel signaling that the new age has come, when God will reign over all the earth (vv. 14–21).[12] Peter then proceeds to proclaim to them Jesus's life, death, and resurrection, which have come about in fulfillment of the promises that God made to David (vv. 22–31). It is important to note that Peter's speech is presented not simply as a sermon but as a prophetic message.[13]

Having reiterated to those present the work of Jesus, Peter brings it back around to explain the events they have just witnessed. Jesus has been raised up and exalted to the right hand of God and there has received the Spirit from the Father. This same Spirit he has poured out upon the apostles before the crowd's very eyes (vv. 32–33). Peter proclaims to the crowd a profound message: that the awesome signs they have just witnessed are a work of Jesus. But these signs are not merely from Jesus: they are God's confirmation of his status as the Davidic King. Peter quotes Psalm 110:1, showing the people that David was not talking about himself because he did not ascend to the right hand of God. However, his descendant Jesus has been raised up to take this position of power and authority, and we know this because he has just poured out the power of the Spirit, which he received upon ascending. Peter uses the event of Pentecost to prove to the crowd that this Jesus, whom they thought proven false by his shameful crucifixion, lives and now has taken the position of the Davidic King. Therefore they are to "know for certain that God has made him both Lord and Christ" (Acts 2:34–36). Peter concludes his speech with a call for repentance, and about three thousand people respond in faith.

In Peter's Pentecost speech we see two aspects of the ascension that have been present in several of our texts so far: the ascension as a prerequisite for Pentecost and the ascension as confirmation of Jesus's Davidic kingship. In the Gospels it is clear that Jesus lived his life in the power of the Holy Spirit. This is most dramatically seen as the Spirit descends upon him at his baptism. But Peter explains that upon Christ's ascension he receives the Spirit from the Father in a different way than he had on earth. Upon receiving the Spirit Christ pours it out upon his disciples, empowering them for their forthcoming mission. Therefore, as we saw in John's Gospel, Christ had to ascend to receive and send the Spirit.

---

[12]See the chapter on Pentecost for more details.

[13]Luke makes this clear by describing Peter's proclamation using the Greek word ἀποφθέγγομαι (*apophthengomai*), which is used of prophetic speeches in the LXX (1 Chron. 25:1; Ps. 58:8; Ezek. 13:9, 19; Mic. 5:11; Zech. 10:2).

The ascension also confirms Jesus's status as the long-expected heir of David. God had made a covenant with David that his throne would be established forever (2 Sam. 7:12–16). This promise seemed unlikely to be fulfilled in the first century. Israel was under the rule of a foreign power and had been for many generations. Yet God fulfilled this promise through Jesus's ascension as he took his place at the right hand of God. In Psalm 110:1, David as a prophet records a conversation between the Lord and another Lord, whom he would exalt. Peter shows us clearly that this was not David speaking of himself because he never ascended to this place of honor. However, this promise has been fulfilled in Christ, who now sits at the right hand of God, taking his place as the Davidic King forever.

Acts 3:19–21

> Repent therefore, and turn again, that your sins may be blotted out, that times of refreshing may come from the presence of the Lord, and that he may send the Christ appointed for you, Jesus, whom heaven must receive until the time for restoring all the things about which God spoke by the mouth of his holy prophets long ago.

Peter mentions the ascension again in his speech at Solomon's Portico. A crowd has gathered around Peter in amazement after seeing him heal a lame beggar in the name of Jesus (3:1–12). The apostle begins speaking to the crowd, telling them this amazing healing was not done through his own power but through Christ whom God exalted. Peter then indicts the crowd for their rejection of this Christ in whose name the lame man was healed (vv. 13–16). Following this exhortation, Peter calls the people to repentance and belief. In verses 19–21 he states three reasons for them to repent: so that their sins may be blotted out, that times of refreshing from the Lord may come, and that God might send Christ again.

The third reason is of particular interest to us because Peter includes a brief comment about Christ's current absence from earth: ". . . Jesus, whom heaven must receive until the time for restoring all the things" (v. 21). Some of the particulars of this section would take us far afield, but one thing we should observe is that Christ's ascension is a necessary part of his saving activity. Peter does not explain why Christ must remain in heaven until the time of restoration of all things, but this is not his point: he explains to the crowd that Christ's current absence on earth is purposeful, and he will come again to complete his work.

Acts 5:30–31

> The God of our fathers raised Jesus, whom you killed by hanging him on a tree. God exalted him at his right hand as Leader and Savior, to give repentance to Israel and forgiveness of sins.

Our final reflection on the ascension in Acts comes during Peter's second appearance before the Jewish Council. In chapter 4 the council commands Peter and John to stop preaching the message of Jesus to the people because the council holds him to have been a false teacher. But Peter and John refuse to listen and are eventually put in prison. Yet they miraculously escape and return to the temple to preach. When the council discovers the disciples renewed proclamation, they have the two brought before them once again. The council asks the disciples why they refuse to cease preaching in the name of Christ. Peter responds that it is better to obey God than man and proceeds to declare the message of Christ to the Jewish leaders (vv. 27–30). We see by their reaction in verse 33 that they take great offense at Peter's declaration and they desire to kill the apostles.

But why is this message so offensive? It is not because Peter accuses them of crucifying Jesus. They would understand this as a godly duty because they see him as one who has led the people astray and whose death was the proper punishment (Deut. 15:1–5). The means of Christ's death would only emphasize this belief for the Jewish leaders because one who has been hung on a tree is accursed by God (Deut. 21:22–23). Peter in no way shies away from this curse and clearly states that Jesus was hung upon a tree, meaning the cross (Acts 5:30). The topic that sends the leaders into a killing frenzy is Peter's continuing theme. Peter has the gall to claim that this one who was cursed by God has been not only raised from the dead but also exalted by God to his right hand and given the titles of Leader and Savior.

With this statement Peter declares the vindication of Jesus. Although Jesus was rejected by Israel, God has declared him to be the long-awaited Messiah who from heaven will grant repentance and the forgiveness of sins to God's people. Peter's mini-sermon makes the outrageous claim that Jesus, who was crucified as a criminal, is in fact the agent God sent to bring about salvation, and the evidence he puts forth for this is Jesus's exaltation, which includes his ascension. Therefore once again, we see that Christ's ascension is the confirmation of his messianic identity and is closely connected to his mission of bringing repentance and forgiveness.

The Ascension in Paul

As we turn to the Pauline Epistles, we first note the scarcity of explicit references to the ascension of Christ within the corpus. The ascension is not prominent in Paul's writing, as there are only two clear references in all thirteen letters. However, if we understand the general theological concerns in Paul's letters and the theological significance of the ascension, the reason for this will become clearer. So far in our study of the ascension two major themes have surfaced: the ascension as confirmation and vindication of Christ's messiahship and the ascension as prerequisite for his sending the Spirit. Neither of these two themes is a major concern in Paul's writings, so it is unremarkable that the ascension itself would move to the background of Paul's thought.

We saw in Acts that Peter repeatedly sets forth Jesus's ascension as the confirmation of his messiahship. However, nowhere in Paul's letter does an overt defense of Jesus's messiahship appear. Thomas Schreiner has shown that the absence of this messianic theme is not necessarily for lack of interest on Paul's part, but it is the result of the occasional nature of his writing.[14] Paul's letters are written to particular churches to address their particular issues and needs. The letters of Paul are not meant to give us an exhaustive account of his theology. It is most likely that none of the churches Paul is writing to have outright questioned that Jesus was the Messiah, and therefore Paul feels no need to defend this point. Instead Jesus's messiahship is assumed throughout his letters, which can be seen by his pervasive use of the title "Christ," the Greek title for the Messiah that became a part of Jesus's name.[15] Because Paul assumes Jesus's messiahship, it is not surprising that he refrains from evoking Christ's ascension.

So far in our study we have seen that both John and Luke speak of the ascension as the prerequisite for the sending of the Spirit at Pentecost. Both of these authors recount history, attempting to show their respective audiences the events that led to the formation of the people of God. John tells of the life and ministry of Jesus, including several references to Jesus's later work at Pentecost. Luke does much the same as he recounts the growth of the early church, narrates the sending of the Spirit, and presents Peter's subsequent explanation of the event. Therefore the necessity of the ascension for the sending of the Spirit fits well within their overall concerns to expound the history of God's deeds through Christ as the foundation of the Christian faith. Paul, on the other hand, has different aims in mind. While John and Luke explain the historical foundation of the faith, Paul expounds and applies the implications of Christ's work to his current situation. Because of this Paul focuses not on the sending of the Spirit but instead on the presence of the Spirit among God's people. Paul focuses more

---

[14]Thomas Schreiner, *Paul: Apostle of God's Glory* (Downers Grove, IL: IVP Academic, 2001), 75–77.
[15]Ibid., 77.

on the current work of the Spirit than on his coming.[16] Given this focus, it is understandable that Paul would not make explicit reference to the ascension in relation to the sending of the Holy Spirit.

Despite the rarity of explicit references, the ascension is implied several times in Paul's writings. Throughout Paul's letters Christ is assumed to be the exalted one who reigns on high. In Philippians 2:9–11 Paul bursts out into doxology as he declares the wonder that Christ has been exalted above all things. In Ephesians 1:20, Paul exhorts his audience to hope in the fact that Christ has been raised from the dead and is seated at the right hand of God until the time when all thing will be put under his feet. We see this again in 1 Corinthians 15 as Paul teaches the Corinthians that Jesus's work will not be completed until he has defeated all his enemies by putting them under his feet, including the final enemy, death itself.

In all of these passages Christ is envisioned as the reigning King over creation, having been given the place of honor by his Father. These sections imply Christ's ascension. We can rightly assume that Paul has a full understanding of the events that led to Christ's exaltation. The ascended Christ himself appeared to Paul on the Damascus Road, revealing to Paul his majesty (Acts 9:1–19). Paul also spent time with the apostles who witnessed Christ's ascension and received from them an account of Jesus's work (9:26–31; 15:1–15). He makes this clear in his first letter to the Corinthians as he writes about Christ's resurrection and makes mention of Jesus's postresurrection appearances (1 Cor. 15:3–8). Paul, then, would understand how Christ came to his position at the right hand of the Father, but does not find it necessary to say so explicitly in many texts. Therefore, as we saw with the sending of the Spirit, Paul is concerned more with the result of the ascension, namely, that Christ now reigns at the right hand of God, than the event itself. Now let us turn to the two texts where Paul does mention the ascension itself.

Ephesians 4:7–8

But grace was given to each one of us according to the measure of Christ's gift. Therefore it says,

"When he ascended on high he led a host of captives,
    and he gave gifts to men." [Ps. 68:18]

---

[16]Gordon Fee agrees: "The Spirit's major role in Paul's view lies with his being *the absolutely essential constituent of the whole Christian life*, from beginning to end." Gordon Fee, *God's Empowering Presence: The Holy Spirit in the Letters of Paul* (Peabody, MA: Hendrickson, 1994), 898, italics original.

Chapter 4 of Ephesians begins with the exhortation that Christians walk in a manner worthy of the calling to which they have been called (Eph. 4:1–2), and that this calling is based on the unity of believers that has been achieved through the work of Christ (4:3–6). But this task has not been given to those who are ill-equipped, since God has given his people grace through Christ: "But grace was given to each one of us according to the measure of Christ's gift. Therefore it says, 'When he ascended on high he led a host of captives, and he gave gifts to men'" (vv. 7–8). Paul's quotation of this verse from Psalm 68 is highly debated, and space does not permit a full discussion of the issues. In that psalm we saw that three themes came together around verse 18: victory as God leads a host of captives, the glory of God as men present him gifts, and the Lord's provision for his people immediately following in verse 19. These themes help us understand Paul's use here.

There are two features of this quotation that must be explained because Paul, inspired by the Holy Spirit, slightly adapts the Old Testament reading to clarify his point. First, he changes the pronouns from the second to the third person. By doing so, Paul makes a strong declaration that Christ is indeed God and that he has now ascended into heaven to take his throne. That means that God's taking his dwelling place on Mount Zion was a foretaste of what Christ would do. Second, Paul changes the action of the verb from "receiving" to "giving." Again, there is much contention over this, but given what we have discussed about the context of the original psalm, Paul develops this citation to include the idea of divine provision, which was present in the original context (Ps. 68:4–7, 19). Therefore Paul is encouraging believers to know that Christ has bestowed gifts to them, including both grace (Eph. 4:7) and church leaders (vv. 11–12), so that they might serve him in unity. And the proof of this fact is that Christ has ascended on high victoriously, echoing the original themes of the psalm and applying them to Christ. Bryan Chapell explains it well:

> Jesus is the risen and ascended Lord, the victor over sin and death. Paul borrows from the imagery of Psalm 68, which metaphorically describes God ascending Mount Zion with his enemies as captives, to portray Jesus as the conquering king. The apostle portrays captives in Christ's victory parade to indicate that Jesus has defeated our spiritual adversaries, making what captivated us in the bonds of sin his own captives. Sin, death, and Satan are now overcome by the power of our King. In this victory march our King also dispenses the gifts of his victory to his people.[17]

---

[17]Bryan Chapell, *Ephesians*, Reformed Expository Commentary (Phillipsburg, NJ: P&R, 2009), 188.

There are other issues that could be considered concerning this verse, its context, and Paul's use of the Old Testament, but they would take us far afield.[18] But given what we have discovered, we can draw two conclusions about Christ's ascension. First, as we saw with Peter's use of Psalm 110:1, Christ's ascension is part of his victory over the powers of this world. Through the cross and resurrection, Jesus triumphed over sin, death, and Satan, and at the ascension he transitioned to his place as victorious King over all creation until his victory is fully worked out and all his enemies are put under his feet. Second, Christ's ascension leads to his showering blessings on his people. In these verses, these blessings include grace and the giving of church leaders, but the blessings are even greater than these. Both of these gifts are intimately connected to the work of the Holy Spirit. It is only by the work of the Spirit that one partakes of the grace offered by Christ and that the leaders function rightly in their given tasks. So while the sending of the Spirit is not primarily in view here, it is the means by which the mentioned blessings are realized among the people of God.

1 Timothy 3:16

Great indeed, we confess, is the mystery of godliness:

> He was manifested in the flesh,
>   vindicated by the Spirit,
>   seen by angels,
>   proclaimed among the nations,
>   believed on in the world,
>   taken up in glory.

The first letter to Timothy is primarily concerned with the upholding of the true teaching, which Paul handed down, in the face of false teaching, which would lead the church astray. Paul is writing to his young disciple and friend, Timothy, whom he left behind in Ephesus to ensure that the church would remain faithful to Paul's teachings (1 Tim. 1:3–4). The issue of maintaining the apostolic teaching pervades the letter as Paul charges Timothy to "guard the deposit entrusted to you" (6:20). It is in this overall context that we must understand 3:16.

In the beginning of chapter 3, Paul sets out for Timothy the requirements for overseers (elders) and deacons, instructing him to be ever vigilant in abid-

---

[18]For further study on this passage, see Frank Thielman, "Ephesians," in *Commentary on the New Testament Use of the Old Testament*, ed. Gregory Beale and D. A. Carson (Grand Rapids: Baker Academic, 2007), 819–25; Harold W. Hoehner, *Ephesians: An Exegetical Commentary* (Grand Rapids: Baker, 2002), 523–30.

ing by the standards of orthodoxy and holiness that these offices require as he seeks to appoint men to these tasks. In verse 15 Paul makes clear that he is writing to Timothy so that he might "know how one ought to behave in the household of God." This exhortation is not merely a call for moral uprightness as an end itself, but also a missional call for the church to function as she ought. The church is the "pillar and buttress of truth," where the revelation of God is upheld and put on display for the world to see. Here Paul declares the inseparability of truth and holiness. There can be no claiming the truth while neglecting holiness, or vice versa.

This same assertion is made in verse 16, where Paul proclaims the "mystery of godliness" by poetically recounting the work of Christ. This mystery is the way of godliness, which was hidden but is now revealed through the Christ, by whom the church was created and continues to function rightly.[19] Paul expounds this mystery in poetic form, which could be taken from an early Christian hymn. The structure and flow of this hymn is highly debated, with no clear scholarly consensus.[20] However, resolving these issues is not essential for our purposes of investigating the ascension.

What is clear is that this hymn moves from the humiliation of Christ to his exaltation. Line 1 speaks of Christ as "manifest in the flesh," referring to his incarnation, and the hymn concludes in line 6 with him "taken up into glory," alluding to his ascension. Paul expresses what he has made clear elsewhere: that Christ came and humbled himself by taking on humanity and has been glorified by the Father. The language of line 6 echoes that of the ascension account in Acts 1, allowing his audience to understand this as the transition between Christ's states of humiliation and exaltation. Paul certainly understands Christ's ascension as an important part of his work, because the apostle includes it in the content of the mystery of godliness, which is laid as the foundation for the church's mission to the world.

The Ascension in Hebrews

So far in our study the ascension of Christ has been primarily connected to his kingly and prophetic roles as he ascends to take his seat at the right hand of the Father and to pour out the Spirit upon his people. The letter to the Hebrews further develops the meaning of the ascension by describing its importance with regard to Christ's role as High Priest who offers himself as the final sacrifice

---

[19]Philip H. Towner, *The Letters to Timothy and Titus*, The New International Commentary on the New Testament (Grand Rapids: Eerdmans, 2006), 276–77.
[20]For details of this debate, see ibid., 276–85.

for sin. Although the author and exact audience of Hebrews are unknown, the general thrust of the book is clear—to establish the supremacy of Christ over the mechanisms of the Sinai covenant to secure salvation and to exhort the audience to maintain their confession of Jesus Christ.[21]

One of the author's chief tactics for accomplishing this is to declare Christ as the great High Priest after the order of Melchizedek and the perfect sacrifice. The author does this by placing these themes in juxtaposition with the imperfections of the old covenant priesthood and sacrifices. The ascension plays a central role in this comparison. Jesus is the High Priest who "has passed through the heavens" (Heb. 4:14), who has entered the "holy place behind the curtain" (6:19), who has been "exalted above the heavens" (7:26), and who has entered into the holy place not made by hands (9:24). Christ's ascension from the earthly realm to the heavenly is essential for his priesthood for "if he were on earth, he would not be a priest at all, since there are priests who offer gifts according to the law" (8:4). Space does not allow us to exhaust the implications of the ascension in Hebrews. For the sake of brevity and clarity, therefore, I will focus on three aspects: the ascension as the necessary qualification for Christ to become the High Priest after the order of Melchizedek, the ascension as Christ's movement into the heavenly sanctuary, and Christ as our forerunner into the presence of the Father.

The first text that we will investigate is Hebrews 8:1–5a. Chapter 8 of Hebrews begins with a brief summary of the previous argument in chapter 7 that establishes Christ as a priest after the order of Melchizedek, which is superior to the Levitical priesthood of the old covenant. Therefore, before we can understand this text, we must discuss Melchizedek.

A shadowy figure who turns up only twice in the Old Testament, Melchizedek first appears in Genesis 14 after Abraham rescues his nephew Lot from captivity. The king of Elam has taken Lot captive in his war against the kings of Sodom and Gomorrah. Upon hearing of his nephew's predicament, Abraham takes all of his able-bodied men and comes to Lot's aid. Uniting with those opposed to the king of Elam, Abraham defeats him and his allies. After this victory Abraham sets out for home, and on the way meets Melchizedek, the king of Salem and priest of God Most High (Gen. 14:18), in the King's Valley (his status of both king and priest is essential in Hebrews).

Melchizedek blesses Abraham, and he, in turn, gives Melchizedek a tenth of all the spoils he has gained from his victory. This is a somewhat peculiar account because it establishes Melchizedek as superior to Abraham. Hebrews 7:7 makes

---

[21]William L. Lane, *Hebrews 1–8*, Word Biblical Commentary (Dallas: Word, 1991), c–ci.

this point explicitly; the superior always blesses the inferior. This expression of superiority is rather shocking. At this point in the story it has been firmly established that Abraham is chosen by God to be the vehicle through which blessing will flow to the nations. Abraham has experienced direct interaction with the Creator of the universe, and yet he acknowledges the superiority of Melchizedek. Then, just as quickly and unexpectedly as he appeared, Melchizedek vanishes from the biblical story without fanfare or comment, only to reappear in Psalm 110 in an unexpected way.

We have already seen that Psalm 110 has special significance with regard to the ascension. The first verse of this psalm is used repeatedly in Acts to connect the ascension with Christ's sitting down at the right hand of God, thereby taking his place as the Davidic King and Messiah.

> The LORD says to my Lord:
> "Sit at my right hand,
> until I make your enemies your footstool." (v. 1)

The psalm goes on to illuminate that this Lord of David will be more than a king; he will be a priest as well.

> The LORD has sworn
> and will not change his mind,
> "You are a priest forever
> after the order of Melchizedek." (v. 4)

This pronouncement would have been rather obscure to its first audience because to this point they were only aware of the Levitical priesthood, which was wholly separate from the kingly line of Judah. Given their position in redemptive history what would the Israelites have understood from this psalm regarding the one after the order of Melchizedek?

Although a full understanding would dawn only with the coming of this great High Priest, three points can be gleaned from the psalm itself. First, this priest will also be a king. We see throughout the psalm that Yahweh is addressing the same person. Therefore the one who sits at the right hand of God is also the same one who will be the Melchizedekian priest (vv. 1, 4). This dual role is also highlighted by the title given to this priesthood. As we saw in the account of Melchizedek in Genesis 14, he is both king and priest; the Holy Spirit through David is invoking the name of this enigmatic figure in order to call to mind his unique standing as both priest and king and to ascribe it to the one spoken of in the psalm.

Second, the psalm is describing a priestly order that is both distinct from and greater than the Levitical priesthood of their day. By naming the order after Melchizedek the psalmist is drawing a distinction from the Levitical line, which was established after the exodus to serve the Lord under the Sinai covenant in the tabernacle and later the temple. However, the priest of Psalm 110 is outside this system and superior to it, as demonstrated by its more ancient pedigree. Melchizedek, in a sense, ministered God's covenant blessings to the patriarch Abraham. This older covenant with Abraham was the foundation for the Sinai covenant, which the Levites administered. Hence in terms of antiquity and place in redemptive history, the priest after the order of Melchizedek surpasses the Levitical priests. In addition to the greater foundation, the Melchizedekian priesthood has a greater duration. The Levitical priests served for a time and then passed away, but the priest of Psalm 110 would retain his status forever.

Third, the order of Melchizedek is founded on a divine oath.

> The LORD has sworn
> and will not change his mind. (v. 4)

The Levitical priesthood was founded on the family line of the tribe of Levi with special prominence given to the family of Aaron. In contrast, because the Melchizedekian priesthood will be established by the very oath of God, no greater foundation could be had. In summary, from Psalm 110 we see that the order of Melchizedek will have a kingly and priestly role, be superior to the Levitical priesthood, and be founded on God's oath.

Hebrews 8:1–5a

> Now the point in what we are saying is this: we have such a high priest, one who is seated at the right hand of the throne of the Majesty in heaven, a minister in the holy places, in the true tent that the Lord set up, not man. For every high priest is appointed to offer gifts and sacrifices; thus it is necessary for this priest also to have something to offer. Now if he were on earth, he would not be a priest at all, since there are priests who offer gifts according to the law. They serve a copy and shadow of the heavenly things.

Although there is a great deal that can be said about the order of Melchizedek from Psalm 110, the means by which it is established and its exact function are left unclear. Only when the author to the Hebrews picks up this theme does its astounding significance become known. One of the key insights of Hebrews is that the ascension was necessary for Christ to assume this priesthood. Hebrews 8:4 demonstrates this clearly, stating that had Christ remained on earth, he could not be a priest at all. The reason given is that priests on earth offer sacrifices according to the law. The law spoken of here is the law laid down in the Sinai covenant, which regulated the offering of sacrifices in the tabernacle and subsequently the temple. However, according to this law, Jesus could not function as a priest because he was not a Levite. Hebrews makes this point in 7:14–16. Jesus was of the tribe of Judah, of the Davidic line specifically; this was required for him to fulfill the promises of a Davidic King who would rule forever (2 Sam. 7:16; Ps. 110:1).

Christ's priesthood, therefore, cannot be of the same type as those who offered sacrifices in the temple because Jesus must perfectly keep the law of Sinai. This is where the order of Melchizedek comes in. God in his providence established a greater priesthood so that Christ could offer a greater sacrifice that brought all other sacrifices to an end, while respecting the Mosaic law. The ascension allowed him to do this. By his ascension Christ passed from the earthly realm, where the law bound the priesthood to the tribe of Levi alone, to the heavenly realm to which the earthly shadows pointed. There, free from the restraints of the Sinai covenant, Christ was able to take up his position as both priest and king forever and lawfully exercise his priestly ministry by presenting his perfect sacrifice before the Father. Therefore, by his ascension Christ entered into the role of the priest in the order of Melchizedek, prophesied in Psalm 110:4, allowing him to secure a greater salvation than was possible through the law of Moses.

Hebrews 9:11–12, 23–24

> But when Christ appeared as a high priest of the good things that have come, then through the greater and more perfect tent (not made with hands, that is, not of this creation) he entered once for all into the holy places, not by means of the blood of goats and calves but by means of his own blood, thus securing an eternal redemption. . . .
>
> Thus it was necessary for the copies of the heavenly things to be purified with these rites, but the heavenly things themselves with better sacrifices than these. For Christ has entered, not into holy places made with hands, which are copies of the true things, but into heaven itself, now to appear in the presence of God on our behalf.

We have established that the ascension was necessary for Christ to take his place as the High Priest after the order of Melchizedek as he passed from the earthly realm; yet the author to the Hebrews goes further. The significance of Christ's ascension is not limited to his movement from the earthly realm, but just as important is his entering into the heavenly realm. Hebrews describes Jesus's new position in several ways: "the inner place behind the curtain" (Heb. 6:19), "in the true tent that the Lord set up, not man" (8:2), "the greater and more perfect tent (not made by hands . . .)" (9:11), and "not into the holy places made with hands . . . but into heaven itself" (9:24).

Through these words, as well as the thorough description of the tabernacle in 9:1–10, the author is invoking the images of the Old Testament Day of Atonement ritual in Leviticus 16. On this appointed day the high priest offered a sacrifice for the sins of the people as a whole (Lev. 16:34). After first offering a sacrifice for his own sin the high priest would enter into the Most Holy Place. This special section of the tabernacle, which was separated from the Holy Place by a veil (Ex. 26:31–33), was to be entered only by the high priest and only on this day and with great precaution, for it was here that the presence of God was manifest. The high priest entered only through a cloud of incense, to avoid looking upon the mercy seat, and thereby preserved his life, for no human can look upon the Lord's presence and live (Lev. 16:12–13; Ex. 33:20). Upon entering, the high priest sprinkled the blood of the sacrifice upon the mercy seat before the presence of the Lord (Lev. 16:15–16). After this he sprinkled blood all around the tabernacle to cleanse and purify it for the pollution of the people's sin (v. 17–19).[22]

The author to the Hebrews draws much from the Day of Atonement in chapters 5–10. Being perfect and sinless, Christ is unlike the Levitical high priests, who had to offer sacrifice for their own sins as well as the people's (Heb. 5:2–3; 7:27). But like the high priest he too offered a sacrifice. His sacrifice, however, was once for all time and would never have to be repeated (7:27; 10:1–14). Christ's crucifixion was the great and perfect sacrifice through which he accomplished the cleansing of all his people. It was through his own blood that he could then enter into the heavenly Most Holy Place where God is in his full glory (9:11–12, 23–24). Once there, Christ, as High Priest, presented the sacrifice that he had accomplished on the cross.[23] I. Howard Marshall makes this point lucidly:

---

[22]For an accessible and fuller treatment of the Day of Atonement, see Gordon Wenham, *Leviticus*, The New International Commentary on the Old Testament (Grand Rapids: Eerdmans, 1979), 227–38.

[23]Some Protestant theologians are uncomfortable speaking in this way because it might allow something like a Roman Catholic doctrine of eucharistic sacrifice. This is not necessarily so if we remember that Christ functions as both the High Priest offering the sacrifice and the sacrifice itself. Christ's sacrifice, his actual death for atonement, was fully accomplished on the cross never to be repeated, but as the High Priest Christ must complete the ritual by presenting his sacrifice before the Father. Given this distinction, it seems possible, following the example of Hebrews, to speak of Christ's presenting his sacrifice before

The work of atonement was not completed until something had been done in heaven that ratified what has been done on the cross; at that point the sacrifice is completed and Christ has no need to "enter heaven to offer himself again and again" as the Jewish high priest did on his annual visit (9:25–28). The act of sacrifice and the offering of sacrifice are thus theoretically distinguishable, but they form a unity, and neither is effective without the other.[24]

What is the means by which Christ enters into the "tent not made by hands"? The answer is his ascension. The ascension is an essential part of Christ's saving accomplishment whereby he brings into God's presence the sacrifice that he made on the cross. We must distinguish between Christ's priestly ministry and his sacrificial work, a crucial part of his priestly ministry. Even as the high priest on the Day of Atonement offered the sacrifice on the altar and then brought the blood of the sacrifice into the Most Holy Place, so it is with Christ. Jesus's sacrifice on the cross was finished; nothing could be added to it. But his priestly ministry is bigger than his sacrifice and involves the presentation of his perfect sacrifice in heaven. The ascension is thus the means whereby Christ's ministry of High Priest is brought to its goal. In that sense, Jesus saves by ascending from earth to heaven.

Hebrews 6:19–20

We have this as a sure and steadfast anchor of the soul, a hope that enters into the inner place behind the curtain, where Jesus has gone as a forerunner on our behalf, having become a high priest forever after the order of Melchizedek.

Hebrews reveals to us yet another implication of Christ's ascension. Christ, having passed beyond the curtain into the holy presence of God the Father as the great High Priest after the order of Melchizedek, has become "a forerunner on our behalf." Christ as our "forerunner" has preceded us into the presence of God. He has made a way through his death, resurrection, and ascension so that we might follow him into this glorious place.[25] Christ came into this world and took to himself the full nature of a human being, becoming fully like us in our weakness (Heb. 2:14–15). In this same manner, as fully God and man, Christ passed beyond the curtain by his ascension (as we saw in Acts 1:11,

---

the Father in the heavenly sanctuary without falling into error regarding its finality. For more discussion of this point, see chapter 8, on Christ's intercession.

[24]I. Howard Marshall, "Soteriology in Hebrews," in *The Epistle to the Hebrews and Christian Theology*, ed. Richard Bauckham et al. (Grand Rapids: Eerdmans, 2009), 271.

[25]Lane, *Hebrews 1–8*, 155.

Christ ascended body and all). By so doing he has blazed a trail that all of those joined to him will follow.

The author to the Hebrews makes this point in order to establish our present hope on a sure foundation. In 6:19 we are said to have a hope that itself enters into the very heavenly presence of God. We should not be too quick to assume that this hope is identical to Jesus. Here hope is the subject of the verb and has passed through the veil where Christ already is.[26] This hope is the assurance and "steadfast anchor" that believers now have secure in the knowledge that Christ, who was in their very likeness and fulfilled the role of a better High Priest, is in the presence of God on their behalf. The believers' hope is set on the firmest foundation, for Christ has ascended and given the privilege of access to God behind the veil that formerly separated humanity from God. We are to live in the hope now that one day we too will come to where Christ has gone before us. He is our forerunner, and his ascension made a way for us also to dwell in God's heavenly presence. As surely as he has died, risen, and ascended, so we will join him in his "Father's house" (John 14:1–3).

The Ascension in 1 Peter 3:22

> . . . [Jesus Christ] who has gone into heaven and is at the right hand of God, with angels, authorities, and powers having been subjected to him.

Unlike the discussion of the ascension in Hebrews, Peter's evocation of the ascension in this verse is not highly interwoven into his argument. Here Christ's ascension, in conjunction with his session and supremacy over all powers and angels, simply serves the function of declaring his kingly authority and honor. Therefore this verse demonstrates continuity with Peter's exposition of the ascension in Acts. Once again the ascension is connected with Christ's session as he takes his rightful place at the right hand of God the Father and his preeminence over created things. First Peter 3:22 presents us with further canonical support for these beautiful truths.

Connecting the Dots

The Ascension as a Work of Christ

As we have seen, the Bible has much to teach us on the importance and glory of Christ's ascension, but before we seek to summarize the saving impact

---

[26]Peter T. O'Brien, *The Letter to the Hebrews*, The Pillar New Testament Commentary (Grand Rapids: Eerdmans, 2010), 241–42.

of this work, we must ask a key question: Is it proper to call the ascension a "work of Christ"? This question necessarily arises because in the account of the ascension the primary actor of the event appears to be God the Father. In his accounts of the ascension Luke records for us that Christ was "carried away" and "lifted up." Both of these verbs are functioning as what is known as the divine passive, meaning that while the one doing the action is not expressly given, the context and type of action imply that it is God. The idea that God is the primary actor in the ascension is also echoed in Acts 5:30–31 and 1 Timothy 3:16.

However, as is often the case when talking about the triune God, things are not that simple. In the Gospel of John, Jesus himself speaks of the ascension as the next step in his ministry: "I have not yet ascended to my Father" (John 20:17). In addition, Paul and the author to the Hebrews depict the ascension as an action of Christ: "he ascended on high" (Eph 4:8), and "a great high priest . . . has passed through the heavens" (Heb. 4:14). In all of these instances Christ himself is the one who is active in the event. Given these two emphases, the best course is to understand the ascension as a cooperative work of the Trinity. The Father lifts Christ up and exalts him above the heavens. Christ himself ascends in accordance with his Father's will and passes through the heavens. And although the Bible does not say so explicitly, it is warranted, by the fact that Christ is the man of the Spirit par excellence, to assume that the Spirit empowers Jesus in the ascension. Allowing this Trinitarian perspective, the ascension can meaningfully be understood as a work of Christ, although we should not forget the actions of the Father and Holy Spirit.

The Ascension as the Linchpin of Christ's Other Saving Works

As we look at Christ's saving work as a whole, the foundational import of the ascension is its function in relation to the other saving events. The ascension confirms the authenticity of Christ's previous works and is a prerequisite for the subsequent works. As we have seen, Jesus alludes to his ascension in John 6, making the implicit claim that if the people were to see the Son of Man ascending to where he was before, then they should believe that he was from God (John 6:61–62). Peter makes a similar point in his speech on Pentecost. After explaining to the crowds that Jesus has ascended, taking his rightful place as the Davidic King of Psalm 110, he declares, "therefore know for certain that God has made him both Lord and Christ, this Jesus whom you crucified" (Acts 2:36). Christ's ascension, then, confirms that he was who he claimed to be. He truly was the Son of God who came into the world to save sinners and restore creation, and proof of this is that after he rose from the dead, he ascended into heaven into the very presence of God to reign.

The ascension is also the prerequisite for the subsequent saving works of Christ: the session, Pentecost, intercession, and the second coming. It is clear from Psalm 110:1 and Acts 2:33–36 that Christ had to ascend in order to sit down at the right hand of the Father, thereby beginning his heavenly session. By his ascension, therefore, Christ was able to take his place as the King over all creation until the time when all things would be wholly subjected to him. The ascension was also necessary for Christ to send the Spirit at Pentecost. Christ makes this claim explicitly in John 16:7: "I tell you the truth: it is to your advantage that I go away, for if I do not go away, the Helper will not come to you. But if I go, I will send him to you." Upon Christ's ascension he received the Spirit from the Father, and then as the great prophet, priest, and king poured out the Spirit upon his church as a blessing (John 7:39; Acts 2:33).

Christ's intercession also required him to ascend. As we will see in chapter 8, Christ's intercession is his current priestly ministry for his people. This heavenly ministry is possible only if Christ takes his position as a priest forever in the order of Melchizedek. That position is not on earth but in heaven, and that position is achieved only by his ascension (Heb. 8:4). Finally, it is clear that Christ could come again only if he went away in the first place. Peter declared this truth before the Sanhedrin in reference to "Jesus, whom heaven must receive until the time for restoring all the things" (Acts 3:21). Although we cannot fully grasp the mystery of God's plan, it does require that Jesus ascend into heaven and once there rule and empower his church so that the kingdom of God might spread. Christ's ascension saves in that every benefit that the church receives from Jesus in heaven would be impossible unless he first ascended to take his position there.

The Ascension and Christ's Perfect Sacrifice

The ascension is essential for the completion of Christ's priestly work. It qualifies him for a greater priesthood and enables him to present in heaven the sacrifice that he accomplished on earth. As we saw from Hebrews 8:1–5, Christ's ascension allowed him to take up the priesthood in the order of Melchizedek so that he could offer a greater sacrifice than those offered under the Sinai covenant. By his ascension beyond the earthly realm he was able to take his sacrifice into the heavenly sanctuary of which the earthly temple was but a mere shadow (Heb. 8:15; 9:11–12, 23–24). Sacrifice in the Old Testament was not completed solely by slaughtering the sacrificial offering but also included the presentation of this offering before God (see Lev. 1–7, 16). We should expect, therefore, that this would also be true of the perfect sacrifice that Christ offered upon the cross. Christ accomplished this through his ascension when he passed behind the heavenly curtain into the presence of God the Father and presented in the heavenly sanctuary what he had accomplished on the cross (Heb. 6:19). After doing so, Christ sat down, signaling that his priestly work of earthly sacrifice and heavenly presentation was complete and perfect (10:12). Consequently because Christ has presented his one perfect sacrifice before God, we have assurance that the sacrificial blood of the Lamb of God has washed away our impurity and that our sins will never again separate us from God.

The Ascension and Divine Reconciliation

Finally, the ascension takes to a new level the reconciliation of humanity and God. After the fall in Genesis 3, Adam and Eve were cast out of the intimate presence of God because of their rebellion. Although we believe that God accepted them in the first promise of redemption (Gen. 3:15), the sweetest fellowship they enjoyed with him in Eden was a thing of the past. While God continued to condescend to interact with his people, Israel, in the Old Testament, the closest relationship was not possible because of the sin that separated a holy God from an unrighteous people. Through his incarnation, life, death, and resurrection Christ destroyed the power of sin and cleansed his people from the iniquity that prevented intimate relationship with God. And, wonderfully this extended even to Old Testament Israel (Heb. 9:15). Nevertheless, the fellowship enjoyed in Eden was never fully recovered.

Then Christ ascended into heaven, taking with him the complete human nature that he had during his incarnation (Acts 1:11). Once there, Christ became the forerunner of humanity (Heb. 6:19–20). Through Christ's ascension (and subsequent saving events) he did everything necessary to reestablish intimate relationship between humanity and divinity. He abolished everything that separated from God those who are now joined to Christ. This is a source of great hope and assurance for humankind because one of our own kind has ascended to the right hand of God thereby making a way for us to be in full relationship to God. This sort of intimacy has not been possible since the time of Eden, and only Christ as the perfect human being could accomplish it. God's people will enjoy this fellowship in its fullness only as resurrected saints on the new earth. But even now "our fellowship is with the Father and with his Son Jesus Christ" (1 John 1:3). This is possible only because Christ died, arose, and ascended to God's right hand (1 John 2:1–2).

Luke gives us the reaction of the apostles upon Christ's ascension: "And they worshiped him and returned to Jerusalem with great joy" (Luke 24:52). Joy and worship should still be our reaction to the ascension today. Karl Barth has put it beautifully:

> The day of the Lord's Ascension makes the devil lament, but the faithful to brighten with joy. For now the pleasant spring comes forth and the beautiful young buds grow up: the vine shoots appear heavy with fruit: the olive trees come into flower: the fig trees bear early fruits: the closely sown fields are stirred by the west wind, imitating the billows of the sea: all things rejoice with us at the Lord's Ascension. Come now and I will sing you the words of David, which he himself proclaimed for us on account of the Lord's Ascension: "O clap your hands, all ye people, shout unto God with the voice of triumph; the Lord has gone up with the sound of a trumpet" to where He was. He has been received up whence He had not been separated. For He who descended is He who ascended above the heavens.[27]

Our Lord has ascended and, as Barth poetically puts it, even the creation rejoices in response. Christ, who came in the full likeness of humanity, lived a faithful and sinless life, was obedient to the point of death on the cross, and rose victorious over the grave, has ascended into heaven to take his rightful place at the right hand of the Father and to reign over his creation. He has moved from his earthly to his heavenly ministry, which he currently executes for the benefit of his people.

Having discussed the glories that the ascension affords, we turn, next, to investigate his heavenly session.

---

[27]Cited in Dawson, *Jesus Ascended*, 70.

Incarnation
Sinless Life
Death
Resurrection
Ascension
Session
Pentecost
Intercession
Second Coming

Chapter

Christ's Session

He made purification for sins. This he did within the course of human history, when, as Aquinas says, "he offered himself on the altar of the cross as a sacrifice to God in satisfaction of the punishment to which man, because of his guilt, was subject." This done, *he sat down at the right hand of the Majesty on high.* The description of the Son, as being now seated signifies the completion of the work of purification. . . . But more than that his position "at the right hand" of God . . . indicates that his is the place of highest honor, that he is not merely on a seat but on a throne, and that he is not just "sitting" but ruling. . . . His session, moreover, is "on high": his exaltation, which started with his resurrection from the grave and continued with his ascension into heaven, is completed by his session. This is the seal of the divine acceptance of his work of purification, for he is now received back to the height from which he descended for our redemption. He who humbled himself for our sakes is now supremely honored.[1]

Jesus's ministry should be viewed in three grand movements of descent, ascent, and descent: from heaven to earth in his incarnation, from earth to heaven in his exaltation, and from heaven to earth again in his second coming. His session is thus to be viewed as the culmination of the central movement of ascent, namely his exaltation—one movement from earth to heaven, beginning with his resurrection and ascension. In his resurrection he defeats our foes

---

[1] Philip Edgcumbe Hughes, *A Commentary on the Epistle to the Hebrews* (Grand Rapids: Eerdmans, 1977), 47, italics original.

and inaugurates the new creation. In his ascension he moves from the limited earthly plane to the unlimited heavenly plane of God himself. And there he "sits." Christ's session has great significance for his threefold office of prophet, priest, and king, as we shall see. He sits at the right hand of God, the place of greatest honor and power in the universe. How fitting for the Son of God our Savior, who humbled himself in crucifixion, now to be exalted to the highest place as Lord of all!

The Event Foretold in the Old Testament

Psalm 110:1

After his resurrection Jesus taught his disciples that the "Law of Moses and the Prophets and the Psalms" were written about him (Luke 24:44). When the New Testament speaks of Christ's sitting at God's right hand, it points back primarily to one Old Testament text—Psalm 110:1:

> The LORD says to my Lord:
> "Sit at my right hand,
> until I make your enemies your footstool."

The Psalms speak about the coming one, the Christ, in a variety of ways. Most psalms that foretell Christ are anchored in the life of Old Testament Israel and first speak of David, or someone else. Few psalms are entirely messianic, and Psalm 110 seems to be one of them.

Verse 4 says something that could not be said of any Old Testament person:

> The LORD has sworn
> and will not change his mind,
> "You are a priest forever
> after the order of Melchizedek."

In the Old Testament, only Melchizedek, the figure who appears in Genesis 14:18–20 and just as quickly disappears, is in "the order of Melchizedek." And in the New Testament, Jesus is the only other priest belonging to that unique order. So Psalm 110:4 is entirely predictive of the future High Priest in the order of Melchizedek—Jesus Christ. Furthermore, only Jesus was appointed a priest by God's oath ("The LORD has sworn . . ."), and only Jesus holds his priesthood "forever" (Heb. 7:21, 23–25). Therefore Psalm 110:4 does not speak of David or Solomon, but speaks only of Jesus.

Verse 1 also predicts the coming one. Jesus himself uses this verse to confound his hearers by asking them how the Messiah could be David's son (descendant) and at the same time David's Lord (Matt. 22:41–46). Jesus quotes verse 1:

> The Lord said to my Lord,
> Sit at my right hand,
>> until I put your enemies under your feet.

Jesus implies that every other Israelite in the time of David's reign had two lords: God in heaven and the Israelite king on earth, namely David. But since Psalm 110 was written by King David, he would have only one Lord—God in heaven. Nevertheless, the first verse reveals that David had two Lords: "The LORD says to my Lord." In this way "David himself, in the Holy Spirit" (Mark 12:36) predicted the deity of his second "Lord," the Messiah.

Notice what the Lord in heaven said to David's Lord, the coming Messiah:

> Sit at my right hand,
> until I make your enemies your footstool. (Ps. 110:1)

David's Lord would sit at God's right hand, the place of honor and authority. And he would do so until God subdued all of his enemies. As we will see, the New Testament reveals that David spoke as a prophet and predicted the Christ's ascension and session—his sitting at the right hand of God.

The Event Predicted in the Gospels

Matthew 22:41–46 and Parallels

All three Synoptic Gospels record an important confrontation between the Pharisees and Jesus near the end of his life:

> Now while the Pharisees were gathered together, Jesus asked them a question, saying, "What do you think about the Christ? Whose son is he?" They said to him, "The son of David." He said to them, "How is it then that David, in the Spirit, calls him Lord, saying,
>
>> "'The Lord said to my Lord,
>> Sit at my right hand,
>>> until I put your enemies under your feet'?

If then David calls him Lord, how is he his son?" And no one was able to answer
him a word, nor from that day did anyone dare to ask him any more questions.
(Matt. 22:41–46)

And as Jesus taught in the temple, he said, "How can the scribes say that the Christ
is the son of David? David himself, in the Holy Spirit, declared,

> "'The Lord said to my Lord,
> Sit at my right hand,
>   until I put your enemies under your feet.'

David himself calls him Lord. So how is he his son?" And the great throng heard
him gladly. (Mark 12:35–37)

But he said to them, "How can they say that the Christ is David's son? For David
himself says in the Book of Psalms,

> "'The Lord said to my Lord,
> Sit at my right hand,
>   until I make your enemies your footstool.'

David thus calls him Lord, so how is he his son?" (Luke 20:41–44)

It is important to note that Jesus does not deny that the Christ is David's
son (descendant). He merely adds another piece of information to that fact—
information that did not fit the Jewish leaders' understanding of the Messiah—he
is also David's Lord. To prove his point Jesus quotes Psalm 110:1, which we
examined above:

> The Lord said to my Lord,
> Sit at my right hand,
>   until I put your enemies under your feet. (Matt. 22:44)

Jesus's opponents are unable to answer the question that he puts to them:
"If then David calls him Lord, how is he his son?" (v. 45). With twenty-twenty
hindsight we answer, "Because the Messiah is both God and a human being in
one person." But this insight is too advanced for Jesus's hearers, including his
disciples, until after his resurrection. Nevertheless, when he teaches them after his
resurrection, they accept the truth of the miracle of the incarnation—God became
a man in Jesus of Nazareth. David's descendant is also his Lord! In addition, Jesus
regards David's words as a prediction: the Christ will sit down at the right hand

of the Lord almighty. It is no wonder that the crowd hears Jesus gladly and that no one asks him any more questions. His words are amazing and confounding!

Matthew 26:64

The Gospels do not record the actual event of Jesus's sitting at God's right hand, his session. But in his trial before Caiaphas Jesus once more predicts his session. The chief priests and Sanhedrin have been seeking false witnesses to testify against Jesus so that they might execute him. After failed attempts two men accuse Jesus of saying, "I am able to destroy the temple of God, and to rebuild it in three days" (Matt. 26:61). When the high priest asks Jesus to defend himself, he refuses to answer.

The high priest then puts Jesus on oath: "I adjure you by the living God, tell us if you are the Christ, the Son of God" (v. 63). Jesus's answer is startling: "You have said so. But I tell you, from now on you will see the Son of Man seated at the right hand of Power and coming on the clouds of heaven" (v. 64). What does Jesus mean when he answers the high priest's question with, "You have said so"? Matthew presents Jesus as answering positively in content though reluctantly in form, as John Nolland explains: "Though formally noncommittal, it is to be taken as an obliquely expressed affirmative."[2] This is confirmed by two things. First, in Mark's version Jesus clearly answers in the affirmative, "I am" (Mark 14:62). Second is the fact that the high priest understands Jesus as answering affirmatively (Matt. 26:65). Perhaps Jesus answers cautiously because "he is not quite the Messiah Caiaphas has in mind."[3]

Jesus's next words combine references to Psalm 110:1 and Daniel 7:13. We have quoted the former text so often that we need only quote the latter:

I saw in the night visions,

> and behold, with the clouds of heaven
> there came one like a son of man,
> and he came to the Ancient of Days
> and was presented before him.
> And to him was given dominion
> and glory and a kingdom,
> that all peoples, nations, and languages
> should serve him;

---

[2] John Nolland, *The Gospel of Matthew*, New International Greek Testament Commentary (Grand Rapids: Eerdmans, 2005), 1131.

[3] D. A. Carson, *Matthew*, The Expositor's Bible Commentary (Grand Rapids: Zondervan, 1984), 555.

> his dominion is an everlasting dominion,
>   which shall not pass away,
> and his kingdom one
>   that shall not be destroyed. (Dan. 7:13–14)

Jesus combines David's prediction that the coming one will sit at God's right hand with Daniel's prediction that "a son of man" will come "with the clouds of heaven" and be given dominion over all peoples forever. D. A. Carson captures the meaning: "Jesus is not to be primarily considered a political Messiah but as the one who, in receiving a kingdom, is exalted high above David and at the Mighty One's right hand, the hand of honor and power."[4]

What do these two sayings have in common? They both speak of divine prerogatives. Only one equal to God can sit at his right hand. And in Scripture only God comes with the clouds of heaven. Only God himself will rule over all nations for all time. Jesus is thus claiming to be divine. It is no wonder that the high priest responds the way he does. He tears his clothes in revulsion at what he considers blasphemy. He shouts, "You have now heard his blasphemy. What is your judgment?" They answer, "He deserves death" (Matt. 26:65–66). Jesus's claim to be the one who will sit at God's right hand leads to the cross.

The Event Preached in Acts

Three passages in the book of Acts speak of Christ's sitting down at God's right hand.

Acts 2:29–36

In his Pentecost sermon, Peter says that David, whose tomb is visible in Jerusalem, was a prophet who predicted Christ's resurrection in Psalm 16:10. David viewed Christ's exaltation to and session at God's right hand as his enthronement, in fulfillment of God's promise. Peter, in his apostolic role as witness to Christ's resurrection, declares, "Being therefore exalted at the right hand of God, and having received from the Father the promise of the Holy Spirit, he has poured out this that you yourselves are seeing and hearing" (Acts 2:33).

Peter cites Psalm 110:1 as proof of the crucified Christ's ascension and session:

> For David did not ascend into the heavens, but he himself says,
>
>> "'The Lord said to my Lord,
>> Sit at my right hand,
>>   until I make your enemies your footstool.'

---

[4] Ibid.

Let all the house of Israel therefore know for certain that God has made him both Lord and Christ, this Jesus whom you crucified." (Acts 2:34–36)

Peter thus interprets Christ's session, inseparable from his resurrection and ascension, as his coronation, as the occasion for his pouring out the Spirit, and as God's official installation of him as Lord and Christ.

Acts 5:27–32

As previously, the apostles are arrested and brought before the Sanhedrin (Acts 5:17–18). This time they are imprisoned for preaching Jesus. But God supernaturally frees them. After taking them again, the council rebukes them for continuing to teach the people about Jesus even after warnings. Peter responds: "We must obey God rather than men. The God of our fathers raised Jesus, whom you killed by hanging him on a tree. God exalted him at his right hand as Leader and Savior, to give repentance to Israel and forgiveness of sins" (Acts 5:29–31).

God's estimation of Jesus differs radically from that of the Jewish leaders. They crucified him and God exalted him. Here the Father's exaltation of Jesus includes his resurrection, ascension, and session. His sitting at God's right hand means his installation as Leader and Savior, not on earth, but in heaven. From this exalted station he bestows divine gifts of repentance and forgiveness.

Acts 7:54–60

Stephen's speech enrages his opponents (Acts 7:54). "But he, full of the Holy Spirit, gazed into heaven and saw the glory of God, and Jesus standing at the right hand of God. And he said, 'Behold, I see the heavens opened, and the Son of Man standing at the right hand of God'" (vv. 55–56). The martyr Stephen tells his foes that he sees the glorified Jesus at God's right hand. He thereby ascribes deity to Christ. His enemies cannot endure such talk. "But they cried out with a loud voice and stopped their ears and rushed together at him. Then they cast him out of the city and stoned him" (vv. 57–58).

I am not sure what to make of the fact that Stephen saw Jesus *standing* at God's right hand.[5] But it is plain that Stephen associates Jesus with heaven and God's glory, and proximity to God (at his right hand). These are ways of identifying Jesus with God. His session thus marks his transition from lowly earthly service

---

[5]For views, see William J. Larkin Jr., *Acts*, The IVP New Testament Commentary (Downers Grove, IL: InterVarsity, 1995), 120–21, note on 7:56.

to exalted heavenly rule. William Larkin summarizes: "Stephen is emphatically confessing Jesus' transcendent place in heaven."[6]

The Event Taught in Paul's Epistles

Romans 8:33–34

Paul, in the strongest preservation passage in the Bible, presents an argument based on God's justice. He asks, "Who shall bring any charge against God's elect?" To which he answers, "It is God who justifies" (Rom. 8:33). God, the Judge of all the earth, has declared us righteous in Christ. No one will bring a charge against us and make it stick, for that would mean overturning God's verdict, which is unthinkable. Again, the apostle asks, "Who is to condemn?" He answers, "Christ Jesus is the one who died—more than that, who was raised—who is at the right hand of God, who indeed is interceding for us" (v. 34).

It is no accident that Paul mentions Christ after asking a question about the last judgment, for Scripture almost evenly assigns the role of Judge to the Father and Son. But in answering his question, Paul does not assign Christ the role of Judge. Instead, he presents him as the Savior of his people. He "is the one who died—more than that, who was raised—who is at the right hand of God, who indeed is interceding for us" (v. 34). Christ, the Judge of all, will not condemn those who trust in him. Rather, he died, arose, sat at God's right hand, and intercedes—all to save them and keep them saved.

Here Paul presents Christ's session as one of his saving events in the midst of his death, resurrection, and intercession to assure true believers of final salvation.

Ephesians 1:15–23

Paul prays that the Ephesian believers might know in their lives "the immeasurable greatness" of God's power toward them. He describes that power in two remarkable ways. It is the power of God "according to the working of his great might that he worked in Christ when he raised him from the dead" (Eph. 1:19–20). This is God's mighty power indeed! It accomplished the central deed of the Christian faith (inseparable from the cross)—raising the crucified one from the dead and thereby unleashing the life that results in the regeneration of God's people and the inauguration of the new creation.

The apostle describes the enormity of God's power in a second way too. It is not only God's power as displayed in Jesus's resurrection. It is also the power

---

[6]Ibid.

that the glorified Christ wields at God's right hand. Paul prays that the Ephesians might know

> the immeasurable greatness of his power toward us who believe, according to the working of his great might that he worked in Christ when he raised him from the dead and seated him at his right hand in the heavenly places, far above all rule and authority and power and dominion, and above every name that is named, not only in this age but also in the one to come. And he put all things under his feet and gave him as head over all things to the church, which is his body, the fullness of him who fills all in all. (vv. 19–23)

Paul waxes eloquent concerning this power by describing it from below and above. Viewed from below, this power is that exercised by Christ who is at God's right hand, "far above" all earthly and heavenly powers, the evil angels. In fact, he is above any other conceivable power, whatever its title, whether present or future (v. 21). Viewed from above, where Christ sits at God's right hand, "all things" are (in the words of Ps. 8:6) "under his feet." Not only so, but God graciously gave the exalted Christ "as head over all things to the church" (Eph. 1:22). This means more than that Christ is the head of his body, the church. He is head over *all things* for the church. He exercises his lordship over the cosmos for the benefit of his people.

Paul refers to Christ's sitting at God's right hand to extol the immensity of the power of God available to the church, including the church at Ephesus. P. T. O'Brien's summary is apt: "It affirms that the decisive demonstration of God's power available to believers occurred in the resurrection and exaltation of Christ, as well as the subjugation of the powers to him and his being given as head over everything to the church."[7] The right hand of God the Father is the place of the greatest honor and authority. When Christ ascends and sits there, he is honored as God and rules from his divine throne. For individual Christians and churches to realize and live in that power is powerful indeed.

Colossians 3:1–4

Paul counters asceticism at Colossae by reminding his readers of their union with Christ. Believers ought not to beat down their bodies in a vain attempt to achieve holiness because they died with Christ to the world (Col. 2:20). For godliness they should not look downward to "self-made religion and asceticism" (2:23). Rather, they should look upward, since they "have been raised

---

[7]Peter T. O'Brien, *The Letter to the Ephesians*, The Pillar New Testament Commentary (Grand Rapids: Eerdmans, 1999), 139.

with Christ," and are therefore to "seek the things that are above, where Christ is, seated at the right hand of God" (3:1).

As they live for God on earth, they are to look to heaven for divine supply. Paul instructs them, "Set your minds on things that are above, not on things that are on earth" (v. 2). What is the apostle's rationale for this command? He explains: "For you have died, and your life is hidden with Christ in God. When Christ who is your life appears, then you also will appear with him in glory" (vv. 3–4).

This is Paul's theme of union with Christ. Though once "separated from Christ . . . having no hope and without God in the world . . . now in Christ Jesus you who once were far off have been brought near by the blood of Christ" (Eph. 2:12–13). Henceforth, Christians are united to Christ, and his saving events become theirs. Perhaps Paul's greatest expression of this is found in Ephesians 2:4–7:

> But God, being rich in mercy, because of the great love with which he loved us, even when we were dead in our trespasses, made us alive together with Christ—by grace you have been saved—and raised us up with him and seated us with him in the heavenly places in Christ Jesus, so that in the coming ages he might show the immeasurable riches of his grace in kindness toward us in Christ Jesus.

Notice that the apostle says that God united us to Christ in his heavenly session; he "seated us with him in the heavenly places in Christ" (v. 6). Union with Christ also dominates Paul's teaching in Colossians 3:1–4. The Colossian Christians are to live as those who have been spiritually joined to Christ in his death, resurrection, ascension, session, and even second coming. That is, by God's grace they not only know Christ relationally in justification and adoption. But by that same grace they know Christ participationally in union with him. They are "in him" and he is "in" them (Gal. 2:20).

As a result, when he died, they died spiritually; sin no longer has the right to dominate them. When he was raised, they were raised to newness of life (cf. Rom. 6:1–12). Paul assumes that when Christ ascended and sat down at God's right hand, spiritually speaking, so did they. Consequently, he could write that their "life is hidden with Christ in God" (Col. 3:3). They have eternal life only "in him," and that life is at God's right hand because that is where "Christ, who is" their "life" is (v. 4). Their spiritual life as Christians is so bound up with Christ, that there is a sense that his second coming is theirs. When he "appears, then" they "also will appear with him in glory" (v. 4).

Douglas Moo's summary is fitting:

This note dominates vv. 1–4, as Paul focuses on the believer's union with Christ. The *past* experience of dying with him and being raised with him is the basis for our *present* status as people whose heavenly identity is real and secure, yet hidden, an identity that will be gloriously manifested in the *future*.[8]

Here Paul assumes that Christ's session is one of his saving deeds, all of which constitute his argument that the Colossian Christians have been joined to Christ. Consequently, they must look "up" to heaven and Christ for victory over sin, not "down" to "asceticism and severity to the body," which "are of no value in stopping the indulgence of the flesh" (2:23).

The Event Taught in Hebrews

Hebrews has much to contribute to our study of the theological significance of the crucified, risen, and ascended Christ's sitting at God's right hand. In at least four passages Hebrews teaches us what Christ's session accomplished.

Hebrews 1:3–14

In the prologue, the author presents the Son of God as prophet, priest, and mainly king. He briefly contrasts him with Old Testament prophets as God's Son by whom God "in these last days . . . has spoken to us" (Heb. 1:2). He also speaks of his priesthood only briefly, anticipating the full exposition in chapters 7–10: "After making purification for sins, he sat down at the right hand of the Majesty on high, having become as much superior to angels as the name he has inherited is more excellent than theirs" (Heb. 1:3–4). The name that Christ inherited as a result of his sitting at God's right hand is "Son," as the Old Testament quotations that follow demonstrate:

> You are my Son;
> today I have begotten you. (Ps. 2:7)

I will be to him a father, and he shall be to me a son. (2 Sam. 7:14)

David had offered to build a house, a temple, for God. God denied his request and instead told him that he, the Lord, would build a "house," a dynasty, for David (2 Sam. 7:11–12). God promised David's son: "I will establish the throne of his kingdom forever. I will be to him a father, and he shall be to me a son"

---

[8]Douglas J. Moo, *The Letters to the Colossians and to Philemon*, The Pillar New Testament Commentary (Grand Rapids: Eerdmans, 2008), 244.

(vv. 13–14). This promise pertained to each of David's sons who reigned and is celebrated in Psalm 2, even in the midst of Gentile rebellion. Although both of these texts speak of the house of David, ultimately they speak of the only son of David who will reign "forever"—the Christ. Jesus Christ is the ultimate son of David. Indeed, as Hebrews 1 makes clear, he is the divine Son of God (Heb. 1:8). The Father proclaims the sonship of his unique divine Son by raising him from the dead and exalting him to his right hand (v. 3).

Our focus is on these words: "After making purification for sins, he sat down at the right hand of the Majesty on high" (Heb. 1:3). Here the author introduces a theme that he will develop in 10:11–14, a passage that we will investigate. The Son's sitting at "the right hand of the Majesty on high" speaks of the finality, perfection, and efficacy of his priestly sacrifice. He, the divine-human Mediator, offers himself once for all time. As such his self-offering is final because, unlike the Old Testament high priests, he sat down, indicating the completion of his sacrifice. His offering is perfect, as is shown by where he sat—at the right hand of God himself. The Father's receiving the Son in this place of honor shows that he is well pleased with his Son's saving accomplishment. The Son's offering is also efficacious, utterly effective to save all who come to him in faith. Nothing else can be required of him or them because his work was final and perfect. It is impossible for sinners to add to the value of the work of Christ.

The writer forms an inclusion in Hebrews 1, with verse 13 corresponding to verse 3 above: "Sit at my right hand until I make your enemies a footstool for your feet" (v. 13). This quotation of Psalm 110:1 is the Old Testament basis for Christ's session, as we have seen. The victorious Christ sits at God's right hand until Christ's return, when his enemies will be finally and utterly vanquished. And this will occur only because "after making purification for sins, he sat down at the right hand of the Majesty on high" (Heb. 1:3).

Hebrews 8:1–7

At this point in his epistle, the writer gives a valuable summary: "Now the point in what we are saying is this: we have such a high priest, one who is seated at the right hand of the throne of the Majesty in heaven, a minister in the holy places, in the true tent that the Lord set up, not man" (Heb. 8:1–2).

Christ is a High Priest in the order of Melchizedek, not of Levi, as the writer has explained in the previous chapter. Nevertheless, when he describes Christ's high priesthood, he compares it with that of the sons of Aaron.[9] Since the Aaronic

---

[9] A big reason for this is his goal to show the superiority of the new covenant, inaugurated by Christ in his death and resurrection, over the one given to Israel at Mount Sinai, and thereby to dissuade his

priests offered "gifts and sacrifices," similarly, "it is necessary for this priest also to have something to offer" (v. 3). The author does not tell us here what Christ the High Priest had to offer, but he makes it plain enough elsewhere.

He offered up himself. (7:27)

Christ . . . through the eternal Spirit offered himself without blemish to God. (9:14)

Christ, having been offered once to bear the sins of many, will appear a second time. (9:28)

We have been sanctified through the offering of the body of Jesus Christ once for all. (10:10)

Christ . . . offered for all time a single sacrifice for sins. (10:12)

By a single offering he has perfected for all time those who are being sanctified. (10:14)

Christ is both High Priest and offering! He offered his own body, even himself, to save from sins "those who draw near to God through him" (7:25). A key contrast between Christ and the Old Testament high priests is the location of their priestly ministries. The Old Testament high priests' ministries took place "on earth," but their offerings were only "a copy and shadow of the heavenly things" (8:4, 5). This is because when God gave Moses instructions concerning the tabernacle of the old covenant, he told him, "See that you make everything according to the pattern that was shown you on the mountain" (v. 5; cf. Ex. 25:40).

Because God ordered that the earthly tabernacle be built according to his heavenly specifications, Israel, out of all the peoples on earth, had an earthly priesthood that corresponded to "the heavenly things" (Heb. 8:5). They alone knew God and worshiped him in truth. Nonetheless, the Old Testament high priests' ministries took place on earth. Now Christ too has offered himself to God on earth. His death and resurrection are the heart of his saving work. But they are not all of it. His priestly work, begun on earth in sacrifice, is continued in heaven. And that all-important transition from earth to heaven occurs in his ascension and is sealed, as it were, in his session at God's right hand.

We are now in a position to understand these verses better: "Now the point in what we are saying is this: we have such a high priest, one who is seated at

---

readers from forsaking Christ and returning to Judaism.

the right hand of the throne of the Majesty in heaven, a minister in the holy places, in the true tent that the Lord set up, not man" (Heb. 8:1–2). Jesus Christ, our High Priest, is no longer on earth. He, having completed his all-important earthly ministry, is seated at God's right hand—even "the throne of the Majesty in heaven," the place of supreme honor. His sitting there indicates that his work completely satisfies God and therefore completely saves his people. He has brought his saving work, accomplished on earth, into the heavenly tabernacle, of which the Old Testament tabernacle and temple were merely "a copy and shadow of the heavenly things" (v. 5).

Christ thus "has obtained a ministry that is as much more excellent than the old as the covenant he mediates is better, since it is enacted on better promises" (v. 6). He is the Mediator of the new covenant, the unique earthly-heavenly Savior. He gave himself for his people in death, arose from the dead, and is seated at God's right hand. His session thus shows the success of his earthly ministry because by means of his session he has taken the fruits of his earthly ministry permanently into God's heavenly presence. Plainly, there never will be anyone like him, our great High Priest!

Hebrews 10:11–18

Again the author appeals to Christ's session to extol his priesthood. He makes a number of contrasts between the Old Testament priests and Christ. He contrasts their posture and the timing, number, and efficacy of their sacrifices.

First, he contrasts their posture. Every Levitical priest "stands daily at his service" (v. 11). But Christ "sat down at the right hand of God" (v. 12). Then the writer contrasts the timing of their sacrifices. Every Levitical priest "repeatedly" offers "the same sacrifices" (v. 11). Christ "offered for all time a single sacrifice for sins" (v. 12). Next he contrasts the number of their sacrifices. Every Levitical priest offers "the same sacrifices" (plural, v. 11). Christ "offered a single sacrifice for sins" (v. 12). Finally, he contrasts the efficacy of their sacrifices. Every Levitical priest offers "sacrifices, which can never take away sins" (v. 11). But Christ "by a single offering . . . has perfected for all time those who are being sanctified" (v. 14).

As a result of these momentous contrasts the writer shows the vast superiority of the new covenant to the old. Unlike the Old Testament priests, Christ "sat down at the right hand of God" (v. 12). Their standing indicated that their work was never done; they had to keep offering the same sacrifices for sin over and over. But Christ's sitting down indicates the finality of his atoning death. Once for all time he made atonement for sins. There is no more need for temple, priests, sacrifices, and the Day of Atonement. From an Old Testament perspective, this is astonishing, for these realities constituted the essence of Israel's religion. But Christ's coming was the goal of Old Testament faith, and now that he has come and done his singular work, the old covenant is fulfilled and eclipsed by the new.

Consequently, Christ's unique sacrifice makes obsolete the multiple Old Testament sacrifices. They were not efficacious as is obvious from their being repeated (cf. 10:1–4). "It is impossible for the blood of bulls and goats to take away sins" (v. 4). But it is possible—no, actual—that the blood of Christ takes away sins. Indeed, "By a single offering he has perfected for all time those who are being sanctified" (v. 14).

Unmistakably, in this context Christ's session underlines the finality and efficacy of his sacrificial death, in contrast to the old covenant sacrifices. William L. Lane's words bear repeating:

> Even his posture declares the sharp difference between Christ and the Levitical priests. His unique sacrifice accomplished, "he sat down . . . at the right hand of God." The allusion to Ps. 110:1 resumes the thesis statement in [Heb.] 8:1–2 and reinforces the image of Christ as the enthroned priest. The concept of Christ's session in the presence of God was first introduced in 1:3, but only now is its significance for the writer's argument clarified. Jesus sits because his sacrifice requires no repetition. His heavenly session attests that the benefits of his sacrificial death endure perpetually. The sacrificial phase of his priestly ministry is completed.[10]

Hebrews 12:1–6

As previously, the author encourages his readers to persevere, this time by pointing them to Jesus. He reminds them of the example of Old Testament heroes and heroines of faith from Hebrews 11, especially verses 39–40: "Therefore, since we are surrounded by so great a cloud of witnesses, let us also lay aside every weight, and sin which clings so closely, and let us run with endurance the race that is set before us" (12:1). He inspires them to run a long-distance race successfully.

But he does more. To the Old Testament figures he adds another—Jesus himself is the goal toward which they must run. He has previously presented Jesus as "the apostle and high priest of our confession" (3:1). Now he adds another role—supreme example. While doing so, he does not leave behind Jesus's other more salvific roles; rather he summarizes them by summoning his

---

[10]William L. Lane, *Hebrews 9–13*, Word Biblical Commentary (Dallas: Word, 1991), 267.

readers to look "to Jesus, the founder and perfecter of our faith" (12:2). Jesus is founder of our faith: "He is the author or originator of true faith"[11]—his death and resurrection alone deliver sinners (2:15). He is also our faith's perfecter: "He has fulfilled God's promises for all who believe, giving faith a perfect basis by his high-priestly work."[12] He saves and keeps to the end all who trust him as Savior and Lord (7:24–25).

The writer's chief purpose here, however, is to point to Jesus not as Savior but as an example for his readers to follow in persevering faith, "looking to Jesus, the founder and perfecter of our faith, who for the joy that was set before him endured the cross, despising the shame, and is seated at the right hand of the throne of God" (12:2). Jesus himself persevered to the end in faith. Those who believe in him are to do no less. At first blush, the author's demands seem rigorist, almost cruel: "In your struggle against sin you have not yet resisted to the point of shedding your blood" (v. 4). How can he possibly demand that they give up their lives rather than turn away from Christ in apostasy? The answer is simple and powerful—because their Lord and Savior did the same thing. He gave up his life rather than be deterred from his God-appointed course. He "endured the cross, despising the shame" (v. 2).

What motivated him to do such a thing? It was "for the joy that was set before him" (v. 2). As runners in a race focus on the prize, Christ focused on the end—joy in the Father's presence—in order to endure the means—crucifixion and shame. All Christians must rejoice in this. Without such perseverance on the part of their Savior, none would be saved. But, praise his holy name! Jesus was faithful and "obedient to the point of death, even death on a cross" (Phil. 2:8). And even as we rejoice, we must realize that God requires nothing less of us. We too must persevere to the end in faith, regardless of the consequences.

Now in speaking of these matters, the author, after describing Christ's humiliation in terms of the cross and its shame, speaks also of his exaltation. He does so in these terms: "Jesus . . . is seated at the right hand of the throne of God" (Heb. 12:2). Whereas in the previous two passages in Hebrews Christ's session has mainly to do with his priesthood, here it pertains chiefly to his royal office. Jesus overcame and sat down at God's right hand—the place of greatest honor. As Jesus says in Revelation 3:21: "I also conquered and sat down with my Father on his throne." Here Jesus finds consummate joy with the Father.

Christ, the prophet, priest, and king, and also the example for his people, strengthens their assurance, as Lane explains:

---

[11]Peter T. O'Brien, *The Letter to the Hebrews*, The Pillar New Testament Commentary (Grand Rapids: Eerdmans, 2010), 454.
[12]Ibid., 455.

The crucified Jesus is the exalted Son. The exemplary fidelity of Jesus and its consequence is stressed to encourage the community, undergoing its own ordeal, in a resolve to persevere in faithfulness. The session at the right hand is the guarantee of the absoluteness of Christ's exaltation, and the utter security of those who have placed their hope in him.[13]

The Event Taught in 1 Peter 3:21–22

Peter speaks of Christ's humiliation and exaltation early in his first epistle (1 Pet. 1:11, 19–21) and again in chapter 3, where he retains the same order: first humiliation (3:18) and then exaltation (3:21–22). In between these verses are some of the most difficult in all of Scripture. In the preceding context, Peter, as he does often in this epistle, encourages his readers to suffer for Christ's sake (vv. 13–17). The reason? "For Christ also suffered once for sins, the righteous for the unrighteous, that he might bring us to God" (v. 18). When Jesus calls his people to suffer, he is not asking them to do something foreign to him. To the contrary, "Christ also suffered for you, leaving you an example, so that you might follow in his steps" (2:21). But, unlike his people's suffering, Christ's is redemptive. "He himself bore our sins in his body on the tree, that we might die to sin and live to righteousness" (2:24).

Similarly, in chapter 3 Christ, like his people, suffers; but unlike them, he suffers vicariously to rescue them: "Christ also suffered once for sins, the righteous for the unrighteous, that he might bring us to God" (3:18). The difficult verses follow. Because they are not crucial for our purposes, rather than give an extended discussion, I will merely interpret them and indicate other views in the notes.

Christ was "put to death in the body but made alive by the Spirit, through whom also he went and preached to the spirits in prison who disobeyed long ago when God waited patiently in the days of Noah while the ark was being built" (3:18–20, NIV). Although each of the four most common views has its weaknesses, this seems to mean that Peter describes "Christ's proclamation of victory and judgment over the evil angels. These evil angels, according to Gen. 6:1–4, had sexual relations with women and were imprisoned because of their sin."[14]

Peter's point, then, is not that Christ descended into hell, but that after his resurrection he proclaimed his victory to the demons at his session at God's right hand. This fits well with the verses that are our main concern,

---

[13]Lane, *Hebrews 9–13*, 415.

[14]Thomas R. Schreiner, *1, 2, Peter, Jude*, The New American Commentary (Nashville: Broadman and Holman, 2003), 185. See pp. 184–90 for views and evaluation of them.

in which Peter writes of "an appeal to God . . . through the resurrection of Jesus Christ, who has gone into heaven and is at the right hand of God, with angels, authorities, and powers having been subjected to him" (1 Pet. 3:21–22). Peter speaks of Christ's resurrection, ascension, and session. Christ suffered on earth, but now he "has gone into heaven" (v. 22). He will never again be humiliated because he has moved from the earthly to the heavenly sphere. Furthermore, he occupies a place of honor and authority in heaven, for he "is at the right hand of God" (v. 22). The apostle underscores Christ's authority at God's right hand when he adds, "with angels, authorities, and powers having been subjected to him" (v. 22).

Here Christ's session marks the epitome of his victorious exaltation. He has triumphed over the evil powers and rules over them all at God's right hand. And his triumph gives his people confidence that they too will triumph, as J. Ramsey Michaels asserts:

> The theme of the passage . . . is vindication. The vindication of Christ lays the basis for the vindication of the Christian believer, and Christ's vindication is total. Peter is bolder than either the early Paul or the author of Hebrews in depicting "angels, authorities, and powers" as *already* in subjection to the risen Lord at God's right hand. . . . Peter knows as well as his readers that the forces of evil have not literally been routed . . . yet he offers them a vision of assurance that Christ in his journey to heaven has broken the back of evil; whatever they may have to suffer, they have no need to be afraid (cf. 3:13), nor even be surprised (cf. 4:12) when they realize that Christ himself was "put to death in the flesh" before he was "made alive in the spirit." Vindication is real, and Christ's vindication belongs precisely to those who suffer.[15]

The Event Taught in Revelation

Revelation 3:21. The letters to the seven churches in first-century Asia Minor follow a recognizable pattern. Toward the end of each letter appears Jesus's promise to "overcomers" or conquerors, those who persevere to the end amid trials and even persecutions. Jesus's promise to the church in Laodicea includes these words: "The one who conquers, I will grant him to sit with me on my throne, as I also conquered and sat down with my Father on his throne" (Rev. 3:21).

Jesus's words contain an important truth—the conquering believers' victory is possible only because of Jesus's prior victory. In the Revelation, Jesus is the Victor, as the following three passages reveal.

---

[15] J. Ramsey Michaels, *1 Peter*, Word Biblical Commentary (Waco, TX: Word, 1988), 220–21.

Revelation 5:5. "Weep no more; behold, the Lion of the tribe of Judah, the Root of David has conquered, so that he can open the scroll and its seven seals." Only the Lion can open the book of God's judgments. This passage precedes the first occurrence of the Revelation's favorite designation for Jesus—the symbol of the Lamb. Before he appears as "a Lamb standing, as though it had been slain," he appears as "the Lion" who "has conquered" (5:5–6).

He is "the Lion of the tribe of Judah," the son to whom Jacob promised the kingship (Gen. 49:9). He is "the root of David." (Rev. 5:5). We might expect the text to say that he is "a shoot from the stump of Jesse," David's father, as Isaiah prophesied (Isa. 11:1). This is true because the Messiah is David's descendant. But Revelation here says that he is "the root of David," reflecting the words of Isaiah 11:10, "the root of Jesse." That is, he is not only David's descendant ("a shoot") as a man, but his source ("the root") as God. Philip Hughes explains, "In short, the incarnation is the event whereby the Root of David becomes the Lion of Judah, or the Root of Jesse becomes the Shoot of Jesse."[16] The Messiah is both God and man in one person. And as such, he is "the Lion of the tribe of Judah, the Root of David" who "has conquered" (Rev. 5:5).

Revelation 17:14. "They will make war on the Lamb, and the Lamb will conquer them, for he is Lord of lords and King of kings." The great evil forces and enemies of God fight the Lamb but of course are unsuccessful. The Lamb defeats them because he is the divine-human conqueror. He is the Lord over all earthly lords and the supreme King over all earthly monarchs. Robert Mounce sums up matters succinctly: "The beast will be overcome because he has met the One to whom all others will ultimately be subordinate. The armies of heaven share his victory as well (cf. Rev. 19:14)."[17]

Revelation 19:11–16. Here the author paints a complex picture of Christ:

> Then I saw heaven opened, and behold, a white horse! The one sitting on it is called Faithful and True, and in righteousness he judges and makes war. His eyes are like a flame of fire, and on his head are many diadems, and he has a name written that no one knows but himself. He is clothed in a robe dipped in blood, and the name by which he is called is The Word of God. And the armies of heaven, arrayed in fine linen, white and pure, were following him on white horses. From his mouth comes a sharp sword with which to strike down the nations, and he will rule them with a rod of iron. He will tread the winepress of the fury of the

---

[16] Philip Edgcumbe Hughes, *The Book of the Revelation*, The Pillar New Testament Commentary (Grand Rapids: Eerdmans, 1990), 79.

[17] Robert H. Mounce, *The Book of Revelation*, The New International Commentary on the New Testament (Grand Rapids: Eerdmans, 1977), 318.

wrath of God the Almighty. On his robe and on his thigh he has a name written, King of kings and Lord of lords.

Here we do not see the Lamb who was slain but a great general riding on his horse into battle. He is the mighty champion who routs his enemies in the last battle. The "armies of heaven" here are not angels, but their clothing—the "fine linen, white and pure"—identifies them as the saints who share in Jesus's victory (cf. 6:11; 7:9; 19:8). Many features of this picture show Jesus to be the conqueror: the white horse symbolizing military triumph, his many crowns, the sword in his mouth, his ruling the nations with the rod of iron, his treading the winepress of God's judgment, and his title "King of kings and Lord of lords."

Plainly—as these three passages show—Jesus is the Victor in the Revelation. Noteworthy for our purposes is that the victory that Jesus wins is also the victory of his people—the saints follow him, also on white horses of victory (19:14). Dennis Johnson agrees: "Just as Christ's white horse promises certain victory, so the white horses of the riders who follow him assure the church that his triumph will be ours as well."[18]

We are now better equipped to understand Jesus's promise to the church in Laodicea: "The one who conquers, I will grant him to sit with me on my throne, as I also conquered and sat down with my Father on his throne" (3:21). Indeed, Jesus conquered! And after he ascended from earth to heaven, he sat down with his Father on his heavenly throne. Here Jesus's session is the epitome of his exaltation. And it is the promise that persevering believers will reign with him.

Hughes hits all the right notes:

> The Lord's promise *to him who overcomes* that he will sit with him on his throne is founded on the reality of the believer's status in Christ and therefore his union with Christ. It is indeed a present reality in that the incarnate Son, who has been raised from the dead and exalted to the transcendental glory, now sits, enthroned, at the Father's right hand in the heavenly places; for this means that all that has happened to him has also happened to our human nature which he took to himself to redeem and glorify. . . . His enthronement is the enthronement of his redeemed who are one with him. In him our glorification is even now a reality. But the promise indicates that there is also a future dimension to this reality.[19]

---

[18]Dennis E. Johnson, *Triumph of the Lamb: A Commentary on Revelation* (Phillipsburg, NJ: P&R, 2001), 275.
[19]Hughes, *The Book of the Revelation*, 68–69, italics original.

Connecting the Dots

Jesus's session saves. After his death, resurrection, and ascension, Jesus sat down at the right hand of God the Father, the place of highest honor and authority in the universe. He did not walk, as in his earthly ministry; stretch out his arms, as on the cross; or lift his hands in priestly blessing, as he was carried to heaven in his ascension (Luke 24:50–51). Instead, he sat down to complete his exaltation begun in his resurrection and ascension. He sat down as prophet, priest, and king. I will use the rubric of the threefold office, but this time in reverse order, which reflects the emphases of Scripture regarding Christ's session.

Jesus Sat Down as the King Par Excellence

In his Pentecost sermon, Peter interprets Christ's session as his coronation, as God's official installation of him as Lord and Christ (Acts 2:32–36). The covenant people rejected their Messiah and crucified him. But God declares his estimation of Jesus by exalting him to God's own right hand. This means his inauguration as Leader and Savior in heaven, from which lofty station he bestows divine gifts of repentance and forgiveness (Acts 5:29–31).

The martyr Stephen in his famous speech indicates that Christ's session marks his transition from lowly earthly service to exalted heavenly rule. Stephen thereby ascribes deity to Christ (Acts 7:55–56). God displayed his power in raising Christ from the dead and seating him at God's right hand. From this glorious position Christ makes immense power available to the church (Eph. 1:19–23).

When believers are spiritually joined to Christ, they are made partakers of his saving events, including his session (specifically in Eph. 2:6), as Paul reminds us in Colossians 3:1–4. The Colossians have been joined to Christ, who is in heaven due to his ascension and session. Because believers are joined to the seated heavenly Christ, they are to look "up" to heaven and him for victory over sin. They are not to look "down" to "asceticism and severity to the body," which "are of no value in stopping the indulgence of the flesh" (2:23).

Though Christ's session pertains to all three of his messianic offices, it especially pertains to his royal office. Jesus overcame our foes and sat down at God's right hand—the position of supreme honor and rule (Heb. 12:1–2). Jesus's session marks the pinnacle of his victorious exaltation. He has triumphed over the evil powers and rules over them all at God's right hand. And his triumph gives his people confidence that they too will triumph (1 Pet. 3:21–22). Jesus's session, the zenith of his royal exaltation, promises persevering believers that they also will reign with him (Rev. 3:21).

Jesus Sat Down as the Priest Par Excellence

In Romans 8:33–34, Paul presents Christ's session as one of his saving events along with his death, resurrection, and intercession. After Paul speaks of bringing charges, condemnation, and justification (vv. 33–34), the mention of Christ's death suggests the legal idea of penal substitution. This means that the messianic office in view is that of priest. This is confirmed by the mention of his priestly intercession. Christ our priest is not only "the one who died" for us; he lives at God's right hand "interceding for us" (v. 34) and so assures us of final salvation.

The succinct but powerful words of Hebrews 1:3, "After making purification for sins, he sat down at the right hand of the Majesty on high," hint at the finality, perfection, and efficacy of the Son's priestly sacrifice. These attributes are made explicit later in Hebrews when the author shows the superiority of Christ and his sacrificial death to the old covenant priests and their sacrifices (Heb. 10:11–14). The Old Testament priests in their service never sat, "but when Christ had offered for all time a single sacrifice for sins, he sat down at the right hand of God" (v. 12). This indicated that his priestly work was complete, perfect, and utterly effective. As a result, amazingly, "by a single offering he has perfected for all time those who are being sanctified" (v. 14)!

In fact, Christ, unlike any other priest, took the fruits of his earthly priestly ministry permanently into God's heavenly presence (Heb. 8:1–8). The writer of Hebrews says it beautifully: "Now the point in what we are saying is this: we have such a high priest, one who is seated at the right hand of the throne of the Majesty in heaven" (8:1).

Jesus Sat Down as the Prophet Par Excellence

We have followed the inverse order of Christ's offices because when Scripture speaks of Christ's session, it puts most emphasis on his royal office, much on his priestly office, and some on his prophetic office. Jesus spoke as a prophet when put on oath by the high priest and asked if he was "the Christ, the Son of God" (Matt. 26:63): "You have said so. But I tell you, from now on you will see the Son of Man seated at the right hand of Power and coming on the clouds of heaven" (Matt. 26:64). With these words, the prophet Jesus predicted his session and second coming.

The risen, ascended, seated Christ pours out the Holy Spirit on the day of Pentecost in fulfillment of Joel's prophecy (Acts 2:33; Joel 2:28–32). In so doing he acts as a heavenly prophet who sends the Spirit to his disciples, enabling them to spread the word of his saving death and resurrection. This is in fulfillment of Jesus's prophetic prediction in Acts 1:8: "But you will receive power when the Holy Spirit has come upon you, and you will be my witnesses in Jerusalem and in all Judea and Samaria, and to the end of the earth."

The writer to the Hebrews affirms the superiority of the Son-prophet to Old Testament mediators of special revelation—prophets and angels (Hebrews 1). Indeed, "in these last days he has spoken to us by his Son" (Heb. 1:2). When in this context the author calls Christ "the radiance of the glory of God" and "the exact imprint of his nature," he also depicts him as revealer. As a ray reveals the sun's glory and as a coin reveals the imprint of its die, so the incarnate Son reveals the invisible God. The point is, as O'Brien explains, that "the Son is uniquely qualified to be the final manifestation of God."[20]

The incarnate, sinless, crucified, risen, and ascended Christ's sitting at God's right hand saves because he fulfills his threefold office of prophet, priest, and king bestowed on him when he received the Spirit at his baptism. But even his session is not the last of his saving works. It is followed by his pouring out the Holy Spirit at Pentecost, which is the subject of our next chapter.

---

[20]O'Brien, *The Letter to the Hebrews*, 56.

Incarnation
Sinless Life
Death
Resurrection
Ascension
Session
Pentecost
Intercession
Second Coming

Chapter 7

Christ's Pentecost

In the first book, O Theophilus, I have dealt with all that Jesus *began to do and teach*, until the day when he was taken up, after he had given commands through the Holy Spirit to the apostles whom he had chosen. (Acts 1:1–2)

F. F. Bruce captures a key implication of this beginning of Luke's second book, Acts, in which Luke refers to his first book, the Gospel of Luke: "As the Gospel tells us what Jesus *began* to do and teach, so Acts tells us what He *continued* to do and teach by His Spirit in the apostles after His Ascension."[1] The ascended Lord Jesus does continue to act and instruct in Acts, as Bruce says. What is Jesus's most momentous deed performed in Acts? From the perspective of the Bible's story, there is no doubt—it is his sending the Holy Spirit at Pentecost.

Christ's pouring out the Spirit at Pentecost saves. Perhaps this truth is the least familiar of the nine that are included in this first section of the book. It is not difficult to understand that the Son of God's saving deeds include his incarnation, sinless life, death, resurrection, ascension, session, intercession, and second coming. But is Pentecost really similar? As our study will show, the answer is yes. Pentecost is *Jesus's* unique, nonrepeatable deed, as unique and nonrepeatable as his dying for our sins and rising again. And Jesus's sending the Spirit in newness and power applies the salvation that he won on the cross and

---

[1] F. F. Bruce, *The Acts of the Apostles* (Grand Rapids: Eerdmans, 1951), 66, italics original.

the empty tomb. Pentecost, as Jesus's saving deed, has powerful ramifications for Christians, the church, and ministry.

The Event Predicted in the Old Testament

The prophet Joel foretold the coming of the Holy Spirit at Pentecost:

> And it shall come to pass afterward,
>   that I will pour out my Spirit on all flesh;
> your sons and your daughters shall prophesy,
>   your old men shall dream dreams,
>   and your young men shall see visions.
> Even on the male and female servants
>   in those days I will pour out my Spirit.
>
> And I will show wonders in the heavens and on the earth, blood and fire and columns of smoke. The sun shall be turned to darkness, and the moon to blood, before the great and awesome day of the LORD comes. And it shall come to pass that everyone who calls on the name of the LORD shall be saved. (Joel 2:28–32)

Joel, as all of the Old Testament prophets, spoke the word of God to his contemporaries. But he also predicted something that would happen in the distant future ("afterward")—God would "pour out" his "Spirit on all flesh" (v. 28). People of both genders, of all ages, and from all socioeconomic classes would receive God's Spirit. The results would include prophesies, dreams, and visions. Moreover, changes would occur in God's creation itself, witnessing the new thing that God was doing. In a word, Pentecost would mark the division between the old covenant and the new.

The Event Predicted in the Gospels

John the Baptist's Prediction

John the Baptist in all four Gospels predicts that the Messiah will baptize the church with the Holy Spirit:

> I baptize with water for repentance, but he who is coming after me is mightier than I, whose sandals I am not worthy to carry. He will baptize you with the Holy Spirit and with fire. (Matt. 3:11)

> After me comes he who is mightier than I, the strap of whose sandals I am not worthy to stoop down and untie. I have baptized you with water, but he will baptize you with the Holy Spirit. (Mark 1:7–8)

> I baptize you with water, but he who is mightier than I is coming, the strap of whose sandals I am not worthy to untie. He will baptize you with the Holy Spirit and with fire. (Luke 3:16)

> I saw the Spirit descend from heaven like a dove, and it remained on him. I myself did not know him, but he who sent me to baptize with water said to me, "He on whom you see the Spirit descend and remain, this is he who baptizes with the Holy Spirit." And I have seen and have borne witness that this is the Son of God. (John 1:32–34)

The Gospels give us four different portraits of Christ; they are not identical. Therefore, few events in Jesus's ministry appear in all four Gospels. Even many significant things do not appear in all four, such as Jesus's genealogy and birth, his temptation, the transfiguration, famous sermons (e.g., the Sermon on the Mount, the farewell discourses, and the Olivet Discourse), Jesus's prayer in Gethsemane, and the Great Commission. Events that appear in all four Gospels, then, are very important. These include Jesus's baptism, the calling of the disciples, the feeding of the five thousand, the cleansing of the temple, the triumphal entry, and Jesus's betrayal, arrest, trials, crucifixion, death, burial, and resurrection. So, when all four Gospels record John the Baptist's prediction of Christ's baptizing the church with the Holy Spirit, that is noteworthy.

Luke, the author of the third Gospel and the book of Acts, includes another reference to Pentecost near the end of his Gospel. Jesus says:

> Everything written about me in the Law of Moses and the Prophets and the Psalms must be fulfilled. . . . Thus it is written, that the Christ should suffer and on the third day rise from the dead, and that repentance and forgiveness of sins should be proclaimed in his name to all nations, beginning from Jerusalem. You are witnesses of these things. And behold, I am sending the promise of my Father upon you. But stay in the city until you are clothed with power from on high. (Luke 24:44, 46–49)

Of course, the promise of the Father to be sent by Jesus is the Holy Spirit. And on the day of Pentecost his faithful followers were indeed "clothed with power from on high" (v. 49), as Acts 2 shows.

The Gospel of John's Witness to the Spirit

John's Gospel says little about Pentecost itself. Other than the Baptist's prediction, he records Jesus's acted prophecy of Pentecost in 20:21–23. But in at least five passages John treats the results of Pentecost. Therefore, a discussion of those passages belongs in this chapter. In his farewell discourses Jesus predicts that the Father and he will send the Spirit to perform vital ministries.

John 14:16–17

> And I will ask the Father, and he will give you another Helper, to be with you forever, even the Spirit of truth, whom the world cannot receive, because it neither sees him nor knows him. You know him, for he dwells with you and will be in you.

After telling the disciples to show their love for him by obeying him, Jesus promises that, when he returns to the Father, he will ask him to send the Holy Spirit to his disciples. The word rendered "Helper" by the ESV is difficult to translate. Perhaps it is best left untranslated (and transliterated from the Greek) as "Paraclete," with the contexts providing the various nuances of its meaning. Jesus is leaving the disciples to return to the Father, but will not abandon them. Instead, at his request the Father will send the Spirit to be with them forever.

The Father answers the Son's prayer at Pentecost when he pours out the Spirit on the church. He is God present with believers and with them forever. Jesus identifies him as "the Spirit of truth" because he will teach the disciples, as Jesus makes clear in three of the next four passages. The world system at odds with God rejects the Spirit because it believes only what it sees, and it cannot see him. The disciples also will not see the Spirit, but they will know him because he will indwell them individually and corporately. He will be in and with them forever.

John 14:25–26

> These things I have spoken to you while I am still with you. But the Helper, the Holy Spirit, whom the Father will send in my name, he will teach you all things and bring to your remembrance all that I have said to you.

Once more as Jesus prepares to leave the disciples, he promises not to leave them alone. The Father will send the Paraclete, identified as the Holy Spirit, when Jesus, the Mediator, returns to the Father. This means that the Holy Spirit will take Jesus's place. Jesus predicts that, after Pentecost, the Spirit will have a teaching ministry among the disciples. He will help them recall the words that Jesus has said to them. Here Jesus pre-authenticates the apostles' preaching and more. By implication he also pre-authenticates the New Testament, which is an application of much of that preaching to particular churches' and individuals' circumstances. Graham Cole agrees: "Thus there is a good case for seeing part of the fulfillment of the teaching about the Paraclete in the formation of the NT."[2]

John 15:26–27

> But when the Helper comes, whom I will send to you from the Father, the Spirit of truth, who proceeds from the Father, he will bear witness about me. And you also will bear witness, because you have been with me from the beginning.

Jesus's return to the Father will mean that Jesus will send the Paraclete from the Father to the disciples. Once more Jesus calls him the Spirit of truth, indicating that he will teach. The Spirit will testify about Jesus, and so will the disciples. The implication is that the Spirit will empower the disciples' witness to Jesus.

John 16:7–11

> Nevertheless, I tell you the truth: it is to your advantage that I go away, for if I do not go away, the Helper will not come to you. But if I go, I will send him to you. And when he comes, he will convict the world concerning sin and righteousness and judgment: concerning sin, because they do not believe in me; concerning righteousness, because I go to the Father, and you will see me no longer; concerning judgment, because the ruler of this world is judged.

Once more the coming of the Paraclete is tied to Jesus's return to heaven. Jesus's return triggers his sending the Spirit to the disciples. It is necessary that Jesus go so the Spirit can come in a new and powerful way at Pentecost. Here the Paraclete plays the role of a prosecuting attorney. The world will be put on trial, just as it put Jesus on trial. His trial was unjust, but this one will be just, because it will be conducted by the Holy Spirit himself, who, as we have seen, is "the Spirit of truth" (John 14:16; 15:26; 16:13).

In fact, the Holy Spirit's putting the world on trial should also be viewed as an extension of Jesus's ministry: "The world . . . hates me because I testify about it that its works are evil" (John 7:7; see also 15:22–24). It is clear that the Spirit will prosecute the guilty world, but the details of the "trial" are not as clear. Andreas Köstenberger's summary represents the majority view: "When the evidence is properly weighed, it turns out that it is the world that is guilty

---

[2]Graham A. Cole, *He Who Gives Life: The Doctrine of the Holy Spirit*, Foundations of Evangelical Theology (Wheaton, IL: Crossway, 2007), 187.

of the sin of unbelief, convicted on the basis of Christ's righteousness . . . and judged together with the supernatural 'ruler of this world.'"[3]

John 16:12–15

> I still have many things to say to you, but you cannot bear them now. When the Spirit of truth comes, he will guide you into all the truth, for he will not speak on his own authority, but whatever he hears he will speak, and he will declare to you the things that are to come. He will glorify me, for he will take what is mine and declare it to you. All that the Father has is mine; therefore I said that he will take what is mine and declare it to you.

Jesus has been teaching his disciples alone in the upper room, having closed the door on the world. He has taught them much concerning the Father, but they cannot bear any more now. Rather, Jesus must return to the Father and send the Spirit of truth to teach them in Jesus's place. The Spirit will teach on Jesus's authority even as Jesus has taught on earth on the Father's authority. In so doing he will bring glory to Jesus, even as Jesus has brought glory to the Father. When Jesus promises that the Spirit "will declare to you the things that are to come," he probably does not have predictive prophecy mainly in mind. Instead, the Spirit will teach about "events following Pentecost. . . . on helping the believing community understand their present situation in light of Jesus' by-then-past revelation of God."[4] This involves teaching Christians the meaning of Jesus's death, resurrection, and ascension, as well as Pentecost and the implications of these great events for their lives.

John 20:21–23

Thus in five passages in Jesus's farewell discourse he teaches about the ministries of the Spirit whom the Father and he will send at Pentecost. In addition John, toward the end of his Gospel, records an acted prophecy of Jesus:

> Jesus said to them again, "Peace be with you. As the Father has sent me, even so I am sending you." And when he had said this, he breathed on them and said to them, "Receive the Holy Spirit. If you forgive the sins of any, they are forgiven them; if you withhold forgiveness from any, it is withheld." (John 20:21–23)

---

[3] Andreas J. Köstenberger, *John*, Baker Exegetical Commentary on the New Testament (Grand Rapids: Baker Academic, 2004), 471. For another view, see D. A. Carson, *The Gospel According to John*, The Pillar New Testament Commentary (Grand Rapids: Eerdmans, 1991), 537–38.
[4] Köstenberger, *John*, 473–74.

Jesus, about to leave the disciples, promises them peace. He then links their ongoing ministry to his unique ministry. Many times the Fourth Gospel says that the Father sent the Son into the world (e.g., John 3:17; 5:38; 7:29; 12:44; 15:21). Now Jesus says that he is sending his disciples into the world on their own redemptive mission, which is an extension of his.

His breathing on the disciples (John 20:22) while saying "Receive the Holy Spirit" symbolically predicts their reception of the Spirit at Pentecost. His breathing on them recalls God's breathing into Adam the breath of life (Gen. 2:7). Christ's action thus portrays Pentecost as the beginning of the new creation of God in the church. When Jesus sends the Spirit to the disciples at Pentecost, he equips them for the ministry of the forgiveness of sins through the preaching of the gospel (John 20:23).

The Event Occurring in the Acts of the Apostles

John the Baptist's Prophecy Again

The coming of the Spirit at Pentecost is so important to the book of Acts that immediately after his introduction, Luke records Jesus's words to his disciples: he "ordered them . . . to wait for the promise of the Father, which, he said, 'you heard from me; for John baptized with water, but you will be baptized with the Holy Spirit not many days from now'" (Acts 1:5).

Luke thus forges a strong link between John the Baptist's prophecy in the beginning of Luke's Gospel (Luke 3:16) and Jesus's words at the end of that Gospel (22:49) and at the beginning of Acts (Acts 1:4–5). The Baptist predicted that the Messiah would baptize the church with the Holy Spirit, and in Acts 2 he does just that. Jesus told his disciples that he would send them the promise of the Father, and in Acts 2 he makes good on his word. The coming of the Holy Spirit at Pentecost is the work of the Messiah Jesus.

Moreover, Jesus's next words about the coming of the Spirit outline the book of Acts. Dennis Johnson is correct: the gospel will spread through three phases "in Jerusalem (chaps. 1–7), through Judea and Samaria (chaps. 8–12), to the last part of the earth (chaps. 13–28)."[5] The disciples are not to try to predict the time of Jesus's return. Rather, he promises them, "You will receive power when the Holy Spirit has come upon you, and you will be my witnesses in Jerusalem and in all Judea and Samaria, and to the end of the earth" (Acts 1:8). Then Jesus ascends to heaven (v. 9).

---

[5]Dennis Johnson, *The Message of Acts in the History of Redemption* (Phillipsburg, NJ: P&R, 1997), 8.

The Day of Pentecost

The Jewish feast of Pentecost after Jesus's death and resurrection was like none other. The "devout men from every nation under heaven" (Acts 2:5), pilgrims who came to Jerusalem from across the Roman Empire, had no idea of the special thing God was going to do on this unique day. God worked through wind and fire. "Suddenly there came from heaven a sound like a mighty rushing wind, and it filled the house where they were sitting" (v. 2). Next, "divided tongues as of fire appeared to them and rested on each one of them" (v. 3). Through wind and fire God grabbed the attention of the apostles. He was preparing to do something momentous through them.

The wind and fire symbolized the coming of the Holy Spirit. The word translated "spirit" (πνεῦμα, *pneuma*) means "breath, wind, or spirit." God sent a mighty wind to indicate that he was about to pour out the Holy Wind of God upon the apostles. God would do this to proclaim the mighty works of Jesus in order to bring many people into his kingdom. How would he accomplish this? By filling the apostles with the Holy Spirit and giving them the ability to speak in languages they did not know, the very languages of the Pentecost pilgrims.

The Jewish pilgrims "were amazed and astonished, saying, 'Are not all these who are speaking Galileans? And how is it that we hear, each of us in his own native language? . . . We hear them telling in our own tongues the mighty works of God'" (vv. 7–8, 11). Peter answered their questions: "This is what was uttered through the prophet Joel" (v. 16). Peter then quoted the entire prophecy of Joel cited above. Given its importance, we repeat it here, as recorded in Acts:

> And in the last days it shall be, God declares,
> that I will pour out my Spirit on all flesh,
> and your sons and your daughters shall prophesy,
>   and your young men shall see visions,
>   and your old men shall dream dreams;
> even on my male servants and female servants
>   in those days I will pour out my Spirit, and they shall prophesy.
> And I will show wonders in the heavens above
>   and signs on the earth below,
>   blood, and fire, and vapor of smoke;
> the sun shall be turned to darkness
>   and the moon to blood,
>   before the great day of the Lord comes, the great and magnificent day.
> And it shall come to pass that everyone who calls upon the name of the
>   Lord shall be saved. (Acts 2:17–21)

Peter proceeded to preach Jesus to them—crucified and risen from the dead, in fulfillment of Old Testament prophecies. "This Jesus God raised up, and of that we are all witnesses. Being therefore exalted at the right hand of God, and having received from the Father the promise of the Holy Spirit, he has poured out this that you yourselves are seeing and hearing" (vv. 32–33).

It is crucial to understand that *Jesus* poured out the Spirit on the church on the day of Pentecost. He was the Messiah, the Christ, the Anointed One. He received the Spirit at his baptism in order eventually to give the Spirit to the church. The four Gospels record the most important of Jesus's saving deeds—his death and resurrection. But the Gospels do not record Jesus's pouring out the Spirit upon the church. That would wait until Acts 2. In fulfillment of Joel 2, God gave signs from heaven, signs for eye and ear, to rivet the people's attention on the apostles.

Peter cited Psalm 110:1 as proof that Jesus is alive at God's right hand (vv. 24–32). Then comes the zinger: "Let all the house of Israel therefore know for certain that God has made him both Lord and Christ, this Jesus whom you crucified" (v. 36). The result? The hearers "were cut to the heart" and asked the apostles what they should do (v. 37). Peter urged them to repent and believe in Jesus (expressed in baptism, v. 38). Three thousand people did (v. 41)!

Christ Gives the Spirit at Pentecost

Twice Joel predicted that Yahweh would send the Spirit. "I will pour out my Spirit on all flesh. . . . I will pour out my Spirit" (Joel 2:28–29; cf. Isa. 44:3; Ezek. 39:29). Although the New Testament largely understands the fulfillment of this prophecy as Jesus's work, the Father also plays an important role. Jesus himself implies this, "And behold, I am sending the promise of *my Father* upon you. But stay in the city until you are clothed with power from on high" (Luke 24:49). In John's Gospel the Spirit is sent by the Father and the Son.[6] Scripture, then, presents Pentecost in Trinitarian terms: the Father and Son send the Spirit to the church in newness and power.

Nevertheless, the giving of the Holy Spirit at Pentecost, predicted by Joel and the four Evangelists, is especially Jesus's deed. It is an act that he performs. It is as much an aspect of his saving work as dying for our sins and rising on the third day. Pentecost is properly understood only as a saving action of the Christ whereby he applies the benefits of his death and resurrection to the church. Pentecost is a unique and unrepeatable redemptive-historical deed of the Messiah. It is important to understand—Pentecost is as singular and unrepeatable

---

[6]See John 14:16, 18, 26, 28; 15:26; 16:7.

a work of Jesus, as is his being "delivered up for our trespasses and raised for our justification" (Rom. 4:25).

Acts does not elaborate on Pentecost. Instead it tells the results of that stunning event—the apostles were equipped by the Spirit to spread the gospel across the first-century world. The Holy Spirit "filled the entire house where" the 120 were (Acts 2:2). Moreover, "they were all filled with the Holy Spirit" (v. 4). The rest of Acts records the apostles and other Christian servants ministering powerfully and effectively, "filled with the Holy Spirit" (4:8, 31; 9:17; 13:9, 52) and "full of the Spirit" (6:3, 5; 7:55; 11:24), two expressions that appear to be synonymous.[7] These expressions point to the Spirit's powerfully equipping the believers to serve their ascended Lord.

The Spirit filled the apostles and enabled them to perform ministries of defending the faith (4:8), preaching (4:31), healing (9:17), supernaturally blinding enemies of the gospel (13:9–11), mercy (6:3–6), standing firm under persecution (7:54–56), and evangelism (11:23–24). Later Paul commands all Christians, "Be filled with the Spirit" (Eph. 5:18). Moreover, after Pentecost the apostles and other believers were guided by the Holy Spirit into the early church's mission. The Spirit directed the church's mission in the lives of individuals (e.g., Barnabas and Paul, Acts 13:2), in wisdom (e.g., at the Jerusalem council, 15:28), and in directing the apostolic mission (e.g., to Macedonia, 16:6–7).

In fulfillment of some of the details of the prophecy of Joel 2:28–32, Acts records the Spirit's leading the early Christians through visions and prophecies. This is seen in the lives of Ananias (Acts 9:10), Cornelius (10:3), Peter (10:10–16), Agabus (11:27–28), Paul and Barnabas (13:1), and Judas and Silas (15:32).

Christ's Sending the Spirit at Pentecost Saves

Christians have erred in two directions concerning Pentecost. Some have minimized its importance. They need to hear the wise words of Herman Bavinck: "After the creation and the incarnation, the outpouring of the Holy Spirit is the third great work of God."[8] Other Christians have missed the unique place of Pentecost in redemptive history and have wrongly regarded it as a pattern encouraging us to seek "a second blessing."[9] Both approaches are wrong.

---

[7] I acknowledge the aid of T. S. Caulley, "Holy Spirit," in Walter A. Elwell, ed., *Evangelical Dictionary of Theology*, 2nd ed. (Grand Rapids: Baker Academic, 2001), 569–70.

[8] Herman Bavinck, *Reformed Dogmatics*, vol. 3, *Sin and Salvation in Christ* (Grand Rapids: Baker, 2006), 500.

[9] Proof of this is beyond the scope of this volume. For solid treatments, see Anthony A. Hoekema, *Holy Spirit Baptism* (Grand Rapids: Eerdmans, 1972); and Sinclair B. Ferguson, *The Holy Spirit*, Contours of Christian Theology (Downers Grove, IL: InterVarsity, 1996), 79–92.

Pentecost is a unique event in which the risen, ascended Lord Jesus baptizes his church with the Holy Spirit once for all time, thereby accomplishing great things. Neither Acts nor the rest of the New Testament specifically tells how Pentecost saves. But if we view Jesus's ministry at Pentecost in light of the Bible's whole story, we learn several ways in which his giving the Spirit applies and extends his saving work:

- At Pentecost the Mediator publicly proclaims the new covenant.
- At Pentecost the risen Lord publicly inaugurates the new creation.
- At Pentecost the Christ publicly bestows the Spirit on the new community.

At Pentecost the Mediator Publicly Proclaims the New Covenant

Jesus is Mediator of the new covenant. The Old Testament promises find their fulfillment in Christ the Mediator of the new covenant. Isaiah (61:8) and Ezekiel (37:26) predict an "everlasting covenant," while Jeremiah (31:31) predicts "a new covenant." They all speak of the same reality characterized by blessing (Isa. 61:9), personal relationship with God, the forgiveness of sins (Jer. 31:33–34), the cleansing of sins, possession of the Spirit, and obedience (Ezek. 36:26–27). All of this is realized in Jesus, the "one mediator between God and men" (1 Tim. 2:5) and is especially revealed in the epistle to the Hebrews.

He is the mediator of a new covenant. (Heb. 9:15)

. . . Jesus, the mediator of a new covenant, and . . . the sprinkled blood. (Heb. 12:24)

The God of peace who brought again from the dead our Lord Jesus, the great shepherd of the sheep, by the blood of the eternal covenant . . . (Heb. 13:20)

Jesus, the Mediator of the new covenant, fulfills the Old Testament prophecies and ushers in the last days.

Jesus ratifies the new covenant by his death and resurrection. Christ's death and resurrection are essential prerequisites to the establishment of the new covenant. In fact, that covenant is ratified at his cross. While instituting the Lord's Supper, Jesus says, "This cup that is poured out for you is the new covenant in my blood" (Luke 22:20). Jesus here uses the figure of speech known as metonymy—the use of a word to signify something else that is closely identified with it. Jesus identifies the cup of the covenant with the covenant itself. When Jesus speaks of "the new covenant in my blood," blood signifies his violent death on the cross. The new covenant is *in* Jesus's blood because his death ratifies the covenant—it officially puts it into effect. Of course, Jesus's saving work is so great that its effects were experienced by Old Testament believers even before Jesus came to die and rise. But he had to actually come, die, and rise in order for the new covenant to be effective both before and after in redemptive history.

Matthew ties forgiveness to the cup and the blood: "And he took a cup . . . saying, '. . . this is my blood of the covenant, which is poured out for many for the forgiveness of sins'" (Matt. 26:27–28). The forgiveness promised by the Old Testament prophets has now been realized because atonement has been accomplished.

Many benefits accrue to the people of God as a result of Jesus's ratifying the new covenant. These include eternal life and strength to serve God. Because he is "the mediator of a new covenant," and because "a death has occurred that redeems them from the transgressions committed under the first covenant," Christians enjoy "the promised eternal inheritance" (Heb. 9:15). Eternal life in resurrected bodies on the new earth is our portion because Jesus our Mediator accomplished his saving work. Since Jesus's death and resurrection are inseparable, the author to the Hebrews asks that "the God of peace who brought again from the dead our Lord Jesus, the great shepherd of the sheep, by the blood of the eternal covenant, equip" the saints for doing God's will as he works in them (Heb. 13:20–21).

Jesus publicly proclaims the new covenant at Pentecost. The work needed to ratify the new covenant was performed by Christ in his death and resurrection. But this grand news was not broadcast until fifty days after his resurrection. Jesus, the Mediator of the new covenant, publicly heralded that covenant at Pentecost. He did this through the Holy Spirit, whom he poured out on his apostles. I say this for three reasons.

First, at Pentecost Jesus fulfilled the prophecy of John the Baptist. John baptized with water and predicted that the Messiah would baptize with the Holy Spirit (Matt. 3:11; Mark 1:7–8; Luke 3:16). Jesus recalled John's prophecy in Acts 1:5: "John baptized with water, but you will be baptized with the Holy Spirit not many days from now." And then Jesus baptized the church with the Spirit at Pentecost. The important point is that this is what the Old Testament prophets had predicted would happen in the last days at the dawning of the new covenant.

> I will pour my Spirit upon your offspring,
>   and my blessing on your descendants. (Isa. 44:3)

> And it shall come to pass afterward,
>> that I will pour out my Spirit on all flesh. . . .
>> . . . I will pour out my Spirit. (Joel 2:28–29)

And I will put my Spirit within you, and cause you to walk in my statutes and be careful to obey my rules. (Ezek. 36:27; cf. 39:29)

Jesus, the Mediator of the new covenant, fulfilled these Old Testament predictions, along with John the Baptist's, on the day of Pentecost. This is possible only because of his death and resurrection, which ratified the new covenant. But God had planned to announce that covenant with a public event. And Pentecost was that event. "Pentecost publicly marks the transition from the old to the new covenant."[10]

Second, Pentecost was Jesus's heralding the new covenant because Pentecost was the fulfillment of the Old Testament type of the tower of Babel. In Genesis 11 we read that "the whole earth had one language and the same words" (v. 1). Audacious humankind tried to build a tower to reach the heavens and make a name for itself to avoid being "dispersed over the face of the whole earth" (v. 4). God in anger confused the language of the people so they could not understand each other and had to disperse as he originally desired (vv. 7–9). Beginning in Genesis 12, God selected one people—Abraham and his descendants—to spread his covenant with the world.

Michael Williams helpfully contrasts Babel and Pentecost:

At Babel, man was confused to ignorance, for he no longer spoke a common language. But at Pentecost, mankind was amazed and confused to knowledge as they heard people from the far-flung corners of the empire communicate with one another. Rather than seeking to ascend a tower to the heavens and make a name for themselves as the people did at Babel, those gathered together at Pentecost praised God because the Spirit descended from heaven. . . . Luke includes in his account of Pentecost a table of nations (Acts 2:8–12), just as the Babel story follows a table of nations (Gen. 10:1–32). At Babel, God came to judge and scatter the nations into many tribes and tongues. At Pentecost, God comes to bless and scatter a new tribe, the church, who will take the gospel of the kingdom to many nations.[11]

Third, Pentecost was a proclamation of the new covenant because Scripture sets Pentecost over against the giving of the law at Mount Sinai. The new covenant

---

[10]Ferguson, *The Holy Spirit*, 57.
[11]Michael D. Williams, *Far as the Curse Is Found: The Covenant Story of Redemption* (Phillipsburg, NJ: P&R, 2005), 260–61.

supersedes the old. The New Testament itself establishes a parallel between the old covenant given at Sinai and the new covenant given by Jesus.

> For you have not come to what may be touched, a blazing fire and darkness and gloom and a tempest and the sound of a trumpet and a voice whose words made the hearers beg that no further messages be spoken to them. For they could not endure the order that was given, "If even a beast touches the mountain, it shall be stoned." Indeed, so terrifying was the sight that Moses said, "I tremble with fear." But you have come to Mount Zion and to the city of the living God, the heavenly Jerusalem, and to innumerable angels in festal gathering, and to the assembly of the firstborn who are enrolled in heaven, and to God, the judge of all, and to the spirits of the righteous made perfect, and to Jesus, the mediator of a new covenant, and to the sprinkled blood that speaks a better word than the blood of Abel. (Heb. 12:18–24)

In this description Mount Sinai (and the giving of the commandments) is contrasted with spiritual Mount Zion (God, angels, saints in heaven, and Jesus). The old covenant is associated with trembling and fear, the new covenant with celebration and joy. Of course, this contrast is not absolute. There is much joy among God's people in the Old Testament (cf. Psalm 100). But the joy of the Old Testament does not compare to the joy experienced by God's New Testament people. Why? The answer is simple: what makes the new covenant new is its Mediator, Jesus.

Sinclair Ferguson sums up the contrasts between Sinai and Pentecost:

> The revelation of God to Moses at Sinai had been accompanied by fire, wind and a divine tongue (Heb. 12:18–21). Moses had ascended the mountain. When he descended he had in his possession the Ten Commandments, the law of God. Christ too had recently ascended. At Pentecost he comes down, not with the law written on tablets of clay, but with the gift of the Spirit to write the law in the hearts of believers by his power to enable them to fulfill the law's commands. Thus the new covenant promise begins to be fulfilled (*cf.* Je. 31:31–34; Rom. 8:3–4; 2 Cor. 3:7–11).[12]

Even more could be said. Yahweh descends on Mount Sinai (Ex. 19:20); Jesus bestows the Spirit who descends on and fills the apostles (Acts 2:3–4). "As Moses experiences the glory and presence of the Lord (Ex. 24:16–18), now all the people of God experience that presence."[13] Plainly, when viewed with a

---

[12]Ferguson, *The Holy Spirit*, 61.
[13]Williams, *Far as the Curse Is Found*, 261.

wide-angle lens, the new covenant broadcast by Jesus at Pentecost replaces the old covenant of Moses at Sinai.

At Pentecost the Risen Lord Publicly Inaugurates the New Creation

The new creation will be fully revealed only in the end. Isaiah predicts that God will "create new heavens and a new earth" (Isa. 65:17; see also 66:22). Jesus foretells a "new world" (literally "regeneration") "when the Son of Man will sit on his glorious throne" and believers "will inherit eternal life" (Matt. 19:28). Paul prophesies the creation's being "set free from its bondage to corruption" to obtain "freedom" when believers will experience "the redemption of [their] bodies" (Rom. 8:21, 23). Peter anticipates "new heavens and a new earth in which righteousness dwells" (2 Pet. 3:13). Finally, John sees in a vision the fulfillment of these many expectations: "Then I saw a new heaven and a new earth, for the first heaven and the first earth had passed away" (Rev. 21:1). At this time "death shall be no more, neither shall there be mourning, nor crying, nor pain anymore, for the former things have passed away" (v. 4). Scripture is plain: the full manifestation of the new heavens and earth is still future. But like every other major eschatological theme, the new creation is "already" as well as "not yet."

Jesus begins the new creation by his resurrection. After showing Christ's preeminence over creation (as its Creator and heir), Paul shows that Christ also is preeminent over his church: "And he is the head of the body, the church" (Col. 1:16, 18). When Paul next says that "he is the beginning" (v. 18), he refers to Genesis 1:1: "In *the beginning*, God created the heavens and the earth." Christ is Lord over the creation because in the beginning he was God's agent in creating it. He is Lord over his church because it is a part of his *re-creation*; he is the beginning of the new creation. He is the source of life for the church specifically as "the firstborn from the dead" (v. 18). Jesus's resurrection enables him to regenerate each of the church's members. In a word, his resurrection initiates the new creation.

Furthermore, "God was pleased . . . through him to reconcile to himself all things" (v. 20). Here "all things" include angels, saved human beings, and the heavens and earth. That angels are involved is shown when verse 16 refers to "all things in heaven . . . invisible, whether thrones or dominions or rulers or authorities." Christ reconciles evil angels by subjugating them to maintain his peaceable kingdom (cf. Col. 2:15). That human beings are reconciled is shown by the two verses that follow Colossians 1:20: "And you, who once were alienated and hostile in mind, doing evil deeds, he has now reconciled in his body of flesh by his death" (vv. 21–22).

That the heavens and earth are reconciled is shown by a comparison of verses 16 and 20: "By him all things were created, in heaven and on earth" (v. 16); "God was pleased . . . through him to reconcile to himself all things, whether on earth or in heaven" (v. 20). As God incarnate Christ reconciled "all things," all created reality. Douglas Moo's comments on Colossians 1:20 are correct: "God's work in Christ has in view a reclamation of the entire universe, tainted as it is by human sin (Rom. 8:19–22)."[14] It is important to note that as Christ is "the beginning" of the new creation in his role of "the firstborn from the dead," he reconciles all things "making peace by the blood of his cross" (Col. 1:18, 20). Christ crucified and risen is the peacemaker who begins the new creation. In light of the Bible's total message this universal reconciliation does not entail an absolute universalism. Not all human beings will be saved. Scripture clearly teaches that eternal punishment in hell awaits the lost.[15]

Jesus publicly inaugurates the new creation at Pentecost. Though the new creation will be fully disclosed only at the end, Christ began the new creation when he died and arose. But it was not *publicly* manifested then. Its public manifestation occurred on the day of Pentecost. I say this for two reasons, found in John 20 and Acts 2. Neither John 20:21–23, which tells of Jesus's acted prophecy, nor Acts 2:1–2, which reports the "mighty rushing wind" of Pentecost, *says* that it points to the new creation. But both of these passages *show* that a reference to the new creation is intended.

Jesus's acted prophecy in John 20:21–23 recalls Genesis 2:7. In the second post-resurrection appearance of Christ to his disciples recorded by John, Jesus promises them peace. He then says, "As the Father has sent me, even so I am sending you" (John 20:21). He thereby connects his followers' ongoing ministry to his unique ministry. That the Father sent the Son into the world is a favorite theme of the Fourth Gospel. Now their risen Lord says that he is sending his disciples into the world on their own redemptive mission as an extension of his.

He then performs a prophetic action to equip them for their mission. John writes: "And when he had said this, he breathed on them and said to them, 'Receive the Holy Spirit. If you forgive the sins of any, they are forgiven them; if you withhold forgiveness from any, it is withheld'" (John 20:22–23). Jesus's breathing on the disciples recalls God's breathing into Adam the breath of life:

---

[14]Douglas J. Moo, *The Letters to the Colossians and to Philemon*, The Pillar New Testament Commentary (Grand Rapids: Eerdmans, 2008), 137.

[15]See Christopher W. Morgan and Robert A. Peterson, eds., *Hell Under Fire* (Grand Rapids: Zondervan, 2004) for a scholarly and compassionate defense of the traditional doctrine of hell.

"Then the LORD God formed the man of dust from the ground and breathed into his nostrils the breath of life, and the man became a living creature" (Gen. 2:7).

Even as God the Creator granted his human creature life by a divine act of in-breathing, so the risen Christ, the re-Creator, by his prophetic act, promises to give spiritual life to his disciples. Jesus symbolically predicts their reception of the Spirit at Pentecost. Christ's action of breathing on his disciples while saying "Receive the Holy Spirit" foretells that Pentecost will be the beginning of the new creation of God.[16] Furthermore, his words, "If you forgive the sins of any, they are forgiven them; if you withhold forgiveness from any, it is withheld" (John 20:23), tie the new age of Pentecost to the apostles' preaching the gospel. When Jesus sends the disciples the Spirit at Pentecost, he equips them for the ministry of forgiving sins through preaching.

The wind of Acts 2:2 recalls Genesis 1:2. The sounds of Pentecost point to another Old Testament connection. Luke says that on the day of Pentecost the disciples were gathered together in the same house. He then reports, "And suddenly there came from heaven a sound like a mighty rushing wind, and it filled the entire house where they were sitting" (Acts 2:1–2). Ferguson notes, "The 'sound like the blowing of a violent wind' echoes the imagery of the powerful operation of the *ruach elohim* [Spirit of God] of creation (Gn. 1:2), suggesting that the event about to take place marks the beginning of a new world order."[17]

Ferguson is perceptive. Luke reports aspects of the events of Pentecost to drive readers to the Old Testament for a full understanding of his message. Here his words remind careful readers of the first words of the Old Testament: "In the beginning, God created the heavens and the earth. The earth was without form and void, and darkness was over the face of the deep. And the Spirit of God was hovering over the face of the waters" (Gen. 1:1–2).

It is important to note that one Hebrew word means, "breath, wind, spirit, or Spirit," and that the same meanings hold true for one Greek word. So, when Luke refers to the "mighty rushing wind" that filled the house, he is symbolically speaking of the mighty Spirit of God that Jesus the Christ was pouring on his apostles. This was as God intended. He sent the mighty wind, he and Jesus sent the Spirit, and by that Spirit God guided Luke to write Acts.

What is the significance of the wind in Acts 2:2 recalling the Spirit of God of Genesis 1:2? Dennis Johnson answers well: "The sound of wind signaled the arrival of the Spirit, who makes the dead alive. The 'wind' was the breath of

---

[16]Ferguson agrees: "Jesus breathed on his disciples as God breathed the breath of life into Adam (Gen. 2:7). The symbolism is that of the beginning of a new creation." *The Holy Spirit*, 65.
[17]Ibid., 60.

God, breathed into the new humanity. Pentecost was a new creation. . . . The coming of the Spirit at Pentecost marked a major step in God's restoration of his creation in the last days."[18]

The rest of the New Testament bears this out. The healings in Acts point forward to the perfect "healing" in the resurrection on the last day. Consider the healing of the lame man in Acts 3:6–8. "At the dawn of the last days, selective and temporary previews of complete, eternal restoration (the leaping of a lame man) provided divine confirmation of the apostles' testimony about Jesus (Acts 4:30; Heb. 2:3–4)."[19] In the Epistles, we learn of regeneration, God's granting spiritual life to those who were spiritually dead (e.g., Eph. 2:1–7). Believers thus now have eternal life in mortal bodies. A day is coming, however, when, following their resurrection, they will have eternal life in immortal bodies (Rom. 8:11; 1 Cor. 15:52–53).

Dennis Johnson is eloquent: "Now things 'fall apart,' and suffering and death dog our steps, but the reversal of cosmic entropy has begun in the resurrection of Jesus. Faith in the name of Jesus, germinating from the Spirit's witness, is the seed from which will grow the restoration of all things."[20] "Not yet" are the new heaven and the new earth. But because Jesus died and rose again, the new creation has "already" begun, and he publicly inaugurated it on the day of Pentecost by sending the Spirit in a new and powerful way.

At Pentecost the Christ Publicly Bestows the Spirit on the New Community

The Gospel of John presents a difficult word: "As yet the Spirit had not been given, because Jesus was not yet glorified" (John 7:39). The best texts read literally, "For the Spirit was not yet because Jesus was not yet glorified." Of course John does not mean that the Holy Spirit did not exist before Jesus's glorification. He also does not deny that the Holy Spirit worked in the world previously, because he records some of that work (e.g., John 1:32–33; 3:6, 8, 34). Rather, John here points to the same reality of which Jesus speaks in John 14:16–17, 26; 15:26; 16:7–15—Jesus on the day of Pentecost giving the Holy Spirit to the people of God in a new and powerful manner. This involves at least four truths.

The fullness of salvation arrives. The people of God were always saved by grace through faith. Before the cross, God provided forgiveness based upon the work of Christ to come. And God circumcised the hearts of believing Israelites by his Spirit (Deut. 10:16; 30:6; Jer. 4:4; Acts 7:51; Rom. 2:28–29). So, Jesus's death and

---

[18]Johnson, *The Message of Acts in the History of Redemption,* 58.
[19]Ibid., 66.
[20]Ibid.

resurrection did not bring salvation for the first time. Instead, his achievement was so great as to be the basis for salvation at any time in redemptive history. Similarly, Pentecost does not represent the beginning of the Holy Spirit's work in the world. Instead, it represents the work of salvation in a grander and fuller way than previously. This is true because the risen, exalted Christ sends the Spirit as *his* Spirit, the Spirit of Christ.

Sinclair Ferguson captures this truth:

> Until the exaltation of Christ, the Spirit of God could not be received in his specific economic identity as the Spirit of the ascended Christ. By means of Christ's exaltation (which for John seems to include his victorious death), he would be. ... During the days of his humiliation the Spirit of Christ was on Christ, and therefore in this sense, "with" the disciples. But at the exaltation, Christ would breathe his Spirit on his disciples. He would now indwell them in his identity as the Spirit of the exalted Saviour.[21]

A huge transition in redemptive history occurred at Pentecost. And this affects believers' relationship with the Son and the Spirit. Faith in Christ was never so explicit. Only "now Jesus can be believed on as the risen, vindicated Lord."[22] And the Spirit comes with newness and power. This is because "beginning with the Pentecost converts themselves, the receiving of the Spirit in full new-covenant blessing has been one aspect of their conversion and new birth."[23] It is with good reason, then, that Herman Bavinck titles a section of his systematic theology "The fullness of salvation as the Spirit's gift."[24] That is exactly what the Spirit of the exalted Christ brings—the fullness of salvation. And that salvation manifests itself in many ways, including heretofore-unprecedented witness.

New power for witness is given. How are we to account for the fact that more people were saved during the week following Pentecost than in Jesus's entire three and one-half years of public ministry? By pointing to the Spirit of Christ's filling and empowering the apostles and their converts. Moses longed for the day of Pentecost: "Would that all the LORD's people were prophets, that the LORD would put his Spirit on them!" (Num. 11:29). Now that day has arrived, and great power has come upon the disciples, enabling them to speak for God and more, as Wayne Grudem aptly summarizes:

---

[21] Ferguson, *The Holy Spirit*, 68.
[22] Cole, *He Who Gives Life*, 195.
[23] Ibid., 196.
[24] Bavinck, *Sin and Salvation in Christ*, 504.

The disciples, however, do not receive this full new covenant empowering for ministry until the Day of Pentecost. . . . This new covenant power gave the disciples more effectiveness in their witness and their ministry (Acts 1:8; Eph. 4:8, 11–13), much greater power for victory over the influence of sin in the lives of all believers (. . . Rom. 6:11–14; 8:13–14; Gal. 2:20; Phil. 3:10), and power for victory over Satan and demonic forces that would attack believers (2 Cor. 10:3–4; Eph. 1:19–21; 6:10–18; 1 John 4:4).[25]

This should come as no surprise because this is the very thing that Jesus promised them: "You will receive power when the Holy Spirit has come upon you, and you will be my witnesses in Jerusalem and in all Judea and Samaria, and to the end of the earth" (Acts 1:8). As a result of the Spirit's coming at Pentecost the apostles and others ministered "filled with the Holy Spirit" (Acts 4:31; 6:5; 7:54; etc.). The filling of the Spirit and the power for evangelism resulted in something else new—a new community of God's people.

The new community is constituted. The making of a new community is already hinted at by the number of persons "among the brothers"—"the company of persons was in all about 120" (Acts 1:15). I. H. Marshall is helpful: "The number 120 . . . was the minimum number of men required to 'establish a community with its own council,' so that these early Christians were able to 'form a new community.'"[26]

Old Testament Israel was supposed to be a light to the nations but largely failed to fulfill that role. Now one Israelite, even Jesus the Christ, the true light of the nations, pours out his Spirit on the Jewish apostles, and they eventually become a light to the nations. Acts records especially Paul's powerful ministry among the Gentiles. Ferguson explains, "On the Day of Pentecost that new community became the sphere in which the eschatological reversal of the effects of sin began to appear in a reconciled people consisting of both Jew and Gentile, possessing one Lord, one faith and one baptism (Eph. 4:1ff.), united by one Spirit."[27]

Christ formed a new community, the New Testament church, when he gave the Spirit at Pentecost. Another important way of speaking of the new community of God's people is with temple imagery. At Pentecost the church becomes God's temple. Herman Bavinck offers this summary:

---

[25] Wayne Grudem, *Systematic Theology: An Introduction to Biblical Doctrine* (Grand Rapids: Zondervan, 1994), 771.

[26] I. Howard Marshall, *The Acts of the Apostles*, Tyndale New Testament Commentary (Grand Rapids: Eerdmans, 1980), 64.

[27] Ferguson, *The Holy Spirit*, 60.

But it was only on the day of Pentecost that he made the church into his temple, a temple he perpetually sanctifies, builds up, and never again abandons. The indwelling of the Holy Spirit confers on the church of Christ an independent existence. It is now no longer enclosed within the circle of Israel's existence as a people and within the boundaries of Palestine but lives independently by the Spirit, who lives within it, and expands over the whole earth and reaches out to all peoples. God by his Spirit now moves from the temple on Zion to take up residence in the body of Christ's church, which is consequently, born on this very day as a mission and world church.[28]

Jesus's central saving deeds were his death and resurrection. They were so efficacious as to produce awesome and permanent effects in other saving deeds. One of those deeds was Pentecost, when Christ baptized his church with the Holy Spirit. Pentecost was Jesus's unrepeatable redemptive-historical act. There he as Mediator publicly heralded the new covenant. As risen Lord he publicly began the new creation. As the Christ he publicly gave the Spirit to his church, thereby constituting it as the new community.

---

[28]Bavinck, *Sin and Salvation in Christ*, 501.

Incarnation
Sinless Life
Death
Resurrection
Ascension
Session
Pentecost
Intercession
Second Coming

Chapter

Christ's Intercession

> Therefore, in order to be the perfect high priest who intercedes for us, [Jesus] must be God as well as man. He must be one who in his divine nature can both know all things and bring them into the presence of the Father. Yet because he became and continues to be man he has the right to represent us before God and he can express his petitions from the viewpoint of a sympathetic high priest, one who understands by experience what we go through.
>
> Therefore, Jesus is the only person in the whole universe for all eternity who can be such a heavenly high priest, one who is truly God and truly man, exalted forever above the heavens.[1]

Wayne Grudem expresses well the unique qualifications of Jesus Christ, our great High Priest, to make intercession for us. And he captures Christ's current ministry in heaven of praying for his people. But Grudem separates Jesus's presentation of his sacrifice from his intercession (although he includes that presentation on the preceding page of his systematic theology). This chapter will join the two aspects of Christ's saving intercession—presenting his finished sacrifice in heaven and praying for us according to the will of God.

The saving work of Christ does not conclude with the ascension, session, and Pentecost. The ascension is the transition from his earthly ministry to his heavenly one. When Christ ascends to heaven and sits at the right hand of God,

---

[1] Wayne Grudem, *Systematic Theology: An Introduction to Biblical Doctrine* (Grand Rapids: Zondervan, 1994), 628.

he assumes his place as our exalted prophet, priest, and king. Specifically, as our priest he is now interceding for us: "Who is to condemn? Christ Jesus is the one who died—more than that, who was raised—who is at the right hand of God, who indeed is interceding for us" (Rom. 8:34). Having made the final sacrifice for sin, our High Priest has now entered into the heavenly tabernacle to perform the second half of his priestly work, to make intercession.

Like his incarnation, sinless life, death, resurrection, and ascension, his intercession saves us, too. Consider the words of Hebrews 7:25: "Consequently, he is able to save to the uttermost those who draw near to God through him, since he always lives to make intercession for them." Jesus is a perfect Savior because he forever lives to intercede for his people. In order to understand Christ's intercession as part of his saving work, we must consider the office of priest and the pictures of sacrifice and sanctuary as they are presented in the Bible. This means that we must study the Old Testament pictures and promises of his intercession, and the New Testament previews and presentations of his intercession. In doing so, we shall discover that Christ saves his people, not only by sacrificing his life for them, but also by offering himself to the Father in their behalf and by effectively praying for them that they might persevere until final salvation.

Old Testament Pictures and Promises of Christ's Intercession

Since Christ's intercession is a function of his high priestly work, we will investigate the Old Testament pictures of the high priest and his work on the Day of Atonement. We will also study the specific promises that the Messiah will be a priest who, having made sacrifice for sins, will make intercession for his people.

Leviticus 16

We read about the work of the high priest's on the Day of Atonement in Leviticus 16. The high priest enters the Most Holy Place once every year to make atonement for his sins and the sins of the people. He is permitted to come before the Lord not "at any time" (v. 2) but only once a year on the Day of Atonement. God provides a specific procedure through his prophet Moses for the high priest to perform.

This procedure begins with the high priest preparing his body for his priestly duties. He first bathes himself and then clothes himself with the priestly garments. These garments are made of linen and include the undergarment, the holy coat, the sash around the waist, and the turban for the head (v. 4).

After the high priest cleans and clothes his body, he then prepares the Most Holy Place for his priestly work. He is required to bring incense into the Most

Holy Place and offer it on the fire before the mercy seat. In this way the whole sanctuary fills with smoke, preventing the high priest from seeing God and forfeiting his life (vv. 12–13).

The final step of the procedure concerns the sin and burnt offerings that the high priest must perform. These offerings contain two important stages. The first stage takes place outside the sanctuary, and the second stage takes place inside the sanctuary in the Most Holy Place. Both the priest's offering for himself and his offering for the people require these two stages.

The high priest first makes the sacrifice outside the sanctuary. He then takes the blood of the sacrifice into the sanctuary and sprinkles the blood on the mercy seat. He does this both in the case of the sacrifice made for his sins and in the case of the sacrifice made for the sins of the people (vv. 14–15).

It is important for us to grasp these two stages of the high priest's work. This is because the most important contribution of this Old Testament picture is that the work of atonement is not complete until the blood of the sacrificial victim, which is slaughtered outside the sanctuary, is carried into the Most Holy Place and offered on the mercy seat in the presence of God. The high priest performs his work without *and* within the sanctuary. He first makes the sacrifice, and then he presents the finished sacrifice in the presence of God. The two stages of his work are inseparable components of the one atonement event.

Such then is the Old Testament picture of the high priest and his work on the Day of Atonement. But where does the Old Testament promise that the Messiah will be a priest who engages in the work of sacrifice and intercession? Having explored the pictures of high priest, sacrifice, sanctuary, and offering, we now turn to the Old Testament promises of the high priest and his work of intercession.

Psalm 110:4

Psalm 110 is the starting point when investigating the Old Testament promise of a priest. The psalm is without question messianic because it promises a Messiah who will be not only a king but also a priest (see New Testament citations of Ps. 110:1, 4, etc.). But how can the Messiah be both king and priest? The Old Testament predicts that the Messiah will be from the line of Judah, but the Old Testament priests are from the line of Aaron. It is thus impossible for a single person to be both king and priest, at least, a priest from the line of Aaron (cf. Heb. 7:14). However, in Psalm 110 David makes it clear that the Messiah will be a priest after another order. He will be "a priest forever after the order of Melchizedek" (v. 4). Melchizedek is the priest-king who mysteriously appears in

Genesis 14:17–24 and does not appear again in the biblical record until Psalm 110. As both priest and king (Gen. 14:18) Melchizedek provides the perfect pattern of the Messiah who will occupy both offices. Of course, this theme is developed at length by the author of Hebrews (Hebrews 7).

The unique contribution of Psalm 110 is that it says the Messiah will be both king and priest. Even though we might expect the Messiah to fulfill the Old Testament offices of prophet, priest, and king, we would not be able to explain from the Old Testament how the Messiah is both king and priest without this psalm. The office of prophet is an occasional office in the Old Testament and not associated with a particular lineage. So it presents no problems in this regard.

It is also important to note that Psalm 110 presents the Messiah enthroned and exalted. Consider verse 1:

> The LORD says to my Lord:
>   "Sit at my right hand,
> until I make your enemies your footstool."

The enthroned king is also the exalted priest.

> You are a priest forever
>   after the order of Melchizedek. (v. 4)

So then, we learn from Psalm 110 that the Messiah will be both an enthroned king and exalted priest. As a priest the Messiah must perform priestly work. Does the Old Testament make promises about the Messiah's priestly work? The key passage that promises the priestly work of the Messiah is the suffering Servant prophecy in Isaiah 52:13–53:12. The prophecy culminates by combining the two stages of Messiah's high priestly work: sacrifice and intercession.

Isaiah 53:12

Isaiah 53:12 says,

> Therefore I will divide him a portion with the many,
>   and he shall divide the spoil with the strong,
> because he poured out his soul to death
>   and was numbered with the transgressors;
> yet he bore the sin of many,
>   and makes intercession for the transgressors.

Isaiah 52:13 and 53:12 form an inclusion. The suffering Servant prophecy begins and ends with the exaltation of the Servant. In between the two exaltation book-ends there is a vivid description of the suffering and sacrifice of the Servant. Thus Isaiah 52:13–53:12 is a prophecy about the humiliation and exaltation of the Lord's Servant. In the terms of Leviticus 16 this suffering Servant prophecy concerns both the Servant's sacrifice outside the sanctuary and his intercession inside the sanctuary. Theologically, the prophecy concerns his priestly work both in the state of humiliation and in the state of exaltation. It is a relevant Old Testament text, then, for our study of Christ's intercession.

Even though Isaiah 52:13 and 53:12 speak of the exaltation of the Lord's Servant, some reputable commentators like Franz Delitzsch[2] have suggested that the phrase "and makes intercession for the transgressors" in 53:12 speaks of the Servant's intercession in the state of humiliation, not exaltation. In terms of Christ's saving work this would mean that the statement refers exclusively to Christ's intercession from the cross (Luke 23:34). However, even though the phrase "he makes intercession for the transgressors" applies to the intercession from the cross in the state of humiliation, Isaiah encourages us to look at the Servant's intercession in a broader sense. This can be seen by looking at the tense of the verbs.

> Yet he *bore* the sin of many
> and *makes intercession* for the transgressors.[3]

In light of the context concerning the Servant's exaltation as a reward for his suffering, it appears that the work of intercession extends beyond his suffering.

Also, if Isaiah is drawing upon the work of the high priest, he would understand that the work of intercession takes place *after*, not during or before, the sacrifice. Edward J. Young observes, "Here again there is reflection upon the priestly work of the servant, who pleads before God the merit and virtue of his atoning work as the only ground of acceptance of the transgressors for whom he dies."[4] Thus Isaiah 53:12 promises the Messiah's intercession for his people as an exalted priest.

The Old Testament provides a composite picture and a clear promise of a coming priest who makes a sacrifice for the sins of the people, and then, having

---

[2]Franz Delitzsch, *Isaiah*, Commentary on the Old Testament (Peabody, MA: Hendrickson, 2006), 522–24.

[3]The ESV is the only major translation that reveals the difference between the Hebrew verb tenses at this point. The KJV, NASB, and NIV disguise the difference between the perfect and imperfect: "Yet he bore [נָשָׂא] the sin of many and made intercession [יַפְגִּיעַ] for the transgressors."

[4]Edward J. Young, *The Book of Isaiah*, vol. 3 (Grand Rapids: Eerdmans, 1972), 359.

made the sacrifice, intercedes for them. As the messianic king he is a descendant from the house of David, but as the messianic priest he is a priest forever after the order of Melchizedek. In holding the office of priest, the Messiah performs his work in a manner comparable to, though not identical to, the work of the high priest on the Day of Atonement. Such work contains two distinct, yet inseparable stages: the sacrifice performed outside the sanctuary and the sacrifice presented inside the sanctuary. Finally, the Old Testament promises a coming suffering Servant who performs the role of both giving his life as a sacrifice and making intercession on the basis of his sacrifice. As we enter the New Testament, then, we observe that the categories for Christ's intercession are ready for apostolic development.

New Testament Previews of Christ's Intercession

The Gospel accounts provide previews of Christ's intercession. While the Gospels focus on Christ's earthly ministry, they anticipate his heavenly ministry. These accounts of Christ's interceding for his people in the days of his flesh (cf. Heb. 5:7) provide a lens for viewing his heavenly intercession as our exalted High Priest.

Luke 22:31–32

In the Gospel of Luke there is an interchange between Jesus and Peter that is not found in the other Gospels. Shortly before Jesus tells Peter that he will deny him three times, Jesus says to Peter, "Simon, Simon, behold, Satan demanded to have you, that he might sift you like wheat, but I have prayed for you that your faith may not fail. And when you have turned again, strengthen your brothers" (Luke 22:31–32). Since Jesus prays for Peter, and praying for others is one aspect of intercession, this passage is relevant to our study of Christ's intercession. It is, however, only a preview because it speaks of Christ's intercession on earth, not his intercession in heaven. But what can we learn about Christ's intercessory prayers for his people from this preview?

First, we learn that the occasion of Christ's intercession is Satan's attack on believers' faith. Since the "you" that appears twice in verse 31 is plural, it is evident that Satan planned to attack the disciples in general. However, the transition from the plural to the singular "you" that appears four times in verse 32 magnifies Satan's assault on Peter in particular. When Jesus is delivered to be crucified, Satan attacks Peter's faith, and he tempts him to deny Christ. Peter then succumbs to Satan's temptation, and he renounces Christ three times. Satan's ultimate goal in tempting Peter to reject Christ is the destruction of Peter's faith. Because of

Satan's opposition, Christ prays that Peter's faith may not fail. Peter's faith does not ultimately fail, precisely because Christ prays for him.

The second truth we learn about Christ's intercession is that it ensures believers' continuance in the faith. We see this in two ways. First, Christ prays for Peter to persevere in the faith, and since the Father always hears his Son (John 11:42), we correctly assume that his request is granted. Second, and perhaps more relevant to the context in Luke, Jesus's words assume that Peter will persevere in the faith. In saying, "When you have turned again," he implies that even though Peter will deny Christ, Peter will later repent and encourage his fellow disciples. Christ's intercession, then, guarantees that Peter will persevere until final salvation.

Thus in Luke 22:31–32 we have a preview of Christ's intercession. In the way that Christ effectively prays for Peter's perseverance because of Satan's attack, he prays continually and effectively for all believers to continue in the faith and arrive at final salvation. This is not the only preview of Christ's intercession in the Gospel of Luke. There is another account, which is more difficult to connect with Christ's heavenly intercession.

Luke 23:34

Luke 23:34 presents a problem for our understanding of Christ's intercession. When Jesus prays for his enemies, he says, "Father, forgive them, for they know not what they do." Jesus intercedes for his assailants from the cross. The allusion to Isaiah 53:12 is unmistakable:

> Yet he bore the sin of many,
>   and makes intercession for the transgressors.

It is also doubtless that Christ's intercession is the function of his priestly role. However, Lutheran and Reformed theologians disagree on the implications of this verse in relationship to the objects of Christ's intercession. Is Christ's intercession particular, that is, for the elect alone (the Reformed view)? Or is Christ's intercession particular *and* universal (the Lutheran view)?

Complicating the issue even further is the fact that John 11:42 teaches that Christ's prayers are always effective. Jesus says that his Father always hears him. When Jesus speaks of the Father hearing him, he means that his Father hears and answers him affirmatively (John 11:41). If we apply Jesus's words in John 11:42 to Luke 23:34, this would mean that everyone for whom Jesus prayed "Father, forgive them" will be forgiven. Since universal salvation is not a biblical teaching,[5] we conclude that the Reformed view is surely correct, though there is still more to consider.

The Reformed view is supported by two additional observations. First, this is the only New Testament text that Lutherans present in favor of a universal intercession. All other New Testament Scriptures speak of a particular intercession. For example, in the two New Testament passages (Rom. 8:34; Heb. 7:25) that use the verb "intercede"[6] the intercession is made exclusively for believers. In Romans 8:34 Christ is now interceding "for us." In context the expression "for us" refers to God's elect (Rom. 8:33). In Hebrews 7:25 Christ intercedes for "those who draw near to God through him." Certainly such language applies only to believers. In any event, the burden of proof is placed on the Lutheran theologian to establish a universal intercession from a single passage alone.

Second, if we consider also that the best and earliest manuscript evidence does not contain Jesus's prayer in Luke 23:34, then we have even stronger grounds for omitting this verse from our exposition of Christ's intercession. Although this verse has a place in church tradition, it should not be the basis of a developed theology about Christ's universal intercession.

We conclude, then, that Luke 23:34 does not require us to believe that in addition to Christ's particular intercession, Christ intercedes universally.

John 14:16

The Upper Room Discourse in the Gospel of John provides a fuller preview of Christ's heavenly intercession than does Luke's account. Although John's preview culminates in Jesus's High Priestly Prayer in John 17, we must be careful not to overlook John 14:16, where Jesus connects the Father's giving of the Holy Spirit with the Son's ministry of intercessory prayer. Jesus says, "And I will ask the Father, and he will give you another Helper, to be with you forever" (v. 16). Since I have already discussed the connection between the ascension of Christ and the gift of the Spirit (cf. John 16:7), I will not repeat that discussion here.[7] However, John 14:16 remains relevant to our treatment of Christ's heavenly intercession. Essentially, Jesus tells his disciples that they will receive the Spirit because he will ask the Father to bestow the Spirit. But when will Jesus ask the Father to give his disciples the Holy Spirit? In light of the aforementioned connection between the ascension and the gift of the Spirit, it seems that Jesus

---

[5]The biblical arguments against universalism are beyond the scope of this chapter. For a refutation of universalism, see J. I. Packer, "Will Everyone Ultimately Be Saved?," in Christopher W. Morgan and Robert A. Peterson, eds., *Hell Under Fire* (Grand Rapids: Zondervan, 2004), 169–94.

[6]Greek, ἐντυγχάνειν (*entynchanein*).

[7]See pp. 158–59.

will offer this prayer in heaven in the state of exaltation (cf. John 7:39; 16:7). In other words, John 14:16 is more than a preview of Christ's heavenly intercession. It is a prediction on the lips of Christ himself that when he ascends to heaven, he will intercede for his people and ask the Father to provide his Holy Spirit to help them.

John 17

The clearest preview of Christ's intercession is found in the so-called High Priestly Prayer in John 17. As we witness the Son of God speaking to his Father, his ministry of intercession is before us in full view. God condescends to us by providing an account of the intra-Trinitarian conversation between the Father and the Son on the eve of Jesus's crucifixion. Even though such is the historical setting in which Jesus offers his prayer, he anticipates his glorification beyond the humiliation of the cross as if he has already accomplished all that his Father gave him to do (vv. 4–5).[8] In this way, Jesus's prayer becomes a powerful preview of his heavenly work of intercession. Specifically, his prayer reveals the content of his intercession for the people the Father entrusts to his care. What does Christ pray for his people? Here we learn that he prays for his followers to experience protection (vv. 11–12, 15), holiness (vv. 17–19), unity (vv. 20–23), and glory (v. 24).

Protection. The first request that Jesus makes for his people is for the Father to keep them safe and secure. In verse 11b he prays, "Holy Father, keep them in your name." Jesus also asks his Father to protect his people from satanic attack (v. 15). Jesus guarded the disciples during his earthly ministry, and he asks for additional protection as he transitions from his earthly ministry to his heavenly ministry. Jesus emphatically denies that this will involve removing the disciples from the world, but he does pray that God will "keep them from the evil one" (v. 15). This first request, then, indicates that Jesus's intercession is concerned with the protection of his followers.

Holiness. In his second request Jesus asks the Father to sanctify his people. Jesus says, "Sanctify them in the truth; your word is truth" (v. 17). In order to sanctify his followers, Christ must first sanctify himself. In verse 19 he continues his prayer, "And for their sake I consecrate myself, that they also may be sanctified in truth."

It is important to recognize that Christ's sanctification differs from our sanctification. Christ's sanctification does not mean that he is a sinner in need of

---

[8]Note the past tense of the verb and participle in v. 4: "I glorified you on earth, having accomplished the work that you gave me to do."

purification. Instead, his sanctification means that he sets himself apart for the divine service his heavenly Father gives him to perform. Like both the high priest and the sacrifice in Leviticus 16, Christ must consecrate himself. From this point of view, Christ is both priest and sacrifice. The single Greek word ἁγιάζω (*hagiazō*) is behind the two English words "sanctify" and "consecrate," and it means "set apart for divine service." As the High Priest, Christ sanctifies himself to perform his priestly work of sacrifice. As the sacrifice, Christ sanctifies his people by means of his death on the cross. The reason that Christ's sanctification impacts his followers is their union with him. In reality they are sanctified in him and by virtue of his sanctification. Furthermore, this sanctification is progressively realized in the life of the believer by means of the Word of God (v. 17). Thus, Christ prays not only that his people might be kept safe and secure, but also that they might be sanctified.

Unity. After Christ asks the Father to keep and to sanctify his people, Jesus makes his third request. He pleads with his Father to unify the believers. Jesus already anticipated this request in verse 11b when he asked the Father to keep his people: "Holy Father, keep them in your name, which you have given me, that they may be one, even as we are one." Christ develops his request further in verses 20–23, where he reveals the pattern and the purpose of the believers' unity.

The pattern of the believers' unity is the unity of the Father and Son. Jesus's prayer is "that they may be one, even as we are one" (vv. 11b, 22b). He prays also in verse 21 "that they may all be one, just as you, Father, are in me, and I in you, that they also may be in us." We can see that the Trinity is the pattern for Christian unity. Even as the Father and Son are one, so Christians must be one with each other in the fellowship of the Father and the Son.

In addition to the pattern of Christian unity, Jesus also states the purpose of the unity for which he prays. The purpose is to bring the world to faith in Christ as the sent Son of the Father. Jesus prays in verse 21 "that the world may believe that you have sent me." He restates God's purpose for Christian unity in verse 23: "so that the world may know that you sent me and loved them even as you loved me." Jesus wants the world to see a unified community of believers in him and to be drawn to the faith on account of such visible love and harmony (cf. John 13:35).

In this way, Christ asks the Father to unify the believers so that the world might come to faith in Jesus Christ as the Son sent by the Father to save the world.

Glory. The fourth and final request that Jesus makes is for the glorification of believers. He expresses his desire in 17:24: "Father, I desire that they also, whom you have given me, may be with me where I am, to see my glory that you have given me because you loved me before the foundation of the world." Jesus began his High Priestly Prayer in verses 1–5 by praying for himself. In particular he prayed that the Father would restore his preincarnation glory: "And now, Father, glorify me in your own presence with the glory that I had with you before the world existed" (v. 5). But even as Jesus began his prayer by praying for his own glorification, he concludes his prayer by praying for the glorification of all believers. The culmination of Jesus's High Priestly Prayer is the request that the Father might bring his people to see the resplendent glory of the Son of God. This beatific vision is the essence of glorification. It means that the believer is forever free to see the Son of God without the inhibitions of sin. Thus Jesus closes his earthly preview of his heavenly intercession by pleading with his Father to reveal his glory to those the Father has given him to save.

The High Priestly Prayer of Jesus is more than the prayer that Jesus offers to his Father on the eve of his crucifixion. It is a revelation of the intra-Trinitarian relationship between the Father and Son and of the Son's deepest desires for his people. As such it is also a preview of the Son's heavenly intercession for all believers. Although he prays this prayer on earth and before his crucifixion, he prays as if he has already been crucified and resurrected. And since the perspective of Christ's prayer extends beyond his earthly life, it informs our understanding of his current work of intercession. The content of Christ's intercessory prayers for his people includes his asking the Father to keep them safe, sanctify them, unify them, and eventually glorify them. Moreover, it is also helpful to realize that Christ's deepest desires for his followers concern the saving purposes of God. When this is understood, it is difficult to avoid the conclusion that the intercession is indeed yet another aspect of Christ's saving work. As we turn from the Gospel previews of Christ's intercession to the New Testament presentations of his intercession, we shall see that the intercession is indeed an integral component of the saving work of Christ.

New Testament Presentations of Christ's Intercession

The New Testament presentation of Christ's intercession is primarily found in the books of Romans and Hebrews, though there are traces of the intercession in 1 John and Revelation. We begin in Romans.

Romans 8:31–34

In Romans 8:34 Paul presents Christ's intercession as a saving event in sequence with his death, resurrection, and ascension. He says: "Who is to condemn? Christ Jesus is the one who died—more than that, who was raised—who is at the right hand of God, who indeed is interceding for us." Verse 34 falls within the wider conclusion of Romans 8:31–39. Here the apostle speaks with an elevated style as he rejoices in the gracious provision of God in the gospel. Christ's death, resurrection, ascension, and intercession parade before us with the assurance that no malicious accusation will stand before the just tribunal of God.

It is also true that in the larger context these events illustrate how believers are assured that God is for us, not against us (cf. 8:31). Indeed, the context is not merely our present justification, but it is also our future glorification. God's grace ensures that his elect will persevere from present justification to future glorification (cf. Rom. 8:30). Most important of all, the basis of this persever-ance is the saving work of Christ, who died, was raised, and intercedes for us. Thomas Schreiner observes, "This intercession should not be separated from his death on behalf of his people; rather, his intercession on behalf of the saints is based on his atoning death."[9] Believers, therefore, shall never be condemned in the sight of a just and holy God, because Jesus Christ intercedes for them on the basis of his death, resurrection, and ascension to the right hand of the Father. Thus in these verses Paul instills a sense of security in believers on the basis of Christ's saving work, both past (death, resurrection, and ascension) and present (intercession).

The meaning of the verb "intercede" with the preposition "for" should be understood in context.[10] Tellingly, Paul also uses this verb with reference to the Holy Spirit in Romans 8:26–27.

> Likewise the Spirit helps us in our weakness. For we do not know what to pray for as we ought, but the Spirit intercedes[11] for us with groanings too deep for words. And he who searches hearts knows what is the mind of the Spirit, because the Spirit intercedes[12] for the saints according to the will of God.

This means that the Holy Spirit prays in behalf of believers, and Christ does the same in verse 34.

There does, however, seem to be a critical difference between the Spirit's intercession and Christ's intercession; the Spirit's work is inside us, whereas Christ's work is outside us at the right hand of God in heaven. A ministry of intercessory prayer is intended. It would be incorrect, however, to reduce Christ's intercessory ministry to prayer, for at least one reason: Paul places Christ's

---

[9]Thomas R. Schreiner, *Romans*, Baker Exegetical Commentary on the New Testament (Grand Rapids: Baker Academic, 1998), 463.
[10]Greek, ἐντυγχάνειν with ὑπέρ.
[11]Greek, ὑπερεντυγχάνει.
[12]Greek, ἐντυγχάνει.

intercession in sequence with his death, resurrection, ascension, and session. Christ is qualified to intercede for us in heaven because he has died, risen, and ascended to the right hand of God. The exact nature of Christ's intercession is developed in more detail by the author of Hebrews.

Hebrews 6:19–20; 7:25; 8:3; 9:11–14, 24

The major contribution of the book of Hebrews to our study of Christ's intercession is that the eternal Son of God assumes a full humanity in order to become the great High Priest of the new covenant. In doing so, Christ, having made the final sacrifice for sins, presents himself to the Father in behalf of his people, and on the basis of his finished sacrifice makes continual and effective intercession for us.

The author of Hebrews develops his treatment of Christ our High Priest in chapter 2 by explaining the priestly purpose of Christ's incarnation: "Therefore he had to be made like his brothers in every respect, so that he might become a merciful and faithful high priest in the service of God, to make propitiation for the sins of the people" (Heb. 2:17). By virtue of his incarnation, Jesus becomes our High Priest who offers his own life as our sacrifice. The author of Hebrews argues from this point that the new covenant surpasses the old covenant because Christ is a better priest who offers a better sacrifice.

Although the author's main emphasis is upon Christ's finished sacrifice, he alludes at various points in his argument to Christ's continual work of intercession on the basis of his completed sacrificial work (6:19–20; 7:25; 8:3; 9:11–14, 24). Having become the final sacrifice for sins, our High Priest rises by means of his indestructible life (7:16), passes through the heavens (4:14), appears in the presence of God in our behalf (9:24), sits down at the right hand of God (1:3), and is now interceding for us (7:25). As a result of his continual and effective work of intercession, he is able to save his people completely. But according to the author of Hebrews, what is involved in Christ's intercession? Is his intercession merely his effective and continual prayers for his people to persevere until final salvation? Or does his intercession also include his self-offering to the Father?

Seeing Christ's self-offering to the Father as a denial of the once-for-all character of Christ's sacrifice, and fearing the Roman Catholic doctrine of eucharistic sacrifice, Protestant theologians commonly dismiss the idea that Christ's intercession includes the self-offering of his completed sacrifice to the Father in the heavenly sanctuary. For example, Schreiner says, "Christ's intercession is based on his final and definitive sacrifice and should not be construed as a continuation of his sacrificial work in God's presence, for such a view would contradict the finality of Christ's sacrifice, which is such a prominent theme in Hebrews."[13] I understand Schreiner's concern. Christ's sacrifice is a finished work (cf. 10:1–18). However, while it is certainly true that Christ's *sacrificial* work is complete on the cross, his *priestly* work does not conclude with his once-for-all sacrifice on Calvary.

In the account of the work of the high priest on the Day of Atonement in Leviticus 16, the high priest does more than make sacrifices. After making sacrifices outside the sanctuary, the high priest then presents those sacrifices inside the sanctuary on the mercy seat. It seems reasonable to conclude that Christ, our High Priest, must also present his finished sacrifice in the presence of God in the heavenly sanctuary. In some sense, then, the sacrificial role of his atonement on the cross has spiritual ramifications for the intercessory role of his atonement in heaven.

However, those who oppose the self-offering of Christ argue that this interpretation pushes too far the continuity between the work of the high priest in the old covenant and his work in the new covenant. Consider, for instance, the comments of F. F. Bruce:

> Aaron certainly carried the sacrificial blood into the holy of holies, but our author deliberately avoids saying that Christ carried His own blood into the heavenly sanctuary. Even as a symbolic expression this is open to objection. There have been expositors who, pressing the analogy of the Day of Atonement beyond the limits observed by our author, have agreed that the expiatory work of Christ was not completed on the cross—not completed, indeed, until He ascended from earth and "made atonement 'for us' in the heavenly holy of holies by the presentation of His efficacious blood." But while it was necessary under the old covenant for the sacrificial blood first to be shed in the court and then to be brought into the holy of holies, no such division of our Lord's sacrifice into two phases is envisaged under the new covenant. When upon the cross He offered up His life to God as a sacrifice for His people's sin, He accomplished in reality what Aaron and his successors performed in type by the twofold act of slaying the victim and presenting its blood in the holy of holies.[14]

In other words, Bruce is concerned at the overinterpretation of the connection between the Aaronic priesthood and Christ's priesthood. Even though the high priest in the Old Testament made the sacrifice outside the sanctuary and

[13]Thomas R. Schreiner, *New Testament Theology: Magnifying God in Christ* (Grand Rapids: Baker, 2008), 395.

[14]F. F. Bruce, *The Epistle to the Hebrews*, The New International Commentary on the New Testament (Grand Rapids: Eerdmans, 1964), 200–201.

then carried the blood of the sacrifice inside the sanctuary in completion of his priestly work, the author of Hebrews never makes this connection, according to Bruce. In fact, if the author of Hebrews were to make this connection, he would undermine the finality of Christ's sacrifice for our sins. This argument by Bruce is later espoused by Philip Hughes in a series of four articles published in *Bibliotheca Sacra*.[15]

As we can see, then, two main arguments are advanced against the position that Christ's intercession includes his self-offering to the Father. First, opponents of this position claim that it undermines the finished work of Christ on the cross. Second, opponents argue that this position overinterprets the implications of the Aaronic priesthood for Christ's priesthood. Even though these are strong objections to the self-offering of Christ made by good and godly scholars, they do not withstand the scrutiny of consistent evaluation and exposition.

Hebrews 6:19–20. When we survey the key passages in the book of Hebrews, we discover that the author certainly teaches that Christ, having finished his sacrificial work on the cross, presents himself in the presence of God, and on the basis of his completed sacrifice he continually and effectively intercedes for his people. Hebrews 6:19–20 says, "We have this as a sure and steadfast anchor of the soul, a hope that enters into the inner place behind the curtain, where Jesus has gone as a forerunner on our behalf, having become a high priest forever after the order of Melchizedek." The author employs the Old Testament language of the tabernacle in order to explain what Christ does for his people *after* his work on the cross is complete.

The "curtain" (v. 19) refers to the curtain that served as a veil between the Holy Place and the Most Holy Place (cf. Ex. 26:31–33; Heb. 9:2–3), and the "inner place behind the curtain" refers to the Most Holy Place, or the Holy of Holies. It is difficult to ignore the author's allusion to the work of the high priest in Leviticus 16:15, which says, "Then he shall kill the goat of the sin offering that is for the people and bring its blood inside the veil and do with its blood as he did with the blood of the bull, sprinkling it over the mercy seat and in front of the mercy seat." This describes the high priestly work of the Aaronic priesthood, but the author uses the same language to describe the priestly work of Jesus. It is true that Hebrews 6:19–20 says nothing of what Christ does when he "enters into the inner place behind the curtain" (v. 19), but we already know from Leviticus 16 about the pattern for the work of the high priest. Does the

---

[15]Philip Edgcumbe Hughes, "The Blood of Jesus and His Heavenly Priesthood in Hebrews," parts 1–4, *Bibliotheca Sacra* (April 1973–January 1974).

author not imply, and consequently desire the reader to infer, the Old Testament background of Christ's priestly work? He does indeed.

Thus, even though Bruce and others allege that this view overinterprets the continuity between the Aaronic priesthood and Christ's priesthood, the author of Hebrews encourages us to think in this way. The comments of Charles Hodge are instructive in this regard: "There is error in pressing the representations of Scripture too far; and there is error in explaining them away."[16] In this case Bruce and others have explained away the Old Testament background for Christ's intercession. Even though we are sympathetic with their reasons for dismissing the Old Testament connection, we must respectfully differ with these otherwise excellent commentators in order to be faithful to the meaning of the texts before us.

Hebrews 7:25. Hebrews 7:25 is a powerful witness to the perfection of Christ's saving work. God says, "Consequently, he is able to save to the uttermost those who draw near to God through him, since he always lives to make intercession for them." Surprisingly, Hebrews 7:25 is the only place in the book of Hebrews to use the verb "intercede."[17] Of course, it would be a fallacy to conclude that this is the only text relevant to our discussion of Christ's intercession in the book of Hebrews. As noted above, when the Greek verb translated "intercede"[18] is used with the preposition "for,"[19] the meaning of the verb is "plead for someone."[20] The word "consequently"[21] at the beginning of the verse indicates the conclusion of an argument.

The argument begins in Hebrews 7:1 and culminates in verse 25. Hebrews 6 concludes with the statement that Christ has become "a high priest forever after the order of Melchizedek" (v. 20). In chapter 7 the author seeks to demonstrate that Christ is a High Priest after the order of Melchizedek and that this high priesthood is superior to the Aaronic high priesthood. After providing several proofs of this, the author concludes that the Aaronic priesthood is inferior to Christ's priesthood because the Aaronic priests "were prevented by death from continuing in office" (v. 23). Christ, however, "holds his priesthood permanently, because he continues forever" (v. 24). By this the author means that Christ's resurrection qualifies him to serve as High Priest forever, and as High Priest

---

[16]Charles Hodge, *Systematic Theology*, vol. 2 (Peabody, MA: Hendrickson, 2003), 593.

[17]Greek, ἐντυγχάνειν.

[18]Greek, ἐντυγχάνειν.

[19]Greek, ὑπέρ.

[20]Greek, ἐντυγχάνειν, "meet, turn to, approach, appeal, petition," in William F. Arndt and F. Wilbur Gingrich, *A Greek-English Lexicon of the New Testament and Other Early Christian Literature*, 2nd ed. (Chicago: University of Chicago, 1979), 270.

[21]Greek, ὅθεν.

he always lives to make intercession for God's people (v. 25). Since Christ is risen, he is able to intercede for his people for all time. Further, since Christ is able to intercede for his people for all time, he is able to save them completely.[22] This verse teaches us to give due weight to the saving significance of Christ's intercession. The intercession of our Lord is a saving event.

Hebrews 8:3. Although some scholars maintain that Christ's intercession in Hebrews 7:25 refers exclusively to prayer, it becomes clear in Hebrews 8:3 and 9:11–14, 24 that Christ's intercession includes more than mere intercessory prayer. Christ has more to offer, namely, his finished sacrifice, to his heavenly Father. Hebrews 8:3 says, "For every high priest is appointed to offer gifts and sacrifices; thus it is necessary for this priest also to have something to offer." Some have argued that this refers to Christ's sacrifice on the cross because the verb "offer" is in the past tense (προσενέγκη, *prosenenkē*). However, the context of this verse reveals that Christ cannot have something to offer on earth because there are priests (the Aaronic priests) who have something to offer on earth (v. 4). Moreover, in verses 1–2 the author is discussing Christ's *present* priesthood in the heavenly tabernacle. Again, it is helpful to remember that even though Christ's *sacrificial* work is finished on earth, his *priestly* work continues in heaven. This priestly work is more than praying for the people for whom he died, but is also the presentation of his finished sacrifice to his Father in their behalf.

It must be understood that Christ's sacrifice is finished. It has been offered once for all time (Heb. 10:10, 14). It does not need to be repeated. However, while Christ's sacrifice is not continual, Christ does continually plead the efficacy of his finished sacrifice. Although we do not know *how* and therefore should not speculate how Christ pleads this finished sacrifice,[23] we know *that* his intercession includes this active presentation of his completed sacrifice. This says more than Hughes[24] and Peter Toon[25] say when they admit that Christ's sacrifice has

---

[22]The expression εἰς τὸ παντελὲς (*eis to panteles*) has been interpreted in two ways: in a temporal sense, "forever," and in a qualitative sense, "completely." I follow William L. Lane in opting for "absolutely," which includes both of the preceding senses. See his, *Hebrews 1–8*, Word Biblical Commentary (Dallas: Word, 1991), 176n v and 189.

[23]Philip Hughes demonstrates the problems with these speculative explanations of how Christ presents his sacrifice to the Father (i.e., the imperishability of Christ's blood, the release of life, eucharistic sacrifice, etc.). Hughes inaccurately concludes, however, that this means that Christ does not present his sacrifice to the Father in heaven. In point of fact, we may know *that* without knowing *how*. Hughes seems to overlook the possibility that the author of Hebrews may assert *that* Christ pleads his finished sacrifice without an explanation of *how* Christ does this. See Philip Edgcumbe Hughes, "The Blood of Jesus and His Heavenly Priesthood in Hebrews," part 1, "The Significance of the Blood of Jesus," *Bibliotheca Sacra* (April 1973): 99–109.

[24]Philip Edgcumbe Hughes, "The Blood of Jesus and His Heavenly Priesthood in Hebrews," part 2, "The High Priestly Sacrifice of Christ," *Bibliotheca Sacra* (July 1973): 197.

[25]Peter Toon, *The Ascension of Our Lord* (Nashville: Nelson, 1984), 60–61.

a perpetual efficacy. This says that Christ is in fact continually and actively pleading the efficacy of his cross work in his intercessory prayers for his people and their preservation.

Hebrews 9:11–14, 24. The author to the Hebrews continues in the vein of intercession in Hebrews 9:11–14 and 24. Verses 11–12 teach that Christ, our High Priest, entered once for all into the heavenly tabernacle "by means of his own blood," thus securing an eternal redemption. Unlike the blood of goats and bulls that purifies the flesh (v. 13), the blood of Christ purifies the conscience (v. 14). These two references to the blood of Christ (vv. 12, 14) refer to his violent, sacrificial death on the cross.[26] This is the sacrifice that Christ accomplished once for all time. It is significant, however, that this sacrifice is also the means[27] by which Christ enters the heavenly sanctuary and secures an eternal redemption (v. 12). Therefore, we cannot reduce the redemptive work of Christ in these verses to refer exclusively to his death on the cross. This does not mean that we must envision Christ literally taking his blood before the Father in order to gain access to the heavenly tabernacle. Nor does this mean that we must develop speculative theories about how Christ employs his blood in order to enter the heavenly tabernacle. And this certainly does not mean that Christ continually repeats his sacrifice in heaven.

This simply means that the death of Christ on the cross is the means by which he enters into the heavenly tabernacle to perform his high priestly work. In the words of Hebrews 12:24, his blood "speaks." His blood has efficacy beyond the cross event, and this efficacy is relevant for his present priestly ministry in heaven. Hebrews 9:12 conveys more than the fact that Christ's blood secures an eternal redemption; it also communicates the truth that his blood is the means by which he begins his continuous work of intercession. Verse 24 elaborates Christ's entry into the heavenly tabernacle: "For Christ has entered, not into holy places made with hands, which are copies of the true things, but into heaven itself, now to appear in the presence of God in our behalf." Wearing the ephod with the stones of remembrance for the sons of Israel, the high priest of the Old Testament represented the people of Israel in the earthly tabernacle (Ex. 39:6–7). In similar fashion, Christ, the High Priest of the New Testament, represents us in the heavenly tabernacle. He appears in the presence of God for us, and he represents our humanity in heaven.

Thus, the author of Hebrews presents to us Christ's presence, his prayer, and his plea as the components of his intercession for our salvation. After making the final sacrifice for sin, Christ ascended to the right hand of God to

---

[26]See the reference to death in v. 15. Leon Morris, *The Apostolic Preaching of the Cross*, 3rd ed. (Grand Rapids: Eerdmans, 1965), 112–28.

[27]Greek, διά + the genitive.

represent us in the presence of God, to pray effectively and continually for us, and to plead for us the merit of his finished sacrifice. Our salvation is forever as safe and secure as Christ, our perfect priest, is in heaven now sitting at the right hand of God.

So then, the New Testament presentations of Christ's intercession from the books of Romans and Hebrews include Christ's presence for us in heaven, his continual and effective prayers for us to persevere until final salvation, and his pleading the merits of his finished sacrifice. Another aspect of Christ's intercession refers to his advocacy for us to his Father. This theme appears in 1 John, and it is an integral component of Christ's intercession.

1 John 2:1–2

John exhorts his audience: "My little children, I am writing these things to you so that you may not sin. But if anyone does sin, we have an advocate with the Father, Jesus Christ the righteous." Jesus is the believers' advocate. Although John's terminology differs from the terminology in Romans and Hebrews, John addresses Christ's intercession in terms of advocacy.

In simplest terms, "advocate"[28] means "one who is called alongside to help."[29] The semantic range of the Greek word includes "advocate," "defender," "intercessor," "helper," "comforter," or "counselor," and because it is difficult to discern its exact meaning in this verse, some translators have chosen to transliterate the word in order to convey the full range of meaning.[30] John's Gospel uses "advocate" ("Helper," esv) for the Holy Spirit (John 14:16–17, 26; 15:26; 16:7), not for Jesus. But in the single occurrence of the term in his epistles (1 John 2:1) he uses "advocate" for Jesus, not for the Holy Spirit. There the word denotes a forensic appeal to the Father, but it also connotes a priestly intercession in light of verse 2: "He is the propitiation for our sins."

First, note in verse 1 that John speaks of forensic appeal to the Father in behalf of believers. John encourages Christians who struggle with sin that Jesus Christ is our advocate "to the Father," "with the Father," or "in the presence of the Father."[31] Christ's advocacy, then, occurs in heaven. When believers sin, the ascended Christ pleads their case in the presence of the Father in the heavenly

---

[28]Greek, παράκλητος (*paraklētos*).

[29]I. Howard Marshall, *The Epistles of John*, The New International Commentary on the New Testament (Grand Rapids: Eerdmans, 1978), 116. See also, Stephen S. Smalley, *1, 2, 3 John*, Word Biblical Commentary (Waco, TX: Word, 1984), 36.

[30]Raymond E. Brown, *The Epistles of John*, The Anchor Bible Commentary (New York: Doubleday, 1982), 215–16.

[31]Compare this construction with πρὸς τὸν θεόν in John 1:1, which speaks of the preincarnate Word in the presence of God.

court. Jesus Christ is different from us in that he is called "the righteous," and therefore his plea before the Father always avails for us.

Second, in addition to forensic appeal, Christ's advocacy includes priestly intercession. Some commentators have suggested[32] that the title "the righteous" or "the Righteous One" may in fact be an allusion to Isaiah 53:11:

> Out of the anguish of his soul he shall see and be satisfied;
> by his knowledge shall the righteous one, my servant,
>   make many to be accounted righteous,
>   and he shall bear their iniquities.

This allusion is difficult to prove. If John is indeed making this allusion, then the reference to Christ's priestly intercession is likely, especially on account of the explicit mention of priestly intercession in Isaiah 53:12, which has been discussed above. Nevertheless, the argument for priestly intercession does not rest on this Old Testament connection.

When John continues in verse 2 with the statement that Jesus Christ is the propitiation for our sins, he connects Christ's legal advocacy with his priestly intercession. It is important in this regard that John uses the present tense with reference to Christ's past propitiation: "He is the propitiation for our sins" (1 John 2:2). Of course, John does not suggest that Christ makes continual sacrifices in heaven, but he does imply that Christ's once-for-all propitiation has continual efficacy. And since this statement follows an affirmation of Christ's active role as the advocate for believers who sin, it implies that Christ advocates for believers on the basis of the perpetual efficacy of his propitiation. So Calvin says: "The intercession of Christ is a continual application of his death for our salvation. That God then does not impute to us our sins, this comes to us, because he has regard to Christ as intercessor."[33]

This means that John echoes the same teaching that we discovered in Hebrews, namely, that Christ's continual work of heavenly intercession is on the basis of the perpetual efficacy of his once-for-all sacrifice on the cross. So, then, rather than destroying the finality of Christ's cross work, Christ's present and perpetual intercessory work in heaven confirms his once-for-all sacrifice on the cross. On the one hand, we must affirm that without Christ's finished work on the cross his intercession would be impossible; but, on the

[32]See F. F. Bruce, *The Book of the Acts*, The New International Commentary on the New Testament (Grand Rapids: Eerdmans), 88; Darrell L. Bock, *Acts*, Baker Exegetical Commentary on the New Testament (Grand Rapids: Baker Academic, 2007), 170–71.

[33]John Calvin, *The First Epistle of John*, Calvin's Commentaries, trans. John Owen (Grand Rapids: Baker, 1999), 171.

other hand, we must also affirm that Christ's finished work on the cross does not nullify the need for his subsequent intercession. As Louis Berkhof states, "The fundamental point to remember is that the ministry of intercession should not be dissociated from the atonement, since they are but two aspects of the same redemptive work of Christ, and the two may be said to merge into one."[34]

The connection between Christ's once-for-all sacrifice and his continual work of intercession is evident in the final New Testament presentation of Christ's intercession in the book of Revelation.

Revelation 5:6

At first glance Revelation 5:6 may seem irrelevant to a study of Christ's intercession. The verse says, "And between the throne and the four living creatures and among the elders I saw a Lamb standing, as though it had been slain, with seven horns and with seven eyes, which are the seven spirits of God sent out into all the earth." Revelation 4–5 contains John's vision of the heavenly throne room of God. In Revelation 5 John describes Jesus as the Lion of the tribe of Judah and the Lamb standing as though it had been slain. The key component of verse 6 in relation to Christ's intercession is that John speaks of Jesus as a sacrificial Lamb in heaven. This indicates that the past, completed, once-for-all sacrifice of Christ on the cross has present significance for believers in heaven as he stands before the throne of God. Hughes correctly says, "The presence of the Lamb bearing the marks of His passion in heaven is itself the perpetual guarantee of our acceptance with God, who gave His Son to be the propitiation for our sins."[35] Again, we have another New Testament confirmation that Jesus intercedes for believers in heaven on the basis of his sacrificial death. This does not mean that Christ must offer his sacrifice again, but it does mean that his past sacrifice is the ground upon which he represents us to the Father. He stands forever in the presence of God as the Lamb that has been slain. This is not a passive role. As we observe in the New Testament, this is an integral component of his active ministry of intercession.

Connecting the Dots

Having studied the Old Testament pictures and promises and the New Testament previews and presentations of Christ's intercession, we are now able to summarize the intercession as a saving event.

---

[34]Louis Berkhof, *Systematic Theology*, 4th ed. (Grand Rapids: Eerdmans, 1996), 402.
[35]Philip Edgcumbe Hughes, "The Blood of Jesus and His Heavenly Priesthood in Hebrews," part 4, "The Present Work of Christ in Heaven," *Bibliotheca Sacra* (January 1974): 33.

Christ's Intercession Is Saving

The Bible teaches that the intercession saves. But exactly how does the heavenly intercession of Christ save us? First, it saves us because *it is the completion of Christ's priestly work*. Christ's intercession is emphatically not the completion of his sacrificial work. His sacrificial work was forever finished on the cross. However, his sacrificial work was not the end of his priestly work. After making the final sacrifice for sins, he rose again, ascended into heaven, sat down at God's right hand, and poured out the Holy Spirit on the church. As a result of these prior saving events, he now makes intercession for the sinners he came to save. If he had not risen from the dead, then he would have been unable to appear in the presence of God in our behalf as intercessor, and if he had not appeared in the presence of God in our behalf, his priestly work would be incomplete. The testimony of Scripture is that Christ has risen and that he has ascended to heaven and appeared in the presence of God in our behalf. And even now the exalted Christ in heaven is making continual and effective intercession for his people, thus guaranteeing our final salvation.

This leads to the second way that the intercession saves. It saves us because *it is one means by which God enables his people to continue in faith and obedience*. It is God's plan that his elect persevere in faith and obedience (Rom. 8:29–30), and one means by which God accomplishes his plan is the intercessory work of his Son (Rom. 8:34). It may seem strange to suggest that Christ needed to do more than die on the cross to ensure believers' final salvation, but the multifaceted problem of sin requires a multifaceted solution. Christ's saving events must address the whole panorama of human sinfulness in order to provide a complete salvation. If Christ's sinless life, death, resurrection, session, and sending the Spirit at Pentecost are necessary for the believer's justification, then what is necessary for the believer's perseverance until final salvation? The biblical answer is, all of these events plus his intercession and return.

Christ's Intercession Involves the Father and the Spirit

The intercession not only saves believers, but also reminds us that we are saved by the work of God the Trinity. The Father, the Son, and the Holy Spirit work together in order to save us from our sins. Gerrit Scott Dawson says, "The intercessions of Jesus represent his role in the Triune God's continual work of sanctifying us."[36] Christ's intercession highlights the relationship between the Father and the Son. It also reminds us that even as Christ intercedes for

---

[36]Gerrit Scott Dawson, *Jesus Ascended: The Meaning of Christ's Continuing Incarnation* (Phillipsburg, NJ: P&R, 2004), 132.

us externally (Rom. 8:34), the Spirit intercedes for us internally (Rom. 8:26). The intercession is the work of Christ, but his ministry of intercession includes interactions with the Father and the Holy Spirit.

Christ's Intercession Is Priestly

In addition to the saving role of the whole Trinity in Christ's intercession, we must keep in mind that the background of Christ's intercession is the work of the high priest on the Day of Atonement (Leviticus 16). The ministry of intercession is a priestly one. Quite naturally, then, most of the New Testament teaching about Christ's intercession is found in the book of Hebrews, which is the only New Testament book to designate Christ as our High Priest. As we have learned, there are echoes of the priestly character of Christ's intercession in Romans, 1 John, and Revelation, too. These references become clear when we understand that Christ's priesthood involves two roles, not one. Those two roles are sacrifice and intercession. Having made the final sacrifice for sin, Christ ascends into heaven, not to make another sacrifice, but to sit down and appear in the presence of God in behalf of his people. His sacrificial work is complete, but his priestly work continues.

Christ's Intercession Is Continual

Christ's intercession is the aspect of his priestly work that continues. Theologians discuss the finished work of Christ, and in doing so they emphasize Christ's sacrifice on the cross. It would be a misunderstanding to conclude from this that all of Christ's saving work is completed. After all, Christ will return to save those who are eagerly waiting for him (Heb. 9:28). Christ has present, ongoing, continual work to perform in heaven. He must plead, pray, and advocate in the Father's presence. This is his intercessory task, and it is an active role. Of course, this does not necessarily mean that Christ is always verbally speaking to his Father in our behalf. It simply means that his intercession is an active and continual role in heaven.

Christ's Intercession Is Effective

Christ's priestly intercession is not only continual, but it is also effective. God the Father listens to his Son, and the Father always answers his Son's requests (John 11:42). This means that Christ's intercessory prayers are always successful. As Jesus prayed for Peter (Luke 22:31–32), he prays for all his people. He prays that the elect will continue in the faith and persevere until final salvation, and God answers his prayers. He is always successful. He always lives to make intercession for us (Heb. 7:25). Jesus Christ is a perfect Savior for his people.

Christ's Intercession Is Particular

Finally, Christ intercedes particularly for believers, not for all people. Even if Luke 23:34 justifies a universal dimension to Christ's intercession, which is unlikely for the reasons mentioned above, the dominant New Testament emphasis is that Christ effectively intercedes for a particular people. When Christ intercedes for his people in heaven, he has specific names on his mind. As the high priest bore the names of the twelve tribes on his chest when he entered the Most Holy Place to intercede for the people of Israel (Ex. 28:12; 39:6–7), so Christ takes the names of his people into the presence of God to make intercession for them.

Christ's saving work is one united work, but it has many aspects. His incarnation and sinless life are necessary prerequisites for his primary deeds of dying and rising again on the third day. His death and resurrection are followed by five necessary results: his ascension, session, giving the Spirit at Pentecost, intercession, and second coming. The final and full results of his saving work will be revealed only at this last aspect, to which we turn next.

Incarnation
Sinless Life
Death
Resurrection
Ascension
Session
Pentecost
Intercession
Second Coming

Chapter

Christ's Second Coming

The expectation of Christ's Second Advent is a most important aspect of New Testament eschatology—so much so, in fact, that the faith of the New Testament church is dominated by this expectation. Every book of the New Testament points us to the return of Christ and urges us to live in such a way as to be always ready for that return. . . . This same lively expectation of Christ's return should mark the church of Jesus Christ today.[1]

Anthony Hoekema speaks wisely. The second coming of the Lord Jesus Christ is vital. Hope in it fills the pages of the New Testament, and it should impact the lives of believers. This is true because the second coming saves. When Christ returns, he brings the final application of his saving work. That work was accomplished in his death and resurrection. But following these events, the second coming triggers the final outworking of the saving purposes of God.

Old Testament Background

The following texts do not make clear predictions of Christ's second coming that all original readers would understand ahead of time. But seen through New Testament eyes, these passages anticipate the second coming.

---

[1] Anthony A. Hoekema, *The Bible and the Future* (Grand Rapids: Eerdmans, 1979), 109–10.

Psalm 110:1

In a most remarkable messianic psalm, David wrote,

> The LORD says to my Lord:
>   "Sit at my right hand,
> until I make your enemies your footstool." (Ps. 110:1)

Jesus says that in this verse "David, in the Spirit, calls him [the Christ] Lord" when David speaks of God telling his Lord to sit at his right hand until God vanquishes his foes (Matt. 22:43). The writer to the Hebrews includes Psalm 110:1 as proof of the divine Son's superiority to the angels:

> And to which of the angels has he ever said,
>
> > "Sit at my right hand
> > until I make your enemies a footstool for your feet?" (Heb. 1:13)

When Jesus ascended to heaven and sat down at God's right hand, the first part of Psalm 110:1 was fulfilled; David's Lord sat in the supreme seat of power and honor in the whole universe. The second part will not be fulfilled until Christ comes again and God subdues all of his foes.

Daniel 7:13–14

> I saw in the night visions,
>
> > and behold, with the clouds of heaven
> >   there came one like a son of man,
> > and he came to the Ancient of Days
> >   and was presented before him.
> > And to him was given dominion
> >   and glory and a kingdom,
> > that all peoples, nations, and languages
> >   should serve him;
> > his dominion is an everlasting dominion,
> >   which shall not pass away,
> > and his kingdom one
> >   that shall not be destroyed.

In his night vision Daniel sees "one like a son of man." The title "son of man" implies the figure's humanity. But what it says of him more than implies his deity.

He comes into the presence of God himself ("the Ancient of Days"). This son of man was granted universal and everlasting dominion. And "all peoples, nations, and languages" will serve him. Daniel thus sets the stage for Jesus to use "son of man" as his favorite self-designation for teaching his humanity and deity.

The Event in the Synoptic Gospels

Matthew 25:31–34

> When the Son of Man comes in his glory, and all the angels with him, then he will sit on his glorious throne. Before him will be gathered all the nations, and he will separate people one from another as a shepherd separates the sheep from the goats. And he will place the sheep on his right, but the goats on the left. Then the King will say to those on his right, "Come, you who are blessed by my Father, inherit the kingdom prepared for you from the foundation of the world."

Jesus predicts his second coming in the famous passage about the sheep and the goats. His second coming, unlike his first, will be glorious. As a King is accompanied by his servants, so Jesus will come "in his glory," accompanied by angels and "sit on his glorious throne" to judge all nations (v. 31). He will function as a shepherd-king who separates the sheep from the goats, believers from unbelievers. King Jesus will banish the goats into everlasting hell: "Depart from me, you cursed, into the eternal fire prepared for the devil and his angels" (v. 41). By contrast, he will bless believers. Mixing familial and royal language, he ushers the sons and daughters of the heavenly Father into their eternal "inheritance," which is "the kingdom" of God (v. 34).

Jesus's return will save because only then will he give his people their inheritance and place in God's final kingdom. That inheritance and kingdom were planned before creation (v. 34), and believers' places therein were assured by the cross and empty tomb, but they will enter into the fullness of their salvation only when their King comes back.

Mark 13:26–27

> And then they will see the Son of Man coming in clouds with great power and glory. And then he will send out the angels and gather his elect from the four winds, from the ends of the earth to the ends of heaven.

Alluding to Daniel 7:13–14, Jesus predicts his visible second coming "with great power and glory" (Mark 13:26). This stands in bold relief against his first coming in weakness and humbleness. The triumphant, returning Son of Man will send his angel-servants to bring his elect from the whole earth to enter into their final salvation.

Teaching in the Gospel of John

John 14:1–3

Let not your hearts be troubled. Believe in God; believe also in me. In my Father's house are many rooms. If it were not so, would I have told you that I go to prepare a place for you? And if I go and prepare a place for you, I will come again and will take you to myself, that where I am you may be also.

Jesus's disciples are justifiably upset because he has told them that one of them will betray him and that he is leaving them to return to the Father: "Where I am going you cannot come" (John 13:33). Jesus brings comforting words: "Let not your hearts be troubled." He encourages their faith: "Believe in God; believe also in me" (John 14:1).

Jesus next explains what he will be doing in their behalf when he leaves: "In my Father's house are many rooms. If it were not so, would I have told you that I go to prepare a place for you?" (John 14:2). Jesus is going to his "Father's house," to ready a place for the disciples to live. By using this warm picture, Jesus assures his disciples of the Father's love for them. They belong to the Father, and he will welcome them into his presence.

Furthermore, Jesus will come back for them. "And if I go and prepare a place for you, I will come again and will take you to myself, that where I am you may be also" (v. 3). Jesus will return for his own and take them back to the Father's heavenly home. What is the purpose of Jesus's second coming according to John's Gospel? He says that it is "that where I am you may be also" (v. 3). Being with Christ in bliss is what heaven is all about (Luke 23:43; Phil. 1:23; 2 Cor. 5:8). And Christ's return saves by making it possible for his followers to be with him forever.

Teaching in the Acts of the Apostles

Acts 1:9–11

And when he had said these things, as they were looking on, he was lifted up, and a cloud took him out of their sight. And while they were gazing into heaven as he went, behold, two men stood by them in white robes, and said, "Men of Galilee, why do you stand looking into heaven? This Jesus, who was taken up from you into heaven, will come in the same way as you saw him go into heaven."

Acts records Jesus's ascension and at the same time gives assurances of his return. In between his resurrection and ascension, Jesus went many times in and out of the Father's presence in heaven. For that reason the record of his ascension in Acts 1 is not for his benefit but for the disciples'. It is God's way of saying that the intermittent appearances of Jesus will stop. The next great event will be his second coming.

The ascension, then, is a public event performed to teach the disciples. "And when he had said these things, as they were looking on, he was lifted up, and a cloud took him out of their sight" (Acts 1:9). As the disciples continue to stare into heaven, two angels, appearing as human beings, told them: "Men of Galilee, why do you stand looking into heaven? This Jesus, who was taken up from you into heaven, will come in the same way as you saw him go into heaven" (vv. 10–11). Here the angels, speaking for God, promise that Christ will return on the clouds of heaven. This is in keeping with the words of Jesus that he will return on clouds (Matt. 24:30; Mark 13:26; Luke 21:27), and the words of his apostles that he will return from heaven (Phil. 3:20; 1 Thess. 1:10; 2 Thess. 1:7).

Acts 3:19–21

> Repent therefore, and turn again, that your sins may be blotted out, that times of refreshing may come from the presence of the Lord, and that he may send the Christ appointed for you, Jesus, whom heaven must receive until the time for restoring all the things about which God spoke by the mouth of his holy prophets long ago.

After God through Peter heals a lame beggar, Peter is careful not to take glory to himself but to give it to Jesus (Acts 3:12–13, 16). Peter then preaches Jesus's death and resurrection to the gathered crowd (vv. 14–15). He admits that they acted in ignorance when they put Jesus to death and rejoices that God used even their ignorance to fulfill what he "foretold by the mouth of all the prophets, that his Christ would suffer" (v. 18). This Christ, promised by the Old Testament, is Jesus who has returned to heaven.

Peter announces the amazing cosmic consequences that Christ's return will bring: "times of refreshing . . . from the presence of the Lord" and "the time for restoring all the things," and these too in fulfillment of prophetic predictions (v. 21). The second coming will mean final salvation for believers ("times of refreshing") and the unveiling of the new heavens and new earth ("restoring all . . . things").

Dennis Johnson insightfully draws the connection between the healing of the lame man and the enormous results of Jesus's return:

> This healing may be thought of as both an X-ray and a preview. As an X-ray, it makes visible to outside observers the unseen inner cure that faith in Jesus produces. Astonishing as it is for a man of forty who has never walked to leap in the temple, the cure of hearts paralyzed in sin is even greater. As a preview, it shows the final completion of Jesus' restorative work, when believers' physical bodies will fully experience the salvation which we already taste in the form of firstfruits (see Rom. 8:18–25). Astonishing as it is for a lame man to leap, it is nothing when compared to the *cosmic* restoration to come—"the restoration of all the things" (Acts 3:21).[2]

Teaching in the Pauline Epistles

Philippians 3:20–21

> But our citizenship is in heaven, and from it we await a Savior, the Lord Jesus Christ, who will transform our lowly body to be like his glorious body, by the power that enables him even to subject all things to himself.

Paul instructs the Philippians both to follow his example and to watch out for "enemies of the cross of Christ" (Phil. 3:17–19). By contrast to the enemies, "our citizenship is in heaven" (v. 20). Philippi, a city in the province of Macedonia, many miles away from Rome, enjoyed the status of being a Roman colony with privileges of Roman citizenship. Even as the Philippians, far from Rome, had Roman citizenship, so believers, far from heaven, have their citizenship there.

From heaven "we await a Savior, the Lord Jesus Christ" (v. 20). This is a clear reference to the second coming. And at his return Jesus will bring us final salvation. This would not be possible had he not died and risen for us. Having performed the work of dying and rising, he applies that work to us when he comes again. "The particular feature of the Lord's saving activity at his parousia here singled out by the apostle is his transformation of our weak mortal bodies into the likeness of his own glorified body."[3]

---

[2]Dennis E. Johnson, *The Message of Acts in the History of Redemption* (Phillipsburg, NJ: P&R, 1997), 65.
[3]Peter T. O'Brien, *The Epistle to the Philippians*, New International Greek Testament Commentary (Grand Rapids: Eerdmans, 1991), 463.

How will he accomplish this work? By changing our weak mortal bodies to be like his glorious immortal body. He "will transform our lowly body to be like his glorious body, by the power that enables him even to subject all things to himself" (v. 21). Christ's omnipotent power—the same power that enables him to subdue the entire universe ("all things," v. 21)—will equip us for everlasting life on the new earth by changing our present bodies into resurrection bodies.

Once again Paul presents Christ's return as a significant aspect of his saving work. "Here, the final saving act of the awaited Saviour from heaven is the transformation of the body."[4]

Colossians 3:1–4

> If then you have been raised with Christ, seek the things that are above, where Christ is, seated at the right hand of God. Set your minds on things that are above, not on things that are on earth. For you have died, and your life is hidden with Christ in God. When Christ who is your life appears, then you also will appear with him in glory.

The backbone running through this passage is union with Christ. Believers have died with him (Col. 2:2; 3:3), been raised with him (1:1), ascended with him (vv. 1, 3), and, in a sense, will even come again with him (v. 4)! Our "second coming" is expressed in the same language of "appearing" as is his second coming: "When Christ who is your life *appears*, then you also *will appear* with him in glory" (v. 4). In what sense will we appear with him?

First John 3:2 helps answer this question: "Beloved, we are God's children now, and what we will be has not yet appeared; but we know that when he appears we shall be like him, because we shall see him as he is." Our redemption and true identity are so bound up with Christ, that we now receive only glimpses of what morally handsome sons or beautiful daughters of God we will be in that day. Our full salvation and who we are in him will be revealed only at his return. In that way, his appearing will mean our appearing. Here yet again our final salvation depends upon Christ's second coming. It is the final manifestation of his saving accomplishment in our behalf.

1 Thessalonians 1:9–10

> . . . you turned to God from idols to serve the living and true God, and to wait for his Son from heaven, whom he raised from the dead, Jesus who delivers us from the wrath to come.

---

[4]Ibid.

Paul rejoices that the Thessalonians, after receiving the gospel, powerfully passed on the saving message to others. The combination of their preaching the gospel and the testimony of their faith in Christ was causing a stir in Macedonia and Achaia (1 Thess. 1:7–8). Specifically, those living near and far reported how the Thessalonians "turned to God from idols to serve the living and true God, and to wait for his Son from heaven" (vv. 9–10).

Paul implies that Christ will bring final salvation when he comes again. The Thessalonians' neighbors bore witness to three things: their turning from idols, their turning to God in order to serve him, and their actively hoping in Christ's return. Specifically, the Thessalonian Christians were waiting for the return from heaven of God's Son, "whom he raised from the dead, Jesus who delivers us from the wrath to come" (v. 10). They were looking for God's Son, a favorite designation of Paul, used only here in 1 Thessalonians. Paul mentions Christ's resurrection because "to the extent that the Thessalonians accepted the resurrection as an act of God, it would give them confidence in the prospect of Christ's coming in power."[5]

Paul names the returning Son of God—Jesus—to connect the returning Savior with the figure of Jesus of Nazareth. The description that follows connects his return with ultimate salvation: "Jesus who delivers us from the wrath to come" (v. 10). Gene Green captures Paul's thought:

> The last part of the verse describes Jesus as the one *who rescues us from the coming wrath*. . . . The wrath of God is an eschatological event that is directed toward those who do not know and obey God (2 Thess. 1:6–10; Rom. 1:18). Paul assures the Thessalonians that they will not suffer this wrath because Jesus, the one who was raised from the dead, will deliver them from it (5:9; cf. Rom. 5:9).[6]

Christ's unique death and resurrection make that deliverance possible. In its fullest sense it will occur when Jesus comes again.

1 Thessalonians 4:14–18

For since we believe that Jesus died and rose again, even so, through Jesus, God will bring with him those who have fallen asleep. For this we declare to you by a word from the Lord, that we who are alive, who are left until the coming of the Lord, will not precede those who have fallen asleep. For the Lord himself will descend from heaven with a cry of command, with the voice of an archangel, and

---

[5]Charles A. Wanamaker, *Commentary on 1 & 2 Thessalonians*, New International Greek Testament Commentary (Grand Rapids: Eerdmans, 1990), 87.

[6]Gene L. Green, *The Letters to the Thessalonians*, The Pillar New Testament Commentary (Grand Rapids: Eerdmans, 2002), 110.

with the sound of the trumpet of God. And the dead in Christ will rise first. Then we who are alive, who are left, will be caught up together with them in the clouds to meet the Lord in the air, and so we will always be with the Lord. Therefore encourage one another with these words.

Though the Thessalonians have a living hope in Christ's return (1 Thess. 1:10), they have misconceptions concerning aspects of it. They mistakenly believe that their deceased members might miss out on the salvation that Jesus will bring. Paul writes to correct their mistaken belief: "But we do not want you to be uninformed, brothers, about those who are asleep, that you may not grieve as others do who have no hope" (4:13). Paul uses "sleep" as a euphemism for the death of believers.

Christians grieve when their loved ones die, but not as unbelievers, who have no hope. Rather, Paul assures his readers, "For since we believe that Jesus died and rose again, even so, through Jesus, God will bring with him those who have fallen asleep" (v. 14). Deceased believers will not miss out on final salvation; Jesus will bring them with him when he returns.

Paul spells out what the second coming will mean for living and dead Christians. "We who are alive, who are left until the coming of the Lord, will not precede those who have fallen asleep" (v. 15). Before we are taken up, the descending Lord Jesus will issue a command "and the dead in Christ will rise first" (v. 16). Then living believers will join resurrected believers in ascending "to meet the Lord in the air, and so we will always be with the Lord" (v. 17). As a result, instead of the Thessalonians being upset when their fellow believers die, they are to "encourage one another with these words" (v. 18).

The foundation for Christian hope is "that Jesus died and rose again" (v. 14). This is the heart of salvation, but it is not its end. That involves Christ's return to apply finally to his own the salvation won by his death and resurrection. Green's words bear repeating:

> The death and resurrection of Christ becomes the paradigm and foundation for the destiny of believers. As Jesus died and was raised, so "God will take with Jesus those who have fallen asleep in him" . . . . The hope in the resurrection of believers is based on the resurrection of Christ, an event that will take place in union *with Jesus.*[7]

2 Thessalonians 1:6–10

God considers it just to repay with affliction those who afflict you, and to grant relief to you who are afflicted as well as to us, when the Lord Jesus is revealed

---

[7] Ibid., 220, italics original.

from heaven with his mighty angels in flaming fire, inflicting vengeance on those who do not know God and on those who do not obey the gospel of our Lord Jesus. They will suffer the punishment of eternal destruction, away from the presence of the Lord and from the glory of his might, when he comes on that day to be glorified in his saints, and to be marveled at among all who have believed, because our testimony to you was believed.

Paul writes to encourage a congregation whose testimony burns bright even while suffering persecution (2 Thess. 1:3–4). They are to persevere, realizing that their suffering will result in their being counted worthy to suffer for God's kingdom (v. 5). And God is not unaware of what they are enduring for his name's sake: "God considers it just to repay with affliction those who afflict you, and to grant relief to you who are afflicted" (vv. 6–7). Christ will bring relief for his own and wrath for his enemies.

These will both occur "when the Lord Jesus is revealed from heaven with his mighty angels in flaming fire" (vv. 7–8). He will punish those "who do not know God and . . . who do not obey the gospel" (v. 8). Their destiny is to "suffer the punishment of eternal destruction, away from the presence of the Lord and from the glory of his might" (v. 9). Unbelievers will suffer everlasting "destruction," the forfeiture of all that is worthwhile about human existence. They will forever be separated from God's grace and his glorious majesty.

So, Paul comforts the persecuted Thessalonians by informing them that the return of Christ will mean terrible and eternal punishment for their adversaries. The apostle also comforts them by promising them relief from affliction when Jesus returns. His return will mean wrath for God's enemies. But his saints, including the Thessalonians, will revel in "the glory of his might" because on "that day" he will "be glorified in his saints, and . . . be marveled at among all who have believed" (vv. 9–10). The second coming will consummate believers' salvation as they stand in amazement and glorify him who saved them by his grace.

Titus 2:11–14

For the grace of God has appeared, bringing salvation for all people, training us to renounce ungodliness and worldly passions, and to live self-controlled, upright, and godly lives in the present age, waiting for our blessed hope, the appearing of the glory of our great God and Savior Jesus Christ, who gave himself for us to redeem us from all lawlessness and to purify for himself a people for his own possession who are zealous for good works.

Paul announces the appearance of God's grace in the person and work of Christ. In fulfillment of God's promise to Abraham—"in you all the families of the earth shall be blessed" (Gen. 12:3)—the gospel has gone to "every tribe and language and people and nation" (Rev. 5:9). Christ's saving death represents his self-giving for us. His primary purpose in this? "To redeem us from all lawlessness and to purify for himself a people for his own possession who are zealous for good works" (Titus 2:11–14). Christ died for us to deliver us from ungodliness and make us his own. He redeemed us and bought us for himself. Consequently, we should be eager to do good.

Christ's saving work, in addition to putting people right with God, is a powerful incentive for godly and sober Christian living: "For the grace of God has appeared . . . training us to renounce ungodliness and worldly passions, and to live self-controlled, upright, and godly lives in the present age" (Titus 1:11–12). The atonement saves and motivates God's people.

Believers are further described as those who are "waiting for . . . the appearing of the glory of our great God and Savior Jesus Christ" (2:13). The second coming will display the glory of the Lord Jesus Christ as never before. Philip Towner says it well: Paul here describes "the future parousia of Jesus Christ as *the* saving/helping epiphany of 'the glory of our great God and Savior.' In his return, God's glory will be fully and finally revealed."[8] He will not come in weakness, as he did in his first coming, to suffer and die. Instead, he will return triumphantly, crushing his foes and bringing final deliverance to his holy people. As a result the prospect of Christ's return is "our blessed hope" (v. 13). Anticipation of that return and the final salvation it brings should fill us with joy. He who died for us and lived again will come in great glory. That will be the greatest day!

Teaching in the General Epistles

Hebrews 9:26–28

> But as it is, he has appeared once for all at the end of the ages to put away sin by the sacrifice of himself. And just as it is appointed for man to die once, and after that comes judgment, so Christ, having been offered once to bear the sins of many, will appear a second time, not to deal with sin but to save those who are eagerly waiting for him.

---

[8]Philip H. Towner, *The Letters to Timothy and Titus*, The New International Commentary on the New Testament (Grand Rapids: Eerdmans, 2006), 758.

The writer to the Hebrews focuses more on Christ's first coming than on his second. In his first coming, the Son as prophet brought God's new covenant revelation (Heb. 1:2). The Son as King ascends and sits down at the Father's right hand, where angels worship him in his coronation (vv. 5–14). Above all, Hebrews stresses that the Son as priest makes "purification for sins" in his crucifixion (v. 3).

As Mediator of the new covenant "by means of his own blood" he secures "an eternal redemption" and an "eternal inheritance" for believers (9:12, 15). How does he accomplish this? Unlike the Old Testament high priests, who offered animal sacrifices in the holy places every year, he "appeared once for all at the end of the ages to put away sin by the sacrifice of himself" (v. 26). He makes final expiation for sins.

The author to the Hebrews warns that "it is appointed for man to die once, and after that comes judgment" (v. 27). Since Adam's fall we all die and there is no chance after death for salvation. It is in this life that we must repent and believe in Christ to be saved. We die once and so did Christ. In his first coming he came to die: he was "offered once to bear the sins of many" (v. 28). In his second coming he will not die but will bring final salvation to his people: he "will appear a second time, not to deal with sin but to save those who are eagerly waiting for him" (v. 28).

More than any other book in Scripture, Hebrews emphasizes that Jesus accomplished salvation "once for all" in his death on the cross (7:27; 9:12, 26, 28; 10:10). And Hebrews correlates his crucifixion and resurrection (7:23–25), which together are the center of his saving accomplishment. But they are not the end of it. He finishes applying the salvation won in his death and resurrection only when he returns "to save those who are eagerly waiting for him" (9:28). I cannot improve on William Lane's words:

> The parousia is not an event that can add anything to the sacrificial office Christ has already fulfilled. The force of sin has been decisively broken by his death. . . . But his appearance will confirm that his sacrifice has been accepted and that he has secured the blessings of salvation for those whom he represented. For those who are the heirs of salvation . . . it will mean full enjoyment of their inheritance. The parousia is thus the key event in the realization of salvation.[9]

1 Peter 1:13

Therefore, preparing your minds for action, and being sober-minded, set your hope fully on the grace that will be brought to you at the revelation of Jesus Christ.

---

[9]William L. Lane, *Hebrews 9–13*, Word Biblical Commentary (Dallas: Word, 1991), 251.

After reminding his readers of the greatness of the salvation that God has prepared for them, Peter exhorts them to mental preparedness and spiritual sobriety: "Therefore, preparing your minds for action, and being sober-minded" (1 Pet. 1:13). Does the apostle have a specific event in mind? Indeed, he does, for he immediately speaks of Christ's return, "the revelation of Jesus Christ" (v. 13).

If we are honest, many of us have mixed feelings about the second coming. We long to see our Savior, but are afraid of giving an account, of being judged, of Christ being ashamed of us, and of losing rewards. But Peter points our minds in another direction: "Set your hope fully on the grace that will be brought to you at the revelation of Jesus Christ" (v. 13). Christ's second coming will mean the greatest outpouring of grace that we have ever seen. God's grace in Christ is past (Eph. 2:8–9), present (Heb. 4:16), and future (here). Jesus will shower us with grace when he comes for us. We need not fear his return but should be eager for the grace he will lavish on us then. And such a prospect is strong motivation to live for him now.

1 John 3:2–3

> Beloved, we are God's children now, and what we will be has not yet appeared; but we know that when he appears we shall be like him, because we shall see him as he is. And everyone who thus hopes in him purifies himself as he is pure.

First John loves to sing of the love of the Father and the Son. It does so in many passages, most famously in 4:7–19. John bursts forth in 3:1, "See what kind of love the Father has given to us, that we should be called children of God; and so we are."

John makes the important distinction between the "already," what God has already done for us in Christ, and the "not yet," the good things that God will yet do for us in the future. "Beloved, we are God's children *now*, and what we will be has *not yet* appeared" (1 John 3:2). Already God the Father has placed us into his family as his adult sons or daughters. This is a supreme demonstration of his love. But there is more to come! Because "what we will be has not yet appeared" (v. 2), we do not know exactly what it shall be.

But this we do know: "When he appears we shall be like him" (v. 3). One way in which Scripture expresses our final salvation is to speak of our conformity to Christ. He is "the firstborn among many brothers" to whose image we will conform (Rom. 8:29). He, the eternal Son of God, redeemed us slaves of sin that we might belong to the same family of God as he (Gal. 4:4–7). He, our older brother, is the one who sanctifies us. As a result we are sanctified, and "he is not ashamed to call" us "brothers" (Heb. 2:11). "Just as we have borne the image of the man of dust [Adam], we shall also bear the image of the man of heaven [Jesus]" in resurrected glory (1 Cor. 15:49).

When will this occur? "When he appears," when he comes again. Christ's return will mean the fulfillment of our salvation as we are conformed to him in perfect holiness and glory. "A coming glimpse of Jesus will complete the redemptive work that the incarnation inaugurated," Robert Yarbrough says well.[10] And this great hope strengthens us now to live for him: "And everyone who thus hopes in him purifies himself as he is pure" (1 John 3:2–3).

Teaching in the Book of Revelation

As befits its name, the last book in the Bible paints an awesome picture of Christ's second coming:

> Then I saw heaven opened, and behold, a white horse! The one sitting on it is called Faithful and True, and in righteousness he judges and makes war. His eyes are like a flame of fire, and on his head are many diadems, and he has a name written that no one knows but himself. He is clothed in a robe dipped in blood, and the name by which he is called is The Word of God. And the armies of heaven, arrayed in fine linen, white and pure, were following him on white horses. From his mouth comes a sharp sword with which to strike down the nations, and he will rule them with a rod of iron. He will tread the winepress of the fury of the wrath of God the Almighty. On his robe and on his thigh he has a name written, King of kings and Lord of lords. (Rev. 19:11–16)

There is no doubt whom these verses describe, for many of the descriptions were used previously in the Apocalypse (and one in John's Gospel). He is faithful and true (Rev. 19:11; see also 3:7, 14); his eyes are like a flame of fire (19:12; also 1:14; 2:18); his name is the Word of God (John 1:1); from his mouth comes a sharp sword (Rev. 19:15; also 1:16); he will rule the nations with a rod of iron (19:15; also 2:27; 12:5); and he is King of kings and Lord of lords (19:16; also 17:14). These verses describe the returning Christ.

Revelation 19:11–16 powerfully speaks of him and his heavenly armies vanquishing his enemies. In the passage that immediately precedes it John speaks of God's people rejoicing at the end:

---

[10]Robert W. Yarbrough, *1–3 John*, Baker Exegetical Commentary on the New Testament (Grand Rapids: Baker Academic, 2008), 179.

Hallelujah!
For the Lord our God
    the Almighty reigns.
Let us rejoice and exult
    and give him the glory,
for the marriage of the Lamb has come,
    and his Bride has made herself ready. (19:6–7)

There will be great blessing for those "who are invited to the marriage supper of the Lamb" (19:9). The Lamb, of course, is another name for Christ, his bride is the church, and the wedding supper and wedding take place at his return.

Other passages in Revelation promise blessing to believers at the end:

> The time [came] . . .
> . . . for rewarding your servants, the prophets and saints,
>   and those who fear your name,
>   both small and great. (11:18)

> Now the salvation and the power and the kingdom of our God and the authority of his Christ have come. . . . They have conquered him by the blood of the Lamb. (12:10–11)

These passages do not explicitly mention the second coming, but we know from other Scripture that the events they describe take place at the return of the Savior. Another text does mention Christ's return: "'Behold, I am coming soon, bringing my recompense with me, to repay everyone for what he has done. . . .' Blessed are those who wash their robes, so that they may have the right to the tree of life" (22:12, 14).

Revelation, then, in agreement with the rest of the New Testament, promises wrath to God's enemies and final salvation to those who have been saved freely by his grace. This final salvation is the application of the first-century achievement of him who is "the firstborn from the dead," who said, "I died, and behold I am alive forevermore," the one "who died and came to life" (1:5, 18; 2:8). Indeed, those who participate in this final salvation are those "ransomed . . . for God from every tribe and language and people and nation" by the blood of the Lamb who was slain (5:9).

How Does Jesus's Second Coming Save?

Scripture teaches us numerous specific ways in which Jesus's second coming saves. Before looking at them, let us survey some general ways.

In Jesus's famous sermon concerning last things in Mark he says that the returning Christ "will send out the angels and gather his elect from the four winds, from the ends of the earth to the ends of heaven" (Mark 13:27). There is no doubt that this means good things for God's people, although we are not given details concerning those things.

Likewise, the writer to the Hebrews, after affirming that Jesus offered himself up once for all time as a sacrifice for sins, writes that he "will appear a second time, not to deal with sin but to save those who are eagerly waiting for him" (Heb. 9:28). Jesus's return means salvation for all who believe in his name.

The reason his second coming means salvation is that those who know him will then experience the greatest outpouring of God's grace that they have ever seen. Peter urges his readers, "Therefore, preparing your minds for action, and being sober-minded, set your hope fully on the grace that will be brought to you at the revelation of Jesus Christ" (1 Pet. 1:13).

The book of Revelation announces that when the time arrives "for the dead to be judged," it also will be the time for "rewarding" God's "servants . . . those who fear" his "name" (Rev. 11:18). Consequently, the end will be a time for praising God. We saints will cry out "Hallelujah!" because "the Lord our God the Almighty reigns," and we will "rejoice and exult and give him the glory." Amazingly, we, the people of God, are the bride of the Lamb and will experience great joy because "blessed are those who are invited to the marriage supper of the Lamb" (19:6–9).

Along with these general statements, Scripture gives at least seven particular ways in which Christ's second coming saves.

Jesus's Return Means Our Being with Him and the Father

Jesus's return saves in that it means being with him and the Father. Jesus himself asserts this in John's Gospel: "In my Father's house are many rooms. If it were not so, would I have told you that I go to prepare a place for you? And if I go and prepare a place for you, I will come again and will take you to myself, that where I am you may be also" (John 14:2–3). Here Jesus likens heaven to a large house with many rooms. He has returned to the Father's house to prepare a place for each believer. The point is that the Father loves us and we will be "right at home" in his heavenly presence. We will not feel out of place; we will belong in our Father's heavenly house.

Paul teaches the same truth when he clears up the Thessalonians' confusion concerning Jesus's return. They had the mistaken idea that their fellow believers who died might miss out on final salvation. But Paul says that they are not to grieve, as the unsaved do, when their loved ones die. They will not miss out on final salvation, but Jesus will raise them from the dead. "Then we who are alive, who are left, will be caught up together with them in the clouds to meet the Lord in the air, and so we will always be with the Lord" (1 Thess. 4:17). Jesus's second coming will mean salvation for living and dead believers. Salvation is here expressed as being with Jesus forever. It is triggered by the second coming at which time all the saints will go to be with the Lord.

Jesus's Return Brings Glory

Paul asserts that Jesus's return will mean glory for Christians. Although we live on earth, "Our citizenship is in heaven." From there "we await a Savior, the Lord Jesus Christ, who will transform our lowly body to be like his glorious body, by the power that enables him even to subject all things to himself" (Phil. 3:20–21). Our mortal bodies are lowly because they are subject to illness and death. At his return Christ will exert his almighty power and cause our lowly bodies to share his resurrection glory. His second coming will mean great glory for all of the redeemed.

God has spiritually joined every believer to his beloved Son, so that his saving benefits become ours. We spiritually died with him, were raised with him, and are presently seated in the heavenly places with him (Col. 2:20; 3:1, 3; Eph. 2:6). We are so united to him that twice Scripture teaches that Christ's second coming will mean a second coming for us, so to speak. "When Christ who is your life appears, then you also will appear with him in glory" (Col. 3:4; see also Rom. 8:19). Paul means that Christians' true identity is only partially revealed now because it is obscured by sin. We are so joined to Christ spiritually that our full identity will be revealed only when Jesus returns. In that sense we will have a "second coming" too. Our Lord's return means the revelation of our true identity, and that involves appearing with him "in glory."

Jesus's Return Brings Eternal Life

Jesus's message concerning the sheep and goats in Matthew 25 is the most famous biblical passage on the eternal destinies of human beings. He teaches powerfully that the sheep will be blessed with a rich inheritance in the final kingdom of God, but the goats will be cursed forever in the fire prepared for the Devil and his angels. Jesus leaves the following words ringing in his hearers' ears: "And these will go away into eternal punishment, but the righteous into eternal life" (Matt. 25:46). As we consider these sobering words, it is important to keep in mind the way Matthew introduces Jesus's teaching: "When the Son of Man comes in his glory, and all the angels with him, then he will sit on his glorious throne" (v. 31). It is the returning King Jesus who will condemn the wicked to hell and bless the righteous with everlasting life.

The Bible concludes on a similar note. Near the end of Revelation, a speaker says, "Behold, I am coming soon, bringing my recompense with me, to repay everyone for what he has done" (Rev. 22:12). The speaker is Jesus, who will come again and reward his people (and punish the wicked). Next, John utters a beatitude: "Blessed are those who wash their robes, so that they may have the right to the tree of life" (Rev. 22:14). Here again Scripture pronounces Christians as "blessed," filled with joy, at the end. Why? Because they have been cleansed by the blood of the Lamb and as a result have "the right to the tree of life." The tree representing eternal life with God was found in the garden of Eden and reappears at the end of the biblical story. Adam and Eve were banished from the garden so that they would not eat from the tree and live forever in a sinful state. At the end all sin will be removed from God's people, and they will have free access to the tree, which symbolizes abundant life (Rev. 22:2).

Jesus's Return Brings Joy

Both Paul and John speak of the consummate joy of the redeemed. As we just saw, John, after recording Jesus's promise to return, speaks of the bliss awaiting the saints: "*Blessed* are those who wash their robes, so that they may have the right to the tree of life" (Rev. 22:14).

Paul's message is similar. After extolling the grace of God that brings salvation, he directs our attention to "the appearing of the glory of our great God and Savior Jesus Christ, who gave himself for us" (Titus 2:11, 13–14). The apostle speaks of the returning Redeemer. How does he describe Christ's "appearing"? It is "our blessed hope" (v. 13). The hope of the Lord and Savior's coming again fills Christians with joy as they anticipate being with him forever.

Jesus's Return Brings Deliverance

Another benefit that Jesus brings at his return is deliverance. This deliverance takes two forms. First, he will deliver his people from any persecution they are enduring. Paul makes this plain in the beginning of 2 Thessalonians: "God considers it just to repay with affliction those who afflict you, and to grant relief to you who are afflicted as well as to us, when the Lord Jesus is revealed from heaven with his mighty angels in flaming fire" (1:6–8). On that day he will come "to be glorified in his saints, and to be marveled at" by all true believers (v. 10). The next passage tells us why.

Second, Christ will deliver his people from eternal punishment. At the beginning of his first letter to the Christians in Thessalonica, the apostle proudly rehearses the testimony of the church in that city. People in surrounding areas "themselves report . . . how you turned to God from idols to serve the living and true God, and to wait for his Son from heaven, whom he raised from the dead, Jesus who delivers us from the wrath to come" (1 Thess. 1:9–10). Because Jesus's (death and) resurrection save, when he comes "from heaven" he will bring final deliverance "from the wrath to come" (v. 10).

Jesus's Return Brings the Kingdom and Our Inheritance

In the same message about the sheep and the goats referred to above, Jesus promises more blessings to the saints at his return. Before he condemns the goats, who are on his left, he gives words of comfort to the sheep, on his right: "Come, you who are blessed by my Father, inherit the kingdom prepared for you from the foundation of the world" (Matt. 25:34). Here Jesus combines familial and royal imagery. God is our Father, and all who trust his Son for salvation become God's children and receive an inheritance. God is also King, as is his Son, and the inheritance of the sons and daughters of God is "the kingdom prepared for" them "from the foundation of the world." We learn from other Scriptures that the final dimension of the kingdom of God, our inheritance, is nothing less than the new heaven and new earth!

Jesus's Return Brings Cosmic Restoration

Peter speaks of Jesus's sufferings to his hearers in Jerusalem and then invites them to repent. What will be the results? That the penitent hearers may know the forgiveness of sins and that "times of refreshing may come from the presence of the Lord, and that he may send the Christ appointed for you, Jesus, whom heaven must receive until the time for restoring all the things" (Acts 3:20–21). Jesus's return will bring many blessings for his people, as we have seen. It will result in God's "restoring all things" according to Old Testament prophetic prediction. Here again the second coming issues forth in the new heavens and new earth foretold by Isaiah (65:17; 66:22–23).

PART *Two*

PICTURES

Introduction to the Pictures of Jesus's Saving Events

Thus far we have seen that we are saved by works—not our own, for they could never save us—but the works of Jesus. The works he accomplished to save us form one unified work that took place in nine events. Each of the previous nine chapters has examined one of those events. Two are essential prerequisites: the incarnation of the Son of God and his sinless earthly life. Without these nobody would be delivered from sin. Nevertheless, neither of them on its own nor both together are sufficient for salvation. They are necessary but not sufficient conditions of deliverance.

The necessary and sufficient conditions of salvation are Jesus's crucifixion and resurrection. They are at the center of his work of rescue. They are distinct events, but Scripture links them as the heart and soul of redemption. They are preceded by two essential preconditions and followed by five essential consequences. The consequences, like the prerequisites, are necessary but not sufficient conditions. As necessary, they had to occur for salvation to reach us and for us to experience it. They are Jesus's ascension, session (sitting at God's right hand), pouring out the Spirit at Pentecost, intercession, and second coming.

Christ's nine events are unlike other events in some ways and just like them in others. The nine events are unlike any others in that they alone rescue sinners from their plight. Only Christ's deeds are redemptive. In another way, however, his deeds are just like any others. No events are self-interpreting. Events need to be interpreted for people to understand them aright. When the first-century Romans heard reports of the early Christians breaking bread and drinking wine together in a ceremony having to do with Jesus's death, they did not immediately understand. They did not make connections with Exodus 24 and Jeremiah 31 and interpret the Lord's Supper as the ratification of the new covenant. Instead, they accused the early believers of cannibalism!

Events need interpretation. Even Jesus's death and resurrection are not self-interpreting. People could have stood at the foot of his cross and not understood its significance. Some did! As George Ladd taught years ago, God's revelation is deed-word revelation.[1] It is deed revelation because the God of creation and providence chooses to act in redemptive history. It is word revelation because he graciously stoops to explain the meaning of his deeds to his covenant people. Thus it is deed-word revelation, divinely given explanation of divine acts.

Scripture interprets Christ's saving accomplishment in two main ways. First, it does so via his threefold office of prophet, priest, and king. These Old Testament offices coalesce in the ministry of the Son of God, who is God's supreme prophet, priest, and king, as presented powerfully in Hebrews 1. The Son is the great prophet through whom "in these last days [God] has spoken to us" (v. 2). He is our great High Priest and "after making purification for sins, he sat down at the right hand of the Majesty on high" (v. 3). Hebrews 1 is chiefly about his coronation as King when he sat down in the place of highest honor and authority in the universe. Christ's threefold office will have to be the subject of another volume; this one treats it only briefly at the end of the chapter on Christ's session.

Second, Scripture interprets Christ's saving work by painting pictures. It uses images, motifs, themes to explain what Jesus did for us. Although there are many such images in Scripture, I count six major ones. These pictures come from six spheres of life: human relationships, the institution of slavery, the court of law, the battlefield, creation, and worship. The picture from the realm of relationships is that of reconciliation or peacemaking. Christ by his death and resurrection establishes peace between human beings and God. The image from the world of slavery is redemption, whereby Christ with his own blood purchases those in the bondage of sin and Satan, liberates them, and claims them for his own. The picture pertaining to law is legal penal substitution. Here Jesus dies to uphold God's justice and to pay the penalty that sins deserved. The image from the domain of warfare is Christus Victor, where the incarnate Son is our champion, who via his cross and empty tomb defeats our enemies of Satan, demons, death, and hell. The picture having to do with creation depicts Christ as the second Adam, who by his death and resurrection overturns the curse brought on by the disobedience of the first Adam. And the

---

[1]George Eldon Ladd, *A Theology of the New Testament* (Grand Rapids: Eerdmans, 1974), 31–32.

image corresponding to worship is Christ as our great High Priest, who offers himself as the final sacrifice for sins.

Each of the following six chapters deals with one of these pictures of the work of Christ. Every chapter traces one theme in Scripture from the Old Testament into the New in the Gospels, Acts, Epistles, and Revelation. The last few pages of each chapter draw together the teaching of its picture. I invite you to come with me on a journey to look at the pictures of Christ's saving accomplishment, that we might better appreciate what he did and respond accordingly.

Reconciler
Redeemer
Legal Substitute
Victor
Second Adam
Sacrifice

Chapter 10

Christ Our Reconciler

I. Howard Marshall, after acknowledging that two leading New Testament scholars give reconciliation a central place in New Testament theology, laments its marginalization by most scholars.[1]

> But now, on the other hand, consider what happens, or rather doesn't happen, in the fullest contemporary English reference work on the Bible, the *Anchor Bible Dictionary*, a work running to six volumes, each of over 1000 pp. With 6000 pp. to play with, the compilers could evidently find no room in volume 5, in between entries on such central themes of the Bible as "Rechabites" and "Recorder" (p. 633), for any mention of reconciliation; there is not even a cross-reference to some other article that would include the topic. Yes, "Redemption" is covered; so too is "Atonement" in a rather broad sweep covering 5 pp. and including one paragraph headed "Reconciliation" (I, 521), but otherwise we shall hunt in vain for mention of the theme.
>
> Even in confessedly evangelical publications, where you would expect to find particular attention devoted to the subject, the coverage is slight. One recent dictionary treats it along with "Forgiveness," but it is forgiveness that gets the major share of the coverage. Another treats it under "Peace." It scarcely figures in the index of the most recent monograph on New Testament theology.[2]

---

[1] I. Howard Marshall, *Aspects of the Atonement: Cross and Resurrection in the Reconciling of God and Humanity* (London: Paternoster, 2007), 99. The two scholars are Peter Stuhlmacher, *Historical Criticism and Theological Interpretation of Scripture: Toward a Hermeneutic of Consent* (Philadelphia: Fortress, 1977); and Ralph P. Martin, *Reconciliation: A Study of Paul's Theology* (Atlanta: John Knox, 1981).
[2] Marshall, *Aspects of the Atonement*, 100–101.

Marshall is right; reconciliation has not received the attention it deserves. With no pretensions that I will remedy the situation, I will devote this chapter to it.

Surprisingly, unlike any of the other major biblical pictures describing Christ's saving work, and unlike the great majority of New Testament themes, reconciliation appears to lack clear Old Testament background.[3] And, although one could cite parables of Jesus as illustrations (e.g., the prodigal son), it remains for Paul to explicate the doctrine. I will exegete his four key passages devoted to the topic before systematizing findings: Romans 5:1–11; 2 Corinthians 5:16–21; Ephesians 2:11–19; and Colossians 1:19–23.

Romans 5:1–11

> Therefore, since we have been justified by faith, we have peace with God through our Lord Jesus Christ. Through him we have also obtained access by faith into this grace in which we stand, and we rejoice in hope of the glory of God. More than that, we rejoice in our sufferings, knowing that suffering produces endurance, and endurance produces character, and character produces hope, and hope does not put us to shame, because God's love has been poured into our hearts through the Holy Spirit who has been given to us.
>
> For while we were still weak, at the right time Christ died for the ungodly. For one will scarcely die for a righteous person—though perhaps for a good person one would dare even to die—but God shows his love for us in that while we were still sinners, Christ died for us. Since, therefore, we have now been justified by his blood, much more shall we be saved by him from the wrath of God. For if while we were enemies we were reconciled to God by the death of his Son, much more, now that we are reconciled, shall we be saved by his life. More than that, we also rejoice in God through our Lord Jesus Christ, through whom we have now received reconciliation.

This reconciliation passage contains much valuable instruction. Reconciliation and justification are brought together in verse 1. What is their relationship? They may simply be two different ways of speaking of God's saving action in Christ, or here reconciliation may be a result of justification. We will be in a better position to address this issue at the end of this chapter.

The text says, "We have peace with God," not vice versa. So it is in every reconciliation passage. But, although Scripture always says "we were reconciled to God" and never "God is reconciled to us," is that meaning implied? Once more, I will address that question at the end of this chapter.

---

[3]Brian Vickers, *Jesus' Blood and Righteousness: Paul's Theology of Imputation* (Wheaton, IL: Crossway, 2006), 163–70, discusses this matter and concludes that it has an Old Testament sacrificial background.

Before treating the famous Adam-Christ parallel in Romans 5:12–21, Paul shares four advantages of justification. Justification views salvation in legal terms. God the Father, acting as Judge, declares righteous all sinners who trust Christ for deliverance. This declaration is based on Christ's death viewed in "negative" and "positive" terms. Viewed negatively, Christ's cross was a propitiation that turned away God's wrath (3:25–26). Viewed positively, Christ's cross was "one act of righteousness" (5:18) credited to the spiritual bank account of believers.

Peace, Joy, and Hope

The benefits of free justification that Paul speaks of here start with reconciliation, peace with God (Rom. 5:1). No longer do our sins alienate us from a holy God because he has made peace through his Son's death on the cross. As a result, we have access to God and his ongoing grace (v. 2). Joy and hope are additional benefits of justification: "We rejoice in hope of the glory of God" (v. 2). The confidence that one day we will see Christ and share his glory creates hope and joy now.

We not only celebrate the thought of being with Christ in the future; we also rejoice in the present, even when we suffer: "More than that, we rejoice in our sufferings, knowing that suffering produces endurance, and endurance produces character, and character produces hope" (vv. 3–4). It is easy to track Paul's thought up to a point. When believers look to the Lord in suffering, they learn persistence. And if they continue to persist, eventually their character changes and they become reliable people. But it is not as easy to understand how "character produces hope" (v. 4). We must read between the lines. Paul seems to imply that, as we see God cultivating our character now, it strengthens our faith in what we cannot see—God's future blessings. As Christians respond to sufferings faithfully, their hope in the future glory of God grows. And such hope does not disappoint us because God has poured his Holy Spirit into our hearts to assure us within that God loves us (v. 5).

God's Incredible Love

Paul says more about God's incredible love (vv. 6–8). The apostle differentiates God's act of love from those of normal human affairs. It is rare for human beings to give their lives for others—such a deed is heroic (v. 7). Moreover, such self-sacrifice, as rare as it is, always is done for those whom we highly esteem. Soldiers fall on grenades to save their friends; no one falls on a grenade to save enemies! But God's love surpasses human love: "For while we were still weak, at the right time Christ died for the ungodly. . . . God shows his love for us in that while we were still sinners, Christ died for us" (vv. 6, 8). We did not earn God's love. He did not give Christ for us because we deserved him. To the contrary, we were "weak," "ungodly," "sinners," unable to rescue ourselves (vv. 6, 8).

A Pattern

Paul's praising God's peerless love forms the center of a pattern that he sketches in Romans 5:1–11. We already saw four gains of justification in verses 1–5: reconciliation, joy, hope, and God's love, in that order. Paul repeats these advantages of justification in reverse order: God's love (vv. 6–8), hope (vv. 9–10), joy (v. 11), and reconciliation (v. 11). This pattern (an inverted parallelism or chiasm) follows the form ABCD DCBA, where the letters stand for ideas.

A Reconciliation (v. 1)

  B Joy (v. 2)

    C Hope (vv. 2–5)

      D God's love (v. 5)

      D God's love (vv. 6–8)

    C Hope (vv. 9–10)

  B Joy (v. 11)

A Reconciliation (v. 11)

We Shall Be Saved

> Since, therefore, we have now been justified by his blood, much more shall we be saved by him from the wrath of God. For if while we were enemies we were reconciled to God by the death of his Son, much more, now that we are reconciled, shall we be saved by his life. (Rom. 5:9–10)

After Paul extols God's amazing love that enflames our hope of eternal glory, he argues for preservation—God's keeping his people saved to the end. It is an awesome demonstration of love that God saves and keeps his saints. It is this preservation that undergirds Paul's affirmation that "hope does not put us to shame" (v. 5). To teach preservation Paul twice uses a Jewish argument from the more difficult to the less difficult. He employs the catchphrase "much more" to signal his use of this argument. In verse 9 he argues in terms of justification, and in verse 10 in terms of reconciliation.

As we saw in chapter 3, "Christ's Death," Paul employs shorthand in verse 9 and longhand in verse 10. The full argument involves an "if" clause followed by a "then" clause, and we find both types of clauses in verse 10. But verse 9 only has a "then" clause. Paul wants readers to supply an "if" clause from the preceding verses: If, when we were guilty before a holy and just God, he justified us through the death of his Son. . . . "Since, therefore, we have now been justified by his blood, much more shall we be saved by him from the wrath of God." As he frequently does in his writings, Paul uses "wrath" to refer to God's future punishment of unbelievers in hell.[4]

Paul's argument proceeds from the harder to the easier: if God did the more difficult thing—justified condemned sinners—he will surely do the easier thing—keep saved to the end those he has justified. This is a strong argument for God's keeping his saints saved. God did the inconceivable and declared the unrighteous righteous through Christ. Now he will do the expected—he will honor his previous verdict and not condemn his justified people.

To emphasize his point, Paul gives a similar argument for preservation. This time, however, he speaks of salvation in terms of reconciliation rather than justification. "For if while we were enemies we were reconciled to God by the death of his Son, much more, now that we are reconciled, shall we be saved by his life" (Rom. 5:9–10). Here Paul writes in longhand, giving both "if" and "then" clauses: if when we were God's enemies he made us his friends by his Son's death, now that we are his friends we can be certain that he will keep us saved by his Son's resurrection. This time Paul does not state what we shall be saved from, but he has already told us in verse 9—God's wrath.

Teaching

The apostle teaches us much about reconciliation in this one verse. First, he gives the need for reconciliation—"we were enemies" (v. 10). Reconciliation is a picture of salvation drawn from the arena of personal relations. And the need of reconciliation is fractured personal relations. We need to be reconciled because we are God's foes due to our sins. We "once were alienated and hostile in mind, doing evil deeds" (Col. 1:21).

Second, Paul gives the remedy for our hostility to God. God acts through Christ to overcome our hostility. Specifically, it is "the death of his Son" and "his life" that rescue us (Rom. 5:9–10). The former, of course, refers to Jesus's

---

[4]He also uses "wrath" similarly in Rom. 1:18; 2:5, 8; 3:5; 9:22; 12:19; Eph. 2:3; 5:6; Col. 3:6; 1 Thess. 1:10; 2:16; 5:9. See Douglas J. Moo, "Paul on Hell," in Christopher W. Morgan and Robert A. Peterson, eds., *Hell Under Fire* (Grand Rapids: Zondervan, 2004), 91–109.

crucifixion. And by means of the latter "a reference to the resurrection of Christ is certainly intended," as Thomas Schreiner explains.[5] This is the only place where reconciliation is attributed to Christ's resurrection; in the other three passages it is always attributed to his death. It is important to note at this point, however, that Paul's references to Christ's blood in verse 9 and his life in verse 10 do not divide the accomplishment of salvation between his death and resurrection. Rather, reminiscent of 4:25, "Christ's death and resurrection are inseparable in effecting salvation."[6] As a result, either (as a metonymy) can stand for Christ's whole saving achievement.

Third, Christ's saving work results in reconciliation, both objective and subjective. When Paul says, "We have peace with God through our Lord Jesus Christ" (Rom. 5:1), he speaks of God's accomplishment in Christ outside of us. No longer are we enemies; now we are friends. And this objective accomplishment has wonderful subjective results. In Christ God has made peace outside of us with the result that we now have peace within our hearts.

Fourth, there are even more positive results. "More than that, we also rejoice in God through our Lord Jesus Christ, through whom we have now received reconciliation." That is, the reconciling work of Christ "our peace" (Eph. 2:14) brings us joy in God himself. It is no accident that Paul begins and ends this passage (Rom. 5:1–11) with peace and joy, as we noted in the preceding pattern (vv. 1, 11).

Fifth, let us not lose sight of Paul's employment of the doctrine of reconciliation in Romans 5:10–11 to underscore our preservation. Douglas Moo is correct (referring to verses 9–10): Paul returns to the idea of hope and this time highlights "the certainty of Christian hope."[7] Twice Paul says unequivocally that we shall be saved (vv. 9, 10). Our heavenly Father loves us and assures us via his promises that guarantee our final salvation in Christ. Judith Gundry Volf aptly summarizes Paul's message:

> In 5:9, 10, Paul draws out the significance of God's gracious love as the guarantee that Christian hope will not disappoint. . . . With the help of two arguments *ad maiori ad minus* [from the greater to the lesser], he shows that God's accomplishment of the scarcely imaginable feat of demonstrating love toward rebellious sin-

---

[5]Thomas R. Schreiner, *Romans*, Baker Exegetical Commentary on the New Testament (Grand Rapids: Baker Academic, 1998), 264.
[6]Ibid.
[7]Douglas J. Moo, *The Epistle to the Romans*, The New International Commentary on the New Testament (Grand Rapids: Eerdmans, 1996), 309.

ners in the cross of Christ guarantees the future salvation of those who are God's
own people in fulfillment of their hope.[8]

Sixth, again we note the apostle's conjoining of justification and reconciliation
in verse 1. But we are not able to discern the relation between the two from this
text. We will have to wait, therefore, to draw conclusions until we have explored
the other three reconciliation passages.

2 Corinthians 5:16–21

> From now on, therefore, we regard no one according to the flesh. Even though
> we once regarded Christ according to the flesh, we regard him thus no longer.
> Therefore, if anyone is in Christ, he is a new creation. The old has passed away;
> behold, the new has come. All this is from God, who through Christ reconciled
> us to himself and gave us the ministry of reconciliation; that is, in Christ God was
> reconciling the world to himself, not counting their trespasses against them, and
> entrusting to us the message of reconciliation. Therefore, we are ambassadors for
> Christ, God making his appeal through us. We implore you on behalf of Christ,
> be reconciled to God. For our sake he made him to be sin who knew no sin, so
> that in him we might become the righteousness of God.

Fear and Love

Paul has been speaking of his motives in preaching the gospel. His aim is to
please the Lord, whether in life or death (2 Cor. 5:6–9). His motives include
"the fear of the Lord" (v. 11) and "the love of Christ" (v. 14).

First, "knowing the fear of the Lord, we persuade others," he writes (v. 11).
Paul knows that each person will "appear before the judgment seat of Christ"
to give an account (v. 10). Therefore, he warns sinners of the coming judgment
and points them to Christ as he is offered in the gospel.

In spite of enemies' attacks on Paul's character and message, he is confident
before the Lord as to his sincerity, a confidence that he hopes the Corinthians
share (v. 12). He wants them to be able to answer his detractors (v. 12). Linda
Belleville comments, "His rivals take pride in the externals or *what is seen*. Paul
takes pride in the internals or *what is in the heart*."[9] Paul uses sarcasm, quoting
words that his attackers used against him as arguments in his favor: "For if we are
beside ourselves, it is for God; if we are in our right mind, it is for you" (v. 13).

---

[8]Judith M. Gundry Volf, *Paul and Perseverance: Staying In and Falling Away* (Louisville: John Knox,
1990), 53.
[9]Linda L. Belleville, *2 Corinthians*, The IVP New Testament Commentary (Downers Grove, IL: Inter-
Varsity, 1996), 147, italics original.

Second, although the apostle is motivated partly by a proper fear of God, he insists that his main motive for ministry is "the love of Christ," displayed in his atoning death (v. 14). This death, motivated by love, in turn motivates Christians to live for him who "died and was raised" (v. 15). I cannot improve on Philip Hughes's evaluation of Paul: "The great compelling motive force in his life since conversion is that of love; not, however, love originating, far less ending, in himself, but the love which originates and ends with God in Christ."[10]

Because he knows Christ and lives for him who was crucified and raised, Paul views people differently than he did before conversion (v. 16). No longer does he evaluate people based on worldly standards and mere externals. The implication, in light of verse 17, is that he now views people in terms of the new creation, based on the gospel and what is inside people. He views Christ differently too (v. 16). Before conversion Paul viewed Jesus superficially and erroneously as a false messiah and crucified heretic whose disciples must be eliminated.[11] Now he views him as the Messiah whose death and resurrection are the only way to know God, and whom he serves with all of his heart, soul, mind, and strength.

A New Creation

Paul then writes: "Therefore, if anyone is in Christ, he is a new creation. The old has passed away; behold, the new has come" (v. 17). It is common to think of the new creation, including "a new heaven and a new earth," as yet future, and that is the case in a number of passages (e.g., 2 Pet. 3:13; Rev. 21:1). But, as is true with every major eschatological theme, this one is "already" and "not yet." Of course, in the fullest sense the new heavens and new earth are still future. But, in a real sense, they have come already because Jesus was raised from the dead. Again Hughes hits the nail on the head:

> Paul now propounds a further consequence . . . of the Christian's identification with Christ in His death and resurrection ([2 Cor. 5] vv. 14, 15): not only does he no longer know any man according to the flesh (v. 16), but also as a man-in-Christ he is in fact a new creation—a reborn microcosm belonging to the eschatological macrocosm of the new heavens and the new earth—for whom the old order of things has given place to a transcendental experience in which everything is new.[12]

---

[10]Philip E. Hughes, *The Second Epistle to the Corinthians*, The New International Commentary on the New Testament (Grand Rapids: Eerdmans, 1962), 192.

[11]I acknowledge being helped by Murray J. Harris, *The Second Epistle to the Corinthians*, The New International Greek Testament Commentary (Grand Rapids: Eerdmans, 2005), 429.

[12]Hughes, *The Second Epistle to the Corinthians*, 201–2.

Next, Paul transitions from the theme of the new creation to that of reconcili-ation: "All this is from God, who through Christ reconciled us to himself and gave us the ministry of reconciliation" (2 Cor. 5:18). "All this is from God." God is the one who already has birthed the new creation by raising his Son from the dead. God is the one who on the last day will usher in the new heaven and earth. And God is the one who initiates reconciliation. Furthermore, Christ is the Mediator of reconciliation, for it is "through" him that God "reconciled us to himself" (v. 18). In this passage, Paul mentions two aspects of reconciliation. First, the unique ministry of reconciliation was Christ's accomplishment alone in his cross (and resurrection). Second, in addition, God "gave us the ministry of reconciliation" based on Christ's unique ministry (v. 18). The two aspects of reconciliation, then, are Christ's atonement and Christians' proclamation of that atonement.

Implied in the fact that God reconciled us to himself is our need for rec-onciliation—our estrangement from him. And once more we observe that the biblical order is "God . . . reconciled us to himself" and never "God reconciled himself to us."

In Christ God Was Reconciling the World

Paul explains in the next verse: "That is, in Christ God was reconciling the world to himself, not counting their trespasses against them, and entrusting to us the message of reconciliation" (v. 19). Again we notice the two aspects of reconciliation: Christ's cross work—"in Christ God was reconciling the world to himself"—and our proclamation—"entrusting to us the message of reconciliation."

What is more, the apostle also gives a key consequence of reconciliation: God's "not counting their trespasses against them" (v. 19). Because of the work of Christ the Mediator, God no longer reckons believers' sins against them; that is, reconciliation through Christ brings forgiveness. Murray Harris explains the imagery and its significance. To "count something to someone" is

> an accountant's expression meaning "put something down on someone's account," came to be used in a pejorative sense, "count/hold something against someone." . . . As a result of the reconciliation achieved by Christ's "becoming sin" (v. 21), God no longer debits believers' accounts with a listing of their trespasses. This non-imputation of sin ("not holding people's transgressions against them") is perhaps the closest Paul or any NT writer comes to defining forgiveness.[13]

---

[13]Harris, *The Second Epistle to the Corinthians*, 444.

There is division over the meaning of "world" in the expression, "In Christ God was reconciling the world to himself" (v. 19). Some hold that this refers to the world of human beings, constituting an expansion of the Old Testament's focus on Israel, and includes believing Gentiles. Others hold that "world" here refers to a cosmic reconciliation, involving even the subduing of demonic powers. Although the latter is a biblical idea, as we will see in Colossians 1, the former is in view here. I say this because of the words surrounding "world." It is preceded by two references to human beings ("us"). And it is followed by the explanation "not counting their trespasses against them," which does not make good sense as a cosmic reference. Harris is correct: "The movement from ἡμᾶς ["us"] (v. 18) to κόσμον ["world"] (v. 19) with regard to the objects of reconciliation is not a movement from the anthropological to the cosmological, but from the narrower to the wider anthropological focus."[14]

Ambassadors for Christ

"The ministry of reconciliation," which is introduced in verse 18 and whose message is mentioned in verse 19—"God . . . gave us the message of reconciliation"—is now explained: "Therefore, we are ambassadors for Christ, God making his appeal through us. We implore you on behalf of Christ, be reconciled to God" (v. 20). Because God acted in his Son's death to reconcile sinners, and because he wants the news of this reconciliation spread, he has made his reconciled people his ambassadors, his envoys sent into the world to broadcast the good news. Remarkably, God makes "his appeal through" these representatives. In fact, it is as if God himself implored sinners through these ambassadors, "On behalf of Christ, be reconciled to God."

Hughes captures the pathos of this verse:

> He *beseeches* his hearers. We cannot fail to detect the strong note of urgency and compassion in the Apostle's language. He sees men as God sees them, in a lost state; he has the word, which, because it is a word of reconciliation, above all else they need to hear; and, because he is proclaiming what God in His mercy and grace has already done for them in Christ, his voice has the authority of the voice of God.[15]

As Hughes implies, in the first instance the ambassadors are the apostles, commissioned by the risen Christ himself. But even as verse 21 has a broader reference, so it is not wrong to apply the words of verse 20 to all of God's

---

[14]Ibid., 443. See this source for details concerning the division and bibliography.
[15]Hughes, *The Second Epistle to the Corinthians*, 210.

reconciled people. It is startling to consider that believers in Christ can plead with sinners to be reconciled to God!

God Made Christ to Be Sin

Frequently verse 21 has been lifted out of its context and made into a general principle of the atonement. This is not wrong as long as we first place it carefully in its context. Paul wrote, "For our sake he made him to be sin who knew no sin, so that in him we might become the righteousness of God." This verse is famous because of Luther's view that it contains "a joyous exchange." Though this view has been challenged by capable evangelicals, I accept it.[16]

Paul extols him "who knew no sin." This, of course, speaks of the sinlessness of Jesus. Only one is qualified to be the "one mediator between God and men," and that is "the man Christ Jesus" (1 Tim. 2:5). Not only did the Son of God become incarnate, but he also lived a perfect life, never sinning against his Father's will. At times, Scripture focuses on Christ's "becoming obedient to the point of death, even death on a cross" (Phil. 2:8). But in 2 Corinthians 5:21, the word "knew" focuses on Christ's whole life of obedience, as Murray Harris underscores: "Paul's main focus is on Christ's freedom from sin as a human being during his whole earthly life."[17]

"For our sake," underlines the grace of God and speaks of the motive of God's working in Christ—to save poor sinners. God "made" the sinless Christ "to be sin." Although Christ's death is not explicitly mentioned here, it is mentioned in verses 14 and 15 and implied in verses 18 and 19. Scholars agree that verse 21 identifies the crucified Christ and human sin, but different views have been proposed as to the specifics of this identification:

1. God made Christ an offering for sin.
2. God treated Christ as a sinner.
3. God made Christ our sin bearer.
4. God treated Christ as if he were sin.[18]

All four views have been held by worthy scholars. The first view has a venerable pedigree, but the word "sin" (ἁμαρτία, *hamartia*) does not mean "offering for sin" anywhere else in the New Testament. The next three views differ in details but seem to be variations on the same theme: in his work of redemption the Son

---

[16]See, e.g., N. T. Wright, "On Becoming the Righteousness of God: 2 Corinthians 5:21," in D. M. Hay, ed., *Pauline Theology Volume 11: 1 and 2 Corinthians* (Minneapolis: Fortress, 1993), 208.
[17]Harris, *The Second Epistle to the Corinthians*, 450.
[18]See ibid., 452–54 for details.

of God became so closely identified with our sins and their ugly consequences that mysteriously it could be said that he was made sin. Harris bears quotation:

> V. 21a stands in stark contrast to v. 19b. Because of God's transference of sinners' sin on to the sinless one, because sin was reckoned to Christ's account, it is now not reckoned to the believer's account. This total identification of the sinless one with sinners at the cross, in assuming the full penalty and guilt of their sin, leaves no doubt that substitution as well as representation was involved.[19]

Paul ends this impressive verse with a reference to justification: "For our sake he made him to be sin who knew no sin, so that in him we might become the righteousness of God." The result of Christ's being made sin is believers' becoming God's righteousness in Christ. Although no one passage fully teaches the imputation of Christ's passive (lifelong) righteousness to believers, Brian Vickers has successfully shown that a cogent case can be made for a cumulative argument for imputation based on Romans 4:3; 5:19; and 2 Corinthians 5:21.[20] I thus end where I began discussing this text—Luther's "a joyous exchange." C. K. Barrett's words are apt:

> It is only as sinless that Christ can, in Paul's view, bear the sins of others. . . . Paul develops the thought in terms of an exchange: Christ was made *sin*, that we might become *God's righteousness*. It is important to observe that the words Paul uses are words describing relationships. . . . Paul does not say, for by definition it would not have been true, that Christ became a sinner, transgressing God's law; neither does he say, for it would have contradicted all experience (not least in Corinth) that every believer becomes immediately and automatically morally righteous, good as God is good. He says rather that Christ became *sin*; that is, he came to stand in that relation with God which normally is the result of sin, estranged from God and the object of his wrath. . . . We correspondingly, and through God's loving act in Christ, have come to stand in that relation with God which is described by the term *righteousness*, that is we are acquitted in his court, justified, reconciled. We are no longer his enemies, but his friends.[21]

Note that Barrett relates verse 21 to the previous verses dealing with reconciliation. What Barrett implies, Vickers makes explicit: "Taken in this way 5:21 does not at all stand awkwardly at the end of the paragraph as a dis-

---

[19]Ibid., 453.
[20]Vickers, *Jesus' Blood and Righteousness*.
[21]C. K. Barrett, *The Second Epistle to the Corinthians*. Harper's New Testament Commentaries (New York: Harper & Row, 1973), 180, italics original.

connected, timeless truth of salvation, but as a powerful summary of the ultimate historical-redemptive event that lies at the heart of Paul's ministry of reconciliation."[22]

Teaching

This passage increases our understanding of reconciliation. Our need for reconciliation is implied in the fact that God reconciled us to himself—overcoming our estrangement from him (vv. 18–19).

We also learn, as a corollary to our first conclusion, that God takes the initiative in reconciliation: "All this is from God, who through Christ reconciled us to himself" (v. 18). We are not surprised to learn that God, who inaugurates the new creation in Christ's resurrection, and who will usher in the new heavens and new earth, also initiates reconciliation (vv. 18–19). And the divine initiative in salvation, of course, is correlative to his grace. When Paul writes, "for our sake" (v. 21), he highlights the grace of God and reminds us that his motive in reconciliation is to rescue helpless sinners.

Christ is the Mediator of reconciliation, for it is "through" him that God "reconciled us to himself" (v. 18) and "in Christ God was reconciling the world to himself" (v. 19).

Paul distinguishes two inseparable aspects of reconciliation. First is Christ's unique accomplishment of reconciliation in his cross (vv. 14–15, 18–19, 21). Second, reconciliation also involves our proclamation of that reconciling atonement. God "gave us the ministry of reconciliation"; he entrusted "to us the message of reconciliation" (vv. 18–19). We may call these the objective and subjective aspects of reconciliation, respectively. It is critical to understand that they are both divine works. God acted objectively in his Son's death to reconcile to himself the world of human beings, even believing Jewish and Gentile sinners. Furthermore, he himself subjectively entreats sinners through his human ambassadors: "On behalf of Christ, be reconciled to God" (v. 20).

Reconciliation through Christ brings forgiveness, God's "not counting" believing sinners' "trespasses against them" (v. 19). Because of the work of Christ, the Mediator of reconciliation, the peacemaker, God no longer reckons believers' sins against them. This means that reconciliation is related to justification, which has to do with the forgiveness of sins (Rom. 4:6–8).

Paul only hinted at the relation between reconciliation and justification in Romans 5:10. Now he expounds on this relation in 2 Corinthians 5:21: "For our sake he made him to be sin who knew no sin, so that in him we might become

---

[22] Vickers, *Jesus' Blood* and *Righteousness*, 180.

the righteousness of God." The placement of verse 21 indicates that, as Hughes brilliantly declares,

> the apostle sets forth the gospel of reconciliation in all its mystery and all its wonder. There is no sentence more profound in the whole of Scripture; for this verse embraces the whole ground of the sinner's reconciliation to God and declares the incontestable reason why he should respond to the ambassadorial entreaty. Indeed, it completes the message with which the Christian ambassador has been entrusted. To proclaim: "Be reconciled to God" is not good news unless it is accompanied by a declaration of the ground on which reconciliation has been effected and is available.[23]

In his death on the cross, the Son of God, who lived a life of perfect obedience, became so closely identified with our sins and their dismal consequences that Paul mysteriously writes that he was made sin. Because God transferred our sin onto the sinless one, it is now not reckoned to our account; instead God's righteousness is so reckoned. Paul's wonderful exchange is the basis of reconciliation—because Christ was made sin, believers become God's righteousness in Christ and are therefore at peace with God. Thus the legal picture of Christ's atonement accomplishing justification here constitutes the basis of God's act of reconciling the world in Christ. And the justification of verse 21—complete with double imputation—not only is a description of the ground of reconciliation but fleshes out the "message of reconciliation" as well.

Ephesians 2:11–19

> Therefore remember that at one time you Gentiles in the flesh, called "the uncircumcision" by what is called the circumcision, which is made in the flesh by hands—remember that you were at that time separated from Christ, alienated from the commonwealth of Israel and strangers to the covenants of promise, having no hope and without God in the world. But now in Christ Jesus you who once were far off have been brought near by the blood of Christ. For he himself is our peace, who has made us both one and has broken down in his flesh the dividing wall of hostility by abolishing the law of commandments expressed in ordinances, that he might create in himself one new man in place of the two, so making peace, and might reconcile us both to God in one body through the cross, thereby killing the hostility. And he came and preached peace to you who were far off and peace to those who were near. For through him we both have access in one Spirit to the Father. So then you

---

[23]Hughes, *The Second Epistle to the Corinthians*, 211.

are no longer strangers and aliens, but you are fellow citizens with the saints and members of the household of God.

Paul's "Flashback" Method

Paul digs a deep pit for sinners—they are spiritually dead, captivated by the world system opposed to God, inadvertently following Satan, enslaved to their passions, and deserving God's wrath—to extol God's magnificent grace that liberates them from such a plight (Eph. 2:1–10). Then he discusses God's grace in relation to Gentiles (vv. 11–19).

Again, Paul shows believing Gentiles in Ephesus their predicament before salvation. They were uncircumcised and thus excluded from the true Israel, the people of God (vv. 11–12). Their major problem was that they were "separated from Christ," that is, far removed from him who alone became to believers "wisdom from God, righteousness and sanctification and redemption" (v. 12; 1 Cor. 1:30). They were "alienated from the commonwealth of Israel and strangers to the covenants of promise," that is, not part of God's only covenant people (Eph. 2:12). Consequently, they had "no hope" and were "without God in the world"; they were hopeless and God-forsaken (v. 12).

In both 2:1–10 and 2:11–19, Paul employs his "flashback" method: he paints bleak pictures of the preconversion state of his readers to help them better appreciate Christ and the salvation that he brings. He does this for at least two reasons. First, the situation of unsaved people is truly desperate. So, Paul does not exaggerate; in fact it is sinners who exaggerate their goodness and need for someone to tell them the truth. This the apostle does. Second, Paul "flashes back" when writing to Christians to teach them not to take the love of God for granted.

A momentous change has occurred, and marvelous words of healing accentuate it: "But now in Christ Jesus you who once were far off have been brought near by the blood of Christ" (v. 13). By God's grace the Ephesian Gentiles are no longer "separated from Christ"; now they are "in Christ Jesus." They have been spiritually united to the Messiah, in whom they previously had no part, even "the historic person, Jesus," as Peter O'Brien explains.[24] By virtue of union with Christ all of his spiritual benefits become theirs, including the forgiveness of sins and eternal life. The Gentiles who "once were far off" from God "have been brought near" to God; they are included in the new covenant and belong

---

[24]Peter T. O'Brien, *The Letter to the Ephesians*, The Pillar New Testament Commentary (Grand Rapids: Eerdmans, 1999), 189–90.

to him. What is the cause of this dramatic change? The change is all attributable to "the blood of Christ," that is, his atoning, sacrificial death (v. 13).

The preceding is background for Paul's treatment of reconciliation. He begins by drawing attention to the person of Christ, the Mediator of every aspect of salvation, including reconciliation. Indeed, Christ is so indispensable to peacemaking that the apostle can say, "He himself is our peace" (v. 14). Christ's person and work are the center of the doctrine of reconciliation, as Andrew Lincoln maintains: "Peace, in v 14, is not merely a concept nor even a new state of affairs, it is bound up with a person. Christ can be said to be not only a peacemaker or a bringer of peace but peace in person."[25]

Racial Reconciliation

What are the results of Christ's reconciliation in terms of Jewish-Gentile relations? He "made us both one and has broken down in his flesh the dividing wall of hostility . . . that he might create in himself one new man in place of the two, so making peace, and might reconcile us both to God" (vv. 14–16). The short answer is that he made believing Jews and Gentiles one in himself. He united them, eliminating the long-standing hostility between them. He inaugurated the new creation by making Jewish and Gentile believers into "one new man in place of two." Notice that Paul's "new man" terminology here is not referring to individual Christians but is a corporate picture of the church composed of reconciled Jews and Gentiles. All of this was a product of his reconciling "us both to God." Christ's reconciling work, which was first of all vertical, also had powerful horizontal results: racial reconciliation between Jews and Gentiles.

But how did the Savior accomplish reconciliation? What did he *do* to bring it about? Paul answers these questions by pointing in different ways to Christ's cross:

You who once were far off have been brought near *by the blood of Christ.* (v. 13)

He . . . has broken down *in his flesh* the dividing wall of hostility. (v. 14)

. . . that . . . he might reconcile us both to God in one body *through the cross.* (v. 16)

Christ brought about reconciliation by dying on the cross. His death was God's means of making peace between believers (both Jews and Gentiles) and God, and as a result with one another.

---

[25] Andrew T. Lincoln, *Ephesians*, Word Biblical Commentary (Dallas: Word, 1990), 140.

How Did Christ Abolish the Law?

Paul uses another metaphor to depict Christ's reconciling work on the cross—that of Christ's abolishing the law: "For he himself is our peace, who has made us both one and has broken down in his flesh the dividing wall of hostility by abolishing the law of commandments expressed in ordinances" (vv. 14–15). Immediately before this Paul says that Christ "has broken down in his flesh the dividing wall of hostility." Although some have taken this to refer to "a vertical barrier . . . in the temple precincts in Jerusalem, preventing Gentiles from proceeding from the outer court . . . into any of the inner courts," it is probably best to understand it as a reference to the Ten Commandments themselves, which served as the real "dividing wall of hostility" between Jews and Gentiles.[26] Christ accomplished reconciliation by dying to abolish the law. What does this mean?

It is not difficult to identify the law to which the apostle refers. It is "the law of commandments expressed in ordinances," that is, the law of Moses as a whole with a focus on the Ten Commandments. In what sense did Christ abolish the Ten Commandments? Various suggestions have been made in order to correlate what is taught here with other Pauline passages, which extol the law and apply it to Christians (e.g., Rom. 7:12; Eph. 6:2). Interpreters, understandably nervous about accusing Paul of antinomianism, have qualified the word "law" so as to focus on the ceremonial rather than the moral law, the wrongful use of the law, or simply one aspect of it.[27] I agree with O'Brien:

> Perhaps it may help to say that what is abolished is the "law-covenant," that is, the law as a whole conceived as a covenant. It is then replaced by a new covenant for Jews *and* Gentiles. . . . But because the old *Torah* as such, that is, the law-covenant, has gone, it can no longer serve as the great barrier between Jew and Gentile.[28]

Although the problem is thorny, this solution has several advantages. It interprets "the law of commandments expressed in ordinances" as a reference to the Torah as a whole and not simply a part (which appears contrived). It interprets "abolished" as "nullified" in line with other statements of Paul ("In 2 Cor. 3:6–15 it [the verb *katargeō*] appears four times [vv. 7, 11, 13, 14] in relation to the old covenant or its glory being 'set aside' in Christ"[29]). And it absolves the apostle from antinomianism, a correct move in light of Ephesians 6:2 and other texts.

---

[26]For the former view, see F. F. Bruce, *The Epistles to the Colossians, to Philemon, and to the Ephesians,* The New International Commentary on the New Testament (Grand Rapids: Eerdmans, 1984), 297. For the latter view, see Lincoln, *Ephesians,* 141.

[27]See O'Brien, *The Letter to the Ephesians,* 196–98 for sources and discussion.

[28]Ibid., 199.

[29]Ibid., 196n167.

In his flesh Christ unified believing Jews and Gentiles by dying to nullify the law as a covenant that divided the two ethnic groups. By his blood he set aside the Mosaic law as a covenant and ratified the new covenant (Matt. 26:28). Via the cross, he, the Mediator of the new covenant (Heb. 9:15), reconciled all believers to God and to one another.

An Amazing Reversal

Not only so but he also "came and preached peace to you who were far off and peace to those who were near" (Eph. 2:17). When and how did Christ do this? I acknowledge a variety of views, but maintain that the sense is this: Christ by the Holy Spirit preached the gospel through his apostles (cf. Eph. 3:7–9; 6:19–20).[30] As a result of many Jews and non-Jews trusting Jesus, the Reconciler, "through him" they "both have access in one Spirit to the Father" (2:18). F. F. Bruce interprets and applies the apostle's words:

> For it is through Christ that Jewish and Gentile believers alike have their access to the Father. . . . Within his family the Father makes no distinction between those children who are Jewish by birth and those who are Gentile. To us the abolition of the barrier separating Jews and Gentiles may not be so revolutionary as it was for Paul and his associates; but there are other divisions within the human family which are equally irrelevant in the sight of God and ought to be irrelevant in his children's sight.[31]

God's grace surprises us: unclean Gentiles now have access to God the Trinity! Paul ends the passage with an inclusion (reversing the situation described in v. 12): "So then you are no longer strangers and aliens, but you are fellow citizens with the saints and members of the household of God" (v. 19). The Gentiles are no longer godless, hopeless, and separated from Christ and his people. Rather, amazingly, they belong to Christ our peace, and to all believers, regardless of their ethnicity.[32]

A Connection to Ephesians 1:9–10

It is important not to abstract Ephesians 2:11–22 from the previous content of the epistle, particularly 1:9–10. Although the technical language of reconciliation

---

[30]For views and discussion, see ibid., 205–8.

[31]Bruce, *The Epistles to the Colossians, to Philemon, and to the Ephesians*, 301.

[32]Paul's use of "reconciliation" in Rom. 11:15 is similar. Speaking of the Jews, he writes, "For if their rejection means the reconciliation of the world, what will their acceptance mean but life from the dead?"

is absent in that passage, the concept is there in cosmic proportions. We will set the verses in their immediate context.

> In him we have redemption through his blood, the forgiveness of our trespasses, according to the riches of his grace, which he lavished upon us, in all wisdom and insight making known to us the mystery of his will, according to his purpose, which he set forth in Christ as a plan for the fullness of time, to unite all things in him, things in heaven and things on earth. (Eph. 1:7–10)

The "mystery of his will" now made known is God's revelation in the preaching of the gospel of what was previously hidden. Though the mystery plainly includes God's bringing the Gentiles into the people of God, it is shortsighted to restrict the mystery to that idea. O'Brien is correct to say:

> This key motif refers to the all-inclusive purpose of God which has as its ultimate goal the uniting of all things in heaven and earth in Christ. . . . It is, therefore, inappropriate to claim that the content of the mystery in Ephesians is defined *solely* in terms of God's acceptance of the Gentiles and their union with Jews on an equal footing in Christ (Eph. 3:3–4).[33]

In its largest terms, the mystery refers to God's purposefully uniting all things in Christ in "the fullness of time." Note that "all things" are here specified as "things in heaven and things on earth." This is comprehensive language for an eschatological uniting of the cosmos in Christ. The words "reconcile," "reconciliation," and "peace" are absent, but the meaning of this cosmic final summing up in Christ overlaps Paul's doctrine of reconciliation. This restoration restores harmony to the universe and this is reconciliation.

Moreover, 1:9–10 provides Paul's framework of a cosmic unification of all things in Christ for understanding the narrower message of 2:11–22. Chrys Caragounis has done the most important work on this, which O'Brien summarizes:

> In his monograph dealing with the mystery in Ephesians, Chrys Caragounis claims that as Paul proceeds to amplify and explain throughout the letter the meaning of bringing all things together, he concentrates on the two main representatives of these spheres, namely, the *powers* representing "the things in heaven," and the *church*, (particularly the unity of Jews and Gentiles in the body of Christ) representing "the things on earth." He further suggests that the two obstacles which need to be overcome before the divine purpose of bringing everything into unity with Christ can be fulfilled are: (a) the rebellion of the

---

[33]O'Brien, *The Letter to the Ephesians*, 110.

powers, and (b) the alienation of Jews from Gentiles (2:11–22, as well as the estrangement of both from God, 2:16). Much of the rest of Ephesians is given over to explaining, with reference to each of these two spheres, the steps in the process that God has taken in order to achieve this supreme goal.[34]

So, placing 2:11–22 in the larger context of 1:9–10, we are ready to draw conclusions concerning Ephesians' teaching concerning reconciliation.

Teaching

The need for reconciliation is alienation from God and his people, as is emphatically communicated in Ephesians 2:12. It involves separation from Christ and the resulting hopelessness and godlessness. In God's plan, this terrible plight serves to highlight the sovereign grace of God in Christ. Christ's work of reconciliation reverses this alienation and makes friends of God out of those estranged from him.

The focus in reconciliation is on the person and work of Christ. "He himself is our peace" (v. 14). Specifically, it is Christ's atoning death—his "blood," "his flesh," "the cross" (vv. 13, 14, 16)—that accomplishes reconciliation between human beings and God and among human beings. Christ's death ratifies the new covenant and so makes the law, conceived as the law covenant that God made with Moses and that served to separate Jews and Gentiles, obsolete.

Christ's work of reconciliation effects momentous change and marvelous healing. By God's grace the Gentiles are no longer "separated from Christ," but "have been brought near" by his blood (vv. 12, 13). This occurs "in Christ Jesus" (vv. 13, 20–21). The application of salvation that corresponds to Christ's cross work of reconciliation is union with Christ. God spiritually joins believing Gentiles to Christ Jesus so that they partake of all of his spiritual benefits.

Reconciliation operates on multiple levels—individual, corporate, and even cosmic (see also Col. 1:19–20). Individual reconciliation brings sinners one at a time into God's family. Corporate reconciliation, the result of individual reconciliation, makes peace between God and groups of people, constituting churches. Cosmic reconciliation serves "to unite all things in him, things in heaven and things on earth" (Eph. 1:10). This universal "uniting" brings harmony or reconciliation to God's universe. It involves subjugation of the powers, as we shall see in Colossians, and the unification of the church, which is emphasized in Ephesians 2.

---

[34]Ibid., 112–13, italics original. Chrys C. Caragounis's work is *The Ephesian* Mysterion: *Meaning and Content* (Lund: Gleerup, 1977).

Racial reconciliation deserves special mention because it is so emphasized in this passage. By virtue of reconciliation, believing Jews and Gentiles are one in Christ and belong to the same people and family of God.

Although not as prominently as in 2 Corinthians 5:18–20, here reconciliation also involves preaching. Here it is Christ, who through his apostles by the Spirit, "preached peace" to Jew and Gentile alike with the result that all believers are incorporated into the one family of God the Father, the people of God, the church (Eph. 2:17–22).

Colossians 1:19–23

> For in him all the fullness of God was pleased to dwell, and through him to reconcile to himself all things, whether on earth or in heaven, making peace by the blood of his cross.
>
> And you, who once were alienated and hostile in mind, doing evil deeds, he has now reconciled in his body of flesh by his death, in order to present you holy and blameless and above reproach before him, if indeed you continue in the faith, stable and steadfast, not shifting from the hope of the gospel that you heard, which has been proclaimed in all creation under heaven, and of which I, Paul, became a minister.

Christ's Supremacy

Paul's teaching on reconciliation follows one of his strongest christological passages, that of Colossians 1:15–18. Strategic to this passage is verse 18, where the apostle says of Christ, "that in everything he might be preeminent." "Everything" means preeminent in creation (vv. 15–17) and in the church and the new creation (vv. 18–20). Christ is "the firstborn" (v. 15), that is, first in rank (cf. Ps. 89:27) over the creation, because he was God's agent in creation, is the heir of the creation, (Col. 1:16), existed prior to the creation, and preserves the creation (v. 17).

Moreover, Christ is also supreme over his body, the church, over which he is head. Paul alluded to Genesis 1:1 in verse 16, where he wrote of Christ, "For by him all things were created, in heaven and on earth." Now he alludes to Genesis 1:1 again when he says, that Christ "is the beginning." This time Paul is speaking not of the creation but of God's new creation. For this reason he immediately follows the words "he is the beginning" with "the firstborn from the dead" (v. 18). It is as the resurrected one that he is the "beginning," the source of the church's eternal life, even as he was the source of the creation's biological life (v. 16). In both spheres, then, creation and new creation, God willed for "his beloved Son" (v. 13) to have first place.

The prerequisite for Christ's supremacy over the church is his incarnation, which results in the preeminent one being divine and human. Paul teaches the incarnation of the Son when he says, "He is the image of the invisible God." Paul means that he is the visible revelation of the invisible God (cf. 1 Tim. 6:16). In becoming a human being Christ perfectly reveals the invisible Father. The incarnate one is God himself because he does God's unique works of creation and providence, shares God's attribute of eternity, and occupies God's place as heir of all things (Col. 1:16–17). Verse 19 states his deity plainly: "For in him all the fullness of God was pleased to dwell." Paul further explains in 2:9, "For in him the whole fullness of deity dwells bodily." The meaning is that almighty God lives in Christ in bodily form; the Son is God incarnate.

Next the apostle introduces the theme of reconciliation: "For in him all the fullness of God was pleased to dwell, and through him to reconcile to himself all things, whether on earth or in heaven, making peace by the blood of his cross" (1:19–20). It is important to point out that this is the closest Scripture comes to giving a definition of reconciliation. Paul here describes it as "making peace." Reconciliation is peacemaking.

A key is the meaning of "all things." What does the apostle mean when he teaches that God was pleased through Christ to reconcile *all things* to himself by Christ's cross? Evaluating the five main views of "all things" will help us to answer this question.[35]

Evaluation of the Five Views of "All Things" in Colossians 1:20

1. *The reconciliation of all things concerns Christ alone.* Interpreters have been out of focus, concentrating on the reconciliation of "all things" instead of on Christ, the reconciler.[36] This view correctly captures the thrust of Colossians 1:15–20: to magnify the Son as paramount over creation and redemption. But this view falls short as an interpretation of verse 20, for it fails to explain the words "all things" in their context.

2. *The reconciliation of all things concerns human beings alone.* Because human beings "exchanged the glory of the immortal God for" idols (Rom. 1:23), the restoration of God's glory, the reconciliation, also concerns human beings only

---

[35] I used my article, "'To Reconcile to Himself All Things': Colossians 1:20," *Presbyterion* 36, no. 1 (2010): 37–46. In what follows I also acknowledge a debt to Peter T. O'Brien, *Colossians, Philemon*, Word Biblical Commentary (Waco, TX: 1982), 54–57.

[36] Franz Mussner, *Christus, das All und die Kirche, Studien zur Theologie des Epheserbriefes*, Trierer Theologische Studien 5 (Trier: Paulinus, 1955).

and does not concern the creation.[37] This view correctly understands the reconciliation of "all things" as pertaining to human beings. This is shown by the immediately following verses: "And you, who once were alienated and hostile in mind, doing evil deeds, he has now reconciled in his body of flesh by his death" (Col. 1:21–22). The Colossian Christians are among those whom Christ reconciled. Therefore, they are part of "all things" in verse 20. But this view fails as a comprehensive description of Colossians 1:20 because it limits "all things" to human beings, as we shall see.

3. *The reconciliation of all things concerns angels alone.* Though the Bible teaches the reconciliation of human beings, "all things" here omits them and instead concerns only evil angels. Because there is no salvation for evil angels, Christ "reconciles" them by subduing them. Their "reconciliation," then, is more properly defined as their subjugation or pacification.[38]

This view correctly understands "all things" in verse 20 as including the invisible creatures, described in verse 16, as "thrones or dominions or rulers or authorities," that is, differentiations of angels. Angels are included in "all things" of verse 20 because their mention in verse 16 is preceded and followed by statements that Christ created "all things," including angels. Furthermore, it is not hard to regard the angels who are "pacified" as created and fallen angels since, although the passage does not mention the fall, it assumes it, as Moo says:

> In speaking of the reconciliation of all things to Christ, the "hymn" presupposes that the Lordship of Christ over all things (vv. 15–18) has somehow been disrupted. Though created through him and for him, "all things" no longer bear the relationship to their creator that they were intended to have. They are therefore in need of reconciliation.[39]

This view correctly appeals to Colossians 2:15 to explain how Christ subjugated the demons: "He disarmed the rulers and authorities and put them to open shame, by triumphing over them in him." The previous verse says that sinners' bond of indebtedness has been erased, being nailed to Christ's cross. This is one of the most powerful presentations of legal penal substitution in Scripture. Apparently, the thought of verse 14 extends to the next verse. By can-

---

[37] Nikolaus Kehl, *Der Christushymnus im Kolosserbrief. Eine motivgeschichtliche Undersuchung zu Kol 1, 12–20,* Stuttgarter biblische Monographien (Stuttgart: Katholisches Bibelwerk, 1967), 163–65.

[38] Hans Schlier, *Principalities and Powers in the New Testament,* Questiones Disputatae (Freiburg: Herder, 1961), 14, 15.

[39] Douglas J. Moo, *The Letters to the Colossians and to Philemon,* The Pillar New Testament Commentary (Grand Rapids: Eerdmans, 2008), 134.

celing our legal debt on the cross Christ "stripped" the demons of their weapons and made them an object of public ridicule. The Greek of the last word of verse 15 is ambiguous. Either it is "triumphing over them in *him*," that is, Christ, with his cross implied (ESV). Or it is "triumphing over them by *the cross*" [lit. "it"] of Christ (NIV). Whether *auto* refers to Christ or his cross does not matter for theology, because in either case the other is implied. Christ pacified the demons (Col. 1:20) by defeating them on the cross (2:15).

Despite its strengths, this view too fails to define "all things" in Colossians 1:20 comprehensively because it omits human beings, the subject of reconciliation immediately following. Human beings too are included in "all things" reconciled, as the next view shows.

4. *The reconciliation of all things concerns personal beings—humans and angels.* The words "all things" in Colossians 1:20 are explained by what immediately follows: "whether on earth or in heaven." "All things . . . on earth" speaks of human beings. "All things . . . in heaven" speaks of angels. Thus Paul's universal reconciliation concerns human beings and angels.[40]

This view improves the two previous views, which held that "all things" speaks of men and women alone or angels alone, respectively. In the context, "all things" refers to both human beings and angels. It pertains to human beings because of verses 21–23, as noted. It pertains to angels because of verse 16, as noted. But the reconciliation of Colossians 1:20 is bigger still. This view is also too narrow in its focus. That is because, as the next view correctly holds, the whole creation is included in Paul's "all things."

5. *The reconciliation of all things concerns human beings, angels, and the whole creation.* This view is espoused by Eduard Lohse and Peter O'Brien.[41] It concerns human beings because of the verses that immediately follow:

> And you, who once were alienated and hostile in mind, doing evil deeds, he has now reconciled in his body of flesh by his death, in order to present you holy and blameless and above reproach before him, if indeed you continue in the faith, stable and steadfast, not shifting from the hope of the gospel. (Col. 1:21–23)

The reconciliation concerns angels because they are among "all things . . . created in heaven" and are further described as "thrones or dominions or rulers

---

[40]Johann Michl, "Die Versöhnung" (Kol 1, 20)," *Theologische Quartalschrift* 128 (1948): 442–62; and Benjamin N. Wambacq, "'per eum reconciliare . . . quae in caelis sunt' Col I, 20," *Revue biblique* 55 (1948): 35–42.

[41]Eduard Lohse, *Colossians and Philemon*, trans. W. R. Poehlmann, R. J. Karris, from 14th German ed., Hermeneia (Philadelphia: Fortress, 1971), 59–61; O'Brien, *Colossians, Philemon*, 55–57.

or authorities" (v. 16). As explained previously, this "reconciliation" is not salvation but subjugation or pacification.

The reconciliation of "all things" also includes the whole creation because even as verse 16 describes "all things . . . created" as including things "in heaven and on earth," so verse 20 describes "all things" reconciled as including things "whether on earth or in heaven." Paul presents a chiasm: "in heaven and on earth" (v. 16), "on earth or in heaven" (v. 20). By doing this the apostle teaches that Christ accomplished a cosmic reconciliation, though that needs to be defined. In fact, five times in verses 16–17 and 20 Paul writes "all things," and each instance refers to the whole creation. O'Brien agrees:

> The "reconciliation of all things" ought to be understood, in our judgment, with Lohse to mean that the "universe has been reconciled in that heaven and earth have been brought back into their divinely created and determined order . . . the universe is again under its head and . . . cosmic peace has returned.[42]

Moo summarizes:

> Colossians 1:20 teaches, then, not "cosmic salvation" or even "cosmic redemption," but "cosmic restoration" or "renewal." Through the work of Christ on the cross, God has brought his entire rebellious creation back under the rule of his sovereign power. Of course, this "peace" is not yet fully established. The "already/ not yet" pattern of New Testament eschatology must be applied to Colossians 1:20. While secured in principle by Christ's crucifixion and available in preliminary form to believers, universal peace is not yet established. It is because of this work of universal pacification that God will one day indeed be "all in all" (1 Cor. 15:28) and that "at the name of Jesus every knee should bow, in heaven and on earth and under the earth, and every tongue acknowledge that Jesus Christ is Lord, to the glory of God the Father" (Phil. 2:10–11). While modern theologians have therefore often greatly exaggerated the implications of v. 20 in the service of an unbiblical universalism, this passage does, indeed, assert a thoroughly biblical universalism: that God's work in Christ has in view a reclamation of the entire universe, tainted as it is by human sin (Rom. 8:19–22). That fallen human beings are the prime objects of this reconciliation is clear from the New Testament generally and from the sequel to this text ([Col. 1] vv. 21–23). But it would be a serious mistake (not always avoided) to limit this "reconciling" work to human beings.[43]

---

[42]O'Brien, Colossians, Philemon, 56.
[43]Moo, The Letters to the Colossians and to Philemon, 136–37.

Conclusion Concerning "All Things" in Colossians 1:20

When Paul writes, "For in him all the fullness of God was pleased to dwell, and through him to reconcile to himself *all things*, whether on earth or in heaven, making peace by the blood of his cross" (Col. 1:19–20), "all things" refers to saved human beings, subjugated demons, and the renewed heaven and earth.

The Place of the Cross?

What is the place of the cross of Christ in this cosmic restoration? As was the case in the previous passages that we explored, the cross is front and center in reconciliation in Colossians 1 too. God was pleased "to reconcile to himself all things, whether on earth or in heaven, making peace *by the blood of his cross*" (v. 20). The cross, therefore, is multidirectional. Taking into account all of Scripture's teaching, the cross is directed toward God himself (in propitiation); toward our enemies, including demons, to defeat them; toward men and women to redeem them; and toward the whole creation to deliver it from "its bondage to decay" and to bring it into "the freedom of the glory of the children of God" (Rom. 8:21). Why will all of these things occur? Why will we be finally saved? Why will the Devil and evil angels not ruin the *shalom* of the new creation but instead be cast into the lake of fire? Why will there be a new heaven and a new earth? All of these questions have the same answer: because the Son of God died and rose again on the third day to accomplish the reconciliation of human beings, angels, and the creation itself, *mutatis mutandis*.

Having explored the cosmic dimension of reconciliation, we may now delve further into the reconciliation of human beings.

"You . . . Once Were Alienated and Hostile in Mind"

After speaking of cosmic reconciliation, Paul returns his attention to the Colossians and their reconciliation: "And you, who once were alienated and hostile in mind, doing evil deeds, he has now reconciled in his body of flesh by his death" (Col. 1:21–22). The apostle gives the need for justification: alienation and hostility in mind that expresses itself in evil deeds. Bruce's words are sobering: "Once they had been estranged from God, in rebellion against him. Sin is not only disobedience to the will of God; it effectually severs men and women's fellowship with him and forces them to live 'without God in the world' (Eph. 2:12)."[44]

Again we see that Christ is the Mediator of reconciliation: "You . . . he has now reconciled in his body of flesh by his death" (Col. 1:21–22). This passage

---

[44]Bruce, *The Epistles to the Colossians, to Philemon, and to the Ephesians*, 77.

specifies how he accomplished the work of reconciliation: God made peace "by the blood of his cross" (v. 20). "You . . . he has now reconciled in his body of flesh by his death" (v. 22). Notice the language of "blood" and "flesh." The accent is on the divine Christ's humanity as the means by which he accomplished reconciliation. He made peace by his atoning death on the cross, giving himself to save those who could not rescue themselves.

Paul adds the goal of reconciliation: "You . . . he has now reconciled . . . in order to present you holy and blameless and above reproach before him" (v. 22). The goal is final and complete sanctification—absolute moral perfection in God's presence, as Moo explains: "While celebrating the new status that believers enjoy—'reconciled' . . .—Paul at the same time reminds us that this new status is not an end in itself but has a further goal in view: that we who are already 'holy' in status should become 'holy' in reality."[45] Note that perseverance to the end in faith is necessary: "if indeed you continue in the faith, stable and steadfast, not shifting from the hope of the gospel that you heard" (v. 23).

Universalism?

An important question remains: Does the reconciliation of all things that concerns men and women speak of absolute universalism, the final salvation of all human beings? Though Colossians 1:20 taken by itself could be used in support of universalism, to do so would be a serious mistake, for at least four reasons.

First, the near context in Colossians 1 does not support universalism. When Paul writes, "He has delivered us from the domain of darkness and transferred us to the kingdom of his beloved Son" (Col. 1:13), he teaches that salvation involves a change of moral sphere. If the Colossians had not undergone this change, they would not be delivered, and their sins would remain unforgiven (v. 14). In addition, immediately after verse 20, Paul says, "And you, who once were alienated and hostile in mind, doing evil deeds, he has now reconciled in his body of flesh by his death, in order to present you holy and blameless and above reproach before him" (Col. 1:21–22). Again a previous state of sin precedes the rescue of those whom Paul addresses. Had they not been rescued from that state of sin, they would have suffered eternal loss.

A second reason for rejecting universalism is the teaching of the entire epistle. In chapter 3, Paul commands: "Put to death therefore what is earthly in you: sexual immorality, impurity, passion, evil desire, and covetousness, which is idolatry. On account of these *the wrath of God is coming*. In these you too once

---

[45]Moo, *The Letters to the Colossians and to Philemon*, 143.

walked, when you were living in them" (vv. 5–7). Here Paul pronounces God's wrath against rebellious human beings.

Third, Colossians 1:20 should not be adduced as a proof text for universalism because of the overall teaching of Paul's letters. In Romans 2, he contrasts the destinies of the saved and lost in a chiasm.

> To those who by patience in well-doing seek for glory and honor and immortality, he will give eternal life; but for those who are self-seeking and do not obey the truth, but obey unrighteousness, there will be wrath and fury. There will be tribulation and distress for every human being who does evil, the Jew first and also the Greek, but glory and honor and peace for everyone who does good, the Jew first and also the Greek. (vv. 7–10)

Not all human beings will inherit "eternal life" and "glory and honor" (vv. 7, 10). Some will suffer "wrath and fury" and "tribulation and distress" (vv. 8, 9).

In Paul's most famous passage on hell, he tells of "the Lord Jesus" being "revealed from heaven with his mighty angels in flaming fire, inflicting vengeance on those who do not know God and on those who do not obey the gospel of our Lord Jesus. They will suffer the punishment of eternal destruction, away from the presence of the Lord and from the glory of his might" (2 Thess. 1:7–9). These hard words cannot be made to support the doctrine of universalism.[46]

Fourth, universalism should not be embraced because of the message of the New Testament as a whole.[47] Consider Jesus's strong words in Matthew 25: "Depart from me, you cursed, into the eternal fire prepared for the devil and his angels" (v. 41); "And these will go away into eternal punishment, but the righteous into eternal life" (v. 46). "Eternal fire" and "eternal punishment" do not indicate salvation, but its opposite.

And at the conclusion of Scripture's story, we read:

> But as for the cowardly, the faithless, the detestable, as for murderers, the sexually immoral, sorcerers, idolaters, and all liars, their portion will be in the lake that burns with fire and sulfur, which is the second death. (Rev. 21:8)

> Blessed are those who wash their robes, so that they may have the right to the tree of life and that they may enter the city by the gates. Outside are the dogs and

---

[46] As Douglas J. Moo argues in "Paul on Hell," in *Hell Under Fire*, ed. Christopher W. Morgan and Robert A. Peterson (Grand Rapids: Zondervan, 2004), 102–9.

[47] See J. I. Packer, "Universalism: Will Everyone Ultimately Be Saved?," in Morgan and Peterson, *Hell Under Fire*, 169–94.

sorcerers and the sexually immoral and murderers and idolaters, and everyone who loves and practices falsehood. (Rev. 22:14–15)

John's words do not indicate that all human beings will forever enjoy God in the New Jerusalem. Quite the contrary, some will be "outside" the city, in the lake of fire, suffering the second death of eternal separation from the gracious presence of God.

Teaching

Colossians 1 furthers our knowledge of reconciliation. It provides the clearest definition of reconciliation in Scripture—"making peace" (Col. 1:20). It spells out the need for reconciliation—alienation and hostility to God expressed in sins (v. 21).

In accord with the three previous passages studied, Christ is the Mediator, for reconciliation is "through him" (v. 20). Work had to be done for reconciliation to occur. That work was done when the Mediator died to reconcile sinners "by the blood of his cross" and "in his body of flesh by his death" (vv. 20, 22).

More clearly than any other passage, this one teaches a cosmic reconciliation. "For in him all the fullness of God was pleased to dwell, and through him to reconcile to himself *all things*, whether on earth or in heaven, making peace by the blood of his cross" (Col. 1:19–20). Here "all things" means saved men and women, subjugated demons, and the new heavens and new earth. It is important to distinguish this cosmic reconciliation from universalism, which Scripture does not support.

Paul gives the goal of Christ's reconciling work: final and complete sanctification of believers (v. 22).

Connecting the Dots

After studying the four key Pauline passages on reconciliation it is time to systematize findings.

Texts

Paul, the biblical theologian of reconciliation, sets forth his teaching in four passages: Romans 5:1–11; 2 Corinthians 5:16–21; Ephesians 2:11–19; and Colossians 1:19–23.

Sphere

Reconciliation is a picture of salvation and of Christ's saving accomplishment drawn from the arena of personal relations. It has to do with enmity and friendship, with enemies and friends. The apostle's choice of vocabulary bears this out: "[In Col. 1:20] Paul uses the word *eirenopoieo*, 'make peace,' a word implying a well-known Greek concept of hostility that requires pacification."[48] On the human level, it sometimes involves a mediator.

Background

New Testament scholars debate the conceptual background of reconciliation. Proposed backgrounds include "Hellenistic military and political settings," "Isaiah 53 and its surrounding context," Paul's "experience on the Damascus Road, and . . . Isaiah," "Isaiah's promises of 'restoration from the alienation of exile,'" "the Levitical sacrifices" being "connected to the death of Christ via the Servant described in Isaiah,"[49] and 2 Maccabees.[50] The last one seems suggestive, although "the evidence for Paul's use of 2 Maccabees is admittedly very thin."[51] Marshall summarizes the evidence:

> The general picture that emerges is clear and consistent. The view of the writer of 2 Maccabees is that when the people fall into sin and apostasy they arouse the wrath of Yahweh. He proceeds to punish them, and on the completion of the punishment his anger is satisfied and he is reconciled to the people. . . . In short, God is reconciled, that is, abandons his anger, as a result of the prayers of the people and their endurance (in themselves or their representatives) of the punishment which he inflicts upon them. Men act in such a way as to induce God to be favourable to them.[52]

The contrast with Paul's teaching is obvious, where atonement is the act of God alone who provides a sacrifice that reconciles enemies, both Jew and Gentile. Distinguishing "catalysts" from "source," I tentatively agree with Marshall: "The point is beyond proof, but there is a high degree of probability that the Jewish martyr tradition, which surfaces in this particular form in 2 Maccabees,

---

[48]Stanley E. Porter, "Peace, Reconciliation," in *Dictionary of Paul and His Letters*, ed. Gerald F. Hawthorne, Ralph P. Martin, and Daniel G. Reid (Downers Grove, IL: InterVarsity, 1993), 698.

[49]Vickers, *Jesus' Blood and Righteousness*, 163–70, 164n12.

[50]I. Howard Marshall, "The Meaning of 'Reconciliation,'" in *Jesus the Saviour: Studies in New Testament Theology* (Downers Grove, IL: InterVarsity, 1990), 261–62, 271.

[51]Ibid., 271.

[52]Ibid., 262.

has provided the catalyst to the development of Paul's use of the category of reconciliation."[53]

Definition

In the closest that Scripture comes to giving a definition of reconciliation, Paul here describes it as "making peace." "For in him all the fullness of God was pleased to dwell, and through him to reconcile to himself all things, whether on earth or in heaven, *making peace* by the blood of his cross" (Col. 1:19–20). Reconciliation is peacemaking. It involves God's taking the initiative to make friends out of his enemies.

Need

Since reconciliation is a picture belonging to the realm of personal relations, the need for reconciliation is fractured relations. We need to be reconciled because we are God's foes, due to our sins. "We were enemies" of God (Rom. 5:10); we once were "alienated and hostile in mind" (Col. 1:21). This alienation and mental hostility expressed themselves in our "doing evil deeds" (v. 21). I will argue below that there is enmity on both God's side and ours. Though the cause of the conflict is entirely our sin and God is without fault, he is not at peace with us until he reconciles himself to us.

Our need for reconciliation—our estrangement from him—is implied every time we read that God reconciled us to himself. Our alienation from God and his people involves separation from Christ and results in hopelessness and godlessness. In God's plan, this terrible plight highlights the grace of God because Christ's saving work reverses this alienation and makes believers into friends of God.

Initiator and Goal

In reconciliation of human relationships, there is sometimes a mediator—an impartial third party. In Paul, God, the offended party, takes the initiative and accomplishes the reconciliation: "All this is from God, who through Christ reconciled us to himself" (2 Cor. 5:18). Amazingly, "Paul is the first attested Greek author to speak of the offended party (God) initiating reconciliation, using the active voice of the verb," Porter reminds us.[54] Indeed, the initiator of reconciliation is always God, sometimes the Father (2 Cor. 5:18–19; Col. 1:20) and sometimes the Son (Eph. 2:14–16).

---

[53]Ibid., 271.
[54]Porter, "Peace, Reconciliation," 695.

God himself is not only the initiator of reconciliation but also its goal, as Porter says: "The Pauline pattern" is "found in 2 Corinthians 5:18–19 . . . in which God is not only the agent or instigator of reconciliation, but is the goal toward whom reconciliation is directed. In all uses of the verb of reconciliation in 2 Corinthians 5 (verses 18, 19 and 20) the object or goal of the action is God."[55]

Before writing of reconciliation in Romans 5:10, Paul speaks of God's motivation for making atonement: "But God shows his love for us in that while we were still sinners, Christ died for us" (v. 8). H. D. McDonald is right: "Therefore, the reconciliation is itself a revelation of God's holy love."[56]

Mediator

Who is the Mediator of reconciliation? Scripture is plain: the peacemaker, the reconciler, the Mediator of reconciliation, is Christ alone. This is most clearly expressed in Ephesians 2:14: "He himself is our peace." Christ is our personal peace, or peacemaker.

Christ must be God and man in one person for reconciliation to occur, as Colossians 1 teaches. His deity is taught by the words, "For in him all the fullness of God was pleased to dwell, and through him to reconcile to himself all things" (Col. 1:19–20). His humanity is underscored by references to "the blood of his cross," "his body of flesh," and "his death."

Every reconciliation passage communicates that Christ is the Mediator of reconciliation. This is done with the use of prepositions; reconciliation was made "through," "by," or "in" Christ.

We have peace with God through our Lord Jesus Christ. (Rom. 5:1)

All this is from God, who through Christ reconciled us to himself and gave us the ministry of reconciliation; that is, in Christ God was reconciling the world to himself. (2 Cor. 5:18–19)

But now in Christ Jesus you who once were far off have been brought near. (Eph. 2:13)

For in him all the fullness of God was pleased to dwell, and through him to reconcile to himself all things. (Col. 1:19–20)

---

[55]Ibid., 696.
[56]H. D. McDonald, *New Testament Concept of Atonement: The Gospel of the Calvary Event* (Grand Rapids: Baker, 1994), 106.

Christ is the Mediator of reconciliation, but he is also much more, as O'Brien expresses while commenting on Ephesians 1:9–10:

> Christ is the one *in whom* God chooses to sum up the cosmos, the one in whom he restores harmony to the universe. He is the focal point, not simply the means, the instrument, or the functionary through whom all this occurs. . . . The emphasis is now on a universe that is centred and reunited in Christ. The mystery which God has graciously made known refers to the summing up and bringing together of the fragmented and alienated elements of the universe ("all things") in Christ as the focal point.[57]

The focus in reconciliation is on the person *and work* of Christ.

Work

Certain things had to happen for reconciliation to occur. They include the reconciler's death and resurrection, with the accent on the former. The focus is on the atonement accomplished by "the death of his Son" (Rom. 5:10), "through the cross" (Eph. 2:16), "by the blood of his cross," and "in his body of flesh by his death" (Col. 1:20, 22). Christ's death ratifies the new covenant and so makes the law, the law covenant that God made with Moses and that served to separate Jews and Gentiles, obsolete.

Romans 5:10 includes both his death and resurrection in his reconciling work: "For if while we were enemies we were reconciled to God by the death of his Son, much more, now that we are reconciled, shall we be saved by his life." It is a mistake to divide Christ's saving accomplishment between his death and resurrection. Rather, Schreiner is correct: Romans 5:11 is reminiscent of 4:25; "Christ's death and resurrection are inseparable in effecting salvation."[58]

Scope

Christ's saving work of reconciliation is so great that it operates on multiple levels—individual, corporate, and cosmic. Individual reconciliation brings sinners one at a time into God's family. Corporate reconciliation makes peace between God and groups of people, constituting churches. Graham Cole's

---

[57] O'Brien, *The Letter to the Ephesians*, 111–12.
[58] Paul's references to Christ's blood in 5:9 and his life in 5:10 do not divide the accomplishment of salvation between his death and resurrection. Rather, reminiscent of 4:25, "Christ's death and resurrection are inseparable in effecting salvation," ibid. As a result, either (as a metonymy) could stand for Christ's whole saving accomplishment.

comment is pithy: "Enmity gives way to embrace."[59] Cosmic reconciliation serves "to unite all things in him, things in heaven and things on earth" (Eph. 1:10). How did this occur? "For in him all the fullness of God was pleased to dwell, and through him to reconcile to himself *all things*, whether on earth or in heaven, making peace by the blood of his cross" (Col. 1:19–20). This universal "uniting" brings harmony or reconciliation to God's universe. It involves subjugation of the powers (Col. 2:14), and the unification of the church (Ephesians 2). But this cosmic reconciliation is not universalism, which contradicts the truth of Scripture.

Aspects

Paul distinguishes two inseparable aspects of reconciliation. First, Christ's unique accomplishment of reconciliation in his cross (2 Cor. 5:14–15, 18–19, 21) and empty tomb (Rom. 5:10) is the foundation of reconciliation. Second, reconciliation also includes Christians' preaching that reconciling atonement. God "gave us the ministry of reconciliation"; he entrusted "to us the message of reconciliation" (2 Cor. 5:18, 19). We may call these the objective and subjective aspects of reconciliation, respectively.

They are both divine works. God acted objectively in his Son's death to reconcile to himself the world of human beings. Furthermore, he himself subjectively entreats sinners through his human witnesses: "We are ambassadors for Christ, God making his appeal through us. We implore you on behalf of Christ, be reconciled to God" (2 Cor. 5:20). In Ephesians 2, reconciliation involves preaching when Christ through his apostles by the Spirit, "preached peace" to Jew and Gentile alike. The result is that all believers, both Jew and Gentile, are incorporated into the one family of God the Father, the church (Eph. 2:17–22).

Moo achieves a healthy balance distinguishing while not separating the two aspects:

> Reconciliation in Paul has two aspects, or "moments": the accomplishment of reconciliation through Christ on the cross . . . and the acceptance of that completed work by the believer. . . . Naturally, while the focus can be on one of these moments or the other, the reconciling activity of God is ultimately one act; and in the present verse [Rom. 5:10] the complete process is in view.[60]

---

[59]Graham A. Cole, *God the Peacemaker: How Atonement Brings Shalom*, New Studies in Biblical Theology (Downers Grove, IL: InterVarsity, 2009), 178.

[60]Moo, *The Epistle to the Romans*, 311–12.

Is God Reconciled Too?

Scripture never says that God reconciled himself to us. Many have concluded, however, that he was reconciled and that this is more basic than his reconciling us to himself.

We needed to be reconciled to God due to our sin and alienation, as argued in the preceding. But does our sin also constitute a barrier on God's side, so that he also needed to be reconciled? The answer must begin with serious consideration of our sin and its effect on a holy and just God. Marshall, after finishing his magnum opus, *New Testament Theology*, penned an essay "The Theology of the Atonement" in a book devoted to Christ's atonement. Early in that essay he affirms, "The reality of final judgment as the active response of God to human sin is an absolutely central part of the predicament from which sinners need to be saved."[61]

This is indeed the biblical starting point. Of course, our sin is the cause of the predicament, both from our side and God's. But it is wrong to assume that our sin has no effect upon God, as John Stott explains.

> Wherever the verb "to reconcile" occurs in the New Testament, either God is the subject (he reconciled us to himself) or, if the verb is passive, we are (we were reconciled to him). God is never the object. It is never said that "Christ reconciled the Father to us." Formally, linguistically, this is a fact. But we must be careful not to build too much on it theologically. . . . It is a mistake to think that the barrier between God and us, which necessitated the work of reconciliation, was entirely on our side, so that we needed to be reconciled and God did not. True, we were "God's enemies," hostile to him in our hearts. But the "enmity" was on both sides. The wall or barrier between God and us was constituted both by our rebellion against him and by his wrath upon us on account of our rebellion.[62]

Stott's conclusion is borne out in Romans 5:10 and 2 Corinthians 5:21. When Paul writes "For if while we were enemies we were reconciled to God by the death of his Son . . ." (Rom. 5:10), does he view the enmity as ours toward God, as God's toward us, or both? Moo answers:

> Paul may mean by this simply that we, rebellious sinners, are hostile to God—violating his laws, putting other gods in his place. But, as Paul has repeatedly affirmed in this letter (cf. [Rom.] 1:18; 3:25), God is also "hostile" toward us—our

---

[61] I. Howard Marshall, "The Theology of the Atonement," in *The Atonement Debate*, ed. Derek Tidball, David Hilborn, and Justin Thacker (Grand Rapids: Zondervan, 2008), 51. His book is *New Testament Theology* (Downers Grove, IL: InterVarsity, 2004).

[62] John Stott, *The Cross of Christ* (Downers Grove, IL: InterVarsity, 2004), 197.

sins have justly incurred his wrath, which stands as a sentence over us (1:19–32), to be climactically carried out on the day of judgment (2:5). Probably, then the "enmity" to which Paul refers here includes God's hostility toward human beings as well as human beings' hostility toward God. Outside of Christ, people are in a situation of "enmity" with God; and in reconciliation, it is that status, or relationship, that changes: we go from being God's "enemies" to being his "children" (cf. Rom 8:14–17).[63]

Moo's conclusion is correct in light of the greater context of Romans, as well as the immediate context of Romans 5:9–10: God as well as human beings needed to be reconciled if we would be saved.

C. K. Barrett's words (on 2 Cor. 5:21) make the same point:

> Paul develops the thought in terms of an exchange: Christ was made *sin*, that we might become *God's righteousness*. It is important to observe that the words Paul uses are words describing relationships. . . . He says rather that Christ became *sin*; that is, he came to stand in that relation with God which normally is the result of sin, estranged from God and the object of his wrath. . . . We correspondingly, and through God's loving act in Christ, have come to stand in that relation with God which is described by the term *righteousness*, that is we are acquitted in his court, justified, reconciled. We are no longer his enemies, but his friends.[64]

Barrett is right: Paul places verse 21 after his discussion of reconciliation in verses 18–20 in order to ground that doctrine in Christ's atonement. Christ took the place of the sinner and bore God's wrath in our place, so we do not have to bear it. This means that mysteriously the work of Christ affected God himself.

I say "mysteriously" for a reason. It is not good for us to pretend to understand the things of God better than we do. Leon Morris reminds us that we understand God's reconciling himself to us only in part.

> Thus we may speak of God as being reconciled. It may be necessary, indeed it is necessary, to use the term carefully, when we apply it to God. But then does not this happen with all our language? . . . When we say that God is reconciled to man, this does not mean that, with various imperfections, He completely alters His attitude to man. Rather it is our groping way of expressing the conviction that, though He reacts in the strongest possible way against sin in every shape and form so that man comes under His condemnation, yet when reconciliation is effected, when peace is made between man and God, then that condemnation is removed,

---

[63]Moo, *The Epistle to the Romans*, 312.
[64]C. K. Barrett, *The Second Epistle to the Corinthians*. Harper's New Testament Commentaries (New York: Harper & Row, 1973), 180, italics original.

God now looks on man no longer as the object of His holy and righteous wrath, but as the object of His love and His blessing.[65]

God's reconciling us to himself, then, is a reflex action of his simultaneous but logically prior reconciliation of himself to us. And—we dare not miss this point while deep in our theologizing—all of this only underscores the marvelous and incomprehensible love of God in Christ. God stoops to reconcile himself to us so that he can reconcile us rebels to him? Exactly. Amazing! That is what the gospel of God's grace is all about.

Relation to Other Doctrines

We have touched upon other themes in our study of the reconciliation passages, especially themes of law and justification and the new creation. I will postpone questions concerning the relation of the six pictures to each other and to these and other themes until I complete a study of the pictures.

---

[65]Leon Morris, *The Apostolic Preaching of the Cross*, 3rd ed. (Grand Rapids: Eerdmans, 1965), 247.

Reconciler
Redeemer
Legal Substitute
Victor
Second Adam
Sacrifice

Chapter 11

Christis Our Redeemer

No word in the Christian vocabulary deserves to be held more precious than Redeemer, for even more than Savior it reminds the child of God that his salvation has been purchased at a great and personal cost, for the Lord has given himself for our sins in order to deliver us from them.[1]

Everett Harrison's words ring true in believers' ears. "Redeemer" is a precious word to us because of who Jesus is and what he did for us. It is good for us to turn our attention to the Redeemer's saving work. Redemption, like most biblical themes, has roots that sink deep into Old Testament soil. God was Israel's Redeemer, even though the nation rebelled against him again and again, as Psalm 78 reminds us. In spite of Israel's sin, unbelief, and wandering heart, God led them to a hard repentance, and

> they remembered that God was their rock,
>> the Most High God their redeemer. (Ps. 78:35)

If only they had not subsequently suffered from chronic theological amnesia!

---

[1] E. F. Harrison, "Redeemer, Redemption," in *Evangelical Dictionary of Theology*, ed. Walter A. Elwell, 2nd ed. (Grand Rapids: Baker Academic, 2001), 994–95.

Redemption in the Old Testament

Three main influences (possibly a fourth) help us to understand better the New Testament teaching.[2]

Liberation in the Exodus

The most important background is the exodus. God's mighty deliverance of his enslaved people from Egypt is a high point of the Old Testament story. It includes the plagues, the Passover, when God spared the Israelite firstborn, and especially the miraculous crossing of the sea.

From the very beginning of the story, God's compassion for his people and willingness to act in their behalf are underscored, as Alan Cole explains: "Above all, He is the God who acts in salvation; 'I have come down to deliver them' is His word for Moses to bear to the Israelites (Ex. 3:8). This introduces the biblical concept of salvation, an area where later biblical passages are largely indebted to the book of Exodus for language and imagery."[3]

God's words to the people, delivered through Moses, speak of God's mighty power accomplishing redemption from Egyptian slavery and "great acts of judgment" on Egypt's gods.

> Say therefore to the people of Israel, "I am the LORD, and I will bring you out from under the burdens of the Egyptians, and I will deliver you from slavery to them, and I will redeem you with an outstretched arm and with great acts of judgment. I will take you to be my people, and I will be your God, and you shall know that I am the LORD your God, who has brought you out from under the burdens of the Egyptians. I will bring you into the land that I swore to give to Abraham, to Isaac, and to Jacob. I will give it to you for a possession. I am the LORD." (Ex. 6:6–8)

Michael Williams accurately distills these words into four promises: "deliverance from oppression. . . . creation of a community. . . . personal relationship. . . . abundance and blessing."[4] Williams correctly concludes that due to these promises and more, "the exodus was not the first act of divine redemption in Scripture, but it was the event that set the pattern."[5]

---

[2]I acknowledge a debt to Leon Morris, "Redemption," in *Dictionary of Paul and His Letters*, ed. Gerald F. Hawthorne, Ralph P. Martin, and Daniel G. Reid (Downers Grove, IL: InterVarsity, 1993), 784–86.

[3]R. Alan Cole, *Exodus*, Tyndale Old Testament Commentaries (Downers Grove, IL: InterVarsity, 1973), 27.

[4]Michael D. Williams, *Far as the Curse Is Found: The Covenant Story of Redemption* (Phillipsburg, NJ: P&R, 2005), 33–34.

[5]Ibid., 23.

God made good on his promises, the most important of which was the exodus event itself. God opened the sea enabling his people to escape the Egyptian forces. And God closed the sea on the enemy, thereby drowning them (Exodus 14). How did God accomplish these things? Brevard S. Childs answers succinctly, "The rescue was accomplished through the intervention of God and God alone."[6] The result was not only the defeat of God's enemies and the redemption of his people. It was also the revelation of God's brilliant character.

The event is told in narrative and celebrated in song. First, the narrative: "Thus the LORD saved Israel that day from the hand of the Egyptians, and Israel saw the Egyptians dead on the seashore. Israel saw the great power that the LORD used against the Egyptians, so the people feared the LORD, and they believed in the LORD and in his servant Moses" (Ex. 14:30–31). Then, selections from the song:

> I will sing to the LORD, for he has triumphed gloriously;
>> the horse and his rider he has thrown into the sea.
> The LORD is my strength and my song,
>> and he has become my salvation;
> this is my God, and I will praise him,
>> my father's God, and I will exalt him.
> The LORD is a man of war;
>> the LORD is his name. (Ex. 15:1–3)

> Who is like you, O LORD, among the gods?
>> Who is like you, majestic in holiness,
>> awesome in glorious deeds, doing wonders?
> You stretched out your right hand;
>> the earth swallowed them.
> You have led in your steadfast love the people whom you have redeemed;
> you have guided them by your strength to your holy abode. (vv. 11–13)

> The LORD will reign forever and ever. (v. 18)

It is fair to say, in the words of Alan Cole, "nevertheless, in spite of the manifold nature of the saving activity of God, it was always the experiences of the exodus itself to which Israel turned back as the supreme example."[7] Indeed, subsequent Scripture frequently returns to the exodus account. If we inquire as to why this is the case, the answer lies close at hand, as Leon Morris explains: "In

---

[6]Brevard S. Childs, *The Book of Exodus*, The Old Testament Library (Louisville: Westminster, 1974), 237.
[7]Cole, *Exodus*, 29.

the Exodus story God's strength and delivering activity in history are brought to the fore as the means of redemption" (cf. Deut. 7:8; 9:26; Ps. 74:2; 77:15).[8]

Redemption of the Firstborn

A second Old Testament influence that serves as background for the New Testament teaching on redemption is the ransoming of the firstborn. This, of course, is a subset of the exodus events, but is important enough to warrant separate treatment. The final plague against the Egyptians was the killing of the firstborn of human beings and animals. Faithful Israelites who obeyed the Lord and applied the blood of the sacrificed Passover lamb to the lintel and two doorposts of their houses were spared this tragedy—their firstborn were not taken by God's judgment.

In two passages in Exodus, God stakes his claim to the firstborn of men and animals:

> When the LORD brings you into the land of the Canaanites, as he swore to you and your fathers, and shall give it to you, you shall set apart to the LORD all that first opens the womb. All the firstborn of your animals that are males shall be the LORD's. Every firstborn of a donkey you shall redeem with a lamb, or if you will not redeem it you shall break its neck. Every firstborn of man among your sons you shall redeem. And when in time to come your son asks you, "What does this mean?" you shall say to him, "By a strong hand the LORD brought us out of Egypt, from the house of slavery. For when Pharaoh stubbornly refused to let us go, the LORD killed all the firstborn in the land of Egypt, both the firstborn of man and the firstborn of animals. Therefore I sacrifice to the LORD all the males that first open the womb, but all the firstborn of my sons I redeem." (Ex. 13:11–15; see also 34:19–20)

How were these firstborn sons redeemed? "The first-born of men were redeemed . . . by the consecration of the Levites to God and the payment of a ransom price."[9]

That is correct, as the following passages reveal:

> And the LORD spoke to Moses, saying, "Take the Levites instead of all the first-born among the people of Israel, and the cattle of the Levites instead of their cattle. The Levites shall be mine: I am the LORD. And as the redemption price for the 273 of the firstborn of the people of Israel, over and above the number

---

[8]Morris, "Redemption," 784.
[9]I. Howard Marshall, "The Development of the Concept of Redemption in the New Testament," in *Jesus the Saviour: Studies in New Testament Theology* (Downers Grove, IL: InterVarsity, 1990), 252n17.

of the male Levites, you shall take five shekels per head; you shall take them according to the shekel of the sanctuary (the shekel of twenty gerahs), and give the money to Aaron and his sons as the redemption price for those who are over." So Moses took the redemption money from those who were over and above those redeemed by the Levites. From the firstborn of the people of Israel he took the money, 1,365 shekels, by the shekel of the sanctuary. And Moses gave the redemption money to Aaron and his sons, according to the word of the LORD, as the LORD commanded Moses. (Num. 3:44–51)

Thus you shall separate the Levites from among the people of Israel, and the Levites shall be mine. And after that the Levites shall go in to serve at the tent of meeting, when you have cleansed them and offered them as a wave offering. For they are wholly given to me from among the people of Israel. Instead of all who open the womb, the firstborn of all the people of Israel, I have taken them for myself. For all the firstborn among the people of Israel are mine, both of man and of beast. On the day that I struck down all the firstborn in the land of Egypt I consecrated them for myself, and I have taken the Levites instead of all the firstborn among the people of Israel. And I have given the Levites as a gift to Aaron and his sons from among the people of Israel, to do the service for the people of Israel at the tent of meeting and to make atonement for the people of Israel, that there may be no plague among the people of Israel when the people of Israel come near the sanctuary. (Num. 8:14–19)

Here is more background for the New Testament's teaching on Christ's work of redemption. God took the tribe of Levi, dedicated to himself in priestly service, in exchange for the redeemed firstborn sons. And Israel had to redeem, by paying five shekels per person, the 273 of the firstborn sons of the people of Israel that exceeded the number of the male Levites.

Isaiah's Theme of a New Exodus

A third aspect of Old Testament background is Isaiah's theme of a new exodus in the release of Israelites from Babylonian exile. Morris explains the source of this idea:

The ancient practice of prisoners in captivity being set free by payment of a ransom or an act of clemency on the part of the ruling authority is notably seen in the exiles being restored by Cyrus' decree (Ezra 1). Isaiah 45:1–25 speaks of a return celebration in which Cyrus is the agent who releases the Babylonian exiles, but the redeemer is God.[10]

---

[10]Morris, "Redemption," 784–85.

Morris speaks wisely. God calls Cyrus his "anointed" one and uses him, although he does not know the Lord, to deliver his people Israel.

> Thus says the LORD to his anointed, to Cyrus, . . .
> "For the sake of my servant Jacob,
>   and Israel my chosen,
> I call you by your name,
>   I name you, though you do not know me.
> I am the LORD, and there is no other,
>   besides me there is no God;
>   I equip you, though you do not know me,
> that people may know, from the rising of the sun
>   and from the west, that there is none besides me;
>   I am the LORD, and there is no other." (Isa. 45:1, 4–6)

Later Isaiah rejoices in the Israelites' coming deliverance by comparing the Babylonian exile to terrible times that preceded—the years of bondage in Egypt and during the Assyrian captivity.

> Awake, awake,
>   put on your strength, O Zion;
> put on your beautiful garments,
>   O Jerusalem, the holy city;
> for there shall no more come into you
>   the uncircumcised and the unclean.
> Shake yourself from the dust and arise;
>   be seated, O Jerusalem;
> loose the bonds from your neck,
>   O captive daughter of Zion.

For thus says the LORD: "You were sold for nothing, and you shall be redeemed without money." For thus says the Lord GOD: "My people went down at the first into Egypt to sojourn there, and the Assyrian oppressed them for nothing. Now therefore what have I here," declares the LORD, "seeing that my people are taken away for nothing? Their rulers wail," declares the LORD, "and continually all the day my name is despised. Therefore my people shall know my name. Therefore in that day they shall know that it is I who speak; here am I."

> How beautiful upon the mountains
>   are the feet of him who brings good news,
> who publishes peace, who brings good news of happiness,

> who publishes salvation,
>> who says to Zion, "Your God reigns."
> The voice of your watchmen—they lift up their voice;
>> together they sing for joy;
> for eye to eye they see
>> the return of the LORD to Zion.
> Break forth together into singing,
>> you waste places of Jerusalem,
> for the LORD has comforted his people;
>> he has redeemed Jerusalem.
> The LORD has bared his holy arm
>> before the eyes of all the nations,
> and all the ends of the earth shall see
>> the salvation of our God. (Isa. 52:1–10)

Indeed, Isaiah promises redemption from captivity, which is nothing less than a new exodus for the captive covenant people. He brings them words filled with comfort and deliverance.

> But now thus says the LORD,
> he who created you, O Jacob,
>> he who formed you, O Israel:
> "Fear not, for I have redeemed you;
>> I have called you by name, you are mine.
> When you pass through the waters, I will be with you;
>> and through the rivers, they shall not overwhelm you;
> when you walk through fire you shall not be burned,
>> and the flame shall not consume you." (Isa. 43:1–2)

Surely, this is cause for much rejoicing and singing.

> And the ransomed of the LORD shall return
>> and come to Zion with singing;
> everlasting joy shall be upon their heads;
>> they shall obtain gladness and joy,
>> and sorrow and sighing shall flee away. (Isa. 35:10)

The prophet Jeremiah agrees heartily with Isaiah's sentiments:

> Thus says the LORD of hosts: The people of Israel are oppressed, and the people of Judah with them. All who took them captive have held them fast; they refuse to let

them go. Their Redeemer is strong; the LORD of hosts is his name. He will surely plead their cause, that he may give rest to the earth, but unrest to the inhabitants of Babylon. (Jer. 50:33–34)

> For the LORD has ransomed Jacob
>   and has redeemed him from hands too strong for him. (Jer. 31:11)

Kinsman Redeemer?

Some scholars view the kinsman redeemer as another point of Old Testament background, while others disagree.[11] Although the New Testament does not seem to cite the kinsman-redeemer concept, it is at least worth mentioning. A close relative was able to redeem property that had been sold by a kinsman or even redeem a kinsman himself who had been sold into slavery. In both cases redemption was accomplished by paying a redemption price to the owner (Lev. 25:25–28, 47–52).

Redemption in the Synoptic Gospels

In the Gospels there appear general statements of redemption as well as the famous "ransom saying" found in Matthew and Mark.

General Statements in the Gospel of Luke

Luke's Gospel speaks four times of redemption. Each is a general reference to the Old Testament hope, and each pertains to a specific time in Jesus's life. Two pertain to Jesus's birth, one to his crucifixion, and one to his second coming. So the overall impression is to present Jesus as the Redeemer in a general way.

Jesus's birth, Zechariah's prophecy (Luke 1:68). Zechariah, an elderly priest, "was chosen by lot to enter the temple of the Lord and offer incense" (Luke 1:9). While doing this, he is visited by the angel Gabriel, who delivers a startling message to him. He and his barren wife Elizabeth are to have a son and to name him John. John will be a great man of God who "will turn many of the children of Israel to the Lord their God, and he will go before him in the spirit and power of Elijah" (vv. 16–17). But because Zechariah doubts Gabriel's words, the angel tells him that he will be unable to talk until John is born.

So it is. At the baby's birth, Elizabeth announces that his name will be John (v. 60). The puzzled listeners ask why they would choose a name shared by none

---

[11]For a source in favor, see John R. W. Stott, *The Cross of Christ* (Downers Grove, IL: InterVarsity, 1986), 176; for a source against, see C. John Collins, "Homonymous Verbs in Biblical Hebrew: An Investigation of the Role of Comparative Philology" (PhD diss., University of Liverpool, 1988), 65–70.

of their relatives. When Zechariah is asked, he responds using a writing tablet, "His name is John" (v. 63). At once the elderly priest is able to speak and blesses God (v. 67). Filled with the Holy Spirit, he prophesies,

> Blessed be the Lord God of Israel,
>> for he has visited and *redeemed* his people. (v. 68)

Here, Zechariah, the father of John the Baptist, Jesus's forerunner, prophesies by the Spirit of God that John's birth constitutes a visitation of God to his people and will result in their redemption from their enemies (v. 71). Joel Green teaches us that Zechariah does so in language reminiscent of the exodus:

> The appearance of the term "redemption" determines the required sense of "to visit" [as in grace rather than in judgment], but also sets Zechariah's vision of salvation squarely in the context of the Exodus. In that paradigmatic act of deliverance, God redeemed his people and created among them a new community, and in scriptural references to this act of deliverance the term Zechariah uses is paramount.[12]

The redemption that Zechariah (and many others) hoped for is thus in line with Old Testament expectations of God's coming to his people to free them from their enemies and give them prosperity. We note that this redemption also includes the forgiveness of sins, which is also mentioned in the context (v. 77). Most important is that Jesus takes the place of God in the Old Testament; he is the Redeemer.

Jesus's birth, Anna's message (Luke 2:38). Luke tells of another witness who spoke of the redemption that Jesus's birth would bring—Anna the prophetess. Like Zechariah, Anna was elderly, in fact, eighty-four years old (Luke 2:36). Also like the elderly priest, Anna was devoted to God's service: "She did not depart from the temple, worshiping with fasting and prayer night and day" (v. 37). In God's providence, Anna was present when Joseph and Mary came to present Jesus in the temple and to restore Mary to full communion with God's people ("their purification," v. 22; see Lev. 12:3–4). Green notes: "We discern in this passage the divine hand orchestrating human movements. Herod's temple was a massive structure; how could it be that she arrived in the right place at just the right moment apart from divine direction?"[13]

---

[12]Joel B. Green, *The Gospel of Luke*, The New International Commentary on the New Testament (Grand Rapids: Eerdmans, 1997), 116.
[13]Ibid., 151.

After Simeon, a devout man "waiting for the consolation of Israel" (Luke 2:25), took baby Jesus in his arms and prophesied that he had seen God's salvation, amazing Joseph and Mary, it was Anna's turn. We do not know her very words, but Luke reports, "And coming up at that very hour she began to give thanks to God and to speak of him to all who were waiting for the *redemption* of Jerusalem" (v. 38). Darrell Bock cites the Old Testament exodus as the inspiration of Anna's (and Luke's) message:

> Along with her praise, Anna addressed the crowd concerning Israel's redemption. The phrase . . . redemption of Jerusalem refers to the redemption of Israel, since the capital stands for the nation. Equivalent to the phrase *consolation of Israel* (2:25), it has OT background in that it refers to God's decisive salvific act for his people (Isa. 40:9; 52:9; 63:4).[14]

Again Luke mentions redemption, as a general reference to salvation that God would bring, even through his infant Messiah. The baby Jesus was the Redeemer! To first-century Jews, this would involve God's intervening in world affairs to deliver Israel from their foes and give them shalom.

Jesus's death and resurrection (Luke 24:21). A similar reference is found at the end of Luke's Gospel in the discussion on the road to Emmaus. Two followers of Jesus were discussing what had recently happened in Jerusalem, when Jesus himself, not recognized by them, joined them (Luke 24:14–15). When he inquired about their topic of discussion, one of them named Cleopas continued the dialogue.

> "Are you the only visitor to Jerusalem who does not know the things that have happened there in these days?" And he said to them, "What things?" And they said to him, "Concerning Jesus of Nazareth, a man who was a prophet mighty in deed and word before God and all the people, and how our chief priests and rulers delivered him up to be condemned to death, and crucified him. But we had hoped that he was the one to *redeem* Israel. Yes, and besides all this, it is now the third day since these things happened." (vv. 18–21)

This is a fascinating resurrection appearance of Jesus to say the least! The risen Christ appears to two followers who do not recognize him. When he asks them the subject of their conversation, they are astonished that he doesn't know about Jesus of Nazareth's crucifixion and death. Readers should not miss the

---

[14]Darrell L. Bock, *Luke 1:1–9:50*, Baker Exegetical Commentary on the New Testament (Grand Rapids: Baker Academic, 1994), 253.

irony: disciples ignorant of the meaning of Jesus's saving work accuse him, who alone knows the truth, of being ignorant of his own death (v. 18). In the process they share their seemingly unfulfilled expectation: "But we had hoped that he was the one to redeem Israel" (v. 21). The disciples go on to tell Jesus the news of the women's and disciples' reports of angels and an empty tomb testifying to his resurrection, something too wonderful for them to believe.

But our main concern here is another general use of redemption, this time expressing the Jewish hope that the Messiah would liberate them from Roman oppression. Bock summarizes well:

> The two share their personal view of Jesus: they were downcast because they had hoped that he was going to redeem Israel. . . . They had hoped that through Jesus, God would work for the nation and deliver it into a new era of freedom. This is the only time that Luke uses . . . *lytroo*, to redeem. . . . What was hoped for included Israel's political release from Rome.[15]

Of course, the two disciples are somewhat mistaken, as Jesus explains. Indeed, Jesus is "the one to redeem Israel" (v. 21). But, they do not perceive how "all the Scriptures" speak of him, and specifically they fail to see that it is "necessary that the Christ should suffer these things and enter into his glory" (vv. 27, 26). They need the risen Christ to explain to them the saving significance of his death and resurrection. We do not blame them for needing such a theology lesson. This is because, as Green explains, "what has happened with Jesus can be understood only in light of the Scriptures, yet the Scriptures themselves can be understood only in light of what has happened to Jesus. These two are mutually informing."[16] But Jesus faults them for not believing the Old Testament. And he could just as easily fault them for not believing his repeated predictions of his death and resurrection (9:22, 44; 18:32–33).

Once more Luke gives a general reference to redemption, in the Old Testament sense of a divine intervention that would deliver God's people from their enemies and usher in a time of prosperity. This will indeed occur at Christ's return to consummate the age, but God's present focus is on his Son, the Redeemer, whose death and resurrection give all believers access to the present spiritual kingdom.

Jesus's return (Luke 21:28). In Luke's version of Jesus's great eschatological discourse, Jesus, after predicting the destruction of the temple, wars and per-

---

[15]Darrell L. Bock, *Luke 9:51–24:53*, Baker Exegetical Commentary on the New Testament (Grand Rapids: Baker Academic, 1996), 1913–14.
[16]Green, *The Gospel of Luke*, 844.

secutions, and the destruction of Jerusalem, foretells the coming of the Son of Man (Luke 21:5–28).

> And there will be signs in sun and moon and stars, and on the earth distress of nations in perplexity because of the roaring of the sea and the waves, people fainting with fear and with foreboding of what is coming on the world. For the powers of the heavens will be shaken. And then they will see the Son of Man coming in a cloud with power and great glory. Now when these things begin to take place, straighten up and raise your heads, because your *redemption* is drawing near. (vv. 25–28)

As background for his second coming, Jesus paints an eschatological picture with four elements: signs in the heavens, anguish and bewilderment among nations, the sea's roaring, and great fear among the people (vv. 25–26). Though the painting is Jesus's own composition, the paints on his palette come from the Old Testament, as Green helpfully points out.[17]

In the center of the painting is Jesus himself: "And then they will see the Son of Man coming in a cloud with power and great glory" (v. 27). It is noteworthy that Jesus depicts his return in the Old Testament language of theophany, as Green explains:

> Throughout his Gospel, Luke repeatedly identifies Jesus as the Son of Man and, more recently, has laid the groundwork for his readers to anticipate the coming of Jesus as Son of Man. Luke 21:27 portrays the most exalted picture yet, however. . . . Drawing explicitly on the language of Dan 7:13—with its analogy between the coming of God "in the clouds" (e.g., Isa 19:1; Ps 18:2–3) and the coming of the Son of Man—this Lukan text depicts the return of Jesus as a theophany. (See Acts 1:9–11, where it is said of Jesus, who had been taken out of sight in a cloud, that he "will come in the same way"—i.e., in a cloud.)[18]

Jesus comes as God himself "with power and great glory" (Luke 21:27). His return means two very different things for those who do not know him and for those who do. The former group will faint "with fear and foreboding of what is coming on the world" (v. 26). Not so the latter. They will "straighten up and raise [their] heads." Why? Jesus answers plainly: "because [their] redemption is drawing near" (v. 28). And it draws near in the person of the returning Christ.

Bock describes the meaning of redemption here:

---

[17]Ibid., 740nn44–47.
[18]Ibid., 740.

Redemption is used in a broad sense: not deliverance from the penalty of sin but deliverance from a fallen world. . . . This is the moment when the consummation of all that has been promised draws near, as Peter declares in Acts 3:19–21 when he speaks of Jesus' return. . . . It looks past forgiveness of sins to the full demonstration of authority. When the Son of Man appears, he will exercise his authority; the time of victory will be here.[19]

Conclusion. Four times Luke refers to redemption: twice with reference to Jesus's birth (Luke 1:68; 2:38) and once each with reference to his crucifixion (and resurrection) and second coming (24:21; 21:28). The most significant conclusion for our study is that in each of Luke's references to redemption Jesus takes the place of God in the Old Testament. Jesus Christ is the divine Redeemer. In addition, redemption is general. Luke does not speak of the means of redemption, as Paul and the writer to the Hebrews do. Instead, he speaks of redemption in a broad Old Testament sense of God's deliverance of his people and of all things. I. Howard Marshall summarizes:

Deliverance requires a deliverer; just as Moses was called a deliverer (Acts 7:35), so Jesus is the deliverer, and the role ascribed to God in the Old Testament is transferred to him. . . . Luke takes up the Old Testament idea of deliverance from tribulation by Yahweh and finds it fulfilled typologically in Jesus Christ who fulfilled Jewish hopes by his incarnation, suffering and entry into glory and who will bring about final redemption . . . at his second coming. The language is that of Old Testament piety, and there is little reflection over the means of redemption.[20]

The Ransom Saying

Jesus's ransom saying in Mark 10:45—"For even the Son of Man came not to be served but to serve, and to give his life as a ransom for many"—with its parallel in Matthew 20:28, is the most famous text treating the theology of Jesus's death in the Synoptic Gospels. Before discussing its theology, we will examine its authenticity, background, and context.[21]

Authenticity. Critical New Testament scholarship has raised considerable doubt on whether Mark 10:45 should be accepted as an authentic saying of Jesus. It is alleged that this saying was created by the early church and read back into

---

[19]Bock, *Luke 9:51–24:53*, 1687.

[20]Marshall, "The Meaning of Redemption," in *Jesus the Saviour*, 240–41.

[21]I am indebted to Sydney H. T. Page, "Ransom Saying," in *Dictionary of Jesus and the Gospels*, ed. Joel B. Green, Scot McKnight, and I. Howard Marshall (Downers Grove, IL: InterVarsity, 1992), 660–62. Page's work there depends upon his "The Authenticity of the Ransom Logion (Mark 10:45b)," in *Gospel Perspectives 1: Studies of History and Tradition in the Four Gospels*, ed. R. T. France and D. Wenham (Sheffield: JSOT, 1980), 137–61.

Jesus's life. I will briefly respond to four arguments advanced against its acceptance. First, it is claimed that the saying ill-suits the preceding context where
Jesus enjoins his disciples to live a life of humble service. But why could Jesus
not present his own life as a model of service and his self-offering in death as
the epitome of his service?[22]

Second, it is claimed that because the main verb—"For even the Son of Man
came"—is in the past tense, it is the work of a later writer reflecting on Jesus's
life. But this overlooks the fact that Jesus many times speaks of his having come
and that customarily these sayings are in the past tense (e.g., Matt. 5:17; 10:34,
35; Mark 1:38; 2:17; Luke 12:49; 19:10).[23]

Third, it is claimed that the saying is inauthentic because it presents an
interpretation of Jesus's death not found elsewhere in the Synoptics. Sydney
Page responds:

> [This saying] is not at all out of character with what Jesus taught about his death.
> There is abundant evidence that Jesus anticipated that his life would end violently
> and that he believed this had been prophesied in Scripture. It is inherently prob-
> able that he would have reflected on the meaning of this. If, as Luke 22:37 sug-
> gests, he did so in the light of Isaiah 53, the authenticity of the ransom saying is
> perfectly credible. That it expressed the mind of Jesus is confirmed by the presence
> of similar ideas in the words over the cup at the Last Supper.[24]

Fourth, and most importantly, it is claimed that the saying's absence from Luke
22:25–27, which otherwise is a close parallel to Matthew 20:25–28 and Mark
10:45, argues against its being authentic. The three passages present the same
main ideas in the same order, although the ransom saying is omitted from Luke.
The claim is that this means that Luke's version is simpler and original and the
others an embellishment of the early church. Matters get complicated here and I
am indebted again to the wisdom of Page, who offers five trenchant observations:

> (1) The Semitic character of the version in the first two gospels suggests that it is
> more primitive than that in Luke. (2) It is unwarranted to assume that the version
> with the richest theology must be secondary. (3) It appears that Luke drew Luke
> 22:24–27 from his special source(s) rather than from either Matthew or Mark,
> and there is no reason to think that he intended to suppress the theology of the
> saying. (4) Luke places his account in a different historical setting than the other

---

[22]Page, "Ransom Saying," 661.
[23]Simon Gathercole does outstanding work on these texts in *The Pre-existent Son: Recovering the Christologies of Matthew, Mark, and Luke* (Grand Rapids: Eerdmans, 2006), 83–176.
[24]Page, "Ransom Saying," 661.

Evangelists, and it is not at all certain that he is describing the same incident. (5) Even if the placing of the saying in its present location is editorial, the saying itself could be genuine.[25]

All things considered, I agree with D. A. Carson: "There are no substantial reasons for denying the authenticity of this saying."[26] I regard it as a saying of Jesus, from which it is proper to draw Christian theology.

Background. Although an essay by C. K. Barrett challenges the consensus that the background of the ransom saying is in Isaiah's fourth Servant Song in 52:13–53:12, there seems to be little reason to reject the traditional view.[27] Again, Page's arguments are cogent:

> It remains likely that the ransom saying was formed on the basis of Isaiah 53. Both combine the ideas of servanthood and atoning death and speak of the servant voluntarily "giving his life." The Greek *lytron* ("ransom") in Matthew 20:28 and Mark 10:45 corresponds to the Hebrew *'asam* ("guilt offering") in Isaiah 53:10, despite the fact that it is not used to translate it elsewhere. Most importantly, both use the phrase "for many" to indicate who benefits from the servant's death.[28]

The wisdom of Page's words will be borne out in the exposition of the ransom saying that follows.

Context. The saying "provides a climax to the section of the Gospel narratives which begins with Peter's confession at Caesarea Philippi."[29] That confession focuses on the person of Christ, "You are the Christ" (Mark 8:29). It is significant that right after Peter's confession, Jesus speaks openly to his disciples about his death and resurrection (8:31). In fact, he does the same thing twice more (9:31; 10:33–34). The ransom saying follows shortly thereafter. Considered in its context, following Jesus's three predictions, the saying reveals his understanding of the meaning of his death. The location of the saying makes perfect sense, and there is no reason to question its authenticity.

---

[25]Ibid.

[26]D. A. Carson, *Matthew*, The Expositor's Bible Commentary (Grand Rapids: Zondervan, 1984), 433. Scot McKnight agrees in his massive study, *Jesus and His Death: Historiography, the Historical Jesus, and Atonement Theory* (Waco, TX: Baylor University Press, 2005), 356–58.

[27]C. K. Barrett, "The Background of Mark 10:45," in *New Testament Essays: Studies in Memory of T. W. Manson*, ed. A. J. B. Higgins (Manchester: Manchester University Press, 1959), 1–18.

[28]Page, "Ransom Saying," 660. For more argumentation, see Ben Witherington III, *The Gospel of Mark: A Socio-Rhetorical Commentary* (Grand Rapids: Eerdmans, 2001), 288–90.

[29]Ibid.

The immediate context sheds light on the ransom saying too. Immediately after Jesus foretells his death and resurrection a third time, James and John ask him for permission to sit at his right hand and at his left in the kingdom of God (Mark 10:37). The two disciples, therefore, display their misunderstanding of Jesus's predictions. Instead of showing concern for him, when he has just said for the third time that he will be crucified, they selfishly think only of themselves and their glory. His mention of Jerusalem apparently triggers their assumption that he is already "the eschatological Lord who goes to Jerusalem to restore the glory of the fallen throne of David."[30]

As the discussion unfolds, Jesus informs James and John that they will share the cup that he must drink and be baptized with the baptism that he will undergo (v. 39). Of course, his redemptive work of drinking the cup of God's wrath and having God's judgment poured upon him in "baptism" is unique and nonrepeatable. And the same is true of his resurrection, as a saving event. But in a lesser sense, when the disciples identify with Jesus's mission, they too will experience suffering now and glory only later. Thus their request for places of honor now is insensitive to Jesus's sufferings and underestimates their own coming suffering.

As always, Jesus submits to his Father, who alone will appoint places of honor in the kingdom to come (v. 40). In so doing, he rebukes James and John for their selfishness. The other ten fare no better, for they are indignant at the two overbold brothers (v. 41). All of this prompts Jesus to lecture the Twelve concerning the ethic of his kingdom. They are not to rule as unsaved leaders do—selfishly lording it over those under their authority. Rather, they are to follow Jesus's example of humble servant leadership. William Lane vividly illustrates the knowledge that Jesus and his followers would have of their Roman overlords, along with the irony of the brothers' brash request:

> It is probable that his most direct contact with the expression of power and authority by the petty rulers of Palestine and Syria and the great lord of Rome was through the coins which circulated in the land. To cite only two examples, the denarius that was used for paying taxes (cf. Ch. 12:16) portrayed Tiberias as the semi-divine son of the god Augustus and the goddess Liva; the copper coins struck by Herod Philip at Caesarea Philippi showed the head of the reigning emperor (Augustus, then Tiberias) with the emperor's name and the inscription: "He who deserves adoration." There is biting irony in the reference to those who give the illusion of ruling (cf. Jn. 19:11) but simply exploit the people over whom they exercise dominion. In their struggle for rank and precedence and the desire to

---

[30]William L. Lane, *Commentary on the Gospel of Mark*, The New International Commentary on the New Testament (Grand Rapids: Eerdmans, 1974), 378.

exercise authority for their own advantage, the disciples were actually imitating those whom they undoubtedly despised.[31]

Not so with his disciples, Jesus insisted. Instead, "whoever would be great among you must be your servant, and whoever would be first among you must be slave of all" (Mark 10:43–44). If the lords with whom the Twelve were familiar were bad examples of leadership, who could serve as a good one? To ask the question is to answer it: "For even the Son of Man came not to be served but to serve, and to give his life as a ransom for many" (v. 45). This is the immediate context of the ransom saying: Jesus presents himself as the example of a servant-leader par excellence. He, who by rights could have demanded to be served, relinquished his rights and instead served his creatures, especially the Twelve. And the embodiment of his servant leadership? His self-giving unto death.

Theology. This brings us to the meaning and theology of the ransom saying: "For even the Son of Man came . . . to give his life as a ransom for many" (v. 45). This statement deserves a detailed examination. Jesus's favorite self-designation, "the Son of Man," was enigmatic to his hearers, combining two Old Testament strains: the mortal, insignificant "son of man" of Psalm 8:4, for example, and the exalted, divine "son of man" of Daniel's prophecy (see Dan. 7:13–14).

Jesus applies both meanings to himself. We see the first humble strain in Matthew 8:20: "And Jesus said to him, 'Foxes have holes, and birds of the air have nests, but the Son of Man has nowhere to lay his head.'" We see the second exalted strain in Jesus's answer to the high priest: "But I tell you, from now on you will see the Son of Man seated at the right hand of Power and coming on the clouds of heaven" (Matt. 26:64). When Jesus says, "For even the Son of Man came . . . to give his life as a ransom for many" (Mark 10:45), he uses "Son of Man" as "an exalted title and implies that Jesus has the right to be served."[32]

Jesus's words "the Son of Man *came*" imply his preexistence and point to his mission and purpose, in this case, to serve and die.[33] Jesus came "to give his life as a ransom." This word (*lytron*) occurs only here in the New Testament. "In extrabiblical sources *lytron* denotes the price paid to free slaves, and it is likely that it has that meaning here, though obviously it is used in a metaphorical sense."[34]

---

[31]Ibid., 382.
[32]Page, "Ransom Saying," 661.
[33]So Gathercole, *The Pre-existent Son*, 167–68.
[34]Page, "Ransom Saying," 661.

The combination of "giving one's life as a ransom" communicates powerfully against its background in Mark and the Psalms, as Marshall explains:

> In Mark 10:45 . . . Jesus serves men by giving his life as a ransom for many. Mark no doubt intends this saying to be seen against the background of 8:37 where the question is raised whether a man can give any exchange for his life. Behind the question lies Psalm 49:7–9: "Truly no man can ransom himself, or give to God the price of his life, for the ransom of his life is costly, and can never suffice, that he should continue to live on for ever, and never see the Pit." What man cannot do has been done by Christ. We are surely justified in discerning here the thought of human mortality as the result of human sin, and in seeing in the death of Christ the ransom "price" paid to God for the redemption of mankind from death.[35]

Here is substitutionary atonement. It includes the idea of voluntariness on Jesus's part because he willingly gives his life for others. As he says in John's Gospel: "For this reason the Father loves me, because I lay down my life that I may take it up again. No one takes it from me, but I lay it down of my own accord" (John 10:17–18).

And at this point we think of verses from Isaiah 53 that inspire Mark 10:45:

> . . . his soul makes an offering for guilt. . . .
> he poured out his soul to death . . .
> yet he bore the sin of many. (Isa. 53:10, 12)

Lane brings many of these strands together to affirm that Jesus's words teach vicarious atonement:

> The ransom metaphor sums up the purpose for which Jesus gave his life and defines the complete expression of his service. The prevailing notion behind the metaphor is that of deliverance by purchase, whether a prisoner of war, a slave, or a forfeited life is the object to be delivered. Because the idea of equivalence, or substitution, was proper to the concept of a ransom, it became an integral element in the vocabulary of redemption in the OT. It speaks of a liberation which connotes a servitude or an imprisonment from which man cannot free himself. In the context of verse 45a, with its reference to the service of the Son of Man, it is appropriate to find an allusion to the Servant of the Lord in Isa. 53, who vicariously and voluntarily suffered and gave his life for the sins of others. The specific thought underlying the reference to the ransom is expressed in Isa.

---

[35]Marshall, "The Meaning of Redemption," 248.

53:10 which speaks of "making his life an *offering for sin*." Jesus, as the messianic Servant, offers himself as a guilt-offering (Lev. 5:14–6:7; 7:1–7; Num. 5:5–8) in compensation for the sins of the people.[36]

The use of the preposition *anti* after "ransom" (λύτρον, *lytron*) reinforces the concept of substitution. "The Son of Man takes *the place* of the many and there happens to him what would have happened to them. . . . In his death, Jesus pays the price that sets men free."[37] The phrase "for many," reflecting Isaiah 53:12 ("he bore the sin of many"), is not a restrictive reference in the sense that Christ's work was for "many" as opposed to "all." Rather, it contrasts, as does the verse in Isaiah, the "one" Servant of the Lord and the "many" for whom he died. Page hits the right note: "Certainly 'many' stands in contrast to 'one' not 'all,' and the basic idea is that the death of Jesus brings benefit to a great number of persons."[38]

Redemption in Acts

Although Acts is replete with gospel preaching, it does not say much concerning redemption proper. In at least one significant passage, Acts 20:28, Luke records Paul's words, "Pay careful attention to yourselves and to all the flock, in which the Holy Spirit has made you overseers, to care for the church of God, which he obtained with his own blood." Paul addressed these words of admonishment to the Ephesian elders, who met him at Miletus. Paul teaches that Christ, as God incarnate, "purchased" the church with his own blood.[39] This is the language of redemption with an emphasis on redemption's price and results, as John Stott reminds us:

> Jesus' lordship over both the church and Christian is attributed to his having bought us with his own blood. Presbyters, for example, are summoned to conscientious oversight of the church on the ground that God in Christ has bought it with his own blood (Acts 20:28). If the church was worth his blood, is it not worth our labour? The privilege of serving it is established by the preciousness of the price paid for its purchase.[40]

Christ is our Redeemer who bought us at an enormous price—his sacrificial death on the cross.

---

[36]Lane, *Commentary on the Gospel of Mark*, 383–84, italics original.
[37]Ibid., 384, italics original.
[38]Page, "Ransom Saying," 662.
[39]Some manuscripts read "Lord" instead of "God." This matters little because both are divine titles.
[40]Stott, *The Cross of Christ*, 181.

Redemption in Paul

Paul treats redemption in many passages. We will study the most important ones.

Romans 3:24

Paul returns to his announced theme of the revelation of the saving righteousness of God in Christ (Rom. 1:16–17; 3:21). He tells how this righteousness has nothing to do with law keeping, is witnessed to by the Old Testament, is received by faith, and is needed by all sinners. Next he speaks of grace and of Christ's atonement, using two motifs: redemption and propitiation. Our current interest is with the former: "For there is no distinction: for all have sinned and fall short of the glory of God, and are justified by his grace as a gift, through the redemption that is in Christ Jesus" (Rom. 3:22–24). Humankind since the fall is on a level playing field due to sin. We are all in trouble with a holy and just God. Wonderfully, God declares sinners righteous freely by his grace, his favor against our merit. On what basis does he do this? On that of Christ's saving work, here described as "the redemption that is in Christ Jesus" (v. 24). Paul will tell us more about redemption elsewhere, but here he teaches that deliverance from what our sins deserve is found in no one else but Jesus Christ. He is the world's only Redeemer.

Romans 8:19–23

Paul urges the believers in Rome to view their present sufferings in comparison to their final glorious salvation (Rom. 8:18). Even God's creation itself yearns for final salvation, which will mean freedom from "its bondage to corruption."

> For the creation waits with eager longing for the revealing of the sons of God. For the creation was subjected to futility, not willingly, but because of him who subjected it, in hope that the creation itself will be set free from its bondage to corruption and obtain the freedom of the glory of the children of God. For we know that the whole creation has been groaning together in the pains of childbirth until now. (Rom. 8:19–22)

In fact, the creation groans, so to speak, as a woman in labor, awaiting that great day. Since bondage is the need for redemption, when Paul speaks of the creation being delivered from bondage, he teaches that there is a sense in which the creation too will be redeemed. In its largest sense, therefore, Christ's redemption is cosmic.

We groan too: "And not only the creation, but we ourselves, who have the firstfruits of the Spirit, groan inwardly as we wait eagerly for adoption as sons, the redemption of our bodies" (v. 23). Now we are the sons and daughters of God (8:14–17) by grace through faith in God's unique Son. But the fullness of our adoption awaits "the redemption of our bodies" in the resurrection. Paul thus teaches that redemption overlaps adoption and that both have a final bodily aspect. We are redeemed already, but our final redemption is still future and that is why we live in hope of it (vv. 24–25). It will be even greater, for it will involve our being raised in bodies that are immortal, imperishable, glorious, powerful, and dominated by the Spirit (1 Cor. 15:42–44, 52–53).

Romans 11:26

In the midst of his discussion of the place of Israel in God's plan, Paul cites Isaiah 59:20:

> The Deliverer will come from Zion,
>   he will banish ungodliness from Jacob. (Rom. 11:26)

We note that the apostle uses the Old Testament title for God—"Deliverer"—and applies it to Christ. Thomas Schreiner agrees: "In the OT 'the deliverer' . . . is certainly Yahweh, but for Paul it is almost certainly Jesus Christ, and the reference is to his second coming."[41]

1 Corinthians 1:30

Paul responds to Greek and Jewish criticisms that the Christian gospel makes God look foolish and weak. "For the foolishness of God is wiser than men, and the weakness of God is stronger than men" (1 Cor. 1:25). He cites as evidence God's having chosen ordinary people to belong to him and to the Corinthian churches (vv. 26–27). In fact, God had a purpose in this: "God chose what is low and despised in the world, even things that are not, to bring to nothing things that are, so that no human being might boast in the presence of God" (vv. 28–29). God alone is worthy of praise for salvation. Paul cites the corroborating words of the prophet Jeremiah spoken centuries earlier: "Let the one who boasts, boast in the Lord" (v. 31, citing Jer. 9:23–24).

Paul goes on to speak of the zenith of the revelation of God's true wisdom: "And because of him you are in Christ Jesus, who became to us wisdom from God, righteousness and sanctification and redemption" (1 Cor. 1:30). Due to God's grace, the Corinthian believers have been spiritually united to Christ and have

---

[41]Thomas R. Schreiner, *Romans*, Baker Exegetical Commentary on the New Testament (Grand Rapids: Baker Academic, 1998), 619–20.

partaken of all of his saving benefits, including justification ("righteousness"), sainthood and godliness ("sanctification"), and deliverance ("redemption"). Paul lists these benefits in apposition to the words "wisdom from God." Christ "became to us wisdom from God," namely, "righteousness and sanctification and redemption."

Anthony Thiselton captures Paul's thought:

> The new *wisdom*, in contrast to the cleverness of the Jewish or Greek sage in acquiring success in various enterprises, and thereby honor or esteem, derives from God's action through Christ which makes it possible to be *in Christ* as the Christian's objective status. Its content now manifests itself in sharing the gifts of *righteousness, sanctification, and redemption. . . .* The four qualities, then, belong together, and *both characterize Christ and are imparted by Christ.*[42]

Paul thus includes redemption as one of the blessings that all believers have from being united to Christ "in whom are hidden all the treasures of wisdom and knowledge" (Col. 2:3).

1 Corinthians 6:19–20

Paul uses multiple arguments to alert the Corinthian Christians to "flee from sexual immorality" (1 Cor. 6:18). Ongoing sexual sin, whether heterosexual or homosexual, excludes people from the kingdom of God (vv. 9–10). We and our bodies are designed for the Lord, not immorality (v. 13). God will raise our bodies (v. 14). Our bodies belong to the Lord (v. 15). We are united to Christ and dare not unite our bodies (and him) to a prostitute (vv. 16–17). Sexual immorality is a sin against one's own body (v. 18). Our bodies are temples of the Holy Spirit (v. 19).

Paul saves his argument based on redemption for last: "You are not your own, for you were bought with a price. So glorify God in your body" (vv. 19–20). Under the next passage, I will summarize more conclusions of recent studies that shed light on the first-century slave-master relationship in the Graeco-Roman world.[43] The main point here is that Christians, regardless of social status, belong to a new Master or Owner, even Jesus Christ. The emphasis of the transaction involving the price of Christ's own blood in 1 Corinthians 6:19–20 is not on freedom but a change of ownership. Dale Martin has shown that the status of a slave was very complex and that after the question as to whether one

---

[42] Anthony C. Thiselton, *The First Epistle to the Corinthians*, The New International Greek Testament Commentary (Grand Rapids: Eerdmans, 2000), 190, italics original.
[43] See ibid., 562–65, for a good summary with bibliography.

was a slave, the most important question was whose slave one was. The status of a slave depended not only upon his or her function, which varied widely from menial labor to household management, but "still more decisively on the character, status, and influence of the one to whom one belonged as a slave."[44]

And we do not want to miss Paul's secondary stress on the redemption price. Again, Thiselton teaches us: "The imagery stresses primarily the new ownership, and secondly a costly act on the part of the new owner which makes the [owner] legitimately and contractually the one to whom the believer now *belongs*."[45] Costly act, indeed. It was nothing less than the redemptive death of the Son of God!

As a result of their being redeemed, believers belong not to themselves, but to Christ, their new Lord, and must live accordingly. Stott drives home Paul's case for sexual purity, emphasizing redemption:

> Our body has not only been created by God and will one day be resurrected by him, but it has been bought by Christ's blood and is indwelt by his Spirit. Thus it belongs to God three times over, by creation, redemption and indwelling. How then, since it does not belong to us, can we misuse it? Instead, we are to honour God with it, by obedience and self-control. Bought by Christ, we have no business to become the slaves of anybody or anything else. Once we were slaves of sin; now we are slaves of Christ, and his service is the true freedom.[46]

1 Corinthians 7:23

Paul instructs Christian readers to live for God in the situations in which they find themselves: "Only let each person lead the life that the Lord has assigned to him, and to which God has called him" (1 Cor. 7:17). Paul describes situations pertaining to religion, economics, and family (vv. 18–40). After repeating, "Each one should remain in the condition in which he was called" (v. 20, cf. v. 24), he then addresses the circumstances of slaves and freedmen (vv. 21–23). Slaves, constituting the majority in the first-century Roman world, belonged to their masters because they were born to a female slave, sold themselves into slavery, were sold into slavery as children, or were kidnapped.[47] Paul counsels Christians who are slaves to accept their situation, but to seek freedom if possible: "Were you a slave when called? Do not be concerned about it. But if you can gain your freedom, avail yourself of the opportunity" (v. 21). Thiselton informs us: "The very large numbers and influence of freedpersons would be proof alone that

---

[44]Ibid., 477, citing Dale B. Martin, *Slavery as Salvation: The Metaphor of Slavery in Pauline Christianity* (New Haven, CT: Yale University Press, 1990), 1–49.

[45]Thiselton, *The First Epistle to the Corinthians*, 477.

[46]Stott, *The Cross of Christ*, 181–82.

[47]Thiselton, *The First Epistle to the Corinthians*, 562–63.

most or very many slaves hoped to gain their freedom in due course. Relatively few spent their entire lives as slaves."[48]

The apostle redefines the status both of Christian slaves and of Christian freedpersons in terms of their relationship to Christ: "For he who was called in the Lord as a slave is a freedman of the Lord. Likewise he who was free when called is a slave of Christ" (v. 22). A Christian slave, while remaining in the household of his master, has a higher status: "*The slave's real status is determined by his or her placement in a different household entirely: the household of Christ. The slave is a freedperson of the Lord and shares in the benefits, status, and obligations* that relationship brings."[49] Christian freedpersons must value their belonging to Christ more highly than their social freedom.

What accounts for this remarkable situation in which believers transcend social status? Paul's answer is loud and clear: "You were bought with a price; do not become slaves of men" (v. 23). Paul refers, of course, to Christ's atonement, which is here viewed as a redemption price. Christ is our Redeemer who purchased us with his death. We henceforth belong to him, our new Master. Thiselton captures the significance of this in its first-century social context:

> The *price* brings the believer into Christ's own possession as his or her Lord, who then takes over responsibility and care of the purchased one. The Christian *belongs to Christ*, not to himself or to herself. This is status and honor, for the slave represents his or her Lord; and it is freedom, for the believer is placed thereby in the hands of the Lord *for his care, his decisions, his directions, his responsibility.*[50]

Galatians 3:13

Because Galatians 3:13 will feature prominently in the chapter on Christ as our legal substitute, I will treat it briefly here. In a legal context, Paul cites the Old Testament's pronouncement of a curse on lawbreakers: "For all who rely on works of the law are under a curse; for it is written, 'Cursed be everyone who does not abide by all things written in the Book of the Law, and do them'" (Gal. 3:10, citing Deut. 27:26). The curse of the law is its threat of punishment against those who violate it. Because all of us have broken God's law, we are under that threat of punishment and in need of redemption. And that is exactly what God provides: "Christ redeemed us from the curse of the law by becoming a curse for us" (Gal. 3:13). Paul supports this point also with an Old Testament quota-

---

[48]Ibid., 564.
[49]Ibid., 560, quoting Martin, *Slavery as Salvation*, 65; italics added by Thiselton.
[50]Thiselton, *The First Epistle to the Corinthians*, 561, italics original.

tion: "For it is written, 'Cursed is everyone who is hanged on a tree'" (v. 13, citing Deut. 21:23).

Christ himself on the cross bears the law's curse, its threat of punishment, that he might deliver us from it. Here legal penal substitution and redemption overlap. Christ, our Redeemer, redeems us by giving himself in "death as a redeeming and atoning self-sacrifice,"[51] receiving the punishment that we lawbreakers deserved. The results are marvelous for all believers, even Gentiles—"Christ redeemed us . . . so that in Christ Jesus the blessing of Abraham might come to the Gentiles, so that we might receive the promised Spirit through faith" (Gal. 3:13–14).

Galatians 4:4–5

Paul tells of the preconversion bondage of his readers in their time of spiritual immaturity: "We also, when we were children, were enslaved to the elementary principles of the world" (v. 3). Amazingly, both unsaved Jews and Gentiles are subject to these "elementary principles" (vv. 3 and 8–9, respectively). What are they? For Jews they involve a legalistic adherence to the law; for Gentiles the fundamental ideas of pagan religions. But both involve the realm of the demonic, as verse 8 bears out: "You were enslaved to those who by nature are not gods."

God's gracious deliverance of believing Jews and Gentiles from such bondage is called redemption. How did God accomplish redemption? "God sent forth his Son, born of woman, born under the law, to redeem those who were under the law, so that we might receive adoption as sons" (4:4–5). "Jesus, God's Son par excellence, is the culmination and focus of all of God's redemptive activity on behalf of humanity," recounts Longenecker.[52] God accomplished redemption by sending his Son from heaven to become a man by being born of the Virgin Mary. He came to deliver those in bondage to the law. He came to make slaves into sons, as verse 7 explains: "So you are no longer a slave, but a son, and if a son, then an heir through God." By God's amazing grace, unsaved Jews and Gentiles, in bondage to demons, become God's sons and daughters and heirs!

Ephesians 1:7

Paul extols the grace of the triune God (vv. 3, 6, 12, 14). Specifically, he praises the Father as elector, the Son as Redeemer, and the Spirit as seal and guarantee (vv. 4–5, 7, 13–14). We will focus on the Son's work. Paul exalts the Father: "In love he predestined us for adoption . . . to the praise of his glorious grace,

---

[51] Richard N. Longenecker, *Galatians*, Word Biblical Commentary (Nashville: Nelson, 1990), 121.
[52] Ibid., 170.

with which he has blessed us in the Beloved" (Eph. 1:5–6). Peter O'Brien wisely comments, "'Beloved' marks out Christ as the supreme object of the Father's love; at Colossians 1:13 he is called 'the Son of his love.'"[53]

Paul teaches us much about Christ's redemption in a few words: "In him we have redemption through his blood, the forgiveness of our trespasses" (Eph. 1:7). Redemption, along with every other aspect of salvation, is found "in him"; God brings his grace to us by joining us to his beloved Son. Paul here specifically ties redemption to Christ's "blood," his atoning death. O'Brien explains, "This abbreviated expression is pregnant with meaning, and signifies that Christ's violent death on the cross as a sacrifice is the *means* by which our deliverance has been won (cf. Rom 3:25). It was obtained at very great cost."[54]

Christ accomplishes redemption—he dies that we might go free. Paul expands our knowledge of redemption through the use of an appositive: "redemption . . . the forgiveness of our trespasses." Christ effects a saving redemption that involves the forgiveness of sins.

All of this is an expression of the magnificent grace of God heaped upon believers: "redemption . . . according to the riches of his grace, which he lavished upon us" (Eph. 1:7–8). Paul uses "riches" and "lavish" to intensify his statement. The apostle strives to find words to depict the vastness of God's love in redemption.

Ephesians 4:30

After telling his readers "to put off your old self . . . and to put on the new self" (Eph. 4:22, 24) Paul applies this principle to specific areas in the following verses. They are to put off lying and to put on truth telling (v. 25). They are to put off stealing and to put on hard work and generosity (v. 28). They are to put off evil speech and to put on edifying speech (v. 29). They are to put off bitterness, sinful anger, and slander and to put on kindness, gentleness, and forgiveness (vv. 30–31).

In the midst of these exhortations, the apostle warns, "And do not grieve the Holy Spirit of God, by whom you were sealed for the day of redemption" (v. 30). This is the only place in Scripture where this exalted title is used, the Holy Spirit of God. This adds earnestness to Paul's admonition and highlights how evil in God's sight are sins of anger and evil speaking, sins that rend the body of Christ. Consistent with Paul's teaching elsewhere, the Holy Spirit is

---

[53]Peter T. O'Brien, *The Letter to the Ephesians*, The Pillar New Testament Commentary (Grand Rapids: Eerdmans, 1999), 104–5.
[54]Ibid., 106.

presented in personal terms. He is a person who can be offended and grieved. He loves us dearly and is wounded when we sin against him by sinning against other members of the church.

We are to understand this command over against verse 27: "Give no opportunity to the devil." These two are opposed to each other. The Evil One would destroy the unity of God's people, and the Holy Spirit is distressed over such disunity. Gordon Fee points out how verses 25–32 depict not only two ways of living but also their respective sources: "The sins that divide and thereby destroy the unity of the body come directly from Satan; to continue in any of them is to grieve the Spirit."[55]

As in some other passages, Paul here teaches that redemption has a future dimension: "And do not grieve the Holy Spirit of God, by whom you were sealed for the day of redemption" (v. 30). Sealing is mentioned in three passages in the New Testament.[56] God the Father is the sealer. He seals believers with the seal of the Holy Spirit. This indicates ownership and protection. The latter is emphasized because the sealing is "for the day of redemption." O'Brien aptly summarizes and applies the apostle's thought:

> The following clause, "by whom you were sealed until [or for] the day of redemption," furnishes the motivation for Paul's exhortation. By sealing believers with his Spirit, whether Gentile or Jewish, God has stamped them with his own character and guaranteed to protect them . . . until he takes final possession of them on "the day of redemption." How ungrateful would they be if they now behave in a manner which grieves the very Spirit by whom they have been marked as God's own.[57]

Ephesians 4:30 should be considered alongside 1:13–14: "In him you also, when you heard the word of truth, the gospel of your salvation, and believed in him, were sealed with the promised Holy Spirit, who is the guarantee of our inheritance until we acquire possession of it, to the praise of his glory." These two passages have at least three important things in common. Both speak of our being sealed with the Spirit, of final salvation, and of the Spirit assuring God's preservation of his people. He is "the guarantee of our inheritance until we acquire possession of it" and the one by whom we are "sealed for the day of redemption" (1:14; 4:30).

---

[55]Gordon D. Fee, *God's Empowering Presence: The Holy Spirit in the Letters of Paul* (Peabody, MA: Hendrickson, 1994), 713.

[56]2 Cor. 1:22; Eph. 1:13; 4:30.

[57]O'Brien, *The Letter to the Ephesians*, 348–49.

Colossians 1:13–14

Paul has just prayed that God would grant the (largely Gentile) Colossian believers wisdom, godliness, fruitfulness, and endurance (Col. 1:9–11). Then he adds, "giving thanks to the Father, who has qualified you to share in the inheritance of the saints in light" (v. 12). When Paul speaks of "a share" (literally) and "inheritance," he borrows Old Testament language used to speak of Israel's inheritance in the Promised Land. Douglas Moo tells the significance:

> [These] words in the Old Testament . . . are often applied to the territories allotted to Israel's tribes in the land of Israel. The translation "inheritance," found in most of the English versions, is a natural extension of meaning: that which is "allotted" is an inheritance. In a move typical of the New Testament "christifying" of the Old Testament "land" theme, Paul applies this language to the spiritual privilege enjoyed by God's new covenant people.[58]

When Paul says that God qualified his readers "to share in the inheritance of the saints in light," he implies that formerly the Colossians were not in the light and did not have an inheritance. Such an implication finds support in what he writes next: "He has delivered us from the domain of darkness and transferred us to the kingdom of his beloved Son, in whom we have redemption, the forgiveness of sins" (vv. 13–14). These two verses are an exposition of the wonderful work of God reported in verse 12—he gave believing Gentiles an inheritance among the people of God.

Christians have been transported from one kingdom into another. They have been delivered from the rule of Satan and to the rule of Christ, as O'Brien illustrates vividly:

> Like a mighty king who was able to remove peoples from their ancestral homes and to transplant them . . . into another realm, God had taken the Colossians from the tyranny of darkness . . . where evil powers rule (Luke 22:53) and where Satan's authority is exercised (Acts 26:18), transferring them to the kingdom in which his beloved Son held sway.[59]

If we ask who made this remarkable transport possible, the answer is the Son of God, our Redeemer. The Father's relationship with his Son is communicated

---

[58] Douglas J. Moo, *The Letters to the Colossians and to Philemon*, The Pillar New Testament Commentary (Grand Rapids: Eerdmans, 2008), 101.

[59] Peter T. O'Brien, *Colossians, Philemon*, Word Biblical Commentary (Waco, TX: Word, 1982), 27–28.

by the words "his beloved Son." In Paul's high christology it is he who redeems us. In him alone we have deliverance.

Paul's words are rooted in the past and applied to the present. Most commentators find background to Paul's teaching in God's deliverance of the Israelites in the exodus or in his freeing them from exile.[60] Perhaps Paul appeals to both. As we saw, the latter was sometimes expressed in terms of the former as a "new exodus." It is important to note that Paul uses the Old Testament language of redemption to speak of God's spiritual deliverance from sin through Christ.

We have seen that redemption sometimes belongs to the future (Rom. 8:23; Eph. 4:30). But here it is a present reality for God's people. The immediate picture that will come to Paul's hearers is the manumission of slaves, as Moo explains:

> *Redemption* taps into a key New Testament image of the effects of Jesus' death on those who belong to him. The language would have brought to mind in the first century the transaction by which a slave paid a price to secure his or her release from slavery. Christ came to "redeem" (*lytroo, apolytroo*) sinners from their slavery to sin by offering his own life as a "ransom" (*lytron*).[61]

In addition, here, as in Ephesians 1:7, redemption is associated with forgiveness. O'Brien cites C. F. D. Moule's observation that this shows "very clearly how entirely moral and spiritual the conception of the kingdom of God or of Christ was for the disciples of Christ."[62]

1 Timothy 2:6

Paul desires that Christians pray for "all people" and for those who govern them in various stations of civic authority, from the emperor to regional and local rulers (1 Tim. 2:1–2). His purpose? That Christians "may lead a peaceful and quiet life, godly and dignified in every way" (v. 2). Such a life is observable to everyone and pleases God. And Paul explains why this is so: because "God our Savior . . . desires all people to be saved and to come to the knowledge of the truth" (vv. 3–4). This is an expression of God's universal salvific will. How is it to be understood? Surely not as teaching universalism, the view that everyone will be saved in the end, for that contradicts the

---

[60]See Moo, *The Letters to the Colossians and to Philemon*, 102–3, for details.

[61]Ibid., 106, italics original.

[62]O'Brien, *Colossians, Philemon*, 28.

teaching of Paul in the Pastorals, in his other epistles, and in the rest of the New Testament.[63]

In the light of the verses that precede it, and in line with Paul's teaching elsewhere, verse 4 opposes exclusivism, whether Jewish or otherwise. William Mounce helps us:

> God's will is the basis of salvation and that which enables salvation . . . but the text does not move into universalism. . . . The force of the statement is directed toward the opponents' sectarian theology. As Jeremias (20) points out, this statement stands in firm opposition to the synagogue's belief that God hates the sinner and wishes to save only the righteous and to the gnostic belief that salvation is only for those "in the know."[64]

Said positively, 1 Timothy 2:4 has Paul's mission to the Gentiles in mind. It is God's will for all, including those who rule, to hear the gospel, believe it, and be saved.

The apostle tells us more about God's will to save all: "For there is one God, and there is one mediator between God and men, the man Christ Jesus, who gave himself as a ransom for all, which is the testimony given at the proper time" (vv. 5–6). Before we begin to examine these words in detail, it is good to see the big picture. Paul affirms exclusivism, biblical universalism, exclusivism again, and then biblical universalism. He affirms the same monotheistic exclusivism as the Old Testament—the unity of God. But the way he uses it in Romans 3:29–30 and here in 1 Timothy 2:5–6 turns it in the direction of biblical universalism. Philip Towner explains:

> But it is his use of it in Rom 3:29–30 in support of the argument for Gentile access to God's justification that explains our text (cf. Gal 3:20; Eph 4:5–6). In Paul's missiology, the formula "God is one" yields the logical corollary, "therefore all have access to his salvation, both Jews and Gentiles." It corrects Jewish or Judaizing exclusivist tendencies. The formula functions similarly here, supplying theological proof for the statement that God wills to save all people.[65]

Paul affirms an additional exclusivism—there is only one Mediator. He then affirms a biblical universalism—this Mediator died "for all." Paul thus gives more reasons for believers to pray for all people.

---

[63]For refutation in the Pastorals, see 1 Tim. 3:6; 4:1; 5:12, 24; 6:9; 2 Tim. 2:25–26. For a spirited rejection of universalism, see J. I. Packer, "Universalism: Will Everyone Ultimately Be Saved?" in *Hell Under Fire*, ed. Christopher W. Morgan and Robert A. Peterson (Grand Rapids: Zondervan, 2004), 169–94. See also pp. 302–4 of this book.

[64]William D. Mounce, *Pastoral Epistles*, Word Biblical Commentary (Nashville: Nelson, 2000), 84–85.

[65]Philip H. Towner, *The Letters to Timothy and Titus*, The New International Commentary on the New Testament (Grand Rapids: Eerdmans, 2006), 180.

First Timothy 2:5–6 instruct us about Christ and his redemptive mission. "There is one mediator between God and men, the man Christ Jesus" (v. 5). Christ is God's sole Mediator for humankind. No one else joins repentant sinners to the living God. As the God-man the Son relates to both God and humankind, and this enables him to function as the sole go-between. Yet this text emphasizes not his deity (which it does not deny) but his humanity—he is "the man Christ Jesus." Towner elucidates this point:

> The emphasis on "the human Christ Jesus" is the high point of this traditional piece. The placement of the *anthropos* ["man"] designation between "mediator" and the tradition cited in v. 6a [the ransom saying of Mark 10:45] is intended to locate the mediating activity of Christ Jesus specifically in his humanity. What Jesus did to execute God's universal will to save he did as a human being, in complete solidarity with the human condition.[66]

What did the man Christ Jesus, the unique Mediator, do to rescue sinners? Paul answers that he "gave himself as a ransom for all" (1 Tim. 2:6). Here the apostle reflects Jesus's famous saying from Mark 10:45: "The Son of Man came . . . to give his life as a ransom for many." This pithy verse in 1 Timothy informs us about Christ's saving work.

First, Jesus gives himself in death; he dies voluntarily, as elsewhere in Paul (cf. Gal. 1:4; 2:20; Eph. 5:2; Titus 2:14). Second, he gives himself "as a ransom." This reflects not only Old Testament background of the first and the second exodus but also, and more immediately, Mark 10:45, as noted. Paul uses a different word for "ransom" than appears in Mark 10:45, but "it expresses the same sense of a ransom payment that secures release (of someone or something)."[67] The man Christ Jesus gave himself in death to pay the price to secure the release of believers from bondage (to Satan, sin, and self). Paul thus combines Christ's being Mediator, the ideal man, and Redeemer in one sentence.

Christ redeems as both representative and substitute. He is representative because he is "the man Christ Jesus." He became a member of the human race to function as Mediator between God and human beings. It is possible that the preposition *anti* on the front of "ransom" (ἀντίλυτρον, *antilytron*) has its classical meaning of "on behalf of." If so, then it also indicates Christ's representation of his people before God. The preposition ὑπέρ (*hyper*, "in place of, for") in "a ransom *for* all" clearly communicates substitution. It is possible that both

---

[66]Ibid., 183.
[67]Ibid., 184. See 184n61 for bibliography concerning the study of the Greek words *lytron* (Mark 10:45) and *antilytron* (1 Tim. 2:6).

prepositions show substitution, in which case, as Mounce says, "at a minimum, there is here the idea of substitution."[68] If both prepositions communicate it, then substitution is emphasized via repetition. Regardless, the idea of representation adheres in the words, "the man Christ Jesus."

The Son of God joined the human race to represent us before God and gave himself in death as a ransom price to buy us out of slavery. He paid the price that we deserved to pay but could not. Every believer may therefore say with Paul, "[He] loved me and gave himself for me" (Gal. 2:20).

Titus 2:14

In order to correct Cretan false teachers who are "upsetting whole families" (Titus 1:10–11), Paul gives a household code in which he instructs older men, older women, younger women, younger men, Timothy in particular, and slaves in living for Christ (2:1–10). Then he turns to one of his favorite themes—God's grace: "For the grace of God has appeared, bringing salvation for all people" (v. 11). God's grace has been revealed in Christ. We expect Paul to speak next about God's grace abounding where sin abounded, saving people, or justifying them (Rom. 5:20; Eph. 2:5, 8; Titus 3:7). But instead of speaking about God's grace and initial salvation, he speaks of God's grace and ongoing salvation or the Christian life. God's grace not only saves us once and for all; it "saves us" every day in enabling us to live for God (1 Cor. 15:10; 2 Cor. 12:9).

Paul writes, "For the grace of God has appeared, bringing salvation for all people, training us to renounce ungodliness and worldly passions, and to live self-controlled, upright, and godly lives in the present age" (Titus 2:11–12). God's grace is universal—it is "for all people"; he wills for everyone to believe the gospel and be taught in Christian living. God's grace not only justifies; it also progressively sanctifies, here as a tutor. It trains us continually to say no to evil actions and desires and to live godly lives. Towner—referring to the adjectives "self-controlled, upright, and godly"—informs us that

> Paul conceives of it [the new life] in the very terms used by Hellenistic ethics to describe the virtuous life. . . . They represent three of the four cardinal virtues of Hellenistic ethics. . . . Together they characterize the life God intends (Christian existence) as one in which the physical appetites are under control, justice is exemplified in behavior, and the knowledge of God is acted on and worked out at the observable level. Paul has refashioned the Greek ideal to reflect Christian truth.[69]

---

[68]Mounce, *Pastoral Epistles*, 90. See 89–90 for discussion and bibliography.
[69]Towner, *The Letters to Timothy and Titus*, 749.

Paul further describes the Christian life as one of hope: "waiting for our blessed hope, the appearing of the glory of our great God and Savior Jesus Christ" (v. 13). Christ's return is a "blessed hope"; it brings joy to those looking forward to it. Paul has used the same word "appearing," denoting an epiphany, in verse 11 to describe God's grace. Now he uses it to depict the second coming as an epiphany, an appearance of God himself, here God the Son. "The epiphany concept again reflects on the parousia as a powerful, divine intervention among humanity to bring help," Towner explains.[70]

Paul tells of "the appearing of the glory of our great God and Savior Jesus Christ" (v. 13). This clause has been the subject of much debate, even among those with a high view of Scripture and of Christ. I will explain the main issue, avoid minor ones that take us away from our study of redemption, summarize the chief reasons for reaching what is nearly a consensus, and point interested readers to helpful bibliography.

William Mounce clearly presents the main issue:

> The key question regarding our verse is whether . . . "our great God and savior Jesus Christ," refers to two persons of the Godhead ("the great God [the Father] and our savior Jesus Christ") or just one ("our great God and savior, Jesus Christ"). If it refers to one person, Jesus, it is a direct statement of the divinity of Christ . . . . The doctrine of Christ's divinity does not rest on this verse. . . . The question is whether in this verse Paul states what he knows to be true, that Jesus is God.[71]

This is very well said. Regardless of the correct understanding of this verse, the Bible plainly and repeatedly teaches the deity of Christ.[72] But does Titus 2:13 refer to the Father and Son or to the Son alone? Mounce allots six pages of scholarly discussion to both sides of this issue.[73] The details go beyond our present study of redemption. Here is his summary of reasons for concluding that the verse refers to Christ alone, a conclusion with which I agree:

> Fortunately the doctrine of Christ's divinity does not rest on this verse. But the question of what Paul is saying here is still important, and it seems that he is making a Christological pronouncement on the divinity of Christ. This is the most natural reading of the text, is required by the grammar, concurs with Paul's use

---

[70]Ibid., 751–52.

[71]Mounce, *Pastoral Epistles*, 426.

[72]For a vigorous defense of this thesis, see *The Deity of Christ*, ed. Christopher W. Morgan and Robert A. Peterson, Theology in Community (Wheaton, IL: Crossway, 2011).

[73]Mounce, *Pastoral Epistles*, 425–31. See also, Towner, *The Letters to Timothy and Titus*, 752–58.

of ἐπιφάνεια "appearing," accounts for the singular use of the phrase "God and savior" in secular thought, and fits the context well.[74]

Our main focus is on Christ's redemptive work in verse 14. Believers long for "the appearing of the glory of our great God and Savior Jesus Christ" (v. 13). We would dread that day if we did not know him. But by his grace we do know him because he "gave himself for us to redeem us from all lawlessness and to purify for himself a people for his own possession who are zealous for good works" (v. 14).

Once more in short compass Paul teaches us much about redemption. First, we note Christ's self-offering—he "gave himself for us" (v. 14). Not under compulsion but voluntarily, our divine Savior delivered himself up to degradation and crucifixion. Second, he did this "for us"; Christ's saving accomplishment is representative and vicarious. "Jesus died as a representative and a substitute. . . . Jesus did this by means of representing humanity in this act and standing in as a substitute for humanity's benefit," as Towner stresses.[75]

Third the purpose of Christ's self-giving is evident—"to redeem us" (v. 14). Repeatedly, Paul describes Christ's saving work as a redemption, a deliverance from enslavement. Fourth, this redemption delivers God's people from "all lawlessness." In this case redemption is not said to be from sin's penalty but from its tyranny. Christ redeems believers from bondage to wickedness.

Fifth, we note a purpose expressed in positive terms as well: "and to purify for himself a people for his own possession who are zealous for good works." This is covenantal terminology, drawn especially from Ezekiel, that speaks of God's choice of and subsequent cleansing of his people that results in their living for him.[76] Significantly, at the end of verse 14, Paul returns to the theme of verses 1–10, as Mounce explains: "The person who is a . . . 'zealot for good deeds,' stands in contrast to the Cretan opponents, who are unfit for any good deed."[77]

Redemption in Hebrews

Hebrews is replete with passages describing Christ's saving deeds. Its second chapter impressively brings together at least three atonement motifs. Its main thrust is Christ as High Priest and sacrifice. But in at least one passage that picture overlaps with redemption.

---

[74]Mounce, *Pastoral Epistles*, 431.

[75]Towner, *The Letters to Timothy and Titus*, 760.

[76]See ibid., 760–65 for detailed exposition.

[77]Mounce, *Pastoral Epistles*, 432.

Hebrews 9:11–15

After describing the furniture in the Old Testament tabernacle, the high priest's annual service in the Most Holy Place, and the inadequacy of Old Testament sacrifices, the writer speaks of the new covenant.

> But when Christ appeared as a high priest of the good things that have come, then through the greater and more perfect tent (not made with hands, that is, not of this creation) he entered once for all into the holy places, not by means of the blood of goats and calves but by means of his own blood, thus securing an eternal redemption. For if the blood of goats and bulls, and the sprinkling of defiled persons with the ashes of a heifer, sanctify for the purification of the flesh, how much more will the blood of Christ, who through the eternal Spirit offered himself without blemish to God, purify our conscience from dead works to serve the living God.
>
> Therefore he is the mediator of a new covenant, so that those who are called may receive the promised eternal inheritance, since a death has occurred that redeems them from the transgressions committed under the first covenant. (Heb. 9:11–15)

Because this passage will feature prominently in the chapter "Christ Our Sacrifice," I will focus here on its message concerning redemption. Here, as frequently elsewhere, the author contends for Christ's superiority to the Old Testament high priests. Christ did not enter the earthly tabernacle, but the heavenly one, the very presence of God (Heb. 9:11, 24). He did not enter the Most Holy Place on earth, but the true holy places in heaven (9:12). He did not offer sacrifices repeatedly, but shed his blood "once for all" (v. 12). He did not carry the blood of animals into God's presence, but "his own blood" (v. 12). He is the Mediator not of the old covenant but of the new covenant (v. 15).

Most important for our present purposes, his self-offering did not secure forgiveness that needed to be repeated, as did that procured on the Day of Atonement. Rather, his "own blood," his self-sacrifice resulting in violent death, secured "an eternal redemption" (v. 12). This is astounding. When considered against the background of the vast number of Old Testament sacrifices, that Christ's single offering accomplishes "an eternal redemption" is nothing short of staggering!

How is this possible? Hebrews 9:11 points us in the right direction when it puts the name "Christ," in the emphatic first position in Greek. The incomprehensible efficacy of Christ's work is wrapped up in the mystery of his person, introduced in Hebrews 1 and 2. The first chapter teaches the deity of Christ as plainly, comprehensively, and emphatically as any place in Scripture. Chapter 2 repeatedly affirms that his incarnation is essential for him to perform his saving work, thus underscoring his humanity (vv. 9, 14, 17). The reason, as far as we can comprehend, that Christ's sacrifice accomplishes an eternal redemption lies in the mystery of his person. As the God-man he performs a work that saves sinners. His deity empowers him to save and his humanity qualifies him to be our representative and substitute. O'Brien is succinct: "The dignity of his person guarantees the incalculable value of his sacrifice."[78]

Shedding light on Christ's saving accomplishment as "an eternal redemption," Lane ties together Christ's death, ascension, and entrance into heaven:

> Christ's entry [into the heavenly sanctuary] was definitive, and it achieved final redemption. . . . In context Christ's death, ascension, and entrance into the heavenly sanctuary are seen retrospectively as a unity. The stress, however, falls on the arrival into the heavenly sanctuary and the achievement of eternal redemption. . . . Christ penetrated "behind the curtain" . . . in order to consummate the work of salvation in the presence of God. . . . Christ's sacrifice on the cross requires no repetition or renewal; his exaltation and entrance into the real sanctuary consecrates the eternal validity of his redemptive ministry.[79]

Hebrews 9:15 returns to the language of redemption: "Therefore he is the mediator of a new covenant, so that those who are called may receive the promised eternal inheritance, since a death has occurred that redeems them from the transgressions committed under the first covenant." This is a corollary to the truths of verse 12. Because Christ achieved "an eternal redemption," he grants an "eternal inheritance," not just the promise of that inheritance, to those whom God has called to salvation. His death ratifies the new covenant and brings about what Jeremiah 31:31–34 promised, especially the forgiveness of sins. Because of his momentous accomplishment, his saving work redeems all believers of all time, even Old Testament saints, as O'Brien explains:

> According to [Heb. 9] v. 12 Jesus' death is the price of deliverance from judgment and guilt that resulted from sin. Now the focus of attention is on redeeming those who sinned *under the first covenant*. Those who pledged their obedience to it and subsequently transgressed failed to keep their promises and were in danger of being cut off from God (Deut. 30:15–20). Jesus identified with the transgressors and died a representative death for them. His redemptive sacrifice is retrospec-

[78]Peter T. O'Brien, *The Letter to the Hebrews*, The Pillar New Testament Commentary (Grand Rapids: Eerdmans, 2010), 324.

[79]William L. Lane, *Hebrews 9–13*, Word Biblical Commentary (Dallas: Word, 1991), 239.

tive in its effects and is valid for all who trusted God for the forgiveness of sins in ancient Israel (see [Heb.] 11:40).[80]

Redemption in 1 Peter

1 Peter 1:18–19

A key passage, 1 Peter 1:18–19 has already appeared in the chapters on Jesus's death and resurrection and will reappear in the chapter "Christ Our Sacrifice." Nevertheless, it also belongs here owing to its powerful message concerning redemption. After reminding his readers of salvation as regeneration, inheritance, strength for trials, joy, and grace, Peter calls them to a life of self-control, hope, holiness, and the fear of the Lord (1 Pet. 1:3–17). He then gives a strong reason why believers should live for God zealously: "knowing that you were ransomed from the futile ways inherited from your forefathers, not with perishable things such as silver or gold, but with the precious blood of Christ, like that of a lamb without blemish or spot" (vv. 18–19).

Peter uses the imagery of redemption and, as clearly as anywhere in the New Testament, gives the ransom price both negatively and positively. Negatively, the price is not "perishable things such as silver or gold." Reference to the readers' "futile ways" inherited from ancestors identifies them as Gentiles (as does 4:1–4). Peter's mention of "silver or gold" may speak of idolatry because of the metals' association with idolatry in the Old Testament (Deut. 29:17; Dan. 5:23).[81] But Peter Davids has a better suggestion:

> The redemption of slaves . . . was also a vital part of their culture. . . . They have been purchased from all this; their release has been paid. Yet the price is not that which would have purchased a slave in the market, silver and gold, for these are corruptible, which means that they rot or perish . . . the price paid for them was something much more precious, something with true value.[82]

Positively, the ransom price is "the precious blood of Christ, like that of a lamb without blemish or spot" (1 Pet. 1:18–19). "Blood" here clearly refers to the Old Testament sacrifices. Christ's blood, his sacrificial death, is the redemption price. He is likened to a spotless lamb, which comparison communicates Christ's sinlessness. Although some commentators identify this

---

[80]O'Brien, *The Letter to the Hebrews*, 327–28, italics original.
[81]So Thomas R. Schreiner, *1, 2 Peter, Jude*, The New American Commentary (Nashville: Broadman and Holman, 2003), 86.
[82]Peter H. Davids, *The First Epistle of Peter*, The New International Commentary on the New Testament (Grand Rapids: Eerdmans, 1990), 71–72.

lamb with those sacrificed at Passover, the reference is probably more general, as Schreiner maintains:

> To sum up, the text is too general to restrict ourselves to any one background, whether Passover, the Suffering Servant text, or the sacrificial cult. It probably is best to think of Peter as seeing the death of Christ as embracing all three ideas. Early Christians saw Passover, the Suffering Servant, and the sacrificial system as fulfilled in the sacrifice of Christ as God's sinless lamb.[83]

Redemption in Revelation

In the chapter on Christ's cross, we dealt with Revelation 1:5–6; 5:6, 9; 7:14; 12:11; 13:8; and 14:3–4. We will study these texts again in the chapter on Christ's sacrifice. Here we examine briefly three of them that have to do with redemption.

Revelation 1:5–6

In his opening doxology, John praises Jesus the Redeemer: "To him who loves us and has freed us from our sins by his blood and made us a kingdom, priests to his God and Father, to him be glory and dominion forever and ever. Amen" (Rev. 1:5–6). We learn several important things about redemption from this. First, it is grounded in Christ's love. Christ shed his blood for us because he loved us.

Second, redemption is liberation, expressed by a different verb here than those used in our previous passages, but one that overlaps some of them in meaning.[84] Our lover "freed us from our sins by his blood." Redemption here is specifically said to be release from sins. Third, redemption's price is Christ's blood.

Fourth, the results of redemption involve believers, as spiritual Israel (cf. Ex. 19:6), sharing in Christ's royal and prophetic offices. Beale is helpful:

> He revealed God's truth by mediating as a priest through his sacrificial death and uncompromising "faithful witness" to the world (1:5a), and he reigned as king ironically by conquering death and sin through the defeat at the cross and subsequent resurrection (1:5). Believers spiritually fulfill the same offices in this age by following the same model, especially by being faithful witnesses by mediating Christ's priestly and royal authority to the world. . . . The remainder of the book will explain exactly how they do this in the midst of suffering brought on by life in a pagan society.[85]

---

[83]Schreiner, *1, 2 Peter, Jude*, 87.
[84]The verb here is λύω (*lyō*), the close friend of every beginning Greek student.
[85]Gregory K. Beale, *The Book of Revelation*, New International Greek Testament Commentary (Grand Rapids: Eerdmans, 1999), 193.

Fifth, Christ is worthy of praise because of his redeeming work. "To him who loves us and has freed us from our sins by his blood . . . to him be glory and dominion forever and ever. Amen" (vv. 5–6). Christ deserves acclaim for his marvelous work; our part is to give him that acclaim and to honor his kingship, by furthering his rule through proclamation.

Revelation 5:6, 9

An elder comforts John, who is crying because no one can open God's scroll of judgment: "Weep no more; behold, the Lion of the tribe of Judah, the Root of David, has conquered, so that he can open the scroll and its seven seals" (Rev. 5:5). John presents Christ as the champion who has conquered, and as David's descendant.[86] John appeals to Jacob's prophecy of Judah and, using its symbol of the king of the beasts, presents Christ as his people's champion (Gen. 49:9).

John expects to see a Lion but is surprised because when he looks, he sees not a Lion but a Lamb: "And between the throne and the four living creatures and among the elders I saw a Lamb standing, as though it had been slain, with seven horns and with seven eyes" (5:6). The Lamb is the main symbol for Christ in Revelation. In twenty-seven out of twenty-eight occurrences it is a symbol for Christ the deliverer. John's looking for a Lion but seeing the Lamb is ironic.[87] It signifies that Christ the Victor triumphed by being the slain victim. The Lamb's seven horns denote great power and seven eyes great wisdom.

The Lamb slain, Christ crucified, is found worthy to open the sealed book of judgment and is adored by living creatures, elders, and innumerable angels (vv. 7–13). Our ears are attuned to the song of praise:

> Worthy are you to take the scroll
>> and to open its seals,
> for you were slain, and by your blood you ransomed people for God
>> from every tribe and language and people and nation,
> and you have made them a kingdom and priests to our God,
>> and they shall reign on the earth. (vv. 9–10)

The Lamb alone is worthy to open the scroll. He "was slain," or "slaughtered," a reference to Christ's shedding his blood on the cross.[88] With his "blood" the

---

[86]See ibid., 1146–47 for argumentation that the Root of David means his descendant rather than his ancestor, as the expression is commonly understood.
[87]Ibid., 352–53.
[88]Greek, σφάζω (*sphazō*), "to slaughter," in William F. Arndt and F. Wilbur Gingrich, *A Greek-English Lexicon of the New Testament and Other Early Christian Literature*, 2nd ed. (Chicago: University of Chicago, 1979), 796.

Lamb "ransomed people for God." Here John paints a picture of redemption with several aspects. First, Christ, the Lion and the Lamb, is the Redeemer of God. Second, although details are lacking, John assumes a state of bondage out of which people must be redeemed. Third, his focus is on the redemption price—the sacrifice of Christ, the Lamb of God, as Beale affirms: "The whole clause 'because you were slain and purchased for God by the price of your blood' emphasizes the redemptive nature of the Lamb's death.' Ἐν τῷ αἵματί σου (*en tō haimati sou*) is an instrumental dative of price."[89]

Fourth, Christ's death redeems effectively. It actually ransoms people so that they belong to God. Fifth, Christ's ransom is purchased for all, in the sense of persons from "every tribe and language and people and nation." This constitutes not absolute universalism but biblical universalism. Christ's death does not save every human being, but saves all of God's people from every people group, language, ethnic group, and country. Sixth, one result of redemption is that Christ's ransomed people belong to God as a kingdom of priests, including believing Jews and Gentiles, in fulfillment of the divine purpose for Old Testament Israel (Ex. 19:5–6).

Revelation 14:3–4

John looks and sees "on Mount Zion . . . the Lamb, and with him 144,000 who had his name and his Father's name written on their foreheads" (Rev. 14:1). Returning to the image of 7:4–9, John sees the totality of the people of God, those who give allegiance to the true Lamb over against the false lamb of 13:11.[90] The names of the Son and of the Father (not "of the beast," 13:16–17) on their foreheads signify belonging and protection. John hears a thunderous voice from heaven "singing a new song before the throne and before the four living creatures and before the elders" (14:3). A "new song" in Scripture is a song of praise for victory (cf. Pss. 40:3; 144:9; Isa. 42:10; Rev. 5:9). Here the song is sung on an escalated scale for victory over sin. Only the 144,000, "who had been redeemed from the earth," could learn that song (14:3). It is sung only by "those who have experienced Christ's redemption."[91]

The redeemed are described as "these who have not defiled themselves with women, for they are virgins. It is these who follow the Lamb wherever he goes. These have been redeemed from mankind as firstfruits for God and the Lamb, and in their mouth no lie was found, for they are blameless" (vv. 4–5). God's

---

[89]Beale, *The Book of Revelation*, 359.
[90]I received help on this passage from ibid., 730–47.
[91]Ibid., 737.

people, redeemed from among humankind, are depicted as being faithful to "God and the Lamb" ("virgins"), as obeying Christ even in suffering ("following" him), and as confessing Christ even under persecution (not "lying"). The saints' being presented to God and to the Lamb as "firstfruits" means that they are dedicated to God, as the firstfruits of the crops were dedicated in the Old Testament (Lev. 23:9–14).

Connecting the Dots

Texts

Unlike reconciliation, which is found only in four key Pauline passages, there are too many passages that pertain to redemption to list. Instead, I will list sections of the Bible where redemption texts are found: the Old Testament, the Synoptic Gospels, Acts, Paul's epistles (Romans, 1 Corinthians, Galatians, Ephesians, Colossians, 1 Timothy, and Titus), Hebrews, 1 Peter, and Revelation.

Sphere

R. David Rightmire describes redemption broadly in terms of social, legal, and religious ideas of the ancient world: "The metaphor of redemption includes the ideas of loosing from a bond, setting free from captivity or slavery, buying back something lost or sold, exchanging something in one's possession for something possessed by another, and ransoming."[92]

Background

Redemption has Old Testament roots in God's deliverance of the Israelites from Egyptian bondage, Israel's redemption of firstborn sons, and Isaiah's message of a new exodus for Jews taken in the Babylonian captivity. The immediate background for people living in New Testament times is the manumission of slaves.

Definition

Redemption in the New Testament is a picture of Christ's saving work that depicts lost persons in various states of bondage and presents Christ as Redeemer, who through his death—expressed in a number of ways—claims people as his own and sets them free.

---

[92]R. David Rightmire, "Redeem, Redemption," *Evangelical Dictionary of Biblical Theology*, ed. Walter A. Elwell (Grand Rapids: Baker, 1996), 664.

Need

The need for redemption is bondage in its different forms. The Israelites suffered Egyptian bondage before the exodus, and citizens of the southern kingdom endured captivity in Babylon and later Persia before Yahweh released them. First-century Israel longed for the Messiah to release them from Roman captivity. The forms of bondage from which Christ delivers people are moral or spiritual. These are frequently implied, but sometimes are explicit, including "the domain of darkness" (Col. 1:13), enslavement "to the elementary principles of the world" (Gal. 4:3), "futile ways inherited from" ancestors (1 Pet. 1:18), "all lawlessness" (Titus 2:13–14), and "our sins" (Rev. 1:6).

Initiator

God always takes the initiative in redeeming his people. This is true of Yahweh: "I am the LORD, and I will bring you out from under the burdens of the Egyptians, and I will deliver you from slavery to them, and I will redeem you with an outstretched arm and with great acts of judgment" (Ex. 6:6). And it is true of Jesus, the Son of Man, who "came not to be served but to serve, and to give his life as a ransom for many" (Mark 10:45). Under this heading belong the references that tell of Jesus's willingness to give himself to redeem us (1 Tim. 2:5–6; Titus 2:13–14; Heb. 9:26; 10:5–10).

In both Testaments the Deity initiates redemption out of love for his people. We see this in the Law: "He [the LORD your God] loved your fathers . . . and brought you out of Egypt with his own presence, by his great power" (Deut. 4:37). We also see it in Scripture's last book: "To him who loves us and has freed us from our sins by his blood . . . to him be glory and dominion forever and ever. Amen" (Rev. 1:5–6). In love, Yahweh delivered Israel from Egypt; in love Christ delivers us with his blood.

Mediator

In the Old Testament, Israel's God is called, "the Most High God their redeemer" (Ps. 78:35). In the New Testament, Paul uses the Old Testament title for God— "Deliverer"—and applies it to Christ (citing Isa. 59:20 in Rom. 11:26). The apostle thereby sets the tone for the whole New Testament, which consistently presents Christ as the Redeemer, the Mediator of redemption. Virtually every redemption text shows this; I will cite two that actually say it:

> For there is one God, and there is one mediator between God and men, the man Christ Jesus, who gave himself as a ransom for all. (1 Tim. 2:5–6)

He entered once for all into the holy places, not by means of the blood of goats and calves but by means of his own blood, thus securing an eternal redemption. . . .

Therefore he is the mediator of a new covenant, so that those who are called may receive the promised eternal inheritance, since a death has occurred that redeems them from the transgressions committed under the first covenant. (Heb. 9:11–15)

Work

Redemption requires work. Yahweh brought the plagues and exodus to redeem the Israelites from Egypt (Deut. 9:26). He moved Cyrus to deliver Judah from captivity (Ezra 1:1–4; Isa. 45:1–6). In the New Testament, redemption is the work of Christ. It is one way in which Scripture describes his saving accomplishment. Psalm 49:7 declares, "Truly no man can ransom another. In Mark 8:37 Jesus asks, "What can a man give in return for his soul," and then in 10:45 he says, "The Son of Man came . . . to give his life as a ransom for many." Marshall's conclusion is unavoidable: "What man cannot do has been done by Christ. We are surely justified in discerning here the thought of human mortality as the result of human sin, and in seeing in the death of Christ the ransom 'price' paid to God for the redemption of mankind from death."[93]

Revelation's imagery is powerful:

I saw a Lamb standing, as though it had been slain. . . .

"For you were slain, and by your blood you ransomed people for God
from every tribe and language and people and nation." (Rev. 5:6, 9)

Voluntariness

A striking difference between the Testaments is Christ's voluntarily suffering as our Redeemer. Lane points to "a sharp contrast between the involuntary, passive sacrifice of animals and the active obedience of Christ who willingly made himself the sacrifice for sins ([Heb.] 9:26; 10:5–10)."[94] This idea is reflected in the ransom saying: "The Son of Man came . . . to give his life as a ransom for many" (Mark 10:45).

Two passages in the Pastoral Epistles that combine statements of Jesus's self-giving with his redemptive work belong here too:

For there is one God, and there is one mediator between God and men, the man Christ Jesus, who gave himself as a ransom for all, which is the testimony given at the proper time. (1 Tim. 2:5–6)

---

[93] Marshall, "The Meaning of Redemption," 248.
[94] Lane, *Hebrews 9–13*, 238.

> Our great God and Savior Jesus Christ . . . gave himself for us to redeem us from all lawlessness and to purify for himself a people for his own possession who are zealous for good works. (Titus 2:13–14)

Our Redeemer willingly gave himself to deliver us from bondage. Scripture sometimes views this as the payment of a price.

Ransom Price

While Morris, who did exemplary work on the biblical words that describe Christ's saving work, may have overemphasized Christ's death as a ransom, others have rejected the ransom idea altogether.[95] Schreiner, citing an important essay by Marshall, strikes just the right balance:

> Some scholars have argued that in the Scriptures redemption always involves the notion of the payment of a price. I. H. Marshall has demonstrated, however, that the idea of a price is not invariably present, though there is always the idea of the cost or effort involved in redemption. In some texts the emphasis is on deliverance, and nothing is said specifically about price (Luke 21:28; Rom. 8:23; Eph. 1:4; 4:30). On the other hand, some scholars are too eager to strike out any notion of price at all.[96]

Schreiner is surely correct. At least eight passages portray Christ's death as the redemption price:

> Pay careful attention to yourselves and to all the flock . . . to care for the church of God, which he obtained with his own blood. (Acts 20:28)

> You are not your own, for you were bought with a price. So glorify God in your body. (1 Cor. 6:19–20)

> You were bought with a price; do not become slaves of men. (1 Cor. 7:23)

> There is one mediator between God and men, the man Christ Jesus, who gave himself as a ransom for all. (1 Tim. 2:5–6)

> He entered once for all into the holy places . . . by means of his own blood, thus securing an eternal redemption. (Heb. 9:12)

---

[95]Leon Morris, *The Apostolic Preaching of the Cross*, 3rd ed. (Grand Rapids: Eerdmans, 1965), 61–62.
[96]Schreiner, *1, 2 Peter, Jude*, 85–86. Marshall's essay is "The Meaning of Redemption," 153–54.

You were ransomed from the futile ways inherited from your forefathers, not with perishable things such as silver or gold, but with the precious blood of Christ. (1 Pet. 1:18–19)

To him who loves us and has freed us from our sins by his blood . . . be glory and dominion forever and ever. Amen. (Rev. 1:5–6)

For you were slain, and by your blood you ransomed people for God. . . . (Rev. 5:9–10)

J. Gresham Machen's words are apt: "We are not saved by the Lord Jesus Christ by some method that cost him nothing."[97] Indeed, we are saved by Jesus by a method that cost him his very life.

Substitution

Some texts present Christ's redemption as a substitution for sinners. The most famous is the ransom saying of Mark 10:45: "For even the Son of Man came not to be served but to serve, and to give his life as a ransom for many." Lane comments:

The ransom metaphor sums up the purpose for which Jesus gave his life. . . . Because the idea of equivalence, or substitution, was proper to the concept of a ransom, it became an integral element in the vocabulary of redemption in the OT. . . . In the context of verse 45a, with its reference to the service of the Son of Man, it is appropriate to find an allusion to the Servant of the Lord in Isa. 53, who vicariously and voluntarily suffered and gave his life for the sins of others. The specific thought underlying the reference to the ransom is expressed in Isa. 53:10 which speaks of "making his life an *offering for sin.*" Jesus, as the messianic Servant, offers himself as a guilt-offering (Lev. 5:14–6:7; 7:1–7; Num. 5:5–8) in compensation for the sins of the people.[98]

The following three texts also teach that Christ's redemption is substitutionary. Readers are referred to earlier pages of this chapter where this was demonstrated for each text:

Christ redeemed us from the curse of the law by becoming a curse for us. (Gal. 3:13)

For there is one God, and there is one mediator between God and men, the man Christ Jesus, who gave himself as a ransom for all. (1 Tim. 2:5–6)

---

[97] *Machen's Notes on Galatians*, 180, cited in Timothy George, *Galatians*, The New American Commentary (np: Broadman and Holman, 1994), 238.

[98] Lane, *Commentary on the Gospel of Mark*, 383–84, italics original.

Our great God and Savior Jesus Christ . . . gave himself for us to redeem us from all lawlessness. (Titus 2:13–14)

While discussing Galatians 3:13, Graham Cole contemplates humanity's inability to rescue itself:

> However, God has acted in Christ to address the human predicament at this point. The divine move is astounding, for a great exchange has taken place. As Jeffrey, Ovey, and Sach suggest, "It is hard to imagine a plainer statement of the doctrine of penal substitution" . . . . Paul is drawing on the language of the marketplace. A price is paid to set a slave free and the price of this redemption is unfathomable.[99]

Cole is right. Christ gave himself vicariously as a ransom price to deliver sinners. He died in their place, paying a ransom that they could not pay. Moreover, redemption was accomplished with his blood.

Christ's Blood

Morris has shown that the word "blood" in the expression "the blood of Christ" depicts Christ's death, even a violent death.[100] This usage of blood occurs frequently when Scripture speaks of Christ's work of redemption.

> In him we have redemption through his blood. (Eph. 1:7)

> He entered once for all into the holy places, not by means of the blood of goats and calves but by means of his own blood, thus securing an eternal redemption. (Heb. 9:12)

> You were ransomed from the futile ways inherited from your forefathers, not with perishable things such as silver or gold, but with the precious blood of Christ, like that of a lamb without blemish or spot. (1 Pet. 1:18–19)

> To him who loves us and has freed us from our sins by his blood . . . be glory and dominion forever and ever. Amen. (Rev. 1:5–6)

> I saw a Lamb standing, as though it had been slain. . . . For you were slain, and by your blood you ransomed people for God. (Rev. 5:6, 9–10)

Morris explains the relation between Jesus's blood and sacrifice:

---

[99]Graham A. Cole, *God the Peacemaker: How Atonement Brings Shalom*, New Studies in Biblical Theology (Downers Grove, IL: InterVarsity, 2009), 172.

[100]Morris, *The Apostolic Preaching of the Cross*, 121–26.

The term blood is not used as often in the New Testament as it is in the Old (it is found ninety-eight times). But, as in the Old, the most frequent single classification is that which refers to violent death. . . . The New Testament writers . . . meant that Christ had died. And if they used the expression in a way that recalls the sacrifices and the blood shed in them, then they meant that the death of Jesus is to be seen as a sacrifice which accomplishes in reality what the old sacrifices pointed to but could not do.[101]

Forgiveness

Because Christ, the Mediator of redemption, voluntarily gave himself as a ransom for sinners, his death procures forgiveness for all who believe. For that reason, Scripture associates redemption and forgiveness:

In him we have redemption through his blood, the forgiveness of our trespasses. (Eph. 1:7)

He has delivered us from the domain of darkness and transferred us to the kingdom of his beloved Son, in whom we have redemption, the forgiveness of sins. (Col. 1:13–14)

Christ's saving work, described as a redemption, is thus closely associated with forgiveness. John Murray goes one step further: "Redemption through Jesus' blood is defined as 'the forgiveness of our trespasses.'"[102]

Past, Present, and Future

When viewed from a temporal perspective, redemption pertains to the past, present, and future. First, the past:

You are not your own, for you were bought with a price. (1 Cor. 6:19–20)

You were ransomed from the futile ways inherited from your forefathers . . . with the precious blood of Christ. (1 Pet. 1:18–19)

These have been redeemed from mankind as firstfruits for God and the Lamb. (Rev. 14:4)

Redemption also pertains to the present: "He has delivered us from the domain of darkness and transferred us to the kingdom of his beloved Son, in

---

[101]Leon Morris, *The Atonement: Its Meaning and Significance* (Leicester: Inter-Varsity, 1983), 62–63.
[102]John Murray, *The Atonement* (Philadelphia: Presbyterian and Reformed, 1962), 22.

whom we have redemption, the forgiveness of sins" (Col. 1:13–14). The deliverance is described as past but the transference to Christ's kingdom is present, as is forgiveness (see also Eph. 1:7).

Redemption pertains to the future as well:

> And not only the creation, but we ourselves, who have the firstfruits of the Spirit, groan inwardly as we wait eagerly for adoption as sons, the redemption of our bodies. (Rom. 8:23)

> And do not grieve the Holy Spirit of God, by whom you were sealed for the day of redemption. (Eph. 4:30)

In sum, Christ purchased a complete redemption for his people, even for everyone who believes in his name. His deliverance pertains to the past, present, and future.

Individual, Corporate, and Cosmic

Christ redeems individuals, the church, and the cosmos. His redemption of individuals is demonstrated in a context of sexual immorality.

> Flee from sexual immorality. Every other sin a person commits is outside the body, but the sexually immoral person sins against his own body. Or do you not know that your body is a temple of the Holy Spirit within you, whom you have from God? You are not your own, for you were bought with a price. So glorify God in your body. (1 Cor. 6:18–20)

There is also a corporate dimension of redemption, as is obvious in the following passages:

> Pay careful attention to yourselves and to all the flock . . . to care for the church of God, which he obtained with his own blood. (Acts 20:28)

> For there is one God, and there is one mediator between God and men, the man Christ Jesus, who gave himself as a ransom for all. (1 Tim. 2:5–6)

> You were slain, and by your blood you ransomed people for God
> from every tribe and language and people and nation. (Rev. 5:9)

As is the case with reconciliation, there is also a cosmic dimension of redemption. Paul refers to this in Romans 8:

For the creation waits with eager longing for the revealing of the sons of God. For the creation was subjected to futility, not willingly, but because of him who subjected it, in hope that the creation itself will be set free from its bondage to corruption and obtain the freedom of the glory of the children of God. For we know that the whole creation has been groaning together in the pains of childbirth until now. (Rom. 8:19–22)

Results

The results of Christ's redeeming work are incredible. All of the categories that have gone before this one inform it. Here we underscore more results that eluded the previous headings. Jesus's death ratifies the new covenant and brings about what Jeremiah 31:31–34 promised, especially the forgiveness of sins, including those of Old Testament saints: "Therefore he is the mediator of a new covenant, so that those who are called may receive the promised eternal inheritance, since a death has occurred that redeems them from the transgressions committed under the first covenant" (Heb. 9:15).

Redemption purchases believers for God so they henceforth belong to him: "You are not your own, for you were bought with a price" (1 Cor. 6:19–20; cf. 1 Cor. 7:23; Rev. 14:4).

At the same time Christ's death frees us from bondage: "So you are no longer a slave, but a son, and if a son, then an heir through God" (Gal. 4:7).

In addition, redemption leads Christians to do good because Christ "gave himself for us to redeem us from all lawlessness and to purify for himself a people for his own possession who are zealous for good works" (Titus 2:14).

Christ redeemed his people that they may fulfill the roles that Old Testament Israel failed to perform: He "has freed us from our sins by his blood and made us a kingdom, priests to his God and Father" (Rev. 1:5–6; cf. 5:9–10).

Christopher Wright sounds a good note on which to end this chapter:

Sin puts us into *slavery*, a bondage from which we need to be released. But *redemption* always comes at a cost. God chose to bear that cost himself in the self-giving of his Son, who came "to give his life as a ransom for many" (Mark 10:45). In him, therefore, we have "redemption through his blood, the forgiveness of sins" (Eph. 1:7). The cross spells freedom and release for captives.[103]

---

[103]Christopher J. H. Wright, *The God I Don't Understand: Reflections on Tough Questions of Faith* (Grand Rapids: Zondervan, 2008), 119, italics original.

Reconciler
Redeemer
Legal Substitute
Victor
Second Adam
Sacrifice

Chapter 12

Christ Our Legal Substitute

It is not surprising that liberal Christians attack the teaching of penal substitution—the idea that Jesus died in the place of sinners to pay the penalty owed to God because of their sins.[1] But some have expressed surprise that evangelical Christians have opposed the doctrine. Joel B. Green and Mark D. Baker ask "pressing questions" about penal substitution that reveal their uneasiness with it:

1. First and centrally we may ask whether the theory of penal substitutionary atonement is faithful to the teaching of Scripture. . . .
2. In what ways is the theory of penal substitution shaped by Western culture in which it has grown and gained its popularity? . . .
3. What will be its fate with the ascendancy of postmodern culture? . . .
4. Is it any surprise that proclamation of the gospel grounded in this theory has tended to fall on deaf ears in other social worlds? . . .
5. Penal substitutionary atonement remains susceptible to misunderstanding and even bizarre caricature. . . .[2]

---

[1] For examples, see Joanne Carlson Brown and Rebecca Parker, "For God So Loved the World?" in *Christianity, Patriarchy, and Abuse: A Feminist Critique*, ed. Joanne Carlson Brown and Carole R. Bohn (New York: Pilgrim, 1989), 26; and Rita Nakashima Brock, "And a Little Child Will Lead Us: Christology and Child Abuse," also in *Christianity, Patriarchy, and Abuse*, 51–53.

[2] Joel B. Green and Mark D. Baker, *Recovering the Scandal of the Cross* (Downers Grove, IL: InterVarsity, 2000), 27–32.

In spite of these reservations, and although some have overemphasized penal substitution and suppressed other equally biblical pictures, it is plain to me that it is a biblical picture. After surveying the Old Testament background, we will investigate penal substitution in Mark 10:45, Paul, 1 Peter, and 1 John, and then treat objections before summarizing.

Old Testament Background for Penal Substitution

As with almost all New Testament teachings, this one has roots that sink deep into Old Testament soil. At least five themes shed light on New Testament teaching.

"A Pleasing Aroma to the Lord": Genesis 8:21; Leviticus 1:9; 2:1–2; 3:3, 5; 4:29, 31

Gordon Wenham profitably studies the first occurrence in Scripture of the phrase he translates "a soothing aroma" (to God)—in reference to Noah in Genesis 8:21:

> Then Noah built an altar to the Lord and took some of every clean animal and some of every clean bird and offered burnt offerings on the altar. And when the Lord smelled the pleasing aroma, the Lord said in his heart, "I will never again curse the ground because of man, for the intention of man's heart is evil from his youth. Neither will I ever again strike down every living creature as I have done." (Gen. 8:20–21)

Wenham explains his line of reasoning:

> A second characteristic of all of the sacrifices is that at least part of each offering is burnt on the altar and makes "a pleasing odour" (rsv) to the Lord (e.g. Lv. 1:9; 2:2; 3:5; 4:31). In what ways do sacrifices please God? The adjective translated "pleasing" (*nihoah*) by RSV comes from the root "rest" and would therefore be better translated "soothing," "pacifying," "quieting." The word suggests divine uneasiness which is quieted by sacrifice.
>
> This understanding of the phrase "pleasing odour" as "soothing aroma" is confirmed by its very first use in the OT in Gn. 8:21, a passage of great significance for the OT view of sacrifice. When Noah left the ark he offered burnt offerings, "then the Lord smelled the soothing aroma, and the Lord said to himself 'I shall not curse the land any further because of man, for the ideas of man's mind are evil from his youth.'"
>
> The comment that "the Lord said to himself" comes immediately after "the Lord smelled the soothing aroma." The obvious implication of the sequence of verbs "the Lord smelled . . . [the Lord] said" is that God's thoughts about mankind were prompted by his appreciation of the sacrifice. . . . God's attitude

to Noah has already been seen to be gracious from the moment "he remembered Noah" (8:1). It can hardly be said that the offering of the sacrifice changed God's attitude to Noah.

However, this is not really what Gn. 8:21 is asserting. . . . It is God's attitude to the rest of mankind that is turned around.[3]

Wenham thus shows that "a pleasing aroma" conveys aspects of Noah's sacrifice toward God and human beings. It both appeases God's anger and cleanses humankind. This is of great consequence for our study. Wenham underlines the importance of his finding not only for Genesis 8:21, but for the study of *all* of the sacrifices: "Looked at in this light, we can view Noah's offering of sacrifice as a prototype of the work of later priests, who made atonement for Israel."[4]

Here are snippets of Levitical instructions concerning burnt offerings, grain offerings, peace offerings, and sin offerings. Every sacrifice is said to be "a pleasing aroma to the LORD."

And the priest shall burn all of it on the altar, as a burnt offering, a food offering with a pleasing aroma to the LORD. (Lev. 1:9)

When anyone brings a grain offering as an offering to the LORD. . . . the priest shall burn this as its memorial portion on the altar, a food offering with a pleasing aroma to the LORD. (2:1–2)

And from the sacrifice of the peace offering. . . . it is a food offering with a pleasing aroma to the LORD. (3:3, 5)

And he shall lay his hand on the head of the sin offering and kill the sin offering. . . . and the priest shall burn it on the altar for a pleasing aroma to the LORD. And the priest shall make atonement for him, and he shall be forgiven. (4:29, 31)

Christopher Wright summarizes Wenham's significant contribution:

Gordon Wenham argues cogently that "soothing aroma" is a highly significant phrase which indicates that sacrifice effects a change in God's attitude towards the worshiper. That is to say, this metaphor expresses a propitiatory, as well as an expiatory function. Yes, sacrifice expiates; it cleanses away the sins and offenses

---

[3]Gordon J. Wenham, "The Theology of Old Testament Sacrifice," in *Sacrifice in the Bible*, ed. Roger T. Beckwith and Martin J. Selman (Grand Rapids: Baker, 1995), 80–81.
[4]Ibid., 81.

for which it is offered. But it does so precisely in order to avert the wrath that those sins and offenses would otherwise inevitably incur.[5]

The Passover Lamb: Exodus 12:13

The sacrifice of the Passover lambs sheds light on Christ as a legal substitute. Pharaoh stubbornly refused to let the Israelites go after each of the first nine plagues. So God brought a tenth and final plague: "The LORD said to Moses, 'Yet one plague more I will bring upon Pharaoh and upon Egypt. Afterward he will let you go from here. When he lets you go, he will drive you away completely'" (Ex. 11:1). This plague, of course, was the slaying of firstborn males in Egypt, both of human beings and of animals (vv. 4–5).

This plague was different from the preceding nine in that it would affect the Israelites too. Certainly the Egyptian oppressors deserved God's judgment, but did the Israelites? God through Ezekiel answers affirmatively:

> And I said to them, Cast away the detestable things your eyes feast on, every one of you, and do not defile yourselves with the idols of Egypt; I am the LORD your God. But they rebelled against me and were not willing to listen to me. None of them cast away the detestable things their eyes feasted on, nor did they forsake the idols of Egypt.
>
> Then I said I would pour out my wrath upon them and spend my anger against them in the midst of the land of Egypt. But I acted for the sake of my name, that it should not be profaned in the sight of the nations among whom they lived, in whose sight I made myself known to them in bringing them out of the land of Egypt. So I led them out of the land of Egypt and brought them into the wilderness. (Ezek. 20:7–10)

God provided a way of escape for the Israelites. They would be spared his judgment on their firstborn if they killed the Passover lamb and applied the blood to the lintel and doorposts of their houses (Ex. 12:21–22). The plague was God's judgment from which his people would be spared if they followed his instructions.

> It is the LORD's Passover. For I will pass through the land of Egypt that night, and I will strike all the firstborn in the land of Egypt, both man and beast; and on all the gods of Egypt I will execute judgments: I am the LORD. The blood shall be a sign for you, on the houses where you are. And when I see the blood, I will pass

---

[5]Christopher J. H. Wright, "Atonement in the Old Testament," in *The Atonement Debate*, ed. Derek Tidball, David Hilborn, and Justin Thacker (Grand Rapids: Zondervan, 2008), 76.

over you, and no plague will befall you to destroy you, when I strike the land of Egypt. (vv. 11–13)

Note that the Lord is the avenger—he will strike dead the firstborn. Note too that God will spare the Israelites when he sees the blood of the Passover lambs properly applied to their houses. Christopher Wright is correct: "The sacrifice of the lamb is the central element. The blood ritual had an apotropaic [averting evil] force in protecting the Hebrew families from the wrath of the destroyer of the firstborn throughout the land. The effect of blood sacrifice in the averting of judgment is clear."[6]

In sum, it is difficult to avoid the conclusion of Steve Jeffrey, Michael Ovey, and Andrew Sach: "The Passover lamb functioned as a penal substitute, dying in place of the firstborn sons of the Israelites, in order that they might escape the wrath of God."[7]

The Character of Yahweh: Exodus 34:6–7

Although Exodus 34:6–7 does not speak of sacrifice, it provides important background for the theme of Christ our legal substitute. The Lord has withdrawn his punishment against his people after the golden calf incident, has reaffirmed his pledge to accompany the Israelites, and now renews his covenant with them (Exodus 32–34).

After Moses's audacious request that God show him his glory, the Lord declares, "I will make all my goodness pass before you and will proclaim before you my name 'The LORD'" (33:19). He then warns Moses that no one may see his "face" and live. So, instead, God will allow Moses to glimpse his "back" (vv. 20–23). God means that Moses will be permitted to see not a full revelation of God's glory (that would be fatal!) but only a small portion of his glory. This occurs in the next chapter.

In obedience to God's instructions, Moses cuts two new tablets for the Ten Commandments and meets God on the mountain. The Lord descends to Moses on the mountain and reveals his name to him.

The LORD, the LORD, a God merciful and gracious, slow to anger, and abounding in steadfast love and faithfulness, keeping steadfast love for thousands, forgiving iniquity and transgression and sin, but who will by no means clear the guilty,

---

[6]Wright, "Atonement in the Old Testament," 73.
[7]Steve Jeffrey, Michael Ovey, and Andrew Sach, *Pierced for Our Transgressions: Recovering the Glory of Penal Substitution* (Wheaton, IL: Crossway, 2007), 34.

visiting the iniquity of the fathers on the children and the children's children, to the third and the fourth generation. (34:6–7)

How does this passage on God's character lay a foundation for New Testament teaching concerning Christ's saving accomplishment? Christopher Wright answers correctly: "The paradox inherent in this self-description, that Yahweh is characterized by compassion, grace, love and faithfulness, and yet does not let sin go unpunished, is only finally resolved on the cross."[8]

The Day of Atonement: Leviticus 16:21–22

The most famous day on Israel's sacrificial calendar—the Day of Atonement recounted in Leviticus 16—also has substitutionary overtones. The context is critical. After reminding Moses of the death of Aaron's two sons for entering the Most Holy Place in disobedience, God instructs Aaron how he should approach the very presence of God (16:1–5). God thus reminds Israel and its high priest of his holiness and wrath.

On the Day of Atonement Aaron is to take two goats, cast lots over them, and treat them differently. The one becomes a sin offering; the other is sent away into the wilderness. Aaron kills the first goat as an offering of purification for the sins of the people and sprinkles its blood on the mercy seat. "Thus he shall make atonement for the Holy Place, because of the uncleannesses of the people of Israel and because of their transgressions, all their sins" (v. 16). In addition, "he shall go out to the altar that is before the LORD and make atonement for it" (v. 18).

As Wenham argues, these priestly offerings have substitutionary implications: "In sacrifice it appears that the worshipper identifies himself with the animal he offers. What he does to the animal, he does symbolically to himself. The death of the animal portrays the death of himself."[9] Aaron slays the goat on behalf of Israel and makes atonement for the people's sins as well as his own (the text repeatedly draws attention to the latter, vv. 6, 11, 17, 24, 33, 34).

The second goat more strongly speaks of vicarious atonement. This is because of the ceremony involved:

And Aaron shall lay both his hands on the head of the live goat, and confess over it all the iniquities of the people of Israel, and all their transgressions, all their sins. And he shall put them on the head of the goat and send it away into

---

[8]Wright, "Atonement in the Old Testament," 75.
[9]Wenham, "The Theology of Old Testament Sacrifice," 77.

the wilderness by the hand of a man who is in readiness. The goat shall bear all their iniquities on itself to a remote area, and he shall let the goat go free in the wilderness. (vv. 21–22)

Allen Ross explains the vicarious meaning of the symbolism: "Aaron laid both hands on the goat to ensure the transference of sin to the goat. He then confessed all of the wickedness and rebellion of Israel—all their sins. And these sins were placed on the goat to bear them away into the wilderness."[10] Wenham is more expansive:

> Another possibility is that the imposition of hands conveys the worshipper's sins to the animal, which then dies in the worshipper's place. This is certainly the most probable interpretation of Lv. 16:21, where in the day of atonement ceremony the high priest lays *both* his hands on the scapegoat's head, confesses "over him all the iniquities of the people of Israel . . . all their sins; and he shall put them upon the head of the goat and send him away into the wilderness."[11]

When the goat is sent away into the wilderness, this portrays the removal of the people's sins, for "the goat shall bear all their iniquities on itself to a remote area" (v. 22).

The two goats involved in the ceremonies on the Day of Atonement, then, are substitutes for the people.

The Lord's Suffering Servant: Isaiah 52:13–53:12

"The interpretation of Isaiah 53, the fourth Servant Song, the song of the Suffering Servant . . . is hotly debated, particularly with respect to the identity of the servant," Sue Groom informs us.[12] Actually, many issues are debated with regard to this important chapter of Isaiah's prophecy.[13]

Isaiah 52:13–53:12 constitutes the fourth of Isaiah's Servant Songs (see also 42:1–9; 49:1–13; 50:4–9). Groom summarizes the content of the four songs while tracing the identity of the Servant:

---

[10]Allen P. Ross, *Holiness to the Lord: A Guide to the Exposition of the Book of Leviticus* (Grand Rapids: Baker Academic, 2002), 320–21.

[11]Wenham, "The Theology of Old Testament Sacrifice," 79, italics original.

[12]Sue Groom, "Why Did Christ Die? An Exegesis of Isaiah 52:13–53:12," in Tidball, Hilborn, and Thacker, *The Atonement Debate*, 96.

[13]For discussion see Brevard S. Childs, *Isaiah*, The Old Testament Library (Louisville: Westminster John Knox, 2001), 407–23; J. Alan Groves, "Atonement in Isaiah 53," in *The Glory of the Atonement*, ed. Charles E. Hill and Frank A. James III (Downers Grove, IL: InterVarsity, 2004), 61–89; and Jeffrey, Ovey, and Sach, *Pierced for Our Transgressions*, 61–67.

[In] the first song . . . the author's thought is predominantly of a collective servant, Israel, destined to carry the light of true religion to the entire world. . . . In the second song, the prophet realizes that only a purified Israel can fulfill its mission; therefore, there is a mission to Israel as well as through Israel. The third song deals with the suffering and shame the servant will experience in execution of his mission. . . . It is not clear whether he is speaking of a collective servant, or an individual and leader in whose person the mission of Israel can be both symbolized and supremely expressed. In the fourth song, the servant is unmistakably an individual, and the prophet perceives that suffering will be not merely incidental to the mission but its organ. He contemplates an individual who will supremely fulfil the mission of Israel through the organ of his own innocent suffering and who will pass through shame and death to exaltation and triumph.[14]

One task remains before we see specifically how the Servant anticipates Jesus Christ's vicarious atonement. That is to set the fourth song in the theological context of Isaiah 40–55, as Chris Wright does: "Salvation and forgiveness come from the sheer grace of Yahweh and his choice to forgive or blot out transgressions (Isa. 43:25)."[15] Israel, which is in covenant relation to Yahweh, cannot obtain forgiveness on its own. On what basis, then, will Yahweh bring salvation and forgiveness? Ringing throughout Isaiah 53 is the message that God will bring salvation and forgiveness through his chosen Servant.

The Servant possesses at least seven unique qualifications to perform his saving work. First, he suffers rejection, oppression, affliction, and such horrible physical pain as to be unrecognizable.

> His appearance was so marred, beyond human semblance,
> and his form beyond that of the children of mankind. (52:14)

> He was despised and rejected by men;
> a man of sorrows, and acquainted with grief. (53:3)

> But he was wounded . . . ;
> he was crushed. . . . (v. 5)

> He was oppressed, and he was afflicted. (v. 7)

> By oppression and judgment he was taken away. (v. 8)

---

[14]Groom, "Why Did Christ Die?," 100.
[15]Wright, "Atonement in the Old Testament," 80.

Second, he is sinless in deed and word:

> ... he had done no violence,
>   and there was no deceit in his mouth. (v. 9)

Indeed, in terms of character, he is "the righteous one, my servant" (v. 11).

Third, the righteous Servant voluntarily gives his life; no one coerces him: "he poured out his soul to death" (v. 12).

Fourth, if we ask whether God plays a part in the innocent Servant's suffering, the answer may surprise us:

> Yet it was the will of the LORD to crush him;
>   he has put him to grief. (v. 10)

God willed the dreadful suffering of his righteous Servant! Though this seems difficult to reconcile with God's righteous character, the reconciliation lies in another theme of this Servant Song—that of vicarious suffering.

Fifth, the willing Servant suffers and dies on behalf of others:

> But he was wounded for our transgressions;
>   he was crushed for our iniquities;
> upon him was the chastisement that brought us peace,
>   and with his stripes we are healed.
> ... and the LORD has laid on him
>   the iniquity of us all. (vv. 5–6)

>   ... who considered
> that he was cut off out of the land of the living,
>   stricken for the transgression of my people? (v. 8)

Sixth, the Servant suffers in the place of others, enduring the suffering that they deserve, as Isaiah says twice:

> ... and he shall bear their iniquities. (v. 11)

> ... yet he bore the sin of many. (v. 12)

Peter Gentry makes the proper connections: "The Lord laid on him the iniquity of us all so that we might go free. This passage clearly teaches penal substitution."[16]

---

[16]Peter J. Gentry, "The Atonement in Isaiah's Fourth Servant Song (Isaiah 52:13–53:12)," *The Southern Baptist Journal of Theology* 11, no. 2 (2007): 33.

Alec Motyer sums up the theology of verse 11:

Isaiah 53:11 is one of the fullest statements of atonement theology ever penned. (i) The Servant knows the needs to be met and what must be done. (ii) As "that righteous one, my servant" he is both fully acceptable to the God our sins have offended and has been appointed by him to his task. (iii) As righteous, he is free from every contagion of our sin. (iv) He identified himself personally with our sin and need. (v) The emphatic pronoun "he" underlines his personal commitment to this role. (vi) He accomplishes the task fully. Negatively, in the bearing of iniquity; positively, in the provision of righteousness.[17]

Seventh, as Jeffrey, Ovey, and Sach point out:

[Another] noteworthy feature of this passage is the phrase "guilt offering" in Isaiah 53:10. The Hebrew word *'asam* underlying this phrase unmistakeably refers to the "guilt offering" described in Leviticus 5–7 as an atoning sacrifice for sin (Lev. 5:16, 18; 7:7). By using the same word here Isaiah plainly intends to ascribe the same significance to the suffering Servant. Isaiah 53:10 thus anticipates something that will become explicit in the New Testament: the animal sacrifices of Leviticus are ultimately fulfilled in the sacrificial death of a person.[18]

Taken all together, then, Isaiah 52:13–53:12 is a powerful prediction of the substitutionary atoning sacrifice of the Christ. Christopher Wright sums up matters well:

His vicarious suffering and death will "bear" the iniquities of those who, having thought he was suffering under the judgment of God for his own sin, now realize that it was actually *our* sorrows, transgressions, iniquities and sins that were laid upon him. The language of sacrificial substitution and of vicarious sin-bearing runs through Isaiah 53 unmistakeably.[19]

Penal Substitution in Mark 10:45: The Ransom Saying

We previously studied the ransom saying of Mark 10:45 in some detail.[20] Now I will briefly review its context and exposition and demonstrate how this text teaches substitution. The ransom saying follows Peter's confession regarding

---

[17]J. Alec Motyer, *The Prophecy of Isaiah: An Introduction and Commentary* (Downers Grove, IL: Inter-Varsity, 1993), 442.
[18]Jeffrey, Ovey, and Sach, *Pierced for Our Transgressions*, 61.
[19]Wright, "Atonement in the Old Testament," 80, italics original.
[20]See pp. 325–31 for discussion of the saying's authenticity, background, context, and theology.

Jesus, and Jesus's three predictions of his death and resurrection (8:29, 31; 9:31; 10:33–34). In its context the saying reveals Jesus's understanding of the meaning of his death.

Instead of showing concern for Jesus, who has just predicted his crucifixion, James and John ask him for the best places in the future kingdom of God (10:37). Jesus informs them that, mirroring his experience, they and their fellow disciples must endure suffering now to enjoy glory later. Their request for glory now, therefore, is insensitive to Jesus's sufferings and underestimates their own suffering.

Jesus rebukes James and John for their selfishness, and the ten are indignant at them (v. 41). Jesus next instructs the Twelve that they are not to rule as unsaved leaders do—selfishly lording it over those under them. Instead, they are to imitate his example of servant leadership (vv. 26–27). Then comes the clincher: "For even the Son of Man came not to be served but to serve, and to give his life as a ransom for many" (v. 45; parallel, Matt. 20:28). In the immediate context, then, Jesus presents himself as the chief example of a servant-leader. And the epitome of his servant leadership is his giving himself unto death.

Though Jesus's favorite self-designation, "The Son of Man," combines two Old Testament themes—the mortal, insignificant "son of man," and the exalted, divine "Son of Man"—in the ransom saying Jesus uses "Son of Man" as "an exalted title and implies that Jesus has the right to be served."[21] Jesus's words "the Son of Man came" underline the voluntariness of his self-giving and point to his mission and purpose, in this case, to serve and die. The purpose for Jesus's coming in this world was "to give his life as a ransom."

For four reasons, Jesus's saying teaches that he will die a substitutionary death. First, the word "ransom" in this context implies substitution. Ben Witherington explains: "The term λύτρον is a mercantile term. It should be translated 'ransom' and refers to the deliverance by purchase of a slave or prisoner of war or of some object one wants back (see Lev. 25:47–55). Very clearly the idea of equivalence, a quid pro quo, is in the background here."[22] That is true as background, but it does not demand that every use of "ransom" implies substitution. But, as used by Jesus in the ransom saying, it does that very thing.

Second, in the saying, "The Son of Man came . . . to give his life as a ransom *for* many," the preposition is also important. Specifically, the use of "for" (ἀντί, *anti*) after "ransom" (λύτρον, *lytron*) reinforces the concept of

---

[21]Sydney H. T. Page, "Ransom Saying," in *Dictionary of Jesus and the Gospels*, ed. Joel B. Green, Scot McKnight, and I. Howard Marshall (Downers Grove, IL: InterVarsity, 1992), 661.

[22]Ben Witherington III, *The Gospel of Mark: A Socio-Rhetorical Commentary* (Grand Rapids: Eerdmans, 2001), 290.

substitution. William Lane clarifies: "The Son of Man takes *the place* of the many and there happens to him what would have happened to them. . . . In his death, Jesus pays the price that sets men free."[23] Witherington agrees: "Here we have enunciated the notion of substitutionary atonement."[24]

Third, the relation of the ransom saying to Isaiah 53 suggests substitution. Traditionally, the following verses from Isaiah have been thought to have inspired Mark 10:45:

> . . . his soul makes an offering for guilt,
> . . . he poured out his soul to death . . .
> yet he bore the sin of many. (Isa. 53:10, 12)

But some have argued that the ransom saying did not have in mind Isaiah's famous chapter. They point to differences in vocabulary between the two. But this misses the point, as Craig Evans argues:

> Mark 10:45 is not a translation of any portion of Isa 52:13–53:12 . . . it is a summary of the task of the Servant. It is true that Jesus has not said that the "son of man" has given his life as a guilt offering; rather he says that the "son of man" has given his life as a ransom. But a ransom for what? Why would a ransom be required? The last part of Isa 53:12 answers this question in saying that the Servant "bore the sins of many, and made intercession for the transgressors." . . . Jesus' life would constitute the ransom that would free Israel from divine penalty; his blood would make the hoped-for new covenant a reality (Mark 14:24).[25]

Evans is correct. While not quoting Isaiah 53, Mark 10:45 is shaped by that Old Testament text.[26] Seeing this reinforces the notion of substitution in Jesus's saying.

Fourth, the saying teaches substitution when viewed alongside similar sayings in Psalm 49:7–9 and Mark 8:37, as I. Howard Marshall argues:

> In Mark 10:45 . . . Jesus serves men by giving his life as a ransom for many. Mark no doubt intends this saying to be seen against the background of 8:37 where the question is raised whether a man can give any exchange for his life. Behind the question lies Psalm 49:7–9: "Truly no man can ransom himself, or give to God the price of his life, for the ransom of his life is costly, and can never

---

[23]William L. Lane, *Commentary on the Gospel of Mark*, The New International Commentary on the New Testament (Grand Rapids: Eerdmans, 1974), 384, italics original.
[24]Witherington, *The Gospel of Mark*, 290.
[25]Craig A. Evans, *Mark 8:27–16:20*, Word Biblical Commentary (Nashville: Nelson, 2001), 121.
[26]For more argumentation, see Witherington, *The Gospel of Mark*, 288–90.

suffice, that he should continue to live on for ever, and never see the Pit." What man cannot do has been done by Christ. We are surely justified in discerning here the thought of human mortality as the result of human sin, and in seeing in the death of Christ the ransom "price" paid to God for the redemption of mankind from death.[27]

These four reasons convince me that Mark 10:45 teaches that Jesus's redemptive death was vicarious. I agree with David Peterson, who after reviewing much of the same evidence, concludes:

> [Jesus] viewed himself as the ultimate "guilt offering" for the sins of the people and the ransom to redeem Israel and the nations from judgement and death (cf. 1 Tim. 2:6). Jesus' whole life was a ministry to others, designed to serve their needs. But ultimately his service to them meant offering himself in death, in perfect obedience to the will of his Father, as a payment for their sins.[28]

Grant Osborne, commenting on the parallel text in Matthew 20:28, is comprehensive and helpful.

> Jesus' atoning sacrifice provides the ultimate model of servanthood. . . . Thus the mercy seat was the place of atonement, and Christ here is seen as the NT counterpart, the means of atonement for all humankind. His blood is the once-for-all sacrifice, the *ransom payment* for sin, the only way atonement can be effected for sinful humanity. Three things happened: the wrath of God was appeased, sins were forgiven, and freedom was purchased.[29]

Penal Substitution in Paul

The major biblical witness to Christ's saving work as a penal substitution is the apostle Paul. At least five passages convey this truth: Romans 3:25–26; 8:1–4; 2 Corinthians 5:21; Galatians 3:13; and Colossians 2:14. Because every text except Romans 8:1–4 has been treated, for the others I will briefly summarize the exposition and focus on how they teach substitution.[30]

---

[27]I. Howard Marshall, "The Meaning of Redemption," in *Jesus the Saviour* (Downers Grove, IL: InterVarsity, 1990), 248.

[28]David Peterson, ed., *Where Wrath and Mercy Meet: Proclaiming the Atonement Today* (Carlisle, Cumbria, UK: Paternoster, 2001), 30.

[29]Grant R. Osborne, *Matthew*, Exegetical Commentary on the New Testament (Grand Rapids: Zondervan, 2010), 744, italics original.

[30]For treatment of the passages, see the following pages, respectively: Rom. 3:25–26 (pp. 375–78); 8:1–4 (pp. 379–81); 2 Cor. 5:21 (pp. 381–84); Gal. 3:13 (pp. 384–89); and Col. 2:14 (pp. 389–91).

Romans 3:25–26

Paul's purpose statement for Romans says that in the gospel "the righteousness of God is revealed" (Rom. 1:17). But instead of talking about the revelation of God's saving righteousness, the apostle begins a long section in which he tells of "the wrath of God" being "revealed from heaven" and concludes with "the whole world . . . accountable to God" (1:18–3:20). Only then does Paul return to his theme: "But now the righteousness of God has been manifested" (3:21).

Furthermore, everyone needs this righteousness, "for all have sinned and fall short of the glory of God" (v. 23). And it is received only "through faith in Jesus Christ" (v. 22). The basis of this saving righteousness is Christ's saving accomplishment described as a redemption and a propitiation (vv. 24–26). Paul simply mentions redemption but unfolds the meaning of propitiation.

As we saw in chapter 3, propitiation and expiation must be distinguished. Both are ways of depicting Jesus's work on the cross, but they are pointed in different directions and have different aims. Propitiation is directed toward God and expiation is directed toward sin. Propitiation is the turning away of God's wrath and expiation is the putting away of sin.

C. H. Dodd's *The Bible and the Greeks*, published in 1935, led to a "critical orthodoxy" that overturned the traditional understanding of the words rendered "propitiation."[31] Largely on linguistic and theological grounds, Dodd maintained that the word in Romans 3:25 should be rendered "means of expiation" and not propitiation. The latter idea he considered unworthy of God, for it was pagan in origin, involving notions of vengeful deities demanding blood. Dodd's work has been successfully challenged by Leon Morris and Roger Nicole, among others.[32]

It is important to note that Scripture teaches that Christ's death accomplishes the expiation of sin (in, e.g., Heb. 9:26). That is not debated. But the meaning of ἱλαστήριον (*hilastērion*) in Romans 3:25 is debated. It is also important to distinguish the biblical portrayal of propitiation from pagan notions. In paganism humans take the initiative to make fickle gods willing to forgive by appeasing (propitiating) them by various means. In Scripture a loving and holy God takes the initiative and propitiates his own justice by bearing the brunt of his wrath against sin to freely forgive his rebellious creatures.

---

[31]C. H. Dodd, *The Bible and the Greeks* (London: Hodder & Stoughton, 1935). This was a reprint of an earlier article, "Ἰλαστήριον, Its Cognates, Derivatives and Synonyms in the Septuagint," *Journal of Theological Studies* 32 (1931): 352–60. The words are *hilasterion* (Rom. 3:25), *hilaskesthai* (Heb. 2:17), and *hilasmos* (1 John 2:2; 4:10).

[32]Leon Morris, *The Apostolic Preaching of the Cross*, 3rd ed. (Grand Rapids: Eerdmans, 1965), 155–78; Roger Nicole, "C. H. Dodd and the Doctrine of Propitiation," *Westminster Theological Journal* 17 (1955): 117–57.

For two reasons I take *hilastērion* in Romans 3:25 to mean propitiation and not merely expiation. First, Paul's argument in Romans has built to this point. The gospel is the revelation of God's saving righteousness (1:16–17). God has revealed his wrath against sinners (1:18–3:20). In 3:21 Paul revisits his theme— the revelation of God's saving righteousness. But if verses 25–26 do not teach that God's wrath was satisfied in Christ's cross, then where did the wrath of 1:18–3:20 go? How can 5:1 say that believers have "peace with God through our Lord Jesus Christ"? How is that possible if God has not dealt with his holy hatred against sin? The answer is that God has punished Christ with the wrath that we sinners deserve. I agree with Douglas Moo: "When to the linguistic evidence we add the evidence of the context of Rom. 1–3, where the wrath of God is an overarching theme (1:18; cf. 2:5), the conclusion that *hilastērion* includes reference to the turning away of God's wrath is inescapable."[33]

Second and more importantly, 3:25–26 teach propitiation and not merely expiation because of the meaning of these very verses. Vital to interpreting the passage is the redemptive historical difference between "former sins" and "the present time" (vv. 25, 26). God put forward Jesus as a *hilastērion* in his blood because in his mercy he had passed over "former sins" (v. 25). The meaning is that up until Jesus's crucifixion, God forgave sins without actually having made atonement for them. The animal sacrifices were a picture of the gospel, and God actually forgave Old Testament saints (see, e.g., Ps. 103:12). But "it is impossible for the blood of bulls and goats to take away sins" (Heb. 10:4). In his forbearance God forgave the Old Testament believers without yet making atonement. He forgave them on the basis of Christ's work to come. But before that, every time a sacrifice was performed, God wrote an IOU to himself, figuratively speaking, anticipating his making atonement through Christ's blood. Paul tells us that this is what Christ did "at the present time." For God to maintain his moral integrity, to "settle accounts" that he had made with himself prior to Christ's death, it was necessary for Christ to die.

Therefore, Romans 3:25–26 says, "God put forward [Christ Jesus] as a propitiation by his blood. . . . to show God's righteousness," and "it was to show his righteousness at the present time, so that he might be just and the justifier of the one who has faith in Jesus." Though the meaning of "righteousness" is debated, Moo argues convincingly that

> "his righteousness" must have reference to some aspect of God's character that
> might have been called into question because of his treating sins in the past with

---

[33]Douglas J. Moo, *The Epistle to the Romans*, The New International Commentary on the New Testament (Grand Rapids: Eerdmans, 1996), 235.

less than full severity, and that has now been demonstrated in setting forth Christ as "the propitiatory." . . . [It means] God's "consistency" in always acting in accordance with his character.[34]

The problem is not what is commonly argued today—how could a loving God condemn anyone? That question is easily answered by reading Genesis 1–3 or Romans 1–3. A loving and holy God could condemn the world for its rebellion. The biblical problem is a much more difficult one—how could a loving and holy God maintain his moral integrity and still pardon sinners? The answer is by displaying Christ "as a propitiation in his blood." God settled accounts accumulated in the Old Testament. He satisfied his holy anger against sin by pouring that anger against Christ, who willingly gave himself for his people.[35]

Amazing results follow. God maintains his moral integrity as God and at the same time saves everyone who believes in Jesus. And believers have peace with God, God's love poured into their hearts, and hope of future glory that does not disappoint (Rom. 5:1–5). It is, then, "at the present time" that we learn that God forgave "former sins" on the basis of Christ's work to come.

It is not difficult to show that propitiation involves legal penal substitution. Romans 1–5 is replete with legal themes, including law, sin, condemnation, and justification. All human beings are condemned before a holy God, including Gentiles who do not have the Ten Commandments.

> For all who have sinned without the law will also perish without the law. (2:12)

> For when Gentiles, who do not have the law, by nature do what the law requires, they are a law to themselves, even though they do not have the law. They show that the work of the law is written on their hearts, while their conscience also bears witness, and their conflicting thoughts accuse or even excuse them. (2:14–15)

Condemnation also includes Jews, who do have God's holy law. In fact, they are worse off than Gentiles because they stand thrice condemned: by natural law (1:18–20), by the law written on the heart (2:15), and especially by the commandments (3:17–25). Paul's words cut deep:

> And all who have sinned under the law will be judged by the law. (2:12)

> You who boast in the law dishonor God by breaking the law. (2:23)

---

[34]Ibid., 240. See the discussion beginning on p. 238.
[35]See the excellent treatment of this passage by D. A. Carson, "Atonement in Romans 3:21–26," in Hill and James, *The Glory of the Atonement*, 119–39.

Paul summarizes his argument from 1:18–3:18 using legal terminology:

> Now we know that whatever the law says it speaks to those who are under the law,
> so that every mouth may be stopped, and the whole world may be held account-
> able to God. For by works of the law no human being will be justified in his sight,
> since through the law comes knowledge of sin. (3:19–20)

The passage dealing with propitiation follows (3:21–26). In the developing argument of Romans, redemption and propitiation meet humankind's need in a way that law keeping could not. Verses 25–26 too are full of legal themes: "righteousness" (twice), "just," and "justifier." And these are the very terms with which Paul presents propitiation. He expressly says that "God put forward [Christ] as a propitiation by his blood. . . . to show God's righteousness. . . . that he might be just and the justifier of" believers (vv. 25–26).

This conjunction of legal themes leads Marshall, speaking of the work of P. T. Forsyth, to reach the following conclusion:

> Here we have an exposition of the matter which takes holiness and wrath seri-
> ously, and that I find to be much more in tune with the teaching of the New
> Testament than the position of the anti-penal thinkers. The essential difference
> is that Forsyth and those like him hold firmly to the biblical teaching about the
> holiness and the wrath of God, which issue in his active judgment of sinners.
> They then embrace that understanding of the work of Christ which sees it as
> the active obedience and expression of holiness in which God himself bears the
> painful consequences of human sin, providing reconciliation with himself. God
> must be seen as both just and the justifier, and this he did by himself bearing the
> judgment or penalty of sin.[36]

D. A. Carson shares my reasons for including Romans 3:25–26 in a chapter on penal substitution:

> In short, Romans 3:25–26 makes a glorious contribution to Christian understand-
> ing of the "internal" mechanism of the atonement. It explains the need for Christ's
> propitiating sacrifice in terms of the just requirements of God's holy character.
> This reading not only follows the exegesis carefully, but it brings the whole of the
> argument from Romans 1:18 on into gentle cohesion.[37]

---

[36]I. Howard Marshall, "The Theology of the Atonement," in Tidball, Hilborn, and Thacker, *The Atonement Debate*, 58.
[37]D. A. Carson, "Atonement in Romans 3:21–26," 138.

Romans 8:1–4

Paul begins Romans 8, "There is therefore now no condemnation for those who are in Christ Jesus" (v. 1). The apostle speaks in legal terms and affirms that Christ completely delivers his people from "condemnation," the penalty of sin for lawbreakers. Paul makes his point emphatically: "There is no condemnation."[38] Believers will not experience God's eternal wrath.

Paul combines the language of the court with that of relationship when he says that this deliverance pertains to those "who are in Christ Jesus." All who died and rose with Christ (Rom. 6:1–11) are spiritually united to him and will not suffer God's condemnation, "since the condemnation which they deserve has already been fully borne for them by Him,"[39] as C. E. B. Cranfield asserts.

Paul explains the basis for this verdict of "no condemnation": "For the law of the Spirit of life has set you free in Christ Jesus from the law of sin and death" (Rom. 8:2). The Holy Spirit has freed believers from the threat of the Mosaic law. He is called "the Spirit of life" because he brings eternal life to those who are spiritually dead. In this manner he sets us free from the law that leads to sin and death. There is a great transfer. The life-giving Spirit liberates us from the dominion of sin and death and delivers us into the dominion of life. Consequently, sin's penalty and power are broken. We will never be condemned (v. 1) and do not need to live in sin anymore (vv. 4b–17).

"For God has done what the law, weakened by the flesh, could not do. By sending his own Son in the likeness of sinful flesh and for sin, he condemned sin in the flesh" (Rom. 8:3). The law of Moses is "weakened by the flesh." Paul means that the law cannot save because fallen human beings cannot obey it. But what the law could not do, God did in Christ, the one he sent "in the likeness of sinful flesh."

Paul chooses his words carefully. If he had written, "Christ came in sinful flesh," then Christ would have been a sinner unable to save others. But if Paul had denied that Christ identified with sinners, Christ again would have been unable to save, because he would not have been near enough to us. Paul hits the golden mean—the Son came "in the likeness of sinful flesh," that is, genuinely sharing with the sinful human condition without committing sin himself.

The Father sent the Son "in the likeness of sinful flesh and for sin." Since the words "for sin" are used regularly in the Septuagint in the sense of "sin offering,"

---

[38] Paul uses the emphatic negative οὐδέν (*ouden*) and places it in the emphatic first position.

[39] C. E. B. Cranfield, *A Critical and Exegetical Commentary on the Epistle to the Romans*, 2 vols., International Critical Commentary (Edinburgh: T&T Clark, 1975), 1:373.

most commentators take them to mean that here.[40] The apostle speaks of Christ's death as a sacrifice that removes sin.

The main thrust of the verse is that "God . . . condemned sin in the flesh." Paul refers to Christ's flesh in which he made a sin offering. Paul continues to use legal language when he tells of "the righteous requirement of the law" (v. 4). But how did God, "by sending his own Son in the likeness of sinful flesh and for sin," condemn sin in the Son's humanity? Moo answers well:

> The condemnation of sin consists in God's executing his judgment on sin in the atoning death of his Son. As our substitute, Christ "was made sin for us" (2 Cor. 5:21) and suffered the wrath of God, the judgment of God upon that sin (cf. . . . Rom. 3:25; Gal. 3:13). In his doing so, of course, we may say that sin's power was broken in the sense that Paul pictures sin as a power that holds people in its clutches and brings condemnation to them. . . . The condemnation that our sins deserve has been poured out on Christ, our sin-bearer; that is why "there is now no condemnation for those who are in Christ Jesus" ([Rom. 8] v. 1).[41]

Repeatedly Moo says that Christ became our legal substitute and paid the penalty for our sins that we could not pay. That is penal substitution written in large letters.

The apostle continues, ". . . in order that the righteous requirement of the law might be fulfilled in us, who walk not according to the flesh but according to the Spirit" (Rom. 8:4). There is great agreement that Romans 8:5–17 tells of the Christian life. Although many hold that Paul's speaking of the fulfilling of the law's requirement in us in verse 4 also refers to our growth in holiness, I disagree. Rather, when Paul writes, "He condemned sin in the flesh, in order that the righteous requirement of the law might be fulfilled in us," he speaks of Christ's fulfillment of the law. I am persuaded by Moo:

> If, then, the inability of the law is to be overcome without an arbitrary cancellation of the law, it can happen only through a perfect obedience of the law's demands. . . . This, of course, is exactly what Jesus Christ has done. As our substitute, he satisfied the righteous requirement of the law, living a life of perfect submission to God. In laying upon him the condemnation due all of us (v. 3b; cf. v. 1), God also made it possible for the righteous obedience that Christ had earned to be transferred to us.[42]

---

[40]See James D. G. Dunn, *Romans 1–9*, Word Biblical Commentary (Waco, TX: Word, 1988), 403.
[41]Moo, *The Epistle to the Romans*, 481.
[42]Ibid., 483.

God's purposes in sending his Son include both to liberate sinners from condemnation (vv. 1–4a), and to transform their lives (v. 4b–17). Christ died not only to justify his people, but also to progressively sanctify them. The ones whom God has declared righteous are identifiable, for they "walk not according to the flesh but according to the Spirit" (v. 4).

I agree with Jeffrey, Ovey, and Sach that "this amounts to an explicit statement of the doctrine of penal substitution."[43] Paul teaches that God who saves people will also keep them to the end (Rom. 8:1). How are we to account for such a bold declaration? Commenting on Romans 8:34, Judith Gundry Volf answers:

> "Christ Jesus is the one who died" (v. 34b). The κατάκριμα [condemnation] due us (5:16, 18) fell upon the crucified Christ: "Sending his Son in the likeness of sinful flesh and for sin, God condemned (κατέκρινεν) sin in the flesh" (8:3). Thus Paul can assure believers already, "there is therefore now no κατάκριμα [condemnation] for those who are in Christ Jesus" (8:1).[44]

Christ suffered and died in our place. He took the condemnation that we deserved to spare us from it. He was our legal substitute.

2 Corinthians 5:21

In one of the most famous Pauline passages on Christ's saving work, the apostle says, "For our sake he made him to be sin who knew no sin, so that in him we might become the righteousness of God" (2 Cor. 5:21). This statement belongs in a chapter on penal substitution for two reasons: its exegesis in context and its function in context. We will examine these in turn.

First, 2 Corinthians 5:21 teaches penal substitution because of its exegesis in its context. Paul draws attention to the one "who knew no sin." This is Jesus, the sinless one, the only one qualified to be the "mediator between God and men"—"the man Christ Jesus" (1 Tim. 2:5). The Son of God became incarnate and never sinned; he lived a perfect life. Scripture sometimes focuses on Christ's "becoming obedient to the point of death, even death on a cross" (Phil. 2:8). But in 2 Corinthians 5:21 the focus of the word "knew" is on Christ's lifelong obedience, as Paul Barnett affirms: "It points first to the sinlessness of his incarnate life ('he knew no sin')."[45]

Gordon Fee, writing on 2 Corinthians 5:21, agrees:

---

[43]Jeffrey, Ovey, and Sach, *Pierced for Our Transgressions*, 87.

[44]Judith M. Gundry Volf, *Paul and Perseverance* (Louisville: Westminster John Knox, 1990), 68.

[45]Paul Barnett, *The Second Epistle to the Corinthians*, The New International Commentary on the New Testament (Grand Rapids: Eerdmans, 1997), 314.

The sinlessness of Christ in his incarnation is here asserted as a nonnegotiable presupposition. . . . Christ "knew no sin." This is the "knowing" that comes from experience, not from mental activity, the kind of "knowing evil" that Adam and Eve experienced that led to human fallenness. It was the fact that Christ did not "know sin" in this way that made it possible for him to be offered as the perfect sacrifice on behalf of others.[46]

The words "*For our sake* he made him to be sin who knew no sin" highlight God's grace and reveal his motive for sending Christ—to save needy sinners. God "made" the sinless Christ "to be sin." Christ's death is not explicitly mentioned here, but it is mentioned in verses 14–15 and implied in verses 18–19. Scholars agree that verse 21 identifies the crucified Christ and human sin, although they differ on how to explain this identification.[47] It is clear that the Son of God in his redemptive work became so closely identified with our sins that mysteriously it could be said that he was made sin, as Harris affirms:

> V. 21a stands in stark contrast to v. 19b. Because of God's transference of sinners' sin on to the sinless one, because sin was reckoned to Christ's account, it is now not reckoned to the believer's account. This total identification of the sinless one with sinners at the cross, in assuming the full penalty and guilt of their sin, leaves no doubt that substitution as well as representation was involved.[48]

Harris is correct. Christ is both our representative and our substitute. He became one of us and so in all of his saving work represents us before God. He is also our substitute, who took our sin that we might gain his righteousness. Paul thus ends 2 Corinthians 5:21 by referring to justification. The result of Christ's being made sin is believers' becoming God's righteousness in Christ. As mentioned earlier, Brian Vickers has argued convincingly that, though no one passage fully teaches the imputation of Christ's lifelong righteousness, a strong cumulative argument for imputation can be made based on Romans 4:3; 5:19; and 2 Corinthians 5:21.[49] Therefore, challenges notwithstanding, I affirm Luther's view that 2 Corinthians 5:21 contains "a joyous exchange."[50]

C. K. Barrett's apt words bear repeating:

---

[46]Gordon D. Fee, *Pauline Christology: An Exegetical-Theological Study* (Peabody, MA: Hendrickson, 2007), 166–67.

[47]See Murray J. Harris, *The Second Epistle to the Corinthians*, The New International Greek Testament Commentary (Grand Rapids: Eerdmans, 2005), 452–54, for views.

[48]Ibid., 453.

[49]Brian Vickers, *Jesus' Blood and Righteousness* (Wheaton, IL: Crossway, 2006).

[50]See, e.g., N. T. Wright, "On Becoming the Righteousness of God: 2 Corinthians 5:21," in *Pauline Theology Volume 11: 1 and 2 Corinthians*, ed. D. M. Hay (Minneapolis: Fortress, 1993), 208.

It is only as sinless that Christ can, in Paul's view, bear the sins of others. . . . Paul develops the thought in terms of an exchange: Christ was made *sin*, that we might become *God's righteousness*. It is important to observe that the words Paul uses are words describing relationships. . . . Paul does not say, for by definition it would not have been true, that Christ became a sinner, transgressing God's law; neither does he say, for it would have contradicted all experience (not least in Corinth) that every believer becomes immediately and automatically morally righteous, good as God is good. He says rather that Christ became *sin*; that is, he came to stand in that relation with God which normally is the result of sin, estranged from God and the object of his wrath. . . . We correspondingly, and through God's loving act in Christ, have come to stand in that relation with God which is described by the term *righteousness*, that is we are acquitted in his court, justified, reconciled. We are no longer his enemies, but his friends.[51]

Note that Barrett relates verse 21 to the previous verses dealing with reconciliation. What Barrett implies, Vickers makes explicit. "Taken in this way 5:21 does not at all stand awkwardly at the end of the paragraph as a disconnected, timeless truth of salvation, but as a powerful summary of the ultimate historical-redemptive event that lies at the heart of Paul's ministry of reconciliation."[52] And this brings us to the second reason this verse teaches penal substitution.

Second, 2 Corinthians 5:21 teaches penal substitution because of the function it plays in its context. This passage teaches much about reconciliation. Our need is implied in that God reconciled us to himself—overcoming our alienation from him (vv. 18–19). God takes the initiative: "All this is from God, who through Christ reconciled us to himself" (v. 18). Christ is the Mediator of reconciliation (vv. 18–19). Paul distinguishes two inseparable aspects. First is Christ's unique accomplishment of reconciliation on the cross (vv. 14–15, 18–19, 21). Second, reconciliation also involves our proclamation of that reconciling atonement (vv. 18–19).

Reconciliation through Christ brings forgiveness, God's "not counting" believing sinners' "trespasses against them" (v. 19). Because of the work of Christ, the peacemaker, the Mediator of reconciliation, God no longer reckons believers' sins against them. Reconciliation, then, is related to justification, which deals with the forgiveness of sins (Rom. 4:6–8).

In Romans 5:1, 10, Paul only hinted at the relation between reconciliation and justification. Now he explains that relation in 2 Corinthians 5:21: "For our

---

[51]C. K. Barrett, *The Second Epistle to the Corinthians*, Harper's New Testament Commentaries (New York: Harper & Row, 1973), 180, italics original.
[52]Vickers, *Jesus' Blood and Righteousness*, 180.

sake he made him to be sin who knew no sin, so that in him we might become the righteousness of God." The placement of verse 21 in its context indicates that, as Philip Hughes explains,

> the apostle sets forth the gospel of reconciliation in all its mystery and all its wonder. There is no sentence more profound in the whole of Scripture; for this verse embraces the whole ground of the sinner's reconciliation to God and declares the incontestable reason why he should respond to the ambassadorial entreaty. Indeed, it completes the message with which the Christian ambassador has been entrusted. To proclaim: "Be reconciled to God" is not good news unless it is accompanied by a declaration of the ground on which reconciliation has been effected and is available.[53]

In his atoning death, the Son of God, who lived sinlessly, was so closely identified with our sins and their miserable consequences that the apostle mysteriously says that he was made sin. Because God transferred our sin onto the sinless one, it is now not reckoned to our account; rather, God's righteousness is reckoned to us. This wonderful exchange is the basis of reconciliation: because Christ was made sin, believers become God's righteousness in Christ and are therefore at peace with God. Thus the legal theme of Christ's saving death accomplishing justification is the basis of God's reconciling the world in Christ. And the justification of verse 21—complete with double imputation— not only is a description of the ground of reconciliation but fleshes out the "message of reconciliation" as well. Our part in "the ministry of reconciliation" is to proclaim the penal substitution of the Son of God as we implore sinners, "be reconciled to God" (vv. 18, 20).

David Peterson sums up matters: "The logic of 2 Corinthians 5 is that God condemns our sin in the death of his sinless Son so that we might be justified and reconciled to him (cf. Rom 8:1–4, 10). This 'great exchange' is a reality for all who are 'in him,' that is, united to Christ by faith."[54]

Galatians 3:13

In one of the most powerful verses describing penal substitution in all of Scripture, Paul writes, "Christ redeemed us from the curse of the law by becoming a curse for us—for it is written, 'Cursed is everyone who is hanged on a tree'" (Gal. 3:13).[55] This verse is located in a section of the epistle replete with the

---

[53]Philip Edgcumbe Hughes, *Paul's Second Epistle to the Corinthians* (Grand Rapids: Eerdmans, 1962), 211.
[54]D. Peterson, *Where Wrath and Mercy Meet*, 38.
[55]After giving my exposition, I will treat a recent challenge to the traditional post-Reformational understanding.

ideas of "curse" and "blessing." Just a few verses before verse 13, Paul cites one of God's promises to Abram in Genesis 12: "I will make of you a great nation, and I will bless you and make your name great, so that you will be a blessing. I will bless those who bless you, and him who dishonors you I will curse, and in you all the families of the earth shall be blessed" (Gen. 12:1–3).

The passage mentions blessing five times and curse once, and this is significant. God delights to bless but is slow to curse. After prohibiting idolatry in the second commandment, the Lord explains, "For I the LORD your God am a jealous God, visiting the iniquity of the fathers on the children to the third and the fourth generation of those who hate me, but showing steadfast love to thousands of those who love me and keep my commandments" (Ex. 20:5–6). Notice that the Lord curses to three and four generations of those who hate him but blesses to the thousandth generation of those who love him. Blessings and curses are thus built into God's covenant with his people.

Another noteworthy Old Testament account is the Israelites' rehearsing the blessings and curses of the law on Mount Ebal and Mount Gerazim, respectively (Deut. 27:12–28:68). I cite the first and last curses:

> "Cursed be the man who makes a carved or cast metal image, an abomination to the LORD, a thing made by the hands of a craftsman, and sets it up in secret." And all the people shall answer and say, "Amen." (Deut. 27:15)

> "Cursed be anyone who does not confirm the words of this law by doing them." And all the people shall say, "Amen." (v. 26)

The blessing section begins this way:

> And if you faithfully obey the voice of the LORD your God, being careful to do all his commandments that I command you today, the LORD your God will set you high above all the nations of the earth. And all these blessings shall come upon you and overtake you, if you obey the voice of the LORD your God. Blessed shall you be in the city, and blessed shall you be in the field. Blessed shall be the fruit of your womb and the fruit of your ground and the fruit of your cattle, the increase of your herds and the young of your flock. Blessed shall be your basket and your kneading bowl. Blessed shall you be when you come in, and blessed shall you be when you go out. (Deut. 28:1–6)

It is certain that God wanted his people never to forget that, depending on their obedience or disobedience to him and his law, they would reap the blessings or curses contained in it. Blessings and curses are a part of biblical religion.

Blessings and curses are not limited to the Old Testament. They also play a role in the New Testament. We see this in Galatians 3:7–14, where Paul educates his readers concerning the blessings of the Abrahamic covenant and the curses of the law. Note the frequency of the words "blessed"/"blessing" and "curse"/"cursed" (in italics):

> And the Scripture, foreseeing that God would justify the Gentiles by faith, preached the gospel beforehand to Abraham, saying, "In you shall all the nations be *blessed*." So then, those who are of faith are *blessed* along with Abraham, the man of faith.
>
> For all who rely on the works of the law are under a *curse*; for it is written, "*Cursed* be everyone who does not abide by all things written in the Book of the Law, and do them." Now it is evident that no one is justified before God by the law for . . . . Christ redeemed us from the *curse* of the law by becoming a *curse* for us—for it is written, "*Cursed* is everyone who is hanged on a tree"—so that in Christ Jesus the *blessing* of Abraham might come to the Gentiles, so that we might receive the promised Spirit through faith. (Gal. 3:8–11, 13–14)

The passage begins and ends with blessing, and in between there are five occurrences of cursing. Paul defines the blessing as the fulfillment of the covenantal promise that God made to Abraham, "In you shall all the nations be blessed" (Gal. 3:8; citing Gen. 12:3). Paul views this promise as fulfilled in the gospel coming to the Gentiles. He writes that Christ died for us "so that in Christ Jesus the blessing of Abraham might come to the Gentiles" (Gal. 3:14). Then he describes an aspect of that blessing: "so that we might receive the promised Spirit through faith" (v. 14). The blessings of the Abrahamic covenant are all the blessings of the gospel, including a relationship with God through Christ, eternal life, receiving the Holy Spirit, and what these entail.

Paul specifies what he means by the curse. It is the threat of the punishment that all lawbreakers deserve: "Cursed be everyone who does not abide by all things written in the Book of the Law, and do them" (v. 10). Within this context of blessing and curse Paul speaks of Christ's atoning death: "Christ redeemed us from the curse of the law by becoming a curse for us" (v. 13).

This is as strong a statement of Christ's being our legal penal substitute as is found in Scripture. Christ delivers sinners from the law's threat of punishment *by becoming* a curse for them! Paul cites Deuteronomy 21:23, which curses the executed person whose body is left hanging on a tree, to prove that Christ died the death of an accursed man: "For it is written, 'Cursed is everyone who is hanged on a tree'" (Gal. 3:13). Christ took the penalty that we lawbreakers deserved—

he became a curse—in order that we might gain the blessing of eternal life. He died an accursed death on the tree to rescue us from the punishment of the law.

Paul's words need to be interpreted in light of his own experience, as Gordon Fee forcefully reminds us. Before Paul's conversion, Deuteronomy 21:23 convinced him that Jesus could not possibly be the Messiah.

> Since Jesus had been "hung on a pole" by the Romans, this for Paul was the sure evidence that God had cursed him; and he whom God had cursed could not possibly be honored as the Jewish Messiah. . . . That this lies at the heart of Paul's pre-Christian understanding of Jesus of Nazareth helps to explain his being described in 1 Tim. 1:13 as at one time "a blasphemer, persecutor, and violent man" . . . . His encounter with Jesus risen from the dead radicalized Paul.[56]

Paul came to a radical new understanding of Deuteronomy 21:23 and Jesus in light of his resurrection. Again, Fee explains:

> What he came to realize, as the argument in Gal. 3:10–14 indicates, is that Christ's having been hanged on a cross did indeed involve God's curse but not on Christ himself. Rather, the whole human race, in its sin and rebellion against the eternal God, came under God's curse and in effect was hung on the cross through the one perfect sacrifice.[57]

Ronald Fung draws out the meaning of Paul's statement that "Christ redeemed us from the curse of the law by becoming a curse *for us*":

> By submitting to the curse of the law on behalf of his people, both Jew and Gentile, Christ redeemed them from the law's curse and condemnation. "He neutralized the curse for them, so that they on whom the curse rightfully falls because of their failure to keep the law, now become free from both its demands and its curse. Christ was able to neutralize the curse because in his death he satisfied the claim of the law."[58]

Christ died vicariously as a legal substitute for all who would believe in him. F. F. Bruce writes succinctly, "The curse which Christ 'became' was his people's curse, as the death which he died was their death."[59]

---

[56] Fee, *Pauline Christology*, 535.
[57] Ibid.
[58] Ronald Y. K. Fung, *The Epistle to the Galatians*, The New International Commentary on the New Testament (Grand Rapids: Eerdmans, 1988), 149–50, citing F. Büchsel, *Theological Dictionary of the New Testament*, ed. Gerhard Kittel, trans. Geoffrey W. Bromiley (Grand Rapids: Eerdmans, 1964), 1:126.
[59] F. F. Bruce, *Commentary on Galatians*, New International Greek Testament Commentary (Grand Rapids: Eerdmans, 1982), 166.

I must interact with a recent interpretation that sees Galatians 3:13 as referring not to Christ's penal substitution but to his suffering Israel's exile on the
cross. Hans Boersma favors this interpretation:

> We need to opt for a national-historical reading of this passage . . . that makes the
> judicial elements subservient to the hospitality that God extends in Jesus Christ.
> . . . When St. Paul quotes the Deuteronomic invocation of the curse, he is assum-
> ing that Israel has, in fact, suffered the curse of the Law in the historical punish-
> ment of exile. In other words, the "curse of the Law" is not some eternal principle
> that results from any and every transgression of the commandment, but it refers
> to the historical judgment of exile against Israel because of its consistent rejec-
> tion of divine hospitality. . . . According to a national-historical interpretation
> of Galatians 3, therefore, St. Paul maintains that in his death Christ has suffered
> Israel's exile. . . . Redemption is not simply the result of punishment, but is the
> result of a punishment that leads to the restoration of new life of the eschaton.[60]

Although Boersma's book accomplishes much good, chiefly in rehabilitating
the much-maligned idea that Christ's atonement was violent, I take issue with
his handling of Galatians 3:13. He misrepresents the traditional exegesis. It takes
the law's curse not as "some eternal principle" but as the historical principle
issuing from the Mosaic law and cited by Paul in Galatians 3:10: "Cursed be
everyone who does not abide by all things written in the Book of the Law, and
do them" (citing Deut. 27:26).

The traditional reading does make "the judicial elements subservient to the
hospitality [Boersma's term for God's sharing his love with us] that God extends
in Jesus Christ." It does not make Christ's atonement an end in itself but God's
means to bring the blessings of the Abrahamic covenant to all believers. And
the traditional view holds that "redemption . . . is the result of a punishment
that leads to the restoration of new life of the eschaton."[61] It does not sever Jesus's
death from his resurrection.

Aside from misrepresentations, Boersma errs when he holds that "in his
death Christ has suffered Israel's exile."[62] There is not a hint of Israel's exile in
Galatians 3 (or anywhere else in the epistle). Rather, the apostle specifically
points to infractions of the Ten Commandments: "For all who rely on works
of the law are under a curse; for it is written, 'Cursed be everyone who does not
abide by all things written in the Book of the Law, and do them'" (v. 10). Is this

---

[60]Hans Boersma, *Violence, Hospitality, and the Cross: Reinterpreting the Atonement Tradition* (Grand
Rapids: Baker Academic, 2004), 175–77.
[61]Ibid.
[62]Ibid., 176.

interpretation individualizing? Yes, but it is also collective, as the church is the aggregate of all who are convicted by the law and trust Jesus to have become a curse for them.

Timothy George deserves quotation:

> While the national and corporate character of the curse truly belongs to the background of this text, we must not allow this fact to blind us to the deeper doctrinal truth Paul was presenting here. What happened outside the gates of Jerusalem just a few decades before Paul wrote Galatians was not merely another episode in the history of Israel. It was an event of universal human, indeed cosmic, significance. While Paul posed the problem, as he had to, in Jewish terms of blessing and curse, law and faith, it is clear from Abraham on that God's dealings with Israel had paradigmatic meaning for all peoples everywhere. . . . Thus when Paul spoke of the curse of the law he was not thinking merely of Jews, anymore than when he showed how one becomes a true child of Abraham through faith he had only Gentiles in mind. Thus the "us" of 3:13—those whom Christ has redeemed from the curse of the law—are not merely Jewish Christians but instead all the children of God, Jews and Gentiles, slaves and freed ones, males and females, who are Abraham's seed and heirs according to the promise because they belong to Christ through faith (3:26–29).[63]

Colossians 2:14

This is another powerful penal substitution text. Paul, a physician of souls, diagnoses two spiritual diseases afflicting lost men and women, including the Colossians before salvation. The first is spiritual death: you "were dead in your trespasses." The second is moral impurity and uncleanness: you "were dead in . . . the uncircumcision of your flesh" (Col. 2:13). The apostle next reveals how God, the divine physician, graciously heals their diseases. His cure for spiritual death is regeneration: "God made [you] alive together with him" (v. 13). His cure for moral impurity is pardon for sin: ". . . having forgiven us all our trespasses" (v. 13).

How did God forgive us all our trespasses? Paul answers, ". . . by canceling the record of debt that stood against us with its legal demands" (v. 14). "Record of debt" translates χειρόγραφον (*cheirographon*), which "refers literally to something that is written by hand and more specifically to the certificate of indebtedness issued by the debtor in his or her own hand as an acknowledgment of debt," as Margaret McDonald explains well.[64]

---

[63] Timothy George, *Galatians*, The New American Commentary (np: Broadman and Holman, 1994), 233.
[64] Margaret Y. MacDonald, *Colossians and Ephesians*, Sacra Pagina 17 (Collegeville, MN: Liturgical Press, 2000), 102.

Paul provides more details concerning this note. The record of debt opposes us "with its legal demands." Paul uses the same expression in Ephesians 2:15, where it is rendered "the law of commandments expressed in *ordinances*." This demonstrates that it refers to the Ten Commandments.

We all signed, so to speak, a handwritten note confessing our disobedience to the commandments. Our record of debt with its legal demands "opposes us" because it exposes us as guilty lawbreakers. In a word, it condemns us. Paul says that God forgave us "by canceling the record of debt that stood against us with its legal demands" (Col. 2:14). The word "cancel" here means "blot out" or "erase" the debt. Though Paul may seem here to say that God merely overlooked our disobedience to the commandments and forgave us, this is not what Paul intends. The next words explain the way God canceled our moral debt: "This he set aside, nailing it to the cross" (v. 14).

Paul thus paints a dramatic picture of legal substitution. God forgave our transgressions by nailing our bill of indebtedness, recording our failure to keep the law, to Jesus's cross. Peter O'Brien summarizes:

> God has not only forgiven us all our sins but he also utterly removed the signed acknowledgment of our indebtedness. . . . This taking away was effected through blotting it out. . . . [the verb] means "to rub out," "wipe away" and so obliterate from sight, as writing on wax or other written records were removed. . . . God has canceled the bond by nailing it to the cross—this is a vivid way of saying that because Christ was nailed to the cross our debt has been completely forgiven.[65]

Paul draws his imagery from the Roman practice of nailing to crosses the charges for which the crucified were being executed, as was the case with Jesus's cross in John 19:19. Moo explains:

> In causing him to be nailed to the cross, God . . . has provided the full cancellation of the debt of obedience that we had incurred. Christ took upon himself the penalty that we were under because of our disobedience, and his death fully satisfied God's necessary demand for due punishment of that disobedience.[66]

Moo is correct. Paul paints a vivid picture of penal substitution. Michael Bird adds, "The penalty and curse of the Torah is undone as its punitive effects are absorbed in the flesh of the Son of God."[67]

---

[65]Peter T. O'Brien, *Colossians, Philemon*, Word Biblical Commentary (Waco, TX: Word, 1982), 126.

[66]Douglas J. Moo, *The Letters to the Colossians and to Philemon*, The Pillar New Testament Commentary (Grand Rapids: Eerdmans, 2008), 211–12.

[67]Michael F. Bird, *Colossians, Philemon*, New Covenant Commentary (Eugene, OR: Cascade, 2009), 81.

Paul abruptly shifts imagery in the next verse: "He disarmed the rulers and authorities and put them to open shame, by triumphing over them in him." God is portrayed as our mighty champion, who through Christ's cross defeats and humiliates the demons. We will further explore Colossians 2:15 and its Christus Victor picture of Christ's saving deeds in the chapter "Christ Our Victor."

Penal Substitution in 1 Peter

In two texts, Peter joins the chorus of biblical witnesses to Jesus's having accomplished penal substitution on the cross.

1 Peter 2:24

Peter's placement of his discussion of Christ's sufferings is indicative of the grace of God. In a section in which Peter discusses submission to authority—citizens to civil government, slaves to masters, and wives to husbands (1 Pet. 1:13–2:6)—he speaks of Christ in the context of slaves (2:21–24). God is concerned for the lowly. Peter presents Jesus as an example of suffering unjustly while doing the will of God: "For to this you have been called, because Christ also suffered for you, leaving you an example, so that you might follow in his steps" (2:21). Peter explains that Christ did not sin in deed or word, even when reviled and suffering (vv. 22–23).

But Peter cannot help himself. Though in context he sets forth Christ chiefly as an example, he is constrained to sound more redemptive notes when talking of Jesus's death: "He himself bore our sins in his body on the tree" (v. 24). Throughout verses 22–25, the apostle has in mind Isaiah 53:9, 7, 4, 11, 5, 6 (in that order). Paul Achtemeier draws attention to Isaiah's influence on verse 24: "Our author sees in Jesus' death a vicarious suffering by which a new life freed from sin is made possible, a theology already nascent in the description of the suffering servant in Isaiah 53 from which this verse is largely drawn."[68]

This is correct, including the emphasis on Jesus suffering vicariously, as J. N. D. Kelly highlights:

> Here, as in Isa. 53:12, "bearing sins" means taking the blame for sins, accepting the punishment due for them, and so securing their putting away. . . . The force of *in his body* is that what Christ did He did as man, sharing our human nature. The implied teaching is that His sufferings and death were vicarious; as our representative He endured the penalties which *our sins* merited.[69]

---

[68] Paul J. Achtemeier, *1 Peter*, Hermeneia (Minneapolis: Fortress, 1996), 203.
[69] J. N. D. Kelly, *A Commentary on the Epistles of Peter and Jude*, Thornapple Commentaries (Grand Rapids: Baker, 1969), 123.

First Peter 2:24, then, is a proof that Jesus is our legal substitute. It is important to realize that the apostle's goal here in teaching substitution is moral: "He himself bore our sins in his body on the tree, that we might die to sin and live to righteousness" (v. 24). Jesus died in our place to remove our sins and also to transform us. It is this latter idea that Peter stresses. He speaks of our "dying" to sin, because Christ has broken its stranglehold over us. He speaks of our "living" to righteousness because Christ, who died in our place, is alive from the dead.

Peter immediately reinforces the idea of substitution with another reference to Isaiah 53: "By his wounds you have been healed" (1 Pet. 2:24). Isaiah had written: "And with his stripes we are healed" (53:5). Peter Davids explains: "This death was vicarious, for it was 'our sins' that he bore. This fact is further underlined in the last clause of the verse (now shifting to Isa. 53:5), that his wounds (the welts and bruises one would have as a result of a blow with a fist or whip) have brought healing to us."[70] We have been healed spiritually by Jesus's suffering wounds. Grudem is clear: "Here again is the idea of the punishment of a substitute: the punishment deserved by us Christ took on himself and thus made us (morally and spiritually) well."[71]

1 Peter 3:18

After urging believers to suffer for doing good, Peter returns to a familiar theme—that of Christ's suffering. He is straightforward: "For Christ also suffered once for sins, the righteous for the unrighteous" (v. 18). When Jesus calls us to suffer, he is not asking us to do something that he has not experienced. He too suffered. In this way our suffering is like his, and Peter implies that Christ is our example in suffering (something he explicitly states in 2:21).

But, more importantly, Christ's suffering is also unlike ours. He suffered "once," and that suffering was unique, which is not true of ours. Jesus's suffering was unique in at least three ways. First, his suffering is once for all time, as Thomas Schreiner explains:

> This interpretation is strengthened by the phrase "once for all" (*hapax*). The suffering of Christ was unique and definitive in that he offered himself as a sin offering once for all. The distinctiveness of Christ's sacrifice is featured here, for even though believers suffer, they do not suffer for the sins of others, nor does their suffering constitute a sacrifice for others.[72]

---

[70]Peter H. Davids, *The First Epistle of Peter*, The New International Commentary on the New Testament (Grand Rapids: Eerdmans, 1990), 113.
[71]Wayne Grudem, *1 Peter*, Tyndale New Testament Commentaries (Grand Rapids: Eerdmans, 1988), 132.
[72]Thomas R. Schreiner, *1, 2 Peter, Jude*, The New American Commentary (Nashville: Broadman and Holman, 2003), 181–82.

Second, the most significant difference between the suffering of Christians and that of Christ's is that, unlike ours, his is redemptive. "Christ also suffered once for sins." Peter gives more detail: "the righteous for the unrighteous" (v. 18). The Greek is instructive, for it reads, "the righteous one for the unrighteous ones." Jesus died for sinners. He died in their place. Peter Davids affirms, "Christ's substitutionary death for those who deserved death comes across clearly."[73] Schreiner brings out the substitutionary force of the apostle's words: "Since Christ suffered as the sinless one (1 John 2:1; 2 Cor. 5:21), his suffering was unique. Indeed, only Christ suffered 'for the unrighteous' (ὑπὲρ ἀδίκων, *hyper adikōn*). His death was vicarious and substitutionary and the basis upon which people become right with God."[74]

Third, because Christ's once-for-all suffering is redemptive, it has great results. "Christ also suffered once for sins, the righteous for the unrighteous, that he might bring us to God" (1 Pet. 3:18). Christ, as Mediator of the new covenant, died a redemptive death for those who were far away from God to take them to God. As Davids expresses it, "Jesus died in order that, so to speak, he might reach across the gulf between God and humanity and, taking our hand, lead us across the territory of the enemy into the presence of the Father who called us."[75]

Therefore, Peter belongs with those who confess Jesus as our penal substitute.

Penal Substitution in 1 John

Two passages in 1 John pertain to propitiation and therefore penal substitution:

> He is the propitiation for our sins, and not for ours only but also for the sins of the whole world. (1 John 2:2)

> In this is love, not that we have loved God but that he loved us and sent his Son to be the propitiation for our sins. (1 John 4:10)

Of course, the matter is debated. Some insist that these references in 1 John speak of expiation, not propitiation.[76] In expiation the cross is directed toward sins to put them away from God's sight; it thus has to do with the purging of sin. In propitiation, the cross is directed toward God's justice, enabling him to "be just and the justifier of the one who has faith in Jesus" (Rom. 3:26). It thus has to do with satisfying God's justice so that he can retain his holy character

---

[73]Davids, *The First Epistle of Peter*, 136.
[74]Schreiner, *1, 2 Peter, Jude*, 182.
[75]Davids, *The First Epistle of Peter*, 136.
[76]See ad loc. R. Alan Culpepper, *The Gospel and Letters of John* (Nashville: Abingdon, 1998); and John Painter, *1, 2, and 3 John*, Sacra Pagina 18 (Collegeville, MN: Liturgical Press, 2002).

and still forgive sinners. My view is that Christ's saving work accomplishes both propitiation and expiation and that the former is especially in view in 1 John 2:2 and 4:10, as their contexts bear out.

1 John 2:2

John writes to prevent his readers from sinning (1 John 2:1). He promotes the active pursuit of holiness, but knows that they will not attain sinless perfection in this life (1:8, 10) and urges daily confession of sin (v. 9). But confession, as important as it is for Christians to enjoy forgiveness, is not the basis of that forgiveness. The basis is the work of Christ. John points to Jesus's person and work when he writes, "But if anyone does sin, we have an advocate with the Father, Jesus Christ the righteous" (2:1).

Jesus, the sinless one, is our advocate and intercessor, as Yarbrough explains: "'Advocate' in the legal sense or 'intercessor' or 'mediator' are therefore apt translations of the word."[77] Jesus is our advocate and Mediator with the Father when we sin. Marshall sums up the sense: Jesus "can, as it were, plead his own righteousness before God and ask that sinners be forgiven on the basis of his righteous act."[78]

John extends this thought into the next verse: "He is the propitiation for our sins" (2:2). In this context *hilasmos* is correctly translated by the ESV as "propitiation." Marshall explains:

> The picture . . . is of Jesus pleading the cause of guilty sinners before a judge who is being petitioned to pardon their acknowledged sins. In order that forgiveness may be granted, there is an action in respect of the sins which has the effect of rendering God favorable to the sinner. We may, if we wish, say that the sins are cancelled out by the action in question. This means that the one action has the double effect of expiating the sin and thereby propitiating God.[79]

John continues: "Jesus Christ the righteous . . . is the propitiation for our sins, and not for ours only but also for the sins of the whole world" (vv. 1–2). There is thus a universalizing sense to Christ's atonement. Yarbrough strikes the right balance when he denies that this entails an absolute universalism and affirms that Christ's death is for the whole world "in the sense that it provides the

---

[77] Robert W. Yarbrough, *1–3 John*, Baker Exegetical Commentary on the New Testament (Grand Rapids: Baker Academic, 2008), 76.
[78] I. Howard Marshall, *The Epistles of John*, The New International Commentary on the New Testament (Grand Rapids: Eerdmans, 1978), 117.
[79] Ibid., 118.

basis throughout all human history for God the Father to extend patience and forgiveness to those who merit his rejection . . . until the day Christ appears."[80]

1 John 4:10

John returns to the idea of propitiation in one of the Bible's greatest passages on God's love. John exhorts his readers to love one another because God is love and because regeneration evidences itself in love for brothers and sisters in Christ (1 John 4:7). The negation is also true: a lack of love is a bad sign because God is love (v. 8). If we ask how God has demonstrated his love supremely, John has a ready answer: "In this the love of God was made manifest among us, that God sent his only Son into the world, so that we might live through him" (v. 9).

But how exactly has Christ revealed God's love? Again, John is not lacking a reply: "In this is love, not that we have loved God but that he loved us and sent his Son to be the propitiation for our sins" (v. 10). This is the fourth time we meet propitiation in the New Testament (along with Rom. 3:25; Heb. 2:17; and 1 John 2:2). Here John appeals to propitiation to define God's love. James Denney's words hit the mark:

> So far from finding any kind of contrast between love and propitiation, the apostle can convey no idea of love to anyone except by pointing to the propitiation—love is what is manifested there; and he can give no account of propitiation but by saying, "Behold what manner of love." For him, to say "God is love" is exactly the same as to say, "God has in His Son made atonement for the sin of the world." If the propitiatory death of Jesus is eliminated from the love of God, it might be unfair to say that the love of God is robbed of all meaning, but it is certainly robbed of its apostolic meaning. It has no longer that meaning which goes deeper than sin, sorrow, and death, and which recreates life in the adoring joy, wonder, and purity of the first Epistle of John.[81]

John's following words motivate Christians to mutual love. Yarbrough writes well: "Christ's costly propitiatory atonement uncaps an artesian well of selflessness in which believers find resources for sacrificial care for each other."[82]

John Stott labors to distinguish the biblical understanding of propitiation from its pagan counterpart. He cites three critical points that, though long, are worthy of quotation:

---

[80]Yarbrough, *1–3 John*, 79. He also argues correctly that this universalizing is compatible with particularity (ibid., 80–81).

[81]James Denney, *The Death of Christ* (London, 1951), 152, cited in Marshall, *The Epistles of John*, 215.

[82]Yarbrough, *1–3 John*, 240.

First, the reason why a propitiation is necessary is that sin arouses the wrath of God. . . . His anger is neither mysterious nor irrational. It is never unpredictable, but always predictable, because it is provoked by evil and evil alone. . . .

Secondly, who makes the propitiation? . . . God himself "presented" (NIV) or "put forward" (RSV) Jesus Christ as a propitiatory sacrifice (Rom. 3:25). It is not that we loved God, but that he loved us and sent his Son as a propitiation for our sins (1 Jn. 4:10). . . . Christ died for us because God loved us. If it is God's wrath which needed to be propitiated, it is God's love which did the propitiating. . . . What the propitiation changed was his dealings with us. . . .

Thirdly, what was the propitiatory sacrifice? . . . And the person God offered was not somebody else, whether a human person or an angel or even his Son considered as somebody distinct from or external to himself. No, he offered himself. In giving his Son, he was giving himself.

So then, God himself is at the heart of our answer to all three questions about the divine propitiation. It is God himself who in holy wrath needs to be propitiated, God himself who in holy love undertook to do the propitiating, and God himself who in the person of his Son died for the propitiation of our sins.[83]

I conclude that 1 John 2:2 and 4:10 are sufficient reasons for the epistle's inclusion among the New Testament witnesses to penal substitution.

Objections to Penal Substitution

I agree with the assessment of Schreiner when he says:

I conclude that the penal substitution view needs defending today because it is scandalous to some scholars. We know that it is scandalous to radical feminists who see it as a form of divine child abuse, or to scholars like Denny Weaver who promote nonviolent atonement. Indeed, among all the views of the atonement, penal substitution provokes the most negative response.[84]

Because penal substitution has been the target of many objections, including some from within the evangelical community, I will deal with the main objections before drawing conclusions.[85]

---

[83]John R. W. Stott, *The Cross of Christ* (Downers Grove, IL: InterVarsity, 1986), 173–75.

[84]Thomas R. Schreiner, "Penal Substitution View," in *The Nature of the Atonement*, ed. James Beilby and Paul R. Eddy (Downers Grove, IL: IVP Academic, 2006), 72.

[85]I learned from Marshall, "The Theology of the New Testament," in Tidball, Hilborn, and Thacker, *The Atonement Debate*, 61–63; Garry Williams, "Penal Substitution: A Response to Recent Criticisms," in *The Atonement Debate*, 172–91; and the most extensive treatment, "Answering the Critics," in Jeffrey, Ovey, and Sach, *Pierced for Our Transgressions*, 205–328.

Objection 1: It Was Not Taught until the Reformation

One objection says that penal substitution was invented by the Reformers. It is true that Luther taught the doctrine, along with Christus Victor,[86] and that it was the prominent atonement motif of John Calvin.[87] But that does not mean that it was unheard of before, as Marshall explains:

> A distinction must be made between the existence of the doctrine and its prominence. The doctrine of penal substitution may not have been prominent before the Reformation, but this is quite different from saying that it was unknown. Thus, while Green and Baker can show how great stress is laid on the doctrine of recapitulation in Irenaeus, they also rightly point out that Irenaeus includes statements of propitiation.[88]

Objection 2: It Is a Product of Western Individualism

Green and Baker claim that penal substitution coheres "fully with the emphasis on autonomous individualism characteristic of so much of the modern middle class in the West."[89] Garry Williams shows that this objection is strange, historically inaccurate, and ironic.

First, it is strange because penal substitution by its very definition relies heavily on corporate categories and denies individualism. "No proponent of penal substitution has ever conceived of it as the transfer of punishment between two wholly unrelated persons."[90] Rather, Christ is viewed as the covenant and corporate head who dies in the place of his people. Christ takes the curse of the covenant on himself to redeem those under its curse (Gal. 3:13). And in its characteristic formulation, penal substitution is combined with union with Christ. To choose three examples, Eusebius of Caesarea, John Calvin, and John Owen all maintain that penal substitution depends on a mystical union between Christ and his people, a far cry from modern individualism.[91]

Second, the charge is historically inaccurate because there are examples of the church fathers employing union with Christ to explain God's justice in penal substitution. Listen to a powerful quotation from Eusebius of Caesarea that Williams adduces:

---

[86]For Luther, see Paul Althaus, *The Theology of Martin Luther* (Philadelphia: Fortress, 1966), 202–11.
[87]For Calvin, see my "Calvin on Christ's Saving Work," in *Theological Guide to Calvin's Institutes*, ed. David W. Hall and Peter A. Lillback (Phillipsburg, NJ: P&R, 2009), 230–32, 245–46.
[88]Marshall, "The Theology of the New Testament," 61–62. Marshall cites Green and Baker, *Recovering the Scandal of the Cross*, 121.
[89]Green and Baker, *Recovering the Scandal of the Cross*, 213.
[90]Williams, "Penal Substitution: A Response to Recent Criticisms," 181.
[91]Ibid., 181–82.

And how can He make our sins His own, and be said to bear our iniquities, except by our being regarded as His body. . . . And the Lamb of God not only did this, but was chastised on our behalf . . . and suffered a penalty . . . He did not owe, but which we owed because of the multitude of our sins. . . . and drew down on Himself the apportioned curse, being made a curse for us. And what is that but the price of our souls? And so the oracle says in our person: "By his stripes we were healed," and "The Lord delivered him for our sins," with the result that uniting Himself to us and us to Himself, and appropriating our sufferings, He can say, "I said, Lord, have mercy on me, heal my soul, for I have sinned against thee."[92]

This is Patristic penal substitution, undergirded by union with Christ, which tells how the sufferings of the One become the salvation of the many. It is not accurate, then, to regard substitution as the product of modern Western individualism.

Third, the charge is ironic because it is the critics of penal substitution who have embraced individualism. Williams illustrates this with a quotation from the Church of England's 1995 Doctrine Commission report, *The Mystery of Salvation*: "In the moral sphere each person must be responsible for their own obligations. Moral responsibility is ultimately incommunicable." Williams explains that this report rejects penal substitution "because the authors endorse this species of individualism."[93] If those prognosticators are correct who predict that we are heading into a postmodern age that will emphasize community, then Williams surprises us: "Penal substitution has a bright future and will preach well."[94]

Objection 3: It Contradicts Jesus's Teaching to Turn the Other Cheek

In reaction to Reformation teaching, Faustus Socinus in the seventeenth century brought arguments against penal substitution that are still used today. One of them was that penal substitution involves retributive justice and this makes God inconsistent with himself. Jesus teaches his followers not to oppose evil but to turn the other cheek when slapped (Matt. 5:39). The idea that God exacts punishment in the cross, therefore, contradicts Jesus's plain teaching.

Steve Chalke, a respected British preacher and author, writing in 2004, agrees and claims that such a view makes God hypocritical: "If the cross has anything to do with penal substitution, then Jesus' teaching becomes a divine case of 'do as I say, not as I do.' I, for one, believe that God practices what he preaches!"[95]

---

[92]Ibid., 182.
[93]Ibid., 182–83.
[94]Ibid.
[95]Steve Chalke, "Cross Purposes," *Christianity* (September 2004): 44, cited in ibid., 173.

Garry Williams decisively answers both Socinus and Chalke by presenting a clear counterexample. It is found in Romans 12, where Paul sharply differentiates how justice works for God's relations with his human creatures and for their relations with each other. Paul, like Jesus, prohibits human beings from taking revenge against their fellows. Does he then urge them to follow God's example? No, just the opposite:

> Repay no one evil for evil. . . . Beloved, never avenge yourselves, but leave it to the wrath of God, for it is written, "Vengeance is mine, I will repay, says the Lord." To the contrary, if your enemy is hungry, feed him; if he is thirsty, give him something to drink; for by so doing you will heap burning coals on his head. Do not be overcome by evil, but overcome evil with good. (Rom. 12:17, 19–21)

Williams drives home the point:

> Thus, Paul denies vengeance in the sphere of relationships between individual people and at the same time ascribes it to God, who shares it in limited part with the ruling authorities. Where Chalke infers that God would never do what he tells us not to do, Paul argues exactly the opposite. God tells us not to do what he does precisely because he does it. God says, "Do as I say, not as I do," and justly so, since he is God and we are not.[96]

Objection 4: It Makes Punishment Impersonal Rather than Personal

Critics view retributive punishment, and penal substitution, which is based on it, as impersonal and therefore less than biblical. Stephen Travis implies as much when he writes, opposing retributive punishment, "The judgment of God is to be seen not primarily in terms of retribution, whereby people are 'paid back' according to their deeds, but in terms of relationship or non-relationship to Christ."[97] Travis views retribution and relationship as incompatible. Therefore, penal substitution is an impersonal transaction whereby God punishes Christ for sinners. And that is an unworthy view of the atonement.

But Travis's view is mistaken. Retributive punishment and relationship are not necessarily opposed. Retribution, according to Hugo Grotius (in *De jure belli ac pacis*), involves two aspects: "an ill which is responsive to an ill" and "the infliction of some kind of proportional pain."[98] But based on these two aspects, punishment can be both retributive and relational. Such is the case where

---

[96] Williams, "Penal Substitution: A Response to Recent Criticisms," 174.

[97] Stephen H. Travis, preface to *Christ and the Judgment of God: Divine Retribution in the New Testament* (Basingstoke, UK: Marshall Pickering, 1986).

[98] Williams, "Penal Substitution: A Response to Recent Criticisms," 178.

punishment is deserved for evil character or behavior and where punishment involves pain. Now separation from the blessed presence of Christ is surely pain. "The category of exclusion from a loving relationship with Christ *is* a relational category," as Williams insists, for "the sinner stands in a relationship of hostile confrontation with Christ."[99]

Objection 5: It Misrepresents God as Needing to Be Appeased before He Forgives

Critics sometimes portray advocates of penal substitution as maintaining that it is the cross of Christ that causes God to abandon his wrath and to extend forgiveness. Though responsible proponents of substitution do not hold this, the accusation continues, as Joel Green demonstrates: "Over against the model of penal substitutionary atonement, then, God's saving act is not his response to Jesus' willing death."[100]

But this is itself a misrepresentation, as Marshall shows:

> The motive for Jesus' death is stated to be the loving purpose of God, and there is not the faintest hint in the New Testament that Jesus died to persuade God to forgive sinners. On the contrary, his death is the way in which God acts in his grace and mercy. Hence the death of Jesus is not a means of appeasing a Father who is unable or unwilling to forgive. It is what God himself does while we are yet sinners. . . . It is true that the wrath of God is operative against sinners who have not accepted the gospel, but it is not true that God's wrath has to be appeased before he will be merciful.[101]

Objection 6: It Pits the Father against the Son

Green and Baker oppose unsophisticated forms of penal substitution when they write, "Any atonement theology that assumes, against Paul, that in the cross God did something 'to' Jesus is . . . an affront to the Christian doctrine of the triune God."[102] They object to views that present God as subject and Christ only as object. But thoughtful proponents of penal substitution do not do this. Listen to Stott: "We must never make Christ the object of God's punishment or God the object of Christ's persuasion, for both God and Christ were subjects not objects, taking the initiative together to save sinners."[103]

---

[99]Ibid., italics original.
[100]Joel B. Green, "Must We Imagine the Atonement in Penal Substitutionary Terms?," in Tidball, Hilborn, and Thacker, *The Atonement Debate*, 158.
[101]Marshall, "The Theology of the New Testament," 62.
[102]Green and Baker, *Recovering the Scandal of the Cross*, 57.
[103]Stott, *The Cross of Christ*, 151.

Stott's words reflect a commitment to the Christian doctrine of the Trinity. This doctrine is the reason why reflective penal substitution advocates do not present matters as Green and Baker imply. The Father, Son, and Holy Spirit are one holy Trinity, and although they must be distinguished, they must never be separated. So, though only Jesus died on the cross, there is a sense in which the cross is the action of all three Trinitarian persons. "In Christ God was reconciling the world to himself" (2 Cor. 5:19). And "Christ . . . through the eternal Spirit offered himself without blemish to God" (Heb. 9:14). The work of salvation in Jesus's death and resurrection is the work of the triune God.

Furthermore, Scripture presents Jesus as both the subject and the willing object of the cross. Jesus is subject, in that he voluntarily goes to die, as the following passages attest:

> He poured out his soul to death. (Isa. 53:12)

> I lay down my life that I may take it up again. No one takes it from me, but I lay it down of my own accord. (John 10:17–18)

> Then I said, "Behold, I have come to do your will, O God." (Heb. 10:7; see v. 9)

Jesus the subject was also the willing object of God's action on the cross as the following passages attest:

> The LORD has laid on him
>   the iniquity of us all. (Isa. 53:6)

> It was the will of the LORD to crush him. (Isa. 53:10)

> . . . Christ Jesus, whom God put forward as a propitiation by his blood. (Rom. 3:24–25)

> By sending his own Son in the likeness of sinful flesh and for sin, he condemned sin in the flesh. (Rom. 8:3)

> For our sake he made him to be sin who knew no sin, so that in him we might become the righteousness of God. (2 Cor. 5:21)

It is striking that the five passages just cited occur in penal contexts. Williams draws a sound conclusion:

There is, therefore, biblical testimony to the action of the Father toward the Son, specifically in laying iniquity on him and condemning it in him. To state what ought to be obvious: he punished the sin that had been transferred to Christ, not Christ regarded in and of himself, with whom in this very act he was well pleased.[104]

In fact, Williams goes on to explain that, as long as we qualify our words, all three persons of the Trinity can be subjects and willing objects of their actions. A denial of this entails the ancient error of modalism.

Furthermore, if we deny that the persons of the Trinity can be at once the willing subject and object of one another's actions, then we must deny not only penal substitution but also the love of each person for the others and the sending of the Son, who comes willingly. Ultimately, the logical implication of the denial that one person of the Trinity can act on another is the denial of the distinction between them—namely, modalism.[105]

Objection 7: It Neglects the Life of Jesus

While speaking against penal substitution, Gregory Boyd confesses: "I frankly struggle to see how it's even relevant to any other aspect of Jesus' life and ministry."[106] Even if Scripture did not provide what Boyd struggles to see, it would be possible for systematic theology carefully to do so. But that is not necessary, because four of the passages studied in this chapter connect Jesus's sinless life with his death on the cross regarded as a penal substitution.

This is the case with Isaiah 53. The Servant is sinless in action, word, and character:

> He had done no violence,
>   and there was no deceit in his mouth. . . .
> [he is] the righteous one, my servant. (Isa. 53:9, 11)

The same sinless Servant suffers in the place of others, enduring the suffering that they deserve, as Isaiah says twice:

> And he shall bear their iniquities.
> . . . yet he bore the sin of many. (vv. 11–12)

Paul, Peter, and John assert the same truth:

---

[104]Williams, "Penal Substitution: A Response to Recent Criticisms," 180.
[105]Ibid., 181.
[106]Gregory A. Boyd, "Christus Victor View," in Beilby and Eddy, The Nature of the Atonement, 100.

For our sake he made him to be sin who knew no sin so that in him we might become the righteousness of God. (2 Cor. 5:21)

For Christ also suffered once for sins, the righteous for the unrighteous, that he might bring us to God. (1 Pet. 3:18)

. . . Jesus Christ the righteous. He is the propitiation for our sins, and not for ours only but also for the sins of the whole world. (1 John 2:1–2)

Note how each apostle speaks of Christ's sinless earthly life. Paul calls Jesus "him . . . who knew no sin" (2 Cor. 5:21), Peter calls him "the righteous" one (1 Pet. 3:18), and John, "Jesus Christ the righteous" (1 John 2:1). Notice also how in these texts the three apostles speak of Christ's life while teaching penal substitution, as earlier pages of this chapter demonstrated. I conclude that this objection to penal substitution is without merit.

Objection 8: It Has No Place for Christ's Resurrection

Opponents of penal substitution insist that, "because of the singular focus on penal satisfaction, Jesus' resurrection is not really necessary according to this model."[107] I admit that proponents of penal substitution have not always given sufficient attention to Jesus's saving resurrection, but the abuse of a doctrine does not disprove the doctrine. I will make an exegetical and a theological argument.

First is the exegetical argument. It is well known that the legal themes of substitution and justification go together. Paul connects them to Jesus's resurrection when he speaks of "Jesus our Lord, who was delivered up for our trespasses and raised for our justification" (Rom. 4:24–25). Because the curse resulting from Adam's sin was penal, bringing death, its reversal is also penal, bringing life. That reversal entails Jesus's vicarious death and resurrection.

Marshall exegetes Romans 4:25:

In the cross God's condemnation of sin is demonstrated and carried out, Christ bears the sin and so God declares that sin has been taken away; and Christ is representatively justified so that those who believe and are united with him share in this justification. Hence, the resurrection is essential to the saving act in that it is not merely God saying that Christ has done what is necessary; rather, God himself has to carry out the act of pardon on the basis of what God has done, and

---

[107]Green and Baker, *Recovering the Scandal of the Cross*, 148.

he does so. Thus Christ was raised for our justification, and, without this raising of Christ, we would not be justified.[108]

Second is the theological argument. The great majority of Reformed theologians have taught that Christ's lifelong obedience to the Father and the law is part of his saving work. As Jeffrey, Ovey, and Sach argue, "This integrates perfectly with the doctrine of penal substitution. The righteousness of Jesus' life was imputed . . . to us, so that we might be justified, or declared righteous by God, and stand pure and blameless before him."[109]

Objection 9: It Cannot Account for the Cosmic Scope of Christ's Death and Resurrection

Under the heading "Penal Substitution and Anemic Salvation," Joel Green writes, "An exaggerated focus on an objective atonement and on salvation as transaction . . . obscures the social and cosmological dimensions of salvation."[110] Critics have complained that substitutionary atonement is so concerned with the salvation of individuals that it detracts attention from the larger biblical story, which involves redemption of the cosmos that God created.

While Scripture insists that an individuals' relationship with God is a matter near to his heart—"the Son of God . . . loved me and gave himself for me" (Gal. 2:20)—Scripture also is concerned with the deliverance of the creation from the curse: "The creation itself will be set free from its bondage to corruption" (Rom. 8:21). What does this deliverance have to do with penal substitution?

Penal substitution has much to do with it! The curse resulting from the fall of our first parents was penal: the curses that God pronounces on the serpent, Adam and Eve, and the ground all were penalties for the primal sin. The result was disorder everywhere, among human beings and in the rest of creation itself. Paul explains, "The creation was subjected to futility" and "the whole creation has been groaning together in the pains of childbirth until now" (Rom. 8:20, 22).

The end of the Bible's story reveals that the curse has been removed: "No longer will there be anything accursed" (Rev. 22:3). What occurred to deliver the creation from God's curse? The biblical answer is that Christ died and arose to remove the penalty on creation. God's remedy for the penal curse on the creation is the penal substitution of his Son. Williams summarizes:

---

[108]I. Howard Marshall, *Aspects of the Atonement: Cross and Resurrection in the Reconciling of God and Humanity* (London: Paternoster, 2007), 90.

[109]Jeffrey, Ovey, and Sach, *Pierced for Our Transgressions*, 213.

[110]Green, "Must We Imagine the Atonement in Penal Substitutionary Terms?," 166.

Penal substitution teaches that on the cross, the Lord Jesus Christ exhausted the disordering curse in our place. It is for this reason that there can be resurrection and new creation, because the obstacle to it has been removed. Penal substitution is therefore the prerequisite for a strong doctrine of the resurrection as the beginning of the new creation, not a detractor from it. If the penalty had not been borne by Christ, then the creation is still under the curse, still disrupted, and incapable of being renewed.[111]

Paul in Romans 8:18–23 ties the final redemption of believers in Christ to the redemption of the creation, as Jeffrey, Ovey, and Sach bring out:

> It is as Christians—"the children of God"—are finally redeemed that the whole of creation will be made new. Accordingly, by setting forth the solution to sin and guilt in individual human lives, penal substitution provides the means by which the whole cosmos will one day be transformed. As Christ endured and exhausted God's judgment in our place and thereby "redeemed us from the curse of the law by becoming a curse for us" (Gal. 3:13), he provided also for the lifting of the curse on the whole of the created order.[112]

Objection 10: It Undermines Moral Development in Believers' Lives

A common criticism of opponents of penal substitution is summed up by Green: "The prevailing model of the atonement, focused as it is on the individual, on a forensic judgment . . . is an obstacle to a thoroughgoing soteriology oriented toward holiness of life. . . . Is the work of salvation as transformation unrelated to the atoning work of Christ?"[113] But such objections overlook the link between substitution and union with Christ, the heart of the application of salvation. Union with Christ is essential to penal substitution, for it establishes the justice of the transfer of our sin to Christ, as John Owen explained:

> He [God] might punish the elect either in their own persons, or in their surety standing in their room and stead; and when he is punished, they also are punished: for in this point of view the federal head and those represented by him are not considered as distinct, but as one; for although they are not one in respect of personal unity, they are, however, one,—that is, one body in mystical union, yea *one mystical Christ*;—namely the surety is the head, those represented by him the members; and when the head is punished, the members also are punished.[114]

---

[111]Williams, "Penal Substitution: A Response to Recent Criticisms," 184.

[112]Jeffrey, Ovey, and Sach, *Pierced for Our Transgressions*, 312.

[113]Green, "Must We Imagine the Atonement in Penal Substitutionary Terms?,"166–67.

[114]John Owen, *A Dissertation on Divine Justice* 2.5, in *Works of John Owen*, 10:598, italics original, cited in Williams, "Penal Substitution: A Response to Recent Criticisms," 181.

Owen is correct. Scripture ties together Christ's atonement and the Christian life by virtue of union with Christ. Romans 6 provides a famous example. Paul recoils in horror at the suggestion of his enemies that his gospel promotes license (Rom. 6:1–2). He asks, "How can we who died to sin still live in it?" He proceeds to explain that the fundamental meaning of Christian baptism is union with Christ in his saving death and resurrection (vv. 3–4). The apostle teaches that Christ's substitutionary death delivers believers from the power of sin as well as its penalty: "We have died with Christ. . . . So you must consider yourselves dead to sin and alive to God in Christ Jesus" (6:8, 11; cf. 3:25–26; 8:1–3).

Williams explains:

> This idea of being united to Christ in his death is integral to penal substitution. Union with Christ explains the justice of the transfer of sin to Christ. . . . If we have died with him as he died, as he bore our penalty for us, so we must reckon ourselves dead to sin. The foundational doctrine of union with Christ forges an indissoluble link between penal substitution and personal sanctification.[115]

Objection 11: It Is Cosmic Child Abuse

A last objection assumes that it is wrong for a parent to inflict pain on a child and that in the traditional Christian understanding the Father inflicted pain on Christ on the cross, thereby giving an unjust example that promotes abuse.

There are a number of problems with this view. First, Jesus was a Son but not a minor when he died. Second, "Jesus died to bring glory to himself (e.g. John 17:1 . . .) and to save his people (e.g. Rom. 5:8 . . .), as well as to glorify his Father. By contract, child abuse is carried out solely for the gratification of the abuser," as Jeffrey, Ovey, and Sach remind us.[116]

Third, this criticism is misplaced because it fails to recognize that the initiation of the cross was the decision of the Trinity. The Son died willingly to rescue the lost. "In Christ God [the Father] was reconciling the world to himself" (2 Cor. 5:19). Marshall illustrates the point well:

> A parent who puts herself into the breach and dies to save her child from a burning house is considered praiseworthy. The God who suffers and dies in the person of Jesus for human sin belongs in the same category. It is true that the concept of

---

[115]Williams, "Penal Substitution: A Response to Recent Criticisms," 184–85. Howard Marshall offers additional help: "For a rebuttal of the objection that salvation by penal substitution does nothing to change the sinner, see my discussion of how the substitution of Christ identifies the believer with him in *New Testament Theology* (Downers Grove, Ill./Leicester: IVP and Apollos, 2004), 223–26."

[116]Jeffrey, Ovey, and Sach, *Pierced for Our Transgressions*, 230.

God the Son suffering and dying is paradoxical and incomprehensible, and we have to recognize that fact, but that is what Scripture says.[117]

Fourth, when opponents of penal substitution use this criticism, they must remember that as originally put forth by radical feminists, it attacked not only penal substitution but the Christian doctrine of the atonement in general. Listen to Joanne Carlson Brown and Rebecca Parker:

> The central image of Christ on the cross as the savior of the world communicates the message that suffering is redemptive. . . . The message is complicated further by the theology that says Christ suffered in obedience to his Father's will. Divine child abuse is paraded as salvific and the child who suffers "without even raising his voice" is lauded as the hope of the world.[118]

If accepted, this argument proves too much. Williams's analysis is correct: as originally made, this criticism of penal substitution attacks

> the general idea that the Father willed the *suffering* of the Son, not the specific idea that he willed the penal substitutionary suffering of the Son. . . . For many feminists, their criticism results in the rejection of Christianity because the religion undeniably involves the idea that God purposed the sufferings of Christ. . . . In the end, if purposed redemptive suffering is regarded as unacceptable, Christianity has to go.[119]

Do not misunderstand. I am not accusing evangelicals and others who use the "divine child abuse" argument of necessarily abandoning the Christian faith. I am pointing out, however, that they have strange bedfellows. If pressed, this argument leads to the rejection not only of penal substitution but of Christianity itself. That fact suggests that its evangelical proponents need to rethink this argument.

Connecting the Dots

After studying Scripture's witness to penal substitution and answering objections to it, we are ready for a systematic summary.

Texts

We have studied the following passages: Genesis 8:21; Exodus 12:13; 34:6–7; Leviticus 1:9; 2:1–2; 3:3, 5; 4:29, 31; 16:21–22; Isaiah 52:13–53:12; Mark 10:45;

---

[117]Marshall, "The Theology of the New Testament," 62–63.
[118]Cited in Williams, "Penal Substitution: A Response to Recent Criticisms," 185.
[119]Ibid., 185–86.

Romans 3:25–26; 8:1–4; 2 Corinthians 5:21; Galatians 3:13; Colossians 2:14; 1 Peter 2:24; 3:18; 1 John 2:2; and 4:10.

Sphere

This picture of Christ's saving accomplishment comes from the sphere of law and involves court, Judge, accuser and accused, verdict, condemnation, justification, and adoption.

Background

The Old Testament background includes "a pleasing aroma to the LORD," the Passover lamb, the character of Yahweh in Exodus 34:6–7, the two goats of the Day of Atonement, and the suffering Servant of the Lord of Isaiah 52:13–53:12.

Definition

Schreiner offers a good definition:

> The Father, because of his love for human beings, sent his Son (who offered himself willingly and gladly) to satisfy God's justice, so that Christ took the place of sinners. The punishment and penalty we deserved was laid on Jesus Christ instead of us, so that in the cross both God's holiness and love are manifested.[120]

Need

Humanity's need for Christ our penal substitute is our guilt before a just and holy God. Because of Adam's original sin and our own actual sins we are condemned before God's judgment seat (Rom. 5:12–19; 1:18–3:30). In a word, the need is our deserving condemnation due to sin.

Initiator

The initiator of penal substitution is always God, sometimes the Father (Isa. 53:10; Rom. 3:25; 8:3; 2 Cor. 5:21; Col. 2:14; 1 John 4:10) and at other times the Son (Isa. 53:12; Mark 10:45; Gal. 3:13; 1 Peter 2:24; 3:18).

Mediator

The Mediator, our penal substitute, is Jesus Christ. This is declared in text after text. I will list five:

---

[120]Schreiner, "Penal Substitution View," 67.

By his knowledge shall the righteous one, my servant,
     make many to be accounted righteous,
     and he shall bear their iniquities. (Isa. 53:11)

For even the Son of Man came . . . to give his life as a ransom for many. (Mark 10:45)

Christ redeemed us from the curse of the law by becoming a curse for us. (Gal. 3:13)

For Christ also suffered once for sins, the righteous for the unrighteous, that he might bring us to God. (1 Pet. 3:18)

He is the propitiation for our sins, and not for ours only but also for the sins of the whole world. (1 John 2:2)

Work

Christ dies in our place, taking the punishment we deserve, that we might be justified and forgiven.

But he was wounded for our transgressions;
     he was crushed for our iniquities;
upon him was the chastisement that brought us peace,
     and with his stripes we are healed.
. . . and the LORD has laid on him
     the iniquity of us all. (Isa. 53:5–6)

For even the Son of Man came . . . to give his life as a ransom for many. (Mark 10:45)

. . . Christ Jesus, whom God put forward as a propitiation by his blood. (Rom. 3:24–25)

By sending his own Son in the likeness of sinful flesh and for sin, he condemned sin in the flesh. (Rom. 8:3)

For our sake he made him to be sin who knew no sin, so that in him we might become the righteousness of God. (2 Cor. 5:21)

And you . . . God made alive together with him, having forgiven us all of our trespasses, by canceling the record of debt that stood against us with its legal demands. This he set aside, nailing it to the cross. (Col. 2:13–14)

He himself bore our sins in his body on the tree. (1 Pet. 2:24)

In this is love, not that we have loved God but that he loved us and sent his Son to be the propitiation for our sins. (1 John 4:10)

Voluntariness

Jesus willingly gives himself in the place of his people. He is not coerced:

He poured out his soul to death. (Isa. 53:12)

For even the Son of Man came . . . to give his life as a ransom for many. (Mark 10:45)

I lay down my life that I may take it up again. No one takes it from me, but I lay it down of my own accord. (John 10:17–18)

Then I said, "Behold, I have come to do your will, O God." (Heb. 10:7, 9)

Substitution

This is the heart of the matter. The Son of God dies in the place of sinners, suffering the penalty for their sins. There is no need to quote again the passages cited in the preceding under "Mediator" and "Work."

Particularity[121]

Substitution implies efficacy, which implies particularity. Christ's vicarious atonement, his suffering the penalty that sinners cannot pay, is efficacious for the following reasons:

Upon him was the chastisement that brought us peace,
    and with his stripes we are healed. (Isa. 53:5)

By his knowledge shall the righteous one, my servant,
    make many to be accounted righteous,
    and he shall bear their iniquities. (Isa. 53:11)

Christ redeemed us from the curse of the law by becoming a curse for us. (Gal. 3:13)

And you . . . God made alive together with him, having forgiven us all of our trespasses, by canceling the record of debt that stood against us with its legal demands. This he set aside, nailing it to the cross. (Col. 2:13–14)

---

[121] For a defense of particular atonement, see the appendix.

He himself bore our sins in his body on the tree. (1 Pet. 2:24)

Christ also suffered once for sins, the righteous for the unrighteous, that he might bring us to God. (1 Pet. 3:18)

God . . . loved us and sent his Son to be the propitiation for our sins. (1 John 4:10)

Christ's substitutionary atonement is effective. Through his death (and resurrection) he actually brings peace, heals, makes many to be accounted righteous, redeems from the law's curse, cancels the record of debt, bears sins in his body, brings people to God, and is the propitiation for sins. And if his saving work is substitutionary and efficacious, there are only two possibilities: either it is universal and everyone is saved, or it is particular and all whom God has chosen are saved. Universalism is incompatible with the Bible's message,[122] so Christ's atonement is vicarious, effective, and particular—he has died to save his people from their sins.

J. I. Packer argues in the same manner for particular or definite atonement:

If the use historically made of the penal substitution model is examined, there is no doubt, despite occasional confusions of thought, that part of the intention is to celebrate the decisiveness of the cross as in every sense the procuring cause of salvation. . . . Once this is granted, however, we are shut up to a choice between universalism and some form of the view that Christ died to save only a part of the human race.[123]

Justification and Adoption

The legal aspects of the application of salvation that correspond to Christ's saving work as penal substitution are justification and adoption. We see the former tethered to penal substitution already in Isaiah 53:

> By his knowledge shall the righteous one, my servant,
>   make many to be accounted righteous,
>   and he shall bear their iniquities. (v. 11)

It is noteworthy that Scripture's key propitiation passage is situated in Romans so as to provide the basis for justification (Rom. 3:25–26). Romans 4:1–8 teaches

---

[122]See J. I. Packer, "Universalism: Will Everyone Ultimately Be Saved?," in *Hell Under Fire*, ed. Christopher W. Morgan and Robert A. Peterson (Grand Rapids: Zondervan, 2004), 169–94.

[123]J. I. Packer, "What Did the Cross Achieve? The Logic of Penal Substitution," *Tyndale Bulletin* 25 (1974): 37, 39. See also the reaffirmation of penal substitution and with it particular atonement in A. T. B. McGowan, "The Atonement as Penal Substitution," in *Always Reforming: Explorations in Systematic Theology*, ed. A. T. B. McGowan (Downers Grove, IL: InterVarsity, 2006), 183–210.

that justification involves the forgiveness of sins. According to Colossians 2:14, the objective work that brings subjective forgiveness is Christ's vicarious penal death.

Adoption, like justification, is a legal picture of salvation applied. Paul teaches that the Father sent the Son to redeem slaves of sin so that he might adopt them (Gal. 4:4–7). How does Paul in the same epistle describe the redemption that brings adoption? As a penal substitution (Gal. 3:13).

Individual, Corporate, and Cosmic Scope

Christ dies as a penal substitute for individuals, for his church, and to deliver the whole creation from the curse of sin (Rom. 8:19–23; 2 Cor. 5:21; 1 John 2:2; 1 Pet. 3:18).

Relation to Other Doctrines

One way to demonstrate the importance of penal substitution is to see its function in relation to other pictures of Christ's saving work. Sometimes it is used to describe other pictures: redemption (Mark 10:45; Gal. 3:13), reconciliation (2 Cor. 5:21), victory (Col. 2:14–15), and sacrifice (Rom. 3:25; 1 Pet. 2:24). We turn, next, to Christ as Victor.

Reconciler
Redeemer
Legal Substitute
Victor
Second Adam
Sacrifice

Chapter 13

Christ Our Victor

In 1931 Gustaf Aulén wrote a book that changed the way people think about—and even speak about—the doctrine of the atonement. His book *Christus Victor* bequeathed its title to those subsequently reflecting on the meaning of Christ's death as a victory. Christ is the champion who through his death and resurrection wins a mighty victory over Satan. Few agree with Aulén's claim to objectivity in his conclusion, but a great many appreciate the service that he rendered:

> I have not had any intention of writing an *apologia* for the classic idea; and if my exposition has shaped itself into something like a vindication of it, I would plead that it is because the facts themselves point that way.... Let it be added, in conclusion, that if the classic idea of the Atonement ever again assumes a leading place in Christian theology, it is not likely that it will revert to precisely the same forms of expression that it has used in the past; its revival will not consist in a putting back of the clock. It is the idea itself that will be essentially the same: the fundamental idea that the Atonement is, above all, a movement of God to man, not in the first place a movement of man to God. We shall hear again the tremendous paradoxes: that God, the all-ruler, the Infinite, yet accepts the lowliness of the Incarnation; we shall hear again the old realistic message of the conflict of God with the dark, hostile forces of evil, and His victory over them by the Divine self-sacrifice; above all, we shall hear again the note of triumph.[1]

---

[1]Gustaf Aulén, *Christus Victor: An Historical Study of the Three Main Types of the Idea of the Atonement*, trans. A. G. Hebert (1931; repr., New York: Macmillan, 1969), 159.

This chapter will explore the New Testament's Christus Victor picture of Christ's saving work. Before doing so, however, it will examine a topic Aulén omitted from his study—the Old Testament motif of God as a warrior who fights for, and sometimes against, his people Israel. The divine warrior of the Old Testament becomes incarnate in Jesus of Nazareth, who is Christ our mighty champion.

Old Testament Background

Although the divine-warrior image fills the Old Testament, I will treat only key passages: the *protoevangelium* of Genesis 3:15, the songs of Moses and Miriam in Exodus 15:1–21, David's defeat of Goliath in 1 Samuel 17, the prophecy of David's Lord in Psalm 110, Jeremiah's prophecy of the Babylonian exile in Jeremiah 21:3–7, and the son of man in Daniel 7:13–14.

Space prohibits even citing all of the Old Testament divine-warrior passages. I will simply select a few texts from the Law, Historical Books, Psalms, and the Prophets as representative of many more:

> And whenever the ark set out, Moses said, "Arise, O LORD, and let your enemies be scattered, and let those who hate you flee before you." And when it rested, he said, "Return, O LORD, to the ten thousand thousands of Israel." (Num. 10:35–36)

> LORD, when you went out from Seir,
>   when you marched from the region of Edom,
> the earth trembled
>   and the heavens dropped,
>   yes, the clouds dropped water.
> The mountains quaked before the LORD,
>   even Sinai before the LORD, the God of Israel. (Judg. 5:4–5)

> O LORD God of hosts,
>   who is mighty as you are, O LORD,
>   with your faithfulness all around you?
> You rule the raging of the sea;
>   when its waves rise, you still them.
> You crushed Rahab like a carcass;
>   you scattered your enemies with your mighty arm. (Ps. 89:8–10)

> The LORD goes out like a mighty man,
>   like a man of war he stirs up his zeal;
> he cries out, he shouts aloud,
>   he shows himself mighty against his foes. (Isa. 42:13)

Who is this who comes from Edom,
  in crimsoned garments from Bozrah,
he who is splendid in his apparel,
  marching in the greatness of his strength?
"It is I, speaking in righteousness,
  mighty to save."
Why is your apparel red,
  and your garments like his who treads in the winepress?
"I have trodden the winepress alone,
  and from the peoples no one was with me;
I trod them in my anger
  and trampled them in my wrath;
their lifeblood spattered on my garments,
  and stained all my apparel.
For the day of vengeance was on my heart,
  and the year of redemption had come." (Isa. 63:1–4)

Then the LORD will go out and fight against those nations as when he fights on a day of battle. (Zech. 14:3)

Genesis 3:15: The Protoevangelium

The first mention of the gospel in Scripture, the *protoevangelium*, is given in terms of conflict and eventual victory for Eve's offspring. After Eve and Adam sin against the Lord, he confronts them, and they make excuses (Gen. 3:1–13). Then the Lord brings judgment against the serpent and our first parents. Our concern is with God's words of judgment to the serpent, because included among them are words of divine promise and hope. God curses the serpent (v. 14) and says,

I will put enmity between you and the woman,
  and between your offspring and her offspring;
he shall bruise your head,
  and you shall bruise his heel. (v. 15)

God will bring discord between the woman, and humankind of whom she is the mother, and the serpent, whom Bruce Waltke accurately labels "only a masquerade for a heavenly spirit."[2] Indeed, he is an instrument of Satan (John 8:44; Rev. 12:9; 20:2). C. John Collins has argued on grammatical grounds that the woman's "offspring" refers to an individual. He will be dealt a blow by

---

[2]Bruce K. Waltke, *Genesis: A Commentary* (Grand Rapids: Zondervan, 2001), 93.

the serpent's offspring, those who follow Satan and who are "seduced into his darkness."[3] But the good news is that the woman's offspring will deal Satan a mortal blow; a wound to the head is more serious than one to the heel.

God promises to act for humankind's benefit by defeating the serpent. "But," Collins asks, "may we go further and call it messianic?" He answers:

> We are within our rights to say that this text envisions an individual who will engage the serpent (really, the Dark Power that used the serpent as its mouthpiece) in combat and defeat him, thus bringing benefits to mankind. That is, he is a champion. We are further entitled to say that he will be a human (an offspring of the woman), but one with power extraordinarily enough to win. The rest of Genesis will unfold the idea of this offspring and lay the foundation for the developed messianic teaching of the prophets. . . . Genesis fosters a messianic expectation, of which this verse is the headwaters.[4]

Collins speaks measured words. Already Genesis 3:15 promises a champion who will defeat Satan and benefit humankind. The rest of Genesis—and the rest of Scripture—will identify him clearly enough.

Exodus 15:1–21: The Songs of Moses and Miriam

The chief Old Testament background for Christus Victor is the divine-warrior motif, which appears for the first time in the song of Moses in Exodus 15. The song says explicitly,

> The Lord is a man of war;
>   the Lord is his name. (Ex. 15:3)

The historical context is Yahweh's deliverance of the Israelites after 430 years of slavery in Egypt. The plagues must be seen as a battle between Israel's God and the gods of Egypt. God specifically stated the purpose of the plagues: "The Egyptians shall know that I am the Lord, when I stretch out my hand against Egypt and bring out the people of Israel from among them" (7:5; cf. 7:17; 8:10, 22; 14:4, 18).

The plagues built toward the tenth and final one as Pharaoh repeatedly hardened his heart and refused to let the Israelites go to worship Yahweh in the wilderness. After Yahweh slayed the firstborn of human beings and animals, Pharaoh

---

[3]C. John Collins, *Genesis 1–4: A Linguistic, Literary, and Theological Commentary* (Phillipsburg, NJ: P&R, 2006), 156.
[4]Ibid., 157.

relented and told Moses and Aaron to lead their people out of Egypt (12:31–32). The exodus followed. Pharaoh then changed his mind again, and he and his armies pursued the Israelites, intent on keeping them in bondage. The Israelites were terrified when they saw hundreds of Egyptian chariots pursuing them.

Moses spoke words of comfort to the people, words that told of Yahweh as their warrior-deliverer: "Fear not, stand firm, and see the salvation of the LORD, which he will work for you today. For the Egyptians whom you see today, you shall never see again. The LORD will fight for you, and you have only to be silent" (14:13–14). Moses stretched out his hand over the sea, the waters parted, and the Israelites went through on dry ground. The Egyptians, not to be denied their slaves, pursued. Moses stretched out his hand again, however, and the waters closed and "covered the chariots and the horsemen; of all the host of Pharaoh that had followed them into the sea, not one of them remained" (14:28).

The songs of Moses and Miriam extol Yahweh the divine warrior and celebrate his great victory over the Egyptians that brought deliverance to the Israelites (chap. 15). Brevard Childs summarizes the songs' focus: "The poem praises God as the sole agent of salvation. Israel did not co-operate or even play a minor role. The figure of Moses is completely omitted. Yahweh alone effected the miracle at the sea."[5]

The songs deserve full quotation, but in the interest of space, I will cite selections.

Then Moses and the people of Israel sang this song to the LORD, saying,

> I will sing to the LORD, for he has triumphed gloriously;
>> the horse and his rider he has thrown into the sea.
> The LORD is my strength and my song,
>> and he has become my salvation;
> this is my God, and I will praise him,
>> my father's God, and I will exalt him.
> The LORD is a man of war;
>> the LORD is his name.
> Pharaoh's chariots and his host he cast into the sea,
>> and his chosen officers were sunk in the Red Sea.
> The floods covered them;
>> they went down into the depths like a stone.
> Your right hand, O LORD, glorious in power,
>> your right hand, O LORD, shatters the enemy.

[5]Brevard S. Childs, *The Book of Exodus*, The Old Testament Library (Louisville: Westminster, 1974), 249.

In the greatness of your majesty you overthrow your adversaries;
  you send out your fury; it consumes them like stubble.
At the blast of your nostrils the waters piled up;
  the floods stood up in a heap;
  the deeps congealed in the heart of the sea.
The enemy said, "I will pursue, I will overtake,
  I will divide the spoil, my desire shall have its fill of them.
  I will draw my sword; my hand shall destroy them."
You blew with your wind; the sea covered them;
  they sank like lead in the mighty waters.
Who is like you, O LORD, among the gods?
  Who is like you, majestic in holiness,
  awesome in glorious deeds, doing wonders?
You stretched out your right hand;
  the earth swallowed them. (Ex. 15:1–12)

And Miriam sang to them,

"Sing to the LORD, for he has triumphed gloriously;
  the horse and his rider he has thrown into the sea." (v. 21)

1 Samuel 17: David and Goliath

In their book surveying the divine-warrior motif in the Old Testament (and Christus Victor in the New Testament), Tremper Longman and Daniel Reid point out a fascinating aspect of the relationship between God and the Israelite army:

> Since God fights for Israel, that nation does not have to worry about the number of its troops or its weapons technology. Indeed, in the ethos of the Old Testament, a large army and superior weapons technology are a liability. Israel cannot boast in its own strength, but only in the power and might of the Lord, who gives victory in spite of overwhelming odds.[6]

A striking example of these principles of holy war is found in the battle of David and Goliath. The Philistines and Israel had drawn up in line of battle on two mountains with a valley in between. An imposing figure stepped forward.

> And there came out from the camp of the Philistines a champion named Goliath of Gath, whose height was six cubits and a span. He had a helmet of bronze on his

---

[6]Tremper Longman III and Daniel G. Reid, *God Is a Warrior*, Studies in Old Testament Biblical Theology (Grand Rapids: Zondervan, 1995), 37.

head, and he was armed with a coat of mail, and the weight of the coat was five thousand shekels of bronze. And he had bronze armor on his legs, and a javelin of bronze slung between his shoulders. The shaft of his spear was like a weaver's beam, and his spear's head weighed six hundred shekels of iron. (1 Sam. 17:4–7)

The Philistines' strategy was to have Goliath, their champion, fight a representative of Israel, easily defeat him, and presumably prevent the losses of their troops that would occur if the two armies fought. The plan looked good as Goliath for forty days taunted Israel to produce someone to fight him. The Israelites to a man were frightened, Saul among them.

However, when David, a mere shepherd deemed too young to fight, visited his brothers and heard the Philistine's taunts, he was offended and moved to action: "Who is this uncircumcised Philistine, that he should defy the armies of the living God?" (v. 26). David insisted on fighting Goliath. When Saul asked his qualifications, David explained: "The LORD who delivered me from the paw of the lion and from the paw of the bear will deliver me from the hand of this Philistine" (v. 37). And Saul was convinced.

Against all appearances (the young man was too small to put on Saul's suit of armor) David withstood Goliath. Armed with his slingshot and five smooth stones, he approached the giant. After Goliath taunted David and promised to give his dead flesh to the birds and the beasts, David famously said:

You come to me with a sword and with a spear and with a javelin, but I come to you in the name of the LORD of hosts, the God of the armies of Israel, whom you have defied. This day the LORD will deliver you into my hand, and I will strike you down and cut off your head. And I will give the dead bodies of the host of the Philistines this day to the birds of the air and to the wild beasts of the earth, that all the earth may know that there is a God in Israel, and that all this assembly may know that the LORD saves not with sword and spear. For the battle is the LORD's, and he will give you into our hand. (vv. 45–47)

Of course, David slung a stone into the forehead of Goliath, who fell facedown, and David used the giant's sword to kill him and sever his head. The Philistines fled, and Israel pursued them in victory and plundered their camp. The divine warrior won a mighty victory for his people through David, the young shepherd.

Psalm 110: David's Lord

Few psalms are purely messianic and futuristic. Psalm 110 appears to be one. Especially God's oath in verse 4, proclaiming someone "a priest forever after the order of Melchizedek," does not fit any mere human descendant of David. Instead it points to the coming one as a divine (and human) figure. "Like Psalms 2 and 72, this psalm goes well beyond the achievements of any merely human heir of David and thus looks forward to the messianic King; in fact, unlike those two psalms, it is almost entirely future in its orientation," according to Collins.[7]

Such teaching usually prompts the question, "Then, what function did the psalm serve in its historical context to its original readers?" I cannot improve Collins's answer: "When the people of God would sing this in faith, they would celebrate God's promises to David, yearn for the day in which the Gentiles receive the light (the coming accomplishment of the Messiah), and seek to be faithful to their calling until that great day."[8]

This psalm uses divine-warrior language to assure David's Lord, the coming one, of great victory and enthronement in heaven. All Israelites, except the king, had two lords: God was their heavenly Lord; and the king in Jerusalem, God's representative on earth, was their earthly lord. But according to the psalm title and according to Jesus (in Matt. 22:43–45 and parallels), David was its author. Now, David as king had only one Lord—God in heaven. Why is it, then, that David in Psalm 110:1 speaks of two Lords?

> The LORD says to my Lord:
> "Sit at my right hand,
> until I make your enemies your footstool."

The answer is that David's second Lord is the coming one, the Messiah as Jesus implied in Matthew 22:43–45. David's second Lord is told to sit at God's right hand, the greatest place of honor and authority, where he will rule with God until God subdues his enemies under him (v. 1). In fact, Yahweh himself will fight for David's Lord and defeat his foes.

> The LORD sends forth from Zion
> your mighty scepter.
> Rule in the midst of your enemies! . . .
> The Lord is at your right hand;
> he will shatter kings on the day of his wrath.
> He will execute judgment among the nations,
> filling them with corpses;
> he will shatter chiefs
> over the wide earth. (Ps. 110:2, 5–6)

---

[7]C. John Collins, note in *ESV Study Bible* on Psalm 110 (p. 1084).
[8]Ibid.

Of course, we need the New Testament to learn details of the fulfillment of this psalm's messianic predictions—that verse 1 foretells Christ's ascension, enthronement (Heb. 1:3, 13), and deity (Matt. 22:43–45)—and to understand in detail about Christ's priesthood like that of Melchizedek (Hebrews 7). But for our present purposes this will suffice: Psalm 110 foretells a coming one, David's Lord, for whom God will fight, and who will reign with him after a great victory.

Jeremiah 21:3–7: The Babylonian Exile

Sadly, because of Israel's unfaithfulness to the Lord, he, the divine warrior who fought for them against their enemies, turned against them. Israel should not have been surprised at this turn of events because God had plainly spelled out their obligations to him in the terms of the covenant. He himself had established the covenant with Israel based on his love and deliverance: "I am the LORD your God, who brought you out of the land of Egypt, out of the house of slavery" (Deut. 5:6). But, though God alone had initiated the covenant, once instituted it obligated Israel to loyalty and obedience to its covenant Lord. God had announced beforehand the respective outcomes of Israel's faithfulness and obedience on the one hand, and its unfaithfulness and disobedience on the other. Israel reaped exactly what it sowed and was alone responsible for turning the divine warrior from protector to enemy.

> The LORD will cause your enemies who rise against you to be defeated before you. They shall come out against you one way and flee before you seven ways. (Deut. 28:7)

> The LORD will cause you to be defeated before your enemies. You shall go out one way against them and flee seven ways before them. And you shall be a horror to all the kingdoms of the earth. (v. 25)

The epitome of God's rejection of his covenant people was the exile, as Longman and Reid explain:

> The reflex of the Exodus is the Exile. If the Exodus shows God's power on behalf of Israel, the Exile displays God's power against Israel. The Exodus is an expression of God's grace; the Exile displays his judgment. In the Exodus event we witness God as Israel's warrior; in the Exile, he is Israel's enemy.[9]

---

[9]Longman and Reid, *God Is a Warrior*, 52.

God rejected his covenant people, Israel, and removed the presence of his glory from their midst. His glory moved in stages—from the cherubim in the Most Holy Place to the threshold of the temple, to the east gate of the temple, to the midst of the city, heading east outside the city.[10]

> Now the glory of the God of Israel had gone up from the cherub on which it rested to the threshold of the house. (Ezek. 9:3)

> Then the glory of the LORD went out from the threshold of the house, and stood over the cherubim. And the cherubim lifted up their wings and mounted up from the earth before my eyes as they went out, with the wheels beside them. And they stood at the entrance of the east gate of the house of the LORD, and the glory of the God of Israel was over them. (10:18–19)

> Then the cherubim lifted up their wings, with the wheels beside them, and the glory of the God of Israel was over them. And the glory of the LORD went up from the midst of the city and stood on the mountain that is on the east side of the city. (11:22–23)

While the prophet Ezekiel ministered to the exiled Judeans in Babylon, Jeremiah served the people in Jerusalem until he was taken by them to Egypt after the fall of the city. The book that bears his name contains many of Jeremiah's sermons but records only two who believed his message: Baruch, his scribe (32:12; 36:4–8; 45:1–5); and Ebed-melech, an Ethiopian who served the king (38:7–13; 39:15–18). The majority response to Jeremiah's summons to repentance and warnings of impending exile was unbelief, and rejection, which included his being beaten and put into stocks, threatened with death, beaten and imprisoned, and thrown into a cistern (18:18; 20:1–2; 26:7–11; 37:13–21; 38:1–6).

Nevertheless, Jeremiah remained faithful to his Lord and brought unpopular messages of judgment, including judgment on Judah. Indeed, the prophet foretold the Babylonian captivity when King Zedekiah sent to him and asked him to inquire of the Lord concerning Nebuchadnezzar, king of Babylon, who was making war against Judah:

> Thus says the LORD, the God of Israel: Behold, I will turn back the weapons of war that are in your hands and with which you are fighting against the king of Babylon and against the Chaldeans who are besieging you outside the walls. And I will bring them together into the midst of this city. I myself will fight against you with outstretched hand and strong arm, in anger and in fury and in great wrath. And I will

---

[10]Ibid., 53.

strike down the inhabitants of this city, both man and beast. They shall die of a great pestilence. Afterward, declares the LORD, I will give Zedekiah king of Judah and his servants and the people in this city who survive the pestilence, sword, and famine into the hand of Nebuchadnezzar king of Babylon and into the hand of their enemies, into the hand of those who seek their lives. He shall strike them down with the edge of the sword. He shall not pity them or spare them or have compassion. (Jer. 21:4–7)

How sad that Yahweh, who formerly fought on behalf of his people, would now himself fight against them (v. 5)! How sad that the same expressions that used to display God's power on behalf of his people—"with an outstretched hand and a strong arm"—were now used to depict the divine warrior's judgment of his own rebellious people! Of course, this is not the final word in the story. God would restore his people from captivity and even make a new covenant with them in the future, both of which Jeremiah prophesies (16:14–17; 23:1–8; 24:4–7; 30:1–33:26).

Daniel 7:13–14: A Son of Man

The story of the divine warrior would be incomplete without consideration of an apocalyptic passage that foretells the coming one. Daniel, in the beginning of the visionary section of his book, reports seeing a terrifying vision of four frightening beasts that came from the sea, a well-known symbol for chaos (Ps. 89:9; 93:3–4). Daniel 7:17 indicates that "these four great beasts are four kings who shall arise out of the earth." Most evangelical interpreters identify the four kings and kingdoms with those of the image in Nebuchadnezzar's dream: Babylon, Medo-Persia, Alexander the Great and Greece, and Rome (2:31–45). The fourth beast deserves special mention because it was "terrifying and dreadful and exceedingly strong" (v. 7). It had ten horns (kings), of which one little one is especially aggressive and makes large boasts.

Along with the horrible beasts (7:1–8), Daniel saw a courtroom in heaven (vv. 9–12). God, the Ancient of Days, occupied the central throne; he ruled supreme in judgment. He is depicted as perfectly pure (with snow-white clothing) and very wise (with pure-white hair). His chariot-throne

> was fiery flames;
> its wheels were burning fire. (v. 9)

Iain Duguid explains that these are "images of the divine warrior's fearsome power to destroy his enemies."[11] An innumerable host served God in heaven and

---

[11] Iain M. Duguid, note in the *ESV Study Bible* on Dan. 7:9–12 (p. 1600).

> the court sat in judgment,
> and the books were opened. (v. 10)

The little horn continued to boast but "the [fourth] beast was killed, and its body destroyed and given over to be burned with fire" (v. 11).

Then Daniel saw one "like a son of man" coming "with the clouds of heaven" (v. 13). This is an unusual combination because "son of man" in the Old Testament usually refers to humanity in its frailty and mortality (e.g., Ps. 8:4 and more than ninety times in Ezekiel to refer to the prophet). But only God rides on a cloud in the Old Testament (Ps. 68:4; 104:3–4; Isa. 19:1; Nah. 1:3). The "son of man" is thus both human and divine. He approaches the Ancient of Days and is presented before him (Dan. 7:13). Tremendous power and adoration are given to the son of man:

> And to him was given dominion
> and glory and a kingdom,
> that all peoples, nations, and languages
> should serve him;
> his dominion is an everlasting dominion,
> which shall not pass away,
> and his kingdom one
> that shall not be destroyed. (v. 14)

Here is a figure distinguished from the Ancient of Days and yet, like him, he is divine. He is both divine and human, the son of man who will reign over the whole world and forever! Everyone will serve him. Jesus's favorite self-designation is Son of Man. He applies the language of Daniel 7:13 to himself in Mark 14. When Jesus stands before the Sanhedrin, the high priest asks him point-blank, "Are you the Christ, the Son of the Blessed?" (Mark 14:61). Jesus replies, "I am, and you will see the Son of Man seated at the right hand of Power, and coming with the clouds of heaven" (v. 62). Jesus here applies to himself the messianic prophecies of Psalm 110:1 and Daniel 7:13. He thus claims to be the son of man of Daniel's prophecy.

The divine warrior and son of man of Daniel 7 are ultimately fulfilled in the returning warrior-king Jesus of Revelation:

Then I saw heaven opened, and behold, a white horse! The one sitting on it is called Faithful and True, and in righteousness he judges and makes war. His eyes are like a flame of fire, and on his head are many diadems, and he has a name written that no one knows but himself. He is clothed in a robe dipped in blood, and the name by which he is called is The Word of God. And the armies of heaven, arrayed in fine linen, white and pure, were following him on white horses. From his mouth comes a sharp sword with which to strike down the nations, and he will rule them with a rod of iron. He will tread the winepress of the fury of the wrath of God the Almighty. On his robe and on his thigh he has a name written, King of kings and Lord of lords. (Rev. 19:11–16)

Christ Our Victor in the Synoptic Gospels

The Old Testament divine-warrior image becomes incarnate in Jesus Christ who is Christus Victor. This theme occurs in the Synoptic Gospels in Jesus's temptation by the Devil, his exorcisms, his parable about binding the strong man, his seeing Satan fall from heaven, his crucifixion, and his predictions of his return.

Jesus's Temptation by the Devil

Mark's narrative is stark: "The Spirit immediately drove him out into the wilderness. And he was in the wilderness forty days, being tempted by Satan. And he was with the wild animals, and the angels were ministering to him" (Mark 1:12–13). Matthew and Luke provide the details. Luke indicates that the three recorded temptations were the culmination of Jesus's being tempted by the Devil over the whole forty days: "And Jesus, full of the Holy Spirit . . . was led by the Spirit in the wilderness for forty days, being tempted by the devil" (Luke 4:1–2).

Satan engages Jesus in one-on-one combat, in direct confrontation, the likes of which we do not see again until Jesus's crucifixion. Why do so at this time? Jesus has just begun his public ministry by being baptized, identifying himself with sinners and foreshadowing his bearing of sin and judgment on the cross. Michael Wilkins comments, "The temptations are a diabolical attempt to subvert God's plan for human redemption by causing Jesus to fall into sin and disobedience, thus disqualifying him as the sinless Savior."[12] The fact that Jesus is tempted over forty days reminds readers of Old Testament Israel's forty years in the wilderness.[13] William Lane shows the significance of Jesus's obedience in the place where Israel disobeyed: "Jesus' obedience to God is affirmed and sustained *in the wilderness*, the precise place where

---

[12]Michael J. Wilkins, note in the *ESV Study Bible* on Matt. 4:1–11 (p. 1825).
[13]There are more parallels. See Joel B. Green, *The Gospel of Luke*, The New International Commentary on the New Testament (Grand Rapids: Eerdmans, 1997), 192, for a list.

Israel's rebellion brought death and alienation, in order that the new Israel of God may be constituted."[14]

Three times the Devil tries to trick Jesus into using his divine powers for personal gain, outside of the will of God. "Satan's aim was to entice Jesus to use powers rightly his but which he had voluntarily abandoned to carry out the Father's mission," as D. A. Carson reminds us.[15] Three times Jesus refuses to succumb, citing texts from Deuteronomy, once again identifying himself as the new Israel. Jesus's answer to the third temptation—the lie that if he would worship Satan, Jesus would be given all the kingdoms and their glory—is telling: "Be gone, Satan! For it is written, 'You shall worship the Lord your God and him only shall you serve'" (Matt. 4:10). And the Evil One does depart (v. 11), but not forever, as Luke reminds us: "And when the devil had ended every temptation, he departed from him until an opportune time" (Luke 4:13).

Joel Green skillfully draws out the cosmic significance of the episode:

> Behind those efforts [of opposition to God in Luke 1–3] stands the devil, who now steps out from behind the curtain for a direct confrontation with the one through whom God would manifest his redemptive will. Behind Jesus, on the other hand, stands the Holy Spirit, so that, through its dramatis personae, 4:1–13 presents a clash of cosmic proportions.[16]

Jesus our champion's entrance into the cosmic battle on earth has begun and will not end until his death and resurrection, in one sense (John 12:31), and not until the last judgment, in another (Rev. 20:10).

Jesus's Exorcisms

Tremper Longman points out an important difference between Christ as Victor and God as divine warrior in the Old Testament: "Jesus' Holy War is different from the Holy War of Israel. While the latter, at the Lord's command, directed their warfare against earthly enemies, Jesus struggled with the forces, the powers and principalities, which stand behind sinful mankind (cf. his miracles and healings)."[17] We could add Jesus's exorcisms.

Jesus's confrontations with demons are too numerous to be studied in detail. I will comment briefly on some representative encounters. That there is a

---

[14]William L. Lane, *Commentary on the Gospel of Mark*, The New International Commentary on the New Testament (Grand Rapids: Eerdmans, 1974), 62.

[15]D. A. Carson, *Matthew*, The Expositor's Bible Commentary (Grand Rapids: Zondervan, 1984), 113.

[16]Green, *The Gospel of Luke*, 192.

[17]Tremper Longman III, "The Divine Warrior: The New Testament Use of an Old Testament Motif," *Westminster Theological Journal* 44 (1982): 303.

heightening of demonic activity when the Son of God begins his public ministry should not surprise us: Christus Victor is doing battle with the enemy! Mark summarizes Jesus's early ministry in these terms: "And he went throughout all Galilee, preaching in their synagogues and casting out demons" (Mark 1:39). Listen to the way Luke introduces Mary of Magdala: "Mary, called Magdalene, from whom seven demons had gone out" (Luke 8:2).

Mark in his first chapter, after recording Jesus's calling his first disciples, tells of his healing a man with an unclean spirit. As Jesus is teaching in a synagogue in Capernaum, the spirit within the man cries out: "What have you to do with us, Jesus of Nazareth? Have you come to destroy us? I know who you are—the Holy One of God" (Mark 1:24). Lane provides helpful background information to this encounter. He distinguishes between the titles of Jesus used by ordinary sick people and those used by demoniacs. The former call Jesus "Lord" (Mark 7:28), "Teacher" (9:17), "Son of David" (10:47–48), or "Rabbi" (10:51). Those possessed by demons use names that identify him as the divine Son of God: "the Holy One of God" (1:24), "the Son of God" (3:11), or "the Son of the Most High God" (5:7). Lane draws a crucial distinction:

> The contrast in address is an important characteristic distinguishing ordinary sickness from demonic possession, and reflects the superior knowledge of the demons. The recognition-formula is not a confession, but a defensive attempt to gain control of Jesus in accordance with the common concept of that day, that the use of the precise name of an individual or spirit would secure mastery over him.[18]

The battle is on and the demons know it. But they are no match for the Son of God, as the following passages attest:

> But Jesus rebuked him, saying, "Be silent, and come out of him!" And the unclean spirit, convulsing him and crying out with a loud voice, came out of him. (Mark 1:25–26)

> And he healed many who were sick with various diseases, and cast out many demons. And he would not permit the demons to speak, because they knew him. (Mark 1:34)

> And Jesus rebuked the demon, and it came out of him, and the boy was healed instantly. (Matt. 17:18)

---

[18]Lane, *Commentary on the Gospel of Mark*, 74.

He rebuked the unclean spirit, saying to it, "You mute and deaf spirit, I command you, come out of him and never enter him again." (Mark 9:25)

And demons also came out of many, crying, "You are the Son of God!" But he rebuked them and would not allow them to speak, because they knew that he was the Christ. (Luke 4:41)

The next section treats one famous encounter involving Jesus, a demon-possessed man, the people, Satan, and the Jewish leaders.

Jesus's Parable about Binding the Strongman

The occasion for Jesus's saying about binding the strongman is his healing a blind and mute man who has a demon. In the power of the Holy Spirit, Jesus heals him and amazes the people, who in turn wonder aloud whether he is the Messiah (Matt. 12:22–23). The Pharisees are angry at the attention Jesus is getting and accuse him of casting out demons by "Beelzebul, the prince of demons" (v. 24).

Jesus uses several arguments to answer to their charge. First, he asks, does Satan fight against himself? "Every kingdom divided against itself is laid waste, and no city or house divided against itself will stand. And if Satan casts out Satan, he is divided against himself. How then will his kingdom stand?" (vv. 25–26). Second, Jesus appeals to Jewish exorcisms, "And if I cast out demons by Beelzebul, by whom do your sons cast them out? Therefore they will be your judges" (v. 27).

After defending himself, Jesus goes on the offensive: "But if it is by the Spirit of God that I cast out demons, then the kingdom of God has come upon you" (v. 28). Jesus's exorcisms do not represent Satan's casting out himself. On the contrary, they represent the powerful in-breaking of God's kingdom.

Jesus then tells a little parable: "Or how can someone enter a strong man's house and plunder his goods, unless he first binds the strong man? Then indeed he may plunder his house" (v. 29). D. A. Carson traces Jesus's line of thought: "Jesus' argument has thus advanced: if Jesus' exorcisms cannot be attributed to Satan (vv. 25–26), then they reflect authority greater than that of Satan. By this greater power Jesus is binding 'the strong man' and plundering his 'house.' So the kingdom of heaven is forcefully advancing."[19]

Lane helpfully views this little parable against the Old Testament background of the contest of champions, such as that between David and Goliath:

The prophets at times described God as the divine warrior. . . . The motif draws upon the older practice of conducting warfare as a contest of champions, as an

---

[19]Carson, *Matthew*, 290.

alternative to the costly commitment of armies in standard combat. . . . Within the gospel tradition Jesus resorts to the metaphor of a contest between champions in response to certain scribes who accused him of collusion with Beelzebul, the prince of demons. . . . In the context of the Beelzebul controversy, the strong man is the demonic prince. The stronger one who vanquishes him is Jesus, who defeats his adversary by the finger of God and releases those who had been enslaved through demonic possession (Luke 11:18–20).[20]

Jesus is the champion who defeats the prince of demons and frees those held captive by him. But even as the divine warrior turned against his own disobedient people in the Old Testament, Christus Victor turns his sword on the wicked Jewish leaders:

> Therefore I tell you, every sin and blasphemy will be forgiven people, but the blasphemy against the Spirit will not be forgiven. And whoever speaks a word against the Son of Man will be forgiven, but whoever speaks against the Holy Spirit will not be forgiven, either in this age or in the age to come. (vv. 31–32)

Only God can make such a statement, and Jesus assumes the divine prerogative: the sin of the Jewish leaders in knowingly ascribing Jesus's exorcisms in the power of the Spirit to Satan is a sin that will never be forgiven.

Jesus is the champion of his people who binds the strong man, plunders his house, "and divides his spoil" (Luke 11:22); he overpowers the demons and frees those who have been possessed by them.

Jesus's Seeing Satan Fall from Heaven

In a saying unique to Luke's Gospel, Jesus says that he saw Satan fall from heaven. Jesus had sent out the seventy-two "ahead of him, two by two, into every town and place where he himself was about to go" (Luke 10:1). They were an advance party whose mission was to proclaim the kingdom and to heal (and to cast out demons, 10:17). He had warned them that they would face difficulties and told them to take no provisions; they were to rely upon the hospitality of those who would receive them.

Jesus knows that the presence of the kingdom will cause division. Those sent are told to bring the peace of God to those who welcome them and to leave in judgment those who reject them. In both cases the kingdom of God has come near, whether in blessing or in judgment. Luke thus highlights the responsibility of the hearers to welcome Jesus's messengers and their message. Green explains,

---

[20]William L. Lane, *Hebrews 1–8*, Word Biblical Commentary (Dallas: Word, 1991), 62.

"The mission of the seventy-two, and especially the question of how they and their message are received, thus serves the larger Lukan themes of the division and reversal that accompany the inauguration of salvation."[21]

After pronouncing woes on the unrepentant Galilean cities that heard his preaching and observed his miracles, he announces the principle that to hear his emissaries is to hear him, to reject his emissaries is to reject him, and to reject him is to reject God (10:16). Jesus then receives back the seventy-two (10:13–20). We are given no report of their mission, but only hear them exclaim, "Lord, even the demons are subject to us in your name!" (10:17). Jesus had granted them the ability to perform exorcisms (cf. 9:1), and they were ecstatic to see this happen.

It is at this point that Jesus says, "I saw Satan fall like lightning from heaven" (10:18). This saying is illumined by two texts, one from each Testament. Luke, who had just used Isaiah's imagery when condemning Capernaum (v. 15; Isa. 14:1–27), wants his readers to think of the same chapter of Isaiah, where it is said of the king of Babylon,

> You said in your heart,
>   "I will ascend to heaven;
> above the stars of God
>   I will set my throne on high." (Isa. 14:13)

Similarly, the Devil made great boasts earlier in Luke's Gospel when tempting Jesus: "And the devil took him up and showed him all the kingdoms of the world in a moment of time, and said to him, 'To you I will give all this authority and their glory, for it has been delivered to me, and I will give it to whom I will. If you, then, will worship me, it will all be yours'" (Luke 4:5–7).

Jesus's statement means that he saw the Evil One, despite all of his pompous boasting, suddenly fall mightily; his power over people is broken. There is no doubt that Jesus's statement concerns the successful exorcisms of the seventy-two. It is hard to decide whether Jesus is speaking of a vision that he saw in the spiritual realm or he is making a strong figurative statement of what happened when his emissaries cast out demons. Green opts for the former and explains.

> Luke portrays Jesus as having a prophetic vision, then, whose content was the future (and ultimate) downfall of Satan, presumably scheduled for the time of the judgment to which he alludes in [Luke 10] vv. 12 and 14. . . . The decisive fall of

---

[21]Green, *The Gospel of Luke*, 415.

Satan is anticipated in the future, but it is already becoming manifest through the mission of Jesus, and, by extension, through the ministry of his envoys.[22]

Whether the visionary interpretation is correct or not, Green is right: Jesus views the successful exorcisms of the seventy-two as a foretaste of the final demise of the Evil One and his minions. "His healing and exorcising may be seen as previews of the battle with the demonic hordes," Longman says.[23] Once more Christ our Victor rejoices in triumph over his foe and ours. But then he goes his disciples one better: "Do not rejoice in this, that the spirits are subject to you, but rejoice that your names are written in heaven" (10:20).

Jesus's Death

The Synoptic Gospels, especially Matthew, include divine-warrior motifs when presenting Jesus's crucifixion and its effects. Already at his arrest we see this. When Peter begins to fight to prevent Jesus's arrest, Jesus replies, "Put your sword back into its place. . . . Do you think that I cannot appeal to my Father, and he will at once send me more than twelve legions of angels? But how then should the Scriptures be fulfilled, that it must be so?" (Matt. 26:52–54). Jesus the Victor has heavenly troops at his disposal, but they are not the means by which the battle will be won at this time. No, Scripture must be fulfilled and the Christ must be crucified (and raised).

Longman and Reid demonstrate convincingly that Matthew presents Jesus's death not only as the obedience of the suffering Servant of Yahweh, but also as the startling manifestation of the Day of Yahweh:

> Here, more emphatically than in Mark, Matthew tells us that Jesus' death was the hour of eschatological travail in which darkness prevailed over the land (Mt 27:45; cf. Zec 14:6). At the moment Jesus gave up his spirit, the temple veil was torn in two (Mt 27:51), the earth shook (27:51; cf. Zec 14:5), the rocks split (Mt 27:51; cf. Zec 14:4), the tombs opened (Mt 27:52), and many saints who had died were raised to life (27:52; cf. Zec 14:5). The last days are telescoped into this epochal moment. The cosmic significance of the cross is set out in bold relief. And its meaning for salvation history is accented by the tearing of the temple veil, thus symbolizing the end of Israel's sacred cult and the coming destruction of the temple. The Roman centurion and his military companions react with terror, like the ancient enemies of Israel's divine warrior (e.g. Ex 15:15; Isa 13:8), and they

---

[22]Ibid., 419.
[23]Longman, "The Divine Warrior," 304.

confess Jesus as Son of God (Mt 27:54). Jesus—tried, obedient, and the focus of the eschatological travail—emerges as triumphant Son of God.[24]

Jesus's Predictions of His Return

In his trial before the Sanhedrin, Jesus is put on oath by Caiaphas, the high priest: "Are you the Christ, the Son of the Blessed?" (Mark 14:61; cf. Matt. 26:63). Jesus answers, "I am, and you will see the Son of Man seated at the right hand of Power, and coming with the clouds of heaven" (Mark 14:62). At this the high priest tears his clothes and accuses Jesus of blasphemy.

Why such a violent response from Israel's spiritual leader? Because Jesus combines two Old Testament texts to present himself as God: David's Lord (in Psalm 110) and the divine son of man of Daniel 7. And both texts, which we previously studied, reverberate with divine-warrior repercussions.

When Jesus says, "You will see the Son of Man seated at the right hand of Power," he identifies himself with the mysterious figure of Psalm 110:1. There the Lord tells this figure,

> Sit at my right hand,
> until I make your enemies your footstool.

The figure is David's second Lord (along with God in heaven) who will sit at God's right hand, the ultimate place of honor and power. God will fight for him and will subdue all of his enemies (vv. 1–2, 5–6).

But remember that Jesus speaks these startling words in the presence of the high priest who is about to condemn him to death. How then, can these great things be said of him? Longman and Reid answer: "In a divine reversal of events, Jesus the victim will be vindicated and exalted to a position of regal glory and honor. And, as the echo of Psalm 110:1a implies, he will remain at the right hand until the Lord makes his enemies a footstool for his feet (Ps 110:1b)."[25] The suffering Servant is the Victor.

When Jesus says, "You will see the Son of Man . . . coming with the clouds of heaven," he identifies himself with the Danielic son of man of 7:13:

> And behold, with the clouds of heaven
> there came one like a son of man.

---

[24]Longman and Reid, *God Is a Warrior*, 132.
[25]Ibid., 128.

As argued previously, "son of man" as used there involves both humanity and deity. It frequently distinguishes human beings from God. Yet only God comes "with the clouds," as the son of man does here. This human-divine figure receives universal power and adoration (v. 14).

Once more, Longman and Reid drive home the significance of Jesus's words:

> By immediately following this echo of Psalm 110 with an allusion to Daniel 7:13, Jesus implies not only his fulfillment of the Davidic promise, but his future epiphany as the mysterious heavenly figure who would come to initiate the kingdom of God. Against the backdrop of Jesus' previous announcement of the coming of the Son of Man and the Day of the Lord, Mark 14:62 suggests an eschatological vindication characterized not only by judicial proceedings but also by divine warfare led by the cloud-riding Son of Man. The irony and arresting boldness of this declaration is that the high priest and elders of Israel, the very ones vested with the responsibility of guarding the traditions and holiness of the nation, would behold the coming of the Son of Man to seal their doom. The old theme of Yahweh the divine warrior coming to bring judgment against Israel is reborn.[26]

Christ is our Victor in the Synoptics. The same is true for the Fourth Gospel, although it is different, as we will see.

Christ Our Victor in the Gospel of John

John's Gospel contains neither a temptation narrative nor exorcisms, features that play an important role in the Synoptic Gospels. Why the omissions? John clears the field that the big battle might stand in bold relief. What is a bigger battle than one-on-one temptation by the Devil in the wilderness? Satan's killing of Jesus and, in turn, being defeated by his death and resurrection.

Satan's Attack on Christ: John 14:30

Of course to say simply that the Devil killed Christ is inadequate. God planned the death of the Son before the creation of the world (1 Pet. 1:20; Rev. 13:8, NIV, NASB). The Trinity was involved in Christ's redemptive death. The Son willingly went to the cross (John 10:18). "In Christ God was reconciling the world to himself" (2 Cor. 5:19). And "Christ . . . through the eternal Spirit offered himself without blemish to God" (Heb. 9:14). But it was Judas who betrayed Jesus. And the Jewish leaders cried out for Jesus's blood (John 19:15). In addition, under God, the Evil One wanted to destroy Christ.

---

[26]Ibid.

In John 14, after telling the disciples that he must return to the Father and promising to send them the Spirit, Jesus alludes to the Devil's evil desire to destroy him: "I will no longer talk much with you, for the ruler of this world is coming. He has no claim on me, but I do as the Father has commanded me, so that the world may know that I love the Father" (John 14:30–31). The reason that Jesus will not talk much more with the disciples is that Satan is coming to work through the betrayer to put Jesus to death. He calls him "the ruler of this world." He does the same in John 12:31 and 16:11 (cf. 1 John 5:19).

In what sense is Satan the ruler of this world? Certainly in a subordinate sense because almighty God is the ultimate ruler of all things. But under God, Satan, the usurper, gained authority when our first parents fell. That is why Paul calls him "the god of this world" (2 Cor. 4:4). Although we do not understand this entirely, he "rules" under God's authority (see Job 1:11–12; 2:4–5; Luke 22:31).

When and how does Satan come? Andreas Köstenberger answers well:

> The "coming of the ruler of this world" is the time of the devil's final assault on Jesus as God's Sent One ([John] 13:2, 27; 14:30; cf. Luke 22:31, 53), the world's final hour in its hostility and unbelief. Yet Satan fails, because with the crucifixion he has lost all grounds of appeal against sinful humanity; redemption has been achieved through Jesus' vicarious sacrifice.... Paradoxically, at the cross the world and its ruler are judged, while Jesus is glorified and salvation is procured for all.[27]

Jesus speaks of this when he says of the Devil, "He has no claim on me" (John 14:30). Satan has no hold on Jesus as he does on sinners. D. A. Carson clarifies:

> *He has no hold on me* is an idiomatic rendering of "he has nothing in me," recalling a Hebrew idiom frequently used in legal contexts, "he has no claim on me," "he has nothing over me." How could he? Jesus is not of this world (8:23), and he has never sinned (8:46). The devil could have a hold on Jesus only if there were a justifiable charge against Jesus. Jesus' death would then be his due, and the devil's triumph.[28]

But, thank God, there is no justifiable charge against the sinless Son of God. Though Satan has no claim on Christ, because Jesus loves the Father, he submits to his will and goes to the cross (John 14:31). In fact, he hastens his move to Gethsemane where he will be arrested, "Rise, let us go from here" (v. 31).

---

[27] Andreas J. Köstenberger, *John*, Baker Exegetical Commentary on the New Testament (Grand Rapids: Baker Academic, 2004), 385.

[28] D. A. Carson, *The Gospel According to John*, The Pillar New Testament Commentary (Grand Rapids: Eerdmans, 1991), 508–9, italics original.

John presents the Evil One as both instigating and empowering the betrayal of Jesus. At the same time, the apostle carefully frames Satan's vile act with statements that Jesus is in control:

> Now before the Feast of the Passover, when Jesus knew that his hour had come to depart out of this world to the Father, having loved his own who were in the world, he loved them to the end. During supper . . . Jesus, knowing that the Father had given all things into his hands, and that he had come from God and was going back to God, rose from supper. He laid aside his outer garments, and taking a towel, tied it around his waist. (John 13:1–4)

As I've written elsewhere: "In fact, Jesus actually teaches that Judas's betrayal is in fulfillment of Psalm 41:9 (John 13:18). God is not the author of sin; Satan and Judas are guilty of the murder of Jesus. Nevertheless, not even this act is out of God's sovereign control."[29]

In between the verses affirming Jesus's control of the situation, we learn of Satan's work in Judas's heart: "The devil had already put it into the heart of Judas Iscariot, Simon's son, to betray him" (13:2). This does not relieve Judas of culpability for betraying his Master. But it traces his rebellious act to its nefarious source—the Evil One himself.

At one point during the Last Supper, which Jesus had with his disciples before the cross, he is "troubled in his spirit" and says, "Truly, truly, I say to you, one of you will betray me" (v. 21). The Eleven are bewildered, and Peter prompts John to ask Jesus of whom he is speaking. "Jesus answered, 'It is he to whom I will give this morsel of bread when I have dipped it.' So when he had dipped the morsel, he gave it to Judas, the son of Simon Iscariot" (v. 26). The next words reveal that the Devil is not only the instigator of Judas's betrayal; he also empowers him to carry out the act: "Then after he had taken the morsel, Satan entered into him" (v. 27).

It was customary for a host to give a tasty morsel to an honored guest. Apparently Jesus was discreet in doing so to Judas; that fact combined with Judas's deceptiveness led the others (Peter and John excepted) not to suspect him of betraying Jesus. (Judas had secretly been a thief, robbing the moneybag of the group, over which he had charge—12:6.) As is his practice, John uses symbolism: "And it was night" (13:30). Night is the time for doing evil. Köstenberger agrees: John's reference "in all likelihood also conveys the notion of spiritual darkness entered by the betrayer."[30]

---

[29]Robert A. Peterson, *Getting to Know John's Gospel: A Fresh Look at Its Main Ideas* (Phillipsburg, NJ: P&R, 1989), 102.

[30]Köstenberger, *John*, 418.

Satan's Defeat by Christ: John 12:31; 16:11

Twice in the Fourth Gospel, Jesus speaks of Satan's defeat. First, in his most extensive section concerning the cross, he includes this theme: "'Now is the judgment of this world; now will the ruler of this world be cast out. And I, when I am lifted up from the earth, will draw all people to myself.' He said this to show by what kind of death he was going to die" (John 12:31–33). Jesus says his anticipated crucifixion (and resurrection) means that the world, conceived as the evil system opposed to God (cf. 1 John 2:15), will be condemned.

Furthermore, Jesus predicts that his cross will mean the defeat of the Devil: "Now will the ruler of this world be cast out" (John 12:31). Regardless of Satan's planning and executing Jesus's demise, God is far greater, as John reminds us in his first epistle: "He who is in you is greater than he who is in the world" (1 John 4:4). Jesus's cross is Satan's defeat, as D. A. Carson explains:

> Although the cross might seem like Satan's triumph, it is in fact his defeat. In one sense Satan was defeated by the outbreaking power of the kingdom of God even within the ministry of Jesus (Luke 10:18). But the fundamental smashing of his reign of tyranny takes place in the death/exaltation of Jesus. This is a brief statement analogous to the apocalyptic scene in Revelation: the followers of the Lamb overcome the dragon "by [i.e. 'on account of'] the blood of the Lamb" (Rev. 12:11). When Jesus was glorified, "lifted up" to heaven by means of the cross, enthroned, then too was Satan dethroned.[31]

Second, Jesus also speaks of Satan's defeat when he foretells the Holy Spirit's coming to convict the world: "And when he comes, he will convict the world concerning sin and righteousness and judgment: concerning sin, because they do not believe in me; concerning righteousness, because I go to the Father, and you will see me no longer; concerning judgment, because the ruler of this world is judged" (John 16:8–11). Though the interpretation of some of the details is debated, Jesus's main message is plain. When he leaves, the Holy Spirit will come to bring conviction to a world that would never see its sin without his ministry. He will convict the world concerning its sin, self-righteousness, and faulty evaluation of spiritual reality.[32]

Köstenberger says it well:

> The world's judgment is demonstrated by the fact that the "ruler of the world" . . . now stands "condemned" (perfect tense in Greek; cf. 1 John 3:8; Heb. 2:14). But if

---

[31]Carson, *The Gospel According to John*, 443.
[32]I am following D. A. Carson's exegesis as summarized in ibid., 534–39.

the celestial ringleader of all evil is condemned, this also includes those who do his bidding, whether demons or human instruments. . . . Hence, John can write in his first epistle that believers *already have* "overcome the evil one" (1 John 2:13–14 . . .). Significantly, this note of ultimate triumph concludes the present farewell discourse: "Take heart, I have triumphed over the world" (16:33; cf. 1 John 5:4).[33]

Indeed, Jesus has triumphed over the world, in spite of Satan's big attack. After surveying two spiritual warfare texts in Acts, we will learn more about *how* Christ's work defeats the Evil One in the rest of the New Testament.

Christ Our Victor in Acts

There are at least two passages in Acts that contribute to our understanding of Christ our Victor, one treating Jesus himself and one his servant Paul.

Acts 10:36–38

Through extraordinary means God brings Peter to Cornelius's house to preach the good news. After acknowledging that God not only works among the Jews, the apostle speaks of "the word that [God] sent to Israel" (vv. 34–36). This involves his "preaching good news of peace through Jesus Christ" (v. 36). At this point while addressing Gentiles, Peter cannot resist to add concerning Jesus—"he is Lord of all" (v. 36).

Peter then appeals to the testimony of Jesus's life, something known to Gentiles: "You yourselves know what happened throughout all Judea, beginning from Galilee after the baptism that John proclaimed: how God anointed Jesus of Nazareth with the Holy Spirit and with power" (vv. 37–38). The apostle refers to Jesus's ministry in both Galilee and Judea and underlines God's equipping Jesus for service by giving him the powerful Holy Spirit at his baptism by John.

Next Peter encapsulates Jesus's ministry in a simple and yet "profound summary of Jesus' life:"[34] "He went about doing good and healing all who were oppressed by the devil, for God was with him" (v. 38). Here is a reminder of Christus Victor at work freeing the oppressed. A good example is Jesus's healing in a synagogue on the Sabbath a woman who was disabled by a demon and was bent over for eighteen years. When the ruler of the synagogue objects, Jesus, appalled at the hypocrisy of the man, who certainly cares for his animals on the Sabbath, rebukes him: "And ought not this woman, a daughter of Abraham whom Satan bound for eighteen years, be loosed from this bond on the Sabbath

---

[33]Köstenberger, *John*, 472–73, italics original.
[34]John B. Polhill, note in the *ESV Study Bible* on Acts 10:38 (p. 2104).

day?" (Luke 13:16). Jesus is the champion who does good, including healings and exorcisms, seven days a week.

Acts 26:17–18

As part of his defense before Herod Agrippa II, Paul tells the story of his conversion. When, as Saul of Tarsus, he asks, "Who are you, Lord?" of the one who knocked him to the ground and who questioned why he was persecuting him, Saul receives the surprise answer of his life: "I am Jesus whom you are persecuting" (Acts 26:14–15). Jesus then proceeds to tell Saul (who will be renamed Paul) what his mission will be. Paul will be Jesus's servant who will bear witness to what Jesus shows him. God will protect Paul, who is to preach to Jews and especially Gentiles.

Jesus then specifies Paul's ministry in terms of his primary audience, the Gentiles, "to whom I am sending you to open their eyes, so that they may turn from darkness to light and from the power of Satan to God, that they may receive forgiveness of sins and a place among those who are sanctified by faith in me" (vv. 17–18). Paul will preach the gospel to enable people to understand God's grace. As a result many will turn to God in Christ and know forgiveness and holiness.

Jesus's emissary Paul will be his agent to redirect people "from darkness to light and from the power of Satan to God" (v. 18). Christus Victor thus continues his work through his Apostle to the Gentiles. We see the opposite effect on Paul's first missionary journey when he is opposed by the sorcerer and Jewish false prophet Bar-Jesus or Elymas on Cyprus. When the sorcerer seeks to turn people away from Christ, Paul explodes:

> "You son of the devil, you enemy of all righteousness, full of all deceit and villainy, will you not stop making crooked the straight paths of the Lord? And now, behold, the hand of the Lord is upon you, and you will be blind and unable to see the sun for a time." Immediately mist and darkness fell upon him, and he went about seeking people to lead him by the hand. (Acts 13:10–11)

Here is a temporary and physical blinding, showing the hearers of the gospel that the sorcerer is spiritually blind. But what Jesus commissions Paul to do is exactly what Jesus did for him, as Ben Witherington explains: Acts 26:18 "indicates that Paul is to do for others what in fact happened to him—to open their eyes so they may turn from darkness to light, from the power of Satan to God."[35] First Thessalonians bears witness to God's using Paul to accomplish

---

[35]Ben Witherington III, *The Acts of the Apostles: A Socio-Rhetorical Commentary* (Grand Rapids: Eerdmans, 1998), 745.

that very thing. At Paul's preaching they "turned to God from idols to serve the living and true God" (1 Thess. 1:9).

The Lord Jesus, our champion, routed the demons in his earthly ministry and continues to do the same through his apostles in the Acts. As we might expect, the apostle Paul will give more instruction in his epistles concerning the Victor's work in the present and the future.

Christ Our Victor in Paul

Spiritual warfare is a major theme in Paul's epistles. He says much about our spiritual enemies, about Christ our champion, and about the results of the victory that he wins for us. Curiously, he does not say as much about how Christ wins the victory. Nonetheless, the note of triumph is unmistakable in Paul.

> For I am sure that neither death nor life, nor angels nor rulers, nor things present nor things to come, nor powers, nor height nor depth, nor anything else in all creation, will be able to separate us from the love of God in Christ Jesus our Lord. (Rom. 8:38–39)

> The God of peace will soon crush Satan under your feet. (Rom. 16:20)

> But thanks be to God, who gives us the victory through our Lord Jesus Christ. (1 Cor. 15:57)

> But thanks be to God, who in Christ always leads us in triumphal procession, and through us spreads the fragrance of the knowledge of him everywhere. (2 Cor. 2:14)

> He has delivered us from the domain of darkness and transferred us to the kingdom of his beloved Son, in whom we have redemption, the forgiveness of sins. (Col. 1:13–14)

Our Enemies

Paul speaks often about spiritual foes, more powerful than we, whose bent is to destroy us. Frequently in this regard he tells of Satan, the arch-enemy of God and his people. Paul has many names for him: "Satan," "the god of this world," "the prince of the power of the air," "the spirit that is now at work in the sons of disobedience," "the devil," and "the evil one."

> The god of this world has blinded the minds of the unbelievers, to keep them from seeing the light of the gospel of the glory of Christ, who is the image of God. (2 Cor. 4:4)

And no wonder, for even Satan disguises himself as an angel of light. (2 Cor. 11:14)

And you were dead in the trespasses and sins . . . following the prince of the power of the air, the spirit that is now at work in the sons of disobedience. (Eph. 2:1–2)

Be angry and do not sin; do not let the sun go down on your anger, and give no opportunity to the devil. (Eph. 4:26–27)

Put on the whole armor of God, that you may be able to stand against the schemes of the devil. (Eph. 6:11)

In all circumstances take up the shield of faith, with which you can extinguish all the flaming darts of the evil one. (Eph. 6:16)

Moreover, he must be well thought of by outsiders, so that he may not fall into disgrace, into a snare of the devil. (1 Tim. 3:7)

God may perhaps grant them repentance leading to a knowledge of the truth, and they may come to their senses and escape from the snare of the devil, after being captured by him to do his will. (2 Tim. 2:25–26)

The apostle also speaks of the world as God's enemy and ours. He does not mean the world simply as created, but as fallen, as the sinful system dedicated to eradicating the knowledge of God. When Paul views this enemy spatially, he calls it the world; when he views it temporally, he calls it this (evil) age.[36]

Yet among the mature we do impart wisdom, although it is not a wisdom of this age or of the rulers of this age, who are doomed to pass away. . . . None of the rulers of this age understood this, for if they had, they would not have crucified the Lord of glory. (1 Cor. 2:6, 8)

The god of this world has blinded the minds of the unbelievers. (2 Cor. 4:4)

. . . the Lord Jesus Christ, who gave himself for our sins to deliver us from the present evil age. (Gal. 1:3–4)

And you were dead in the trespasses and sins in which you once walked, following the course of this world. (Eph. 2:1–2)

---

[36] He uses the same Greek word αἰών (aiōn) in both cases. See William F. Arndt and F. Wilbur Gingrich, *A Greek-English Lexicon of the New Testament and Other Early Christian Literature*, 2nd ed. (Chicago: University of Chicago, 1979), 27–28.

Paul varies his vocabulary to speak of other adversaries—evil rulers, powers, authorities, and spiritual forces of evil. People in the first century were more aware of these evil spiritual powers than are many in the twenty-first century West. Presumably they are to be equated with the demons and unclean spirits of the Gospels and, in turn, with the fallen angels.

> For I am sure that neither death nor life, nor angels nor rulers, nor things present nor things to come, nor powers, nor height nor depth, nor anything else in all creation, will be able to separate us from the love of God in Christ Jesus our Lord. (Rom. 8:38–39)

> Then comes the end, when he delivers the kingdom to God the Father after destroying every rule and every authority and power. (1 Cor. 15:24)

> For we do not wrestle against flesh and blood, but against the rulers, against the authorities, against the cosmic powers over this present darkness, against the spiritual forces of evil in the heavenly places. (Eph. 6:12)

> He disarmed the rulers and authorities and put them to open shame, by triumphing over them in him. (Col. 2:15)

Another foe is death personified. Whether fallen human beings live few years or many, they are alike in this—they cannot avoid this persistent antagonist. All die.

> The last enemy to be destroyed is death. (1 Cor. 15:26)

> When the perishable puts on the imperishable, and the mortal puts on immortality, then shall come to pass the saying that is written:

> > "Death is swallowed up in victory."
> > "O death, where is your victory?
> > O death, where is your sting?"

> The sting of death is sin, and the power of sin is the law. But thanks be to God, who gives us the victory through our Lord Jesus Christ. (1 Cor. 15:54–57)

Our Champion

For Paul, Christ is the mighty Victor, who defeats our adversaries in his death and resurrection. God the Father stands behind this, for he has freed us from Satan's kingdom: "He has delivered us from the domain of darkness and transferred us to the kingdom of his beloved Son, in whom we have redemption, the forgiveness of sins" (Col. 1:13–14). "God the Father's bestowal of the inheritance on his new covenant people takes the form of a rescue and transfer operation," as Douglas Moo puts it.[37]

Paul does not go into detail to tell us *how* God in Christ defeats our foes. In one place he extols "the Lord Jesus Christ, who gave himself for our sins to deliver us from the present evil age, according to the will of our God and Father" (Gal. 1:3–4). It is plain that Christ's giving himself in crucifixion delivers us from our foes, but Paul does not tell us more about how this works.

In another place the apostle exults in God's power, displayed preeminently in Christ's resurrection and sitting at God's right hand. He prays that the Ephesians may know

> what is the immeasurable greatness of his power toward us who believe, according to the working of his great might that he worked in Christ when he raised him from the dead and seated him at his right hand in the heavenly places, far above all rule and authority and power and dominion, and above every name that is named, not only in this age but also in the one to come. (Eph. 1:19–21)

Again, it is clear that the Father's raising the Son and seating him at his right hand are the supreme displays of power from which the readers are to draw confidence. And we can imply that Christ's forever being "far above all rule and authority and power and dominion" means that the evil powers are subject to him, the Victor. But Paul does not here connect Jesus's resurrection and session and Christ's defeating our foes.

The closest Paul comes to explaining how Christ our champion defeats our enemies by his death and resurrection is in Colossians 2:13–15. But his explanation will surprise some.

> And you, who were dead in your trespasses and the uncircumcision of your flesh, God made alive together with him, having forgiven us all our trespasses, by canceling the record of debt that stood against us with its legal demands. This he set aside, nailing it to the cross. He disarmed the rulers and authorities and put them to open shame, by triumphing over them in him. (vv. 13–15)

In order to treat properly the Christus Victor theme of verse 15, I must set it in its context. Paul gives two spiritual problems for which we sinners desper-

---

[37]Douglas J. Moo, *The Letters to the Colossians and to Philemon*, The Pillar New Testament Commentary (Grand Rapids: Eerdmans, 2008), 102.

ately need solutions. First is spiritual death: you "were dead in your trespasses." Second is moral impurity: you "were dead in . . . the uncircumcision of your flesh" (v. 13). The apostle then shows how God solves our problems. His solution for spiritual death is regeneration: "God made [you] alive together with him" (v. 13). His solution for moral impurity is pardon for sin: ". . . having forgiven us all our trespasses" (v. 13).

Paul goes into detail concerning this second solution. God granted total forgiveness of our trespasses "by canceling the record of debt that stood against us with its legal demands" (v. 14). "The standard meaning for" *cheirographon* "is 'certificate of indebtedness,' a document recording debts that one is obliged to pay, what we would call an 'IOU.'"[38] This IOU opposes us "with its legal demands." This refers to the Ten Commandments, as is shown by the fact that Paul uses the same expression in Ephesians 2:15, where it is rendered "the law of commandments expressed in *ordinances.*"

The apostle's picture is vivid, as C. F. D. Moule shows: "I owe God obedience to his will. Signed, mankind."[39] Paul says that God cancelled our record of debt. The word "cancel" (*exaleiphō*) here "means to 'rub out,' 'wipe away,' and so obliterate from sight."[40] Did God simply wipe away our moral debt and forgive us? No, Paul answers: "This [our debt] he set aside, nailing it to the cross" (Col. 2:14). Here is an impressive picture of penal substitution. God forgave all of our sins by nailing the certificate of indebtedness, the recording of our failure to obey God's commandments, to Jesus's cross. Paul draws his imagery from the Roman practice of nailing to crosses the charges for which the crucified were being executed, as was the case with Jesus's cross in John 19:19.

Paul suddenly changes imagery in the next verse and speaks of Christus Victor: "He disarmed the rulers and authorities and put them to open shame, by triumphing over them in him" (Col. 2:15). The apostle portrays God as the mighty conqueror, who through Christ's cross routs and disgraces the demons.

The imagery comes from the triumphal Roman military procession, in a lavish parade in which the victorious Roman army would march ahead of their defeated foes—including king, some surviving warriors, and spoils—through the streets of Rome to cheers for victors and jeers for the defeated.[41] Second Corinthians 2:14–16 uses this imagery:

---

[38]Ibid., 209.

[39]C. F. D. Moule, *The Epistles of Paul the Apostle to the Colossians and to Philemon*, Cambridge Greek Testament Commentary (Cambridge: Cambridge University Press, 1968), 97.

[40]Peter T. O'Brien, *Colossians, Philemon*, Word Biblical Commentary (Waco, TX: Word, 1982), 126.

[41]I received help from Scott Hafemann's note in the *ESV Study Bible* on 2 Cor. 2:14 (p. 2226).

But thanks be to God, who in Christ always leads us in triumphal procession, and through us spreads the fragrance of the knowledge of him everywhere. For we are the aroma of Christ to God among those who are being saved and among those who are perishing, to one a fragrance from death to death, to the other a fragrance from life to life.

The only occurrences of the same verb (*thriambeuō*) occur in these two texts; it is translated "leads in triumphal procession" in 2 Corinthians 2:14 and "triumphing" in Colossians 2:15. We will benefit from background information from Murray Harris:

> At the head of the procession came the magistrates and the senate, followed by trumpeters and some spoils of war such as vessels of gold or beaks of ships. Then came the flute players, ahead of white oxen destined to be sacrificed in the temples, along with some representative captives from the conquered territory, including such dignitaries as the king, driven in chains in front of the ornate chariot of the general, the *triumphator* ("the one honored by the triumph"), who wore a garb of Jupiter . . . and carried a scepter in his left hand. A slave held a crown over his head. The victorious soldiers followed, shouting *"Io triumphe!"* (Hail, triumphant one!). As the procession ascended the Capitoline Hill, some of the leading captives . . . were taken aside into the adjoining prison to be executed. Sacrifices were offered upon arrival at the temple of Jupiter Capitolinus. Livy informs us of the two purposes of a triumph: to thank the gods who had guaranteed the victory and to glorify the valor of the *triumphator*.[42]

It is easy to see this background reflected in 2 Corinthians 2, and it helps us understand the use of the word "fragrance" (*osmē*) there (vv. 14, 16). Harris adds that sometimes "included in the victory procession . . . were those who burned incense along the triumphal route, others who carried and displayed spices brought from the conquered regions, and yet others who scattered garlands of flowers and sprinkled perfume along the streets."[43]

Paul wrote, "He [God] disarmed the rulers and authorities" (Col. 2:15). The word translated "disarmed" means "stripped" and when used of human warriors refers to the conquered being stripped of either their clothes or their weapons. In the former case, the stress would be on embarrassment; in the latter, on subjection. It comes down to a matter of emphasis because each idea implies

---

[42]Murray J. Harris, *The Second Epistle to the Corinthians*, The New International Greek Testament Commentary (Grand Rapids: Eerdmans, 2005), 243–44.
[43]Ibid., 246.

the other, for the conquered are humiliated and are without weapons. And this is the same for the conquered demons; they are embarrassed and powerless.

God in Christ put the defeated spiritual powers "to open shame" (v. 15). The only other New Testament use of this word informs its meaning here. Matthew writes of Joseph with respect to Mary: he was "a just man and unwilling *to put her to shame*, resolved to divorce her quietly" (Matt. 1:19). If we ask how God shamed the demons, Paul answers "by triumphing over them in him" (Col. 2:15).

God led a triumphal procession over the evil powers; he routed them. The last word in the verse is ambiguous. It could be translated "him," as in the ESV, meaning that God triumphed over the powers in Christ (the crucified). Or it could be translated "it," as in the NIV, meaning that God triumphed over the powers in the cross (of Christ). Either translation implies the other, because verse 14 mentions the cross.

This, then, is the clearest statement in Paul that Christus Victor defeated the spiritual forces of evil in the heavenly places by his cross. Peter O'Brien captures the sense well:

> The "principalities and powers" who have been conquered and are drawn along in God's triumphal procession are not related to God or Christ as Paul and the other Christians are. God parades these powerless "powers" and "principalities" to make plain to all the magnitude of the victory.... Their period of rule is finished; they must worship and serve the victor. These authorities are not depicted as gladly surrendering but as submitting against their wills to a power they cannot resist. They have been pacified (1:20), overcome and reconciled, yet not finally destroyed or appeased. They continue to exist, opposed to man and his interests (Rom. 8:38, 39). But they cannot finally harm the person who is in Christ, and their ultimate overthrow, although in the future, is sure and certain (1 Cor. 15:24–28).[44]

What is the implied connection between Colossians 2:14 and 15? It seems that by nailing our bond of indebtedness to Christ's cross (v. 14) God defeated the demons (v. 15). F. F. Bruce is correct:

> Not only has he blotted out the record of their indebtedness but he has subjugated those powers whose possession of the damning indictment was a means of controlling them. The very instrument of disgrace and death by which the hostile forces thought they had him in their grasp and had conquered him forever was turned on them into the instrument of their defeat and disablement.[45]

---

[44]O'Brien, *Colossians, Philemon*, 129.
[45]F. F. Bruce, *The Epistles to the Colossians, to Philemon, and to the Ephesians*, The New International Commentary on the New Testament (Grand Rapids: Eerdmans, 1984), 110–11.

That is, the Christus Victor motif, in verse 15, is subservient to penal substitution, in verse 14:

> And you, who were dead in your trespasses and the uncircumcision of your flesh, God made alive together with him, having forgiven us all our trespasses, by canceling the record of debt that stood against us with its legal demands. This he set aside, nailing it to the cross. He disarmed the rulers and authorities and put them to open shame, by triumphing over them in him. (Col. 2:13–15)

Results

Awesome results follow from Christ's victorious death and resurrection. Because of his saving accomplishment "the creation itself will be set free from its bondage to corruption and obtain the freedom of the glory of the children of God" (Rom. 8:21). Furthermore, because of Christ's conquest believers are safe in his love: "For I am sure that neither death nor life, nor angels nor rulers, nor things present nor things to come, nor powers, nor height nor depth, nor anything else in all creation, will be able to separate us from the love of God in Christ Jesus our Lord" (Rom. 8:38–39).

In addition, Christians have access to the mighty power of God that raised Christ and seated him "at his right hand in the heavenly places, far above all rule and authority and power and dominion, and above every name that is named, not only in this age but also in the one to come" (Eph. 1:20–21). Finally, Jesus's conquest assures the final victory of God and his people, and the ultimate defeat of his and our foes. "Then comes the end, when he delivers the kingdom to God the Father after destroying every rule and every authority and power. For he must reign until he has put all his enemies under his feet. The last enemy to be destroyed is death" (1 Cor. 15:24–26).

Christ Our Victor in Hebrews

The chief focus of Hebrews is on Christ our great High Priest and sacrifice, not on Christus Victor. Nevertheless, in at least three passages, this theme is addressed.

Hebrews 1:13 and 10:13: His Enemies Will Be Made His Footstool

We included Psalm 110:1 among the Old Testament divine-warrior passages:

> The LORD says to my Lord:
>   "Sit at my right hand,
> until I make your enemies your footstool."

We saw that David's second Lord is the coming one, the Messiah, and that the psalm uses divine-warrior language to assure him of great victory and rule. The Lord himself will fight for him and defeat his foes (vv. 2, 5–6). He is told to sit at God's right hand, the greatest place of honor and authority, until God subdues his enemies under him (v. 1).

Twice Hebrews quotes Psalm 110:1 with reference to Jesus. The first occurrence is in chapter 1, in which the author shows Christ's superiority to Old Testament mediators of revelation, prophets and angels (Heb. 1:1–14). He then applies that message by showing that the message of Christ, the gospel, is superior to "the message declared by angels" (the law; cf. Acts 7:53; Gal. 3:19). Therefore, his readers dare not reject the gospel, for to do so is to commit spiritual suicide (Heb. 2:1–4).

The writer uses multiple arguments to show Christ's superiority to angels. He has a superior name, Son (1:4–5), and is worshiped by angels when, after ascending, he sits at God's right hand (v. 6). The angels are mere servants of God, but the Son is divine King (vv. 7–9). The Son was God's agent in creation and is immutable (vv. 10–12). In contrast to angels who are "ministering spirits" (v. 14), the Son is told by God, "Sit at my right hand until I make your enemies a footstool for your feet" (v. 13; Ps. 110:1).

The psalm is used to fortify the author's argument for the superiority of the divine Son. He is God's co-regent and awaits the full revelation of the fact that he is Christus Victor. God neither tells angels to sit at his right hand nor promises to subdue their enemies before them in the future. But he does both things for his Son, as O'Brien summarizes:

> With the citation of Psalm 110:1 the climax of the series of Old Testament texts is reached. . . . As the climactic and final quotation in the series Psalm 110 receives particular emphasis. The rhetorical question which introduces it is given prominence, while the text serves to underscore what has been argued in the preceding verses, namely, that angels are inferior to the exalted Son and can never share his position or glory. That the Son is enthroned eternally in the place of honour guarantees his superiority to all else in creation.
>
> The language of the psalm, "*Sit at my right hand,*" (v. 1), has already been alluded to in the opening paragraph where the Son of God is said to have *sat down at the right hand of the Majesty in heaven* (1:3). Now it is explicitly quoted in relation to the king's enthronement, and with it the promise of victory over all his enemies. Accordingly, the citation of Psalm 110 celebrates Christ's *present*

position as the enthroned one, while at the same time pointing forward to the *eschatological* fulfillment of his rule.[46]

The second time Hebrews quotes Psalm 110:1 with reference to Jesus is in chapter 10. Christ's sacrifice is far better than those of the Old Testament (Heb. 10:1–14). Old Testament sacrifices were not efficacious and were therefore repeated perpetually because they did not make perfect the worshipers (vv. 1–4). By contrast, Christ does away with the Old Testament sacrifices by doing God's will and offering himself (vv. 5–9).

"And by that will we have been sanctified through the offering of the body of Jesus Christ once for all" (v. 10). This replaces the Old Testament pattern where priests stood and offered the same sacrifices every day, which were necessarily ineffective because repeated. "But when Christ had offered for all time a single sacrifice for sins, he sat down at the right hand of God" (v. 12). Christ's "single sacrifice" supersedes those of the old covenant. Unlike Old Testament priests, "he sat down" after offering himself, thereby demonstrating the finality of his work.

The place where he sat—"at the right hand of God"—shows that his offering was perfect and efficacious. It was perfect because a holy God accepted it. It was efficacious because it made all other sacrifices obsolete. The next verse testifies to its efficacy: "For by a single offering he has perfected for all time those who are being sanctified" (v. 14).

I omitted one phrase from the quotation of Psalm 110 in Hebrews 10:13: "But when Christ had offered for all time a single sacrifice for sins, he sat down at the right hand of God, waiting from that time *until his enemies should be made a footstool for his feet*" (vv. 12–13). Once again, we see that the exalted King awaits the final results of his work—for every foe finally to be vanquished.

Two points stand out. First, Christ's royal and priestly functions are combined here, as O'Brien underscores:

> The sequence of atonement followed by the heavenly session recalls the intro-duction of Hebrews (1:3), while the allusion to Psalm 110 uses the same formula found in this opening, *at the right hand* of God. This reference to Psalm 110:1 . . . reinforces the image of the kingly Messiah as the enthroned priest. Although the notion of Christ's session in the presence of God was introduced in the exordium (1:3), only now is its significance for our author's argument clarified. Christ's tak-ing his seat is the sure sign that his sacrifice is finished. The "worth of his sacrifice

---

[46]Peter T. O'Brien, *The Letter to the Hebrews*, The Pillar New Testament Commentary (Grand Rapids: Eerdmans, 2010), 77–78, italics original.

and the dignity of his person are further indicated in that he has taken his seat not merely in the presence of God but at 'God's right hand.'"[47]

Second, the final judgment, when Christ's enemies will be made his footstool, is only the outworking of what he has already accomplished as Christus Victor. Philip Hughes explains:

> In the description of Christ as *waiting* for the subjugation of all his enemies . . . there is no shadow of uncertainty regarding the outcome of this period of waiting. The complete defeat of his enemies is assured, for the supreme exaltation by which the redemption he accomplished on earth as the incarnate Son has been crowned spells the doom of every opponent of his authority. . . . The cross of Christ is the conquest of Satan (Jn. 12:31; 16:11). That is precisely why it is the place of our salvation. Future judgment is only the application of the final judgment that has already taken place at Calvary.[48]

Hebrews 2:14–15: He Destroys the Devil and Delivers His People

The principal Christus Victor passage in Hebrews is 2:14–15. Before and after it are other atonement motifs. Christ is the second Adam, who in his suffering of death and exaltation restores the creational glory and dominion forfeited by our first parents in the fall (v. 9). And, he is our great High Priest, who made atonement on the cross and continues to make intercession in heaven "to help those who are being tempted" (vv. 17–18).

In our text, the writer begins with the incarnation, as he does for each of the three atonement pictures (cf. vv. 9, 17), this time picking up the word "children" from Isaiah 8:18, which he has just cited: "Since therefore the children share in flesh and blood, he himself likewise partook of the same things" (Heb. 2:14). By becoming a human being, Jesus shared in humanity. As Lane expresses it: "This assertion grounds the bond of unity between Christ and his people in the reality of the incarnation. In the incarnation the transcendent Son accepted the mode of existence common to all humanity."[49] His incarnation is an essential prerequisite to his death and resurrection. It is true, as Aulén emphasized, that the Christus Victor theme lays stress on the Redeemer's deity. But the scriptural presentation of Christus Victor also highlights his humanity, as here. The One who defeated the Devil and delivers his people is God and man in one person.

---

[47]Ibid., 355–56, italics original.
[48]Philip Edgcumbe Hughes, *A Commentary on the Epistle to the Hebrews* (Grand Rapids: Eerdmans, 1977), 402, italics original.
[49]Lane, *Hebrews 1–8*, 60.

Why was the incarnation necessary? Why did the divine Son become a man? So he could die on the cross. He is the mighty Victor, who attains two goals: by dying he breaks the power of the Devil who held sway over death; and through this same death he rescues those who lived in bondage to the fear of judgment.

First, he became incarnate "that through death he might destroy the one who has the power of death, that is, the devil" (v. 14). The Devil and death are powerful foes, as O'Brien makes plain:

> The mention of the devil as the tyrant shows the depth of the human plight. He "did not possess control over death inherently but gained his power when he seduced humankind to rebel against God" (Gen. 3). Death is the rebel's henchman who bludgeons humanity into submission. Tragically human beings, destined to rule over creation (Ps. 8:5–7), are slaves, paralysed by the fear of death.[50]

Bruce underlines the paradox of Christ's death as a victory for people living in the first century (or twenty-first!).

> If ever death had appeared to be triumphant, it was when Jesus of Nazareth, disowned by His own nation, abandoned by His disciples, executed by the might of imperial Rome, breathed His last on the cross. . . . His faithful followers had confidently expected that He was the destined liberator of Israel; but He had died—not like Judas of Galilee or Judas Maccabeus, in the forefront of the struggle against Gentile oppressors of Israel, but in evident weakness and disgrace—and their hopes died with Him. If ever a cause was lost, it was His; if ever the powers of evil were victorious, it was then.[51]

Appearances notwithstanding, Christ our Victor's death vanquishes the Evil One by already depriving him of his power and will one day result in his being cast into "the lake of fire and sulfur" to suffer eternal punishment (Rev. 20:10). It is difficult to conceive how, by dying, Christ defeats the Devil, and most commentators avoid the issue. Thankfully, Hughes nobly attempts what is ultimately mysterious:

> The power of death is held by the devil only in a secondary and not in an ultimate sense. . . . Scripture, as Aquinas observes, clearly teaches that death, like all else, is under God's control . . . and the clinching proof of this is the conquest of death and Satan by the incarnate Son. Besides, the devil is a creature—finite and futile

---

[50]O'Brien, *The Letter to the Hebrews*, 114–15.

[51]F. F. Bruce, *The Epistle to the Hebrews*, The New International Commentary on the New Testament (Grand Rapids: Eerdmans, 1964), 49.

in his rebellion, and subject to judgment and destruction. . . . Death is the awful reality of divine judgment, not satanic victory.

We should carefully consider *whose* death it was that achieved this triumph and *what kind of* death it was that he died. . . . The spectacle of the cross is not that of any man enduring the pains of death, but of the incarnate Son of God in his pure innocence suffering a death which is not his due. . . . In Christ, the Son of man and only law-keeper, dying in the place of man the guilty law-breaker, the justice and love of God prevail together.

Thus the death of Christ for us was the defeat of the devil; but it is not the end of the story, for it was followed by his resurrection. . . . If Good Friday had not been followed by Easter, that is, if Christ were still dead and buried, then he would be no savior, for Satan, not he, would have been the victor and the power of death would have remained in full force. But the victory is Christ's and, as the next verse declares, he is indeed our all-powerful deliverer.[52]

Second, because Christ is our all-powerful deliverer, our Christus Victor, his dying delivers his people from death and hell. "He himself likewise partook of the same things, that through death he might . . . deliver all those who through fear of death were subject to lifelong slavery" (Heb. 2:14–15). The Devil "has the power of death" as the usurper who deceived Adam and Eve and occasioned the fall. The "death" spoken of here is not only physical death, but also spiritual death, which involves the "fear" that "has to do with punishment" (1 John 4:18). Such fear of death enslaves those who do not know the Lord. Christ the Redeemer, through his death and resurrection, delivers from this bondage all who believe in him. He is his people's mighty champion.

Lane rightly grounds this passage both in the Old Testament divine-warrior tradition's contest of champions, illustrated by David and Goliath, and especially in Jesus's parable about binding the strong man. Lane explains: "The writer to the Hebrews affirms that the Son of God assumed humanity in order to become their champion and to secure their release. Through his death, he crushed the antagonist who had the power of death and so brought deliverance to the captives."[53]

Christ Our Victor in 1 Peter

In at least one passage, Peter implies Christ's victory over the demons. The apostle compares Christian baptism to Noah's ark, "in which a few, that is, eight persons, were brought safely through water" (1 Pet. 3:20). Similarly, "baptism

---

[52]Hughes, *A Commentary on the Epistle to the Hebrews*, 112–13.
[53]Lane, *Hebrews 1–8*, 62–63.

. . . now saves you" (v. 21). Both the ark and baptism signify salvation through the waters of judgment. Peter clarifies: baptism saves "not as a removal of dirt from the body but as an appeal to God for a good conscience" (v. 21). That is, the mere application of water in baptism does not save; one must sincerely believe the gospel (signified in baptism as a visible word from God) to be saved. Does this saving faith in baptism have an object? Is there an objective side to the rite? Peter's answer is yes on both counts: ". . . an appeal to God for a good conscience, through the resurrection of Jesus Christ" (v. 21). One must believe that Jesus (died and) arose in order to be saved.

The apostle does not stop at the mention of Jesus's name: ". . . the resurrection of Jesus Christ, who has gone into heaven and is at the right hand of God" (vv. 21–22). Peter, having spoken of Jesus's death in verse 18, here speaks of his resurrection, ascension, and session. In this context, Peter adds: ". . . with angels, authorities, and powers having been subjected to him" (v. 22).

Peter here speaks of Christus Victor with an accent on his exaltation. He emphasizes Jesus's entrance into heaven and his reigning at the right hand of God. Here again a New Testament writer appeals to Psalm 110:1. Peter Davids argues:

> This is also derived from Ps. 110:1, along with Ps. 8:6, for if Jesus is now seated in the place of power, his enemies must be under his feet. The idea that the affairs of this world are controlled by various spiritual forces . . . is common in Paul . . . . Either these powers or Satan as the arch-power is seen as the force behind evil, idolatry, and persecution . . . and thus the power behind the suffering of the Christians to whom Peter is writing. In ascending Jesus goes through the "air" or the heavens . . . triumphantly and sits by God the Father enthroned over them.[54]

Thomas Schreiner agrees with this line of argument and helpfully draws out the application that Peter intends for his readers.

> The point is that Jesus reigns over all the hostile angelic powers. Contextually, it would make little sense to emphasize that Jesus ruled over good angels. The message for Peter's readers is clear. In their suffering Jesus still reigns and rules. He has not surrendered believers into the power of the evil forces even if they suffer unto death. Jesus by his death and resurrection has triumphed over all demonic forces, and hence by implication believers will reign together with him.[55]

---

[54]Peter H. Davids, *The First Epistle of Peter*, The New International Commentary on the New Testament (Grand Rapids: Eerdmans, 1990), 146–47.

[55]Thomas R. Schreiner, *1, 2 Peter, Jude*, The New American Commentary (Nashville: Broadman and Holman, 2003), 197–98.

Furthermore, if we take into account the New Testament's tension between eschatological realities fulfilled and those still to come, we gain a proper perspective on life, including current trials. Because of the work of Christus Victor, the best is yet to come, as Davids reminds us:

> Peter is well aware . . . that while Jesus may now sit and potentially control the powers, he has yet to bring them all decisively into subjection (cf. 5:8, where the devil can still hurt Christians). But this already–not yet tension is found throughout the NT. That is why some of the passages cited refer to victory over the powers to the cross, some to the resurrection and ascension, and some to the future return of Christ, for what was potentially won at the cross began to be exercised in the resurrection and will be consummated in the return of Christ.[56]

Christ Our Victor in 1 John

John's letters acknowledge an impressive array of enemies of God and his people: the Evil One, the Devil (1 John 2:13–14; 3:8, 10–11; 5:18–19), the world (2:15–17; 5:19), antichrist(s) (2:18, 22; 4:3; 2 John 7), false prophets (1 John 4:1), the spirit of the antichrist (4:3), and deceivers (2 John 7).

John differentiates between "the children of God" and "the children of the devil": "By this it is evident who are the children of God, and who are the children of the Devil: whoever does not practice righteousness is not of God, nor is the one who does not love his brother" (1 John 3:10). He distinguishes those who belong to God and those under the Devil's power: "We know that we are from God, and the whole world lies in the power of the evil one" (5:19).

He identifies those who believe that Jesus is the Son of God as those who overcome the world by faith: "For everyone who has been born of God overcomes the world. And this is the victory that has overcome the world—our faith. Who is it that overcomes the world except the one who believes that Jesus is the Son of God?" (5:4–5).

Once, he speaks of Christus Victor: "The reason the Son of God appeared was to destroy the works of the devil" (3:8). Not only did Christ come "to take away sins" (v. 5), by shedding his "blood" (1:7) and thereby making propitiation for sins (2:2; 4:10). He also came "to destroy the works of the devil" (3:8).

Robert Yarbrough explains two senses in which Christ destroyed the Devil's works (v. 8) by his triumphant death and resurrection:

---

[56]Davids, *The First Epistle of Peter*, 147.

First, death itself has been destroyed. This is implicit in every Johannine reference to eternal life (1:2; 2:25; 3:15; 5:11, 13, 20), and it is explicit in 3:14: "We know that we have passed from death to life." . . . Second, "works" hostile to God, or characteristic of the devil, have been destroyed. . . . In essence they correspond to Paul's "works of darkness" (Rom. 13:12) or "works of the flesh" (Gal. 5:19) or "evil work" (2 Tim. 4:18). Such works are the stuff of the sin that John so steadily decries throughout his epistle and mentions twice in this verse alone. Because Christ is victorious over the devil in death, he can mentor daily ethical victory in the lives of his followers who would otherwise be "held in slavery by their fear of death" (Heb. 2:15 NIV).[57]

And Christ's victory also extends to Christians. Köstenberger shows that the spiritual warfare theme of the Fourth Gospel extends to John's letters, that Christ's victory is evident in both, and how that victory extends to his people:

John's letters, therefore, contain all the same ingredients of the cosmic trial motif as does the gospel. One finds terminology related to witness, the world, truth, and references to the battle between God's Christ and Satan. While focused on Jesus, who has "overcome the world" (John 16:33), and destroyed "the devil's work" (1 John 3:8), this cosmic conflict has also engulfed believers, who have the victory by their faith in the victorious Son of God, who has broken the power of the evil one. Thus John's opening words in the gospel are proved true: "The light shines in the darkness, and the darkness has not overcome it."[58]

Christus Victor thus appears in the Synoptic Gospels, John, Acts, Paul's letters, Hebrews, 1 Peter, 1 John, and finally Revelation, to which we now turn.

Christ Our Victor in Revelation

Dennis E. Johnson, bridging Revelation's occasion and purpose in the first century and its relevance for the twenty-first century, asserts:

Revelation is addressed to a church that is under attack. Its purpose . . . is not to satisfy idle eschatological curiosity or feed a hunger for revenge but to fortify Jesus' followers in steadfast hope and holy living. . . . The dragon's [Satan's] assault on the church comes in different forms and from different quarters in different places and times. . . . But always, in every age and place, the church is under attack. Our

---

[57]Robert W. Yarbrough, *1–3 John*, Baker Exegetical Commentary on the New Testament (Grand Rapids: Baker Academic, 2008), 188–89.

[58]Andreas J. Köstenberger, *A Theology of John's Gospel and Letters*, Biblical Theology of the New Testament, ed. Andreas J. Köstenberger (Grand Rapids: Zondervan, 2009), 456.

only safety lies in seeing the ugly hostility of the enemy clearly and clinging fast to our Champion and King, Jesus.[59]

Johnson is right. Revelation is filled with conflict between the enemies of God and his people. In fact, nowhere else does Scripture identify our chief Enemy so comprehensively as in 12:9: "The great dragon was thrown down, that ancient serpent, who is called the devil and Satan, the deceiver of the whole world" (cf. 20:2). Thankfully, Revelation is also replete with ultimate victory for the redeemed. I will illustrate both conflict and victory together.

Conflict and Victory

The one who conquers, I will grant him to sit with me on my throne, as I also conquered and sat down with my Father on his throne. (Rev. 3:21)

And the great dragon was thrown down, that ancient serpent, who is called the devil and Satan, the deceiver of the whole world—he was thrown down to the earth, and his angels were thrown down with him. And I heard a loud voice in heaven, saying, "Now the salvation and the power and the kingdom of our God and the authority of his Christ have come, for the accuser of our brothers has been thrown down, who accuses them day and night before our God. And they have conquered him by the blood of the Lamb and by the word of their testimony, for they loved not their lives even unto death." (Rev. 12:9–11)

And I saw what appeared to be a sea of glass mingled with fire—and also those who had conquered the beast and its image and the number of its name, standing beside the sea of glass with harps of God in their hands. (Rev. 15:2)

They will make war on the Lamb, and the Lamb will conquer them, for he is Lord of lords and King of kings, and those with him are called and chosen and faithful. (Rev. 17:14)

Notice that in the first quotation Jesus shares his victory with overcomers. In the second quotation, the saints triumph over the Devil "by the blood of the Lamb," which means the atoning death of Christ. In the third, human beings have conquered the great opponent of God, the beast. And in the fourth, God's enemies oppose the Lamb, who defeats them because he is God almighty. Let us learn more about the blood of the victorious Lamb.

---

[59]Dennis E. Johnson, *Triumph of the Lamb: A Commentary on Revelation* (Phillipsburg, NJ: P&R, 2001), 16, 19.

The Lion Is the Lamb: Revelation 5:5–6, 9

In a vision depicting the heavenly throne room, an elder consoles John, who is weeping because no one is found worthy to open a scroll containing God's purposes for history: "Weep no more; behold, the Lion of the tribe of Judah, the Root of David, has conquered, so that he can open the scroll and its seven seals" (Rev. 5:5). John presents Jesus both as the Lion, Christus Victor who has triumphed in his resurrection from the dead, and as David's descendant.[60]

Christ is "the Lion of the tribe of Judah" who "has conquered" (v. 5). John appeals to Jacob's prophecy concerning Judah in Genesis 49:9 to present Christ as the ruler and champion of his people.

> Judah, your brothers shall praise you;
>> your hand shall be on the neck of your enemies;
>> your father's sons shall bow down before you.
> Judah is a lion's cub;
>> from the prey, my son, you have gone up.
> He stooped down; he crouched as a lion
>> and as a lioness; who dares rouse him?
> The scepter shall not depart from Judah,
>> nor the ruler's staff from between his feet,
> until tribute comes to him;
>> and to him shall be the obedience of the peoples. (Gen. 49:8–10)

Israel's (Jacob's) final blessings on his sons contain predictive elements, and so it is with his last words to Judah. Judah will rule (Gen. 49:8). Israel compares him to the fierce king of the beasts (v. 9). God will establish a dynasty for him with a great empire (v. 10). As Johnson notes:

> God's selection of David as king in place of the Benjamite Saul set the fulfillment of Israel's prophecy in motion. Though the exile would make it seem that David's dynasty had been cut off, like a tree sawn down, leaving only root and stump, Isaiah foresaw a fresh shoot from the stump of David's father Jesse, a fruitful branch springing from a root that seemed lifeless and hopeless (Isa. 11:1, 10).[61]

---

[60]See G. K. Beale, *The Book of Revelation*, The New International Greek Testament Commentary (Grand Rapids: Eerdmans, 1999), 1146–47 for argumentation that the Root of David means his descendant rather than his ancestor, as the expression is commonly understood.

[61]Johnson, *Triumph of the Lamb*, 105.

Of course, these prophecies were fulfilled in "Jesus Christ, the son of David" (Matt. 1:1). Upon first meeting Jesus, Nathanael spoke better than he knew: "Rabbi, you are the Son of God! You are the King of Israel!" (John 1:49).

John is told to behold the conquering Lion, but, shockingly, when he looks he sees not a Lion but a Lamb. Charles Hill captures the moment: "After being told about the triumphant Lion, the Root of David, it must have been a shock for John to look and see a Lamb, looking as though slain!"[62] Christ in his resurrection conquers our foes and thereby delivers us. John develops this idea elsewhere in Revelation (6:16; 17:14; 19:15–21), but only here relates it to Christ's saving work.

"And between the throne and the four living creatures and among the elders I saw a Lamb standing, as though it had been slain, with seven horns and with seven eyes, which are the seven spirits of God sent out into all the earth" (5:6). This is the dominant symbol for Christ in Revelation—the Lamb. In fact, in all of its twenty-eight occurrences in Revelation but one—a simile in 13:11—it is a symbol for Christ the Redeemer. His seven horns denote great might and seven eyes great wisdom. What is the significance of John's looking for a Lion but seeing the Lamb? Beale answers: "Christ as a Lion overcame by being slaughtered as a Lamb, which is the critical event in ch. 5."[63] This is very ironic; it signifies that Christus Victor triumphs by being slain as a victim. The Lamb slain, Christ crucified, is found worthy to open the sealed book of judgment and is adored by living creatures, elders, and innumerable angels (vv. 7–13).

The Returning Warrior-King: Revelation 19:11–16

Our study of Christus Victor has always pointed to the end, when God will win the ultimate victory through him. Revelation celebrates that victory in a classic passage:

> Then I saw heaven opened, and behold, a white horse! The one sitting on it is called Faithful and True, and in righteousness he judges and makes war. His eyes are like a flame of fire, and on his head are many diadems, and he has a name written that no one knows but himself. He is clothed in a robe dipped in blood, and the name by which he is called is The Word of God. And the armies of heaven, arrayed in fine linen, white and pure, were following him on white horses. From his mouth comes a sharp sword with which to strike down the nations, and he will rule them with a rod of iron. He will tread the winepress of the fury of the

---

[62]Charles E. Hill, "Atonement in the Apocalypse of John," in *The Glory of the Atonement*, ed. Charles E. Hill and Frank A. James III (Downers Grove, IL: InterVarsity, 2004), 196.

[63]Beale, *The Book of Revelation*, 352.

wrath of God the Almighty. On his robe and on his thigh he has a name written, King of kings and Lord of lords. (Rev. 19:11–16)

This time Christ is portrayed not as the slain Lamb, but as the divine warrior-king who comes riding a white horse to destroy his enemies. As was evident "in the victory parade granted to Julius Caesar upon his return from a successful campaign . . . white horses symbolize triumphant military achievement," Johnson points out.[64] The intention of this one "called Faithful and True" (witness; cf. 1:5; 3:14) is not in doubt, for John declares, "In righteousness he judges and makes war" (v. 11). He is all-knowing (his "eyes are like a flame of fire"; cf. 1:14) and in complete control ("on his head are many diadems").

His "name written that no one knows but himself" points to the fact that "the infinite being of the Son of God can never be fully known."[65] His "robe dipped in blood" points not to his atoning death but in another direction, as Beale explains:

> The rider is portrayed as "clothed with a garment sprinkled with blood," which is a clear allusion to the description of God judging the nations in Isa. 63:1–3: "with garments of red colors . . . garments like the one who treads in the winepress . . . their juice is sprinkled on my garments." John thus affirms Isaiah's prophecy of God as a warrior and identifies Christ as that divine warrior.[66]

Notice that the rider, also called "the Word of God" (the revealer of God [cf. John 1:1, 14] whose judgment fulfills biblical prophecy), is accompanied by "the armies of heaven" arrayed for battle (Rev. 19:14). These are the saints who share in his great victory. Johnson interprets the next few images from the Old Testament and applies them to John's hearers:

> John's visions are for Christians who have experienced or will soon experience the atrocities of which human evil and injustice are capable. The vision of the righteous judge who will not spare the wicked is precisely what they and we need to sustain their persistent and nonviolent response to their oppressors. The sharp sword proceeding from Christ's mouth (19:15) . . . is the implement of righteous vengeance by which he will strike down the nations (cf. Isa. 11:4). It is drawn together with the "iron rod" with which the Messiah (Ps. 2:9) . . . will rule or

---

[64]Johnson, *Triumph of the Lamb*, 270.
[65]Dennis Johnson, note in the *ESV Study Bible* on Rev. 11:12 (p. 2491).
[66]Beale, *The Book of Revelation*, 957.

shatter the nations. When Christians are victimized by injustice and cannot fight back, they must not despair. The strong and righteous Judge is coming.[67]

John returns to the imagery of Yahweh, the victorious warrior in Isaiah 63, who will trample his enemies as a person in a winepress tramples grapes, to depict the returning Christ as destroying his and our foes: "He will tread the winepress of the fury of the wrath of God the Almighty" (Rev. 19:15). The Old Testament divine warrior has become Christus Victor. And there is no doubt of his successful defeat of his enemies because of his identity; he is "King of kings and Lord of lords" (v. 16), that is supreme ruler.

Christus Victor is coming back to redeem his people and to judge his enemies. As completely as anywhere in Scripture, Revelation 19:11–21 pictorially describes that judgment. "Our confidence of victory is reaffirmed by a macabre dinner invitation that an angel now issues to the carrion-eating birds," Johnson writes.[68] "Come, gather for the great supper of God, to eat the flesh of kings, the flesh of captains, the flesh of mighty men, the flesh of horses and their riders, and the flesh of all men, both free and slave, both small and great" (vv. 17–18).

There follows the final battle. God's enemies are routed: the beast and false prophet are captured and consigned to the lake of fire (v. 20), a fate they will share with Satan and the resurrected wicked (20:10–15). As for the rebellious kings of the earth and their armies, they "were slain by the sword that came from the mouth of him who was sitting on the horse, and all the birds were gorged with their flesh" (19:21). So much for God's enemies!

Connecting the Dots

Lane concludes, "Champion Christology provided a fresh interpretation of the incarnation from the perspective of the tradition that God or Jesus is the champion who rescues those enslaved by the prince of death (cf. Isa. 49:24–26; Luke 11:21–22)."[69]

Texts

We have studied the following passages: Genesis 3:15; Exodus 15:1–21; 1 Samuel 17; Psalm 110; Jeremiah 21:3–7; Daniel 7:13–14; Matthew 4:10; 12:22–29; Mark 1:12–13, 24; 14:61–62; Luke 4:13; 10:17–20; John 12:31; 13:2, 27; 14:30–31; 16:11; Acts 10:36–38; 26:17–18; Colossians 1:13–14; 2:14–15; Hebrews 1:13; 2:14–15;

---

[67]Johnson, *Triumph of the Lamb*, 272.
[68]Ibid., 275.
[69]Lane, *Hebrews 1–8*, 67.

10:13; 1 Peter 3:20–22; 1 John 3:8; and Revelation 3:21; 5:5–9; 12:9–11; 15:2; 17:14; 19:11–16.

Sphere

This picture of Christ's saving accomplishment comes from the sphere of conflict and combat between God and his enemies. In the Old Testament this picture appears as divine warfare theology and in the New Testament under the image of Christus Victor.

Background

The Old Testament background includes the protoevangelium of Genesis 3:15, the songs of Moses and Miriam (Ex. 15:1–21), David and Goliath (1 Samuel 17), the predictions concerning David's Lord (Psalm 110), the Babylonian exile (Jer. 21:3–7), and the son of man (Dan. 7:13–14).

Definition

Christ our champion is the New Testament picture of Jesus as the incarnation of Yahweh, the divine warrior of the Old Testament. The mighty Son of God who became a human being defeats foes that are far more powerful than we through his death and resurrection. His work as Christus Victor brings us partial victory now and complete deliverance in the resurrection and new earth.

Need

Humanity's need for Christ our conqueror consists of the many and terrible enemies arrayed against us. These include the Devil, demons, the world (viewed as a system set against God and his people), human enemies (John 13:2, 27; 2 John 7), death, and hell.

Initiator

God takes the initiative in defeating his and our foes. He appears as Yahweh the divine warrior in the Old Testament and as Christ our Victor in the New Testament. The Father (1 Cor. 15:57; Col. 1:13–14; 2:14–15; Heb. 1:13), Son (Acts 10:38; Heb. 2:14–15; 1 John 3:8; Rev. 17:14; 19:11–16), and Holy Spirit (Matt. 12:28; Acts 10:37–38) all play roles. But the focus is on Christ our conqueror and his incarnation, death, resurrection, ascension, session, and return.

Mediator

Viewed from the perspective of the conflict between Satan and God, the Mediator is Christ Jesus, "Lord of lords and King of kings" (Rev. 17:14; 19:16), our mighty champion, Christus Victor.

Work

Christus Victor's work includes his incarnation (Heb. 2:14), his earthly ministry—including successful endurance of Satan's temptations and the exorcisms (Matt. 4:1–11; 12:22–29)—especially his death (John 12:31–33; Col. 2:14–15; Heb. 2:14–15; Rev. 12:11) and resurrection (1 Cor. 15:4, 54–57; Eph. 1:19–22; Rev. 5:6–9), his ascension to God's right hand (Eph. 1:19–22; 1 Pet. 3:21–22), his session (Rev. 3:21), and his return (Rev. 19:11–16).

Present and Future Results

Jesus, our mighty champion, has won a great victory now and will win an even greater one in the future. Now, because of his conquest believers are safe in his love (Rom. 8:38–39), have access to God's mighty power exhibited in Christ's resurrection and session (Eph. 1:20–21), and need not fear the Evil One (1 John 4:4).

At his return, he will utterly vanquish his and our enemies (Rev. 19:11–16), including death: "For he must reign until he has put all his enemies under his feet. The last enemy to be destroyed is death" (1 Cor. 15:25–26). As a result his people will be raised from the dead and will mock death (vv. 54–57). Due to his saving accomplishment "the creation itself will be set free from its bondage to corruption and obtain the freedom of the glory of the children of God" (Rom. 8:21).

Relation to Other Doctrines

It is significant that in Colossians 2:14–15, the key Pauline text on the Christus Victor theme and the only place where he explains *how* Christ wins the victory, that theme is subservient to penal substitution.

Scope

As was true of other pictures of Christ's saving deeds, Christus Victor pertains to believers, the church, and the whole creation. Graham Cole says beautifully:

> The Scriptures are obviously addressed to us as creatures. Paul did not write his letters to angels, principalities and powers. As a consequence, we can lose sight of the wider canvas. . . . If we lose sight of the bigger picture, we can shrink the achievement of Christ's work down to how it affects us at the personal level alone.

Yet the New Testament draws the veil aside on occasion to reveal that God has a cosmic point to make. Paul writes to the Ephesians: *His intent was that now, through the church, the manifold wisdom of God should be made known to the rulers and authorities in the heavenly realms*, according to his eternal purpose which he accomplished in Christ Jesus our Lord. In him and through faith in him we may approach God with freedom and confidence (Eph. 3:10–12).[70]

---

[70]Graham A. Cole, *God the Peacemaker: How the Atonement Brings Shalom*, New Studies in Biblical Theology (Downers Grove, IL: InterVarsity, 2009), 129–30, italics original.

Reconciler
Redeemer
Legal Substitute
Victor
Second Adam
Sacrifice

Chapter 14

Christo Our Second Adam

With 1 Corinthians 15 and Romans 5 in mind, Herman Ridderbos speaks of the importance of including Christ as second Adam in an investigation of his saving accomplishment:

> So Christ is the Firstfruits of them that slept. In him the resurrection of the dead dawns, his resurrection represents the commencement of the new world of God.
>
> Nowhere is this more clearly voiced than in the passages in which Christ is set over against Adam. Paul speaks in 1 Corinthians 15:45ff. of Adam as "the first man," and of Christ as "the last (*ho eschatos*) Adam," the "second man." . . . Christ is thereby designated as the Inaugurator of the new humanity. . . .
>
> Christ as second man and last Adam is the one in whose resurrection this new life of the re-creation has already come to light and become reality in this dispensation. . . . Adam and Christ stand over against one another as the great representatives of the two aeons, that of life and that of death.[1]

Christ as second Adam is the most neglected of the six pictures of his saving work that I am treating. It is profitable to trace this picture through Scripture before summarizing.

---

[1] Herman Ridderbos, *Paul: An Outline of His Theology* (Grand Rapids: Eerdmans, 1975), 56–57, italics original.

Old Testament Background: The First Adam

It is no surprise that the background for Christ as second Adam is the first
man, Adam.

Adam and Eve Are Richly Blessed by God

Adam and Eve are special creations of God and the first parents of the human
race. God is portrayed as the divine potter, working with clay, who directly
fashions the first man, using dust from the ground: "Then the LORD God formed
the man of dust from the ground and breathed into his nostrils the breath of life,
and the man became a living creature" (Gen. 2:7). Although other creatures are
said to have the breath of life (1:30; 6:17; 7:15, 22) and are called living creatures
(1:20–21, 24, 28; 8:17), God is pictured as intimately giving life by in-breathing
only to the first man. And God personally creates the first woman from the rib
of the man (2:21–22). Adam and Eve are very special.

In fact, of all of God's creatures our first parents alone are made in his image:

> So God created man in his own image,
>   in the image of God he created him;
>   male and female he created them. (Gen. 1:27)

Derek Kidner describes the image of God in Adam or Eve in this manner: "This
living creature, then . . . is an expression or transcription of the eternal, incorporeal creator in terms of temporal, bodily, creaturely existence."[2] Theologians
have spoken of the image of God as including aspects of human constitution,
functions, and relationships.[3]

Bruce Waltke provides a pithy summary of a lengthy and influential article
by J. A. Clines on the image of God:

> First, the term *image* refers to a statue in the round, suggesting that a human being
> is a psychosomatic unity. Second, an image functions to express, not to depict;
> thus, humanity is a faithful and adequate representation, though not a facsimile.
> . . . Third, an image possesses the life of the one being represented. Fourth, an
> image represents the presence of the one represented. Fifth, inseparable from the
> notion of serving as a representative, the image functions as ruler in the place of

---

[2]Derek Kidner, *Genesis*, Tyndale Old Testament Commentaries (Downers Grove, IL: InterVarsity,
1967), 51.
[3]For discussion, see Anthony A. Hoekema, *Created in God's Image* (Grand Rapids: Eerdmans, 1986),
11–101.

the deity. . . . Finally, in the context of Genesis, the image refers to the plurality of male and female within the unity of humanity.[4]

What an honor for human beings to be made like God in these many ways!

Indeed, Adam and Eve are greatly blessed by God. They are made for God and each other (1:26; 2:20–25), are given dominion over the other creatures (1:26, 28), are told to be fruitful and multiply (1:28), and are put into a marvelous garden filled with delights that they are to enjoy (2:8–9). Psalm 8, which begins and ends by extolling God for his majesty displayed in all creation, rejoices in his goodness to our first parents. Though seemingly insignificant when compared to the vastness of God's heavens, they are made "a little lower than the heavenly beings and crowned . . . with glory and honor" (Ps. 8:5). They are given dominion over all of the other works of God's "hands"; and everything else is put "under" their "feet" (v. 6–8).

Adam and Eve Tragically Fall into Sin

But Edenic purity and bliss are not to last, for, as absurd as it seems, the first man and woman rebel against their Lord. The crafty serpent, an instrument of Satan (Rev. 12:9; 20:2), uses a subversive and distorting strategy. He first questions God's word—"Did God actually say, 'You shall not eat of any tree in the garden'?", then denies it—"You will not surely die" (Gen. 3:1, 4). The serpent proceeds to impugn God's motives by implying that he is keeping good things from Adam and Eve (v. 5).

Our first parents are enticed: "So when the woman saw that the tree was good for food, and that it was a delight to the eyes, and that the tree was to be desired to make one wise, she took of its fruit and ate, and she also gave some to her husband who was with her, and he ate" (v. 6). Derek Kidner says, "The pattern of sin runs right through the act, for Eve listened to a creature instead of the Creator, followed her impressions against her instructions, and made self-fulfilment her goal."[5] Their sin is disobedience to the word of God, unfaithfulness to their covenant Lord, and rebellion in their hunger for power, revealing unwillingness to accept their creaturely status. Adam is complicit with his wife in the primal sin and, because he is the covenant head, receives the ultimate blame for it (Gen. 3:9–12; Rom. 5:12, 18–19).

The Results of Adam's Sin Are Disastrous

The results of Adam's primal disobedience are catastrophic. The curses of Genesis 3 are well known: pain and sorrow in childbirth, in the marital relationship, in

---

[4]Bruce K. Waltke, *Genesis: A Commentary* (Grand Rapids: Zondervan, 2001), 65–66, italics original.
[5]Kidner, *Genesis*, 68.

tilling the soil, and in death. These are all the more tragic when viewed against the backdrop of prefall life for Adam and Eve, as D. A. Carson notes:

> The Bible begins with God creating the heavens and the earth (Gen. 1–2). Repeatedly, God's verdict is that all of his handiwork is "very good." There is no sin and no suffering. The garden of Eden brings forth food without the sweat of toil being mixed into the earth. But the first human rebellion (Gen. 3) marks the onset of suffering, toil, pain, and death. A mere two chapters later, we read the endlessly repeated and hauntingly pitiful refrain, "then he died . . . then he died . . . then he died . . . then he died."[6]

Death is indeed the major consequence emphasized in Genesis 1–3. There God warns, "In the day you eat of it [the tree of the knowledge of good and evil] you shall surely die" (2:17). Satan denies this: "You will not surely die" (3:4). But, as certainly as God's word is true, when they eat they die. As a result of their sin they will one day die physically (5:5); but Genesis lays emphasis on their spiritual death, their alienation from their Maker. This is seen in their immediate responses. Feeling shame at their nakedness (v. 7), "the man and his wife hid themselves from the presence of the Lord God" (v. 8).

C. John Collins explains:

> In the light of what happens (the actions and changed attitudes of the humans), we can see that the part of the semantic range of "death" that is present here is spiritual death, estrangement from God. Physical mortality, which 3:19 predicts, is a consequence of the humans' disrupted condition—which even those who have been morally recovered will have to undergo.[7]

In Romans 5, the apostle Paul affirms that the death spoken of in Genesis 3 is both physical and spiritual:

> Sin came into the world through one man, and death through sin. (Rom. 5:12)

> Many died through one man's trespass. (v. 15)

> The judgment following one trespass brought condemnation. (v. 16)

---

[6]D. A. Carson, *How Long, O Lord? Reflections on Suffering and Evil,* quoted in Christopher W. Morgan and Robert A. Peterson, *Suffering and the Goodness of God,* Theology in Community (Wheaton, IL: Crossway, 2008), 122.
[7]C. John Collins, *Genesis 1–4: A Linguistic, Literary, and Theological Commentary* (Phillipsburg, NJ: P&R, 2006), 175.

Because of one man's trespass, death reigned through that one man. (v. 17)

One trespass led to condemnation for all men. (v. 18)

By the one man's disobedience the many were made sinners. (v. 19)

The apostle repeatedly teaches that Adam's primal sin has resulted in death and condemnation for the human race. The race is helpless in its sin and cries out for a Redeemer, which is just what a gracious God promises.

The Protoevangelium

The grace of God is evident in the fact that even within God's curse of the serpent, God makes the first promise of redemption, the protoevangelium, in Genesis 3:15:

> I will put enmity between you and the woman,
>> and between your offspring and her offspring;
> he shall bruise your head,
>> and you shall bruise his heel.

God will bring hostility between the woman, along with all humankind (Adam names her "Eve, because she was the mother of all living" [3:20]), and the serpent ("only the New Testament will unmask the figure of Satan behind the serpent [Rom. 16:20; Rev. 12:9; 20:2]").[8] Collins has argued on grammatical grounds that the woman's "offspring" refers to an individual.[9] He will be dealt a blow by the serpent's offspring, those who follow Satan in sin. But the good news is that the woman's offspring will deal Satan a mortal blow; a wound to the head is more serious than one to the heel.

Collins aptly summarizes what we may conclude from Genesis 3 concerning the woman's seed:

> Here we have a promise of a specific human who will do battle with the evil power that spoke through the serpent, and at cost to himself will defeat the enemy, *for the sake of humans* (that is, not for himself). We may conclude the following about this figure:
>
> - While human, he is also a special person (with supernatural *power* to win).
> - His work is that of a champion (he fights *on behalf of* others).
> - He will inflict a decisive defeat on the Evil One.[10]

---

[8]Kidner, *Genesis*, 70–71.
[9]Collins, *Genesis 1–4*, 156.
[10]Ibid., 176, italics original. Some regard Eccles. 7:29 and Hosea 6:7 (esv) as additional Old Testament allusions to the fall.

This is correct. Collins is careful not to draw out of Genesis 3 more than what is there. Only the New Testament provides the details concerning the identity of the seed of the woman, and to the New Testament we now turn.

The Second Adam in Luke's Gospel

Waltke effectively argues that Genesis cries out for a second man to undo the results of the first:

> Humanity must return to the garden without sin and without death. That will require the second Adam, who by clothing us with his righteousness will take us into the garden. The first Adam, representing all people, fails and brings death upon all. The active obedience of the last Adam satisfies God's demands and gives the faithful eternal life (Rom. 5:12–19; 1 Cor. 15:45–49). The story of paradise regained is true only through Christ. The coming heavenly Adam, who bears the curse of toil, sweat, thorns, conflict, death on a tree, and descent into dust, will regain the garden, tearing apart the veil of the temple on which the cherubim were sewn (Ex. 26:1; Matt. 27:51; Heb. 6:19; 9:3; Rev. 22:1–3, 14).[11]

We gain our first New Testament glimpse of the second Adam in Luke's Gospel.

Jesus's Genealogy (Luke 3:38)

Matthew (1:2–16) and Luke (3:23–38) both give genealogies of Jesus. While it is not difficult to discern the major purpose of each of these genealogies, their differences continue to perplex scholars.[12] Our present concern is with the unique ending of Luke's genealogy of Jesus. Luke begins: "Jesus, when he began his ministry, was about thirty years of age, being the son (as was supposed) of Joseph, the son of Heli" (Luke 3:23). Luke concludes the genealogy, "the son of Enos, the son of Seth, the son of Adam, the son of God" (v. 38).

In the context, Luke frames the genealogy with verses that portray Jesus's special relationship to both God and humanity.[13] At Jesus's baptism, which immediately precedes the genealogy, the Father proclaims to him from heaven, "You are my beloved Son; with you I am well pleased" (v. 22). And in verse 38 Adam is also called "the son of God," a reminder of Jesus's divine sonship. Jesus's solidarity with humankind is also underscored twice. By undergoing baptism himself,

---

[11]Waltke, *Genesis*, 104.

[12]For discussion, see Darrell L. Bock, *Luke 1:1–9:50*, Baker Exegetical Commentary on the New Testament (Grand Rapids: Baker Academic, 1994), 918–23.

[13]I owe this insight to Joel B. Green, *Gospel of Luke*, The New International Commentary on the New Testament (Grand Rapids: Eerdmans, 1997), 189.

Jesus identifies with sinners needing forgiveness (v. 21). And his genealogy is traced to the first man (v. 38).

Jesus is thus "the son of Adam, the son of God" (v. 38). Darrell Bock underscores the uniqueness of this:

> The genealogical table ends with the mention of Adam, the first man created by God in Gen 1. He is made in God's image. According to Genesis, from him all the human race descends. It is probably this connection that allows Luke to conclude the list with the unprecedented words τοῦ θεοῦ (*tou theou,* son of God). No example of such an ending exists in genealogies in the OT, Pseudepigrapha, Qumran writings, or rabbinic literature. Nearly all commentators see an identification of Jesus with all humanity in this reference. This universal perspective fits the Lucan concern for Gentiles.[14]

Luke, therefore, just before the beginning of Jesus's public ministry, introduces him as the second Adam. Joel Green draws out the import of Luke's tracing Jesus's genealogy to Adam: "Jesus is thus rooted securely in the past of God's covenantal interaction with God's people, and his ancestral credentials as God's redemptive agent are asserted. The reference to Adam as son of God presents the divine origin of the human race and indicates Jesus' solidarity with all humanity."[15]

Luke also accomplishes something else; he builds a bridge between the first Adam, mentioned last in his genealogy of Jesus, and Jesus's temptation, which immediately follows. The result is an implied contrast between the two Adams and the testing they underwent, as Graham Cole points out:

> The Lucan account of the temptations is also preceded by a genealogy (Luke 3:23–38). This genealogy goes all the way back to Adam, who is described significantly as "the son of God" (Luke 3:38). It is not too speculative to see in the Lucan account of the temptations an allusion to Adam's test in the paradise of God as God's son, and subsequent failure in contrast to the testing of this son of Adam, Jesus, who in a very different setting—not a garden but a wilderness—does not fall to temptation.[16]

Jesus's Temptation (Luke 4:1–13)

Commentators correctly point to Israel's forty-year temptation in the wilderness as important background for Jesus's temptation by Satan for forty days.

---

[14]Bock, *Luke 1:1–9:50,* 359–60, italics original.

[15]Ibid.,189.

[16]Graham A. Cole, *God the Peacemaker: How Atonement Brings Shalom,* New Studies in Biblical Theology (Downers Grove, IL: InterVarsity, 2009), 108.

But, viewed from the perspective of the ending of Jesus's genealogy, Jesus can also be seen as the second Adam. The first Adam was tested by Satan in the beautiful garden of Eden with one test and failed. The second Adam was tested by Satan in the wilderness with three tests and passed. Jesus, the faithful second Adam and Israel, refused to use his divine powers outside of the Father's will. Empowered by the Holy Spirit (4:1), he resolutely denied himself, and employed Deuteronomy to reject the Tempter's enticements.

Bock helpfully labels the three temptations:

- Temptation of Bread and God's Care (4:3–4)
- Temptation of Rule through False Worship (4:5–8)
- Temptation to Test God's Providence (4:9–12)

Luke does not seem to develop an Adam christology throughout his Gospel. But we can safely say that the one whose genealogy Luke traces to Adam and who, as second Adam, proved to be faithful when tested where our first father had failed, is the same one who goes to the cross, rises from the dead, and ascends to heaven (Luke 23–24). It remains for Paul and the author to the Hebrews to fill in the picture of Christ as second Adam.

The Second Adam in Paul's Epistles

Paul is the master teacher of the theme of Christ the second Adam. Scholars debate the extent of Adam christology in Paul. I follow Fee in rejecting both minimalist and maximalist positions and opt for a middling one instead.[17] Paul teaches that Christ is the second Adam in at least six important passages: Romans 5:12–19; 8:29; 1 Corinthians 15:20–22, 42–49; 2 Corinthian 4:4–6; and Colossians 1:15, 18. Although many New Testament scholars include Philippians 2:5–8, I follow Peter O'Brien's rationale for not doing so.[18]

Romans 5:12–19

While presenting Christ's work as the basis for justification, Paul gives Scripture's *textus classicus* for original sin. It is important to note, however, that original sin is not the main theme of Romans 5:12–21; justification is. Paul frames his presentation of faith in Christ as the means of sinners' receiving pardon from

---

[17]See the discussion in Gordon D. Fee, *Pauline Christology: An Exegetical-Theological Study* (Peabody, MA: Hendrickson, 2007), 513–23.

[18]Peter T. O'Brien, *The Epistle to the Philippians*, The New International Greek Testament Commentary (Grand Rapids: Eerdmans, 1991), 263–68.

God (Rom. 3:27–4:25) with pictures of Christ's saving accomplishment (in 3:25–26 and 5:18–19). In the former passage he extols Christ's work of redemption and especially propitiation. In the latter passage he extols Christ's "one act of righteousness" and "obedience." What is the apostle's point? He wants to guard that fact that faith is the means, not the basis, of justification. Not just any faith saves, but faith in Christ's atonement. Faith is only as good as its object, and faith that saves has as its object Christ's atonement.

The flow of thought. It is imperative to see how 5:18–19 fits into the flow of thought of verses 12–19. In verse 12, Paul begins a comparison that he leaves unfinished: "Therefore, just as sin came into the world through one man, and death through sin, and so death spread to all men because all sinned. . . ." He presents sin and death as intruders who break into God's good world as a result of Adam's primal sin. Consequently, "death spread to all men because all sinned" (v. 12). These words will not be fully explained until verses 18–19. But Paul does not finish his thought. If he did, he would speak of the second Adam's obedience countering that of Adam and bringing righteousness and life. But that too will wait until verses 18–19.

Instead, in the next two verses he argues that only Adam's sin explains the domination of sin over humanity from the fall in Eden to the giving of the law at Sinai: "For sin indeed was in the world before the law was given, but sin is not counted where there is no law" (v. 13). This verse is very difficult, and I will give my understanding and point readers to two outstanding commentaries for more information.[19] Paul acknowledges that there was sin during the time between the garden of Eden and God's giving of the law at Mount Sinai. "Sin is not counted where there is no law" should not be understood absolutely, for it would not only contradict Old Testament history before the giving of the law in Exodus 20 (e.g., Genesis 6 and 19!), but also clash with Romans 1:18–32, where Gentiles without the law are condemned for rebellion against God. Romans 2:12 is conclusive: "All who have sinned without the law will also perish without the law."

Paul appears to use an unstated comparison: "Sin is not counted where there is no law" as it is counted where there is law. In other words, the law is a sin-detector, enabling sin to be seen for what it is—an offense against a holy God (cf. 5:20). The next verse, then, means that even though the law magnifies sin, death still ruled as a cruel master from the time of Adam to that of Moses. Why

---

[19]C. E. B. Cranfield *The Epistle to the Romans*, International Critical Commentary, 2 vols. (Edinburgh: T&T Clark, 1975), 1:281–83; Douglas J. Moo, *The Epistle to the Romans*, New International Commentary on the New Testament (Grand Rapids: Eerdmans, 1996), 329–32.

choose those two times? Because Adam sinned against an express prohibition of God, and Moses's law enabled sinners to do the same. Death reigned "even over those whose sinning was not like the transgression of Adam" (5:14), that is, a deliberate violation of a divine sanction.

Paul's argument seems to be that the fact of death could be explained by tallying the actual sins committed by people between the times of Adam and Moses. But more is required to explain the rule of death over the same period—even Adam's original sin. The apostle concludes verse 14 by introducing a key principle that lays a foundation for verses 18–19: "Adam . . . was a type of the one who was to come," that is, Christ, the second Adam.

Adam is a type of Christ. Paul does not immediately pursue the typology of the two Adams, but puts distance between them first. He wants to make plain that Christ is not like Adam in every way, so in the next three verses he tells how they are dissimilar.

> But the free gift is not like the trespass. For if many died through one man's trespass, much more have the grace of God and the free gift by the grace of that one man Jesus Christ abounded for many. And the free gift is not like the result of that one man's sin. For the judgment following one trespass brought condemnation, but the free gift following many trespasses brought justification. For if, because of one man's trespass, death reigned through that one man, much more will those who receive the abundance of grace and the free gift of righteousness reign in life through the one man Jesus Christ. (Rom. 5:15–17)

The first Adam brought sin and death, the second Adam grace and life (v. 15). The first Adam brought condemnation, the second Adam justification (v. 16). The first Adam brought the reign of death, the second Adam the reign of life (v. 17).

Finally, Paul, having sufficiently distinguished the two Adams, is ready to tell how they are similar and, in the process, to finish the unfinished comparison of verse 12: "Therefore, as one trespass led to condemnation for all men, so one act of righteousness leads to justification and life for all men. For as by the one man's disobedience the many were made sinners, so by the one man's obedience the many will be made righteous" (vv. 18–19).

Underlying Paul's teaching is his assumption that one of the ways Adam is "a type of the one who was to come" is as a covenant head. Adam and Christ are the two covenant heads of their respective races. Adam is the covenant head of all humankind; Christ the covenant head of the race of the redeemed. Though Eve sinned first, she is not mentioned in Romans 5 or 1 Corinthians 15. Instead, Adam is. He stands for humankind, and his fall is the fall of the race. Repeatedly, Paul teaches that Adam's one sin brought death and condemnation to all:

> Therefore, just as sin came into the world through one man, and death through sin. . . . (Rom. 5:12)

> For if many died through one man's trespass. . . . (v. 15)

> For the judgment following one trespass brought condemnation. . . . (v. 16)

> For if, because of one man's trespass, death reigned through that one man. . . . (v. 17)

> Therefore, as one trespass led to condemnation for all men. . . . (v. 18)

> For as by the one man's disobedience the many were made sinners. . . . (v. 19)

Paul presents Adam as the representative of the human race, whose primal sin brought God's verdict of condemnation and resulted in death, both physical and spiritual. In the last five of the six verses just mentioned, the ellipses are completed with statements about Christ, the second Adam.

Adam's sin and Christ's "one act of righteousness." Paul uses three words to express Adam's fall: "sin" (vv. 12, 14, 16), "trespass" (vv. 15–18), and "disobedience" (v. 19). He uses two words to describe the work of the second Adam that countered the first man's sin: "one act of righteousness" (v. 18) and "obedience" (v. 19). What is the meaning of this "one act of righteousness"? Since it is the same word translated "justification" in verse 16, should it not be translated the same way here? What justifies (no pun intended) rendering it "one act of righteousness"? Douglas Moo answers these questions well:

> Gk. δικαιώματος [*dikaiōmatos*]. In light of the fact that this word is used in v. 16 to refer to justification, it is not surprising to find that many commentators insist that this must be its meaning here also: it was through the "one sentence of justification," or "the sentence of justification procured by the one man," that righteousness of life is "for" all people (e.g. Godet; S-H; Morris). But there are two reasons to prefer the translation "righteous act," as a reference to Christ's "obedience" (cf. v. 19). First, if, as we think likely, ἑνὸς [*henos*] refers to Christ, it is awkward to speak of justification or a sentence of justification as being "of Christ." Second, and more important, the strict parallelism between the first and second clauses suggests that, as παράπτωμα [*paraptōma*] refers to something Adam did, so δικαίωμα [*dikaiōma*] will refer to something Christ did. While

giving the same word two different meanings within the space of three verses may appear dubious, it is, in fact, the meaning of v. 16 that is unusual.[20]

Christ's "one act of righteousness," since it corresponds to Adam's "one trespass," refers to something Christ did, something he accomplished, but what? Romans commentators disagree. Cranfield argues, "By Christ's *dikaioma* . . . Paul means not just His atoning death but the obedience of His life as a whole, His loving God with all His heart and soul and mind and strength, and His neighbor with complete sincerity, which is the righteous conduct God's law requires."[21] Thomas Schreiner disagrees: "Paul is probably thinking here only of Christ's work on the cross . . . but it is possible that his whole life is in view."[22] My judgment, based on the word's usage, and especially its usage here, is that Christ's "one act of righteousness" refers to his lifelong obedience with an emphasis on his "becoming obedient to the point of death, even death on a cross" (Phil. 2:8).

Universalism? When Paul writes "so one act of righteousness leads to justification and life for all men" (Rom. 5:18), does he teach that all of humankind will be saved? This, the claim of universalists, represents a misunderstanding of Paul's words. In verse 19 he says "by the one man's obedience *the many* will be made righteous." Does Paul contradict himself in the space of two verses? Does he teach that all (and not many) human beings are influenced by the two Adams in verse 18 and that many (and not all) are influenced by them in the next verse?

The answer is no. Paul does not compare "all men" with "the many." Instead, he contrasts the two Adams and their enormous effects upon their two races. Adam ruins his race and Christ rescues his. That is, Paul does not oppose "all" to "many" in verses 18–19. Rather, he contrasts each Adam and his influence on his race, designated by "all" in verse 18 and "many" in verse 19. Paul contrasts Adam's "one trespass" with its effect on "all men" and Christ's "one act of righteousness" with its effect on "all men" in verse 18. It is "one man's disobedience" bringing condemnation and "one man's obedience" bringing justification to "many" in verse 19. It is not Paul's purpose to give the number of the lost or the redeemed in these verses. He does that elsewhere, teaching that all human beings are fallen in Adam, and all believers are saved in Christ.

---

[20]Moo, *The Epistle to the Romans*, 341n127, italics added.
[21]Cranfield, *The Epistle to the Romans*, 289, italics original.
[22]Thomas R. Schreiner, *Romans*, Baker Exegetical Commentary on the New Testament (Grand Rapids: Baker Academic, 1998), 287.

Paul extols the obedience of the second Adam. Here, then, Paul exalts the work of the second Adam. His lifelong obedience resulting in death counters Adam's primal disobedience, as Cranfield correctly notes:

> The use of παρακοή [*parakoē*] and ὑπακοή [*hypakoē*] in this verse makes explicit the fact that Adam's παράπτωμα [*paraptōma*] and Christ's δικαίωμα [*dikaiōma*] are both to be understood in relation to the revealed will of God, the one as disobedience to it, the other as obedience. For Christ's ὑπακοή [*hypakoē*] compare Phil 2:8. The term covers His whole life, not just His passion and death.[23]

I would only underscore, as Cranfield's reference to Philippians 2:8 implies, that the Savior's lifelong obedience culminates in and is fulfilled in his cross.

His "one act of righteousness" reverses God's verdict of condemnation for "those who receive the abundance of grace and the free gift of righteousness" (Rom. 5:17). Instead of sinners being condemned in Adam, they are justified in Christ, declared righteous before the throne of God. James Dunn, commenting on verses 18–19, draws out the comparison between the two Adams:

> At this point the features of Adam Christology are most sharply drawn, with Christ's work described precisely as an antithesis to Adam's—the deed which accords with God's will set against the trespass which marked humankind's wrong turning, the act defined as obedience precisely because it is the reversal of Adam's disobedience. The inaugurating act of the new epoch is thus presented as a counter to and cancellation of the inaugurating act of the old, Christ's right turn undoing Adam's wrong turn.[24]

Indeed, it is difficult to overemphasize the importance of the two Adams in Romans 5. Philip Hughes does not do so when he writes, "Indeed, these two figures are presented as uniquely pivotal in the history of mankind in such a way that the destiny of every person is determined by reference to them."[25] Moo is more expansive:

> The actions of Adam and Christ, then, are similar in having "epochal" significance. But they are not equal in power, for Christ's act is able completely to overcome the effects of Adam's. Anyone who "receives the gift" that God offers in Christ finds security and joy in knowing that the reign of death has been completely and finally overcome by the reign of grace, righteousness, and eternal life

---

[23]Cranfield, *The Epistle to the Romans*, 291.

[24]James D. G. Dunn, *Romans 1–8*, Word Biblical Commentary (Dallas: Word, 1988), 297.

[25]Philip Edgcumbe Hughes, *The True Image: The Origin and Destiny of Man in Christ* (Grand Rapids: Eerdmans, 1989), 128.

(cf. vv. 17, 21). The power of Christ's act of obedience to overcome Adam's act of disobedience is the great theme of this paragraph.[26]

Romans 8:29

Romans 8:28–39 is the longest and strongest passage on the perseverance of the saints in Scripture. Paul bases God's preservation of his people on four bulwarks: God's plan (Rom. 8:28–30), sovereignty (vv. 31–32), justice (vv. 33–34), and love (vv. 35–39). The familiar verse 28 introduces this passage: "And we know that for those who love God all things work together for good, for those who are called according to his purpose." Paul expresses confidence that God will ultimately direct all that happens for the good of those who love him. Paul qualifies the lovers of God by describing them as the ones called in line with God's purpose. In context (vv. 18, 22, 26) he means that God will use everything, even present struggles, for the ultimate well-being of his people, those who know and love him, those whom he has effectively summoned to himself in the gospel.

But how do we know this? Verses 28–30 explain: "For those whom he foreknew he also predestined to be conformed to the image of his Son, in order that he might be the firstborn among many brothers. And those whom he predestined he also called, and those whom he called he also justified, and those whom he justified he also glorified." We know that God will work all for the ultimate good of his people because he has planned, has accomplished, and will finally accomplish their greatest good—their salvation.

Paul uses five simple past-tense verbs (aorist) to describe salvation. God is the subject and his people are the object of each verb. God foreknew, predestined, called, justified, and glorified his own. Paul means that God set his covenant love upon his people, chose them for salvation, effectively summoned them to himself through the gospel, declared them righteous in Christ, and caused them to see and share in his glory. This last event is still future but is so certain in God's plan that Paul describes it also as a simple past event. God's foreloved, chosen, called, and justified saints are as good as glorified already!

Paul uses a literary device called climax to connect the five verbs. "*Climax* consists in taking up the key word of the preceding member in the following one."[27] Here is the progression revealing the climax: "Those whom he foreknew he also predestined. . . . And those whom he predestined he also called, and those whom he called he also justified, and those whom he justified he also

[26]Moo, *The Epistle to the Romans*, 315.

[27]Robert Funk, ed., *A Greek Grammar of the New Testament and Other Early Christian Literature* (Chicago: University of Chicago Press, 1961), 261, italics original. See Judith M. Gundry Volf, *Paul and Perseverance* (Louisville: Westminster John Knox, 1990), 68.

glorified" (vv. 29–30). The verbs are links in a chain, inseparably joined and guaranteeing believers their final salvation. Those whom God foreknows will infallibly be glorified.

Paul amplifies only one of the links in the chain—that pertaining to predestination: "For those whom he foreknew he also predestined to be conformed to the image of his Son, in order that he might be the firstborn among many brothers" (v. 29). The apostle gives one goal of predestination—conformity to Christ. The words "the image of his Son" evoke Adam's creation in the image of God in Genesis 1:26–27. Thus Paul presents Christ as the second Adam. In fact, whenever Scripture presents Christ as the image of God or the image to which we will conform, it assumes his humanity. The very designations "image" or "image of God" when used of Christ always presents him as human. Fee affirms that "the use of this language for Christ in itself always presupposes his humanity."[28]

However, in passages where Christ is called "the image of God" or "the image," his deity is also sometimes communicated. Fee agrees, although his pithy words, describing Romans 8:29, need unpacking: "Deeply embedded in such language are the twin emphases, first that the eternal Son of God perfectly bears the divine image and, second, that he did so in his own identity with us in our humanity."[29] Fee means that "the image of his Son" implies both Christ's deity and his humanity. We will look briefly here at passages that we will examine in more detail below. Two texts emphasize the fact that Christ is the divine image of God. Paul tells how the Devil blinds the minds of the unbelievers, to prevent them "from seeing the light of the gospel of the glory of Christ, who is the image of God" (2 Cor. 4:4). When the Holy Spirit works through the preaching of the gospel, he reveals the divine glory of Christ in his capacity as "the image of God." Christ shares the divine glory; as the image of God he is divine.

It is the same in Colossians 1. There Paul calls Christ, "the image of the invisible God" (v. 15). This too is a divine title, as the immediately following words show: "the firstborn of all creation." Paul, relying on Old Testament texts such as Psalm 89:26–27, means that Christ holds the highest rank, that of God himself, over the whole creation. The next verse in Colossians explains why: "For by him all things were created, in heaven and on earth, visible and invisible, whether thrones or dominions or rulers or authorities—all things were created through him and for him" (Col. 1:16). As the true image Christ holds first place over creation because he was the Father's agent in creating all things.

---

[28] Fee, *Pauline Christology*, 520.
[29] Ibid., 521.

When Paul, then, writes, "For those . . . he also predestined to be conformed to the image of his Son" (Rom. 8:29), he speaks of Christ as the divine image of God to whom believers will be conformed. This is their final adoption, which he spoke of in verse 23: "We wait eagerly for our adoption as sons, the redemption of our bodies." When we are conformed to Christ's image in resurrected glory, then, it will be evident that he is "the firstborn among many brothers" (v. 29). He will have first place in God's family, as our unique older brother and Redeemer. In fact, the one who here appears as the image of God and older brother, in another place is said himself to accomplish that conformity. He "will transform our lowly body to be like his glorious body, by the power that enables him even to subject all things to himself" (Phil. 3:21). Paul ascribes divine power to Christ.

In summary, in Romans 8:29 Christ appears as the Son of God and second Adam (the divine image) to whose likeness the Trinity will bring us into conformity in final salvation when God raises us from the dead and transforms us.

1 Corinthians 15:20–22

God used one passage, above all others, to draw me to Christ as a twenty-one-year-old seeker in 1969—1 Corinthians 15:12–19. I was struck by the stark honesty of Paul's words. There he candidly states the implications that would follow if there were no resurrection from the dead and therefore if Christ were not raised. The apostles' preaching and their hearers' faith would be worthless (1 Cor. 15:14). The apostles would be false witnesses of God (v. 14). The Corinthian believers' faith would be to no avail, and their sins would not be forgiven (v. 16). Those who would die trusting Christ would go to hell (v. 17). And Christians would be very pitiful (v. 18).

Jesus is alive! But, in one of the most significant contrasts in Scripture, the apostle declares, "But in fact Christ has been raised from the dead, the firstfruits of those who have fallen asleep" (v. 20). After weighing the cataclysmic effects of Christ's not being resurrected, Paul asserts the central fact of the Christian faith: Jesus is alive! And thus the ruinous implications of his not being raised are not to be dreaded because they are not true. In fact, the apostle makes plain in verses 1–11 that he is confident that most of the Corinthians believe in Jesus's resurrection. That is not the problem. Rather, as Paul explains, "Now if Christ is proclaimed as raised from the dead, how can some of you say that there is no resurrection of the dead?" (v. 12). Paul thus argues for the resurrection of believers by showing the Corinthians their inconsistency in believing in Jesus's resurrection while questioning whether believers will be raised.

Jesus was raised and believers will be raised also. That is because he is "the firstfruits of those who have fallen asleep." Richard Gaffin, based upon a study of the word in the LXX, points to the organic sense of "firstfruits":

> It refers to the "firstfruits" offerings of grain, wine, cattle, and the like, appointed by Moses. The point of these sacrifices is that they are not offered up for their own sake, as it were, but as representative of the total harvest, the entire flock, and so forth. They are a token expression of recognition and thanksgiving that the whole has been given by God.... "Firstfruits" expresses the notion of organic connection and unity, the inseparability of the initial quantity from the whole.[30]

"Firstfruits" is one of Paul's ways of affirming that the salvation that Christ has purchased is "already" and "not yet." *Already* believers enjoy the forgiveness of sins and eternal life. But they still need to confess their sins, and they have eternal life in mortal bodies. *Not yet* are they sinless and in resurrected bodies. They will obtain both of those blessings in the future, however, and God's present blessings assure that. Paul thus speaks of the Holy Spirit, already given to believers as God's "guarantee" (or "down payment"), "seal," and "firstfruits" of final salvation (Rom. 8:23; 2 Cor. 1:21–22; 5:5; Eph. 1:13–14; 4:30). As "firstfruits" the Spirit is a token, promising that resurrected believers will enjoy the life of the Trinity for eternity on the new earth.

Similarly, the risen Christ is the "firstfruits," God's guarantee of the resurrection of believers on the last day. In fact, Christ is more than a guarantee; he is also God's pledge that the saints will be raised in imperishable, immortal, glorious, powerful, spiritual bodies (1 Cor. 15:42–44, 50–53). This is true because of the organic connection between "firstfruits" and the whole, as Gaffin explains:

> [The word "firstfruits"] brings into view Christ's resurrection as the "firstfruits" of the resurrection-harvest, the initial portion of the whole. His resurrection is the representative beginning of the resurrection of believers.... The term seems deliberately chosen to make evident the organic connection between the two resurrections. In the context, Paul's "thesis" over against his opponents is that the resurrection of Jesus has the bodily resurrection of "those who sleep" as its necessary consequence. His resurrection is not simply a guarantee; it is a pledge in the sense that it is the actual beginning of the general event.[31]

Adam brought death, Christ resurrection. Next the apostle draws a powerful contrast between the two Adams: "For as by a man came death, by a man has

---

[30]Richard Gaffin, *Resurrection and Redemption*, 2nd ed. (Phillipsburg, NJ: P&R, 1987), 34.
[31]Ibid., 34–35.

come also the resurrection of the dead. For as in Adam all die, so also in Christ shall all be made alive" (1 Cor. 15:21–22). Adam's primal sin in the garden of Eden brought sin and death into the world of humanity (Rom. 5:12). Since then, every descendant of Adam is born a sinner and eventually dies:[32]

> Behold, I was brought forth in iniquity,
>> and in sin did my mother conceive me. (Ps. 51:5)

For everything there is a season, and a time for every matter under heaven:

>> a time to be born, and a time to die. (Eccles. 3:1–2)

Because of one man's trespass, death reigned through that one man. (Rom. 5:17)

For the wages of sin is death. (Rom. 6:23)

It is appointed for man to die once, and after that comes judgment. (Heb. 9:27)

Just as the first Adam brought death to humankind, so the second and last Adam brings the reversal of death, even resurrection: "By a man has come also the resurrection of the dead" (1 Cor. 15:21). Christ, a genuine human being like Adam, was raised from the grave. As "the firstfruits of those who have fallen asleep" (v. 20), he is the pioneer, the one who goes before his people in resurrection. Not only does he precede them, but his resurrection life is the cause of their resurrection. Thus while Paul's use of second-Adam imagery here obviously emphasizes Christ's humanity, it also reflects his deity. As Adam's original sin causes the death of his children, so Christ's victory over the grave will cause his people to live forever in resurrected bodies.

For emphasis verse 22 repeats the thought of verse 21 and adds an important feature: "For as in Adam all die, so also in Christ shall all be made alive." All who are "in Adam," that is, related to him as covenant head, die because he died. In a similar way, all who are "in Christ," that is, related to him as covenant head, "shall be made alive" in resurrection because he arose.

Being "in Adam" or being "in Christ." Roy Ciampa and Brian Rosner elucidate the significance of humankind's being "in Adam" and believers' being "in Christ":

To be *in Adam* is to be part of the group which finds in Adam its representative and leader, which finds its identity and destiny in Adam and what he has brought

---

[32]Enoch and Elijah excepted.

about for his people. To be *in Christ* is to be part of the group which finds in Christ its representative and leader, which finds its identity and destiny in Christ and what he has brought about for his people. All humans who have not yet found redemption through faith in Christ remain *in Adam*. Those who have entered into the promise of new life, the life of Christ, are *in Christ*, and will find that their initial experience of the newness of life was but a foretaste of the ultimate restoration of life that awaits them in the resurrection.[33]

Christ as second Adam is covenant head and Lord of the new creation, which includes the race of the redeemed now. Fee underlines the importance of 1 Corinthians 15:21–22 in the Pauline corpus:

> This is the first use of the Adam-Christ analogy in Paul's extant letters. . . . It is a commonplace with Paul, for whom Christ stands at the beginning of the new humanity in a way analogous to, but not identical with, the way Adam stood at the beginning of the old order, both temporally and causally. . . . Paul means that those who are "in Christ," those who have entered the new humanity through grace by means of his death and resurrection, will just as certainly "be made alive"; they will be raised from the dead into the *shared life* of the risen One. Thus Christ is the firstfruits; he is God's pledge that all who are his will be raised from the dead. The inevitable process of death begun in Adam will be reversed by the equally inevitable process of "bringing of life" begun in Christ.[34]

Paul's Adam christology, then, exalts the risen Christ as the head of the new humanity and brings great assurance of final bodily redemption to all believers. In the verses immediately following 1 Corinthians 15:21–22, the apostle includes among Christ's benefits a restoration of the original rule over the creation that God gave Adam and Eve. Paul alludes to Psalm 8:6: "You have given him dominion over the works of your hands; you have put all things under his feet" (which in turn reflects Gen. 1:26). Although this dominion was greatly marred when Adam's sin brought sin and death to humankind, the second Adam restores that dominion by rising from the dead, giving life to his people, and giving the kingdom to God the Father on the last day. When the second Adam returns for his risen people, even "those who belong to Christ" (1 Cor. 15:23), Psalm 8:6 will ring true forever: "For 'God has put all things in subjection under his feet'" (1 Cor. 15:27).

---

[33]Roy E. Ciampa and Brian S. Rosner, *The First Letter to the Corinthians*, The Pillar New Testament Commentary (Grand Rapids: Eerdmans, 2010), 763, italics original.
[34]Gordon D. Fee, *The First Epistle to the Corinthians*, The New International Commentary on the New Testament (Grand Rapids: Eerdmans, 1987), 750–51, italics original.

1 Corinthian 15:42–49

The Corinthians are confused concerning the resurrection of the dead on at
least two counts. Because some within the congregation doubt the doctrine
(v. 12), Paul defends it (in vv. 12–34). But they have an additional problem.
Because they cannot imagine what resurrected bodies would look like, Paul
describes the nature of those bodies in broad outlines (in vv. 35–49). Though
there is considerable scholarly discussion over the precise problem concerning
the resurrection of the dead that Paul treats, the main idea is clear enough.[35]

Illustrations from nature. Paul begins by using two sets of illustrations from
nature that he will apply to the resurrection. First, "the analogy of the seed
(vv. 36–38) illustrates from their everyday experience that one living thing,
through death, can have two modes of existence."[36] His emphasis is on wheat, for
example, being sown as a seed but coming to life in a very different form. Second,
Paul illustrates from the natural world by stating that God gives animals, birds,
and fish the bodies that he deems appropriate. In fact, God adapts all kinds of
"bodies," including those of sun, moon, and stars, to their existence (vv. 39–41).

Paul then applies the illustrations to the resurrection. His basic point is that
there is continuity between our present bodies and our resurrection bodies. But,
in addition, there will be discontinuity—wonderful newness. There is continuity:
one plants a kernel of wheat, and nothing else, to get wheat. But there is also
discontinuity: similar to the difference between the appearance of the kernel
and the wheat, human beings' bodies are "sown" in death as "perishable," "in
dishonor," and "in weakness." But the same bodies are raised as "imperishable,"
"in glory," and "in power" (vv. 42–43).

Paul continues, "It is sown a natural body; it is raised a spiritual body. If
there is a natural body, there is also a spiritual body" (v. 44). The antithesis
between "natural" and "spiritual" bodies "has been the cause of great confusion
in the history of interpretation."[37] Paul is not here distinguishing between the
physical and the spiritual. Rather, taking a cue from his usage of "natural" and
"spiritual" in 2:14–3:3, we learn that "the distinction has to do with the difference between ordinary human life and life empowered by God's Spirit. The
adjectives Paul uses describe 'not what something is composed of, but what it
is animated by.'"[38] Christians' resurrected bodies will not be "spiritual" in the

---

[35] Anthony C. Thiselton, *The First Epistle to the Corinthians*, The New International Greek Testament
Commentary (Grand Rapids: Eerdmans, 2000), discusses three main positions, each having permuta-
tions, before adding a fourth (1169–78).
[36] Fee, *The First Epistle to the Corinthians*, 779.
[37] Ciampa and Rosner, *The First Letter to the Corinthians*, 816.
[38] Ibid., 817, citing N. T. Wright, *The Resurrection of the Son of God* (Minneapolis: Fortress, 2003), 352.

sense of being nonphysical. Such an idea makes no sense in a chapter in which Paul contends for the bodily resurrection of Jesus, who is the "firstfruits," the pledge and guarantee, of our bodily resurrection (1 Cor. 15:20). No, "spiritual" does not mean incorporeal. Instead, it has to do with the Holy Spirit. Geerhardus Vos said it well:

> This adjective *Pneumatikon* [spiritual] expresses the quality of the body in the eschatological state. Every thought of immaterialness, or etherealness or absence of physical density ought to be kept carefully removed from the term. . . . Paul means to characterize the resurrection state as the state in which *Pneuma* [Spirit] rules.[39]

Vos is correct. When Paul describes resurrection bodies as spiritual, he means bodies animated and empowered by the Holy Spirit.

"The last Adam became a life-giving Spirit." Paul returns to his Adam-Christ analogy of verses 21–22, but now with a different slant to fit this context: "Thus it is written, 'The first man Adam became a living being'; the last Adam became a life-giving spirit" (v. 45). This time Paul does not emphasize the common humanity of Adam and Christ; rather, he emphasizes the difference between their bodies. Adam's, fitted for life on the present earth, was perishable and mortal. Christ's, fitted for life on the new earth, is imperishable and immortal.

The apostle alludes to Genesis 2:7 in the LXX, which uses ψυχή (*psychē*, "a living being") to describe what Adam became at creation. By contrast, Christ, the last Adam, "became a life-giving spirit" (πνεῦμα, *pneuma*). Paul uses these two words because they are cognate nouns of the two adjectives he employed in the previous verse—ψυχικόν (*psychikon*) and πνευματικόν (*pneumatikon*), respectively. Fee explains the significance of Paul's contrast of the two Adams in context:

> The overriding urgency in this passage is to show in an analogical way that the two kinds of bodies "sown" and "raised" in [1 Cor. 15] v. 44 are already represented in the two archetypal "Adams." The first Adam, who became a "living *psyche*," was thereby given a *psychikos* body at creation, a body subject to decay and death. This Adam, who brought death into this world (vv. 21–22), thus became the representative man for all who bear his *psychikos* likeness. The last Adam, on the other hand, whose "spiritual (glorified) body" was given at his resurrection, not only

---

[39]Geerhardus Vos, *The Pauline Eschatology* (1930; repr., Grand Rapids: Baker, 1979), 166–67, italics original.

became the representative Man for all who will bear his *pneumatikos* likeness, but he himself is the source of the *pneumatikos* life as well as the *pneumatikos* body.[40]

We have stressed the differences between the Adam-Christ analogies in verses 21–22 and in 45. But there is also a vital similarity—both point to Christ as the source of resurrection life: "So also in Christ shall all be made alive" (v. 22); "The last Adam became a life-giving spirit" (v. 45). An essential aspect of Christ's saving work is his becoming the life-giver based on his resurrection. As the risen second Adam, he gives eternal life to sinners now in regeneration, and he will give eternal life to the redeemed on the last day by raising their bodies and transforming them, fitting them for their new environment on the new earth. As Fee expresses it:

> In referring to Christ as a "life-giving πνεῦμα [*pneuma*]," Paul envisions the risen Christ as assuming the *eschatological* role that God played at the beginning. As God breathed life in the first Adam, so that Adam (and all his progeny) would become living beings, created in God's image, so Christ is now asserted to be the one who will breathe life into the dead so that they too shall live. Thus the risen Christ is seen to share in an otherwise unshared divine prerogative, as the Living One who gives life to others.[41]

Although the matter is debated, I believe that when Paul calls Christ "a life-giving spirit," the last word should be capitalized—"a life-giving Spirit." I am persuaded by the exegesis of Richard Gaffin, who concludes, "At his resurrection the personal mode of Jesus' existence as the last Adam was so decisively transformed by the Holy Spirit that Paul says he has become life-giving Spirit."[42] The identification of the risen Christ with the Spirit is economic, not ontological, but "the change in Christ's person at his resurrection is as real as and commensurate with the transformation to be experienced by the rest of the harvest."[43]

Paul next underscores the proper order of our natural and spiritual bodies. Even as Adam preceded Christ, and hence his natural body preceded Christ's spiritual body, so it is for believers: our present bodies are first and our resurrection bodies second. It is possible that some super-spiritual Corinthians had an overly realized eschatology, but we do not know for sure.

---

[40]Fee, *The First Epistle to the Corinthians*, 789, italics original.

[41]Fee, *Pauline Christology*, 118–19, italics original.

[42]Gaffin, *Resurrection and Redemption*, 85–88. For rejection of this view, see Fee, *Pauline Christology*, 118–19.

[43]Gaffin, *Resurrection and Redemption*, 89.

The man from heaven. Paul continues his contrast of the two Adams: "The first man was from the earth, a man of dust; the second man is from heaven" (v. 47). According to Genesis, God created Adam "of dust from the ground" (2:7). Christ too is a human being; he has humanity in common with Adam. That is why Paul calls him "the second man."

But what does the apostle mean when he says, "The second man is from heaven" (v. 47)? Is he claiming that Jesus "came to earth in" heavenly flesh, as Menno Simons taught, following other Anabaptist teachers? Of course not, for this would undermine his whole argument in this chapter that Christ is "the last Adam" and "the second man" (vv. 45, 47). Christ's humanity, as ours, was received from his mother. "The second man is from heaven" in that he now has a glorified resurrection body that pertains to heaven. He embodies and represents a different order of existence from Adam.

Paul next contrasts the respective races of the two Adams: "As was the man of dust, so also are those who are of the dust, and as is the man of heaven, so also are those who are of heaven" (v. 48). Make no mistake about it: as surely as we bear the imprint of the first Adam, so we will bear the imprint of the second Adam. Thiselton's words bear quotation:

> Humanity as such finds its model in the first *Adam*, who was created from the earth's soil (Gen. 2:7, Hebrew and LXX) and shares the mortality and fragility of what belongs to those whose σῶμα [*sōma*] is made from that which disintegrates into dust in the grave. . . . The *raised Christ*, however, belongs to, indeed provides the model for, a different order of existence. Raised by God through the agency of the Holy Spirit, the second man exhibits those qualities that come from heaven and shape the character and nature of the form in which those "in" Christ . . . will be raised.[44]

Paul closes this section by repeating and expanding his last thought: "Just as we have borne the image of the man of dust, we shall also bear the image of the man of heaven" (1 Cor. 15:49). Once more the apostle contrasts the tremendous effects of the two Adams on their people. And once more he appeals to the early chapters of Genesis, this time to 1:26–27; 5:3. We, like Adam, in our current mode of existence have bodies capable of sickness and death. The good news, however, is that just as surely as we are "in Adam" and share his weakness now, so also by God's grace we are "in Christ" and will share his likeness in resurrection bodies fitted for the new mode of existence.

---

[44]Thiselton, *The First Epistle to the Corinthians*, 1286, italics original.

Although Paul does not mention glory in conjunction with our sharing Christ's image, it is implied, as Ciampa and Rosner point out in a quotation that forms a fitting ending to our discussion of this passage:

> In [1 Cor.] 11:7 Paul tied together the ideas of God's image and glory . . . and in [chap. 15] v. 48 he distinguished between the splendor or glory of heavenly and earthly bodies. In v. 43 he spoke of human bodies being sown in dishonor and raised in glory. The concepts of glory and *image* are probably linked throughout these texts such that we are to understand that *the image of the earthly man* lacks the glory with which it was previously created and is now an image of impermanence, weakness, ignobility, and of earthy humanness, while *the image of the heavenly man* reflects God's glory in its incorruptible, powerful, honorable, and spiritual nature (cf. vv. 42–44). We spend these lives in bodies that reflect Adam's state after the fall; we will spend the rest of eternity in bodies that reflect Christ's state after his resurrection from the dead.[45]

2 Corinthians 4:4–6

In the immediately preceding passage, Paul contrasts the glory of the new covenant with that of the old. Even though Moses's face was so glorious that the Israelites insisted he veil it, when compared to the glory of the new covenant in Christ, "what once had glory has come to have no glory at all, because of the glory that surpasses it" (2 Cor. 3:10). Amazingly, new covenant believers "with unveiled face, beholding the glory of the Lord, are being transformed into the same image from one degree of glory to another" (v. 18). But who is this Lord, whose glory we behold? Paul Barnett answers well:

> Paul's "mirror" analogy suggests that we see the "glory of the Lord" *indirectly*, "mirrored," as it were in "the face of Jesus Christ," "the image of God." Thus, Paul's language transcends a local dispute between Paul and the Corinthian church. Here is the revelation of the glory of God to humankind, in the human face— glorified, to be sure, but human nonetheless—of Jesus Christ, the image of God.[46]

The quotation also shows why this passage is included among those treating the second-Adam motif—because, although it does not mention Adam, it presents

---

[45]Ciampa and Rosner, *The First Letter to the Corinthians*, 824, italics original. See also Richard B. Gaffin Jr., "The Glory of God in Paul's Epistles," in *The Glory of God*, ed. Christopher W. Morgan and Robert A. Peterson (Wheaton, IL: Crossway, 2010), 133–52.

[46]Paul Barnett, *The Second Epistle to the Corinthians*, The New International Commentary on the New Testament (Grand Rapids: Eerdmans, 1997), 206, italics original.

Jesus as the image of God, which of course echoes Adam's creation in Genesis 1. In fact, Paul quotes from that chapter in 2 Corinthians 4:6.

As Paul begins chapter 4 he does something he feels forced to do often in this epistle—defend himself against opponents who would discredit him and his ministry. In spite of their charges, he has not grown lax in his ministry, eschews dishonesty and trickery, does not tamper with the gospel, and remains open before God and human beings (vv. 1–2).[47] "But Paul," we can almost hear his critics bark, "if your new covenant gospel is so glorious and luminous, why don't all receive it?" The apostle has a ready answer: "In their case the god of this world has blinded the minds of the unbelievers, to keep them from seeing the light of the gospel of the glory of Christ, who is the image of God" (v. 4).

Satan blinds minds. The gospel is luminous, Paul insists, and if people do not accept it, it is not because it lacks glory, as Hughes makes plain: "The fault . . . is not in the gospel, but in those who have failed to discern its glory. . . . The veil is over their hearts and minds (3:14ff.), not over the gospel. It is not Paul's gospel but they who stand condemned."[48] And the deeper reason for their unbelief is Satan's blinding their minds, keeping them from accepting the truth (4:4). Paul and his fellow apostles do not preach themselves, as their opponents falsely charge, but they preach "Jesus Christ as Lord." The apostles are merely servants of the Word and of those to whom they minister (v. 5).

Is not God more powerful than Satan? How do we explain the fact that some do believe the gospel? Paul explains that saving faith is the result of a supernatural work, as supernatural as God's creating light out of the darkness in the beginning. This same creator-God "has shone in our hearts to give the light of the knowledge of the glory of God in the face of Jesus Christ" (v. 6). That is, the Creator does a work of re-creation when people are converted, as Harris asserts:

> Conversion is the flooding of the darkened human heart by divine light. Whereas "the god of this age" blinds the mind (v. 4), the God of the ages shines in the heart. Paul's thought moves from the physical creation . . . to the spiritual re-creation . . . from nature to grace. The God of redemption is none other than the God of creation.[49]

---

[47]I acknowledge help from Murray J. Harris, *The Second Epistle to the Corinthians*, The New International Greek Testament Commentary (Grand Rapids: Eerdmans, 2005), 320.

[48]Philip E. Hughes, *The Second Epistle to the Corinthians*, The New International Commentary on the New Testament (Grand Rapids: Eerdmans, 1962), 125.

[49]Harris, *The Second Epistle to the Corinthians*, 335.

Paul has hard words for those who do not believe: "And even if our gospel is veiled, it is veiled only to those who are perishing" (v. 3). He refuses to criticize the gospel or God who stands behind it. Unbelief is due to satanic blinding and indicates that, as long as it lasts, unbelievers are heading for hell.

The second Adam is God and man. The apostle has much to teach concerning the second Adam. His humanity is evident, as in every second-Adam passage. After all, the very picture of Christ the second *Adam* underscores Jesus's humanity. But in addition, this passage brings out his deity in at least three ways. First, as we saw, believers gaze upon "the glory of the Lord" Jesus and are progressively transformed by that gazing into greater degrees of glory (3:18).

Second, Paul asserts that the preaching of the gospel is a revelation of divine glory, "the glory of Christ, who is the image of God" (4:4). Harris is helpful: "As God's εἰκών [*eikōn*], Christ both shares and expresses God's nature. He is the precise and visible representation of the invisible God (Col. 1:15 . . .)."[50]

Third, Paul is explicit: the gospel contains "the knowledge of the glory of God in the face of Jesus Christ" (2 Cor. 4:6). These three references to divine glory in Jesus presuppose that he has the divine glory in order to be able to impart it to others, as Fee explains: "What we have . . . is the true image of God being borne by the one who *shares the divine glory*, the one who, when turned to in devotion and obedience, transforms believers by his Spirit into the true image of God that humanity was created for in the first place."[51]

The context, then, stretches from the Exodus narrative to the ministry of Paul and the other apostles. In between stands the conversion of Paul himself. It is instructive to compare God's glory revealed to Moses, to Saul of Tarsus, and to those who believe the gospel, as Barnett shows:

> In response to Moses' request God revealed his glory to him, but he was not permitted to see the face of God (Exod 32:18–23; cf. [2 Cor. 4] v. 6). On the Damascus Road, Paul too, saw the glory of God. But there was a shape to it. Paul beheld "the image (*eikon*) of God," the glorified Christ. In the heavenly Christ the invisible God, who cannot be seen, has perfectly and fully revealed himself (cf. Col 1:15). The glorified Christ is the ultimate and eschatological revelation of God. There is nothing more that can or will be seen of God.
>
> What Paul saw with his eyes in that unique moment he now "sets forth" by means of "the truth" of the gospel ([2 Cor. 4] v. 2) addressed to the ears of his hearers . . . by means of which the light of God comes into darkened hearts (v. 6).

---

[50]Ibid., 331.
[51]Fee, *Pauline Christology*, 520, italics original.

Light from the glorified Christ streams into the heart through hearing the gospel. God's revelatory "image," the heavenly Christ, shown to the apostle, becomes the revelation of God for those who hear and receive the gospel.[52]

Colossians 1:15, 18

Despite the fact that this passage does not call Christ the second Adam, that theme is present. I say that because the passage is laced with vocabulary pertaining to creation from Genesis 1: "the image" (Col. 1:15), "creation" (v. 15), "created" (v. 16, twice), "heaven and earth" (v. 16), and "beginning" (v. 18). And more specifically, Paul uses that vocabulary to designate Christ by themes from Genesis 1: once when he replaces Adam, "the image of the invisible God, the firstborn of all creation" (v. 15), and another time when he presents him as the re-Creator, "the beginning" (v. 18).

It is important to note that the antecedent of "he" (or more precisely "who") in verse 15 is "his beloved Son" from verse 13. All that this passage says about Christ as preeminent in creation and new creation is predicated of him as the Father's "beloved Son." Two themes in particular stand out as we contemplate Christ as second Adam.

First, the beloved Son is "the image of the invisible God, the firstborn of all creation" (v. 15). The Son is called "the image" of God, a description that harkens back to humankind's creation in God's image in Genesis. Fee draws a noteworthy conclusion: "In v. 15 the first thing said about the Son is that he is the εἰκών [eikōn] (image) of the invisible God; in a strophe that is all about the relation of the Son to the original creation, the first thing said about him is that he replaces Adam (Gen. 1:26–27) as the true image-bearer of God."[53]

As applied to Christ here and in its other use in Paul ("the light of the gospel of the glory of Christ, who is the image of God," 2 Cor. 4:4) "image" concerns his role as revealer of God. The incarnate Son reveals "the invisible God." Ralph Martin is right: "The new Adam as God's Son and image reflects the divine glory in a unique way."[54] Other New Testament writings contain this theme:

> No one has ever seen God; the only God, who is at the Father's side, he has made him known. (John 1:18)

---

[52]Barnett, *The Second Epistle to the Corinthians*, 219–20.
[53]Fee, *Pauline Christology*, 299. Fee is in the minority of scholars when he holds that Christ (rather than the Father) is responsible for the new creation in Col. 3:10, where Paul speaks of believers' having "put on the new self, which is being renewed in knowledge after the image of its creator."
[54]Ralph P. Martin, *Colossians and Philemon*, The New Century Bible Commentary (Marshall, Morgan, and Scott, 1973; Grand Rapids: Eerdmans, 1978), 59.

Whoever has seen me has seen the Father. (John 14:9)

He is the radiance of the glory of God and the exact imprint of his nature. (Heb. 1:3)

Pauline scholars point to an additional source of his theme of Christ as the divine image revealing God—the Hellenistic Jewish wisdom tradition. These texts make use of Genesis 1 and apply "image" to "wisdom." O'Brien summarizes: "According to Proverbs 8:22, Wisdom was with the Lord at the beginning of his work, the creation of the world, while in Wisdom 7:25 the divine Wisdom which is personified, is described as the 'image' . . . of God's goodness, i.e. the one who reveals the goodness of God."[55]

When Paul in Colossians 1:15 presents the *incarnate* Son as revealer of God, he lays emphasis on his humanity; he is the second man, the last Adam. At the same time, the apostle highlights, as strongly as anywhere in Scripture, the Son's deity. He holds first place over creation because he was God's agent in creation (vv. 15–16). He is also the goal of creation, for "all things were created through him and *for* him" (v. 16). He is eternal and performs the divine work of providence (v. 17). All the fullness of deity dwells in him (v. 19; cf. 2:9). In sum, Paul presents God's beloved Son as both divine and human second Adam here.

Fee's words bear repeating:

These new concerns are to identify the Son as the *messianic* Son of God ([Col. 1] v. 13), who also has the rights of primogeniture with regard to the whole of creation, which also came into existence through him. Thus, Paul's emphasis with his use of εἰκών [*eikōn*] in this passage is on the incarnate Son of God as the *divine* image-bearer, who in eternity past was both the agent and the goal of the created order.[56]

Second, Paul also teaches that the Father's beloved Son is the second Adam when, after saying that "he is the head of the body, the church," he calls him "the beginning, the firstborn from the dead" (v. 18). Genesis 49:3 (LXX), which combines "firstborn" and "beginning," provides Old Testament background: "Reuben, you are my *first-born*, my strength, and the *beginning* of my children."[57] Martin (citing Lohse) notes, "This combination suggests . . . that the first-born is the founder of a people (as in Rom. 8:29)."[58] Lexical study confirms this conclusion, as Harris relates, "Jesus is the head of the church inasmuch as he

---

[55] Peter T. O'Brien, *Colossians, Philemon*, Word Biblical Commentary (Waco, TX: Word, 1982), 43.
[56] Fee, *Pauline Christology*, 521, italics original.
[57] Cited in Martin, *Colossians and Philemon*, 59.
[58] Ibid.

is its ἀρχή [*archē*] . . . its originating cause and the source of its life (cf. Acts 3:15; Rev. 22:13)."[59]

Even as "in the beginning, God created the heavens and the earth" (Gen. 1:1), so Christ is "the beginning" of the new people of God. He is the re-Creator, the source of the church's life. The apostle specifies by means of an appositive, "the firstborn from the dead" (Col. 1:18). Adam was the first human being, a special creation of God. The second Adam too is a human being but is also divine and as the risen one is the source of the new creation of God. The result? Jesus holds the highest rank over the new creation by virtue of his resurrection (v. 18). O'Brien captures the import of Paul's words:

> At Colossians 1:18 when it is said of Christ that he is the "beginning," it does not mean he is the "beginning of God's creation" . . . or its first cause, points that might have applied in the first part of the hymn, but rather as the One who is "the firstborn from the dead" he is the founder of a new humanity. At Genesis 49:3 the two terms "firstborn" and "beginning" appear together to describe the firstborn as the founder of a people. . . . The resurrection age has burst forth and as the first who has risen from among those who had fallen asleep . . . he is the first-fruits who guarantees the future resurrection of others (1 Cor. 15:20, 23)[60]

Of course, this emphasis on Christ's resurrection is not intended to downplay the saving virtue of his death. Consequently, in the verses that follow, Paul presents Christ as the one who reconciles "to himself all things . . . making peace by the blood of the cross," and as he who "has now reconciled" the Colossian believers "in his body of flesh by his death" (1:20, 22).

The Second Adam in Hebrews 2:5–10

After demonstrating the superiority of the Son of God to Old Testament mediators of revelation (prophets and especially angels), the writer to the Hebrews applies that contrast to his hearers. Even as the Son's message (the gospel) is superior to the angels' message (the law, Acts 7:53; Gal. 3:19), so rejecting his message brings more dire consequences than rejecting theirs (Heb. 2:1–4)! To turn away from Jesus, after professing faith in him, is to commit spiritual suicide.

---

[59]Murray J. Harris, *Colossians and Philemon*, Exegetical Guide to the Greek New Testament (Grand Rapids: Eerdmans, 1991), 48.

[60]O'Brien, *Colossians, Philemon*, 50.

Psalm 8 in Hebrews 2

Next the writer deals with a theological problem posed as a question: How is the idea of the superiority of Christ, the divine King, to angels compatible with the abasement involved in his incarnation, suffering, and especially death on a cross? The author begins his answer by saying that God did not subject the world to come to angels. From a Jewish perspective, this implied that God has subjected the present world to angels. O'Brien summarizes the evidence:

> The biblical evidence for the angelic administration of the world goes back to the Song of Moses:
>
> > "When the Most High gave to the nations their inheritance,
> >   when he separated the sons of Adam,
> > he established boundaries for the nations
> >   according to the number of the angels of God" (Deut. 32:8 LXX)
>
> This reading implies that the administration of the nations had been parcelled out among a number of angelic powers. The establishment of boundaries for the nations "according to the number of the angels of God" implies that the nations of the world had been subjected to the angels.[61]

There is thus a sense in which God subjected the present world to angels (under him, certainly), but not the world to come. No, the new heavens and new earth will be under the authority of the Son (pointing back to Heb. 1:13), the second Adam (and his people) (pointing ahead to 2:9–10). Then he quotes Psalm 8:4–6. The psalm is so important to understanding the passage at hand that I will quote it in full before summarizing its message.

> O Lord, our Lord,
>   how majestic is your name in all the earth!
> You have set your glory above the heavens.
>   Out of the mouth of babies and infants,
> you have established strength because of your foes,
>   to still the enemy and the avenger.
> When I look at your heavens, the work of your fingers,
>   the moon and the stars, which you have set in place,
> what is man that you are mindful of him,
>   and the son of man that you care for him?

---

[61] Peter T. O'Brien, *The Letter to the Hebrews*, The Pillar New Testament Commentary (Grand Rapids: Eerdmans, 2010), 93. O'Brien points to more evidence in Dan. 10:20–21; 12:21.

Yet you have made him a little lower than the heavenly beings
 and crowned him with glory and honor.
You have given him dominion over the works of your hands;
 you have put all things under his feet,
all sheep and oxen,
 and also the beasts of the field,
the birds of the heavens, and the fish of the sea,
 whatever passes along the paths of the seas.
O Lord, our Lord,
 how majestic is your name in all the earth!

At first glance the psalm's main theme appears to be the great creational blessings that God bestowed on Adam and Eve. The psalm contains that theme, but close inspection reveals a larger theme—God's majesty revealed in creation, especially the creation of humankind. The psalm begins and ends glorying in the greatness of God's character revealed (vv. 1, 9). Verses 2–4 twice move from the macro level to the micro. God's glory is above the heavens, yet he has chosen to silence his enemies through the mouths of the insignificant (v. 2). His heavenly creation is vast, yet he cares for puny human creatures (vv. 3–4). God blessed Adam and Eve with great creational blessings: he "crowned them with glory and honor" by making them royal representatives. They rule under him and for him over the rest of the earthly creation (vv. 5–8, reflecting Gen. 1:26). Their exalted status is that "of creature-sovereign with responsibility for the ordering of the creation for God."[62]

Hebrews 2 quotes Psalm 8:4–6:

What is man, that you are mindful of him,
 or the son of man, that you care for him?
You made him for a little while lower than the angels;
 you have crowned him with glory and honor,
 putting everything in subjection under his feet. (Heb. 2:6–8)

The writer's point is that God subjects the world to come not to angels but to Jesus, the second Adam, a point he will shortly make, and to all Jesus's people. The quotation shows God's astounding care for humankind, displayed in great creational blessings. These include being crowned with "glory and honor" (a "kingly" status, only temporarily below the angels) and accompanying dominion over the lower creation (animals, birds, and fish are listed in Ps. 8:7–8).

---

[62]William L. Lane, *Hebrews 1–8*, Word Biblical Commentary (Dallas: Word, 1991), 46.

The Fall and the Second Adam

The writer to the Hebrews calls attention to the awesome range of human dominion: "Now in putting everything in subjection to him, he left nothing outside his control" (2:8). The author then introduces a problem, that "at present, we do not yet see everything in subjection to him" (v. 8). What has happened? The fall, not mentioned in Psalm 8 but implied in its references to "foes," "the enemy," and "the avenger" (Ps. 8:2), has intervened. O'Brien is perceptive: "The psalmist was amazed at the great gulf between man's insignificance and his lofty position as ruler over creation. The author of Hebrews, however, reflects on the disparity between man's position as ruler and his present lack of control over creation."[63] Humankind does not represent God well while ruling over the other creatures. Fallen men and women cannot even rule themselves! The result is endless hatred, fights, and wars.

Just when the situation seems hopeless and the creational blessings of Psalm 8 seem lost forever, the author to the Hebrews provides hope with his first mention of the name of Jesus: "But we see him who for a little while was made lower than the angels, namely Jesus" (Heb. 2:9). He draws out the implication of what he had already proclaimed in 1:2—God "appointed" his Son "heir of all things." Does this mean that Psalm 8 is a messianic psalm that predicts Jesus's coming? No, it means that the writer to the Hebrews presents Jesus as the second Adam who "steps into" Psalm 8, so to speak, because he is the ideal man. When the Son of God becomes a human being, the words of the psalm that originally described Adam and Eve now pertain to him. By virtue of his incarnation, Jesus becomes the "last Adam," the "second man" (1 Cor. 15:45, 47).

Thus, he "for a little while was made lower than the angels" (Heb. 2:9). The words "for a little while" are important because they express a partial answer to the big question, How are Christ's incarnation and suffering compatible with his superiority to angels? Part of the answer is, because the Son of God's state of humiliation (which includes his incarnation and suffering) is not the end. It is the pathway to his state of exaltation. This state was officially inaugurated when he sat at God's right hand in heaven, at his enthronement as David's divine Son (the major theme of Hebrews 1).

Technically, Psalm 8 spoke only of Adam and Eve, and then the Son of God when he became incarnate as the second Adam. Every other human being was born a sinner and did not fulfill the mandate of the psalm. Jesus, however, did just that. He temporarily "was made lower than the angels," in his state of humiliation (Heb. 2:9). But now we see him "crowned with glory and honor because

---

[63]O'Brien, *The Letter to the Hebrews*, 97.

of the suffering of death, so that by the grace of God he might taste death for everyone" (v. 9). Jesus the second Adam has overcome so as to restore the lost glory and honor and dominion.

Why is it necessary for the Son of God to become the second Adam? F. F. Bruce answers: "As mankind's true representative . . . He must share in the conditions inseparable from man's estate; only so could He blaze the trail of salvation for mankind and act effectively as His people's high priest in the presence of God."[64]

How does he overcome? By "the suffering of death" he experiences death for humankind; he is the only Savior of the world. The second Adam dies to restore the lost creational blessings. As a result, he himself has entered into those blessings; he is "crowned with glory and honor" (v. 9). That is the main theme of Hebrews 1— the exaltation of Jesus to God's right hand, where he began his heavenly rule. The ideal man has regained the royal dominion forfeited by our first parents. "In Jesus we see exhibited humanity's true vocation," as William Lane puts it.[65]

Has he done so only for himself? No, indeed, for "by the grace of God he" tasted "death *for everyone*" (v. 9). He died and arose for others, for God's "children," whom he came to deliver from Satan and the fear of death (vv. 14–15). The second Adam's ministry was undertaken in fulfillment of the plan of God. For that reason, "it was fitting that he, for whom and by whom all things exist . . . should make the founder of their salvation perfect through suffering" (v. 10).

A Son Who Has Been Made Perfect Forever

Hebrews has a christological theme found nowhere else in Scripture—the Son's being made perfect to execute the office of Savior. It occurs in three texts:

> For it was fitting that he, for whom and by whom all things exist, in bringing many sons to glory, should make the founder of their salvation perfect through suffering. (2:10)

> Although he was a son, he learned obedience through what he suffered. And being made perfect, he became the source of eternal salvation to all who obey him, being designated by God a high priest after the order of Melchizedek. (5:8–10)

> For the law appoints men in their weakness as high priests, but the word of the oath, which came later than the law, appoints a Son who has been made perfect forever. (7:28)

---

[64]F. F. Bruce, *The Epistle to the Hebrews*, The New International Commentary on the New Testament (Grand Rapids: Eerdmans, 1964), 36.
[65]Lane, *Hebrews 1–8*, 48.

The Son's being made perfect has to do with his earthly ministry. God did not send his Son to earth as an adult to die and rise. Instead, he caused the Virgin Mary to conceive and bear a son. That son grew up and at thirty engaged in a three-and-a-half-year public ministry. The point of the passages teaching Jesus's perfection is that his sinless life has a role to play in his work of salvation. As the second Adam he had to undergo human life without sin from conception to adulthood in order to be qualified to save his people from their sins. His living a sinless life was a prerequisite to his saving death and resurrection. In that sense, his sinless earthly life saves too.

The second Adam's being made perfect is one of three qualifications for his work as Savior. First, he had to be God. Second, he had to become a human being. Third, he had to be tried and found true, "made perfect," through suffering. Bruce puts God's making Christ perfect in a nutshell: "It was His making Jesus, through His sufferings, perfectly qualified to be the Savior of His people."[66] That is why the writer says, "For it was fitting that" the Creator God "in bringing many sons to glory, should make the founder of their salvation perfect through suffering" (2:10). Christ submits to the suffering that consists in death and rises for others—to bring "many sons to glory." The second Adam restores creational rule to his followers. They too in this life begin to reign as God's representatives. Their reign will be complete only in resurrected bodies on the new earth.

Answering the Big Question

Only now are we prepared to answer the big question that Hebrews 2:5–11 addresses: How does Christ's supremacy over angels fit with the condescension of his incarnation, suffering, and especially death on a cross? Said differently, how do we get from chapter 1 (with its focus on the Son's superiority to angels) to chapters 7–10 (with their focus on Christ's high priesthood and sacrifice)?

Hebrews 2 contains several answers. First, Christ's abasement was not a result of things gone awry; God did not lose control. Rather, Christ's suffering and death fulfilled God's plan. The writer to the Hebrews stresses that it is the Creator who works in and through Christ to effect salvation: "For it was fitting that *he, for whom and by whom all things exist*, in bringing many sons to glory, should make the founder of their salvation perfect through suffering" (v. 10). The One who made Jesus perfectly qualified to redeem through suffering is the God of creation and providence. And the Son came to die according to God's will: "I have come to do your will, O God" (10:7, 9). "It is precisely through Christ's

---

[66]Bruce, *The Epistle to the Hebrews*, 43. O'Brien agrees with this "vocational understanding of the perfecting of Christ," *The Letter to the Hebrews*, 107–8.

temptation, suffering, and death that he was and is able to help human beings, and so carry out the work for which God exalted him," Ellingworth explains.[67]

Second, the condescension is temporary; only "for a little while" was Christ "made lower than the angels" (2:9). It is true that the Son died in order to save us, but he also arose and returned to the Father. Indeed, very early Hebrews says, "After making purification for sins, he sat down at the right hand of the Majesty on high" (1:3). And later the writer says, "We have a great high priest who has passed through the heavens, Jesus, the Son of God" (4:14). Lane is succinct: "The humiliation to which he submitted was only temporary; it lasted for 'a brief while' and has already been exchanged for exaltation glory."[68]

How Does the Second Adam Save?

A summary of the ways in which the second Adam saves his people in Hebrews 2:5–10 is in order. In verse 9, the writer strings together Christ's redemptive-historical events: his incarnation (he "was made lower than the angels"), crucifixion ("the suffering of death" in which he tasted "death for everyone"), and exaltation (he was "crowned with glory and honor"). Following the author's first mention of redemption in 1:3 ("after making purification for sins"), 2:9 sets the stage for his presentation of Jesus as Christus Victor (vv. 14–15) and High Priest (vv. 16–18). The latter points readers forward to the book's main treatment of Christ's saving work as a sacrifice in chapters 7–10.

The introduction of the concept of Christ as "the *founder* of their salvation" in verse 10 is key. Although this word's meaning is debated, I agree with Ellingworth's conclusion:

> Ἀρχηγός [*archēgos*] in the NT always refers to Christ (12:2; Acts 3:15; 5:31), and always in contexts which speak of his death and resurrection or exaltation. . . . In the LXX ἀρχηγός [*archēgos*] most often translates the Hebrew *ros* (e.g., Ex. 6:14) . . . in the general sense of "leader" or "ruler"; this may be all that ἀρχηγός [*archēgos*] means in Hebrews. . . . Hebrews' use of πρόδρομος [*prodromos*] (6:20) of Christ suggests that ἀρχηγός [*archēgos*] may have kept alive the Hellenistic metaphor or a pioneer opening a path on which others can follow. This suits both the immediate context here . . . and the development in 3:7–4:11 of the theme of God's wandering people. The metaphor itself could owe much to Jesus' practice of calling disciples to follow him (e.g., Mk. 2:14; Jn. 1:43), and of walking ahead of them (Mk. 10:32; Lk. 19:28). . . . The entire phrase . . . is well translated by the

---

[67]Paul Ellingworth, *The Epistle to the Hebrews*, The New International Greek Testament Commentary (Grand Rapids: Eerdmans, 1993), 144.
[68]Lane, *Hebrews 1–8*, 48.

NEB as "the leader who delivers them," and more traditionally by REB as "the pioneer of their salvation."[69]

The Son of God who became the second Adam is the leader and "perfecter of our faith, who for the joy that was set before him endured the cross, despising its shame, and is seated at the right hand of the throne of God" (Heb. 12:2). The royal heir (1:2) has occupied his throne, and "those who are to inherit salvation" (1:14) will not fail to follow their leader there, because he "tasted death for" them. Through their pioneer, who is now crowned with glory and honor, God will bring "many sons to glory" (2:10).

Connecting the Dots

Texts

We have studied the following passages: Genesis 1:26–28; 2:7, 21–22; 3:1–19; Luke 3:38; 4:1–13; Romans 5:12–19; 8:29; 1 Corinthians 15:20–22, 42–49; 2 Corinthians 4:4–6; Colossians 1:15, 18; Hebrews 2:5–10.

Sphere

This picture of Christ's saving accomplishment comes from the sphere of God's special creation of the first man (and woman) in his image with dominion over the lesser creation.

Background

The Old Testament background consists of Adam, the first man, created, tempted, and fallen.

Definition

The second Adam is the New Testament picture of Christ's saving work in which, through his "one act of righteousness" (Rom. 5:18), he restores humankind's lost glory, honor, and rule over the earth.

Need

Humanity's need for the second Adam is that the catastrophic fall of the first Adam brought sin and death into the world of humankind and disorder into God's good creation.

---

[69]Ellingworth, *The Epistle to the Hebrews*, 160–61. See these pages for views and literature.

Initiator

The second Adam comes of his own volition and according to the plan of God and rescues Adam's fallen descendants as God, through him, brings "many sons to glory" (Heb. 2:10).

Mediator

The Mediator is the second man and the last Adam (1 Cor. 15:45, 47), the incarnate Son and true image (2 Cor. 4:4; Col. 1:15) of God, who "for a little while was made lower than the angels" by becoming a man of flesh and blood. He is "the beginning, the firstborn from the dead" (Col. 1:18), and thus "the firstborn among many brothers" (Rom. 8:29). Now through the One "crowned with glory and honor" (Heb. 2:9), God will bring "many sons to glory" (Heb. 2:10).

Work

The second Adam's work includes his incarnation (Heb. 2:9, 14, 17), his earthly ministry—including temptations (Luke 4:1–13) and suffering through which he was made "perfect" (Heb. 2:10; 5:9; 7:28)—especially his death (Rom. 5:19; Heb. 2:9) and resurrection (1 Cor. 15:20–22, 45; Col. 1:18; Heb. 2:9), his ascension (Heb. 2:9), and his return (1 Cor. 15:20–23).

Present and Future Results

The accomplishments of the second Adam bring present and future results to his people. Through his work we are now justified (Rom. 5:18) and experience partial restoration of the image of God (Eph. 4:24; Col. 3:10). At his second coming, he will raise us to eternal life on the new earth (1 Cor. 15:20–23), at which time we will be declared righteous (Rom. 5:19), be completely conformed to his image (Rom. 8:29; 1 Cor. 15:42–49), and enjoy restored glory, honor, and dominion (Heb. 2:9–10).

Reconciler
Redeemer
Legal Substitute
Victor
Second Adam
Sacrifice

Chapter 15

Christy Our Sacrifice

The discomfort and repugnance I note are directed particularly at the doctrine most strongly associated with the cross: penal substitutionary atonement. . . . It has nourished much authentic Christian piety. But I would not be writing this book and you would probably not be reading it if this theology were not under fierce attack, indicted for many offenses. Indictments presuppose that enough evidence has been presented to demand a trial. And it appears that there are more than enough reasons to be uncomfortable with the doctrine of substitutionary atonement.

First, such doctrine always trades in the language of sacrifice. Increasing numbers of people find this language empty, literally unintelligible, or actively offensive. The first time I visited the Kali temple in Calcutta, I literally stepped in pools of blood from a sacrificed goat. I felt revulsion, and yet I saw the irony in that reaction. I have attended worship services all my life in which people talked and sang about blood shed for me. I never walked away with any on my shoes before. If I was uncomfortable with the abstract idea, why did I shrink from the reality?[1]

So begins Mark Heim's book *Saved from Sacrifice: A Theology of the Cross*. As the title of his book suggests, he offers an alternative understanding of Jesus's cross, in his case, one written from the perspective of René Girard's scapegoat theory. He opposes the idea that Jesus is our sacrifice whose sufferings are

---

[1] S. Mark Heim, *Saved from Sacrifice: A Theology of the Cross* (Grand Rapids: Eerdmans, 2006), 21–23.

redemptive: "I unequivocally advocate a reversal of polarity in our common theology of the cross. We are not reconciled to God and each other by a sacrifice of innocent suffering offered to God."[2]

We will trace the Bible's theology of sacrifice from the Old Testament, culminating in the New Testament's vision of "a sacrifice of innocent suffering offered to God," even the self-sacrifice of Christ, who rescues all who trust him. I will conclude by responding to objections to the idea that Christ's suffering on the cross is a redemptive sacrifice. Scripture is clear on that point:

> Yet it was the will of the LORD to crush him;
>> he has put him to grief;
> when his soul makes an offering for guilt,
>> he shall see his offspring; he shall prolong his days;
> the will of the LORD shall prosper in his hand. (Isa. 53:10)

Behold, the Lamb of God, who takes away the sin of the world! (John 1:29)

Christ loved us and gave himself up for us, a fragrant offering and sacrifice to God. (Eph. 5:2)

But when Christ appeared as a high priest of the good things that have come, then through the greater and more perfect tent . . . he entered once for all into the holy places . . . by means of his own blood, thus securing an eternal redemption. (Heb. 9:11–12)

Christ Our Sacrifice Anticipated in the Old Testament

It is true that the Old Testament mentions sacrifice prior to God's giving the Mosaic law—consider Cain and Abel (Gen. 4:3–5), Noah (Gen. 8:20), Abraham (Gen. 22:9, 13), and a covenant-making ceremony between Jacob and Laban (Gen. 31:54). But Willem VanGemeren makes a key point: "It is significant that the offerings mentioned or alluded to prior to the Mosaic legislation are either dedicatory or communal, not expiatory."[3]

We will, therefore, focus our attention on four key aspects of sacrifice in the Old Testament: the Passover lamb, the Levitical offerings, the Day of Atonement, and Isaiah's suffering Servant.

---

[2] Ibid., 320.

[3] Willem A. VanGemeren, "Offerings and Sacrifices in Bible Times," in *Evangelical Dictionary of Theology*, 2nd ed., ed. Walter A. Elwell (Grand Rapids: Baker Academic, 2001), 855.

The Passover Lamb: Exodus 12:13

The sacrifice of the Passover lambs prefigures "Christ, our Passover lamb," who "has been sacrificed" (1 Cor. 5:7). Pharaoh repeatedly refused to let the Israelites go after each of the first nine plagues. Consequently, God brought a tenth and final plague: "The LORD said to Moses, 'Yet one plague more I will bring upon Pharaoh and upon Egypt. Afterward he will let you go from here. When he lets you go, he will drive you away completely'" (Ex. 11:1). This plague involved the slaying of firstborn males in Egypt, both of human beings and animals (11:4–5). Enns is perceptive here: "The death of the Egyptian firstborn takes us back to the first chapter of Exodus. In 11:4, Moses warns Pharaoh that God is coming at midnight to kill the firstborn of Egypt. This is clearly retribution for Pharaoh's attempt to kill the male children of Israel in chapter 1."[4]

This plague, unlike the preceding nine plagues, affected the Israelites too. The Egyptian oppressors deserved God's judgment, and, Ezekiel reminds us, so did the idolatrous Israelites: "And I said to them . . . do not defile yourselves with the idols of Egypt; I am the LORD your God. But they rebelled against me and were not willing to listen to me. None of them cast away the detestable things their eyes feasted on, nor did they forsake the idols of Egypt" (Ezek. 20:7–8).

Nevertheless, out of grace and faithfulness to his covenant, God provided the Israelites a way of escape. "Yahweh, proving his Presence to his people, was about to provide freedom for them by a mighty blow from which he was solicitous to give them protection," as Durham states.[5] What was that way of escape that would produce freedom? Make no mistake; the Passover involved a sacrifice:

> Then Moses called all the elders of Israel and said to them, "Go and select lambs for yourselves according to your clans, and kill the Passover lamb. Take a bunch of hyssop and dip it in the blood that is in the basin, and touch the lintel and the two doorposts with the blood that is in the basin. None of you shall go out of the door of his house until the morning." (Ex. 12:21–22)

Their firstborn would not be killed if they killed the Passover lamb and smeared the blood on the lintel and doorposts of their houses. God would spare his people the judgment of the final plague if they obeyed him:

> It is the LORD's Passover. For I will pass through the land of Egypt that night, and I will strike all the firstborn in the land of Egypt, both man and beast; and on all the gods of Egypt I will execute judgments: I am the LORD. The blood shall be a

---

[4]Peter Enns, *Exodus*, The NIV Application Commentary (Grand Rapids: Zondervan, 2000), 246.
[5]John I. Durham, *Exodus*, Word Biblical Commentary (Waco, TX: Word, 1987), 164.

sign for you, on the houses where you are. And when I see the blood, I will pass over you, and no plague will befall you to destroy you, when I strike the land of Egypt. (vv. 11–13)

Plainly the Passover sacrifice saved the believing Israelites from the Lord's judgment. J. A. Motyer's words prompt reflection:

> At three points in chapter 12 the safety of those within the blood-marked houses is brought to the fore. In verses 8–10 their sense of the safety is evident in that on Passover night they were feasting; in verse 13 this is undergirded with a divine promise, *I will pass over you.* . . . *No destructive plague will touch you*; and in verses 22–23 there is a formal statement that behind the blood-marked doors they were guaranteed safety for no destroyer could enter. Objectively, they were made safe (or saved) by the blood of the lamb. The Lord saw the blood and passed over.[6]

Sacrifice became a formal part of Israel's national and religious life with the erection of the tabernacle and the institution of the offerings, to which we now turn.

The Levitical Offerings: Leviticus 1–6

The first six chapters of Leviticus describe the five major offerings of Israel: the burnt offering, the grain offering, the peace (fellowship) offering, the sin (purification) offering, and the guilt (reparation, trespass) offering.[7] I will briefly describe each one and tells its significance.

The burnt offering (Leviticus 1). Presented by any Israelite, the burnt offering was taken from the cattle, sheep and goats, or birds (by the poor). The worshiper brought a male animal without defect, placed his hand on its head. "It shall be accepted for him to make atonement for him" (1:4). After the worshiper slaughtered it, the priests placed its various parts on the altar of burnt offering and splashed its blood all around the altar. The entire animal was burned "with a pleasing aroma to the Lord" (v. 9).

Jay Sklar explains the significance:

---

[6] J. A. Motyer, *The Message of Exodus*, The Bible Speaks Today (Downers Grove, IL: InterVarsity, 2005), 133–34, italics original.

[7] I acknowledge a debt to my colleague Jay Sklar, *Leviticus*, Tyndale Old Testament Commentaries (Downers Grove, IL: InterVarsity, forthcoming); Sklar, *Sin, Impurity, Sacrifice, Atonement: The Priestly Conceptions* (Sheffield, UK: Sheffield Phoenix, 2005); VanGemeren, "Offerings and Sacrifices in Bible Times," 855–57; and Richard E. Averbeck, "Offerings and Sacrifices," in *Evangelical Dictionary of Biblical Theology* (Grand Rapids: Baker, 1996), 574–81.

[It] was the most costly sacrifice. . . . Unlike [the other] offerings . . . no one ate any of the burnt offering: it was all given to the Lord.

The reason becomes clear once we understand the burnt offering's purposes. At least two may be identified. The first is atonement (v. 4). . . . The burnt offering atoned for sinful offerers as they came before the Lord's holy presence. . . . Only a full (and costly) ransom payment would suffice.

The burnt offering's second purpose is to underscore the offerer's prayers. . . . In either case—whether praise or petition—the burnt offering served as an exclamation point.[8]

The grain offering (Leviticus 2). Cooked or uncooked, the grain offering often accompanied burnt offerings and was presented by all Israelites, including priests. It usually had four components: fine flour, oil, frankincense, and salt, but no leaven or honey. The priest offered a part of it on the burnt offering altar and the rest became his portion to eat.

Since grain offerings often accompanied burnt offerings, they had a common purpose (see the preceding). But Leviticus 2:13 adds, "You shall not let the salt of the covenant with your God be missing from your grain offering; with all your offerings you shall offer salt." Sklar explains the significance:

This chapter . . . highlights an element . . . which would have been full of meaning to an ancient Israelite: *the salt of the covenant* (v. 13). Salt represented the permanence of the covenant Israel had just entered into with the Lord (Exod 20–24). By requiring the Israelites to add salt to their offerings, the Lord provided them a way to constantly affirm their covenant relationship with him. This affirmation would have greatly encouraged the people by reminding them of the Lord's steadfast commitment to be their covenant king.[9]

The peace (fellowship) offering (Leviticus 3). The peace offering, which could be presented by any Israelite, and which had as a last stage a communal meal enjoyed by the worshiper and his family, signified a state of well-being between the Lord and his people. Its presentation was similar to that of a burnt offering, including the priest's manipulation of the blood. But there was an important difference from the burnt offering: in a peace offering, only the fat parts of the animal were burned on the altar. The rest was divided between priests and their families, and the worshiper.

Sklar explains the significance:

---

[8]Sklar, *Leviticus*, on Lev. 1:2–17.
[9]Ibid., on Lev. 2:1–16, italics original.

In ancient Israel, the closest relationship that could exist between non-relatives was a covenant relationship. By entering into a covenant, two parties were making their relationship official as well as pledging faithfulness to certain responsibilities involved. . . . Israelites often confirmed a covenant relationship by sharing a meal with the other covenant partner(s). The fellowship offering functioned as this type of meal. . . . As a celebration, the offering underscored for Israelites that their covenant partner was none other than the Lord, their redeeming God, who had rescued them from Egypt and was now dwelling in their midst.[10]

The sin (purification) offering (Lev. 4:1–5:13). The sin offering was the primary expiatory offering required of every Israelite and was taken from the herd or flock. It was presented for ritual cleansing, for unintentional sin against God's law, and at the festivals. In general, the worshiper placed his hand on the head of the animal, which was slaughtered, and the priest performed the blood rites, then burned the fat on the altar. By means of this offering, worshipers received forgiveness. It involved very detailed blood manipulation that differed when it was made for the priest and the congregation, versus when it was made for the leader and common people. The underlying principle was that "the blood penetrated the tabernacle complex as far as the contamination did."[11]

Sklar explains the significance:

> This [offering] underscores that the sin of those in authority is viewed as more serious than that of those they lead. . . .
>
> Even more than its emphasis on a leader's responsibility, however, this section underscores both the purity and the mercy of the Lord. Ancient Israelites thought of sin as something that was defiling, not only to themselves, but also to the Lord's holy dwelling place, the Tent of Meeting. . . . Due to the Lord's great purity, he could not permit such defilement to exist in the midst of his holy camp (cf. Lev 15:31). But due to his great mercy, he could not help but provide a way for his people to deal with this defilement: the purification offering. With this offering the animal's lifeblood served to ransom sinners from the Lord's just punishment as well as to cleanse the defilement of their sin.[12]

The guilt (reparation, trespass) offering (Lev. 5:14–6:7). The guilt offering was an expiatory offering like the sin (purification) offering, but whereas that offering focused on sin as defiling, this one focused on sin as breaking covenant loyalty. It could be presented by any Israelite who had defrauded God (by unintention-

---

[10]Ibid., on Lev. 3:1–17.

[11]Averbeck, "Offerings and Sacrifices," 577.

[12]Sklar, *Leviticus*, on Lev. 4:1–5:13.

ally profaning a holy item) or another Israelite, and was presented as payment for damages of a fine after the guilty party made full restitution plus a fifth. It was similar to the sin-offering ritual, with two differences. First, the offerer had to bring a more costly male animal, rather than a female one, because of the seriousness of covenant infidelity. Second, in the sin offering the blood was put on the horns of the altar to cleanse it (4:5–7), but here it was splashed around the altar (7:2). The word for this offering occurs in Isaiah 53:10, as we will see.

Sklar explains the significance:

> This law reminded the Israelites of the importance of showing due respect to their holy king by showing due respect to his holy property. To do so was to demonstrate covenant loyalty; to do otherwise was to demonstrate utter disregard for the covenant king. . . .
>
> This law [also] addresses two [more] sins. First, an Israelite has committed *a breach of faith against the Lord* by using his holy name in a false oath. . . .
>
> At the same time, the Israelite has also been unfaithful to a fellow covenant brother or sister through fraud.[13]

Summary. The sacrificial system, including the five main sacrifices, was a part of God's special revelation to Israel. The surrounding peoples had altars, priests, and sacrifices. But Israel alone knew the Lord as their God who delivered them from Egyptian bondage, made them a nation, gave them a land, and regulated their worship, first in tabernacle and later in temple. Because Yahweh wanted his people always to remember his holiness, their sin, and his grace, he ordained the priesthood and the sacrifices.

I conclude by quoting Dan Reid, who accentuates two features of the sacrifices, the laying on of hands and the blood:

> In sacrifices involving the slaying of an animal . . . there is evoked a strong sense of substitution or representation of the animal's life for the person or community, particularly symbolized in the action of placing hands on the head of the animal.
>
> The shedding of blood had particular atoning significance. Israelites were reminded that "life is in the blood," and blood was not to be consumed (Lev 17:11; Deut 12:23; *Jub.* 21:17–19; 1QapGen 11:17) but was reserved for God alone, the giver and Lord of life. Blood evoked the presence of a numinous power in animate life, and in cultic sacrifice it could symbolize expiation of sin or a purification from an unclean condition.[14]

---

[13]Ibid., on Lev. 5:14–6:7, italics original.
[14]Dan G. Reid, "Sacrifice and Temple Service," in *Dictionary of New Testament Background* (Downers Grove, IL: InterVarsity, 2000), 1036–37.

The Day of Atonement: Leviticus 16

The foremost day on the sacrificial calendar of Israel is the Day of Atonement, which is recounted in Leviticus 16. It is difficult to overstate its importance, as R. K. Harrison reminds us: "This chapter comprises the ceremonial and theological pivot upon which the entire book of Leviticus turns."[15] The context is crucial: after reminding Moses of the death of Aaron's two sons for entering the Most Holy Place in disobedience, God instructs Aaron (and subsequent high priests) how he should approach God (vv. 1–5). The Lord thus reminds the people and its high priest of his holiness, wrath, and mercy. The chapter contains three sections treating the Day of Atonement: an overview of Aaron's duties (vv. 1–10), a description of the three sacrificial rites to be observed (vv. 11–28), and the institutionalization of the ritual, including instructions for Israel's spiritual preparation (vv. 29–34). Our concern is with the three rites discussed in verses 11–28.

The Day of Atonement included three sacrifices: a sin offering of a bull for Aaron and his family, a sin offering of two male goats, and the burnt offering of two rams, one for himself and one for the people. We will investigate each in turn.

The sin offering of a bull. First, Aaron was to approach the mercy seat in the Most Holy Place only after having made "atonement for himself and for his house" with a sin offering of a bull (vv. 6, 11). We may be surprised to learn that, next, Aaron was to make an incense cloud:

> And he shall take a censer full of coals of fire from the altar before the Lord, and two handfuls of sweet incense beaten small, and he shall bring it inside the veil and put the incense on the fire before the Lord, that the cloud of the incense may cover the mercy seat that is over the testimony, so that he does not die. (vv. 12–13)

What was the purpose of this? Wenham answers:

> Entry into the holy of holies is fraught with danger. To protect himself from the wrath of God, the high priest has to prepare a censer full of hot charcoal taken from the altar of burnt offering in the outer court and put it in fine incense. The smoke of the incense was to *cover the mercy seat*, so that the high priest would not be killed (vv. 12–13). The most obvious explanation is given by Hertz: "the

---

[15]R. K. Harrison, *Leviticus,* Tyndale Old Testament Commentaries (Downers Grove, IL: InterVarsity, 1980), 166.

purpose of the incense-smoke was to create a screen which would prevent the High Priest from gazing upon the Holy Presence."[16]

Then Aaron was to take his finger and sprinkle some of the bull's blood on the east side of the mercy seat seven times (v. 14).

The sin offering of two goats. Second, Aaron was to make a sin offering of two male goats. He was instructed to take two live goats, cast lots over them, and treat them differently. The one became a sin offering; the other was sent away into the wilderness. Aaron was to kill the first goat as an offering of purification for the sins of the people and sprinkle its blood on the mercy seat, as he did with the bull's blood. "Thus he shall make atonement for the Holy Place, because of the uncleannesses of the people of Israel and because of their transgressions, all their sins" (v. 16). He was to make atonement for the tent of meeting (vv. 16–17). In addition, "he shall go out to the altar that is before the Lord and make atonement for it" (v. 18). Israel's sin defiled the very dwelling place of God, with its altar and Holy Place. God in grace and mercy made atonement for these, as well as for the sins of the people.

What about the second goat?

> And Aaron shall lay both his hands on the head of the live goat, and confess over it all the iniquities of the people of Israel, and all their transgressions, all their sins. And he shall put them on the head of the goat and send it away into the wilderness by the hand of a man who is in readiness. The goat shall bear all their iniquities on itself to a remote area, and he shall let the goat go free in the wilderness. (vv. 21–22)

The symbolism is that of substitutionary sacrifice, as Allen Ross explains: "Aaron laid both hands on the goat to ensure the transference of sin to the goat. He then confessed all of the wickedness and rebellion of Israel—all their sins. And these sins were placed on the goat to bear them away into the wilderness."[17]

When the goat was sent away into the wilderness, this depicted the taking away of the sins of the people, for "the goat shall bear all their iniquities on itself to a remote area" (v. 22). Therefore, two goats involved in the rites on the Day of Atonement were sacrifices that served as substitutes for the people.

---

[16]Gordon J. Wenham, *The Book of Leviticus*, The New International Commentary on the Old Testament (Grand Rapids: Eerdmans, 1979), 231, italics original. He cited J. H. Hertz, *Leviticus*, The Pentateuch and Haftorahs (London: Oxford University Press, 1932), 156.

[17]Allen P. Ross, *Holiness to the Lord: A Guide to the Exposition of the Book of Leviticus* (Grand Rapids: Baker Academic, 2002), 320–21.

Burnt offerings of rams. Third, Aaron was to have selected from the herd "a ram for a burnt offering" for himself (v. 3). He was also to have taken "from the congregation of the people of Israel two male goats for a sin offering, and one ram for a burnt offering" (v. 5). After the sacrifice involving the two goats, and after leaving his linen garments in the Holy Place and bathing, he was to "come out and offer his burnt offering and the burnt offering of the people and make atonement for himself and for the people" (v. 24).

Sklar presents the Day of Atonement as the answer to the big problem of the Israelites' sin and impurity, which defiled both themselves and God's dwelling place:

> The Israelites were faced with a serious problem: the holy Lord now dwelt in their midst, but their sins and impurities defiled his holy dwelling. True, they would have atoned for many of these properly (Leviticus 4–5, 11–15), but they would have missed many others, which then, defiled the tabernacle more and more. . . . How could the holy Lord continue in their midst without bringing his justice to bear against them? By means of a regular atonement ceremony—the Day of Atonement—that would cleanse and remove the Israelites' sins and impurities so they could continue in covenant fellowship with him.
>
> Three rites formed the heart of the ceremony, each making atonement in its own way. . . . Taken together, these rites fully atoned for the Israelites; their sins and impurities were no longer there; the slate was completely clean (cf. Ps. 103:12). The holy God who is offended by sin and impurity is also the compassionate and gracious God who delights to cleanse and forgive it.[18]

Indeed, the holy God of Israel is full of compassion and grace, and no Scripture passage shows that better than the one to which we now turn.

Isaiah's Suffering Servant: Isaiah 53:10

The most profound Old Testament passage on the redemptive death of the Messiah is Isaiah's fourth Servant Song—Isaiah 52:13–53:12. It paints various pictures of the Servant's death, including sacrifice. His death involves horrible suffering:

> His appearance was so marred, beyond human semblance,
>   and his form beyond that of the children of mankind . . . (52:14)

> He was despised and rejected by men;
>   a man of sorrows, and acquainted with grief;

---

[18]Sklar, *Leviticus*, on Lev. 16:1–34.

and as one from whom men hide their faces
>he was despised, and we esteemed him not. (53:3)

He was oppressed, and he was afflicted. (v. 7)

By oppression and judgment he was taken away. (v. 8)

Ironically, along with great suffering, the Servant's death is also depicted as a great victory. This is evident in the structure of the Servant Song. The central section, which treats the terrible suffering of the Servant, is bordered by statements of his exaltation:

Behold, my servant shall act wisely;
>he shall be high and lifted up,
>and shall be exalted. (52:13)

Therefore I will divide him a portion with the many,
>and he shall divide the spoil with the strong. (53:12)

In addition, the death of the Servant is portrayed as a sacrifice. This may be hinted at in verse 7, where he is likened to a lamb and a sheep:

He was oppressed, and he was afflicted,
>yet he opened not his mouth;
like a lamb that is led to the slaughter,
>and like a sheep that before its shearers is silent,
>so he opened not his mouth.

That his death is a sacrifice is made explicit in verse 10, which declares that he died as "an offering for guilt." This verse is so important to our purposes that we will examine it in detail:

Yet it was the will of the LORD to crush him;
>he has put him to grief;
when his soul makes an offering for guilt,
>he shall see his offspring; he shall prolong his days;
the will of the LORD shall prosper in his hand.

Add to the Servant's appalling suffering, his sinlessness (vv. 9, 11), and readers are surprised to learn that "it was the will of the LORD to crush him," and "he has put him to grief" (v. 10). The sufferings of "the righteous one my servant" (v. 11) are the will of God. How can this be? The answer is that the Servant suffered willingly (v. 12) and that he suffered for others—his suffering was vicarious (vv. 5–6, 8, 11–12).

Next Isaiah identifies the Servant's sufferings with the guilt (reparation) offering of Leviticus 5: "when his soul makes an offering for guilt" (v. 10). Peter Gentry helps us grasp the significance of this:

> The use of the term אשם is significant. The life of the servant is given as a "guilt" or "reparation offering," not a burnt or purification/sin offering. . . . New studies have cast light on this offering. . . . First, this offering emphasizes making compensation or restitution for the breach of faith or offense. . . . Isaiah is explaining here how restitution is made to God for the covenant disloyalty of Israel and her many sins against God. . . . Second, this offering provides satisfaction for every kind of sin, whether inadvertent or intentional. That is why Isaiah in 54:1–55:13 can demonstrate that the death of the Servant is the basis of forgiveness of sins not only for Israel but also for all the nations.[19]

Harry Orlinsky strongly protests this interpretation:

> [It] would have been the greatest injustice of all, nothing short of blasphemy, that the lawless be spared their punishment at the expense of the law-abiding. Nowhere in the Hebrew Bible did anyone preach a doctrine—which would have superseded the covenant!—which allowed the sacrifice of the innocent in place of and as an acceptable substitution for the guilty.[20]

I respectfully disagree with Orlinsky, a noteworthy Jewish scholar. There is one place the Hebrew Bible teaches that the Messiah will accomplish a penal substitutionary atonement—Isaiah 53:10. And that is exactly Alan Groves's conclusion to a painstaking study:

> Isaiah 53, therefore, is using the language of "bearing guilt" in a unique and most unusual fashion. If the foregoing argument is correct, then for the Servant to "bear guilt" is for him to make atonement. . . . It is precisely by means of the revelation of the *extraordinary* nature of the purification of which Isaiah spoke that the

---

[19]Peter J. Gentry, "The Atonement in Isaiah's Fourth Servant Song (Isaiah 52:13–53:12)," *The Southern Baptist Journal of Theology*, 11, no. 2 (2007): 36.

[20]Harry M. Orlinsky, "The So-Called 'Servant of the Lord' and 'Suffering Servant' in Second Isaiah," in *Studies in the Second Part of the Book of Isaiah*, SVT, XIV (Leiden: Brill, 1967), 68, cited by J. Alan Groves, "Atonement in Isaiah 53," in *The Glory of the Atonement*, ed. Charles E. Hill and Frank A. James III (Downers Grove, IL: InterVarsity, 2004), 68.

prophecy makes its most distinctive contribution to redemptive history. . . . The Torah knew no atonement that produced the universal and permanent purification envisioned in Isaiah. . . . Rather, it would be accomplished by a *new* thing (Is 48:7) . . . the astounding suffering of one righteous Israelite (Is 52:13–53:12), who bore the sins of others.[21]

The passages that we previously studied provide important background for understanding Jesus's saving work as a sacrifice in the New Testament. The New Testament at times even refers to them (e.g., 1 Cor. 5:7; Heb. 9:6–14). But Isaiah 53 is the only one that actually predicts the Messiah's saving work in sacrificial terms.

As Isaiah 53:10 continues, the prophet shares a benefit of Christ's saving accomplishment:

> He shall see his offspring; he shall prolong his days;
> the will of the LORD shall prosper in his hand.

The Servant's humiliation will be followed by exaltation. The song more than hints at his resurrection when it indicates that the suffering Servant lives after dying, as Gentry explains:

> Among the benefits given to the Servant for his atoning death is no less than resurrection. "There is no doubt," says C. Westermann, "that God's act of restoring the Servant, the latter's exaltation, is an act done upon him after his death and on the far side of the grave." This must be the meaning of "he will see his offspring, he will prolong his days" granted this context.[22]

We have investigated four accounts of sacrifice in the Old Testament: the Passover lamb, the offerings of Leviticus 1–7, the Day of Atonement, and Isaiah's suffering Servant. We now turn to the New Testament.

Christ Our Sacrifice in the Synoptic Gospels

VanGemeren is accurate: "Following the crucifixion and ascension of Jesus, the apostles applied the OT language of sacrifice and expiation to Jesus' sacrifice of himself."[23] Three passages in the Synoptic Gospels present Jesus's death as

---

[21]Groves, "Atonement in Isaiah 53," 87–89, italics original.
[22]Gentry, "The Atonement in Isaiah's Fourth Servant Song," 37. J. Alec Motyer agrees, *The Prophecy of Isaiah: An Introduction and Commentary* (Downers Grove, IL: InterVarsity, 1993), 440–41.
[23]Willem A. VanGemeren, "Offerings and Sacrifices in Bible Times," 857.

an atoning sacrifice. They are the three versions of one of Jesus's sayings at the Last Supper:

> And he took a cup, and when he had given thanks he gave it to them, saying, "Drink of it, all of you, for this is my blood of the covenant, which is poured out for many for the forgiveness of sins. I tell you I will not drink again of this fruit of the vine until that day when I drink it new with you in my Father's kingdom." (Matt. 26:27–29)

> And he took a cup, and when he had given thanks he gave it to them, and they all drank of it. And he said to them, "This is my blood of the covenant, which is poured out for many. Truly, I say to you, I will not drink again of the fruit of the vine until that day when I drink it new in the kingdom of God." (Mark 14:23–25)

> And likewise the cup after they had eaten, saying, "This cup that is poured out for you is the new covenant in my blood." (Luke 22:20)

Because they are parallel passages, we will look at them together.

Matthew 26:27–29

Jesus gathers with his disciples for a last meal before his crucifixion. It is a Passover meal in most ways similar to any they have ever observed, but in two striking ways dissimilar. Most things are familiar because they have partaken of a Passover meal yearly for as long as they can remember. As they grew up, their fathers played the role of president of the feast, the role that Jesus now plays. They are familiar with every element that Jesus observes. But now he says two things that they have never heard at a Passover ceremony. Their fathers never said, "Take, eat; this is my body" (Matt. 26:26). No president of the feast ever stated over the third cup, "Drink of it, all of you, for this is my blood of the covenant, which is poured out for many for the forgiveness of sins" (Matt. 26:27–28). But these are the shocking words that Jesus uses.

Our concern is especially with the cup. Three Old Testament passages inform our understanding: Exodus 24:8; Jeremiah 31:31–34; and Exodus 12. Jesus uses metonymy, associating his blood with the vessel holding the wine: "This cup that is poured out for you is the new covenant in my blood" (Luke 22:20). The cup stands for the wine that Jesus identifies with his blood, his violent death. He alludes to the words of Moses, when he ratified the covenant on the mountain with the elders of Israel, in Exodus 24:8: "And Moses took the blood [of the burnt offerings and peace offerings] and threw it on the people and said, 'Behold the blood of the covenant that the LORD has made with you in accordance with all these words.'" The allusion is unmistakable, for Jesus says, "This is my blood of the covenant" (Matt. 26:28).

Donald Carson draws out the sacrificial import of Jesus's words:

> Jesus understands the violent and sacrificial death he is about to undergo. . . . as the ratification of the covenant he is inaugurating with his people, even as Moses in Exodus 24:8 ratified the covenant of Sinai by the shedding of blood. "Covenant" is thus a crucial category. . . . The event through which Messiah saves his people from their sins ([Matt.] 1:21) is his sacrificial death.[24]

Luke (and Paul, 1 Cor. 11:25) specifies, "This cup that is poured out for you is the *new* covenant in my blood" (Luke 22:20). Luke connects the cup (and Jesus's blood) to the new covenant prophesied by Jeremiah 31:31–34. Jesus refers to one feature of that prophecy in Matthew's account of the Supper. Jeremiah prophesied, "For I will forgive their iniquity, and I will remember their sin no more" (Jer. 31:34). Jesus says over the cup, "This is my blood of the covenant, which is poured out for many for the forgiveness of sins" (Matt. 26:28). Jesus, then, views his passion as the sacrifice ratifying the new covenant predicted by the prophets.

Jesus also intends for us to understand the Lord's Supper as the fulfillment of the Passover, because he instituted the Supper at that Jewish feast (Matthew 17–19). "Luke's scene draws on the meaning of the Passover just as it contributes to a reinterpretation of Passover," Joel Green points out.[25] Craig Keener traces Jesus's strategy:

> By reinterpreting a familiar ritual (the Passover, an annual celebration of how God delivered Israel from slavery in Egypt), Jesus gave them a new way of looking at God's purposes, which would make sense once he had risen. . . .
>
> In the context of the Passover, Jesus shows that his own mission provides a new act of redemption (vv. 17–20, 26). . . . By identifying his own mission with the Passover, Jesus indicates that he has come to enact the new redemption and new exodus promised by the biblical prophets.[26]

It is no wonder, then, that Paul writes, "Christ, our Passover lamb, has been sacrificed" (1 Cor. 5:7).

---

[24]D. A. Carson, *Matthew*, The Expositor's Bible Commentary (Grand Rapids: Zondervan, 1984), 537.
[25]Joel B. Green, *The Gospel of Luke*, The New International Commentary on the New Testament (Grand Rapids: Eerdmans, 1997), 758.
[26]Craig S. Keener, *Matthew*, The IVP New Testament Commentary (Downers Grove, IL: InterVarsity, 1997), 367.

At the institution of the vital ongoing rite that Jesus gave the church, he interprets his death in sacrificial terms, viewing it as the confluence of three Old Testament streams of revelation. Carson is correct: "Jesus understands the covenant he is introducing to be the fulfillment of Jeremiah's prophecies and the antitype of the Sinai covenant. His sacrifice is thus foretold both in redemptive history and in the prophetic word."[27]

Christ Our Sacrifice in John

Two passages in the Fourth Gospel contribute to our understanding of Jesus our sacrifice: John 1:29, 36 and 17:19. I will briefly treat them.

John 1:29, 36

After the prologue, John structures the rest of his first chapter around the days of a week. He devotes a section to John the Baptist's testimony (1:19–28) and then introduces the next three sections in the same manner, "The next day . . ." (vv. 29, 35, 43), and begins the second chapter, "On the third day . . ." (2:1). The author appears to do this in order to imply that Jesus miraculously changed water to wine on the Sabbath, showing his replacement of Jewish water purifications with the new wine of the kingdom of God.[28]

The Evangelist tells how John the Baptist, on the second day of this week, saw Jesus approaching and said, "Behold, the Lamb of God, who takes away the sin of the world!" (1:29). On the following day, we learn, John the Baptist and two of his disciples saw Jesus walking by and John exclaimed, "Behold, the Lamb of God!" (v. 36). Thus John the Evangelist early in his Gospel, through John the Baptist's witness, proclaims Jesus's sacrificial atoning death. J. Ramsey Michaels agrees: "'Lamb' evokes the image of sacrifice, and John's words seem to refer to Jesus' death on the cross as an atoning sacrifice for the whole world."[29]

Jesus is "the Lamb of God, who takes away the sin of the world!" (v. 29). Although scholars have attempted to identify Jesus with particular Old Testament sacrificial animals, including the Passover lamb, the suffering Servant of Isaiah 53, the scapegoat, the victorious lamb of the apocalypses, and many more, Leon Morris is correct:

---

[27]Carson, *Matthew*, 538.

[28]For argumentation, see D. A. Carson, *The Gospel According to John*, The Pillar New Testament Commentary (Grand Rapids: Eerdmans, 1991), 168.

[29]J. Ramsey Michaels, "Atonement in John's Gospel and Epistles," in Hill and James, *The Glory of the Atonement*, 107.

"God's Lamb" is too indefinite an expression for us to confine the meaning to any particular lamb. . . .

We may fairly conclude that John has in mind the offering of Christ as a sacrifice. No other lamb than a sacrificial lamb takes away sin, and that is the critical point.

John intended by the expression to express his conviction that in Jesus Christ there is fulfilled all that is foreshadowed in all the sacrifices. The term is sacrificial. But it refuses to be bound to any one sacrifice. It is a most satisfying concept that Jesus did accomplish the perfect sacrifice which completely removed the sin of the world. He is the complete embodiment of all the truth to which the sacrificial system pointed.[30]

I cannot improve on Morris's words. I only add, in agreement to him, that when the Evangelist adds "of God" to "the Lamb," he indicates that God alone, not human beings, provides this ultimate sacrifice that removes from his sight the sins of believing Jews and Gentiles.[31]

John 17:19

After the farewell discourse, John uniquely presents Jesus's final prayer. "Parting" or "final" prayer are better designations for it than the traditional label "High Priestly" Prayer, because John's Gospel does not portray Jesus as a High Priest, and because the "High Priestly" Prayer does not encompass all of the prayer's contents. But based on verse 19, Jesus's prayer does contain priestly elements.

Jesus prays that the Father would protect his disciples from the Devil while they are in the world (v. 15). They do not belong to the world any more than he does, but he wants them in the world (v. 16). Next he prays for their progressive sanctification: "Sanctify them in the truth; your word is truth" (v. 17). God's Word is one vital means that he uses to turn believers increasingly from sin to holiness. Again Jesus speaks of the ministry of his disciples (and their disciples, v. 20) in the world. He wants them not to withdraw from unbelievers but rather to live among them and, by loving them and living holy lives, point them to himself.

Do his disciples' efforts make them holy? The answer, of course, is negative. Once they come to know Jesus, they are actively involved in living for him, but it is his work on their behalf that constitutes the foundation of their pilgrimage. And John here describes that work in priestly terms: "And for their sake I

---

[30]Leon Morris, *The Apostolic Preaching of the Cross*, 3rd ed. (Grand Rapids: Eerdmans, 1965), 141, 143.
[31]Ibid.

consecrate myself, that they also may be sanctified in truth" (v. 19).[32] In the Old Testament, priests were consecrated for service; that included making offerings to Yahweh, and animals were consecrated for sacrifice. Even so, Jesus consecrates himself as both priest and sacrifice.

Implied is that he will offer up himself on the cross. Note that Jesus states that it is "for their sake" that he sets himself apart for his work. His consecration unto death is the basis for their consecration in God's Word. Carson summarizes:

> If Jesus consecrates himself to perform the Father's will, he consecrates himself to the sacrifice of the cross. . . . The point is intimated in this verse by the fact that Jesus sanctifies himself *for them* (*hyper auton*): the language is evocative of atonement passages elsewhere (e.g. Mk. 14:24; Lk. 22:19; Jn. 6:51; 1 Cor. 11:24). It is also evocative of Old Testament passages where the sacrificial animal was "consecrated" or "set apart" for death—indeed, of language where consecration becomes synonymous with the sacrificial death itself (e.g. Dt. 15:19, 21). . . .
>
> Thus in language that applies equally well to the consecration of a sacrifice and the consecration of a priest, Jesus is said to consecrate ("sanctify") himself. His sacrifice cannot be other than acceptable to his Father and efficacious in its effect, since as both victim and priest he who is one with the Father ([John] 1:1; 14:9–10) voluntarily sets himself apart to perform his Father's will (cf. Heb. 9:14; 10:9–10).[33]

Christ Our Sacrifice in Paul

For two reasons, I will not cover in detail every passage in Paul's letters that pertains to Christ's death as a sacrifice. First, it would prove unwieldy if I studied everywhere that he speaks, for example, of the "blood" of Christ: Romans 3:25; 5:9; 1 Corinthians 10:16; Ephesians 1:7; 2:13; and Colossians 1:20. Second, I have already written a number of pages on some of these texts, for example, on Romans 3:24–26 in the chapters on the cross and on "Christ Our Legal Substitute." Therefore, I will skip some of these texts and make brief comments on others, while highlighting their sacrificial emphases.

Specifically, I will show that Paul presents Christ as replacing the mercy seat in Romans 3:25, his death as a sin offering in 8:3, Christ himself as the Passover lamb in 1 Corinthians 5:7, and his death as "a fragrant offering and sacrifice to God" in Ephesians 5:2.

---

[32]The same word is used for both Jesus's and the disciples' consecration—ἁγιάζω (*hagiazō*). The ESV translates it "consecrate" with reference to Jesus and "sanctify" with reference to his disciples to distinguish his work from theirs.

[33]Carson, *The Gospel According to John*, 567, italics original.

Romans 3:25

Paul encloses his presentation of the means of justification—faith (in Rom. 3:27–4:25)—with statements of the basis of justification in 3:25–26 and 5:18–19. Faith is the instrument, the means, by which sinners reach out and take hold of the salvation offered in the gospel. Faith, however, is not the basis of salvation. It may be politically correct to maintain that as long as someone sincerely believes in God, it does not matter what one specifically believes. But it is not correct according to Paul. He is firm on the content of saving faith:

> If you confess with your mouth that Jesus is Lord and believe in your heart that God raised him from the dead, you will be saved. For with the heart one believes and is justified, and with the mouth one confesses and is saved. (Rom. 10:9–10)

> Now I would remind you, brothers, of the gospel I preached to you, which you received, in which you stand, and by which you are being saved, if you hold fast to the word I preached to you—unless you believed in vain.
>
> For I delivered to you as of first importance what I also received: that Christ died for our sins in accordance with the Scriptures, that he was buried, that he was raised on the third day in accordance with the Scriptures. (1 Cor. 15:1–4)

There is no lack of clarity in Paul's epistles regarding the content of saving faith—plainly it is faith in Jesus Christ alone that rescues. In Romans 5:18–19 the object of faith is Jesus's "one act of righteousness," his "obedience" that counters Adam's "one trespass," his "disobedience."

And in 3:24–26 it is Christ's "redemption," his "propitiation by his blood" that delivers believers.[34] The words "by his blood" point to Old Testament sacrificial imagery. The word "propitiation" (ἱλαστήριον, hilastērion) also is a part of that imagery. In fact, "ἱλαστήριον is primarily a cultic term, drawing on the sacrificial terminology of Leviticus," as Thomas Schreiner explains.[35] Specifically, "propitiation" corresponds to the "mercy seat" that is frequently mentioned in Leviticus 16 with regard to the Day of Atonement, although some dispute this. Space precludes answers to the six objections to this idea, which has an impressive pedigree going back to Luther and Calvin, even to Origen.[36]

The chief objection to "mercy seat" as the meaning of "propitiation" is the lack of an early Christian tradition to that effect. But this objection is not con-

---

[34]For discussion, see pp. 84–87 and 375–78 in the chapters on "Christ's Death," and "Christ Our Legal Substitute."

[35]Thomas R. Schreiner, *Romans*, Baker Exegetical Commentary on the New Testament (Grand Rapids: Baker Academic, 1998), 192.

[36]See ibid., 193–94 for discussion.

clusive, because, as Douglas Moo argues, "In this, as in so many other areas, Paul may have been the theological innovator; and the lexical data, combined with the theological appropriateness of the image, make it likely that Paul intends such an allusion."[37]

What is Paul's point in teaching that Christ's saving accomplishment includes God's putting him forward publicly as a "mercy seat"? Moo is succinct: "Christ, Paul implies, now has the place that the 'mercy seat' had in the Old Covenant: the center and focal point of God's provision of atonement for his people."[38] Schreiner, answering the objection that if Christ is identified as the mercy seat, the symbolism is contradictory, is more expansive:

> That Jesus functioned as the priest, victim, and the place where the blood is sprinkled should not trouble us. Paul is attempting to communicate that Jesus fulfills the sacrificial cultus, and the fulfillment transcends the cult. The sprinkling of Jesus' blood makes it possible for believers to meet with God. . . . What Jesus accomplished on the cross transcended previous categories and constituted their fulfillment.[39]

Romans 8:3

As we saw previously, Romans 8:1–4 teaches penal substitution.[40] "For God has done what the law, weakened by the flesh, could not do. By sending his own Son in the likeness of sinful flesh and for sin, he condemned sin in the flesh" (v. 3). When Paul says that the Mosaic law is "weakened by the flesh," he means that the law cannot save because sinful human beings cannot obey it. But what the law was unable to do, God did in his own Son, whom he sent "in the likeness of sinful flesh" (v. 3). The Father, by sending his Son to identify with sinners and share in their humanity, "condemned sin in the flesh." Paul means that God judged sin in his Son's atoning death. Christ took the penalty that our sins deserve to bring us forgiveness. And he did all of this "in order that the righteous requirement of the law might be fulfilled in us" (v. 4). Though this is debated, my understanding is that it refers to Christ's perfect fulfillment of the law's demands, which God, in grace, transfers to us.

What exactly does the apostle mean when he says that God sent his "Son in the likeness of sinful flesh and *for sin*?" The words "for sin" are used regularly in the Septuagint in the sense of "sin offering," and because that idea fits so well

---

[37]Douglas J. Moo, *The Epistle to the Romans* (Grand Rapids: Eerdmans, 1996), 236.
[38]Ibid.
[39]Schreiner, *Romans*, 194.
[40]See pp. 379–81 in the chapter "Christ Our Legal Substitute."

in this context, many commentators take them to mean that here.[41] The apostle speaks of Christ's death as a sacrifice that removes sin. Schreiner captures Paul's thought:

> Some scholars see a general reference to sin here, so that the phrase means "with reference to sin" or "to deal with sin" . . . . But Wright . . . has shown that the phrase περὶ ἁμαρτίας refers to a sin offering in forty-four of its fifty-four LXX occurrences. . . . This meaning makes good sense in the context. . . . God judicially condemned sin "in the flesh" by sending his own Son in the likeness of sinful flesh as a sin offering. The sacrificial death of the Son of God, therefore, was the means by which sin was condemned.[42]

1 Corinthians 5:7

"Christ, our Passover lamb, has been sacrificed." Paul rebukes the Corinthians for tolerating a bizarre case of sexual immorality—"a man has his father's wife" (5:1), something expressly forbidden by the law (Lev. 18:8). The apostle is upset because such sin "is not tolerated even among pagans" (1 Cor. 5:1). He commands excommunication of the offender with a view toward reclaiming him if he repents (vv. 3–5).

Paul is concerned about the effects of the Corinthians' tolerating open sin upon the congregation as a whole. He appeals to an apparent proverbial saying: "Do you not know that a little leaven leavens the whole lump?" (v. 6). Paul does not speak of yeast, which was uncommon, but of a bit of leftover fermented dough that would be added to the next batch. The image is similar to our saying, "One rotten apple ruins the whole barrel."

Paul then continues his ethical exhortation by making an allusion to the Passover festival: "Cleanse out the old leaven that you may be a new lump, as you really are unleavened" (vv. 6–7). Gordon Fee sheds light on the background and Paul's application:

> Because of the fermentation process, which week after week increased the dangers of infection, the Israelites were commanded once a year to purge their homes of all leaven (Exod. 12:14–20). During the Feast they would bake only unleavened bread, from which dough they would then start up the process again after the Feast. Thus in the NT leaven became a symbol of the process by which an evil

---

[41] See James D. G. Dunn, *Romans 1–8*, Word Biblical Commentary (Waco, TX: Word, 1988), 422. Contra, see C. E. B. Cranfield, *The Epistle to the Romans*, The International Critical Commentary (Edinburgh: T&T Clark, 1975), 382.

[42] Schreiner, *Romans*, 403. His reference is to N. T. Wright, *Christian Origins and the Question of God*, vol. 1, *The New Testament and the People of God* (Minneapolis: Fortress, 1992), 220–25.

spreads insidiously in a community until the whole has been infected by it (cf. Mark 8:15). So it was in Corinth. Their problem was that they were not taking this matter seriously, either the evil itself or their danger of being thoroughly contaminated by it.[43]

In the midst of Paul's ethical exhortation using Passover imagery, which he continues in 1 Corinthians 5:8, he speaks of Christ: "For Christ, our Passover lamb, has been sacrificed" (v. 7). He thus shifts from talking about the Feast to talking about the sacrificial animal to teach the significance of the sacrifice of Christ himself.

Anthony Thiselton draws out the apostle's implications:

> But *the death of Christ* corresponds to the sacrifice of the Passover lamb. Here, for Paul, the old is abolished and the blood of the Passover lamb ratifies the promises of redemption *from* bondage (where "Egypt" symbolizes the bondage of human existence without Christ) *to* a new purity and freedom *by* a costly act. This is not to read *into* Paul any "theory of the atonement," for the transparently clear reference here to *sacrifice* (θύω [*thyō*]) is complemented by the language of *redemption* (ἀγοράζω [*agorazō*]) in 6:20, and *covenant promise, identification*, and the shedding of *Christ's blood* in 11:25–26.[44]

Here again, then, Paul views the saving work of Christ in light of Old Testament sacrifices, this time the Passover lamb. Fee calls attention to his point: "The slaying of the lamb is what led to the Jews' being 'unleavened.' So too with us, Paul says. Our Lamb has been sacrificed; through his death we have received forgiveness from the past and freedom for new life in Christ."[45]

Ephesians 5:2

Paul instructs the believers in Ephesus "to put off your old self, which . . . is corrupt through deceitful desires . . . and to put on the new self, created after the likeness of God in true righteousness and holiness" (Eph. 4:22–24). Next, he applies the pattern of taking off and putting on to various areas: take off lying and put on truth telling (v. 25); take off sinful anger and put on not sinning while being angry (v. 26–27); take off stealing and put on honest labor (v. 28); take off evil speech and put on edifying speech (v. 29); take off bitterness, anger, slander, and malice and put on compassion and forgiveness (vv. 31–32).

---

[43]Gordon D. Fee, *The First Epistle to the Corinthians* (Grand Rapids: Eerdmans, 1987), 216.

[44]Anthony C. Thiselton, *The First Epistle to the Corinthians*, The New International Greek Testament Commentary (Grand Rapids: Eerdmans, 2000), 405–6, italics original.

[45]Fee, *The First Epistle to the Corinthians*, 218.

The apostle uses God's forgiveness in Christ as the measure of Christians' eagerness to forgive one other when wronged: "Forgiving one another, as God in Christ forgave you" (v. 32). This leads Paul to write, "Therefore be imitators of God, as beloved children" (5:1). God the Father's love for us in adopting us as sons and daughters inspires us to imitate God and so love each another. Next Paul writes, "And walk in love, as Christ loved us" (v. 2). His thought moves from imitating the Father to imitating Christ. Christians' lives are to be characterized by love, because Christ loved them first.

Paul, when speaking of Christ's love for his people, easily thinks of his sacrificial death: "And walk in love, as Christ loved us and gave himself up for us, a fragrant offering and sacrifice to God" (v. 2). Christ's love is supremely shown by his dying voluntarily on behalf of his people. Peter O'Brien highlights the voluntariness of Christ's self-sacrifice: "The verb 'gave over,' together with the reflexive pronoun 'himself,' indicates that Christ took the initiative in handing himself over to death. He went to the cross as the willing victim."[46]

Love was his motivation. He "gave himself up for us" because he "loved us." Moreover, his self-giving is portrayed in the terms of Old Testament sacrifice: "a fragrant offering and sacrifice to God." The background does not involve a specific sacrifice, as in the previous three passages that we studied. O'Brien explains:

> The sacrificial nature of Christ's death is made explicit in the appositional phrase *as a fragrant offering and sacrifice to God*. The two terms "offering and sacrifice," which are probably a hendiadys and appear in Psalm 40:6 (LXX 39:7), include all kinds of sacrifices, both grain and animal. . . . The final phrase, "for a fragrant aroma," which was used in the Old Testament of all the main types of sacrifice in the Levitical ritual, indicates what is well pleasing to God.[47]

Christ's self-offering "for us" fully pleases God the Father. The Father favorably accepts the self-sacrifice of his beloved Son.

Christ Our Sacrifice in Hebrews

The book of Hebrews is a literary and theological masterpiece that has more to say about Christ as High Priest and sacrifice than the rest of the New Testament combined. We will investigate five passages.

---

[46]Peter T. O'Brien, *The Letter to the Ephesians*, The Pillar New Testament Commentary (Grand Rapids: Eerdmans, 1999), 355.
[47]Ibid.

Hebrews 1:3

The first chapter of Hebrews is chiefly about Christ's coronation as divine Davidic King who sits at God's right hand. It begins by talking about Christ as prophet (vv. 1–2). Although it has only one sentence on Christ as priest, it is a powerful one: "After making purification for sins, he sat down at the right hand of the Majesty on high" (v. 3). Anticipating the content of chapters 9 and 10, the author implies that Christ, our great High Priest, makes Old Testament rites of purification obsolete.

The need for salvation is here viewed as defilement from which we needed to be cleansed or purified. William Lane helpfully sketches the Old Testament background:

> Here sin is viewed as defilement which must be purged. This understanding has its roots in the LXX, where καθαρίζειν [*katharizein*] and its cognates relate to the removal of the defilement of sin, either in association with the altar (cf. Exod 29:37; 30:10; Lev 16:19) or the people (Lev 16:30). The uncleanness of the people of Israel was acknowledged before the Lord at the altar, and it was from this defilement that they had to be cleansed by the sprinkling of the blood of the sacrificial animal. The blood covered and obliterated the sins upon the altar (cf. Exod 30:10: καθαρισμός [*katharismos*]. The purification of the people was similarly achieved by blood in an act of expiation (cf. Lev 16:30). Purity is the essential condition for participation in the cultic life. The defilement of sin erects a barrier to the approach of God which must be removed. . . . That the writer to the Hebrews draws upon this conceptual framework for interpreting the death of Christ is confirmed by chaps. 9 and 10, where the categories of defilement and purgation are foundational to the argumentation.[48]

Lane is correct: purification was central to Old Testament worship. And yet, according to Hebrews, the very repetition of the sacrifices bears witness to their lack of efficacy. "The same sacrifices that are continually offered every year" could never make perfect the worshipers (Heb. 10:1). Jeremiah predicted that the forgiveness of sins would be an essential mark of the new covenant (31:34). How would final purification be accomplished? How would Jeremiah's prophecy of a day of complete forgiveness be fulfilled? The answer to both questions lies in the work of Christ our High Priest.

As Hebrews later makes clear, this took place "once for all when he offered up himself" in death on the cross (7:27). In a characteristic contrast between old and new covenants, the author lauds the purifying power of Christ's blood:

---

[48]William L. Lane, *Hebrews 1–8*, Word Biblical Commentary (Dallas: Word, 1991), 15.

For if the blood of goats and bulls, and the sprinkling of defiled persons with the ashes of a heifer, sanctify for the purification of the flesh, how much more will the blood of Christ, who through the eternal Spirit offered himself without blemish to God, purify our conscience from dead works to serve the living God. (9:13–14)

The writer to the Hebrews, then, cannot wait until later in his book to speak of the cleansing power of the Son of God's blood. He extols it at the very beginning of his sermon: "After making purification for sins, he sat down at the right hand of the Majesty on high" (1:3). He will wait to draw out the implications of his opening statement of Christ's work. He will then speak of its finality and perfection. These are implied in where he sat—at God's right hand, as Philip Hughes states: "The description of the Son as being now seated signifies the completion of the work of purification . . . . His session, moreover, is 'on high' . . . . This is the seal of divine acceptance of his work of purification."[49]

Another astounding result of Christ's unique accomplishment is that, unlike Old Testament sacrifices considered in themselves, his was efficacious, as O'Brien reminds us:

By making purification for sins the Son accomplished something which no one else could achieve. The forgiveness he has won is permanent, and, because the barrier between God and humanity has been removed, it results in entry into the presence of God himself. Such a provision on our behalf, which has perfectly dealt with the defilement of sin, calls forth from us a response of wholehearted gratitude.[50]

To these apt words, believing hearts can only say, "Amen!"

Hebrews 2:17–18

If Hebrews 1 introduces the saving work of Christ, then Hebrews 2 develops it. It does so using the pictures of Christ as second Adam (vv. 9–13), Christus Victor (vv. 14–15), and finally priest (vv. 16–18). The first two pictures begin with a statement of the incarnation of the Son; this is the essential prerequisite for his death and resurrection (vv. 9, 14).

It is the same for his priesthood. "For surely it is not angels that he helps, but he helps the offspring of Abraham" (v. 16). Alluding to Isaiah 41:8–10, the

---

[49]Philip Edgcumbe Hughes, *A Commentary on the Epistle to the Hebrews* (Grand Rapids: Eerdmans, 1977), 47.
[50]Peter T. O'Brien, *The Letter to the Hebrews*, The Pillar New Testament Commentary (Grand Rapids: Eerdmans, 2010), 58.

writer points to the solidarity between Christ and the people of God. How was this solidarity achieved? By the incarnation: "Therefore he had to be made like his brothers in every respect" (Heb. 2:17). The author will later "insist on his sinless character, which sets him apart from other men and women (4:15; 7:26). For now, however, the stress is on the total identification of the incarnate Son with his brothers and sisters," as O'Brien asserts.[51] The writer emphasizes the words "in every respect" by putting them in the emphatic first position in their clause. His point, as Lane shows, is to affirm "that Jesus shared a full and true human existence."[52]

Christ became one of us to perform a divine rescue, and here that rescue is portrayed in priestly language: "Therefore he had to be made like his brothers in every respect, so that he might become a merciful and faithful high priest in the service of God" (2:17). Christ's solidarity with Jewish and Gentile believers, through the incarnation, is the foundation of his priesthood. Here for the first time in the epistle, Christ is called High Priest. As with other priests, his priesthood involved "the service of God." Christ had a ministry to perform and the writer next mentions two key aspects of that ministry.

But first it is good for us to dwell a little on the description of two qualities of Christ our High Priest—he was merciful and faithful. As is often the case, the author introduces categories (probably by alluding to 1 Sam. 2:35) that he will develop later. In this case, what is entailed in these two qualities "is explained in the exposition that follows, as the writer addresses himself first to the quality of faithfulness ([Heb.] 3:1–4:14), and then to the quality of compassion (4:15–5:10)," Lane observes.[53] Indeed, Hebrews will insist first that "Christ is faithful over God's house as a son" (3:6) and then that "we do not have a high priest who is unable to sympathize with our weaknesses" (4:15).

The author speaks of two aspects of Christ's high priestly service to God: sacrifice and help. First, Christ's ministry involved his self-giving in sacrifice: "Therefore he had to be made like his brothers in every respect, so that he might become a merciful and faithful high priest in the service of God, to make propitiation for the sins of the people" (2:17). We have studied propitiation in some detail in the chapter "Christ Our Legal Substitute" and will only summarize the discussion here.[54] The meaning of the verb ἱλάσκεσθαι (*hilaskesthai*) is debated. Does it mean "expiate" (RSV), "propitiate" (ESV), or, more generally, "make atonement" (TNIV)?

---

[51] Ibid., 119.
[52] Lane, *Hebrews 1–8*, 64.
[53] Ibid., 64–65.
[54] See pp. 375–78, 393–407. See also 84–87.

There are two questions: What does this verse mean, and how does its teaching fit in the broader theological context of Hebrews? O'Brien tackles them in reverse order, incorporating important research:

> Within the discourse as a whole, Koester has correctly observed that the notion of atonement has to do with the restoration of a relationship marred by sin, and this encompasses both expiation, the removal of sin, and propitiation, the averting of divine wrath. Our author assumes that divine wrath threatens his listeners, just as it threatened Moses' generation (3:7–4:13; 10:26–31; 12:29). Christ's sacrifice not only sets aside sin (9:26) and purifies people (1:3; 9:13–14); it also delivers men and women from judgment (10:26–31; 12:29) because wrath is averted. Here at 2:17, however, Hebrews does not indicate how this forgiveness and removal of wrath take place. The answer is reserved for the later expository chapters.[55]

It is proper, therefore, based on Hebrews as a whole, to summarize the first aspect of Christ's high priestly ministry as "to make propitiation for the sins of the people" (2:17). Lane speaks concisely: "The making of propitiation for sins exhibits the primary concern of the high priestly office with the reconciliation of the people to God. The concept implies sacrifice, and in this context the propitiatory work of the Son consisted in the laying down of his life for others (cf. vv 10, 14, 18)."[56]

Second, Christ's ministry as High Priest involved his giving help to others: "For because he himself has suffered when tempted, he is able to help those who are being tempted" (2:18). The writer has been speaking of Christ's atonement, which involved his tremendous suffering. Because he successfully endured a lifetime of suffering and temptation culminating in the cross, he is equipped to help others when tempted. His making propitiation is an immeasurable help because it brings the forgiveness of sins to all believers, including the audience of Hebrews that was being tempted to turn away from the gospel under persecution.

Moreover, as a merciful and faithful divine-human High Priest, Christ, seated at God's right hand, gives his people mercy and enabling grace to help them persevere in trials:

> Since then we have a great high priest who has passed through the heavens, Jesus, the Son of God, let us hold fast our confession. For we do not have a high priest who is unable to sympathize with our weaknesses, but one who in every respect

---

[55]O'Brien, *The Letter to the Hebrews*, 121–22. The reference is to C. R. Koester, *The Dwelling of God: The Tabernacle in the Old Testament, Intertestamental Literature, and the New Testament* (Washington, DC: Catholic Biblical Association), 121–22.

[56]Lane, *Hebrews 1–8*, 66.

has been tempted as we are, yet without sin. Let us then with confidence draw near to the throne of grace, that we may receive mercy and find grace to help in time of need. (Heb. 4:14–16)

Hebrews 7:23–27

Although this passage mentions Christ's sacrifice only near the end, I include it because it deals with his saving priestly work throughout. As is his custom, the writer contrasts Christ's priesthood with that of the Mosaic dispensation. This time the author has in mind the implications of David's prediction, "You are a priest forever" (Ps. 110:4; Heb. 7:21): "The former priests were many in number, because they were prevented by death from continuing in office, but he holds his priesthood permanently, because he continues forever" (7:23–24). In contrast to the Levitical priests, whose ministries were cut short by their mortality, the resurrected and ascended Christ has a permanent priesthood. Hebrews contrasts the plurality of the Aaronic priests with the singularity of Christ. Their mortality necessitated that son succeed father, grandson succeed son, and so forth. But no one will ever succeed Christ, because "he continues forever" (v. 24). Hebrews thus reminds us that Christ's saving work, even in its priestly expression, centers in his death *and* resurrection.

Hebrews reaches the awesome conclusion: "Consequently, he is able to save to the uttermost those who draw near to God through him, since he always lives to make intercession for them" (v. 25). This is a strong affirmation of God's preservation of his saints (ironically in a book containing Scripture's two most famous warning passages in 6:4–12 and 10:26–39). The High Priest who "offered up himself" (7:27) is alive after death! Accordingly, he presents his sacrifice perpetually in the presence of God in heaven. And that sacrifice always prevails for those who "draw near to God through him," the only "mediator between God and men" (1 Tim. 2:5). Says Lane, "Since Jesus exercises an eternal and final priesthood, he is able to mediate an eternal and ultimate salvation."[57] F. F. Bruce is eloquent, "His once-completed self-offering is utterly acceptable and efficacious; His contact with the Father is immediate and unbroken; His priestly ministry on His people's behalf is never-ending; and therefore the salvation which He secures to them is absolute."[58]

Once again (as in Heb. 2:17), Hebrews draws attention to Christ's qualifications to be High Priest, this time using five adjectives: "For it was indeed fitting that we should have such a high priest, holy, innocent, unstained, separated

---

[57]Ibid., 188.
[58]F. F. Bruce, *The Epistle to the Hebrews*, The New International Commentary on the New Testament (Grand Rapids: Eerdmans, 1964), 155.

from sinners, and exalted above the heavens" (7:26). Uniquely, our High Priest is sinless (communicated by the first three adjectives) and exalted to God's throne (communicated by the last two adjectives).

Consequently, "He has no need, like those high priests, to offer sacrifices daily, first for his own sins and then for those of the people" (v. 27). Since he is absolutely morally pure and has no sins, he has no need to make sacrifices for them. Instead, "he did this once for all when he offered up himself" (v. 27). "He was able to make the definitive sacrifice because he was the sinless high priest described in v 26," Lane explains. Since he "once for all" time "offered up himself," there is no need to offer any more sacrifices. His is finished, perfect, and efficacious. Again Lane comes to our aid:

> The unique surrender of Christ's life is considered under the image of sacrifice: ἑαυτὸν ἀνενέγκας [heauton anenenkas], "he offered himself." In the LXX the verb ἀναφέρειν [anapherein] is a technical term meaning "to offer a sacrifice, to make an offering." . . . The writer presents Christ as performing an essentially priestly function when he offered his life to God.[59]

As we saw in our survey of the Old Testament sacrifices, there is only one occasion when the high priest makes atonement for his own sins—on the Day of Atonement. O'Brien illumines this point:

> The basis for the comparison between Christ and the Levitical high priests is the ritual of the Day of Atonement, for only on this occasion was it prescribed that the high priest should make an atonement first for his own sins and then for those of the people (Lev. 16:6–10). This twofold sacrifice on the Day of Atonement was decisive for our author's typology. . . .
> The ongoing need for the Levitical high priest to make atonement both for himself and his people serves to highlight the utter inadequacy of the old system. By contrast, effective atonement was achieved through the definitive sacrifice of the perfect Son of God who offered himself without blemish for the sins of the people.[60]

Hebrews 9:11–28

Once again Hebrews contrasts Christ with the high priests of the old covenant. Unlike those who went into a tent on earth once a year on the Day of Atonement, "when Christ appeared as a high priest of the good things that have come,

---

[59]Lane, *Hebrews 1–8*, 193.
[60]O'Brien, *The Letter to the Hebrews*, 282.

then [he entered] through the greater and more perfect tent (not made with hands, that is, not of this creation)" (Heb. 9:11). Christ, our High Priest, went into heaven itself, the very presence of God. That is, "he entered once for all into the holy places" (v. 12). Christ went into the true holy places in heaven, of which the Most Holy Place on earth was a type.

Furthermore, unlike the Levitical high priests, he approached God not "by means of the blood of goats and calves but by means of his own blood" (v. 12). His blood, his sacrificial death, was the antitype to which the Old Testament sacrifices pointed. Astoundingly, his self-offering, accomplished on earth and presented in heaven, secured "an eternal redemption" (v. 12). It is difficult to estimate the number of sacrifices performed in the Old Testament. Their very repetition signified their lack of efficacy (10:1–4). By contrast, by his single sacrifice the Son of God did the work necessary to save his people forever.

Hebrews extols the saving virtue of Christ's blood, his violent sacrificial death:

> . . . Jesus, the mediator of a new covenant, and . . . the sprinkled blood that speaks a better word than the blood of Abel. (12:24)

> So Jesus also suffered outside the gate in order to sanctify the people through his own blood. (13:12)

> Now may the God of peace who brought again from the dead our Lord Jesus, the great shepherd of the sheep, by the blood of the eternal covenant . . . (13:20)

Tirelessly, Hebrews acclaims Christ's sacrifice by showing its superiority to those offered by the Aaronic priests:

> For if the blood of goats and bulls, and the sprinkling of defiled persons with the ashes of a heifer, sanctify for the purification of the flesh, how much more will the blood of Christ, who through the eternal Spirit offered himself without blemish to God, purify our conscience from dead works to serve the living God. (9:13–14)

Once more we read that Christ offered himself to God. Once more we learn of his blood saving, in this case purifying dirty consciences. Once more we are reminded of his sinlessness, this time referring not to his character as priest but to his sacrifice, for he offered himself "without blemish."

But for the only time in Scripture, Hebrews here teaches that Christ sacrificed himself "through the eternal Spirit." Despite some dissenters, this is a reference to the Holy Spirit and, as Lane says, "indicates what makes Christ's sacrifice absolute and final."[61] O'Brien is correct: "It seems better, then, to conclude that the Holy Spirit anointed Jesus as high priest for every aspect of his ministry, including his sacrificial death."[62]

The results of Christ's Spirit-anointed self-offering are spelled out: to "purify our conscience from dead works to serve the living God" (v. 14). Here "conscience" speaks of human beings in terms of their God-given faculty for distinguishing good and evil. Here the author is indicating that the definitive sacrifice of Christ, the Mediator of the new covenant, fulfills Jeremiah's promise that that covenant would involve a work on believers' "hearts" (Jer. 31:33). Christ's atoning death cleanses dirty consciences and renews hearts so people are liberated to "serve the living God."

Next the author declares: "Therefore he is the mediator of a new covenant, so that those who are called may receive the promised eternal inheritance" (Heb. 9:15). Because Christ mediates the new covenant and entered heaven itself to secure "an eternal redemption" (v. 12), those whom God summons to himself through the gospel "receive the promised eternal inheritance" (v. 15). The next words are nothing short of astonishing: ". . . since a death has occurred that redeems them from the transgressions committed under the first covenant" (v. 15). As we have seen, God ordained the Old Testament sacrificial system to provide forgiveness and purification for his people Israel. And yet "it is impossible for the blood of bulls and goats to take away sins" (10:4). God forgave and cleansed believing Israelites who trusted him to do what he promised through the animal sacrifices. But those sacrifices were not the ultimate basis for the people's forgiveness and cleansing. They looked forward to "the Lamb of God, who takes away the sin of the world" (John 1:29).

It was Christ, the Mediator of the new covenant whose sacrifice redeemed Old Testament saints "from the transgressions committed under the first covenant" (Heb. 9:15). This means that Christ's atoning sacrifice not only saves all who come after him and trust him as Lord and Savior, but it also saves all who came before him and believed the gospel communicated through the sacrifices. O'Brien says it well: Christ's "redemptive sacrifice is retrospective in its effects and is valid for all who trusted God for the forgiveness of sins in ancient Israel."[63]

The writer then launches into a discussion that I will only summarize. The majority of commentators take διαθήκη (*diathēkē*) to mean "will," as in "last

---

[61] William L. Lane, *Hebrews 9–13*, Word Biblical Commentary (Dallas: Word, 1991), 240. For argumentation (with bibliography) that it refers to Christ's divinity, see Hughes, *A Commentary on the Epistle to the Hebrews*, 358–59.

[62] O'Brien, *The Letter to the Hebrews*, 324–25.

[63] Ibid., 328.

will and testament," in verses 16–17. A will takes effect only when the one who made it dies. A significant minority of commentators, who have influenced me, understand *diathēkē* to have the same meaning here that it does everywhere else in Hebrews—covenant. In this case verses 16–17 would speak of an ancient Near Eastern covenant, which required the death of a sacrifice to be established. God himself takes an oath of self-malediction in Genesis 15! In either case a *diathēkē*—whether it means "will," or "covenant"—is enacted only if a death takes place.[64]

Similarly, the old covenant involved death: the shedding of animal blood to bring forgiveness (vv. 18, 22). In fact, after receiving the Ten Commandments, Moses inaugurated the covenant with the words, "This is the blood of the covenant that God commanded for you" (v. 20, citing Ex. 24:8;), and by performing sacrifices and sprinkling the blood on the book of the covenant, the people, the tabernacle, and its vessels (Heb. 9:19–21). The words of verse 22 function as an axiom that sums up the preceding ideas and transitions to the following ones: "Indeed, under the law almost everything is purified with blood, and without the shedding of blood there is no forgiveness of sins." Sacrificial blood was essential under the old covenant, and it is the same for the new covenant.

It is shocking to read that the heavenly realities themselves needed purification: "Thus it was necessary for the copies of the heavenly things to be purified with these rites, but the heavenly things themselves with better sacrifices than these" (v. 23). In fact, it is so shocking that this verse has spawned many views. Paul Ellingworth lists eight of them![65] Hebrews moves from speaking of the purification of the earthly tabernacle to the purification of the heavenly realities to which the tabernacle pointed.

Before focusing on what the passage teaches, I need to do two preliminaries. First, we must review some Old Testament background concerning the contaminating effects of Israel's sin, with the aid of Sklar:

> The Israelites' sins and impurities defile not only themselves, but also the Lord's sanctuary. . . . This created a serious problem, for defiling a king's home was viewed as a treasonous act that was to be met with swift justice. . . .
>
> The Lord, however, was Israel's redeeming king, who always desired to continue in covenant fellowship with his people. He therefore provided the rites of this day—"the Day of Atonement" ([Lev.] 23:27)—to make full atonement

---

[64]See ibid., 328–32 for discussion and bibliography.

[65]Paul Ellingworth, *The Epistle to the Hebrews*, The New International Greek Testament Commentary (Grand Rapids: Eerdmans, 1993), 477.

for their sin and impurity, in this way removing the threat of his justice, and assuring the Israelites they could continue in covenant fellowship with him.[66]

Second, the writer would have us remember his previous words, speaking of Christ:

> Now if he were on earth, he would not be a priest at all, since there are priests who offer gifts according to the law. They serve a copy and shadow of the heavenly things. For when Moses was about to erect the tent, he was instructed by God, saying, "See that you make everything according to the pattern that was shown you on the mountain." But as it is, Christ has obtained a ministry that is as much more excellent than the old as the covenant he mediates is better, since it is enacted on better promises. (Heb. 8:4–6)

This passage lays down a fundamental principle for understanding 9:23–24: the priests, tabernacle, and even its furniture are earthly copies and shadows of the original and realities, which are Christ and his heavenly liturgy.

I am persuaded that Lane's treatment of this text is correct:

> The additional statement that the heavenly prototypes of the earthly tabernacle and its cultus required cleansing "by better sacrifices than these" clearly implies that the heavenly sanctuary had also become defiled by the sin of the people. Although this implication has been dismissed as "nonsense" . . . , it is consistent with the conceptual framework presupposed by the writer in 9:1–18. His thinking has been informed by the Levitical conception of the necessity for expiatory purification. Sin as defilement is infectious. An individual assumes his part in the community through social relationships and cultic acts. Consequently, the effects of his defilement contaminate society (e.g., Lev 21:15; cf. Heb 12:15–16), the sanctuary where God met with his people (cf. Lev 16:16; 20:3; 21:33; Num 19:20), and even the inanimate vessels used in the cultus (cf. [Heb. 9] v 21).[67]

I, like others, avoided this interpretation for some time, regarding it as nonsensical and impossible. Heaven needed to be purified?! But that is exactly what Hebrews is teaching as it extols the sacrifice of our great High Priest. Even as the sins of the Israelites defiled the Most Holy Place in God's earthly sanctuary, so that atonement had to be made for it, so also our sins defiled the Most Holy Place in God's heavenly sanctuary, so that atonement had to be made for it.

---

[66]Sklar, *Leviticus*, on Lev. 16:1–34.
[67]Lane, *Hebrews 9–13*, 247.

"Better sacrifices" (the plural is explained by attraction to the plural τούτοις, *toutois* in v. 23a) refers to Christ's once-for-all self-offering.

Hear Lane again:

> That the effects of sin also extend to the heavenly world is a corollary of the solidarity that the writer perceives between ultimate reality in heaven and its reflection on earth. . . . As defilement reaches beyond the individual to taint society and earthly cultus, it also pollutes heavenly reality.
>
> The full, perfect, and sufficient sacrifice of Christ purified the heavenly sanctuary from the defilement resulting from the sins of the people. . . . The superior sacrifice demanded was provided by the self-oblation of Christ.[68]

This interpretation is confirmed by verse 24, which defines "the heavenly things" from verse 23: "For Christ has entered, not into holy places made with hands, which are copies of the true things, but into heaven itself, now to appear in the presence of God on our behalf." "The heavenly things" are "heaven itself," even "the presence of God." The crucified, risen, ascended Christ appears there "on our behalf."

Once again, Hebrews shows the supremacy of Christ over his Old Testament priestly counterparts:

> Nor was it to offer himself repeatedly, as the high priest enters the holy places every year with blood not his own, for then he would have had to suffer repeatedly since the foundation of the world. But as it is, he has appeared once for all at the end of the ages to put away sin by the sacrifice of himself. (vv. 25–26)

Unlike the high priest on the Day of Atonement, Christ performed only one, nonrepeatable sacrifice. Also unlike the high priest on the Day of Atonement, Christ offered "the sacrifice of himself" on the cross. Consequently, his sacrifice, unlike theirs, put away sin. It accomplished expiation—the removal of sin.

Not to be missed is that the author says that Christ's atonement was made "at the end of the ages" (v. 26). O'Brien explains, "This singular event has occurred at the decisive, final moment of history, *the culmination of the ages.* Christ's self-offering is sufficient and final for all history—past, present, and future."[69]

The writer rounds off his passage thus: "And just as it is appointed for man to die once, and after that comes judgment, so Christ, having been offered

---

[68] Ibid., 247–48.
[69] O'Brien, *The Letter to the Hebrews*, 340.

once to bear the sins of many, will appear a second time, not to deal with
sin but to save those who are eagerly waiting for him" (9:27–28). Death and
judgment are inevitable. Every human being dies once, Christ included. But
for him that means that his sacrifice is unrepeatable. He is like other human
beings in dying once; but he is unlike them in that his death made atonement
for sins: he died "to bear the sins of many." These words are reminiscent of
Isaiah 53:

> Therefore I will divide him a portion with the many,
>> and he shall divide the spoil with the strong,
> because he poured out his soul to death
>> and was numbered with the transgressors;
> yet *he bore the sin of many*,
>> and makes intercession for the transgressors. (Isa. 53:12)

Christ, Isaiah's suffering Servant, died a redemptive death. His offering of himself is the unique sacrificial event of the ages.

The priestly theme is continued through Hebrews 9:28, as Lane underscores:

> The writer's distinctly priestly perspective is evident in the formulation of v 28b
> as well. The reference to Christ's return to those who wait for him draws its force
> in this context from the analogy with the sequence of events on the Day of Atone-
> ment. The people waited anxiously outside the sanctuary until the high priest
> emerged from the Most Holy Place after he had fulfilled his office (cf. Lev 16:17).
> His reappearance provided assurance that the offering he had made had been
> accepted by God. . . .
>
> The parousia is not an event that can add anything to the sacrificial office
> Christ has already fulfilled. The force of sin has been decisively broken by his
> death. . . . But his appearance will confirm that his sacrifice has been accepted
> and that he has secured the blessings of salvation for those whom he represented.
> For those who are the heirs of salvation . . . it will mean full enjoyment of their
> inheritance.[70]

Hebrews 10:10–14

The author begins chapter 10 by demonstrating the inadequacy of the law with
its sacrificial system. The law merely foreshadows the new covenant blessings
brought by Christ, our great High Priest. Its repeated sacrifices, especially on the
Day of Atonement, can never "make perfect those who draw near" in worship

---

[70]Lane, *Hebrews 9–13*, 250–51.

(10:1). For, if they could have, they would have "ceased to be offered" (v. 2). But their very repetition broadcasts the impotence of "the blood of bulls and goats to take away sins" (v. 4).

The writer then employs Psalm 40:6–8 (viewing David as a type of Christ) as an address of the Son of God to the Father to show the necessity for the Son's incarnation, specifically his assuming a human body that he can offer in sacrifice (Heb. 10:5–7). By using four terms for sacrifice ("probably intended to cover all the main types of offerings prescribed in the Levitical system"[71]) Hebrews expresses God's dissatisfaction with the sacrifices in themselves, a frequent theme of the Old Testament prophets (1 Sam. 15:22; Isa. 1:10–13; Jer. 7:21–24). God desires heartfelt worship. "Sacrifices in themselves are powerless to please God or secure a proper relationship between God and his people," Lane asserts.[72]

What sacrifices cannot do, the incarnate divine Son does. The psalmist tells of a speaker who realizes that his body is given him by God to perform his will. Hebrews identifies the Son of God as that speaker who at his incarnation utters Psalm 40:6–8 to the Father. The Son identifies with his people by willingly taking a human body with which he will perform God's will (Heb. 10:5–7). Christ abolishes the Old Testament sacrifices, associated with the Mosaic law (and thereby abolishes that law), to accomplish God's will (vv. 8–9) in his body. And the next verse explains how.

Hebrews 10:1–9 has built to this point: "And by that will [of God] we have been sanctified through the offering of the body of Jesus Christ once for all" (v. 10). Here is a magnificent statement of the unique and efficacious sacrifice of Christ. Bruce makes an important point: "The offering of His body is simply the offering of Himself."[73] By doing God's will and offering himself in his body once for all time there results the definitive sanctification of his people. This is a once-for-all consecration, constituting them the saints of God. Flowing from it is their progressive sanctification, their gradual growth in holiness, which is spoken of in verse 14.

Ellingworth underlines the importance of this verse, "The importance of the statement is stressed by the use, for the first time in the epistle (cf. 13:1, 21), of the full name 'Jesus Christ.'"[74] Note that Jesus Christ's sacrifice is superior to the Levitical sacrifices for several reasons. First, his sacrifice is "once for all," and theirs were endlessly repeated. Second, his personal offering of his own body is effective over against the ineffective offering of animals. Consequently,

---

[71] O'Brien, *The Letter to the Hebrews*, 349.
[72] Lane, *Hebrews 9–13*, 263.
[73] Bruce, *The Epistle to the Hebrews*, 236.
[74] Ellingworth, *The Epistle to the Hebrews*, 505.

there is a finality and efficacy to his work and to what depends upon it—the sanctification of his people.

Lane captures the sense of this weighty verse:

> In the sacrifice of his body on the cross, Christ freely and fully made the will of God his own. Consequently, his sacrifice requires no repetition. It embodied the totality of obedience and eradicated the disparity between sacrifice and obedience presupposed by Ps 40:6–8. . . . By virtue of the fact that he did so under the conditions of authentic human, bodily existence and in solidarity with the human family, the new people of God have been radically transformed and consecrated to his service.[75]

The argument advances. Hebrews 10:5–10 argues that Christ's one sacrifice supersedes the many repeated Old Testament sacrifices; verses 11–14 argue that the one High Priest of the new covenant supersedes the many priests of the old covenant. "And every priest stands daily at his service, offering repeatedly the same sacrifices, which can never take away sins. But when Christ had offered for all time a single sacrifice for sins, he sat down at the right hand of God" (vv. 11–12). I will mention four sharp contrasts.

First, the very posture of the unique priest of the new covenant contrasts dramatically with the posture of the priests of the old covenant. They stood, indicating that their work was not done; he sat, indicating that his work was finished (vv. 11–12). Second, they "daily" performed their priestly service (v. 11); he "offered *for all time* a single sacrifice" (v. 12). Third, they offered "repeatedly the same sacrifices" (v. 11); he offered "a single sacrifice for sins" (v. 12). Fourth, their sacrifices were not efficacious—they "can never take away sins" (v. 11); his sacrifice "has perfected" his people "for all time," as verse 14 teaches.

The author says that Christ, having made his unique and unrepeatable sacrifice, and having sat at God's right hand, waits "from that time until his enemies should be made a footstool for his feet" (v. 13). His session does not render him inactive. To the contrary, it enables him to engage actively in his heavenly new covenant ministry of intercession and help. He will do so until, according to Psalm 110:1, God overthrows his enemies forever. Christ sits as God's enthroned priest; there is no doubt as to the outcome: "For the future he has only to wait for the complete subjugation of every power that resists the gracious redemptive purposes of God," as Lane declares.[76]

---

[75]Lane, *Hebrews 9–13*, 266.
[76]Ibid., 267.

Hebrews 10:14 is another blockbuster (along with 9:12, 15, 23; 10:10): "For by a single offering he has perfected for all time those who are being sanctified." This is a tremendous statement of the efficacy of Christ's sacrifice. It brings together two ideas in wonderful theological complementarity. On the one hand, believers contribute nothing to their salvation—it is all of grace and all of Christ, for by his self-offering "he has perfected" them "for all time." On the other hand, they are identifiable; those for whom this sacrifice has availed "are being sanctified." Attridge agrees:

> The description of the recipients of that perfection as "those who are being sanctified" . . . reinforces the connection between perfection and sanctity that was established in the previous pericope. Yet the present tense used here nuances the relationship, suggesting that the appropriation of the enduring effects of Christ's act is an ongoing present reality. . . . The creative tension between what Christ is understood to have done and what remains for his followers to do begins to emerge with particular clarity.[77]

This verse, then, further emphasizes the decisive character of the completed work of the Mediator of the new covenant, as Hughes relates: "The sacrifice of himself in our place on the cross was the sacrifice to end all sacrifices (cf. v. 26 below)."[78] And it ties that work to his people in such a way as to make their final salvation certain. Bruce declares, "The sacrifice of Christ has purified His people from the moral defilement of sin, and assured them of permanent maintenance in a right relation with God."[79]

The author situates his discussion of the superiority of Christ's sacrifice and priesthood by reminding his readers of his citation (in 8:7–12) of Jeremiah's new covenant prophecy. The quotations and applications of parts of Jeremiah 31:33–34 in the four following verses of Hebrews 10 (vv. 15–18) accentuate two results of Christ's priestly sacrifice. These are, by declaration from the Lord, obedience from the heart—"I will put my laws on their hearts, and write them on their minds"—and the forgiveness of sins—"I will remember their sins and their lawless deeds no more" (vv. 16–17). Verse 18 is an aphorism giving emphasis to forgiveness: "Where there is forgiveness of these, there is no longer any offering for sin."

---

[77] Harold W. Attridge, *Hebrews*, Hermeneia (Philadelphia: Fortress, 1989), 281.

[78] Hughes, *A Commentary on the Epistle to the Hebrews*, 400.

[79] Bruce, *The Epistle to the Hebrews*, 241.

Conclusion

The teaching of Hebrews concerning Christ our sacrifice is so massive and detailed that it is very difficult to summarize. The following words of David Peterson do the job better than I can:

> Hebrews consistently portrays the atoning work of Christ as the fulfilment of the Day of Atonement ritual. At the heart of this portrayal is the presentation of Christ as the sinless savior, who "bears the sins of many" in his death, and delivers those who are cleansed and sanctified by his "blood" from the awesome judgement of God. Allusions to the fulfilment of other blood rituals help to expand the picture. Jesus' death and heavenly exaltation accomplish an eternally effective redemption from sin and its consequences, inaugurating all the benefits of the New Covenant. Since he continues for ever as a heavenly high priest, he is always able to apply the benefits of his once-for-all sacrifice to those who draw near to God through him. One sacrifice replaces the many sacrifices of the Old Covenant used to maintain people in a relationship with God.[80]

Christ Our Sacrifice in 1 Peter

The apostle Peter also speaks of Christ our sacrifice in three passages. Since we have treated all three elsewhere, here I will summarize, with emphasis on the sacrificial elements.[81]

1 Peter 1:2

In the salutation to his first epistle, the apostle Peter portrays salvation as the work of the Trinity. He writes "to those who are elect . . . according to the fore-knowledge of God the Father, in the sanctification of the Spirit, for obedience to Jesus Christ and for sprinkling with his blood" (1:1–2).

Christians, including Peter's recipients, are chosen according to the Father's foreknowledge, sanctified by the Holy Spirit, and sprinkled with Jesus's blood. When he speaks of "the sanctification of the Spirit," he means the sanctification produced by the Holy Spirit. This is not the Spirit's progressive sanctifying work, but his initial sanctifying work in which he sets people apart from sin and unto God, constituting them saints (cf. 1 Cor. 6:11).

This initial sanctification is "for obedience to Jesus Christ," that is, it results in obedience to Christ. The obedience of which Peter speaks is evangelical

---

[80]David Peterson, ed., *Where Wrath and Mercy Meet: Proclaiming the Atonement Today* (Carlisle, Cumbria, UK: Paternoster, 2001), 55.

[81]See the chapters on the death of Christ, Christ our Redeemer, and Christ our legal substitute.

obedience, faith in Jesus. At times Peter uses "obedience" and "obey" to signify obeying the gospel, regarded as a command to believe in Christ (1:22; 3:1), and hence accepting Christ. And at times Peter uses "disobey" to signify disobeying the gospel command and hence rejecting Christ (4:17). Evangelical obedience also has results—sprinkling with Jesus's blood. "Blood" harkens back to the Old Testament sacrificial system, and "Jesus' blood" refers to his death as a sacrifice. Ramsey Michaels instructs us: "To be sprinkled with Jesus' blood was to be cleansed from one's former way of living and released from spiritual slavery by the power of his death."[82]

Peter Davids effectively relates Peter's words to their Old Testament background:

> Surely acquaintance with the OT would remind these readers of the blood sprinkled on the people after their acceptance of the old covenant at Sinai, which blood sealed the covenant (Exod. 24:7–8). And the fact that in Exodus this sprinkling follows the acceptance of the covenant by the people with their pledge of obedience (Exod. 24:3), as well as the fact that in some of the passion traditions Jesus' blood is specifically connected with this covenant initiation (Mark 14:24), probably explains the sprinkling's *following* the obedience of the people. The people who have responded to the gospel proclamation have been properly brought into a covenant relationship with God, and that covenant is not the old one of Sinai but the new one based on the blood of Christ himself.[83]

The apostle says only a little about the blood of Christ here, but what he says is important and sets the tone for his letter. Schreiner recaps: "Believers enter the covenant by obeying the gospel and through the sprinkled blood of Christ, that is, his cleansing sacrifice.[84]

1 Peter 1:18–19

Leading up to Peter's chief passage on Christ's atoning sacrifice, the apostle urges his hearers to spiritual alertness and sobriety and exhorts them to fully trust in the abundant outpouring of God's grace that will occur at Jesus's return (1:13). He urges them as God's children to obey their heavenly Father and not to give in to the evil desires that dominated their lives before they came to know the Lord (v. 14). Rather, with the help of Leviticus 11:44—"Be holy, for I am

---

[82]J. Ramsey Michaels, *1 Peter*, Word Biblical Commentary (Waco, TX: Word, 1988), 12–13.

[83]Peter H. Davids, *The First Epistle of Peter*, The New International Commentary on the New Testament (Grand Rapids: Eerdmans, 1990), 49.

[84]Thomas R. Schreiner, *1, 2 Peter, Jude*, The New American Commentary (Nashville: Broadman and Holman, 2003), 56.

holy"—he exhorts them to holiness in all that they do. They are to bear a family resemblance to their Father in godliness (1 Pet. 1:15–16).

Peter returns to the pilgrim motif with which he began his letter (1:1; cf. 2:11) and commands his audience to live in the fear of God their Father: "And if you call on him as Father who judges impartially according to each one's deeds, conduct yourselves with fear throughout the time of your exile" (1:17). Then he adds another reason for circumspect living: ". . . knowing that you were ransomed from the futile ways inherited from your forefathers, not with perishable things such as silver or gold, but with the precious blood of Christ, like that of a lamb without blemish or spot" (vv. 18–19). The apostle here speaks the language of sacrifice and redemption. His readers were delivered from a pagan lifestyle (cf. 4:3), and not by earthly riches but by something far more valuable—"the precious blood of Christ."

Peter uses a metaphor identifying Jesus with sacrificial lambs from the Old Testament. There are two points of comparison. First, both had to be "without blemish or spot." This ensured that Old Testament saints' sacrifices were costly to them, showing how highly they esteemed the Lord. Of Christ, "without blemish or spot" speaks of his moral perfection, which qualifies him to be *the* sacrifice for sin (cf. John 1:29). J. N. D. Kelly draws out Peter's comparison:

> At this point the imagery he employs . . . changes and becomes frankly sacrificial; Christ is likened to "a lamb without blemish or stain," i.e. a sacrificial victim. The first adjective (*amomos*) . . . recalls the Jewish requirement that such an offering must be faultless; the second (*aspilos*) does not occur in the LXX, but is added so as to emphasize that in Christ's case the faultlessness which makes the victim acceptable must be understood in terms of sinlessness and holy consecration (Heb. ix.14).[85]

Second, both gave their "blood." God ordained that the animals be sacrificed upon the altar; their blood stood for their atoning death. Similarly, Christ's blood, his atoning death, delivers sinners, as Schreiner relates:

> L. Morris rightly argues that blood does not involve the release of life, as if life is somehow mystically transmitted by the spilling of blood. Instead, the shedding of blood indicates that Christ poured out his life to death for sinners.

---

[85]J. N. D. Kelly, *A Commentary on the Epistles of Peter and Jude,* Thornapple Commentaries (Grand Rapids: Baker, 1969), 74–75.

What Peter teaches is that the blood of Christ is the means by which believers are redeemed.[86]

The exact Old Testament background is debated. Some claim that the Passover lamb is in view, but I agree with Schreiner: "Some scholars try to restrict the background imagery here to exodus tradition, but the references above indicate that Peter referred to sacrificial language more generally."[87]

Joel Green brings out a much-neglected aspect of 1 Peter 1:19:

> The author's qualification of Christ's blood as "precious" marks a profound, if easily overlooked theological move. Reckoned by human criteria, Jesus' death on a tree (2:24) was anything but honorable, so mention of his passion could easily evoke valuations of humiliation and scorn. In a manner consistent with his emphasis on God's choice of Jesus (1:20) and the subsequent declaration of Jesus as rejected among humans but "chosen and precious (or honored)" before God (2:4, 6), Peter declares that Jesus' death, however ignominious in the Roman world, actually bears divine approval. The imagery Peter borrows from Israel's economy of sacrifice thus portrays the honorable death of Jesus as effective in wiping away sin and its effects.[88]

Green's words are apt. Although the world cursed God's Christ, to us he is indeed precious because he redeemed us with his "precious blood."

1 Peter 2:21–24

With an eye on Isaiah 53, Peter exhorts his readers, especially slaves, to suffer injustice patiently, and by so doing to follow Christ's example (1 Pet. 2:21–23; cf. Isa. 53:9, 7):

> For to this you have been called, because Christ also suffered for you, leaving you an example, so that you might follow in his steps. He committed no sin, neither was deceit found in his mouth. When he was reviled, he did not revile in return; when he suffered, he did not threaten, but continued entrusting himself to him who judges justly.

---

[86]Schreiner, *1, 2 Peter, Jude*, 85. The reference is to Leon Morris, *The Apostolic Preaching of the Cross*, 114–18.

[87]Ibid., 86. For argument that Peter was alluding to the Passover lamb, see Davids, *The First Epistle of Peter*, 72–73.

[88]Joel B. Green, *1 Peter*, The Two Horizons New Testament Commentary (Grand Rapids: Eerdmans, 2007), 42.

Peter employs Jesus's suffering on the cross as an example for Christians to follow, but that easily leads the apostle to contemplate more redemptive themes. Considering the topic of suffering, Jesus is secondly our example, but he is first of all our suffering Savior, whose matchless suffering rescues us: "He himself bore our sins in his body on the tree, that we might die to sin and live to righteousness" (1 Pet. 2:24; cf. Isa. 53:4, 11). Peter does not write that Christ "offered" our sins on the tree, but that he "bore" them to or on the tree. The apostle thereby paints a picture of Jesus carrying our sins away in his death.

How should we understand Peter's reference to Jesus's dying on a "tree"? Ramsey Michaels answers:

> Ξύλον [ksylon], lit., "wood," was used in ancient literature (especially the LXX and Jewish literature) to refer to a stake or gallows . . . . It becomes in the New Testament an almost technical word for the cross of Jesus (Acts 5:30; 10:39; Gal 3:13; cf. *Barn.* 5:13), particularly in the expression ἐπὶ ξύλου [epi ksylou], "on a cross," based in all likelihood on the LXX of Deut 21:23 (see Gal 3:13, its earliest Christian occurrence).[89]

When Peter says "tree," he likely alludes to the curse of the Deuteronomy passage, and yet his emphasis is not there, "but rather on the removal of sins which the cross of Christ accomplished."[90]

Isaiah 53 was more on Peter's mind than Deuteronomy 21:23 when he penned this passage. Throughout 1 Peter 2:21–25, the apostle has in mind Isaiah's famous chapter. He quotes verses 9, 7, 4, 12, 5, and 6, in that order. A question naturally comes to readers' minds, why this order? Green answers:

> The sequence of Peter's affirmations does not replicate the order of the source material in Isaiah 53. Instead, his order follows that of the passion accounts, moving from Jesus' trials (during which he remained silent while he was mocked and beaten) to the cross and its significance. Apparently, Peter found in Isaiah a commentary on Jesus' passion which he then organized in relation to the events of Jesus' suffering and death.[91]

Now, as we saw when investigating Isaiah 53, that chapter contains sacrificial references in verse 10, but not in the verses that Peter quotes here. Davids explains, "What we have is a generalized picture in which Isa. 53:12 is assimilated to the sacrificial language of the OT."[92] I agree, except that I would broaden

---

[89]Michaels, *1 Peter*, 148.
[90]Ibid.
[91]Green, *1 Peter*, 85.
[92]Davids, *The First Epistle of Peter*, 112.

Davids's words to include all of the allusions to Isaiah 53 mentioned above and in the order of passion accounts, as Green has noted.

Peter applies Christ's atonement to his audience, "He himself bore our sins in his body on the tree, that we might die to sin and live to righteousness." God desires holy lives in his people, and that was one reason Christ died for them. Peter, sounding like Paul in Romans 6, wants believers to know that, because Jesus bore their sins, they are now dead to sin.

Conclusion

So, then, how does Peter portray Christ's death as an atoning sacrifice in his first epistle? Green answers perceptively:

> These texts [treating Old Testament sacrifices] portray atonement as redemption through the substitution of an animal for a human being and as purification of the sanctuary and, by extension, of the community of God's people. . . .
>
> For Peter, two ingredients of the sacrifice are especially developed. In this system, the life of an unblemished animal substitutes for blemished human life. Accordingly, Peter affirms that Jesus "committed no sin, nor was deceit found in his mouth" ([1 Pet. 2] v. 22; see 1:19: "a lamb without blemish or defect"). Moreover, in the rite of sacrifice, the laying of hands on the beast's head signals the importance of "identification" or "representation"—with sinners identifying themselves with the beast and the beast now representing sinners in their sin. According, Jesus "bore our sins . . . on the tree" ([chap. 2] v. 24).[93]

Christ Our Sacrifice in 1 John

John's first epistle has at least one important text pertaining to Christ our sacrifice—1 John 1:7.[94] I will sketch the theological context before we explore that text. John writes to discourage his readers from sinning: "My little children, I am writing these things to you so that you may not sin" (1 John 2:1). Nevertheless, he knows that they will sin: "If we say that we have no sin, we deceive ourselves, and the truth is not in us" (1:8). He repeats, "If we say we have not sinned, we make him a liar, and his word is not in us" (v. 10). Because some sin is inevitable, he instructs them on how to deal with sin in the Christian life: "But if anyone does sin, we have an advocate with the Father, Jesus Christ the righteous," and "if we confess our sins, he is faithful and just to forgive us our sins and to cleanse us from all unrighteousness" (v. 9; 2:1).

---

[93]Green, *1 Peter*, 88–89.

[94]Two texts dealing with propitiation in 1 John (2:2; 4:9–14) were treated in the chapter "Christ's Death."

The question arises, What is the state of affairs when Christians do not sin? When they do sin, they need their "advocate . . . Jesus Christ the righteous" and God's forgiveness and cleansing. But what about when they do not sin? Do they need Jesus then? Or do they somehow stand on their own before God? John answers these questions for us: "But if we walk in the light, as he is in the light, we have fellowship with one another, and the blood of Jesus his Son cleanses us from all sin" (1:7).

It might surprise some to learn that even when we are not aware of sinning, the basis of our relationship with God is "the blood of Jesus his Son," that is, his atoning sacrifice. And even when we live authentically as Christians—"walk in the light"—Jesus's blood "cleanses us from all sin." John "means that in the cross of Christ our sin is effectively and repeatedly . . . removed," as Smalley explains.[95] Jesus's blood purifies us from the beginning to the end. There is no other atonement, no other remedy for sin. And as a result of Christ's sacrifice, "we have fellowship with one another" as fellow believers. This horizontal fellowship is based on the vertical fellowship of 1:3: "Our fellowship is with the Father and his Son Jesus Christ."

It is worthwhile for us to meditate on John's reference to "the blood of Jesus." Robert Yarbrough comes to our aid by placing the expression in the context of the Old Testament:

> This ["the blood of Jesus"] refers to his atoning death and not to some magical quality of his blood per se. . . . Since the saving efficacy of Jesus's blood in the NT "derives its meaning particularly from the sacrifices of the Day of Atonement" in the OT (F. Laubach, NIDNTT 1:223; cf. Lev. 1), John's assertion is a reminder of the OT substructure of his theology and his understanding of Jesus's ministry. . . . Jesus's death cleanses from the sin that is frankly depicted and thereby explicitly defined in much OT narrative, law, prophecy, and wisdom. While walking in the dark makes a mockery of fellowship (1 John 1:6), walking in the light facilitates fellowship and preserves believers from the ravaging effects of sin (1:7), from which no one in this life can claim to be completely immune (1:8, 10; 2:1).[96]

John's words, therefore, are a great encouragement to believers: "But if we walk in the light, as he is in the light, we have fellowship with one another, and the blood of Jesus his Son cleanses us from all sin" (1:7). Especially strengthening

---

[95]Stephen S. Smalley, *1, 2, 3 John*, Word Biblical Commentary (Waco, TX: Word, 1984), 25.
[96]Robert W. Yarbrough, *1–3 John*, Baker Exegetical Commentary on the New Testament (Grand Rapids: Baker Academic, 2008), 57.

for us pilgrims is John's word that Jesus's atoning self-offering "cleanses us from *all* sin." Christ's is an efficacious sacrifice, and therefore ours is a joyful life (v. 4).

Christ Our Sacrifice in Revelation

We have already investigated five passages in which Revelation tells of Jesus the Lamb who was slain and who saves his people by his blood.[97] Here I will offer brief comments that accent Christ our sacrifice.

Revelation 1:5–6

Jesus deserves never-ending praise for his great love demonstrated in dying for sinners. "To him who loves us and has freed us from our sins by his blood . . . be glory and dominion forever and ever." The mention of "his blood" has its roots in Old Testament priests' making atonement for sins by the sprinkling of blood. Jesus's sacrificial death delivers believers by releasing them from their sins.

Revelation 5:6, 9

John, told to behold the Lion, is surprised when he sees not a Lion but a Lamb. "And between the throne and the four living creatures and among the elders I saw a Lamb standing, as though it had been slain" (5:6). This is the principal symbol for Jesus in Revelation—the Lamb. Indeed, in every occurrence but one, it is a symbol for Christ our sacrifice. It is noteworthy that John looks for a Lion but sees the Lamb. Christ the Victor triumphs by being slaughtered as a Lamb. He is worthy to open the sealed book of judgment and is praised by many (vv. 7–13):

> Worthy are you to take the scroll
>> and to open its seals,
> for you were slain, and by your blood you ransomed people for God
>> from every tribe and language and people and nation. (v. 9)

Only the Lamb is worthy to open the scroll. He "was slain," or "slaughtered,"[98] a reference to Jesus's bloody death. By the Lamb's "blood" he "ransomed people for God." The redemption price is the sacrificial death of Christ, the Lamb of God. Christ's redemptive death is efficacious to redeem; it actually ransoms people for God from "every tribe and language and people and nation."

---

[97] In the chapter "Christ's Death."

[98] Greek, *sphazō*, "to slaughter," in William F. Arndt and F. Wilbur Gingrich, *A Greek-English Lexicon of the New Testament and Other Early Christian Literature*, 2nd ed. (Chicago: University of Chicago, 1979), 796.

Revelation 7:14

John gives a description of the saints: "They have washed their robes and made them white in the blood of the Lamb." This speaks of their being purified through Christ's sacrifice.

Revelation 12:11

John pictures a great battle in heaven between the archangel Michael, with his angels, and a dragon, a symbol for the Devil (v. 7). When the Devil is defeated and thrown out of heaven into the world, victory is announced (v. 10). Though this means war on earth, there is rejoicing in heaven over the saints. Here is their testimony: "And they have conquered him by the blood of the Lamb and by the word of their testimony, for they loved not their lives even unto death" (v. 11). Martyred Christians triumph over Satan by "the blood of the Lamb," Christ's atoning sacrifice.

Revelation 13:8

The beast from the sea, a counterfeit christ, blasphemes and attacks the saints, with the result that people worship it and the dragon, Satan (Rev. 13:1–7). Indeed, "all who dwell on earth will worship it, everyone whose name has not been written before the foundation of the world in the book of life of the Lamb who was slain" (v. 8).

The book of life is as the census register of the city of God. It records the names of those chosen for salvation, for "only those who are written in the Lamb's book of life" will enter the eternal city of God (21:27). God will shield them from eternal death (3:5), the beast's deceptions (17:8), and the lake of fire (20:15).

When John calls it "the Lamb's book of life" (21:27) and "the book of life of the Lamb who was slain" (13:8), he signifies that the book belongs to Jesus because he made atonement for his peoples' sins. Thus in all five passages, Jesus is the slaughtered Lamb, who died as an atoning sacrifice to cleanse sinners.

Conclusion

Gregory Beale's comments on 1:5 can serve as a summary of Revelation's teaching as a whole:

> Christ expressed his love by redeeming his people from their sins through his *death* ("blood"). People are released from their bondage to the power and penalty of sin by identifying by faith with Jesus' sacrificial death. This suggests a priestly function, since OT priests accomplished sanctification and atonement for Israel

by sprinkling the blood of sacrificial animals. . . . Here, as in Hebrews, Christ is portrayed as both priest and sacrifice.[99]

Connecting the Dots

Texts

We have studied the following passages: Exodus 12:13; Leviticus 1–6, 16; Isaiah 53:10; Matthew 26:27–29; John 1:19, 36; 17:19; Romans 3:25; 8:3; 1 Corinthians 5:7; Ephesians 5:2; Hebrews 1:3; 2:17–18; 7:23–27; 9:11–28; 10:14–18; 1 Peter 1:2, 18–19; 2:21–24; 1 John 1:7; Revelation 1:5–6; 5:6, 9; 7:14; 12:11; 13:8.

Sphere

This picture of Christ's saving work comes from the sphere of the Old Testament cultus, involving the tabernacle or temple, priests, altars, sacrifices, and blood.

Background

The Old Testament background includes the Passover Lamb, Levitical sacrifices, the Day of Atonement, and Isaiah's suffering Servant.

Definition

This picture portrays Jesus as the fulfillment of the Old Testament sacrificial system. He is both the great High Priest and sacrifice of the new covenant. By making a self-offering of his body and his blood (atoning death), he saves forever all who come to God through him. Because of his death and resurrection, he also has an ongoing priestly ministry of intercession for his people (Heb. 7:23–25).

Need

Humanity's need for Christ our sacrifice is our moral uncleanness and impurity before a holy and just God. We are all defiled and in need of cleansing and forgiveness promised in Jeremiah 31:34 (Heb. 10:17).

Initiator

Christ our sacrifice comes of his own volition and according to God's plan (Heb. 10:5–10) to live a sinless life as "a lamb without blemish or spot" (1 Pet. 1:19) and to give himself in death so as to bear our sins "in his body on the tree" (2:24).

---

[99]G. K. Beale, *The Book of Revelation*, The New International Greek Testament Commentary (Grand Rapids: Eerdmans, 1999), 191.

The initiative was all of the Father and the Son, "who through the eternal Spirit offered himself without blemish to God" (Heb. 9:14).

Mediator

Christ our sacrifice is "the Lamb of God, who takes away the sin of the world" (John 1:29), our "great high priest" (Heb. 4:14; cf. 8:1; 9:11), the Mediator of the new covenant (Heb. 8:6; 9:15; 12:24).

Work

Christ was the High Priest of the new covenant who became a human being (Heb. 10:5, 10), "suffered when tempted" (2:18), and "once for all . . . offered up himself" to God (7:27; 9:14) as a sacrifice (9:26; 10:12) "to bear the sins of many" (9:28).

Voluntariness

Christ displayed his love supremely when he "gave himself up for us, a fragrant offering and sacrifice to God" (Eph. 5:2). Hebrews 10:5–10 emphatically teaches the willingness of the Son of God to come into the world to do God's will by offering his body once for all.

Scope

Remarkably, Christ by offering himself "once for all" (Heb. 7:27; 9:12; 10:10) made "purification for sins" (1:3), saving believers of the new covenant as well as redeeming Old Testament saints "from the transgressions committed under the first covenant" (9:15). His unique sacrifice "purified . . . the heavenly things" from the pollution of our sins (9:23–24).

Substitution

It is noteworthy that Joel Green, who wrote "Must We Imagine the Atonement in Penal Substitutionary Terms?"[100] and answered his title in the negative, found substitutionary atonement in Peter's presentation of Christ our sacrifice:

> These texts [treating Old Testament sacrifices] portray atonement as redemption through the substitution of an animal for a human being . . . .
> . . . Moreover, in the rite of sacrifice, the laying of hands on the beast's head signals the importance of "identification" or "representation"—with sinners iden-

---

[100]Joel B. Green, "Must We Imagine the Atonement in Penal Substitutionary Terms?," in *The Atonement Debate*, ed. Derek Tidball, David Hilborn, and Justin Thacker (Grand Rapids: Zondervan, 2008), 153–71.

tifying themselves with the beast and the beast now representing sinners in their sin. According, Jesus "bore our sins . . . on the tree" ([1 Pet. 2] v. 24).[101]

This comports with our findings in many other texts: Exodus 12:13; Leviticus 16; Isaiah 53:10; Romans 3:25; 8:3; Hebrews 2:17; Revelation 5:9. Sacrifice seems to imply substitution.

Past, Present, and Future Results

The priestly service of Christ our sacrifice avails for Old Testament believers (Heb. 9:15), new covenant saints (1:3; 9:14, 26; 10:10), and all of the people of God forever (7:23–25; 9:12, 28; 10:14). His self-sacrifice produces forgiveness (Matt. 26:28; Heb. 10:17–18), redemption (1 Pet. 1:18–19; Rev. 5:9), purification (John 17:19; Heb. 1:3; 9:14; 10:14; 1 John 1:7), and a life of godliness and service to God (1 Pet. 2:24; Heb. 9:14). Christ's ongoing intercession guarantees final salvation (Heb. 7:23–25).

---

[101]Green, *1 Peter*, 88–89.

Conclusion

It is time to bring things together, highlight salient points, and draw conclusions. We will do this with the aid of a couple of figures and a table. But before we look at the illustrations, it is important to underscore three points. First, we hold together in our minds and hearts the person and work of Christ. This book assumes the high christology of John's Gospel, Paul's epistles, Hebrews, and Revelation. It assumes the theological conclusions of the great christological councils culminating in Chalcedon. Without apology, it does christology "from above," affirming that the second person of the Trinity, the eternal Son, the Word, the light, truly became incarnate in Jesus of Nazareth.

Second, in light of the book's focus on Christ's saving events, we affirm that it is Jesus who saves through those events. We do not separate the person and work of Christ. The work saves only because he accomplished it. And, as the chapter on the incarnation emphasizes—his becoming a man does not save in and of itself. Jesus had to perform various deeds to save his people from their sins.

Third, because the separation of Christ's saving work into nine events tends to focus on their multiplicity, we emphasize their unity. There is *one* saving work of Christ. All nine events can thus be viewed as *the* Christ-event.

The table and two figures that follow will help us synthesize and better understand Christ's saving events, the biblical pictures that interpret them, and the directions in which his work points.

Christ's Saving Events

Figure 1 briefly summarizes the saving significance of each of Christ's events, organized according to descending or ascending movements. Notice the lines that come from heaven to earth and vice versa.

Figure 1. Christ's nine saving events

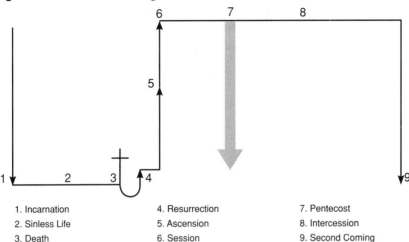

1. Incarnation
2. Sinless Life
3. Death
4. Resurrection
5. Ascension
6. Session
7. Pentecost
8. Intercession
9. Second Coming

A Movement from Heaven to Earth

The first movement in the work of Christ is his coming from heaven to earth. This coming is not simply a temporary appearance of God, as in the theophanies or even the Christophanies of the Old Testament. No, this is much more—the incarnation of the Son of God. Astoundingly, the eternal, almighty God became a human being. God the Son left the glory of heaven and the fellowship of the Father and Holy Spirit to become "the last Adam," "the second man" (1 Cor. 15:45, 47). God permanently took to himself genuine humanity! If we ask why the Son should do this, Scripture has a ready answer: "God sent forth his Son, born of woman, born under the law, to redeem those who were under the law, so that we might receive adoption as sons" (Gal. 4:4–5). God became a man to undertake a rescue mission that would lead to the God-man's death and resurrection.

Three events cluster between this first coming from heaven to earth and his returning to heaven: Christ's sinless life, crucifixion, and resurrection. Like his incarnation, Christ's spotless life is an essential precondition for his saving death and resurrection. Although Christ was "in every respect . . . tempted as we are," the great news is that he was "without sin" (Heb. 4:15). He was, as God said through Isaiah, "the righteous one, my servant" (53:11). This qualified him "who knew no sin" to give himself for others "so that in him" they "might become the righteousness of God" (2 Cor. 5:21).

The central saving deeds of God's Son are his death and resurrection. The death of the sinless incarnate one saves in all of these ways. It reconciles sinners to God, redeems them from bondage to sin, pays the penalty for their sins, triumphs over their foes, undoes the disobedience of the first Adam, and purifies defiled human beings. All of that is to say, it saves them from their sins!

His death should not be separated from his resurrection because together they constitute the essence, the core, the center of his saving accomplishment. If he had not died, he could not have risen, and if he had not risen, his death would not save. "But thanks be to God, who gives us the victory through our Lord Jesus Christ" by raising him from the dead "on the third day in accordance with the Scriptures" (1 Cor. 15:4, 57). Jesus's resurrection, the last event in this first movement from heaven to earth, signals his mighty conquest of Satan, of Satan's demons, and of all the other foes of God.

A Movement from Earth to Heaven

The first movement from heaven to earth is followed by Christ's going from earth to heaven in his ascension. He not only accomplished salvation on earth in his death and resurrection as the God-*man*, but also continues to minister in heaven in his intercession as the God-*man*. The ascension moves Christ from the limited earthly plane to the transcendent heavenly one. The incarnation enabled the Son to partake of flesh and blood "that through death he might destroy . . . the devil, and deliver" his people (Heb. 2:14–15). The ascension ensures that one who still partakes of flesh and blood has gone to heaven "as a forerunner on our behalf" (6:20). As a result, "we have . . . a sure and steadfast anchor of the soul, a hope that enters into the inner place behind the curtain" (v. 19). From heaven, the exalted Lord and Prince bestows gifts of "repentance . . . and forgiveness of sins" (Acts 5:31).

The ascension enabled the session, Christ's sitting at "the right hand of the Majesty on high" (Heb. 1:3). He sat as prophet, priest, and especially king. As heavenly prophet he equips his servant with his Spirit to spread his Word and advance the kingdom. As priest, he sat down, demonstrating the completion, perfection, and efficacy of his sacrifice (10:12). As enthroned king, he reigns on high with his Father and awaits the time when "his enemies should be made a footstool for his feet" (10:13; cf. 1:13; Ps. 110:1).

Pentecost is as much Christ's saving deed as are his death and resurrection. He is the "Christ," or Anointed One, because he received the Spirit at his baptism so that after ascending, he would dispense the Spirit to the church. In fulfillment of Old Testament prediction, the exalted Lord baptized his church by pouring out the Holy Spirit on it (Joel 2:28–32; Acts 2:17, 18, 33). He thereby publicly proclaimed the new covenant and began the new creation.

The only ongoing work of Christ among the nine, his intercession, has two aspects. First, as crucified, risen, and ascended one, he prays for his people with understanding and compassion and grants them "mercy and . . . grace to help in time of need" (Rom. 8:34; Heb. 4:15–16). Second, because of "the power of an indestructible life" he is priest forever and thus "is able to save to the uttermost those who draw near to God through him, since he always lives to make intercession for them" (7:16, 24–25).

A Second Movement from Heaven to Earth

The first movement was from heaven to earth in the incarnation of the Son. The second movement was from earth to heaven in Christ's ascension. The third movement will be from heaven to earth in Christ's second coming. In the first movement the Son brought a little piece of heaven to earth, so to speak, namely himself. In the second movement Christ brought a little piece of earth to heaven, again himself, because his incarnation is permanent. In the third movement he will bring heaven down to earth, as Revelation reveals: John saw "the holy city Jerusalem coming down out of heaven from God" to earth (Rev. 21:10). Christ's second coming brings final salvation. "Christ, having been offered once to bear the sins of many, will appear a second time, not to deal with sin but to save those who are eagerly waiting for him" (Heb. 9:28). The returning Christ will initiate the resurrection of the dead, the last judgment, and the eternal state.

Christ's Saving Events Listed

Here are Christ's nine saving events with representative Scripture references:

1. Incarnation (Luke 2:11; Gal. 4:4–5; Heb. 2:14–15)
2. Sinless life (2 Cor. 5:21; Heb. 5:8–10; 1 Pet. 3:18)
3. Death (Gal. 3:13; Heb. 10:14)
4. Resurrection (Rom. 4:25; 1 Cor. 15:21–22; 1 Pet. 1:3)
5. Ascension (John 14:2–3; Acts 5:31; Heb. 9:24)
6. Session (Col. 3:1–3; Heb. 1:3; 10:11–12)
7. Pentecost (John 20:22–23; Acts 1:5)
8. Intercession (Rom. 8:34; Heb. 7:25)
9. Second coming (Matt. 25:46; 1 Thess. 1:9–10; 1 Pet. 1:13)

Christ's Saving Events Related

There are four key points: (1) All nine events constitute one saving work of Christ. (2) Christ's death and resurrection are *the* saving events par excellence.

(3) Those saving events are preceded by two essential prerequisites, and (4) they are followed by five essential results.

First, all nine events constitute one saving work of Christ. Each event is important in its own right and should be appreciated as such. Yet Christ's saving work consists of all nine events. We should, then, have a holistic view of his salvation that includes everything from his incarnation to his return. It is all his saving work, and it is all one.

Second, although all nine events are necessary to salvation, two are central and inseparable. Christ's death and resurrection are the heart and soul of his saving accomplishment. Sometimes Scripture combines the two (John 10:17–18; Acts 2:22–24; Rom. 4:25; 10:9–10; 1 Cor. 15:3–4; 2 Cor. 5:15; Phil 3:10; Heb. 1:3; 1 Pet. 1:11), but usually it uses shorthand and merely mentions one, implying the other.[1]

Third, there are two essential preconditions to Christ's death and resurrection: his incarnation and sinless life. His incarnation is essential because he had to become a man to die and rise again. His atonement counts for human beings because it was accomplished by a human being. His sinless life is essential because it qualified him to die for others. Had he sinned, he would have been disqualified from being Savior.

Fourth, there are five essential results that follow Christ's death and resurrection: his ascension, session, sending the Spirit at Pentecost, intercession, and second coming. His ascension saves in that it transported him from the limited earthly realm to the transcendent heavenly one to appear in God's presence for us. His session saves in that, sitting at God's right hand, he rules and saves from on high. His work at Pentecost saves in that he, the Anointed One, poured out the Spirit on the church to extend the kingdom of God. His intercession saves in that he perpetually presents his sacrifice in God's presence and prays for the saints. His second coming saves in that he will come again in great glory and power to vanquish his foes and bring final salvation to his own.

Biblical Pictures of Christ's Work

A chapter was devoted to each of the six major pictures that Scripture paints to interpret the significance of Christ's accomplishment. Here we view all six pictures together. Note that selected Scripture passages are given for each one (table 3).

---

[1] John Calvin makes this point, *Institutes of the Christian Religion*, ed. John T. McNeill, trans. Ford Lewis Battles, 2 vols. (Philadelphia: Westminster, 1960), 1:521 (2.16.13).

Table 3. Biblical pictures of Christ's saving work

Christ As	Sphere	Need	His Work	Result	Passages
Reconciler	Relations	Alienation	Makes peace	Peace	Rom. 5:10; 2 Cor. 5:18–20; Eph. 2:12–17; Col. 1:20–23
Redeemer	Slavery	Bondage	Delivers	Freedom	1 Cor. 6:20; Heb. 9:15; 1 Pet. 1:19
Legal substitute	Law	Condemnation	Pays penalty	Justification	Rom. 3:25–26; Gal. 3:13; Col. 2:14
Victor	Warfare	Enemies	Defeats foes	Victory	Col. 2:15; Heb. 2:14–15; Rev. 5:5
Second Adam	Creation	Disorder	Obeys	Restoration	Rom. 5:18–19; 1 Cor. 15:22; Col. 1:18
Sacrifice	Worship	Defilement	Makes sacrifice	Purification	Eph. 5:2, 25–26; Heb. 9:12, 14; 10:14

A Summary of the Pictures

The picture of reconciliation comes from the sphere of interpersonal relations. We need to be reconciled to God because of alienation, or the disruption of relations. Christ is portrayed as the peacemaker who by his death and resurrection reconciles God to human beings and human beings to God. The result is peace between God and us.

The theme of redemption comes from the sphere of the master-slave relationship. We need to be redeemed because we are in bondage to sin and Satan. Christ is portrayed as the Redeemer, who by his death and resurrection delivers us from spiritual slavery. As a result we experience the freedom of the sons or daughters of God.

The picture of legal substitution comes from the sphere of law. We need to be justified because of the guilt of Adam's original sin and of our own actual sins. Christ is portrayed as our legal substitute, who by his death and resurrection propitiates God and pays the penalty for our sins. The result is that a holy and just God declares righteous all who trust Christ.

The theme of Christus Victor comes from the sphere of warfare. We need to be delivered because we have spiritual enemies far more powerful than we. Christ is portrayed as our champion who by his death and resurrection defeats our foes. As a result there is real victory in the Christian life.

The picture of re-creation comes from the sphere of creation. We need to be restored because Adam's fall brought sin, death, and disorder into the world of humankind. Christ is portrayed as the second Adam, who by his obedience unto death and resurrection reverses the effects of Adam's sin. The result is the restoration of our lost glory and dominion.

The theme of sacrifice comes from the sphere of worship. We need to be cleansed because we are defiled by our sin. Christ is portrayed as the great High Priest who offers himself as a sacrifice and lives forever. As a result believers are purified.

The Pictures Portray the Same Reality

It is important to keep in mind that the six pictures do not talk of six different realities. Rather, they are six different ways of talking about the same reality—the salvation that Christ accomplished. Why, then, does Scripture offer six major pictures? The answer seems to lie, as Leon Morris suggested years ago, in the Bible's depiction of sin. The multiplicity of images of salvation corresponds to the multiplicity of the images of sin.[2] The many ways of speaking about our plight correspond to the many ways God in his grace comes to our aid. Sin is so odious to God that he depicts it in a variety of ways, as the discussion of the need for each picture in the preceding shows.

Each need, each way of describing sin, corresponds to God's way of overturning sin in Christ's work. So, God overturns sin as alienation with Christ's reconciliation. He overcomes bondage with Christ's redemption. He overturns guilt with Christ's propitiation. He overcomes our mighty enemies with a mightier champion's victory. He overturns Adam's disobedience with the second Adam's obedience. He overcomes our spiritual defilement with Christ's purifying blood. But the key point here is that these are multiple ways of communicating the same truth—Jesus saves sinners through his death and resurrection!

Each Picture Is Important

Every one of the six major pictures is notable. Certainly, Scripture contains more than six pictures of Christ's accomplishment. John McIntyre, in *The Shape of Soteriology*, lists thirteen images: ransom, redemption, salvation, sacrifice, propitiation, expiation, atonement, reconciliation, victory, punishment/penalty, satisfaction, example, and liberation.[3] Although I am unsure as to the exact number and would combine some items on his list, his point is well taken: Scripture presents Christ's saving work using more than six themes.

What are my criteria for identifying major pictures? Acknowledging help from Henri Blocher,[4] I have four: (1) appearance across the biblical canon with roots in

---

[2] Leon Morris, *The Cross in the New Testament* (Grand Rapids: Eerdmans, 1965), 395.
[3] See the list in the introduction to part 2.
[4] Henri Blocher, "Biblical Metaphors and the Doctrine of the Atonement," *Journal of the Evangelical Theological Society* 47, no. 4 (December 2004): 639–40.

the Old Testament, (2) occurrence in a good number of passages, (3) theological significance, and (4) recognition in historical theology. Using these criteria, I conclude that there are six main pictures. My chief point at present is that each of these pictures is important to gain a good understanding of the cross and empty tomb. Thus it is a mistake to champion one picture by downplaying the import of the others. To gain a full-orbed appreciation of the work of Christ, one must explore all six pictures. I would cite second Adam/new creation as the most neglected picture of the six in my experience in both academy and church. I hope that this book contributes to redressing that neglect.

Penal Substitution Is Foundational

Although every picture is valuable and none is to be ignored, I conclude that penal substitution is foundational to the others. Those who heard me read papers at two recent annual meetings of the Evangelical Theological Society will be surprised at this conclusion. In those papers I regarded legal substitution as a biblical theme, but in my efforts to promote all six pictures, I questioned whether any one of them is a "master metaphor." I do not like that terminology and will qualify my statement, but I now regard substitution as foundational to a doctrine of Christ's saving work.

I am jealous to underscore my last point: all six pictures are biblical and therefore important. It is a mistake to defend one image by minimizing the others. And it is a mistake to ignore any of the images. Nevertheless, after completing this study of Christ's saving events and giving considerable thought to the biblical pictures, I conclude that penal substitution should be regarded as foundational.

I have nine reasons for this stance, which I will spread across four categories: redemptive history, pictures of Christ's work, prominence, and the Godward direction.

Redemptive history. First, an argument can made from the flow of redemptive history. Isaiah 53 teaches legal substitution (in vv. 5–6, 10–12).[5] Christopher Wright's words are apt:

> [Jesus's] vicarious suffering and death will "bear" the iniquities of those who, having thought he was suffering under the judgment of God for his own sin, now realize that it was actually *our* sorrows, transgressions, iniquities and sins that were laid upon him. The language of sacrificial substitution and of vicarious sin-bearing runs through Isaiah 53 unmistakeably.[6]

---

[5]See pp. 368–71 for argumentation.
[6]Christopher J. H. Wright, "Atonement in the Old Testament," in *The Atonement Debate*, ed. Derek Tidball, David Hilborn, and Justin Thacker (Grand Rapids: Zondervan, 2008), 80, italics original.

Furthermore, Isaiah 52:13–53:12 exerts a powerful influence upon the New Testament writers.[7]

Second, though Jesus predicts his death and resurrection three times in the first two Gospels, in only one place does he interpret its significance—in the ransom saying of Mark 10:45 (parallel, Matt. 20:28). As I argued previously, this saying teaches both redemption and penal substitution.[8] I. Howard Marshall, interpreting the ransom saying in light of similar sayings in Psalm 49:7–9 and Mark 8:37, agrees:

> Jesus serves men by giving his life as a ransom for many. Mark no doubt intends this saying to be seen against the background of 8:37 where the question is raised whether a man can give any exchange for his life. Behind the question lies Psalm 49:7–9: "Truly no man can ransom himself, or give to God the price of his life, for the ransom of his life is costly, and can never suffice, that he should continue to live on for ever, and never see the Pit." What man cannot do has been done by Christ. We are surely justified in discerning here the thought of human mortality as the result of human sin, and in seeing in the death of Christ the ransom "price" paid to God for the redemption of mankind from death.[9]

Third, Hebrews 2:17 (propitiation) and 9:23 (Christ's blood purifying heaven) constitute an inclusion underscoring substitution. William Lane highlights the substitutionary character of our great High Priest's self-giving: "The making of propitiation for sins exhibits the primary concern of the high priestly office with the reconciliation of the people to God. The concept implies sacrifice, and in this context the propitiatory work of the Son consisted in the laying down of his life for others (cf. [chap. 2] vv 10, 14, 18)."[10]

Hebrews 9:23 teaches the astounding truth that Christ's sacrifice purifies heaven itself! Once more, listen to Lane: "The full, perfect, and sufficient sacrifice of Christ purified the heavenly sanctuary from the defilement resulting from the sins of the people. . . . The superior sacrifice demanded was provided by the self-oblation of Christ."[11]

---

[7]The second edition of the United Bible Societies' *Greek New Testament* lists forty-one New Testament passages in its "Index of Quotations" for Isa. 52:13–53:12.

[8]See pp. 325–31 for argumentation.

[9]I. Howard Marshall, "The Meaning of Redemption," in *Jesus the Saviour* (Downers Grove, IL: InterVarsity, 1990), 248.

[10]William L. Lane, *Hebrews 1–8*, Word Biblical Commentary (Dallas: Word, 1991), 66.

[11]William L. Lane, *Hebrews 9–13*, Word Biblical Commentary (Dallas: Word, 1991), 247–48.

Thus early in Hebrews (2:17) and later (9:23) the author sounds strong substitutionary notes. He intends for us to understand Christ our High Priest and sacrifice within this substitutionary framework.

Pictures of Christ's work. Most of the other pictures of the work of Christ include legal substitution. Fourth, therefore, although redemption is more than substitution, it includes it. We have shown this for the "ransom saying" (Mark 10:45); we add Galatians 3:13: "Christ redeemed us from the curse of the law by becoming a curse for us." Graham Cole brings out the substitutionary force of this text:

> God has acted in Christ to address the human predicament at this point. The divine move is astounding, for a great exchange has taken place. As Jeffrey, Ovey, and Sach suggest, "It is hard to imagine a plainer statement of the doctrine of penal substitution" .... Paul is drawing on the language of the marketplace. A price is paid to set a slave free and the price of this redemption is unfathomable.[12]

Fifth, penal substitution is the basis for reconciliation according to 2 Corinthians 5:21: "For our sake he made him to be sin who knew no sin, so that in him we might become the righteousness of God."[13] The preceding three verses all mention reconciliation. Linda Belleville admits that the exact interpretation of God's making Christ "sin" in verse 21 is difficult but insists that the big idea is clear:

> If our debts are not posted to our account [according to v. 19], it is because someone else has legally assumed them—much as the scapegoat did on the Day of Atonement (Lev 16) and the guilt offering did on other occasions (Lev 4–5). This is why God can make overtures of friendship toward those who are otherwise his enemies.
>
> If the exact point of "made sin" is lost to us, the thrust is clear. So closely did Christ identify with the plight of humanity that their sin became his sin.[14]

Sixth, to my surprise, although Scripture says much about spiritual warfare and presents the Christus Victor theme in a number of New Testament

---

[12]Graham A. Cole, *God the Peacemaker: How Atonement Brings Shalom,* New Studies in Biblical Theology (Downers Grove, IL: InterVarsity, 2009), 172. He refers to Steve Jeffrey, Michael Ovey, and Andrew Sach, *Pierced for Our Transgressions: Recovering the Glory of Penal Substitution* (Wheaton, IL: Crossway, 2007), 89.

[13]See pp. 282–89 and 381–84 for argumentation.

[14]Linda L. Belleville, *2 Corinthians,* The IVP New Testament Commentary (Downers Grove, IL: InterVarsity, 1996), 159.

passages, when it tells *how* Christus Victor saves, it subordinates that theme to legal substitution in Colossians 2:14–15 and Revelation 5:5–9.[15] Graham Cole is right: "Christus Victor needs the explanatory power of substitutionary atonement."[16]

Seventh, sacrifice is strongly colored by substitution.[17] All of the following passages dealing with the Old Testament background to Christ's sacrifice or his actual sacrifice imply substitution: Exodus 12:13; Leviticus 16; Isaiah 53:10; Romans 3:25; 8:3; Hebrews 2:17; 1 Peter 2:24; 3:18; and Revelation 5:9.

I want to be clear. I am not reducing redemption, reconciliation, Christus Victor, and sacrifice to penal substitution. Rather, I am arguing that when the biblical writers spoke of Christ's atonement, substitution came readily to mind. It is spread across the other pictures in a manner that suggests that it is foundational.

Prominence. Eighth, legal substitution is prominent in Scripture. Its roots sink deep into Old Testament soil: Exodus 12:13; Leviticus 1:9; 2:1–2; 3:3, 5; 4:29, 31; 16:21–22; and Isaiah 53:5–6, 10–12. And substitution is prominent in the New Testament: Romans 3:25–26; 8:1–4; 2 Corinthians 5:21; Galatians 3:13; Colossians 2:14; Hebrews 2:17; 1 Peter 2:24; 3:18; 1 John 2:2; 4:10; and Revelation 5:9.

The Godward direction. Ninth, penal substitution is the most important aspect of the most profound direction of Jesus's death and resurrection, as the next section argues.

Directions of Christ's Work

A fruitful way of considering Christ's saving accomplishment is to construe it in terms of the directions to which it points. When we do so, we find that it points in three directions: toward God himself (an upward direction), toward our enemies (a downward direction), and toward the whole creation (a believer's horizontal dimension) (see fig. 2).

---

[15]See pp. 389–91, 441–46, and 455–57 for argumentation.

[16]Graham A. Cole, *God the Peacemaker: How Atonement Brings Shalom*, New Studies in Biblical Theology (Downers Grove, IL: InterVarsity, 2009), 184. Henri Blocher agrees, "Agnus Victor: The Atonement as Victory and Vicarious Punishment," in *What Does It Mean to Be Saved? Broadening Evangelical Horizons of Salvation* (Grand Rapids: Baker, 2002), 67–91.

[17]See pp. 365–71, 375–81, 391–93, 541–43, 545, and 548–49 for argumentation. In addition, the second-Adam motif in Romans 5:18 involves legal language ("one act of righteousness") that may imply substitution.

Figure 2. Christ's saving works as three directions

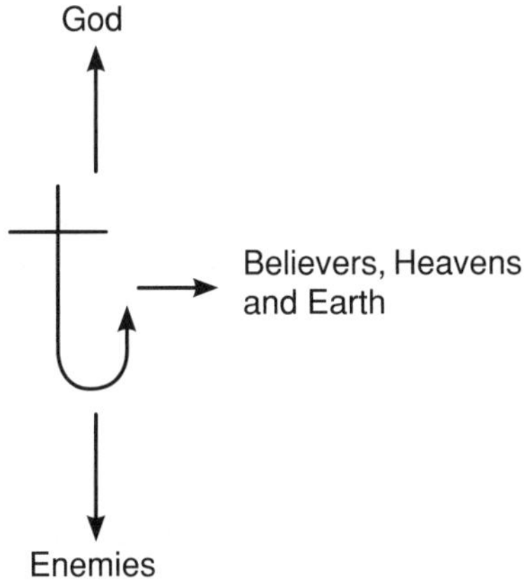

Christ's Saving Work Is Directed toward God Himself

Most profoundly, the death and resurrection of Christ are directed toward God. Incredibly, the work of Christ affects the life of God himself. Included here are penal substitution, the Godward aspect of reconciliation, an aspect of sacrifice, the second-Adam motif, and possibly redemption.

Penal substitution. Substitution is directed primarily toward God himself. God propitiates his own justice by bearing the brunt of his wrath in Christ. Because substitution brings us forgiveness, it also has a horizontal direction. A downward direction is implied in Colossians 2:14–15, where substitution drives Christus Victor.

Reconciliation. Reconciliation occurs in all three directions. Most profoundly God reconciles himself in the death and resurrection of Christ. As a result, human beings are reconciled to God along with the creation (Col. 1:20). God's enemies are "reconciled" in the sense of being subjugated (Col. 1:20; 2:15).

Sacrifice. As we saw, the Levitical sacrifices were intended to make atonement for both the people and the sanctuary (because the people's sins defiled it). Corresponding to this, Hebrews 9:22–23 teaches that Christ's death purifies the heavenly sanctuary itself (because our sins defiled it). In this sense, sacrifice has an upward direction.

Second Adam. Even as Adam's disobedience was directed toward God, so was the second Adam's obedience.

Redemption? Scripture never tells us to whom the redemption price is paid. Certainly the ransom-to-Satan view was wrongheaded. I have always resisted deducing a direction for redemption.[18] But if we were to do so, it would be to God. Plainly, there is a horizontal dimension in that people are redeemed.

Christ's Saving Work Is Directed toward Our Enemies

It is the genius of the Christus Victor theme that it directs Christ's death and resurrection toward our foes. Christ's work routs the Devil, his demons, the "world," death, and hell. At least two other themes have a downward aspect. By "the blood of" Christ's "cross," God reconciles "all things," which in context includes "thrones," "dominions," "rulers," and "authorities" (Col. 1:16, 20). Christ reconciles the demons by subduing them, thereby maintaining peace in his kingdom (cf. 2:15). Redemption may be vertical, is certainly horizontal, and has downward overtones. We are delivered from "the domain of darkness" (Col. 1:13) and from enslavement "to the elementary principles of the world" (Gal. 4:3).

Christ's Saving Work Is Directed toward Human Beings and the Creation

Human beings. All the themes of the work of Christ pertain to human beings because, as God told Joseph, "You shall call his name Jesus, for he will save his people from their sins" (Matt. 1:21). The various pictures are different ways of expressing Jesus's saving his people. Reconciliation means peacemaking, and Christ's death and resurrection make peace with God and then with people. In redemption God purchases the human slaves of sin at the cost of Christ's blood. Legal substitution propitiates God and brings forgiveness to the guilty who believe. Christ our Victor's work is primarily directed at our spiritual foes, but it is horizontal in that it delivers us from their clutches. As second Adam, Christ obeys God to restore the image of God in us, and glory and dominion to us. Christ our sacrifice purifies believers with his blood.

The creation. The horizontal dimension of Christ's saving work includes the creation. Scripture predicts that there will be new heavens and a new earth (Isa. 65:17–25; 66:22–23; Matt. 19:28; Rom. 8:20–22; 2 Pet. 3:10–13; Revelation 21–22). Given the fall, why will this be? The answer is, because of the cross and the empty tomb! The work of Christ has cosmic effects. This is evident because "God was pleased . . . to reconcile to himself all things, whether on earth or in heaven, making peace by the blood of his cross" (Col. 1:19–20). Christ's work redeems God's world, for "the creation itself will be set free from its bondage to corruption and obtain the freedom of the glory of the children of God" (Rom. 8:20–22). Penal substitution and second Adam images also play roles in the deliverance of the cosmos, because even as the curse was a legal penalty

---

[18]John R. W. Stott takes the same tack, *The Cross of Christ* (Downers Grove, IL: InterVarsity, 1986), 175.

imposed due to Adam's disobedience, so lifting the curse is a penal event owing to the second Adam's obedience.[19]

Conclusion

All three directions are important, the upward, horizontal, and downward. Christ's saving accomplishment, which centers in his death and resurrection, affects God himself, human beings and the creation, and our spiritual enemies.

The horizontal. The direction or dimension involving the salvation of human beings is more prevalent in Scripture than the others. The six pictures involve scores of passages that tell of God's rescuing us sinners through the Mediator's work. And some of those pictures teach that because of Christ's saving work there will be new heavens and a new earth (Rom. 8:19–22; Col. 1:19–20). I will argue below that this dimension, like the downward direction, is a derivative of the upward.

The upward. The upward dimension directed toward God is the most fundamental and profound. Christ's work influences the life of God himself. As the summaries at the end of the "picture" chapters have shown, the initiative for the work of Christ belongs to God the Trinity. That means God acts through the cross and empty tomb to influence himself. He satisfies his justice, reconciles himself, is pleased with the second Adam's obedience, and purifies heaven. God in Christ affects God.

This is profound for several reasons. First, it reflects the greatness of God's grace in the initiative and the accomplishment of salvation. This story was not conceived on earth by human beings. It was conceived in heaven by God. What kind of a world religion posits that God becomes a man to die in order to satisfy the demands of his own character and thereby save his creatures? A divinely revealed, unique, and gracious one!

A second reason is the mystery of the incarnation itself. If we cannot fully understand the incarnation, how will we fully understand the cross and empty tomb? Third, the concept of God's entering into covenant with Abraham and eventually with us in the new covenant provides a framework for understanding how covenant keepers or breakers influence God. But, at the end of the day, we confess we are out of our depth trying to understand God's influencing himself through Christ's cross and empty tomb because, although Christ is a

---

[19]See the dissertation by Lee Tankersley, "The Courtroom and the Created Order: How Penal Substitution Brings about New Creation" (PhD diss., Southern Baptist Theological Seminary, 2010).

covenant-keeping man, he also is God. These things are beyond understanding. They are too much for us. What shall we do? We will be very grateful for them!

This upward element is foundational to the horizontal and downward ones. Without the Godward direction of the work of Christ, the other two directions would not exist. They are very important but derivative of the influence of Christ's work on God himself. Because God propitiates himself, he defeats our foes and rescues us and the creation. I agree with Sinclair Ferguson: "A comprehensively biblical exposition of the work of Christ recognizes that the atonement, which terminates on God (in propitiation) and on man (in forgiveness), also terminates on Satan (in the destruction of his sway over believers). And it does this last precisely because it does the first two."[20] I do not disagree, but would add that the atonement terminates on man and Satan because it terminates on God. In my terminology: both the horizontal and downward aspects depend on the upward aspect.

The downward. Christus Victor is a derivative of the Godward direction. Ferguson says it well. His reference is to Gustaf Aulén's *Christus Victor*, the book whose title became a label for a view of the atonement.

> In this respect, Gustav Aulén's view was seriously inadequate. He displaced the motif of penal satisfaction with that of victory. But, as we have seen, in Scripture the satisfaction of divine justice, the forgiveness of our sins, and Christ's defeat of Satan are not mutually exclusive but complementary. Each is an essential dimension of Christ's work. Each is vital for our salvation, and each provides an aspect of the atonement from which the other aspects may be seen with greater clarity and richness. Moreover, these aspects are interrelated at the profoundest level. For the New Testament the dramatic aspect of the atonement involves a triumph that is secured through propitiation. Aulén therefore failed to recognize that in setting the dramatic view over against the penal view of the atonement he inevitably enervated the dramatic view of its true dynamic.[21]

I began this book by stating that Christ's saving work is profound, massive and magnificent. I end in the same way. The work of Christ is massive; hundreds of pages on his events and the biblical pictures do not exhaust his saving work.

---

[20]Sinclair Ferguson, "Christus Victor et Propitiator: The Death of Christ, Substitute and Conqueror," in *For the Fame of God's Name: Essays in Honor of John Piper*, ed. Sam Storms and Justin Taylor (Wheaton, IL: Crossway, 2010), 185.
[21]Ibid.

It is profound. Giving an attentive ear to God's self-revelation, we can learn a lot. But our knowledge takes us only so far. We cannot fully comprehend the incarnation. How shall we plumb the depths of the cross and empty tomb? We understand in part and, awaiting the day when we shall understand in full, we worship, serve, and witness. Full understanding will have to wait, "for now we see in a mirror dimly, but then face to face. Now I know in part; then I shall know fully, even as I have been fully known" (1 Cor. 13:12).

The saving work of Christ is magnificent. It pleases God, saves human beings, and vanquishes their foes. Christ's death and resurrection even deliver the creation itself!

> Such knowledge is too wonderful for me;
> it is high; I cannot attain it. (Ps. 139:6)

Oh, the depth of the riches and wisdom and knowledge of God! How unsearchable are his judgments and how inscrutable his ways!

> "For who has known the mind of the Lord,
> or who has been his counselor?"
> "Or who has given a gift to him
> that he might be repaid?" (Rom. 11:33–35)

Appendix

The Extent of the Atonement

Particular Atonement Is an Implication of Substitutionary Atonement

Although we agree with Wesley against his successors that Scripture teaches substitutionary atonement, we agree with them against Wesley that substitutionary atonement fits better with limited than with unlimited atonement.[1] Unlimited atonement is the view that Christ died to make possible the salvation of every human being. Over against this is the view of limited atonement: Christ died to save only the elect. We prefer to label our position particular or definite atonement. Although certain benefits of Christ's death come to everyone, and although God adopts a posture of love toward a world that hates him, Christ's atonement was designed not merely to make salvation possible, but actually to secure the salvation of those whom God has chosen. It is, therefore, specifically designed to save a definite or particular people.

Weak Calvinist Arguments

Calvinists have not always argued well for limited atonement. For example, Calvinists have adduced passages of Scripture that say Christ died for the church (Eph. 5:25), the sheep (John 10:15), and others as evidence for limited atonement. But this line of reasoning is not persuasive.[2] It only stands to reason that

---

[1] This appendix is taken with permission from Robert A. Peterson and Michael D. Williams, *Why I Am Not an Arminian* (Downers Grove, IL: InterVarsity, 2004), 201–13.
[2] For more discussion of weak Calvinist proofs for limited atonement (and weak Arminian proofs for unlimited atonement), see Millard J. Erickson, *Christian Theology*, 2nd ed. (Grand Rapids: Baker, 1998), 843–51.

Scripture, when talking about Christ's sheep or his church, would say Christ died for them. That does not mean that he did not die for others. But this argument could be strengthened if some Scripture passages indicated that some are excluded.

Another less-than-convincing argument for limited atonement involves deduction from other doctrines. For example, some argue from particular election to particular atonement. God chose some people, and not all, for salvation. Therefore, he sent his Son to atone for those he chose. However, four-point Calvinists agree with the premise but don't reach the same conclusion. They hold to unconditional election but reject limited atonement because they maintain that the Bible teaches unlimited atonement. It is necessary that a doctrine fit a theological system to be true; it is not sufficient, however. To be true, a doctrine must pass not only a test of logical coherence but also a test of empirical fit with the Bible's data. To be true, limited atonement must not only be systematically consistent with Calvinism; it must also be taught in Scripture.

Our experience shows that such arguments for limited atonement only convince those convinced already. What is needed is for a case to be made from Scripture, and not just from systematic theology.

Our Case for Particular Atonement

Although substitutionary atonement is taught in numerous places in both Testaments, particular atonement is not as prominent. It is, however, implied in a number of passages that speak of Christ's substitutionary death. I will present from Scripture three pieces of evidence for definite atonement: Trinitarian harmony, exclusion passages, and efficacy passages.

First, we argue on the basis of Trinitarian harmony from Ephesians 1:3–14. The passage divides thematically as follows: Ephesians 1:3–6, the Father's election; Ephesians 1:7–12, the Son's redemption; and Ephesians 1:13–14, the Spirit as seal.

If we follow the pronouns through the passage, a strong case can be made for Trinitarian harmony in salvation. The Father "chose us . . . before the creation" for sanctification and "predestined us to be adopted as his sons" (Eph. 1:4–5).[3] Paul says about the Son, "In him we have redemption through his blood, the forgiveness of sins" (Eph. 1:7). The continuity of pronouns indicates that the people whom God chooses for salvation are the same ones Christ redeems

---

[3]Unless otherwise indicated, Scripture quotations in this appendix are from the New International Version, 1984 edition.

through his substitutionary atonement. The Son works in harmony with his Father. And even as the Father does not choose every human being for salvation, so the Son does not atone for everyone's sins. He atones for the sins of the elect.

The Spirit too, as God's seal on believers, works in concert with the Father and Son. The same people whom the Father predestined (Eph. 1:5) the Son redeemed (Eph. 1:7) and were sealed with the Spirit (Eph. 1:13). The three divine persons work in harmony in salvation. But an unlimited atonement sets the Son against the Father and Spirit. For, in such a scenario, the Father chooses a particular people, and he only sets the seal of the Spirit on believers, but the Son dies to redeem everyone. Robert Letham, who labels limited atonement "effective atonement" and unlimited atonement "provisional atonement," sounds the alarm: "The doctrine of the Trinity requires . . . effective atonement. . . . This is by far the most serious problem with provisional atonement. It introduces disorder into the doctrine of God. The Father and the Holy Spirit have different goals from the Son."[4] Ephesians 1:3–14, therefore, presents the Father, Son, and Spirit working in unison to save their people, and this implies a definite or limited atonement.

John shows the same harmony in the work of salvation between the Father and the Son when he reports the Son's prayer to the Father for those whom the Father gave him, that is, those whom the Father chose. Although the Son was Lord over all, he gave eternal life only to those the Father gave him (John 17:2). The Son revealed the Father only to those the Father gave him (John 17:6). The Son is in accord with the Father: "I pray for them. I am not praying for the world, but for those you have given me, for they are yours" (John 17:9).

The Son predicts his substitutionary atonement: "For them I sanctify myself, that they too may be truly sanctified" (John 17:19). Jesus consecrates himself to his priestly work of dying on the cross for the people the Father gave him, the elect. Why? That they might become saints, sanctified by the Son's priestly consecration at Calvary.

Finally, the Son asks the Father to bring to heavenly glory the ones whom the Father had given him (John 17:24). John portrays a harmony between the Father and Son. The Son works as Mediator and Redeemer for the ones the Father gave him, the people he chose for salvation. To them alone the Son reveals the Father and gives eternal life; for them alone he prays; he asks the Father to take them alone to heaven. And for them alone the Son consecrates himself in death in order to sanctify them in salvation (John 17:19). This implies a particular atone-

---

[4]Robert Letham, *Work of Christ*, Contours of Christian Theology (Downers Grove, IL: InterVarsity, 1993), 237.

ment, designed to save those whom the Father gave to the Son. An unlimited atonement, by contrast, would disrupt the harmony between Father and Son and put them at odds: the Father choosing some and the Son dying to save all.

Our second piece of evidence for particular atonement is the occurrence of exclusions in substitutionary-atonement passages. It is true that for biblical passages to say that Jesus died for the church or his sheep does not prove that he did not die for others. But for those same passages to contain exclusionary elements is another matter. In John 10, Jesus twice says that he lays down his life for the sheep (John 10:11, 15). And yet he declares to the Jewish leaders, "You do not believe because you are not my sheep" (John 10:26). That is, Jesus follows his statements about dying for his sheep by a stark denial that some are his sheep. It would be difficult to maintain that he lays down his life to save them, for he has just excluded them from the number of his sheep.

Exclusions also appear in John 17. Though the Father gave Jesus "authority over all people," Jesus gives eternal life only to those the Father gave him (John 17:2). And, although God loves the world (John 3:16), in John 17 Jesus does not pray for "the world"; he prays for those the Father gave him (John 17:9). And, as we saw above, the Son makes atonement for the same people (John 17:19). In light of the exclusions in John 17:2 and 9, it is implied that Jesus's consecration of himself for "them (John 17:19), includes those the Father gave him and excludes "the world" (John 17:9). That is, within the context of Jesus's prayer, he excludes some from eternal life. When he speaks of dying for the elect, we are correct in excluding from those whom the Father gave him those whom Jesus himself excludes.

Our third piece of evidence for particular atonement concerns the efficacy of the cross. Does Scripture present Christ's substitutionary atonement as *potential*, making possible the salvation of all, or as *effective*, securing the salvation of God's people? I will argue for the latter based on Revelation 5:9. Christ, the Lion and the Lamb, takes the scroll and is worshiped as the elders and living creatures prostrate themselves before him and sing this song:

> You are worthy to take the scroll
>   and to open its seals,
> because you were slain,
>   and with your blood you purchased men for God
>   from every tribe and language and people and nation.
> You made them to be a kingdom and priests to serve our God,
>   and they will reign on the earth. (Rev. 5:9–10)

The Lamb was "slain," that is, slaughtered in his sacrifice on the cross. John explains what the Lamb's unique sacrifice accomplished: with his blood he purchased human beings.

Notice the results of the Lamb's redeeming work. The song says, "With your blood you purchased men for God *from* every tribe and language and people and nation" (Rev. 5:9). The italicized word is supplied in translation. This is a partitive construction: the preposition "from" introduces the whole out of which what precedes is a part. So translations must supply a word (marked here by italics) to indicate the part:

- "You purchased men for God *from* every tribe." (NIV)
- "You ransomed for God saints *from* every tribe." (NRSV)
- "You ransomed people for God *from* every tribe." (ESV)
- "You bought men for God *of* every race." (JB)
- "You . . . purchased for God . . . men *from* every tribe." (NASB)
- "You bought for God people *from* every tribe." (CEV)

The point is that Jesus via his substitutionary atonement redeemed a part of the human race out of the bigger whole, "every tribe and language and people and nation." Christ's atonement here is not potential, but actual; his blood purchases people for God from among the nations. The words "tribe and language and people and nation" refer to the same entity—humankind from the perspectives of people group, tongue, location, and political entity, respectively. Here John helps us understand the meaning of Christ's dying for "the world" and "all" in Scripture. Christ ransoms people out of "every tribe and language and people and nation," that is, from out of the world. This verse does not teach a universal but a particular atonement. It doesn't say that Christ died for every human being; it says that he died for people from every nation. The concept of "world" here, therefore, is collective rather than distributive. Christ died for the world—understood as all without distinction, not all without exception. Such an interpretation is impossible because Christ's blood actually delivers people out of every tribe and so on.

This suggests that we are justified in understanding world in other atonement passages in a collective rather than a distributive sense. The Lamb redeemed persons from "every tribe and language and people and nation." He died to redeem persons in "every tribe," including Masai, Zulu, Yoruba, Xhosa, Tutsi, and Hutu. He died to redeem persons in "every language," including Japanese, Korean, Indonesian, and Tagalog. He died to redeem persons among "every people," including those born in mainland China, Taiwanese- and American-born Chinese, among others. He died to redeem persons in "every nation," including Mexico, Brazil, Peru, and Chile.

To recapitulate: we believe in particular substitutionary atonement because Scripture implies it when it speaks of Father, Son, and Spirit working harmoniously to save the people of God (Eph. 1:3–14; John 17:2, 6, 9–10, 19, 24; cf. 1 Pet. 1:1–2). We hold to definite atonement because sometimes when the Bible speaks of Christ's saving death, it excludes some persons (John 10:11, 15, 26; 17:2, 9, 19). We teach limited atonement because Scripture describes the cross as effective, not making salvation possible for all, but actually securing salvation for multitudes (Rev. 5:9; cf. 1 Pet. 1:18–19).

Arminian Objections to Particular Atonement

Arminian arguments for unlimited atonement and criticisms of limited atonement overlap. We will examine four important ones and thereby clarify our case for definite atonement.[5]

First, Arminians point to passages that say Christ died for "the world" or "all" in an attempt to prove unlimited atonement. Representative among these are:

> We all, like sheep, have gone astray,
>   each of us has turned to his own way;
> and the LORD has laid on him
>   the iniquity of us all. (Isa. 53:6)

> We have put our hope in the living God, who is the Savior of all men, and especially of those who believe. (1 Tim. 4:10)

> He is the atoning sacrifice for our sins, and not only for ours but also for the sins of the whole world. (1 John 2:2)

The pronouns "we" and "us" in Isaiah 53:6 refer not to all people but to Israelites. This is confirmed by Isaiah's reference to "my people," the nation of Israel, in Isaiah 53:8. Isaiah 53:6 means all we Israelites have strayed like sheep and the Lord has laid on the suffering Servant the iniquity of all us Israelites. Thus, contextually considered, Isaiah 53:6 is not a good proof text for unlimited atonement.

The same is true for 1 Timothy 4:10. Ironically, this verse does not refer to Christ or his cross. We say this because of the way the word *Savior* is used in the

---

[5]These examples are from H. Orton Wiley, *Christian Theology*, 3 vols. (Kansas City, MO: Beacon, 1941), 2:296; and Erickson, *Christian Theology*, 846–49.

Pastoral Epistles, where it occurs ten times. When it refers to God the Father, it appears without Christ's name: "God our Savior" (1 Tim. 1:1; 2:3; Titus 1:3; 2:10; 3:4) and "the living God, who is the Savior of all men" (1 Tim. 4:10). But when it refers to Christ, his name is used: "our Savior, Christ Jesus" (2 Tim. 1:10), "Christ Jesus our Savior" (Titus 1:4), "our great God and Savior, Jesus Christ" (Titus 2:13), and "Jesus Christ our Savior" (Titus 3:6). Because *Savior* appears without qualification in 1 Timothy 4:10, it speaks of God the Father and not of Christ and thus is not a good proof text for unlimited atonement.

First John 2:2 is a better proof text, for it speaks of Christ's being "the atoning sacrifice for our sins, and not only for ours but also for the sins of the whole world." A universal dimension of Christ's work is plainly in view. The apostle John, a Jewish Christian, says that Christ's atonement was not only for his fellow Jews but also for Gentiles. We say this because of the only other reference to "the whole world" in 1 John: "We know that we are children of God, and that the whole world is under the control of the evil one" (1 John 5:19). Here "the whole world" is in contrast to "children of God" and refers not to every person but to sinners viewed collectively as God's enemies. First John 2:2 means that Christ atoned for "the whole world," that is, for the world viewed as a whole, for Gentiles as well as Jews, but not necessarily for each and every Jew or Gentile.

Second, Arminians cite as evidence for unlimited atonement texts that teach that some for whom Christ died will perish. These include Romans 14:15; 1 Corinthians 8:11; and 2 Peter 2:1. The first two references are not good proofs for unlimited atonement. Paul deals with the same theme in Romans 14 and 1 Corinthians 8—Christian freedom in the matter of eating or not eating certain foods. Paul appeals to stronger Christians who have no scruples about eating "unclean" (nonkosher) foods (Rom. 14:15) or foods sacrificed to idols (1 Cor. 8:11). In both cases he warns them against flaunting their Christian liberty to the hurt of weaker believers: "Do not by your eating destroy your brother for whom Christ died" (Rom. 14:15); "So this weak brother, for whom Christ died, is destroyed by your knowledge" (1 Cor. 8:11). There is not clear evidence that the destruction spoken of in Romans 14:15 and 1 Corinthians 8:11 refers to hell. In fact, it is likely that those two verses warn of the "judgment" mentioned elsewhere in 1 Corinthians—not damnation but fatherly discipline involving weakness, sickness, or death (1 Cor. 11:30, 32). Erickson, who holds to unlimited atonement, agrees.[6]

Second Peter 2:1 is a difficult text for those who support limited atonement because it seems to teach that Christ died for false prophets: "But there were

---

[6]Erickson, *Christian Theology*, 850.

also false prophets among the people, just as there will be false teachers among you. They will secretly introduce destructive heresies, even denying the sovereign Lord who bought them." Wayne Grudem summarizes the best Calvinist treatment, that of John Gill in 1735:

> When Peter speaks of false teachers who bring in destructive heresies, "even denying the Master who bought them" (2 Peter 2:1), it is unclear whether the word "Master" (Gk. δεσπότης) refers to Christ (as in Jude 4) or to God the Father (as in Luke 2:29; Acts 4:24; Rev. 6:10). In either case, the Old Testament allusion is probably to Deuteronomy 32:6, where Moses says to the rebellious people who have turned away from God, "Is not he your Father who has bought you?" (author's translation). Peter is drawing an analogy between the past false prophets who arose among the Jews and those who will be false teachers within the churches. From the time of the exodus onward, any Jewish person would have considered himself or herself one who was "bought" by God in the exodus and therefore a person of God's own possession. In this sense, the false teachers arising among the people were denying God their Father, to whom they rightfully belonged. So the text means not that Christ redeemed these false prophets, but simply that they were rebellious Jewish people (or church attenders in the same position as the rebellious Jews) who were rightly owned by God because they had been brought out of the land of Egypt (or their forefathers had), but they were ungrateful to him. Christ's specific redemptive work on the cross is not in view in this verse.[7]

Third, Arminians contend that divine commands to preach the gospel to every person—including Matthew 28:19–20 and Acts 1:8—are incompatible with the idea of a limited atonement and imply an unlimited atonement. We agree that God commands us to take the gospel to the ends of the earth and to every person in it. We are embarrassed that at times Reformed Christians have not been as zealous as others to propagate the gospel. But we deny that there is a necessary connection between Calvinism and a lack of evangelistic zeal. Indeed, we cite as evidence of the compatibility of belief in limited atonement and a fire for spreading the gospel Jonathan Edwards, George Whitefield, Asahel Nettleton, Charles H. Spurgeon, and Francis Schaeffer.

Fourth, Arminians argue that limited atonement contradicts scriptural declarations of God's universal love in John 3:16–17, Romans 5:8, and elsewhere. This too, by implication they claim, is an argument for unlimited atonement. Romans 5:8 is not a good text to show God's universal love because in context it speaks of God's love for Christians before they believed. It is easily harmonized

---

[7] Wayne Grudem, *Systematic Theology* (Grand Rapids: Zondervan, 1994), 600.

with the Calvinistic idea of God's unique love for the elect. But John 3:16–17 teaches that God loves all sinners, a truth unfortunately not endorsed by all Calvinists. Scripture compels us to teach that God loves people in three different senses. First, he loves each person by virtue of common grace. This love preserves the human race but does not save anyone. Second, he loves his elect by planning their salvation, accomplishing it in Christ, and applying it to them by the Holy Spirit. Also, we hold that God loves people in a third sense, the one we would attribute to John 3:16–17. Although the world hates God, the Bible depicts God's posture toward all sinners as one of love, as D. A. Carson explains:

> *God's salvific stance toward his fallen world.* God so loved the world that he gave
> his Son (John 3:16). I know that some try to take κόσμος ("world") here to refer
> to the elect. But that really will not do. All the evidence of the usage of the word in
> John's Gospel is against the suggestion. True, *world* in John does not so much refer
> to bigness as to badness. In John's vocabulary *world* is primarily the moral order in
> willful and culpable rebellion against God. In John 3:16 God's love in sending the
> Lord Jesus is to be admired not because it is extended to so big a thing as the world,
> but to so bad a thing: not to so many people, as to such wicked people. . . . On
> this axis, God's love for the world cannot be collapsed into his love for the elect.[8]

Carson distinguishes this sense from "God's particular, effective, selecting love toward his elect,"[9] the second sense of God's love for people listed above. We agree that Scripture speaks of the saving love of God for human beings in these two distinguishable senses: God's gracious posture toward a world that hates him and God's special effective love for his chosen ones. We admit that Calvinists have not always admitted the first sense and sometimes have resorted to forced exegesis of passages such as John 3:16.

We agree, therefore, with Arminians that John 3:16 and similar texts speak of God's love for every person. We understand these passages to teach that God assumes a saving posture toward his fallen world. When asked how we reconcile these passages with those that teach God's special love for the elect, we admit that our theology contains rough edges. But we would rather have an imperfect theology and be faithful to the whole witness of Scripture than to mute the voice of some texts as Calvinists have sometimes done (John 3:16 and similar passages) and as Arminians do (the texts that teach God's special love for the elect). Carson sounds a needed word of caution:

---

[8] D. A. Carson, *The Difficult Doctrine of the Love of God* (Wheaton, IL: Crossway, 2000), 17, italics original.
[9] Ibid., 18.

If the love of God is exclusively portrayed as an inviting, yearning, sinner-seeking, rather lovesick passion, we may strengthen the hands of Arminians, semi-Pelagians, Pelagians, and those more interested in God's inner emotional life than in his justice and glory, but the cost will be massive. There is some truth in this picture of God, as we shall see, some glorious truth. Made absolute, however, it not only treats complementary texts as if they were not there, but it steals God's sovereignty from him and our security from us. . . .

If the love of God refers exclusively to this love for the elect, it is easy to drift toward a simple and absolute bifurcation: God loves the elect and hates the reprobate. Rightly positioned, there is truth to this assertion; stripped of complementary biblical truths, that same assertion has engendered hyper-Calvinism. I use the term advisedly, referring to groups within the Reformed tradition that have forbidden the free offer of the Gospel.[10]

We affirm that biblical passages dealing with the cross are of two types. Some speak of God's loving stance toward an evil world and others speak of his effective love only for the elect. We choose to hold the two types of atonement passages in creative tension—as Scripture does. The alternative to doing so is to blunt the force of one of the two types of atonement texts. But these two solutions are rationalistic because they affirm some biblical data and suppress other equally biblical data.

Furthermore, we do not regard this problem as insoluble for the mind of God. If we are correct that God has revealed both types of atonement passages in his Word, then they do not pose a problem for God. But we admit that our present state of knowledge prohibits us from explaining how God can love all persons savingly in the one sense and only loves some savingly in another sense.

---

[10]Ibid., 22.

Bibliography

Articles and Essays

Averbeck, Richard E. "Offerings and Sacrifices." In *Evangelical Dictionary of Biblical Theology*, edited by Walter A. Elwell, 574–81. Grand Rapids: Baker, 1996.

Barrett, C. K. "The Background of Mark 10:45." In *New Testament Essays: Studies in Memory of Thomas Walter Manson*, edited by A. J. B. Higgins, 1–18. Manchester, UK: Manchester University Press, 1959.

Blocher, Henri. "Agnus Victor: The Atonement as Victory and Vicarious Punishment." In *What Does It Mean to Be Saved? Broadening Evangelical Horizons of Salvation*, 67–91. Grand Rapids: Baker, 2002.

———. "Biblical Metaphors and the Doctrine of the Atonement." *Journal of the Evangelical Theological Society* 47, no. 4 (December, 2004): 639–40.

Boyd, Gregory A. "Christus Victor View." In *The Nature of the Atonement*, edited by James K. Beilby and Paul R. Eddy, 23–49. Downers Grove, IL: InterVarsity, 2006.

Brock, Rita Nakashima. "And a Little Child Will Lead Us: Christology and Child Abuse." In *Christianity, Patriarchy, and Abuse: A Feminist Critique*, edited by Joanne Carlson Brown and Carole R. Bohn, 42–61. New York: Pilgrim, 1989.

Brown, Joanne Carlson, and Rebecca Parker. "For God So Loved the World?" In *Christianity, Patriarchy, and Abuse: A Feminist Critique*, edited by Joanne Carlson Brown and Carole R. Bohn, 1–30. New York: Pilgrim, 1989.

Carson, D. A. "Atonement in Romans 3:21–26." In *The Glory of the Atonement: Biblical, Theological, and Practical Perspectives*, edited by Charles E. Hill and Frank A. James III, 119–39. Downers Grove, IL: InterVarsity, 2004.

Caulley, T. S. "Holy Spirit." In *Evangelical Dictionary of Theology*, 2nd ed., edited by Walter A. Elwell, 568–73. Grand Rapids: Baker Academic, 2001.

Chalke, Steve. "Cross Purposes." *Christianity* (September 2004): 44–48.

Dodd, C. H. "Ἱλαστήριον: Its Cognates, Derivatives and Synonyms in the Septuagint." *Journal of Theological Studies* 32 (1931): 352–60.

Farrow, Douglas. "Ascension and Atonement." In *The Theology of Reconciliation*, edited by Colin E. Gunton, 67–91. London: T&T Clark, 2003.

Ferguson, Sinclair. "Christus Victor et Propitiator: The Death of Christ, Substitute and Conqueror." In *For the Fame of God's Name: Essays in Honor of John Piper*, edited by Sam Storms and Justin Taylor, 171–89. Wheaton, IL: Crossway, 2010.

Gentry, Peter J. "The Atonement in Isaiah's Fourth Servant Song (Isaiah 52:13–53:12)." *The Southern Baptist Journal of Theology* 11, no. 2 (2007): 20–47.

Green, Joel B. "Must We Imagine the Atonement in Penal Substitutionary Terms?" In *The Atonement Debate: Papers from the London Symposium on the Theology of Atonement*, edited by Derek Tidball, David Hilborn, and Justin Thacker, 153–71. Grand Rapids: Zondervan, 2008.

Groom, Sue. "Why Did Christ Die? An Exegesis of Isaiah 52:13–53:12." In *The Atonement Debate: Papers from the London Symposium on the Theology of Atonement*, edited by Derek Tidball, David Hilborn, and Justin Thacker, 96–114. Grand Rapids: Zondervan, 2008.

Groves, J. Alan. "Atonement in Isaiah 53." In *The Glory of the Atonement: Biblical, Theological, and Practical Perspectives*, edited by Charles E. Hill and Frank A. James III, 61–89. Downers Grove, IL: InterVarsity, 2004.

Harrison, E. F. "Redeemer, Redemption." In *Evangelical Dictionary of Theology*, 2nd ed., edited by Walter A. Elwell, 993–95. Grand Rapids: Baker Academic, 2001.

Hilborn, David. "Atonement, Evangelicalism and the Evangelical Alliance: The Present Debate in Context." In *The Atonement Debate: Papers from the London Symposium on the Theology of Atonement*, edited by Derek Tidball, David Hilborn, and Justin Thacker, 15–33. Grand Rapids: Zondervan, 2008.

Hill, Charles E. "Atonement in the Apocalypse of John." In *The Glory of the Atonement: Biblical, Theological, and Practical Perspectives*, edited by Charles E. Hill and Frank A. James III, 190–208. Downers Grove, IL: InterVarsity, 2004.

Hughes, Philip Edgcumbe. "The Blood of Jesus and His Heavenly Priesthood in Hebrews," parts 1–4. *Bibliotheca Sacra* 130, no. 518—131, no. 521 (April 1973–January 1974): 130:99–109, 195–212, 305–14; 131:26–33.

Köstenberger, Andreas J. "The Deity of Christ in John's Letters and the Book of Revelation." In *The Deity of Christ*, edited by Christopher W. Morgan and Robert A. Peterson. Wheaton, IL: Crossway, 2011.

Longman, Tremper, III. "The Divine Warrior: The New Testament Use of an Old Testament Motif." *Westminster Theological Journal* 44 (1982): 290–307.

———. "Soteriology in Hebrews." In *The Epistle to the Hebrews and Christian Theology*, edited by Richard Bauckham, Daniel R. Driver, Trevor A. Hart, and Nathan Mac-Donald, 253–80. Grand Rapids: Eerdmans, 2009.

———. "The Theology of the Atonement." In *The Atonement Debate: Papers from the London Symposium on the Theology of Atonement*, edited by Derek Tidball, David Hilborn, and Justin Thacker, 49–68. Grand Rapids: Zondervan, 2008.

McGowan, A. T. B. "The Atonement as Penal Substitution." In *Always Reforming: Explorations in Systematic Theology*, edited by A. T. B. McGowan, 183–210. Downers Grove, IL: InterVarsity, 2006.

Michaels, J. Ramsey. "Atonement in John's Gospel and Epistles." In *The Glory of the Atonement: Biblical, Theological, and Practical Perspectives*, edited by Charles E. Hill and Frank A. James III, 106–18. Downers Grove, IL: InterVarsity, 2004.

Moo, Douglas. "Paul on Hell." In *Hell Under Fire: Modern Scholarship Reinvents Eternal Punishment*, edited by Christopher W. Morgan and Robert A. Peterson, 91–109. Grand Rapids: Zondervan, 2004.

Morris, Leon. "Redemption." In *Dictionary of Paul and His Letters*, edited by Gerald F. Hawthorne, Ralph P. Martin, and Daniel G. Reid, 784–86. Downers Grove, IL: InterVarsity, 1993.

Nicole, Roger. "C. H. Dodd and the Doctrine of Propitiation." *Westminster Theological Journal* 17 (1955): 117–57.

Packer, J. I. "Universalism: Will Everyone Ultimately Be Saved?" In *Hell Under Fire: Modern Scholarship Reinvents Eternal Punishment*, edited by Christopher W. Morgan and Robert A. Peterson, 169–94. Grand Rapids: Zondervan, 2004.

———. "What Did the Cross Achieve? The Logic of Penal Substitution." *Tyndale Bulletin* 25 (1974): 3–45.

Page, Sydney H. T. "The Authenticity of the Ransom Logion (Mark 10:45b)." In *Gospel Perspectives: Studies of History and Tradition in the Four Gospels*, vol. 1, edited by R. T. France and D. Wenham, 137–61. Sheffield: JSOT, 1980.

———. "Ransom Saying." In *Dictionary of Jesus and the Gospels*, edited by Joel B. Green, Scot McKnight, and I. Howard Marshall, 660–62. Downers Grove, IL: InterVarsity, 1992.

Peterson, Robert A. "Calvin on Christ's Saving Work." In *A Theological Guide to Calvin's Institutes: Essays and Analysis*, edited by David W. Hall and Peter A. Lillback, 226–47. Phillipsburg, NJ: P&R, 2008.

Porter, Stanley E. "Peace, Reconciliation." In *Dictionary of Paul and His Letters*, edited by Gerald F. Hawthorne, Ralph P. Martin, and Daniel G. Reid, 695–99. Downers Grove, IL: InterVarsity, 1993.

Reid, Daniel G. "Sacrifice and Temple Service." In *Dictionary of New Testament Background*, edited by Craig A. Evans and Stanley E. Porter, 1036–50. Downers Grove, IL: InterVarsity, 2000.

Rightmire, R. David. "Redeem, Redemption." In *Evangelical Dictionary of Biblical Theology*, edited by Walter A. Elwell, 664–65. Grand Rapids: Baker, 1996.

Schreiner, Thomas R. "Penal Substitution View." In *The Nature of the Atonement: Four Views*, edited by James K. Beilby and Paul R. Eddy, 67–98. Downers Grove, IL: InterVarsity, 2006.

Thielman, Frank. "Ephesians." In *Commentary on the New Testament Use of the Old Testament*, edited by G. K. Beale and D. A. Carson, 813–33. Grand Rapids: Baker Academic, 2007.

VanGemeren, Willem A. "Offerings and Sacrifices in Bible Times." In *Evangelical Dictionary of Theology*, 2nd ed., edited by Walter A. Elwell, 855–57. Grand Rapids: Baker Academic, 2001.

Wenham, Gordon J. "The Theology of Old Testament Sacrifice." In *Sacrifice in the Bible*, edited by Roger T. Beckwith and Martin J. Selman, 75–87. Grand Rapids: Baker, 1995.

Williams, Garry. "Penal Substitution: A Response to Recent Criticisms." In *The Atonement Debate: Biblical, Theological, and Practical Perspectives*, edited by Derek Tidball, David Hilborn, and Justin Thacker, 172–91. Grand Rapids: Zondervan, 2008.

Wright, Christopher J. H. "Atonement in the Old Testament." In *The Atonement Debate: Biblical, Theological, and Practical Perspectives*, edited by Derek Tidball, David Hilborn, and Justin Thacker, 69–82. Grand Rapids: Zondervan, 2008.

Wright, N. T. "On Becoming the Righteousness of God: 2 Corinthians 5:21." In *Pauline Theology*. Vol. 2, *1 and 2 Corinthians*, edited by David M. Hay, 200–208. Minneapolis: Fortress, 1993.

Commentaries

Achtemeier, Paul J. *1 Peter*. Hermeneia. Minneapolis: Fortress, 1996.

Akin, Daniel L. *1, 2, 3 John*. New American Commentary. Nashville: Broadman and Holman, 2001.

Attridge, Harold W. *Hebrews*. Hermeneia. Philadelphia: Fortress, 1989.

Barnett, Paul. *The Second Epistle to the Corinthians*. The New International Commentary on the New Testament. Grand Rapids: Eerdmans, 1997.

Barrett, C. K. *The Second Epistle to the Corinthians*. Harper's New Testament Commentaries. New York: Harper & Row, 1973.

Beale, G. K. *The Book of Revelation*. The New International Greek Testament Commentary. Grand Rapids: Eerdmans, 1999.

Beasley-Murray, George R. *The Book of Revelation*. New Century Bible Commentary. London: Marshall, Morgan, and Scott, 1974.

———. *John*. Word Biblical Commentary. Waco, TX: Word, 1987.

Belleville, Linda L. *2 Corinthians*. The IVP New Testament Commentary. Downers Grove, IL: InterVarsity, 1996.

Bird, Michael F. *Colossians, Philemon*. New Covenant Commentary. Eugene, OR: Cascade, 2009.

Bock, Darrell L. *Luke 1:1–9:50*. Baker Exegetical Commentary on the New Testament. Grand Rapids: Baker, 1994.

———. *Luke 9:51–24:53*. Baker Exegetical Commentary on the New Testament. Grand Rapids: Baker, 1996.

Brown, Raymond E. *The Epistles of John*. The Anchor Bible Commentary. New York: Doubleday, 1982.

————. *The Gospel According to John I–XII.* The Anchor Bible Commentary. Garden City, NY: Doubleday, 1966.

Bruce, F. F. *The Acts of the Apostles: The Greek Text with Introduction and Commentary.* Chicago: InterVarsity, 1952.

————. *The Epistle to the Galatians.* New International Greek Testament Commentary. Grand Rapids: Eerdmans, 1982.

————. *The Epistle to the Hebrews.* The New International Commentary on the New Testament. Grand Rapids: Eerdmans, 1964.

————. *The Gospel of John: Introduction, Exposition, and Notes.* Grand Rapids: Eerdmans, 1983.

Calvin, John. *The First Epistle of John.* Calvin's Commentaries. Translated by John Owen. Grand Rapids: Baker, 1999.

Carson, D. A. *The Gospel According to John.* The Pillar New Testament Commentary. Grand Rapids: Eerdmans, 1991.

————. *Matthew.* The Expositor's Bible Commentary. Grand Rapids: Zondervan, 1984.

Chapell, Bryan. *Ephesians.* Reformed Expository Commentary. Phillipsburg, NJ: P&R, 2009.

Childs, Brevard S. *The Book of Exodus: A Critical, Theological Commentary.* The Old Testament Library. Louisville: Westminster Press, 1974.

————. *Isaiah.* The Old Testament Library. Louisville: Westminster John Knox, 2001.

Ciampa, Roy E., and Brian S. Rosner. *The First Letter to the Corinthians.* The Pillar New Testament Commentary. Grand Rapids: Eerdmans, 2010.

Cole, R. Alan. *Exodus.* Tyndale Old Testament Commentaries. Downers Grove, IL: InterVarsity, 1973.

Collins, C. John. *Genesis 1–4: A Linguistic, Literary, and Theological Commentary.* Phillipsburg, NJ: P&R, 2006.

Cranfield, C. E. B. *A Critical and Exegetical Commentary on the Epistle to the Romans.* 2 vols. International Critical Commentary. Edinburgh: T&T Clark, 1975.

Davids, Peter H. *The First Epistle of Peter.* The New International Commentary on the New Testament. Grand Rapids: Eerdmans, 1990.

Delitzsch, Franz. *Isaiah.* Commentary on the Old Testament. Peabody, MA: Hendrickson, 2006.

Denney, James. *The Death of Christ.* New York: A. C. Armstrong, 1903.

DeSilva, David A. *Perseverance in Gratitude: A Socio-Rhetorical Commentary on the Epistle "to the Hebrews."* Grand Rapids: Eerdmans, 2000.

Dodd, C. H. *The Interpretation of the Fourth Gospel.* Cambridge: Cambridge University Press, 1953.

Dunn, James D. G. *Romans.* 2 vols. Word Biblical Commentary. Dallas: Word, 1988.

Durham, John I. *Exodus.* Word Biblical Commentary. Waco, TX: Word, 1987.

Ellingworth, Paul. *The Epistle to the Hebrews.* The New International Greek Testament Commentary. Grand Rapids: Eerdmans, 1993.

Enns, Peter. *Exodus.* The NIV Application Commentary. Grand Rapids: Zondervan, 2000.

Evans, Craig A. *Mark 8:27–16:20*. Word Biblical Commentary. Nashville: Nelson, 2001.

Fee, Gordon D. *The First Epistle to the Corinthians*. The New International Commentary on the New Testament. Grand Rapids: Eerdmans, 1987.

Fung, Ronald Y. K. *The Epistle to the Galatians*. The New International Commentary on the New Testament. Grand Rapids: Eerdmans, 1988.

George, Timothy. *Galatians*. The New American Commentary. Nashville: Broadman and Holman, 1994.

Goldingay, John E. *Daniel*. Word Biblical Commentary. Dallas: Word, 1987.

Green, Gene L. *The Letters to the Thessalonians*. The Pillar New Testament Commentary. Grand Rapids: Eerdmans, 2002.

Green, Joel B. *The Gospel of Luke*. The New International Commentary on the New Testament. Grand Rapids: Eerdmans, 1997.

Grudem, Wayne. *1 Peter*. Tyndale New Testament Commentaries. Grand Rapids: Eerdmans, 1988.

Harris, Murray J. *Colossians and Philemon*. Exegetical Guide to the Greek New Testament. Grand Rapids: Eerdmans, 1991.

———. *The Second Epistle to the Corinthians*. The New International Greek Testament Commentary. Grand Rapids: Eerdmans, 2005.

Harrison, R. K. *Leviticus*. Tyndale Old Testament Commentaries. Downers Grove, IL: InterVarsity, 1980.

Hoehner, Harold W. *Ephesians: An Exegetical Commentary*. Grand Rapids: Baker, 2002.

Hughes, Philip Edgcumbe. *The Book of the Revelation*. The Pillar New Testament Commentary. Grand Rapids: Eerdmans, 1990.

———. *A Commentary on the Epistle to the Hebrews*. Grand Rapids: Eerdmans, 1977.

———. *Paul's Second Epistle to the Corinthians*. The New International Commentary on the New Testament. Grand Rapids: Eerdmans, 1962.

Johnson, Dennis E. *Triumph of the Lamb: A Commentary on Revelation*. Phillipsburg, NJ: P&R, 2001.

Keener, Craig S. *Matthew*. The IVP New Testament Commentary. Downers Grove, IL: InterVarsity, 1997.

Kelly, J. N. D. *A Commentary on the Epistles of Peter and Jude*. Thornapple Commentaries. Grand Rapids: Baker, 1969.

Kidner, Derek. *Genesis*. Tyndale Old Testament Commentaries. Downers Grove, IL: InterVarsity, 1967.

———. *Psalms 1–72*. Tyndale Old Testament Commentaries. London: InterVarsity, 1975.

———. *Psalms 73–150*. Tyndale Old Testament Commentaries. London: InterVarsity, 1975.

Köstenberger, Andreas J. *John*. Baker Exegetical Commentary on the New Testament. Grand Rapids: Baker Academic, 2004.

Lane, William L. *Commentary on the Gospel of Mark*. The New International Commentary on the New Testament. Grand Rapids: Eerdmans, 1974.

———. *Hebrews 1–8*. Word Biblical Commentary. Dallas: Word, 1991.

————. *Hebrews 9–13*. Word Biblical Commentary. Dallas: Word, 1991.

Larkin, William J., Jr. *Acts*. The IVP New Testament Commentary. Downers Grove, IL: InterVarsity Press, 1995.

Lincoln, Andrew T. *Ephesians*. Word Biblical Commentary. Dallas: Word, 1990.

Lohse, Eduard. *Colossians and Philemon*. Translated by W. R. Poehlmann and R. J. Karris, from the 14th German edition. Hermeneia. Philadelphia: Fortress, 1971.

Longenecker, Richard N. *Galatians*. Word Biblical Commentary. Nashville: Nelson, 1990.

MacDonald, Margaret Y. *Colossians and Ephesians*. Sacra Pagina 17. Collegeville, MN: Liturgical Press, 2000.

Marshall, I. Howard. *The Acts of the Apostles*. Tyndale New Testament Commentary. Grand Rapids: Eerdmans, 1980.

————. *The Epistles of John*. The New International Commentary on the New Testament. Grand Rapids: Eerdmans, 1978.

Martin, Ralph P. *Colossians and Philemon*. The New Century Bible Commentary. Grand Rapids: Eerdmans, 1978. First published 1973 by Marshall, Morgan, and Scott.

Michaels, J. Ramsey. *1 Peter*. Word Biblical Commentary. Waco, TX: Word, 1988.

Moo, Douglas J. *The Epistle to the Romans*. The New International Commentary on the New Testament. Grand Rapids: Eerdmans, 1996.

————. *The Letters to the Colossians and to Philemon*. The Pillar New Testament Commentary. Grand Rapids: Eerdmans, 2008.

Morris, Leon. *The Gospel According to John*. The New International Commentary on the New Testament. Grand Rapids: Eerdmans, 1971.

Motyer, J. Alec. *The Message of Exodus*. The Bible Speaks Today. Downers Grove, IL: InterVarsity, 2005.

————. *The Prophecy of Isaiah: An Introduction and Commentary*. Downers Grove, IL: InterVarsity, 1993.

Moule, C. F. D. *The Epistles of Paul the Apostle to the Colossians and to Philemon*. Cambridge Greek Testament Commentary. Cambridge: Cambridge University Press, 1968.

Mounce, Robert H. *The Book of Revelation*. The New International Commentary on the New Testament. Grand Rapids: Eerdmans, 1977.

Mounce, William D. *Pastoral Epistles*. Word Biblical Commentary. Nashville: Nelson, 2000.

Nolland, John. *The Gospel of Matthew*. New International Greek Testament Commentary. Grand Rapids: Eerdmans, 2005.

O'Brien, Peter T. *Colossians, Philemon*. Word Biblical Commentary. Waco, TX: 1982.

————. *The Epistle to the Philippians*. The New International Greek Testament Commentary. Grand Rapids: Eerdmans, 1991.

————. *The Letter to the Ephesians*. The Pillar New Testament Commentary. Grand Rapids: Eerdmans, 1999.

————. *The Letter to the Hebrews*. The Pillar New Testament Commentary. Grand Rapids: Eerdmans, 2010.

Osborne, Grant R. *Matthew*. Exegetical Commentary on the New Testament. Grand Rapids: Zondervan, 2010.

Painter, John. *1, 2, and 3 John*. Sacra Pagina 18. Collegeville, MN: Liturgical Press, 2002.

Ross, Allen P. *Holiness to the Lord: A Guide to the Exposition of the Book of Leviticus*. Grand Rapids: Baker Academic, 2002.

Schreiner, Thomas R. *1, 2 Peter, Jude*. The New American Commentary. Nashville: Broadman and Holman, 2003.

———. *Romans*. Baker Exegetical Commentary on the New Testament. Grand Rapids: Baker, 1998.

Sklar, Jay. *Leviticus*. Tyndale Old Testament Commentaries. Downers Grove, IL: InterVarsity, forthcoming.

Smalley, Stephen S. *1, 2, 3 John*. Word Biblical Commentary. Waco, TX: Word, 1984.

Thiselton, Anthony C. *The First Epistle to the Corinthians*. The New International Greek Testament Commentary. Grand Rapids: Eerdmans, 2000.

Towner, Philip H. *The Letters to Timothy and Titus*. The New International Commentary on the New Testament. Grand Rapids: Eerdmans, 2006.

Waltke, Bruce K. *Genesis: A Commentary*. Grand Rapids: Zondervan, 2001.

Wanamaker, Charles A. *Commentary on 1 & 2 Thessalonians*. New International Greek Testament Commentary. Grand Rapids: Eerdmans, 1990.

Wenham, Gordon. *Leviticus*. New International Commentary on the Old Testament. Grand Rapids: Eerdmans, 1979.

Witherington, Ben, III. *The Acts of the Apostles: A Socio-Rhetorical Commentary*. Grand Rapids: Eerdmans, 1998.

———. *The Gospel of Mark: A Socio-Rhetorical Commentary*. Grand Rapids: Eerdmans, 2001.

Yarbrough, Robert W. *1–3 John*. Baker Exegetical Commentary on the New Testament. Grand Rapids: Baker Academic, 2008.

Young, Edward J. *The Book of Isaiah*, vol. 3. Grand Rapids: Eerdmans, 1972.

Other Books

Althaus, Paul. *The Theology of Martin Luther*. Philadelphia: Fortress, 1966.

Arndt, William F., and F. Wilbur Gingrich. *A Greek-English Lexicon of the New Testament and Other Early Christian Literature*, 2nd ed. Chicago: University of Chicago Press, 1979.

Aulén, Gustaf. *Christus Victor: An Historical Study of the Three Main Types of the Idea of the Atonement*. Translated by A. G. Hebert. 1931. Reprint, New York: Macmillan, 1969.

Barth, Karl. *Church Dogmatics*. Edited by G. W. Bromiley and T. F. Torrance. New York: T&T Clark, 2009.

Bavinck, Herman. *Reformed Dogmatics*. Vol. 3, *Sin and Salvation in Christ*. Grand Rapids: Baker, 2006.

Beckwith, Roger T., and Martin J. Selman, eds. *Sacrifice in the Bible*. Grand Rapids: Baker, 1995.

Beilby, James, and Paul R. Eddy, eds. *The Nature of the Atonement: Four Views*. Downers Grove, IL: IVP Academic, 2006.

Berkhof, Louis. *Systematic Theology*. 2nd ed. Grand Rapids: Eerdmans, 1996.

Boersma, Hans. *Violence, Hospitality, and the Cross: Reinterpreting the Atonement Tradition*. Grand Rapids: Baker Academic, 2004.

Calvin, John. *Institutes of the Christian Religion*. Edited by John T. McNeill. Translated by Ford Lewis Battles. Philadelphia: Westminster, 1960.

Caragounis, Chrys C. *The Ephesian* Mysterion: *Meaning and Content*. Lund: Gleerup, 1977.

Carson, D. A. *How Long, O Lord? Reflections on Suffering and Evil*. Grand Rapids: Baker, 1990.

Chalke, Steve, and Alan Mann. *The Lost Message of Jesus*. Grand Rapids: Zondervan, 2003.

Cole, Graham A. *God the Peacemaker: How Atonement Brings Shalom*. New Studies in Biblical Theology. Downers Grove, IL: InterVarsity, 2009.

———. *He Who Gives Life: The Doctrine of the Holy Spirit*. Foundations of Evangelical Theology. Wheaton, IL: Crossway, 2007.

Culpepper, R. Alan. *The Gospel and Letters of John*. Nashville: Abingdon, 1998.

Dawson, Gerrit Scott. *Jesus Ascended: The Meaning of Christ's Continuing Incarnation*. Phillipsburg, NJ: P&R, 2004.

Dodd, C. H. *The Bible and the Greeks*. London: Hodder & Stoughton, 1935.

Farrow, Douglas. *Ascension and Ecclesia*. Grand Rapids: Eerdmans, 1999.

Fee, Gordon. *God's Empowering Presence: The Holy Spirit in the Letters of Paul*. Peabody, MA: Hendrickson, 1994.

———. *Pauline Christology: An Exegetical-Theological Study*. Peabody, MA: Hendrickson, 2007.

Ferguson, Sinclair B. *The Holy Spirit*. Contours of Christian Theology. Downers Grove, IL: InterVarsity, 1996.

Funk, Robert, ed. *A Greek Grammar of the New Testament and Other Early Christian Literature*. Chicago: University of Chicago Press, 1961.

Gaffin, Richard. *Resurrection and Redemption*, 2nd ed. Phillipsburg, NJ: Presbyterian and Reformed, 1987.

Gathercole, Simon. *The Pre-existent Son: Recovering the Christologies of Matthew, Mark, and Luke*. Grand Rapids: Eerdmans, 2006.

Green, Joel B., and Mark D. Baker. *Recovering the Scandal of the Cross*. Downers Grove, IL: InterVarsity, 2000.

Grudem, Wayne. *Systematic Theology: An Introduction to Biblical Doctrine*. Grand Rapids: Zondervan, 1994.

Gundry Volf, Judith M. *Paul and Perseverance: Staying In and Falling Away*. Louisville: John Knox, 1990.

Heim, S. Mark. *Saved from Sacrifice: A Theology of the Cross*. Grand Rapids: Eerdmans, 2006.

Hoekema, Anthony A. *The Bible and the Future*. Grand Rapids: Eerdmans, 1979.

———. *Created in God's Image*. Grand Rapids: Eerdmans, 1986.

———. *Holy Spirit Baptism*. Grand Rapids: Eerdmans, 1972.

Hughes, Philip Edgcumbe. *The True Image: The Origin and Destiny of Man in Christ*. Grand Rapids: Eerdmans, 1989.

Jeffrey, Steve, Michael Ovey, and Andrew Sach. *Pierced for Our Transgressions: Recovering the Glory of Penal Substitution*. Wheaton, IL: Crossway, 2007.

Johnson, Dennis E. *The Message of Acts in the History of Redemption*. Phillipsburg, NJ: P&R, 1997.

Kehl, Nikolaus. *Der Christushymnus im Kolosserbrief. Eine motivgeschichtliche Undersuchung zu Kol 1, 12–20*. Stuttgarter biblische Monographien 1. Stuttgart: Katholisches Bibelwerk, 1967.

Koester, C. R. *The Dwelling of God: The Tabernacle in the Old Testament, Intertestamental Literature, and the New Testament*. Washington, DC: Catholic Biblical Association, 1989.

Köstenberger, Andreas J., ed. *A Theology of John's Gospel and Letters*. Biblical Theology of the New Testament. Grand Rapids: Zondervan, 2009.

Ladd, George Eldon. *A Theology of the New Testament*. Grand Rapids: Eerdmans, 1974.

Letham, Robert. *The Work of Christ*. Contours of Christian Theology. Downers Grove, IL: InterVarsity, 1993.

Longman, Tremper, III, and Daniel G. Reid. *God Is a Warrior*. Studies in Old Testament Biblical Theology. Grand Rapids: Zondervan, 1995.

Macleod, Donald. *The Person of Christ*. Contours of Christian Theology. Downers Grove, IL: InterVarsity, 1998.

Marshall, I. Howard. *Aspects of the Atonement: Cross and Resurrection in the Reconciling of God and Humanity*. London: Paternoster, 2007.

———. *Jesus the Saviour: Studies in New Testament Theology*. Downers Grove, IL: InterVarsity, 1990.

———. *New Testament Theology*. Downers Grove, IL: InterVarsity; Leicester: Apollos, 2004.

Martin, D. B. *Slavery as Salvation: The Metaphor of Slavery in Pauline Christianity*. New Haven, CT: Yale University Press, 1990.

Martin, Ralph P. *Reconciliation: A Study of Paul's Theology*. Atlanta: John Knox, 1981.

McDonald, H. D. *The New Testament Concept of Atonement: The Gospel of the Calvary Event*. Grand Rapids: Baker, 1994.

McKnight, Scot. *Jesus and His Death: Historiography, the Historical Jesus, and Atonement Theory*. Waco, TX: Baylor University Press, 2005.

Morgan, Christopher W., and Robert A. Peterson, eds. *The Deity of Christ*. Theology in Community. Wheaton, IL: Crossway, 2011.

———. *The Glory of God*. Theology in Community 2. Wheaton, IL: Crossway, 2010.

———. *Hell Under Fire: Modern Scholarship Reinvents Eternal Punishment*. Grand Rapids: Zondervan, 2004.

———. *Suffering and the Goodness of God*. Theology in Community 1. Wheaton, IL: Crossway, 2008.

Morris, Leon. *The Apostolic Preaching of the Cross*, 3rd ed. Grand Rapids: Eerdmans, 1965.

———. *The Atonement: Its Meaning and Significance*. Leicester: Inter Varsity, 1983.

———. *The Cross in the New Testament*. Grand Rapids: Eerdmans, 1965.

Murray, John. *The Atonement*. Philadelphia: Presbyterian and Reformed, 1962.

Mussner, Franz. *Christus, das All und die Kirche, Studien zur Theologie des Epheserbriefes*. Trierer Theologische Studien 5. Trier: Paulinus, 1955.

Owen, John. *The Works of John Owen*. Vol. 2. Edited by William H. Goold. London: Banner of Truth, 1965.

Packer, J. I. *Knowing God*. Downers Grove, IL: InterVarsity, 1973.

Peterson, David, ed. *Where Wrath and Mercy Meet: Proclaiming the Atonement Today*. Carlisle, Cumbria, UK: Paternoster, 2001.

Peterson, Robert A. *Getting to Know John's Gospel: A Fresh Look at Its Main Ideas*. Phillipsburg, NJ: Presbyterian and Reformed, 1989.

———. *Hell on Trial: The Case for Eternal Punishment*. Phillipsburg, NJ: P&R, 1995.

Ridderbos, Herman. *Paul: An Outline of His Theology*. Grand Rapids: Eerdmans, 1975.

Schlier, Hans. *Principalities and Powers in the New Testament*. Questiones Disputatae 3. Freiburg: Herder, 1961.

Schreiner, Thomas. *New Testament Theology: Magnifying God in Christ*. Grand Rapids: Baker, 2008.

———. *Paul: Apostle of God's Glory*. Downers Grove, IL: IVP Academic, 2001.

Sklar, Jay. *Sin, Impurity, Sacrifice, Atonement: The Priestly Conceptions*. Sheffield, UK: Sheffield Phoenix, 2005.

Stott, John R. W. *The Cross of Christ*. Downers Grove, IL: InterVarsity, 1986.

Stuhlmacher, Peter. *Historical Criticism and Theological Interpretation of Scripture: Toward a Hermeneutic of Consent*. Philadelphia: Fortress, 1977.

Tankersley, Lee. "The Courtroom and the Created Order: How Penal Substitution Brings about New Creation." PhD diss., Southern Baptist Theological Seminary, 2010.

Tidball, Derek, David Hilborn, and Justin Thacker, eds. *The Atonement Debate: Papers from the London Symposium on the Theology of Atonement*. Grand Rapids: Zondervan, 2008.

Toon, Peter. *The Ascension of Our Lord*. Nashville: Nelson, 1984.

Travis, Stephen H. *Christ and the Judgment of God: Divine Retribution in the New Testament*. Basingstoke, UK: Marshall Pickering, 1986.

Vos, Geerhardus. *The Pauline Eschatology*. Grand Rapids: Baker, 1979. First published 1930.

Waltke, Bruce K. *An Old Testament Theology*. Grand Rapids: Zondervan, 2007.

Wilcock, Michael. *The Message of Revelation*. The Bible Speaks Today. Downers Grove, IL: InterVarsity, 1975.

Williams, Michael D. *Far as the Curse Is Found: The Covenant Story of Redemption.* Phillipsburg, NJ: P&R, 2005.

Wright, N. T. *Christian Origins and the Question of God.* Vol. 1, *The New Testament and the People of God.* Minneapolis: Fortress, 1992.

———. *Christian Origins and the Question of God.* Vol. 2, *The Resurrection of the Son of God.* Minneapolis: Fortress, 2003.

———. *Surprised by Hope.* New York: Harper One, 2008.

General Index

Aaron, 75, 507
Aaronic priesthood, 49, 133, 194–95,
    229, 240–43, 529
abandonment, of Son, 70
Abraham, 44–45, 501
Abrahamic covenant, 33, 92–93, 174,
    385–86
Achtemeier, Paul, 391
active obedience, of Christ, 47
Acts
    Christus Victor in, 437–39
    redemption in, 331
    second coming in, 254–56
    session of Christ in, 188–90
actual sins, 41, 408, 472, 555
Adam
    as covenant head, 472–73
    death through, 471, 479–80
    from dust of the ground, 131–32,
        146, 264, 485
    sin of, 90–91, 101, 131, 145, 403,
        465, 473–74, 481, 518, 555, 556
    tested by Satan, 470
    as type of Christ, 472–73
Adam and Eve
    banished from the garden, 268
    creation of, 36, 464–65, 493, 498
Adam christology, 90, 470, 475, 481.
    See also second Adam
adoption, 33–34, 333, 411–12
adversaries, 441
advocate
    Christ as, 109, 245, 394, 544
    Holy Spirit as, 109

Agabus, 215
alienation, 89, 555
all things, reconciliation of, 147–48,
    294, 297–301, 304
already/not yet, 223, 263, 283, 300,
    453, 479
ambassadors for Christ, 285–86, 309
"Amen," 137–38, 149
Anabaptists, 485
Ananias, 46, 81, 215
anchor, 178
ancient Near Eastern covenant, 531
Ancient of Days, 253, 424
angels, 147, 298–99, 447, 492, 494
animal sacrifices, 376, 503–4, 506, 540
Anna (prophetess), 30, 321–22
antichrist(s), 453, 546
antinomianism, 292
apostles, as Spirit-filled, 215
Apostles' Creed, 151
apostolic preaching, 45, 125–26
apostolic teaching, 170
ark, as baptism, 451–52
Arminians, 571–75
ascension of Christ, 16, 151–82, 255,
    552
    as essential result of death and
        resurrection, 554
    as saving work, 23–24
asceticism, 191–93, 203
assurance, 178
atonement, 14. See also substitution
    completeness of, 100
    extent of, 109, 411, 566–75

as redemption price, 336
as violent, 388
Attridge, Harold W., 537
Aulén, Gustaf, 37, 413, 449, 564
authorities, 441, 443–46
authority, 391

Babel, tower of, 218
Babylonian exile, 318, 353, 354, 414,
    421–23, 460
Baker, Mark D., 362, 397, 400
baptism, 451–52
Bar-Jesus, 438
Barnabas, 215
Barnett, Paul, 47, 486, 488
Barrett, C. K., 287, 311, 327, 382–83
Barth, Karl, 182
Bavinck, Herman, 215, 224, 225–26
Beale, Gregory K., 113, 115, 137, 350,
    352, 457, 458, 546–47
"bearing guilt," 64
Belleville, Linda, 282, 559
Berkhof, Louis, 247
Bethlehem, as means to Calvary, 39–40
biblical universalism, 342, 352
binding of strong man, 428–29, 451
Bird, Michael, 390
blessed hope, 261, 268, 345
blessings, 170, 385–86, 495
Blocher, Henri, 556
blood, 82, 112, 506
    of bulls and goats, 197
    of Christ, 105, 197, 244, 302, 349,
        517, 518, 540–41, 544
    of the covenant, 513–14
    of the Lamb, 114–15, 268, 351–52,
        546
    and redemption, 95, 338, 358–59
Bock, Darrell, 322, 323, 324–25, 469
bodies
    belong to God, 334
    immortal, imperishable, and
        glorious, 333
    transformation of, 256–57
Boersma, Hans, 93n37, 388
bondage, to sin, 67, 105, 346, 352,
    353, 354, 361, 555
book of life, 115, 546
Boyd, Gregory A., 14, 402

bread from heaven, 157
breath of life, 212, 221–23
Brown, Joanne Carlson, 407
Bruce, F. F., 50, 125, 141–42, 206,
    240–42, 293, 301, 387, 445, 450,
    495, 535, 537
Buddhism, 12
burnt offerings, 229, 503, 509

Caiaphas, 77–78, 187
Cain and Abel, 501
Caird, C. B., 82
Calvin, John, 26, 27, 130, 246, 397,
    518
Calvinism, and evangelistic zeal, 573
captivity, redemption from, 318–19
Caragounis, Chrys, 294
Carson, D. A., 74, 125, 157, 188, 327,
    378, 426, 429, 434, 436, 466,
    514, 515, 517, 574–75
chain of salvation, 476–77
Chalcedon, 550
Chalke, Steve, 14, 398–99
champion christology, 459. *See also*
    Christus Victor
Chapell, Bryan, 169
child abuse, penal substitution as,
    406–7
children of God, 52, 453
children of the devil, 453
Childs, Brevard S., 315, 417
Christ-event, 550
Christian freedom, 572
Christian life, 261, 346, 543–44, 555
    and penal substitution, 406
christology, from above, 13, 27, 550
Christus Victor, 14, 37, 98, 116, 351,
    391, 397, 413–62, 524, 555,
    559–60, 562, 564
church
    and Christus Victor, 461–62
    mission to the world, 171
church leaders, 169, 170
Ciampa, Roy, 480–81, 486
citizenship in heaven, 256, 267
city of God, 115
cleansing, 505, 547
climax (literary device), 476
Clines, J. A., 464

Cole, Alan, 315
Cole, Graham, 210, 308–9, 358, 461–
   62, 469, 559
Collins, C. John, 62, 415–16, 420, 466,
   467–68
common grace, 574
condemnation, 377, 379, 408
confession of sin, 394
consecration, 517
Cornelius, 215
corporate reconciliation, 295, 308
corporate redemption, 360
corporate scope, of penal substitution,
   412
cosmic reconciliation, 294, 295, 300–
   301, 308–9
cosmic redemption, 332, 360–61,
   404–5
cosmic restoration, 269
cosmic salvation, 148, 562
cosmic scope, of penal substitution, 412
covenant, 385, 531
Cranfield, C. E. B., 140, 379, 474, 475
creation, 489, 493, 555
   groaning of, 332
   redemption of, 562
cross, 12–13, 15, 304
   efficacy of, 569–71
   and intercession of Christ, 243–44
   and reconciliation, 288, 295, 301,
     302, 306, 309
curse(s), 82, 92–93, 384–89, 404, 465
   from Adam's sin, 403
   of hanging from tree, 542–43
   of the law, 336–37
   lifting of, 562–63
curtain, 241
   torn in two, 68
Cyrus, 355

Damascus Road, 168
Daniel, 423–24
darkness, 31, 438, 562
   at death of Christ, 70
   domain of, 562
   of unbelief, 487–88
David
   children of, 52
   and Goliath, 414, 418–19, 429, 451

persecution and vindication of, 62
   as type of Christ, 535
Davidic covenant, 165
Davidic king, 155, 156, 162, 164–65,
   173, 179, 523
Davids, Peter, 106, 107, 145, 349, 392,
   393, 452, 453, 542–43
David's Lord, prophecy of, 154–55,
   185–86, 419–21, 432, 460
Dawson, Gerrit Scott, 248
Day of Atonement, 176–77, 228–29,
   232, 240, 249, 367–68, 408,
   507–9, 528, 533, 534, 538, 547
day of Pentecost. See Pentecost
day of redemption, 339
Day of Yahweh, 431
death, 102, 472
   through Adam, 471, 479–80, 481
   and fall, 466–67
   as last enemy, 441, 446, 450–51,
     460, 461
death of Christ, 61–116, 431–32
   as centerpiece of saving work, 23,
     61, 553–54
   not separated from resurrection,
     551–52
debt, 97, 390, 443
deed-word revelation, 17
defilement, 523
definite atonement, 411
definitive sanctification, 535
Delitzsch, Franz, 231
deliverance, 268–69, 334, 337. See also
   redemption
Deliverer, 333, 354
demons, 298–99, 460
   disarming of, 97–98
   on moral uprightness of Christ, 57
   superior knowledge of, 427
Denney, James, 395
descent, ascent, and descent, 183
Devil, 460. See also Satan
   defeat of, 37, 102, 114, 450–51, 546
divine passive, 179
divine rescue, 525
divine warrior, 414, 431, 432, 446,
   458–59, 460
Dodd, C. H., 85, 124, 143, 375
dominion, 101, 481, 498, 499
   of second Adam, 493–95, 498, 555

dominions, 562

double imputation, 384

downward direction, of work of Christ, 560, 564

Duguid, Iain, 423

Dunn, James, 140, 475

Durham, John I., 502

earthly realm, 175, 176, 184

earthly tabernacle, 244, 347, 532

earth-to-heaven movement, 552–53

Eden, 470

Edwards, Jonathan, 573

efficacy, of Christ's death, 114

Elijah, 67

Ellingworth, Paul, 497, 531, 535

Emmaus, road to, 322–23

end of the ages, 533

enemies, 306, 453, 460, 461
    as Christ's footstool, 448–49
    defeat of, 459
    on moral uprightness of Christ, 57
    and saving work of Christ, 562

enmity, 305, 309, 310

Enns, Peter, 502

enslavement, 346

epiphany, 345

eternal life, 123, 125, 134, 143–46, 217, 267, 379

eternal punishment, 260, 268, 280, 303–4

eternity, 137

eucharistic sacrifice, 176n23, 239

Eusebius, 397

evangelical obedience, 104

Evans, Craig A., 373

"every tribe," 570

Evil One, 439, 450, 453

evil powers, 411, 443–45

exaltation, state of, 34–35, 83, 156, 171, 494
    and Christus Victor, 452
    and intercession, 231
    of servant, 65, 512

exclusions, in substitutionary atonement passages, 569, 571

exclusivism, of Paul, 342

exile, 353

exodus, 67, 314–16, 354, 355, 416–18

exorcisms, 426–28, 430

expiation, 85–87, 103, 109, 111, 375–77, 393, 526, 533

Ezekiel, 422

faithful witness, Jesus Christ as, 112, 137, 149

fall, 465–67, 471, 498

fallen angels, 441

false prophets, 453

false shepherds, 73

Farrow, Douglas, 159

fear of death, 102, 451

fear of the Lord, 282, 349

Fee, Gordon, 38, 145–46, 168n16, 381–82, 387, 477, 483, 484, 489–90, 520, 521

fellowship, 544

feminism, 407

Ferguson, Sinclair, 219, 222, 224, 225, 564

"filled with the Holy Spirit," 215

final salvation, 88–89, 145, 233, 248, 265, 266, 549 553, 554

fire, 213

firstborn, 112, 135, 138, 149–50, 220–21, 265, 296, 476, 477, 490–91, 499

firstborn (exodus), 65
    redemption of, 314, 316–17, 353, 502
    slaying of, 316, 365–66, 502

firstfruits, 131, 353, 479, 483

"flashback" method, of Paul, 290

flesh of Christ, 302, 304

food offerings, 96

footstool, 448–49

forerunner, Christ as, 177

forgiveness, 75, 189, 217, 288, 383, 443, 547, 549
    and Pentecost, 221–22, 223
    and redemption, 341, 359
    and resurrection, 140–41

Forsyth, P. T., 378

four-point Calvinism, 567

fragrance, 444

fragrant offering, 96, 522

friendship, 305

Fung, Ronald, Y. K., 387

Gaffin, Richard, 478–79
Gathercole, Simon, 66, 67
genealogies, of Jesus, 468–69
Gentiles, 93, 290–95, 342, 377
Gentry, Peter, 370, 511
George, Timothy, 389
gifts, bestowed by Christ, 169
Girard, René, 500
glorification, 267, 476–77
　　and intercession of Christ, 236–37,
　　　238
glory, 486, 499, 555
　　of second Adam, 493, 495, 498
goats, 367–68, 508
God
　　as avenger, 366
　　character of, 366–67, 408
　　condescension of, 35
　　faithfulness of, 153
　　glory of, 153
　　holiness of, 367
　　as initiator and goal of
　　　reconciliation, 306–7
　　justice of, 190
　　love of, 110–11, 278–79, 338, 354,
　　　395, 573–75
　　majesty in creation, 493
　　power of, 190–91, 442
　　promises of, 315
godliness, 261, 334, 344, 549
God-man, 32, 45, 103, 147, 163, 343,
　　　348, 551, 552
Good Shepherd, 73–74
good works, 21–22, 361
gospel, glory of, 487–88
Gospels
　　on ascension of Christ, 156–60
　　on Christus Victor, 425–37
　　on death of Christ, 66–79
　　on redemption, 320–31
　　on resurrection of Christ, 121–25
　　on sacrifice of Christ, 512–17
　　on second coming of Christ, 253–54
　　on session of Christ, 185–88
grace, 48, 169, 170, 263, 338, 344, 526
grain offering, 504
grain of wheat dying, 78–79
Green, Gene, 258, 259
Green, Joel B., 14, 321, 323, 324, 397,

　　400, 404, 426, 429–31, 541,
　　　543–44, 548
　　on penal substitution, 362
Groom, Sue, 368–69
Grotius, Hugo, 399
Groves, J. Alan, 64, 511
Grudem, Wayne, 224–25, 227, 392,
　　　573
guilt offering, 74, 505–6, 511

hanging on a tree, 81–82, 93, 386
Harris, Murray, 284–85, 286–87, 382,
　　　444, 487–88, 490
Harrison, Everett, 313
Harrison, R. K., 507
harvest, 79
healing, 14, 123, 223
hearts, renewal of, 530
heaven, purification of, 531–32
heavenly realm, 175, 176, 184
heavenly tabernacle, 134, 195–96, 244,
　　　347, 529, 532–33
heaven to earth movement, 551–52,
　　　553
Hebrews
　　on ascension of Christ, 171–78
　　on intercession of Christ, 239–45
　　redemption in, 346–49
　　sacrifice in, 522–38
　　on session of Christ, 192–99
Heim, Mark, 500
hell, 280, 303, 451, 460
　　deliverance from, 102
　　as second death, 124, 143
Helper, Holy Spirit as, 209
Hertz, J. H., 507–8
High Priestly Prayer, 75, 234, 235–37,
　　　516
Hill, Charles E., 457
Hodge, Charles, 242
Hoekema, Anthony, 251
holiness, 58, 110, 134, 235–36, 349,
　　　394, 516, 535
Holy Spirit
　　as firstfruits, 479
　　giving of, 16, 124–25, 126, 158,
　　　180, 204, 206, 207, 209, 214,
　　　216, 554
　　grieving of, 338–39

intercession of, 238
as Paraclete, 209–10
and sacrifice of Christ, 529–30
and sanctification, 538
as "Spirit of life," 379
holy war, 426
hope, 51, 178, 259, 278, 281, 345, 349
horizontal dimension, of work of
Christ, 560, 562, 563
horizontal fellowship, 544
hostility toward God, 280
hour, 78–79
household code, 344
Hughes, Philip Edgcumbe, 39–40, 57,
201, 202, 241, 243n23, 247, 283,
285, 289, 384, 449, 450–51, 475,
487, 536
Humiliation, state of, 34–35, 156, 171,
494
and intercession, 231
as temporary, 497
of servant, 65, 512

image of Christ, 264, 486
image of God, 464–65, 477–78, 498,
499
immortal bodies, 257
impurity, 547
imputation, 140, 287, 382, 384
"in Adam," 480–81, 485
incarnation of Christ, 16, 27–40, 60,
297, 499
and Christus Victor, 449–50
as essential precondition to death
and resurrection, 554
mystery of, 563
and redemption, 33–34
as saving work of Christ, 23–24
"in Christ," 94, 480–81, 485
indebtedness, 97, 390, 443
indestructible life, 133
individualism, 397–98
individual reconciliation, 295, 308
individual redemption, 360
individual scope, of penal substitution,
412
inherent sin, 41
inheritance, 134, 269, 340, 348
intercession, 16, 103, 134, 141, 227–
50, 549, 553

and ascension, 180
as continual, 249
as effective, 249
and efficacy of cross, 243–44
as essential result of death and
resurrection, 554
as particular, 233–34, 250
as priestly, 249
as saving work of Christ, 23–25, 248
interpersonal relations, 555
irony, in Gospel of John, 77
Islam, 12
Israel
disobedience of, 425
temptation in wilderness, 425, 469

Jacob, 501
Jeffrey, Steve, 366, 371, 381, 404, 405,
406
Jeremiah, 422–23
Jesus Christ
baptism of, 328, 468
became sin, 381–84
as beginning of new people of God,
490–91
cosmic lordship of, 112, 135–36,
191
defeat of Evil One, 436–37
deity of, 347–48, 449
descent from heaven, 157–58, 485
divine sonship of, 468
exorcisms of, 426–28
as first and the last, 136–37
as firstfruits, 483
as founder of salvation, 497–98
as fulfillment of law, 292–93, 380
as fulfillment of Old Testament, 152,
547
glory of, 488
as High Priest, 38, 49–50, 58–59,
75, 100, 103–4, 116, 133–34,
141–42, 236, 347, 449, 524,
525–28, 547, 548, 558–59
and ascension, 171–76, 180
and intercession, 249
and session, 204
humanity of, 48, 162–63, 449, 485
as image of God, 488, 489, 499
as King, 99, 203

as "life-giving Spirit," 484
as the light, 30–32
love of, 96, 283, 522
obedience of, 49, 91, 425, 471
as "our peace," 281, 291, 295, 307
as Passover lamb, 514–15, 520–21
power of, 191
prayers of. *See* intercession
as prophet, 68, 204–5
righteousness of, 56
rules over church, 133
sanctification of, 235–36
saving works of, 22–26
standing at God's right hand, 189
story of redemption, 15–16
suffering of, 49, 51, 63, 105–6, 392, 393, 496
superiority to angels, 447
supremacy of, 296–97
as supreme example, 197–98
temptation of, 425–26, 469–70
three-fold office of, 99, 112, 203
as Victor, 76–77, 102, 202. *See also* Christus Victor
vindication of, 166
as Word, 31, 32–33
Jewish martyr tradition, 305
Jews and Gentiles
forgiveness for, 75
reconciliation of, 291–93, 296, 305
redemption from bondage, 337
Johnson, Dennis E., 82n23, 202, 212, 222–23, 256, 454–55, 456, 458, 459
John the Baptist, 207–8, 212, 217–18, 321, 515
Jonah, 120–21
joy, 182, 268, 278, 281
"joyous exchange" (Luther), 46, 286, 287, 289, 382, 384
Judah, line of, 229
Judaism, 12
Judas, 215
Judas Iscariot, 76
justification, 64, 88–89, 90–91, 287, 334, 476
and holiness of Christ, 58
and intercession of Christ, 238
and penal substitution, 411–12

and reconciliation, 272–80, 282, 288–89, 301, 383–84
and resurrection, 127–28, 139–40
through second Adam, 472

kaleidoscopic view (atonement), 14
Keener, Craig, 514
Kelly, J. N. D., 391, 540
key of David, 53, 59
Kidner, Derek, 154, 464, 465
kingdom of God, 269
King of kings and Lord of lords, 459, 461
kinsman redeemer, 330
Koester, C. R., 103, 526
Köstenberger, Andreas, 210–11, 434, 435, 436–37, 454

lake of fire, 303–4
Lamb, 74–75, 111, 113–15, 201–2, 247, 265, 349–50, 351–53, 355, 457, 515–16, 530, 569–71. *See also* Passover lamb
blood of, 455, 545–46
as spotless, 540
lament psalms, 62
Lane, William L., 197, 198–99, 262, 328, 330–31, 348, 355, 357, 373, 425, 427, 428–29, 449, 451, 459, 495, 523, 524, 525, 526, 527–28, 529, 532–34, 535–36, 558
Larkin, William, 190
last Adam, 36, 90, 101–2, 116, 131–32, 494, 551. *See also* second Adam
last judgment, 190
Last Supper, 513–14
law, 218–19
as sin-detector, 471–72
sphere of, 408, 555
Law and the Prophets, 67
law covenant, 292–93, 308
lawlessness, 354, 361
Lazarus, 124, 144
leaven, 520–21
legal substitution, 116, 555, 557
Letham, Robert, 22, 59
Levitical priesthood, 174–75, 194, 196, 316–17, 503–6, 529, 547
liberation, redemption as, 350

life-giver, Jesus as, 123–24
"life-giving Spirit," 484
light, Jesus as, 30–32
"likeness of sinful flesh," 379–80, 519
limited atonement. *See* particular
    atonement
Lincoln, Andrew, 291
Lion of the Tribe of Judah, 113, 201,
    247, 351, 456–57, 545
Lohse, Eduard, 299, 490
Longenecker, Richard N., 93, 337
Longman, Tremper, III, 418, 421, 426,
    431, 432–33
Lord's Supper, 514
love, 110–11, 395, 522
Luke
    on redemption, 320–25
    on second Adam, 468–70
Luke/Acts, dual ascension accounts of,
    160–62
Luther, Martin, 46, 93, 286, 287, 382,
    397, 518
Lutherans, on universal intercession of
    Christ, 233

Machen, J. Gresham, 357
Macleod, Donald, 41
Mann, Alan, 14
manumission of slaves, 341, 353
Marshall, I. Howard, 176–77, 305,
    310, 325, 356, 373, 378, 394,
    397, 400, 403, 406, 558
    on ransom saying, 330
    on reconciliation, 276–77
    on resurrection, 14–15, 127–28
Martha, 123–24
Martin, Dale, 334
Martin, Ralph, 489, 490
Mary (at resurrection), 159
Mary (mother of Jesus), 44, 159
Mary Magdalene, 122, 427
master-slave relationship, 555
McDonald, H. D., 307
McDonald, Margaret, 389
McIntyre, John, 556
McKnight, Scot, 327n26
Mediator, 107, 135
    and Christus Victor, 461
    and exclusivism, 342–43

of new covenant, 393, 530, 548
and reconciliation, 305, 306–7, 383
and redemption, 354–55
and righteousness, 59
Melchizedek, 49, 133, 155, 172–75,
    177, 180, 184, 194, 229–30, 232,
    242
mercy, 48, 525–26
mercy seat, 229, 507, 517, 518–19
Messiah, 42, 154–55, 156, 162, 173,
    387
    as David's son, 185–86, 201
    Paul on, 167
    sacrifice and intercession of, 228,
    229–30
Michael (archangel), 546
Michaels, J. Ramsey, 104, 106, 200,
    515, 539, 542
military messiah, 162
ministry of reconciliation, 284, 285,
    288–89, 309, 384
Moo, Douglas J., 86–87, 97, 148, 192–
    93, 221, 281, 298, 300, 302, 309,
    310–11, 340, 341, 376, 380, 390,
    442, 473–74, 475, 519
moral impurity, 389, 443
Morris, Leon, 74–75, 82, 85, 94–95,
    311–12, 315, 317–18, 356, 358–
    59, 375, 515–16, 540, 556
Mosaic covenant, 33, 174–75
Mosaic law, 175, 379, 472, 519
Moses, 67
    lifting up bronze servant, 72
    sees part of God's glory, 366
Most Holy Place, 70, 176–77, 228–29,
    241, 347, 367, 507
Motyer, J. Alec, 29, 65, 120, 371, 503
Moule, C. F. D., 341, 443
Mounce, Robert, 112, 114, 201
Mounce, William, 342, 344, 345, 346
Mount Ebal, 385
Mount Gerazim, 385
Mount Sinai, 218
Mount Zion, 154, 219
Murray, John, 359
mystery, 294
    of godliness, 171
    of incarnation, 563
mystical union, 397

nations, blessing of, 93
natural body, 482–85
Nebuchadnezzar, 422–23
Nettleton, Asahel, 573
new age, 150, 222
new birth, 143–46
new community, 216, 223–26
new covenant, 33, 107, 196, 216–20,
    292, 308, 347, 348, 393, 486–87,
    530, 536–37, 547
new creation, 137–38, 143–50, 184,
    212, 216, 220–23, 283–84, 288,
    296, 489n53
new earth, as imperishable and
    immortal, 482–83
new exodus, 317–20, 341, 353
new heaven and new earth, 132, 139,
    144, 146–50, 220, 283, 492
new man, 291
new self, 521
new song, 352
New Testament
    presentations of Christ's intercession,
        237–47
    previews of Christ's intercession,
        232–37
    on sinlessness of Christ, 43–53
Nicole, Roger, 85, 375
Noah, 199, 363–64, 451–52
Nolland, John, 187

obedience, 104, 538–39
obedience of Christ, 47, 49, 91
O'Brien, Peter T., 102, 103, 144, 191,
    205, 290, 294–95, 299, 300, 308,
    338, 339, 340, 348, 390, 445,
    447, 448, 450, 490, 491, 492,
    494, 521, 524, 525, 526, 528,
    530
offerings, 503–6
offspring
    of serpent, 415–16
    of woman, 415–16
old covenant, 219, 448, 528, 531, 536
old self, 521
Old Testament
    on ascension of Christ, 152–56
    on death of Christ, 62–67
    on divine warrior, 414–25

on first Adam, 464–68
on intercession of Christ, 228–32
on penal substitution, 363–71
on Pentecost, 207
on redemption, 314–20
on resurrection of Christ, 117–21
on second coming of Christ, 251–53
on session of Christ, 184–85
on sinlessness of Christ, 42–43
Old Testament priests, 112, 133, 141,
    196–97, 347
Old Testament sacrifices, 448, 501–2,
    523–24, 528–29, 530, 535, 543
"one act of righteousness," 90, 91, 127,
    139, 278, 471, 473–75, 498, 518
Origen, 518
original sin, 91, 408, 470, 472, 555
Orlinsky, Harry, 511
Ortlund, Raymond, 28n2
Osborne, Grant, 374
Ovey, Michael, 366, 371, 381, 404,
    405, 406
Owen, John, 397, 405–6

pacification, 298, 300, 305
Packer, J. I., 61, 411
Page, Sydney H. T., 325n21, 326–27,
    331
Paraclete, Holy Spirit as, 209–10
Parker, Rebecca, 407
parousia. See second coming of Christ
particular atonement, 566–75
particular intercession, 233–34, 250
particularity, of penal substitution,
    410–11
passive obedience of Christ, 47
Passover lamb, 350, 365–66, 408, 502–
    3, 514–15, 520–21, 541, 547
Paul, 215
    on ascension of Christ, 166–71
    on Christus Victor, 439–46
    on intercession of Christ, 237–38
    mission to Gentiles, 342
    on penal substitution, 374–91
    on reconciliation, 277
    on redemption, 332–46
    on resurrection, 126–33
    on sacrifice, 517–22
    on second Adam, 470–91

on second coming, 256–61
on session of Christ, 190–93
peace, 212, 221, 291
peace (fellowship) offering, 504–5
peacemaking, 89, 297, 306
peace with God, 142–43, 278, 281, 289, 555
penal substitution, 14, 93, 97, 204, 362–412, 519, 550
and deliverance of cosmos, 562
as foundational picture of salvation, 557–60
and resurrection, 403–4
upward movement of, 561
Pentecost, 16, 79, 125, 126, 158, 180, 204, 206–26, 552
as essential result of death and resurrection, 554
and fullness of salvation, 223–24
as saving work of Christ, 23–25
as singular and unrepeatable, 214, 216
"perfect through suffering," 48–49, 495–96, 499
persecution, 260, 268
perseverance, 135, 198, 260, 302, 476
and intercession of Christ, 233, 238, 248
Peter, 215
Christ's prayer for, 233
at Cornelius's house, 437
Pentecost sermon of, 79, 118, 126, 155, 163–64, 188–89, 203
speech at Solomon's Portico, 165
Peterson, David, 374, 538
physical death, 102, 124, 143, 451, 466
pictures, of work of Christ, 16–17, 273–75, 554–64
pilgrim motif, 104, 540
plagues, 355, 416, 502
pleasing aroma, 363–65, 408
Porter, Stanley E., 306–7
powers, 426, 441, 443–46
predestination, 476–77
preservation, 128, 279–80
price. *See* ransom price; redemption price
principalities, 426, 461
progressive sanctification, 535

propitiation, 38, 51, 85–87, 103, 109, 111, 246, 278, 332, 375–77, 378, 393–96, 518, 525–26
protection, Christ's intercession for, 235
protoevangelium, 414, 415–16, 460, 467–68
providence, 132, 147
purification, 99–100, 505, 523, 530, 531–32, 548, 549

racial reconciliation, 296
ransom, 343, 355, 358, 545
ransom price, 349, 356–57, 358
ransom saying, 66–67, 325–31, 371–74, 558
reconciliation, 46, 87–89, 128, 276–312, 353, 555
of all things, 147–48, 221, 294, 297–301, 304
and ascension of Christ, 181
and justification, 272–80, 282, 288–89, 301, 383–84
and resurrection, 142–43
upward movement of, 561
and vicarious suffering, 370
re-creation, 487, 555
redemption, 116, 313–61, 549, 555
through blood of Christ, 94, 105, 114
as past, present, and future, 359–60
upward movement of, 561–62
redemption price, 82, 95, 114, 336
redemptive history, and legal substitution, 557
Reformation, 397
regeneration, 96, 132, 134, 223
Reichenbach, Bruce R., 14
Reid, Dan, 418, 421, 431, 432–33, 506
reparation. *See* guilt offering
repentance, gift of, 189
representation, 343–44, 382, 473, 543
resurrected bodies, 482–86
resurrection, 124
assurance of, 132
from second Adam, 480
resurrection of Christ, 117–50, 478, 491
as centerpiece of saving work, 23, 61, 553–54

neglect of, 14–15
and penal substitution, 403–4
and reconciliation, 281
retributive punishment, 399–400
Revelation
    Christus Victor in, 454–59
    death of Christ in, 111–15
    redemption in, 350–53
    sacrifice in, 545–47
    second coming of Christ in, 264–65
    session of Christ in, 200–202
reversal, 83
Ridderbos, Herman, 463
righteousness, 87
righteousness of God, 85, 87, 375–77, 384
Righteous One, 46, 51, 54, 63, 81, 246
right hand of God, 100, 448
Rightmire, R. David, 353
Roman Catholic Church, on eucharistic sacrifice, 176n23, 239
Root of David, 113
Rosner, Brian, 480–81, 486
Ross, Allen, 368, 508

Sach, Andrew, 366, 371, 381, 404, 405, 406
sacrifice of Christ, 74, 75–76, 96, 116, 448, 500–549, 556
    and ascension, 180–81
    as finished, 243, 533, 537
    as pleasing aroma, 363–65
    and substitution, 560
    sufficiency of, 106–7
    upward movement of, 561
sacrifice of Passover lamb, 365–66, 502–3
sanctification, 104, 235–36, 302, 334, 344, 516, 535–36
    and Holy Spirit, 538
    precedes sacrifice, 76
Satan, 439–40, 546
    attack on Christ, 433–37
    blinding of, 487–88
    falling from heaven, 429–31
    as ruler of this world, 434
    and temptation of Adam and Eve, 470
    and temptation of Christ, 425–26, 469–70

and temptation of Peter, 232
    victory over, 76–77, 413, 436–37
saving faith, 518
scapegoat, 74, 500
Schaeffer, Francis, 573
Schreiner, Thomas R., 14, 105, 129, 142, 167, 281, 308, 333, 350, 356, 392, 396, 408, 452, 474, 518–19, 520, 540–41
second Adam, 38, 101–2, 116, 131–32, 145, 146, 449, 463–99, 524, 555
    and deliverance of cosmos, 562
    obedience of, 471, 475, 556
    as true image, 499
    upward movement of, 561
second blessing, 215
second coming of Christ, 251–69, 345, 553
    as essential result of death and resurrection, 554
    Jesus's predictions of, 432–33
    as saving work of Christ, 23–25, 265–69
second death, 124, 143, 304
second man, 36, 90, 116, 131–32, 485, 494, 499, 551. See also second Adam
seed, 482
self-control, 344, 349
self-offering, and intercession, 239–41
Servant, 35, 42, 54, 63–65, 80–81, 331, 408, 431. See also suffering Servant
    bearing guilt, 511–12
    and holiness and justification, 58
    humiliation and exaltation of, 512
    lives after death, 119–20
    as victorious, 72, 510
servant leadership, 66, 329, 372
service to God, 525, 549
session of Christ, 16, 99–100, 180, 183–205
    as essential result of death and resurrection, 554
    as saving work of Christ, 23–25
    and threefold office of Christ, 203
sexual immorality, 334–35, 360
sheep and goats, 253, 267, 269
Silas, 215

Simeon, 30
Simons, Menno, 485
sin
    biblical depictions of, 556
    in Christian life, 543–44
    and condemnation, 408
    confession of, 107–9
    disastrous results of, 465–67
    dominion of, 379, 471
    penalty and power of, 379, 406
    tyranny of, 346
sinless life of Christ, 16, 41–60, 286,
    349, 496, 510
    as essential precondition to death
        and resurrection, 554
    as saving work, 23–24
sin offering, 229, 505, 506, 507–8,
    519–22
Sklar, Jay, 503–6, 509, 531–32
slavery, 334–36, 341, 361, 555
Smalley, Stephen S., 108
Socinus, Faustus, 398–99
Son, 193, 491–92, 495–96
Song of Miriam, 414, 416–18, 460
Song of Moses, 414, 416–18, 460
son of David, 193–94
Son of God, 47, 70, 427
    come down from heaven, 131, 146
Son of Man, 71–72, 188, 252–53, 324,
    329, 355, 372, 414, 423–25,
    432–33, 460
soothing aroma, 363–65, 408
spiritual blindness, 438
spiritual body, 482–85
spiritual death, 96, 102, 389, 443, 451,
    466
spiritual slavery, 555
spiritual warfare, 439, 454, 555
Spurgeon, Charles H., 573
Stephen, 45–46, 81, 189, 203
Stott, John, 12, 15, 94–95, 310, 331,
    335, 395–96, 400–401
subjugation, of powers, 295, 298, 300,
    309, 449, 536
substitution, 330–31, 343–44, 357–
    58, 410, 548. *See also* penal
    substitution
    and particular atonement, 566
    and union with Christ, 405–6

suffering, 106, 260, 278, 372
    of Christ, 49, 51, 105–6, 496
    of second Adam, 495
    unjust, 391
suffering Servant, 80, 119, 231–32,
    368–71, 509–12, 534, 547

tabernacle, 99, 176–77, 195–96, 241,
    347, 503, 547
temple, 70, 99, 547
Ten Commandments, 97, 292, 377,
    388, 390, 443, 531
theophany, 324
Thiselton, Anthony, 141, 334, 335–36,
    485, 521
"times of refreshing," 255–56, 269
tongues, at Pentecost, 213
Toon, Peter, 151, 243
Towner, Philip, 261, 344–46
transfiguration, 67
transformation, of mortal bodies,
    256–57
Travis, Stephen, 399
tree, as term for cross, 105, 387,
    542–43
tree of life, 268
Trinity
    and intercession of Christ, 248–49
    and particular atonement, 567–69,
        571
    and penal substitution, 400–402,
        406
    and salvation, 538
    and work of Christ, 179
triumphal march, 97–98, 443–45

uncleanness, 96
unintentional sin, 505–6
union with Christ, 94, 192–93, 203,
    257, 397–98, 405–6
unity, Christ's intercession for, 236
universal dimension, to work of Christ,
    572
universal intercession, 233–34
universalism, 91, 148, 233–34, 302–4,
    309, 341, 394, 411, 474
upper room, 211
Upper Room Discourse, 158, 234
upward direction, of work of Christ,
    560, 563

VanGemeren, Willem, 501, 512
vertical fellowship, 544
vicarious atonement, 367, 392. *See also* substitution
Vickers, Brian, 277n3, 287, 382–83
victory over powers, and ascension of Christ, 170
vindication of Christ, 199–200
violence, of atonement, 388
virgin birth, 28, 33, 44
visions and prophecies, 215
Volf, Judith Gundry, 281, 381
voluntariness
    of penal substitution, 410
    of redemption of Christ, 355–56
    of sacrifice of Christ, 548
Vos, Geerhardus, 483

walking in the light, 108
Waltke, Bruce K., 120, 415, 464
warfare, sphere of, 555
Wenham, Gordon, 363–65, 367, 507–8
Westermann, C., 512
Whitefield, George, 573
wilderness, 425, 469, 508
Wilkins, Michael, 425
Williams, Garry, 397–98, 399, 400, 401–2, 404–5, 406, 407

Williams, Michael, 218, 314
wind, of Pentecost, 213, 221, 222
wisdom of God, 333–34
wisdom tradition, 490
Witherington, Ben, 372, 438
witness, 138, 149, 224–25
Word, Jesus as, 31, 32–33
world
    as enemy of God, 440, 453, 460
    as Jews and Gentiles, 75
    reconciliation of, 285
    subjected to second Adam, 493
    on trial, 210–11
worship, 534–35, 556
wrath of God, 37, 85–86, 111, 149, 258, 278, 280, 302–3, 367, 375–77, 379, 400
Wright, Christopher, 361, 364, 366, 369, 371, 557

Yarbrough, Robert W., 108, 109–10, 264, 394, 395, 453–54, 544
Young, Edward J., 231

Zechariah (father of John the Baptist), 29, 320–21

Scripture Index

Genesis
book of—416, 469
1—469, 489, 490
1–2—466
1–3—377, 466
1:1—296, 491
1:2—222
1:20–21—464
1:24—464
1:26—465, 481, 493
1:26–27—477, 485, 489
1:26–28—498
1:27—464
1:28—464, 465
1:30—464
2:7—131, 146, 212, 221,
    222, 222n16, 464,
    483, 485, 498
2:8–9—465
2:17—466
2:20–25—465
2:21–22—464, 498
3—181, 450, 465, 466,
    467, 468
3:1—465
3:1–13—415
3:1–19—498
3:4—465, 466
3:5—465
3:6—465
3:9–12—465
3:14—415
3:15—181, 414, 415,
    416, 459, 460, 467

3:19—466
3:20—467
4:3–5—501
5:3—485
5:5—466
5:7—466
5:8—466
6—471
6:1–4—199
6:17—464
7:15—464
7:22—464
8:1—364
8:17—464
8:20—501
8:20–21—363
8:21—96, 363, 364, 407
10:1–32—218
11:1—218
11:4—218
11:7–9—218
12—218
12:1–3—385
12:3—93, 110, 261, 386
14—172, 173
14:17–24—230
14:18—172, 230
14:18–20—184
15—531
19—471
22:9—501
22:13—501
31:54—501
49:3—490, 491

49:8—456
49:8–10—456
49:9—113, 201, 351,
    456

Exodus
1—502
3:8—314
6:6—354
6:6–8—314
6:14—497
7:5—416
7:17—416
8:10—416
8:22—416
11:1—502
11:4—502
11:4–5—502
12—513
12:4–5—365
12:5—105
12:8–10—503
12:11–13—366, 503
12:13—365, 407, 502,
    503, 547, 549, 560
12:14–20—520
12:21–22—365, 502
12:22–23—503
12:31–32—417
13:11–15—316
14—315
14:4—416
14:13–14—417
14:18—416

14:28—417
14:30–31—315
15—416, 417
15:1–3—315
15:1–12—417–18
15:1–21—414, 416, 459, 460
15:3—416
15:11–13—315
15:15—431
15:18—315
15:21—418
19:5–6—114, 352
19:6—350
19:20—219
20—471
20–24—504
20:5–6—385
24—273
24:3—539
24:7–8—539
24:8—513, 514, 531
24:16–18—219
25:40—195
26:1—468
26:31–33—176, 241
28:12—250
29:37—523
30:10—523
32–34—366
32:18–23—488
33:19—366
33:20—176
33:20–23—366
34:6–7—366, 367, 407, 408
34:19–20—316
39:6–7—244, 250
40:12–15—75

Leviticus
1—503, 544
1–6—503, 547
1–7—181, 512
1:3—105
1:4—503, 504
1:9—96, 363, 364, 40, 503, 560
1:10—105

2—504
2:1–2—363, 364, 407, 560
2:2—363
2:13—504
3—504
3.1—105
3:1–17—505n10
3:3—363, 364, 407, 560
3:5—363, 364, 407, 560
3:6—105
4–5—509, 559
4:1–5:13—505
4:5–7—506
4:29—363, 364, 407, 560
4:31—363, 364, 407, 560
5–7—371
5:14–6:7—331, 357, 505, 506n13
5:16—64, 371
5:18—64, 371
7:1–7—331, 357
7:2—506
7:7—371
11–15—509
11:44—539
12:3–4—321
15:31—505
16—176, 181, 228–29, 231, 236, 240, 241, 249, 367, 507, 518, 547, 549, 559, 560
16:1–5—367, 507
16:1–10—507
16:1–34—509n18
16:2—228
16:3—509
16:4—228
16:5—509
16:6—367, 507
16:6–10—528
16:11—367, 507
16:11–28—507
16:12–13—176, 229, 507
16:14—508
16:14–15—229

16:15—241
16:15–16—176
16:16—367, 508, 532
16:16–17—508
16:17—367, 534
16:17–19—176
16:18—367, 508
16:19—523
16:21—368
16:21–22—367, 368, 407, 508, 560
16:22—368, 508
16:24—367, 509
16:29–34—507
16:30—523
16:33—367
16:34—176, 367
17:11—506
18:8—520
20:3—532
21:15—532
21:33—532
23:9–14—353
23:27—531
25:25–28—320
25:47–52—320
25:47–55—372

Numbers
3:44–51—317
5:5–8—331, 357
8:14–19—317
10:35–36—414
11:29—224
19:20—532
21—72, 73
21:4–6—72
21:9—73

Deuteronomy
4:37—354
5:6—421
7:8—316
9:26—316, 355
10:16—223
12:23—506
15—76
15:1–5—166
15:19—76, 517

15:21—76, 517
21:22–23—81, 166
21:23—82, 93, 105, 337, 386, 387, 542
27:12–28:68—92, 385
27:15—385
27:26—336, 385, 388
28:1–6—385
28:7—421
28:25—421
29:17—349
30:6—223
30:15–20—348
32:6—573
32:8—492

Judges
5:4–5—414

1 Samuel
2:35—525
15:22—535
17—414, 418, 459, 460
17:4–7—419
17:26—419
17:37—419
17:45–47—419

2 Samuel
7—154
7:11–12—193
7:12–16—165
7:13–14—194
7:14—193
7:16—175

1 Chronicles
25:1—164n13

Ezra
1—317
1:1–4—355

Job
1:11–12—434
2:4–5—434

Psalms
2—45, 118, 127, 194, 420

2:1–2—80
2:7—193
2:9—458
8—36, 101, 465, 492–93, 494
8:1—493
8:2—493, 494
8:2–4—493
8:3–4—493
8:4—329
8:4–6—36, 101, 492, 493
8:5—102, 465
8:5–7—450
8:5–8—493
8:6—191, 452, 481
8:6–8—101, 465
8:7–8—493
8:9—493
16—118, 119, 126, 127
16:8–11—118
16:10—188
18:2–3—324
22—61, 62
22:1—62
22:7—62
22:8—62
22:16—62
22:18—62
22:22—62
22:24—62
22:25—62
22:27—62
23:6—119
31:5—71
39:7—522
40:3—352
40:6—522
40:6–8—535, 536
41:9—435
49:7—355
49:7–9—330, 373, 558
51:5—480
58:8—164n13
68—153–54, 169
68:4—153, 424
68:4–7—153, 169
68:11–14—153
68:15–16—153, 154

68:17—153
68:18—153, 154, 168, 169
68:19—153, 154, 169
68:20–22—153
68:24–27—153
68:29—153
68:30—153
68:31–32—153
72—420
74:2—316
77:15—316
78:35—313, 354
89:8–10—414
89:26–27—477
89:27—135, 135n16, 296
89:37—135n16
89:9—423
93:3–4—423
100—219
103:12—86, 376, 509
104:3–4—424
110—154, 155, 156, 162, 173, 174, 179, 184, 185, 229, 230, 414, 419, 420n7, 421, 432, 447, 448, 459, 460
110:1—154, 155, 164, 165, 170, 173, 175, 180, 184, 185, 186, 187, 188, 194, 197, 214, 229, 230, 252, 420, 424, 432, 446, 447, 448, 452, 536, 552
110:1a—432
110:1b—432
110:1–2—432
110:2—420, 447
110:3—447
110:4—133, 155, 173, 174, 175, 184, 229, 230, 419, 527
110:5–6—420, 432, 447
118:22—126n9
130:3—21
139:6—565

143:2—21
144:9—352

Proverbs
8:22—490

Ecclesiastes
3:1–2—480
7:29—467

Isaiah
1:10–13—535
7:14—28, 28n2, 39
8:18—449
9:6—29, 39
9:7—29
10:21–22—29
11:1—201, 456
11:4—458
11:10—201, 456
12—407
13:8—431
14:1–27—430
14:9–17—65, 120
14:12—65
14:13—430
19:1—324, 424
28:16—129
29:23—120
35:10—319
40–55—369
40:9—322
41:4—136
41:8–10—524
42:1–9—368
42:10—352
42:13—414
43:1–2—319
43:10–13—135n16
43:25—369
44:3—214, 217
44:6—136
45:1—318
45:1–6—355
45:1–25—317
45:4–6—318
45:22—34
45:22–25—34
48:7—64

48:12—136
49:1–13—368
49:24–26—459
50:4–9—368
52:1–10—318–19
52:9—322
52:13—64, 72, 116, 231, 510
52:13–53:12—63, 64, 230, 327, 368, 371, 373, 407, 408, 509, 512, 558, 558n7
52:14—63, 369, 509
52:15—64, 116
53—42, 61, 63, 64, 72, 80, 81, 106, 119, 156, 305, 326, 327, 330, 357, 368, 369, 371, 373, 391, 392, 402, 511, 512, 515, 534, 541, 542, 543, 557
53:1—42
53:2—42
53:3—63, 369, 510
53:3–4—42
53:4—105, 391, 542
53:5—63, 106, 369, 391, 392, 410
53:5–6—64, 119, 370, 409, 511, 557, 560
53:6—391, 401, 571
53:7—63, 74, 105, 369, 391, 510, 541
53:7–8—80
53:8—63, 64, 369, 370, 510, 511, 571
53:9—43, 51, 54, 56, 63, 105, 370, 391, 402, 510, 541
53:10—63, 64, 65, 116, 119, 120, 327, 330, 330–31, 357, 370, 371, 373, 401, 408, 501, 506, 509, 510, 511, 512, 542, 547, 549, 560
53:10c—120
53:10–12—119, 557, 560

53:11—43, 54, 58, 63, 64, 81, 105, 116, 246, 370, 371, 391, 402, 409, 410, 411, 510, 511, 542, 551
53:11–12—402, 511
53:12—43, 64, 65, 116, 119, 120, 230, 231, 233, 246, 330, 331, 370, 373 391, 401, 408, 410, 510, 511, 534, 542
54:1–55:13—511
55:10–11—92
59:20—333, 354
61:8—216
63—459
63:1–3—458
63:1–4—415
63:4—322
65:16—137, 138, 149
65:17—138, 149, 150, 220, 269
65:17–25—562
66:2—150
66:22—220
66:22–23—269, 562

Jeremiah
4:4—223
7:21–24—535
9:23–24—333
16:14–17—423
21:3–7—414, 421, 459, 460
21:4–7—423
21:5—423
23:1–8—423
24:4–7—423
30:1–33:26—423
31—273
31:11—320
31:31–34—219, 348, 361, 513, 514, 537
31:33—530
31:33–34—216
31:34—514, 523, 547
50:33–34—320

Ezekiel
9:3—422
10:18–19—422
11:22–23—422
13:9—164n13
13:19—164n13
18:18—422
20:1–2—422
20:7–8—502
20:7–10—365
26:7–11—422
32:12—422
34:2–4—73
36:4–8—422
36:26–27—216
36:27—218
37:13–21—422
37:26—216
38:1–6—422
38:7–13—422
39:15–18—422
39:29—214, 218
45:1–5—422

Daniel
2:31–45—423
5:23—349
7—424, 432
7:1–8—423
7:7—423
7:9—423
7:9–12—423
7:10—424
7:11—424
7:13—187, 324, 424,
   432, 433
7:13–14—156, 188, 252,
   253, 329, 414, 423,
   424, 459, 460
7:14—424, 433
7:17—423
9:26—65
10:20–21—492n61
12:21—492n61

Hosea
6:7—467

Joel
2—214

2:28—207
2:28–29—214, 218
2:28–32—204, 207, 215,
   552
2:32—129

Jonah
1:1–3—120
1:15—121
1:17—120, 121

Micah
5:11—164n13

Nahum
1:3—424

Zechariah
10:2—164n13
12:10—65
13:7—65
14:3—415
14:4—431
14:5—431
14:6—431

Matthew
book of—70
1:1—457
1:2–16—468
1:19—9, 445
1:20—30
1:21—30, 514, 562
1:22–23—28
3:11—207, 217
3:15—41
3:17—44
4:1–10—59
4:1–11—425n12, 461
4:10—426, 459
4:11—426
4:13—426
5:17—326
5:39—398
8:3—108
8:20—329
9:13—66
10:34—326
10:35—326

12:22–23—428
12:22–29—459, 461
12:24—428
12:25–26—428
12:27—428
12:28—428, 460
12:28–29—37
12:29—428
12:39–40—121
16:16—44
16:17—44
16:21—68, 121
17–19—514
17:5—44
17:18—427
17:22–23—68, 121
19:28—68, 220, 562
20:18–19—68, 121
20:25–28—326
20:28—325, 327, 372,
   374, 558
21:42—126n9
22:41–46—155, 185,
   186
22:43—252
22:43–45—420, 421
22:44—186
22:45—186
23:37–38—68
24:2—68
24:30—255
24:30–31—68
25—267, 303
25:31—253, 267
25:31–34—253
25:31–36—68
25:34—253, 269
25:41—253, 303
25:46—149, 267, 303,
   553
26:17–20—514
26:20–25—68
26:26—513, 514
26:27–28—217, 513
26:27–29—513, 547
26:28—293, 514, 549
26:31—65
26:36–46—48
26:52–54—431

26:61—187
26:63—187, 204, 432
26:64—187–88, 204, 329
26:65—187
26:65–66—188
27—62
27:35—62
27:39—62
27:39–43—16
27:43—62
27:45—431
27:45–50—69
27:51—431, 468
27:52—431
27:54—432
28:5–10—122
28:19–20—573

Mark
book of—44, 70
1:7–8—208, 217
1:12–13—425, 459
1:24—44, 54, 57, 427, 459
1:25–26—427
1:25–28—44
1:34—427
1:38—326
1:39—427
2:14—497
2:17—66, 326
3:11—427
5:7—427
7:28—427
8:15—521
8:29—327, 372
8:31—1, 23, 68, 121, 327, 372
8:37—330, 355, 373, 558
9:12—81
9:17—427
9:25—428
9:31—15, 23, 68, 121, 327, 372
10:26–27—372
10:32—497
10:32–34—15, 121

10:33–34—23, 68, 327, 372
10:35–37—66
10:37—328, 372
10:38–40—66
10:39—328
10:40—328
10:41—66, 328, 372
10:43–44—66, 329
10:45—40, 66, 67, 116, 325, 326, 327, 329, 330, 343, 343n67, 354, 355, 357, 361, 363, 371, 372, 373, 374, 407, 408, 409, 410, 412, 558, 559
10:45a—330, 357
10:47–48—427
10:51—427
12:16—328
12:35–37—186
12:36—154n4, 185
13:26—253, 255
13:26–27—253–54
13:27—266
14—424
14:23–25—514
14:24—373, 517, 539
14:61—424, 432
14:61–62—459
14:62—187, 424, 432, 433
15:33–39—69
15:38—70
15:39—70
16:6–8—122

Luke
book of—43, 70
1–3—426
1:9—320
1:16–17—320
1:31—30
1:35—13, 44, 53, 54, 56
1:54—30
1:60—320
1:63—321
1:67—321
1:68—320–21, 325

1:68–69—29
1:71—321
1:77—321
2:11—30, 39, 553
2:22—321
2:25—322
2:29—573
2:30—30
2:32—30
2:36—321
2:37—321
2:38—30, 321, 322, 325
3:16—208, 212, 217
3:21—469
3:22—468
3:23—468
3:23–38—468, 469
3:38—468, 469, 498
4:1—470
4:1–2—425
4:1–12—59
4:1–13—426, 469, 498, 499
4:3–4—470
4:5–7—430
4:5–8—470
4:9–12—470
4:13—459
4:24—573
4:41—428
5:32—66
8:2—427
9:1—430
9:21–22—162
9:22—68, 121, 323
9:30–31—67
9:31—67, 116
9:43–45—162
9:44—68, 323
10:1—429
10:12—430
10:13–20—430
10:14—430
10:15—430
10:16—430
10:17—429, 430
10:17–20—459
10:18—430, 436
10:20—431

11:18–20—429
11:21–22—459
11:22—429
11:31–32—429
12:49—326
13:16—438
18:31–33—121
18:31–34—162
18:32–33—68, 323
19:10—66, 326
19:28—497
20:41–44—186
21:5–28—324
21:25–26—324
21:25–28—324
21:26—324
21:27—255, 324
21:28—323–25, 356
22:19—517
22:20—216, 513, 514
22:24–27—326
22:25–27—326
22:31—232, 434
22:31–32—232, 233,
  249
22:32—232
22:37—326
22:49—212
22:53—340, 434
23–24—470
23:34—231, 233, 234,
  250
23:43—254
23:44–49—69
23:46—71
23:47—70
24:5–9—122
24:14–15—322
24:18—323
24:18–21—322
24:21—322, 323, 235
24:26—81, 323
24:27—323
24:44—184, 208
24:46–49—161, 208
24:49—161, 208, 214
24:50–51—161, 203
24:50–53—160
24:51—161

24:52—182
24:53—161

John
book of—30, 44, 70,
  122, 209
1:1—31, 245n31, 264,
  458, 517
1:1–3—32
1:3—123
1:7—31
1:9—31, 39
1:10—32
1:10–11—31
1:11—32
1:12—3, 123
1:14—13, 31, 39, 458
1:16—32
1:18—32, 489
1:19—547
1:19–28—515
1:29—33, 74, 75, 116,
  134, 501, 515, 530,
  540, 548
1:32–33—223
1:32–34—208
1:35—515
1:36—74, 116, 515, 547
1:43—497, 515
1:49—457
2:1—515
2:11—32
2:19—23, 33
2:19–22—15, 74n16,
  121, 123
3:2—257
3:6—223
3:8—134, 223
3:11–15—72
3:14—72
3:14–15—73
3:16—569, 574
3:16–17—573, 574
3:17—212
3:18—73
3:34—223
3:36—125
5:21—123, 144
5:24—31

5:25ff.—144
5:28–29—124, 143
5:38—212
6:1–21—157
6:26–31—157
6:27—144
6:32–40—157
6:35—144
6:41–50—157
6:51—517
6:53—157
6:54–59—157
6:60—157
6:61–62—156, 179
6:63–65—157
6:66—44
6:67—44
6:68–69—44, 54, 57
7:7—210
7:29—212
7:38—158
7:39—158, 180, 223,
  235
8—44
8:12—31
8:23—434
8:34—32
8:34–36—67
8:36—32
8:44—45
8:46—45, 57, 434
9:5—31
9:28–29—73
9:34—73
9:38–41—31
9:40–41—31, 73
10:11—32, 73, 569, 571
10:11–18—73, 123
10:12–13—73
10:14—73
10:15—73, 566, 569,
  571
10:16—74
10:17—32, 74
10:17–18—15, 23, 39,
  74n16, 121, 123, 330,
  401, 410, 554
10:18—74, 77, 433
10:26—569, 571

10:28—124
10:28–29—144
10:36—75, 76
11:4—32, 123
11:6—123
11:15—123
11:21—123
11:22—123
11:23—123
11:23–27—123
11:24—123
11:25—123, 124, 143
11:25–26—15, 124, 143
11:26–27—124
11:32—123
11:40—32
11:41—233
11:42—233, 249
11:43–44—124, 144
11:47–50—78
11:50—78
11:51–52—78
11:52—78
11:53—78
12:6—435
12:20–21—78
12:23—71
12:23–24—78
12:25—79, 125
12:26—79
12:27—79
12:31—77, 116, 426,
    434, 436, 449, 459
12:31–33—436, 461
12:32—72
12:32–33—71
12:44—212
12:44–50—31
12:48—109
13–17—158
13:1—79
13:1–2—76
13:1–4—435
13:2—434, 435, 459,
    460
13:12—454
13:18—435
13:21—435
13:26—435

13:27—76, 434, 435,
    459, 460
13:30—435
13:33—254
13:35—236
14—434
14:1—254
14:1–3—178, 254
14:2—254
14:2–3—266, 553
14:3—254
14:6—22, 112, 124
14:9—490
14:9–10—517
14:12—124
14:16—109, 210, 214n6,
    234, 235
14:16–17—124, 209,
    223, 245
14:18—214n6
14:18–20—124
14:19—1, 125
14:20—125
14:25–26—209
14:26—109, 214n6, 223,
    245
14:28—214n6
14:30—433, 434
14:30–31—77, 434, 459
14:31—434
15:21—212
15:22–24—210
15:26—109, 210, 214n6,
    223, 245
15:26–27—210
16—158
16:4–7—158
16:7—109, 180, 214n6,
    234, 235, 245
16:7–11—210
16:7–15—223
16:8–11—436
16:11—77, 434, 436,
    449, 459
16:12–15—211
16:13—210
16:33—77, 437, 454
17—234, 235–37, 569
17:1—79, 406

17:1–5—237
17:2—568, 569, 571
17:4–5—235
17:5—237
17:6—568, 571
17:9—568, 569, 571
17:9–10—571
17:11b—235, 236
17:11–12—235
17:15—235, 516
17:16—516
17:17—76, 235, 236,
    516
17:17–19—75, 235
17:18—76
17:19—75, 76, 116, 235,
    515, 516, 517, 547,
    549, 568, 569, 571
17:20—516
17:20–23—235, 236
17:21—236
17:22b—236
17:23—236
17:24—235, 236, 568,
    571
18:44—415
19:11—328
19:15—433
19:19—97, 390, 443
19:26—111
19:28—71
19:28–30—69
19:30—71
19:37—65
20:11–18—122
20:17—159, 179
20:21—221
20:21–23—209, 211,
    221
20:22—212
20:22–23—221, 553
20:23—212, 222
20:30–31—124

Acts
book of—45, 79, 80, 83,
    125, 126, 163, 188,
    212, 254, 331
1—255

1–7—212
1:1—161
1:1–2—160, 206
1:4–5—212
1:5—212, 217, 553
1:6—162
1:6–11—160
1:7—162
1:8—162, 204, 212, 225, 573
1:9—162, 212, 255
1:9–11—254, 324
1:10–11—255
1:11—163, 177, 181
1:15—225
1:22—79, 79n21
2—161, 208, 212, 214
2:1–2—221, 222
2:1–6—164
2:2—213, 215, 222
2:3—213
2:3–4—219
2:4—215
2:5—213
2:7–8—213
2:7–13—164
2:8–12—218
2:11—213
2:14–21—164
2:16—213
2:17—552
2:17–21—213
2:18—552
2:22–24—23, 554
2:22–31—164
2:23—79
2:23–24—83
2:24—15, 125
2:24–32—214
2:24–36—79n21
2:25–28—118
2:29–32—118
2:29–36—188
2:32—15, 125
2:32–33—25, 126, 164, 214
2:32–36—163–65, 180, 203
2:33—79n21, 180, 188, 204, 552

2:34–35—155
2:34–36—164, 189
2:36—79, 83, 126, 129, 179, 214
2:37—126, 214
2:38—214
2:38–41—126
2:41—214
3:1–12—165
3:6–8—223
3:12–13—255
3:13—45, 80, 83
3:13–16—165
3:14—45, 54, 56, 81
3:14–15—83, 255
3:15—15, 79, 79n2, 125, 491, 497
3:16—255
3:18—80, 255
3:19–21—165, 255–56, 325
3:20–21—269
3:21—165, 180, 255, 256
3:26—79, 79n21, 80
4:1–2—15, 125
4:1–23—45
4:8—215
4:10—15, 79n21, 125, 126, 139
4:10–12—126
4:11—126
4:11–12—22
4:12—139
4:25–27—45
4:27—45, 54, 56, 80
4:27–28—80
4:29–30—45, 54, 81
4:30—45, 56, 223
4:31—215, 225
4:33—79n21
5:17–18—189
5:27–30—166
5:27–32—189
5:29–31—189, 203
5:30—15, 79n21, 81, 105–6, 125, 166, 542
5:30–31—79, 152, 166, 179

5:31—79n21, 497, 552, 553
5:33—166
6:3—215
6:3–6—215
6:5—215, 225
7:35—325
7:51—46, 223
7:51–52—55
7:52—45, 46, 56, 81
7:53—447, 491
7:54—189, 225
7:54–56—215
7:54–60—189–90
7:55—215
7:55–56—189, 203
7:57–58—189
7:59—125
8–12—212
8:34—80
8:34–35—80
8:35—80
9:1–19—168
9:10—215
9:17—215
9:26–31—168
10:3—215
10:10–16—215
10:34–36—437
10:36—437
10:36–38—437, 459
10:37–38—437, 460
10:38—437, 460
10:39—106, 542
10:40—79n21
11:23–24—215
11:24—215
11:27–28—215
13–28—212
13:1—215
13:2—215
13:9—215
13:9–11—215
13:10–11—438
13:23—126, 140
13:27—80
13:27–28—83
13:29—81
13:30—79n21, 83

13:33—15, 79n21, 126
13:34—15, 79n21, 126
13:34–37—119
13:37—15, 79n21, 126
13:37–38—140
13:38—140
13:38–39—127
13:39—21, 81
13:52—215
15:1–15—168
15:28—215
15:32—215
16:6–7—215
16:31—22
17:2–3—15, 126
17:3—79n21, 80
17:18—15, 126
17:31—15, 79n21, 126
20:28—82, 116, 331,
    356, 360
22:14—46, 56
22:14–15—46, 55, 81,
    438
26:17–18—438, 459
26:18—340, 438
26:22–23—79n21, 80

Romans
book of—237, 245, 249
1–3—86, 87, 376, 377
1–5—377
1:16–17—85, 86, 332,
    376
1:17—375
1:18—85, 86, 88n34,
    258, 280n4, 310, 376,
    378
1:18–20—377
1:18–32—471
1:18–3:18—378
1:18–3:20—86, 375, 376
1:18–3:30—408
1:19–32—311
1:23—297
2:5—86, 88n34, 280n4,
    311, 376
2:7—303
2:7–10—303
2:8—88n34, 149, 280n4,
    303

2:9—149, 303
2:10—303
2:12—377, 471
2:14–15—377
2:15—377
2:23—377
2:28–29—223
3:5—88n34, 280n4
3:17–25—377
3:19–20—378
3:21—21, 85, 86, 332,
    375, 376
3:21–26—378
3:22—85, 375
3:22–24—332
3:23—85, 375
3:24—332
3:24–25—401, 409
3:24–26—84, 84n26, 85,
    103, 109, 375, 376,
    517, 518
3:25—85, 86, 109n40,
    310, 338, 375,
    375n31, 376, 380,
    395, 396, 408, 412,
    517, 518, 547, 549,
    560
3:25–26—86, 116,
    127, 139, 278, 374,
    374n30, 375, 376,
    378, 406, 408, 411,
    471, 518, 555, 560
3:26—86, 376, 393
3:27–4:25—471, 518
3:29–30—342
4:1–8—411
4:3—287, 382
4:3–5—140
4:6–7—140
4:6–8—288, 383
4:22—127
4:23—127
4:23–25—140
4:24—127
4:24–25—84n27, 127,
    403
4:25—15, 23, 84n26,
    127, 129, 142, 215,
    281, 308, 308n58,
    403, 553, 554

5—90, 466, 472, 475
5:1—86, 88, 277, 278,
    279, 281, 307, 376,
    383
5:1–5—88, 279, 377
5:1–11—142, 277, 279,
    281, 304
5:2—88, 278, 279
5:2–5—88, 279
5:3–4—278
5:4—278
5:5—88, 278, 279, 463
5:6—279
5:6–8—88, 278, 279
5:6–10—84n26
5:6–11—88
5:7—278
5:8—35, 279, 307, 406,
    573
5:9—88, 89, 128, 143,
    258, 279, 280, 281,
    308n58, 517
5:9–10—88, 128, 142,
    279, 280, 281, 311
5:10—15, 87–89, 116,
    128–29, 142, 143,
    279, 280, 281, 306,
    307, 308, 308n58,
    309, 310, 383, 555
5:10–11—281
5:11—88, 279, 281, 308
5:12—90, 131, 145, 465,
    466, 471, 472, 473,
    480
5:12–19—408, 468, 470,
    471, 498
5:12–21—278, 470
5:13—471
5:14—90, 472, 473
5:15—90, 466, 472, 473
5:15–17—472
5:15–18—473
5:16—90, 381, 466, 472,
    473, 474
5:17—90, 467, 472, 473,
    475, 476, 480
5:18—90, 91, 127, 278,
    381, 467, 473, 474,
    498, 499

5:18–19—89–91, 116, 139, 140, 465, 471, 472, 474, 475, 518, 555
5:19—60, 91, 287, 382, 467, 473, 474, 499
5:20—344, 471
5:21—476
6—406, 543
6:1–2—406
6:1–11—379
6:1–12—192
6:3–4—406
6:3–10—84n26
6:8—84, 406
6:11—406
6:11–14—225
6:23—480
7:4—84n26
7:12—292
8:1—379, 380, 381
8:1–3—406
8:1–4—374, 374n30, 379, 384, 408, 519, 560
8:1–4a—381
8:2—379
8:2–4—84n26
8:3—379, 381, 401, 408, 409, 519, 547, 549, 560
8:3b—380
8:3–4—84n27, 219
8:4—380, 381, 519
8:4b–17—379, 381
8:5–17—380
8:10—384
8:11—223
8:13–14—225
8:14–17—311, 333
8:18—332, 476
8:18–23—405
8:18–25—256
8:18–39—142
8:19—267
8:19–22—148, 221, 300, 332, 360–61, 563
8:19–23—332, 412
8:20—404

8:20–22—562
8:21—147, 220, 301, 404, 446, 461
8:22—404, 476
8:23—220, 333, 341, 356, 360, 478, 479
8:24–25—333
8:26—249, 476
8:26–27—238
8:27—141
8:28—476
8:28–30—476
8:28–39—476
8:29—363, 470, 476, 477, 478, 490, 498, 499
8:29–30—248, 477
8:30—238
8:31—238
8:31–32—476
8:31–34—237
8:31–39—238
8:32—61, 84, 84n26
8:33—190, 234
8:33–34—142, 190, 204, 476
8:34—26, 84n26, 141, 190, 204, 228, 234, 237, 238, 248, 249, 381, 553
8:34b—381
8:35–39—476
8:38—445
8:38–39—439, 441, 446, 461
9:22—88n34, 280n4
10:1—129
10:2—129
10:3–7—129
10:8—129
10:8–13—129
10:9—129, 130
10:9–10—15, 130, 518, 554
10:11—129
10:13—129
11:15—293n32
11:26—333, 354
11:33–35—565

12—399
12:17—399
12:19—88n34, 280n4
12:19–21—399
14—572
14:9—84n26
14:15—84n26, 572
16:20—439, 467

1 Corinthians
1:17–18—84n26
1:23—84n26
1:25—333
1:26–27—333
1:28–29—333
1:30—26, 290, 333
1:31—333
2:2—84, 84n26
2:6–8—440
2:14–3:3—482
5:1—520
5:3–5—520
5:6—520
5:6–7—520
5:7—502, 512, 517, 520, 521, 547
5:8—521
6:9–10—334
6:11—538
6:13—334
6:14—334
6:15—334
6:16–17—334
6:18—334
6:18–20—95, 360
6:19—334
6:19–20—84n27, 334–35, 356, 359, 361
6:20—521, 555
7:17—335
7:18–40—335
7:20—335
7:21—335
7:21–23—335
7:22—336
7:23—335–36, 356, 361
7:24—335
8—572
8:11—84n26, 572

10:16—84n26, 517
11:7—486
11:24—517
11:25—514
11:25–26—521
11:30—572
11:32—572
12:3—129
13:12—565
15—146, 168, 463, 472
15:1–4—518
15:1–11—478
15:3—84n26, 130
15:4—461, 552
15:3–4—15, 22, 83, 117, 130–31, 145, 554
15:3–8—168
15:10—344
15:12—478, 482
15:12–19—130, 478
15:12–34—482
15:14—131, 478
15:14–22—15, 130–31
15:14–15—84n26
15:16—478
15:17—15, 131, 141, 478
15:17–19—131
15:18—478
15:19—131
15:20—131, 145, 478, 480, 483, 491
15:20–22—145–46, 470, 478, 498, 499
15:20–23—499
15:21—480
15:21–22—131, 145, 480, 481, 483, 484, 553
15:22—484, 555
15:23—481, 491
15:24—147, 441
15:24–26—446
15:24–28—445
15:25–26—461
15:26—441
15:27—481
15:28—300
15:35–49—482

15:36–38—482
15:39–41—482
15:42–43—132, 145, 146, 482
15:42–44—132, 333, 479, 486
15:42–49—470, 482, 498, 499
15:43—486
15:44—482, 483
15:45—36, 90, 102, 131, 483, 484, 485, 494, 499, 551
15:45ff.—463
15:45–49—468
15:47—36, 90, 102, 131, 146, 485, 494, 499, 551
15:47–49—15, 131, 146
15:48—132, 146, 485, 486
15:49—132, 146, 264, 485
15:50–53—479
15:52–53—132, 145, 223, 333
15:54–57—441, 461
15:57—439, 460, 552
16:22—129

2 Corinthians
1:21–22—479
1:22—339n56
2—444
2:14—439, 444
2:14–16—443–44
2:16—444
3:6–15—292
3:7—292
3:7–11—219
3:10—486
3:11—292
3:13—292
3:14—292
3:14ff.—487
3:18—486, 488
4—487
4:1–2—487
4:2—488

4:3—488
4:4—434, 439, 440, 477, 487, 488, 499
4:4–6—470, 486, 489, 498
4:5—487
4:6—487, 488
5—384
5:5—479
5:6–9—282
5:8—254
5:10—282
5:11—282
5:12—282
5:13—282
5:14—282, 283, 286
5:14–15—288, 309, 382, 383
5:15—23, 283, 286, 554
5:16—283
5:16–21—277, 282, 304
5:17—283
5:18—284, 285, 286, 288, 306, 307, 309, 383, 384
5:18–19—46, 288, 306, 307, 309, 382, 383
5:18–20—46, 87, 84n27, 296, 311, 555
5:18–21—46
5:19—284, 285, 286, 288, 307, 309, 383, 401, 406, 433, 559
5:19b—287, 382
5:20—285, 288, 307, 309, 384
5:21—46, 47, 55, 56, 58, 84n27, 140, 284, 285, 286, 287, 288, 289, 309, 310, 311, 374, 374n30, 380, 381, 382, 383, 384, 393, 401, 403, 403, 408, 409, 412, 551, 553, 559, 560
5:21a—287, 382
7:1—108
10:3–4—225
11:14—440
12:9—344

Galatians
1:3–4—440, 442
1:4—84n27, 343
2:16—21
2:20—38, 84n26, 192, 225, 343, 344, 404
3—388
3:7–11—93
3:7–14—92, 386
3:8—93, 386
3:8–11—386
3:10—336, 386, 388
3:10–14—387
3:13—26, 34, 82, 92, 93, 106, 116, 336, 337, 357, 358, 374, 374n30, 380, 384, 385, 386, 388, 389, 397, 405, 408, 409, 410, 412, 412, 542, 553, 555, 559, 560
3:13–14—93, 337, 386
3:14—93, 386
3:16–29—33
3:19—447, 491
3:20—342
3:26–29—389
4:3—337
4:4—33
4:4–5—33, 39, 337, 551, 553
4:4–7—95, 263, 412
4:7—337, 361
4:7–9—95
4:8–9—337
4:10—84n26
5:1—95
5:19—454
6:14—13, 84n26

Ephesians
1:3—94, 337
1:3–6—94, 567
1:3–14—94, 567, 568, 571
1:4—356
1:4–5—337, 567
1:5—568
1:5–6—338

1:6—94, 337
1:7—84n26, 85, 94–95, 116, 337–38, 341, 358, 359, 360, 361, 517, 567, 568
1:7–8—338
1:7–10—294
1:7–12—94, 567
1:9–10—293, 294, 295, 308
1:10—295, 309
1:12—94, 337
1:13—568
1:13–14—94, 337, 339, 339n56, 479, 567
1:14—94, 337, 339
1:15–23—190
1:19–20—190
1:19–21—225, 442
1:19–22—461
1:19–23—191, 203
1:20—168
1:20–21—25, 446, 461
1:21—147, 191
1:22—191
2—295, 309
2:1—132
2:1–2—440
2:1–3—132
2:1–7—223
2:1–10—290
2:3—88n34, 280n4
2:4—61
2:4–5—132, 144
2:4–7—15, 132, 144, 192
2:5—132, 344
2:5–6—132
2:6—192, 203, 267
2:8—344
2:8–9—22, 263
2:11–12—290
2:11–19—277, 289, 290, 304
2:11–22—293, 294, 295
2:12—290, 293, 295, 301
2:12–17—555
2:12–13—192

2:13—290, 291, 295, 307, 517
2:13–16—84n26, 87
2:14—89, 281, 291, 295, 307
2:14–15—292
2:14–16—291, 306
2:15—97, 390, 443
2:16—291, 295, 308
2:17—293
2:17–22—296, 309
2:18—293
2:19—293
2:20–21—295
3:3–4—294
3:7–9—293
3:10–12—462
3:19—61
4:1ff.—225
4:1–2—169
4:3—354, 562
4:3–6—169
4:5–6—342
4:7—169
4:7–8—168–70
4:8—153, 179, 225
4:11–12—169
4:11–13—225
4:22—338
4:22–24—95, 521
4:24—338, 499
4:25—95, 338
4:26–27—95, 440
4:27—339
4:28—95, 338
4:29—95, 338
4:30—338, 339, 341, 356, 360, 479
4:30–31—338, 339n56
4:31–32—95, 96
5:1—96, 522
5:1–2—95
5:2—95–96, 116, 343, 501, 517, 521, 522, 547, 548, 555
5:6—88n34, 280n4
5:18—215
5:25—521, 566
5:25–26—555

5:25–32—339
5:26—108
5:26–27—521
5:28—521
5:29—521
5:31–32—521
5:32—522
6:2—292
6:10–18—225
6:11—440
6:12—97, 147, 441
6:16—440
6:19–20—293

Philippians
1:23—254
1:27—34
2:1–4—34
2:3—35
2:4—36
2:5–8—34, 34–36, 84,
    470
2:5–9—24
2:6—34
2:6–7—39
2:7—35
2:8—35, 47, 84n26, 91,
    198, 286, 381, 474,
    475
2:9—35, 39
2:9–11—35, 129, 168
2:10–11—34, 300
2:13–16—84n27
3:10—23, 84n26, 225,
    554
3:17–19—256
3:20—255, 256
3:20–21—256, 267
3:21—145, 257, 478
4:2—34, 36

Colossians
1—132, 148, 477
1:1—257
1:3—257
1:4—257
1:9–11—340
1:12—340
1:13—148, 296, 302,

338, 354, 489, 490,
    562
1:13–14—340–41, 359,
    360, 439, 442, 459,
    460
1:14—302
1:15—97, 470, 477, 488,
    489, 490, 498, 499
1:15–16—132, 137, 490
1:15–17—132, 133, 296
1:15–18—296, 298
1:15–20—297
1:16—133, 147, 220,
    221, 296, 299, 300,
    477, 489, 490, 562
1:16–17—147, 297, 298,
    300
1:17—132, 147, 296,
    490
1:18—15, 132, 133, 135,
    138, 148, 149, 220,
    221, 296, 470, 489,
    490, 491, 498, 499,
    555
1:18–20—296
1:19—147, 297, 490
1:19–20—89, 147, 148,
    295, 297, 301, 304,
    306, 307, 309, 562,
    563
1:19–22—84n27, 87
1:19–23—277, 296, 297,
    304
1:20—84n26, 89, 147,
    148, 220, 221, 297,
    302, 303, 304, 305,
    306, 308, 491, 517,
    561, 562
1:20–23—555
1:21—148, 280, 304,
    306
1:21–22—220, 298, 301,
    302
1:21–23—148, 299, 300
1:22—84n26, 89, 302,
    304, 308, 491
1:23—302
2:2—257
2:3—334

2:9—147, 297, 490
2:13—96, 389, 443
2:13–14—409, 410
2:13–15—96, 442, 446
2:14—84n26, 97, 116,
    298, 309, 374,
    374n30, 389, 390,
    408, 412, 443, 445,
    446, 555, 560
2:14–15—412, 459, 460,
    461, 560, 561
2:15—98, 116, 147, 220,
    298, 299, 391, 441,
    442, 443, 444, 445,
    446, 555, 561, 562
2:20—84n26, 191, 267
2:23—191, 193, 203
3:1—192, 267
3:1–3—553
3:1–4—25, 191, 193,
    203, 257
3:2—192
3:3—192, 257, 267
3:3–4—192
3:4—192, 267
3:5–7—302–3
3:6—88n34, 149, 280n4
3:10—489n53, 499

1 Thessalonians
1:7–8—258
1:9—439
1:9–10—257–58, 269,
    553
1:10—25, 88n34, 255,
    258, 259, 269, 280n4
2:16—88n34, 280n4
4:13—259
4:14—25, 84n26, 259
4:14–18—258
4:15—259
4:17—259, 267
4:18—259
5:9—88n34, 258, 280n4
5:10—84n26

2 Thessalonians
1:3–4—160
1:5—260

1:6–7—260
1:6–8—268
1:6–10—258
1:7—255
1:7–8—260
1:7–9—303
1:8—260
1:8–9—149
1:9—260
1:9–10—260
1:10—268

1 Timothy
1:1—572
1:2–3—572
1:3–4—170
1:13—387
1:15—40
2:1–2—341
2:2—341
2:3–4—341
2:4—342
2:5—216, 286, 343, 381, 527
2:5–6—342, 343, 354, 355, 356, 357, 360
2:6—341, 343, 374
2:6a—343
3—170
3:6—342n63
3:7—440
3:15—171
4:1—342n63
4:10—571, 572
5:12—342n63
5:24—342n63
6:9—342n63
6:16—297
6:20—170

2 Timothy
1:8–9—22
1:10—572
2:8—25
2:11—84n26
2:25–26—342n63, 440
4:18—454

Titus
1:3—572

1:4—572
1:10–11—344
2:1–10—344, 346
2:10—572
2:11—268, 344
2:11–12—261, 344
2:11–14—260, 261
2:13—261, 345, 346, 572
2:13–14—84n27, 268, 354, 356, 358
2:14—108, 343, 344, 346, 361
3:4—572
3:4–5—22
3:6—572
3:7—344

Hebrews
book of—47–50, 98, 193, 237, 245, 262, 495, 526, 538
1—37, 38, 39, 47, 99, 103, 205, 274, 347, 494, 495, 496, 524
1:1–2—523
1:1–4—99
1:1–14—447
1:2—99, 193, 205, 262, 274, 494, 498
1:3—23, 37–38, 98, 98n42, 99, 100, 103, 116, 194, 197, 204, 239, 262, 274, 421, 448, 490, 497, 523, 524, 526, 547, 548, 549, 552, 553, 554
1:3–4—193
1:3–14—193
1:4–5—447
1:5—99
1:5–14—262
1:6—447
1:7–9—447
1:8—47, 99, 194
1:10–12—447
1:13—194, 252, 421, 446, 447, 459, 460, 492, 552

1:14—447, 498
2—36, 38, 39, 47, 101, 103, 239, 347, 492, 493, 524
2:1–4—447, 491
2:3–4—223
2:5–10—491, 497, 498
2:5–11—496
2:6–8—36, 101, 493
2:7—102
2:8—101, 494
2:8–9—100
2:9—36, 39, 102, 116, 348, 449, 494, 495, 497, 499, 524
2:9–10—499
2:9–13—524
2:10—48, 49, 102, 495, 496, 497, 498, 499, 526, 558
2:11—264
2:12—62
2:14—37, 39, 102, 348, 436, 449, 450, 461, 499, 524, 526, 558
2:14–15—36–38, 100, 102, 116, 177, 449, 451, 459, 460, 461, 495, 497, 524, 552, 553, 555
2:15—102, 198, 454
2:16—524
2:16–17—36, 37
2:16–18—497, 524
2:17—38, 39, 100, 103, 109n40, 111, 116, 239, 348, 375n31, 395, 449, 499, 525, 526, 527, 549, 558, 559, 560
2:17–18—98n42, 449, 524, 547
2:18—103, 104, 526, 548, 558
3—38
3:1—197
3:1–4:14—525
3:6—47, 525
3:7–4:11—497

3:7–4:13—526
4:12—92
4:14—47, 103, 172, 179,
　239, 497, 548
4:14–15—24
4:14–16—47, 527
4:15—48, 55, 56, 525,
　551
4:15–16—58, 59, 103,
　553
4:15–5:10—525
4:16—48, 70, 263
5–10—176
5:2—26
5:2–3—176
5:7—48, 232
5:8—49
5:8–10—48, 59, 495,
　553
5:9—499
5:9–10—49, 58
6:4–12—527
6:19—172, 176, 178,
　181, 241, 468
6:19–20—177–78, 181,
　239, 241
6:20—242, 497, 552
7—155, 172, 230, 242,
　421
7–10—38, 193, 496, 497
7:1—242
7:7—172
7:14—229
7:14–16—175
7:16—133, 141, 239,
　553
7:21—184, 527
7:23—133, 242
7:23–24—527
7:23–25—141, 184, 262,
　547, 549
7:23–27—98n42, 527,
　547
7:24—133, 141, 242,
　527
7:24–25—2, 133–34,
　198, 553
7:25—103, 134, 141,
　195, 228, 234, 239,

242, 243, 249, 527,
　553
7:26—50, 103, 172, 525,
　528
7:27—49, 141, 176, 195,
　262, 523, 527, 528,
　548
7:28—48, 495, 499
8—172
8:1—204, 548
8:1–2—194, 196, 197,
　243
8:1–5—180
8:1–5a—172, 174
8:1–7—194
8:1–8—204
8:2—176
8:3—195, 239, 243
8:4—17, 175, 180, 195,
　243
8:4–6—532
8:5—195, 196
8:6—196, 548
8:7–12—537
8:15—180
9–10—99, 119, 176, 523
9:1–18—532
9:2–3—241
9:3—468
9:6–14—512
9:11—176, 347, 529,
　548
9:11–12—175, 176, 180,
　244, 501
9:11–14—239, 243, 244
9:11–15—347, 355
9:11–28—98n42, 528,
　547
9:12—87, 100, 244, 262,
　347, 348, 356, 358,
　529, 530, 537, 548,
　549, 555
9:13—244
9:13–14—524, 526, 529
9:14—195, 244, 401,
　433, 517, 530, 540,
　548, 549, 555
9:15—86, 87, 181, 216,
　217, 262, 293, 347,

348, 361, 530, 537,
　548, 549, 555
9:16–17—531
9:18—531
9:19–21—531
9:20—531
9:21—532
9:22—531
9:22–23—561
9:23—531, 533, 537,
　558, 559
9:23a—533
9:23–24—175, 176, 180,
　532, 548
9:24—172, 176, 239,
　243, 244, 347, 533,
　553
9:24–26—100
9:25–26—533
9:25–28—177
9:26—38, 85, 119, 262,
　354, 355, 375, 526,
　533, 548, 549
9:26–28—261
9:27—262, 480
9:27–28—534
9:28—25, 195, 249, 262,
　266, 534, 548, 549,
　553
9:28b—534
10—448, 534
10:1—523, 534
10:1–4—197, 448, 529
10:1–9—535
10:1–14—176, 448
10:1–18—240
10:2—99, 534
10:4—86, 197, 376, 530,
　534
10:5—548
10:5–7—535
10:5–9—448
10:5–10—354, 355, 536,
　547, 548
10:7—401, 410, 496
10:8–9—535
10:9—401, 410, 496
10:9–10—517
10:10—119, 195, 243,

262, 448, 535, 537,
548, 549
10:10–14—98n42, 534
10:11—99, 196, 536
10:11–12—25, 536, 553
10:11–14—99, 194, 204,
536
10:11–18—196
10:12—100, 181, 195,
196, 204, 448, 536,
548, 552
10:13—446, 448, 460,
536, 552
10:14—25, 100, 195,
196, 204, 243, 448,
535, 536, 537, 549,
553, 555
10:14–18—547
10:15–18—537
10:16–17—537
10:17—547
10:17–18—549
10:18—537
10:26—537
10:26–31—526
10:26–39—527
11—197
11:13—29
11:22—67
11:39–40—197
11:40—349
12:1—197
12:1–2—203
12:1–6—197
12:2—198, 497, 498
12:4—198
12:15–16—532
12:18–21—219
12:18–24—219
12:24—216, 244, 529,
548
12:29—526
13:1—535
13:12—529
13:20—216, 529
13:20–21—217
13:21—535

1 Peter
book of—50, 104, 349,
363, 391, 451, 538
1:1—105–6, 540
1:1–2—104, 538, 571
1:2—107, 116, 538, 547
1:3—134, 144, 145, 553
1:3–17—349
1:4—134
1:11—23, 29, 81, 199,
554
1:13—262, 263, 266,
539, 553
1:13–2:6—391
1:14—539
1:15–16—540
1:17—105, 540
1:18—354
1:18–19—104, 105, 116,
134, 349, 357, 358,
359, 540, 547, 549,
571
1:18–21—134
1:19—105, 107, 541,
543, 547, 555
1:19–21—199
1:20—135, 433, 541
1:20–21—139
1:21—135
1:22—104n47, 539
2:4—541, 542
2:5—542
2:6—541, 542
2:7—542
2:9—542
2:11—105, 540
2:12—542
2:21—106, 199, 391,
392
2:21–23—43, 50, 55,
105, 541
2:21–24—105, 391, 541,
547
2:21–25—542
2:22—51, 105, 543
2:22–23—56, 391
2:22–25—391
2:24—50, 105, 106, 107,
116, 199, 391, 392,

408, 410, 411, 412,
541, 542, 543, 546,
549, 560
2:25—81
3—199
3:1—104n47, 539
3:13—200
3:13–17—199
3:18—26, 51, 55, 56, 58,
59, 106, 107, 116,
199, 392, 393, 403,
408, 409, 411, 412,
452, 553, 560
3:18–20—199
3:20—451
3:20–22—460
3:21—452
3:21–22—26, 199, 200,
203, 452, 461
3:22—178, 200, 452
4:1–4—349
4:3—540
4:12—200
4:17—104n47, 539
5:8—453

2 Peter
1:15—67
1:18—67
2:1—572, 573
3:10–13—562
3:13—150, 220, 283

1 John
book of—51, 107, 111,
237, 245, 249, 363,
393, 395, 453, 543
1:2—454
1:3—108, 181, 544
1:4—108, 545
1:5—109
1:6—109, 544
1:7—107, 108, 109, 111,
116, 453, 543, 544,
547, 549
1:8—110, 394, 543
1:8–10—107, 109, 544
1:9—108, 394, 543
1:10—110, 394, 543,
544

2:1—51, 55, 56, 58, 59,
  109, 110, 245, 393,
  394, 403, 543, 544
2:1-2—51, 181, 245,
  394, 403
2:2—108, 109, 109n40,
  110, 111, 116, 245,
  246, 375n31, 393,
  394, 395, 396,
  408, 409, 412, 453,
  543n93, 560, 571,
  572, 572
2:13-14—437, 453
2:15—37, 436
2:15-17—77, 453
2:18—453
2:20—51, 55, 56
2:22—453
2:22-23—111
2:25—454
2:27—51
3:1—263
3:2—52, 263
3:2-3—263, 264
3:3—52, 57, 263
3:5—52, 55, 453
3:5-6—52, 55, 57, 58,
  59
3:6-7—52
3:7—52, 55, 57, 59
3:8—52, 436, 453, 454,
  460
3:9—52
3:10—52, 453
3:10-11—453
3:14—454
3:15—454
4:1—453
4:3—453
4:4—225, 436, 461
4:7—395
4:7-8—110
4:7-19—263
4:8—395
4:9—110, 395
4:9b—111
4:9-14—110, 543n93
4:10—109n40, 110, 111,
  116, 375n31, 393,

394, 395, 396, 408,
  410, 411, 453, 560
4:11—111
4:12—111
4:13—111
4:14—111
4:18—102, 451
5:4—437
5:4-5—453
5:11—454
5:13—51, 454
5:18-19—453
5:19—434, 453, 572
5:20—454

2 John
7—453, 460

Jude
4—573

Revelation
book of—52, 111, 135,
  200, 237, 249, 264,
  350, 353, 454, 545
1—52
1:4—137
1:4-5—112, 135-36
1:5—112, 116, 138, 139,
  149, 150, 265, 350,
  458, 546
1:5a—350
1:5-6—112, 350, 351,
  354, 357, 358, 361,
  545, 547
1:6—354
1:13-16—136
1:14—264, 458
1:16—264
1:17-18—136, 137n20
1:18—135, 136, 139,
  265
2-3—52, 135
2:1—52
2:8—53, 137, 137n20,
  265
2:12—53
2:13—138, 149
2:18—53, 264

2:27—264
3:1—53
3:5—115, 546
3:7—53, 56, 57, 58, 264
3:11—458
3:14—53, 135, 137-39,
  138n21, 149-50, 264,
  458
3:21—198, 200, 202,
  203, 455, 460, 461
4-5—247
5—113, 247, 457
5:5—201, 351, 456, 555
5:5-6—201, 456
5:5-9—460, 560
5:6—112, 113, 116, 247,
  350, 351, 355, 358,
  457, 545, 547
5:6-9—461
5:7-13—113, 351, 457,
  545
5:9—95, 261, 265, 350,
  351, 352, 355, 360,
  456, 545, 547, 549,
  560, 569, 570, 571
5:9-10—113, 351, 357,
  358, 361, 569
5:10—456
6:10—573
6:11—202
6:16—113, 457
7:4-9—352
7:9—202
7:14—114, 116, 350,
  546, 547
11:3—138, 149
11:18—265, 266
12:5—264
12:7—114, 546
12:9—415, 455, 465,
  467
12:9-11—455, 460
12:10—114, 546
12:10-11—265
12:11—114, 115, 116,
  350, 436, 461, 546,
  547
13:1-7—115, 546

13:8—115, 116, 350, 433, 546, 547
13:11—113, 115, 352, 457
13:16-17—352
14:1—352
14:3—352
14:3-4—350, 352
14:4—359, 361
14:4-5—352
15:2—455, 460
17:4—455
17:6—138, 149
17:8—115, 546
17:14—113, 201, 264, 457, 460, 461
19:6-7—265
19:6-9—266

19:8—202
19:9—265
19:11—264
19:11-16—201, 264, 424-25, 457, 458, 460, 461
19:11-21—459
19:12—264
19:14—201, 202, 458
19:15—264, 458, 459
19:15-21—113, 457
19:16—264, 459, 461
19:17-18—459
19:20—459
19:21—459
20:2—415, 455, 465, 467
20:10—102, 426, 450

20:10-15—459
20:15—115, 546
21—163
21-22—139, 150, 562
21:1—146, 220, 283
21:4—220
21:6—137n20
21:8—149, 303
21:10—553
21:27—115, 546
22:1-3—468
22:2—268
22:3—404
22:13—137n20, 268, 491
22:14—265, 268 468
22:14-15—304
22:15—149

The Theology in Community Series

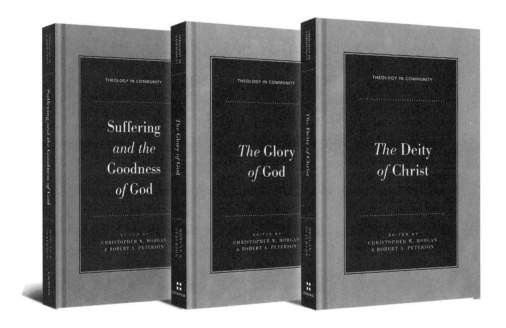

EDITED BY

CHRISTOPHER W. MORGAN
& ROBERT A. PETERSON